Comedy Quotes from the Movies

Comedy Quotes from the Movies

*Over 4,000 Bits of Humorous
Dialogue from All Film Genres,
Topically Arranged and Indexed*

by
LARRY LANGMAN
and
PAUL GOLD

McFarland & Company, Inc., Publishers
Jefferson, North Carolina, and London

791.43
C732

British Library Cataloguing-in-Publication data are available

Library of Congress Cataloguing-in-Publication Data

Comedy quotes from the movies : over 4000 bits of humorous dialogue
from all film genres, topically arranged and indexed / [compiled] by
Larry Langman and Paul Gold.
    p. cm.
  Includes indexes.
  ISBN 0-89950-863-4 (lib. bdg. : 50# alk. paper) ∞
  1. Motion pictures – Quotations, maxims, etc. 2. Comedy films –
Quotations, maxims, etc. I. Langman, Larry. II. Gold, Paul,
1932-   .
PN1994.9.C58   1994
791.43 – dc20   92-56659
                                                                      CIP

Manufactured in the United States of America

McFarland & Company, Inc., Publishers
  Box 611, Jefferson, North Carolina 28640

Table of Contents

Preface and
Acknowledgments

The compilers of this book have tried to bring together some of the funniest, wittiest and more outrageous snatches of dialogue on film during the last 60 years. We have gathered more than 4,000 entries, chiefly from American features.

We decided to include lines and dialogue from dramas as well as comedies, as long as they met our simple criteria – they had to be funny. If these quotations conjure up affectionate memories for the reader, so much the better. One of our aims was to offer proof of the vast treasure of forgotten or overlooked comedy buried within these films. Another aim was to recall the many personalities – stars and other players – who delivered these gems.

If the reader occasionally notices a title that is unfamiliar, the film is probably a short one- or two-reeler. In the early days of the talkies, many studios issued short comedies to fill out their programs or to test promising comics. Many famous comedians and comediennes, including Eddie Cantor, Bob Hope, and the comedy team of George Burns and Gracie Allen, appeared in these shorts. In addition, the reader may find several punch lines repeated in another part of the book. We deliberately included these to demonstrate how comics borrowed from each other over the years or, in the case of Abbott and Costello, often repeated their own material from one picture to the next.

Since many comics and comedy teams more or less play themselves from one film to the next, we have omitted the names of characters with two exceptions: where the names help to clarify who is addressed or is speaking and where the film is based on a famous or popular work. In such cases, the actor's or actress' name is placed in parentheses beside the character name.

Entries are arranged by categories, which are presented alphabetically. Within each category, entries appear chronologically based on the date of release of each film. (If several films within a category were released the same year, they are listed alphabetically.) A title index and a name index follow the body of the book.

Any work of this scope requires the contribution of several people. Therefore, we wish to thank film collector William Shelley for the use of his collection of early sound films; Spencer Fisher, Daniel Finn and Edgar Borg for their editorial suggestions; and Irving Lin of Abest International for keeping our computers functioning. Most of all we wish to pay tribute to all the performers, writers, directors and other creative talents who allowed us to enter briefly their world of laughter.

Introduction

Sound comedy owes much to the silent era as well as to the theater, burlesque, vaudeville, early radio and other forms of show business. Hollywood displayed an uncanny ability to adapt its comedies quickly to sound, especially after nearly three decades of silents which depended largely on sight gags and visual effects. (Many of the silents did have comic title cards as well, consisting of dialogue or narration.)

With the advent of sound, almost overnight, stage comics like Mae West (who allegedly rescued Paramount from bankruptcy), the Marx Brothers and Jimmy Durante lent their talents to the screen. Radio personalities like Amos 'n' Andy and Lum and Abner made the plunge into sound comedies, but many could not duplicate the success on film that they had enjoyed over the air. Together with veteran silent screen comedians like Will Rogers, Buster Keaton and Laurel and Hardy, these performers from the stage and radio joined new screen talents to help make comedy one of the most popular and innovative film genres.

Romantic and so-called "screwball" comedy introduced such actors and actresses as Fred MacMurray, Clark Gable, Carole Lombard, Claudette Colbert and Irene Dunne, while silent screen performers like William Powell and Myrna Loy displayed a penchant for comedy as well as drama. Western and historical satires, featuring Will Rogers, Wheeler and Woolsey, and Laurel and Hardy, also flourished during the first decade of sound.

Several comics familiar to audiences today appeared in early movie shorts, which were designed to serve as a springboard for future full-length films. Bob Hope, for instance, made forgettable shorts which gave little hint of his comic abilities. George Burns and Gracie Allen fared better, but Burns was abrasive and abusive to Allen in these early shorts. Only in their later features did Burns take on a warmer persona. Ventriloquist Edgar Bergen and his popular dummy Charlie McCarthy turned out some very funny shorts that were hampered only by their staginess and cheap production values. Giants like W. C. Fields were as funny in their shorts as in their later features.

Except for Mae West's bawdy innuendoes and double entendres, screen comedy from the 1930s through the 1950s rarely gave rise to controversy. Bob Hope occasionally jabbed at political parties and politicians, but he discreetly pulled his punches. The anarchic Marx Brothers satirized war, the wealthy and the powerful, but for the most part their barbs, though hilarious at times, were generally drowned out by the brothers' more out-landish antics.

The predominant major targets of screen humor were romance, love, marriage, divorce and general male-female relationships: tried-and-true topics popularized on stage and in print. The sashaying Mae West, for instance, satirized sex while the Dickensian W. C. Fields poked fun at domestic life. Other, more specific targets, such as the blundering cop, the dumb blonde, the silly salesperson, the wisecracking domestic, the wimpy manager and the domineering mother-in-law, gained popularity and quickly sank into stereotypes. Comedy ran the gamut from the lowly pun to the insult to the witticism.

The early sound comedies may not have been controversial, but they offered interesting insights into the social mores of the period. With their often lavish sets of large mansions, nightclubs and resorts, coupled with the carefree spending of the rich, many urban comedies provided a welcome respite to their Depression-weary audiences. Other urban comedies depicted the working class (often a mix of well-integrated WASPs and immigrants) as poor but content, struggling yet happy. Rural comedies may have portrayed their characters as slow-moving and slow-thinking yokels, but these rustics often lived better and got the upper hand over their city cousins. City life may be faster and city folk more sophisticated, but rural life was preferred and country people were unencumbered by artifice.

Some films reflected the social or class stratification: the cabby, policeman or maid frequently exchanged quips with their betters, but they rarely mingled. Blacks and other minorities might have been present, but they were usually stereotyped and relegated to the background. Racism flourished on screen, a condition which simply echoed the period. Some academics and politically oriented persons have recently attacked early Hollywood for conspiring against certain groups, but in fact the movie capital was rather even-handedly guilty of stereotypes: it offered a negative portrayal of virtually *all* minorities.

Comedies of the forties often adhered to conventional attitudes of other genres: patriotism was in; communism was out; hoodlums fought enemy agents; minorities, except for blacks, were integrated into the military where they cracked jokes or were the butt of jokes; wartime wives of different classes learned to live together; and servants occasionally accompanied their masters into uniform. Democracy moved forward—at least on the screen. Abbott and Costello led in popularity during the war years, followed by the Bob Hope–Bing Crosby "Road" comedies, and by Red Skelton and the ebullient newcomer Danny Kaye. Comediennes like Rosalind Russell, Martha Raye and Joan Davis continued to be popular, while new faces such as Betty Hutton began to enthrall wartime audiences. Meanwhile, the social satires of writer-director Preston Sturges contrasted sharply with the lighter, slapstick comedy of the war years.

Hollywood cut back on the production of comedies during the fifties, perhaps because audiences could see the best comics at home on television. The comedies reverted to an earlier period and conventional subject matter. Slapstick, chases and domestic comedy dominated the genre. As the more familiar comics like Mae West and W. C. Fields faded from the screen, newer faces were prepared to replace them. Dean Martin and Jerry Lewis superseded Bud and Lou and Stan and Ollie. Spencer Tracy and Katharine Hepburn made up the chief romantic comedy team. Judy Holliday and Marilyn Monroe starred in some of the most scintillating comedies of the period. By the end of the decade, sex comedies became prevalent, thanks to the talents of such as Rock Hudson and Doris Day in movies such as *Pillow Talk* (1959).

Sex in film comedy has always been with us; it particularly flourished in the early thirties under such practitioners as Mae West and Jean Harlow – until the Hays Office clamped down on the more blatant examples of the genre in the mid-thirties. By the 1960s the sexual revolution that was sweeping the country infiltrated the screen, chiefly in the form of an explosion of raunchy language. As a result a censorship-rating system for films was instituted. A flood of sex comedies followed, and the genre has remained popular through the nineties.

Black comedies like *Dr. Strangelove* and *Little Murders* were especially appealing among younger audiences. The spy satire also emerged, dominated by the James Bond films from England. American studios soon hopped on the bandwagon with individual entries and several series, including Dean Martin's Matt Helm and Charles Coburn's Flint films. Sex and action, both treated lightly and filmed in exotic locales, took precedence over plot, theme and characterization in these colorful capers.

Original comics like Woody Allen, who has challenged Bob Hope as king of the one-liners, brought their distinctive humor to the screen in the 1970s. Writer Neil Simon offered us a string of domestic comedies. Elaine May and Mel Brooks were two other writer-performer-directors who enriched the comedy genre.

Later, comics who had honed their skills in television invaded films. The unique talents of Steve Martin, Bill Murray, John Candy, John Belushi, Eddie Murphy, Chevy Chase and others brightened many films. Those who worked the stand-up comedy circuit, like Whoopi Goldberg, Billy Crystal and Robin Williams, found the film format a comfortable and highly profitable medium. By the 1980s no topic was sacrosanct. Jokes and sketches about ethnicity, religion and the Holocaust had reached the screen with little or no protest.

No survey of screen comedy would be complete without acknowledging the contributions of two very diverse and talented groups: the character players and the screenwriters. The unique delivery of such kooky actors as Patsy Kelly, Eric Blore, Mischa Auer, Eugene Pallette, Helen Broderick, Donald Meek, Franklin Pangborn and Margaret Hamilton can be fully appreciated only aurally *and* visually. Legendary screenwriters like George S. Kaufman, S. J. Perelman, Ben Hecht, Norman Krasna, Frank Tashlin, Billy Wilder and scores of others often provided complex situations and sparkling dialogue. Kaufman and Perelman wrote for the Marx Brothers; Hecht was coauthor of *The Front Page;* and Krasna, Tashlin and Wilder both directed and wrote popular comedies over several decades.

While collecting and organizing quotations for this book, the compilers became reacquainted with several comedians and comedy teams long forgotten. Wide-mouthed Joe E. Brown, whose best films were released in the early thirties, often portrayed the lovesick or bragging dupe who finally overcame a series of hurdles to win the love of the heroine. Eddie Cantor, once as well known for his singing as for his comedy, made several lively movie shorts and full-length and musical comedies. Particularly worthwhile are his "Kid" series (*Kid Boots, Kid from Spain, Kid Millions*). Bert Wheeler and Robert Woolsey, a popular comedy team that gained fame on Broadway before moving to Hollywood, remain perennially fresh and audacious. Wheeler wisecracked his way to the heroine's heart while Woolsey, in dark-rimmed glasses and cigar locked between his fingers, demolished pomposity and authority, much in the style of Groucho Marx. Unfortunately, Robert Woolsey died in 1938, thereby bringing to an end a popular comedy team.

Screen comedy has come a long way from the one-reel shorts of Mack Sennett, who virtually invented the genre in 1912 at Keystone Studios. But his slapstick and classic chases live on in the films of Mel Brooks, Blake Edwards and other contemporary writers and directors who, along with other personalities from vaudeville, the Broadway stage, silent films, radio and television, have lifted audiences into wacky worlds of fantasy, helped them to forget their troubles and, most of all, made them laugh.

Comedy Quotes
from the Movies

Accidents

1 Eddie Cantor denies to a doctor that he has ever had an accident, but then admits that once "a bull pitched me over a fence." "Don't you call that an accident?" the doctor asks. "No," Cantor insists. "The darn bull did it on purpose." – *Insurance* (1930)

2 An attractive woman bends over to show dentist W. C. Fields where a small dog has bitten her on her ankle. "You're rather fortunate it wasn't a Newfoundland," Fields quips. – *The Dentist* (1932)

3 W. C. Fields drives his car onto a millionaire's estate and into a statue of Venus de Milo, demolishing it. "She walked right in front of the car," Fields charges. – *It's a Gift* (1934)

4 W. C. Fields, directing his stock players from backstage, falls off a platform and causes a commotion. "Oh, are you hurt?" his daughter asks. "No," he replies. "I had the presence of mind to fall on my head." – *The Old-Fashioned Way* (1934)

5 The Three Stooges are tricked into thinking a house contains buried treasure. As they begin their search, Curly falls down a staircase leading to the cellar. "Did you find anything?" Larry asks. "Yeah," comes the reply. "I found the first step everyone tells you to watch out for." "Well, don't lose it," Larry returns. – *Cash and Carry* (1937)

6 Wealthy financier Edward Arnold accidentally trips and goes tumbling down a flight of stairs in his Fifth Avenue mansion. His butler, at the foot of the stairs, greets the supine Arnold: "I see you're down early this morning, sir." – *Easy Living* (1937)

7 Bert Wheeler and Robert Woolsey, impersonating officers of the law after crashing their stolen airplane onto a private estate, are questioned by their hostess Margaret Dumont. "Have an accident?" "No, we just had one, thanks," Wheeler quips. – *High Flyers* (1937)

8 Assistant newsreel cameraman Chic Chandler, assigned to a South Pacific island, tries his hand at magic during a native feast and accidentally swallows a lighted cigarette. "Boy," he announces to the other guests, "am I hot tonight!" – *Mr. Moto Takes a Chance* (1938)

9 Professor Higgins (Rex Harrison) uses marbles to improve Eliza's (Wendy Hiller) speech. "Oh," she exclaims, "I've swallowed one!" "Don't worry," he calmly responds. "I've plenty more." – *Pygmalion* (1938)

10 Ruthless Communist police chief Oscar Homolka explains to foreign reporters in Moscow why they cannot speak with the official press spokesman: "The former head of the press department was a victim last night of a traffic accident. He apparently, shall we say, did not watch his step." – *Comrade X* (1940)

11 Smalltime hoodlum Abner Biberman accidentally crashes his car into a police patrol wagon. "Imagine bumping into a load of cops!" he exclaims. "They come rolling out like oranges." – *His Girl Friday* (1940)

12 Joan Davis comes rushing across the street and crashes into Lou Costello. "What are you – blind?" Costello exclaims. "I hit you, didn't I?" quips Davis. – *Hold That Ghost* (1941)

13 Actor John Barrymore has fallen down during rehearsals. While he is resting, someone approaches and asks: "Have an accident?" "No thanks," Barrymore replies. "I just had one." – *Playmates* (1941)

14 When a nightclub waiter accidentally dumps a large salad over the head of wealthy Douglass Dumbrille, onlooker Zero Mostel uses his finger to scoop up some salad from the victim's suit. "You dress in good taste," Mostel quips. – *DuBarry Was a Lady* (1943)

15 Stan Laurel accidentally sprays white paint on a painting. "My Van Dyck!" the owner cries. "Do you realize you've ruined my beautiful picture, 'The Height of Spring'? What am I going to do?" "You can call it 'The Depth of Winter,'" suggests Laurel. – *The Big Noise* (1944)

16 Joan Davis: "I went to cooking school, but they threw me out for burning something." Eddie Cantor: "What did you burn?" Davis: "The school." – *Show Business* (1944)

17 Lou Costello smashes his car into the rear of a parked car. "Why, you blithering idiot!" rails the angry owner. "I just got this car out of the repair shop! Now just look at it!" "Well," replies Costello, "send it back to the repair shop. The rest will do it good." – *Abbott and Costello in Hollywood* (1945)

18 Lou Costello backs up his car and smashes into an expensive limousine. "What's the idea of bumping into me?" the irate owner bellows. "Can't you see where you're going? Are you blind?" "I hit you, didn't I?" – *The Noose Hangs High* (1948)

19 Waiter Lou Costello accidentally drops a cake of soap into a stew and unknowingly serves it to the pirate Captain Kidd (Charles Laughton), who soon emits bubbles whenever he speaks. The tavern owner later asks how the captain is enjoying the food. "Oh," Costello replies, "he's bubbling over." – *Abbott and Costello Meet Captain Kidd* (1952)

20 Bing Crosby, Bob Hope and Dorothy Lamour are stranded on an uncharted island after a shipwreck, and Hope gets caught in a trap that leaves him dangling from a tree. "Let's get the sap out of the tree," quips Crosby. – *Road to Bali* (1952)

21 Ranch foreman Dean Martin clumsily smashes a valuable antique chair in the home of business tycoon Agnes Moorehead. "My antique chair!" Moorehead exclaims. "I'm glad it was only an old one," returns Martin. – *Pardners* (1956)

22 Garbage collector Lou Costello enters a home to pick up some refuse and creates a disturbance. "Oh, be careful," the owner calls out from another room. "Don't knock over any of those jars of jelly." "Don't worry," Costello returns, "I'm in enough jam already." – *The 30-Foot Bride of Candy Mountain* (1959)

23 Clumsy police Inspector Clouseau (Peter Sellers) steps on his valuable violin which he had placed on the floor next to his bed. "No matter," he says resignedly to his wife. "When you've seen one Stradivarius you've seen them all." – *The Pink Panther* (1964)

24 A shapely blonde, stepping out of a hotel pool and accidentally drenching Matt Helm (Dean Martin), offers her apologies. "You're really a sport about it," she says. "I'm surprised you didn't take umbrage." "Oh," he quips, "I take a belt now and then." – *The Silencers* (1966)

25 Secretary Candice Bergen describes her employer's medical insurance coverage: "We got this medical plan that's really neat – if you get run over by an armadillo." – *T. R. Baskin* (1971)

26 Billy Pilgrim's (Michael Sacks) wife is killed in a car accident on the way to visit Billy in a hospital. Their daughter learns the tragic news from her boyfriend. "She had some kind of accident with a car and got carbon-monoxide poisoning," he explains gently. "She drives a Cadillac," the puzzled daughter says in disbelief. – *Slaughterhouse Five* (1972)

27 British agent James Bond (Roger Moore) retrieves an important clue, a golden bullet, which he accidentally swallows during a fight. He later takes it to a government laboratory where a scientist cannot identify the object. "You mean there's no way to trace that bullet?" Bond asks. "You have no idea what it went through to get here." – *The Man with the Golden Gun* (1974)

28 After Inspector Clouseau (Peter Sellers) accidentally causes his former boss, Herbert Lom, to fall into a lake, he rescues him and administers mouth-to-mouth resuscitation to Lom. An elderly woman witnessing the incident attacks Sellers with her umbrella. "Pervert!" she shouts as she knocks him off Lom's semi-conscious body. – *The Pink Panther Strikes Again* (1976)

29 John Belushi, watching his neighbor's house burn down, asks the firefighters, who don't have enough water pressure, what else can be done. "I know what we can do," an onlooker says. "What?" "Get some marshmallows." – *Neighbors* (1981)

30 Tom Cruise's girlfriend Rebecca De Mornay reaches into his car for her sweater and accidentally releases the emergency brake – causing the expensive sports car to slowly dip into a nearby

lake. Later, at a repair shop, the manager addresses Cruise and his pals: "Who's the U-Boat commander?" – *Risky Business* (1983)

31 Head of Westmoreland Industries Jonathan Winters receives a phone call from one of his plant foremen who informs Winters of a Class One emergency involving a radioactive cloud emanating from the plant. "It doesn't sound good," Winters affirms. "What are the workers doing?" "They're glowing." – *Say Yes* (1986)

32 Police detective Leslie Nielsen reveals to girlfriend Priscilla Presley how a young woman he once loved died in a tragic blimp accident over the Rose Bowl on New Year's Day. "Goodyear?" she asks. "No," Nielsen replies, "the worst." – *The Naked Gun* (1988)

33 Four children accidentally reduced to microscopic size must survive in the entanglements of their front lawn – which is now a virtual jungle fraught with danger. They are tossed off the back of an ant and come crashing to the ground. "When we crashed," an eight-year-old says excitedly, "my entire life flashed before me!" He then adds: "It didn't take too long." – *Honey, I Shrunk the Kids* (1989)

34 Billy Crystal's wife wants to send their teenage daughter to a private art school, claiming she has talent. "Talent?" he questions. "She was in one play and she fell off the stage. That's not talent, that's gravity." – *City Slickers* (1991)

Actors and Actresses

35 Aline McMahon to Onslow Stevens about an aspiring thespian: "Miss Walker is a young woman who has a chance of becoming the world's worst actress." – *Once in a Lifetime* (1932)

36 Comics Frank Mitchell and Jack Durant have high hopes about their future in Hollywood. "Believe me," Mitchell says to movie star Bebe Daniels, "we're going to get ahead."

"Well," she replies, "you can use one." – *Music Is Magic* (1935)

37 A disgruntled actress, dissatisfied with her summer-stock work, complains to director Erik Rhodes that he misled her when he promised she "would get rich so quick" that it would make her head swim. "Have I become rich?" she challenges him. "Maybe not," he replies, "but your head swims." – *Chatterbox* (1936)

38 Struggling, mediocre actress Glenda Farrell returns from Atlantic City and tells her boyfriend, Herbert Marshall, a critic's remarks on her stage performance: "'Miss Walker [Farrell] gave a performance that was up to her usual standards. She was never any better.'" – *Breakfast for Two* (1937)

39 Herbert Marshall offers a toast to Glenda Farrell, a struggling, mediocre actress: "To my little Sarah Bernhardt." "Oh," Farrell objects, "I want to be a *famous* actress!" – *Breakfast for Two* (1937)

40 Struggling young actresses at a boarding house are elated that one of their group has finally found work in a nightclub chorus line. "She hasn't worked in so long," cracks Eve Arden, "that if she does get the job, it will practically amount to a comeback." – *Stage Door* (1937)

41 Ham actor and amateur sleuth Jack Oakie, forever boasting about his alleged expertise at capturing criminals, enrages a serial killer who sends him a death threat – including a notation that he disliked Oakie's last film. "That's going too far!" Oakie protests. – *Super-Sleuth* (1937)

42 Willie Best, servant to actor and self-appointed sleuth Jack Oakie, learns that a serial killer has sent his boss a death threat. "He must o' didn't like your last picture," Best supposes. – *Super-Sleuth* (1937)

43 An aspiring actress accosts publicity agent Jack Oakie, trying to impress him with her thespian talents: "I shot an arrow into the air, it landed but I know not where–" "You must lose an awful lot of arrows that way," Oakie comments as he dashes out of sight. – *Annabel Takes a Tour* (1938)

44 The police, mistaking a ham actor for a murderer, handcuff him. "Take them off," the actor insists. "You've no right to do this." "They must have seen your last picture," cracks movie director Jack Carson. – *Crashing Hollywood* (1938)

45 Broadway producer Bing Crosby asks Ned Sparks, his cigar-chomping public relations man, if there were any callers. "Only some child actors," Sparks answers. "I threw them down the stairs, and it did my heart good to hear them bounce." – *The Star Maker* (1939)

46 Publicity agent Frank Faylen, watching rehearsals for producer Alan Mowbray's new play, comments on the leading lady: "She's been eating scenery for fifteen years and hasn't hiccupped yet." – *Curtain Call* (1940)

47 Lucille Ball, playing herself, accepts an invitation to a military academy prom. Instead of an expected rousing reception at the train depot, she is greeted by a lone, stray dog. "I don't mind the bands playing," she says to her manager, "but if they don't stop shoving, I'll scream!" – *Best Foot Forward* (1943)

48 During World War II, patriotic radio and film star Martha Raye wants to follow the G.I.s overseas. "You haven't got a chance," a fellow entertainer replies. "And even if you could," adds another, "what could you do with a million soldiers?" "Are you kiddin'?" Raye retorts. – *Four Jills in a Jeep* (1944)

49 Strolling player Gene Kelly, infatuated with Judy Garland and planning to use a contraption of mirrors to hypnotize her, is reminded by a fellow actor: "The last person you hypnotized hasn't woken up yet." "That was a mistake," explains Kelly. "I happened to pick a man with sleeping sickness." – *The Pirate* (1948)

50 Drama critic George Sanders introduces his latest protégée, Miss Caswell (Marilyn Monroe), to accomplished actress Bette Davis: "Miss Caswell is an actress, a graduate of the Copacabana School of Dramatic Arts." – *All About Eve* (1950)

51 Young ambitious actress Anne Baxter is taken backstage to Broadway star Bette Davis' dressing room and relates her sad tale about losing her husband in World War II. She then tells about following her idol – Bette Davis – across the country from San Francisco to New York, all the while friendless and alone. "What a story!" Davis' gal Friday Thelma Ritter exclaims, smelling a rat. "Everything but the bloodhounds snappin' at her rear end." – *All About Eve* (1950)

52 "Do you like Shakespeare?" part-time actress Judy Holliday asks corporate tycoon Paul Douglas. "Well, I've read a lot of it." "Well, take my advice," Holliday suggests, "don't play it. It's so tiring. They never let you sit down unless you're a king." – *The Solid Gold Cadillac* (1956)

53 Movie actress Janis Paige explains to members of the press why she's throwing in the towel: "I've really had it! *The Girl from Sleepy Lagoon, The Cowboy and the Mermaid, Neptune's Mother*. I never got a chance to dry off!" – *Silk Stockings* (1957)

54 Dentist Walter Matthau introduces his girlfriend Goldie Hawn to television actor Jack Weston, one of his patients. "An actor?" she says, surprised. "Isn't that an insecure profession?" "Only financially," Weston replies. – *Cactus Flower* (1969)

55 "Are you appearing anywhere now?" Goldie Hawn asks actor Jack Weston. "Sure," he replies. "You can catch me every Friday at eleven o'clock at the State Unemployment Office." – *Cactus Flower* (1969)

56 Dance-hall hostess Shirley MacLaine relates to famous Italian actor Ricardo Montalban how impressed she was with a scene in which he consoles a crying woman by kissing each of her fingers. He doesn't remember it. "I'll never forget it," she continues. "And then you said, 'Without love, life has no meaning.'" "The things I say for money," replies Montalban. – *Sweet Charity* (1969)

57 "You know what your trouble was?" retired vaudeville comic George Burns says to ex-partner Walter Matthau. "You always took the jokes too seriously. They were just jokes. We did comedy on the stage for 23 years. I don't think you enjoyed it once." – *The Sunshine Boys* (1975)

58 A writer, after viewing excerpts from films by popular Hollywood swashbuckler Alan Swann (Peter O'Toole), snickers at the star's ludicrous costume dramas on the screen. "That's not acting," he declares. "That's kissing and jumping and drinking and humping." – *My Favorite Year* (1982)

59 Popular screen swashbuckler Peter O'Toole, drinking heavily and carousing during rehearsals of a television show, is reminded that he is an actor. "I am not an actor!" he protests. "I am a movie star!" – *My Favorite Year* (1982)

60 Actor Dustin Hoffman's fiery temper has made him a pariah to directors. His agent, Sydney Pollack, cannot find any work for him and explains why. "Are you saying nobody in New York will work with me?" Hoffman asks. "Oh, no, that's too limiting," Pollack replies. "Nobody in Hollywood wants to work with you either." – *Tootsie* (1982)

61 College professor Alan Alda discovers that sweet, demure screen heroine

Michelle Pfeiffer is in reality a coarse and testy actress. "Why, you're two people!" he blurts out. "If all I could be is two different people," she fires back, "I'd be out of business." – *Sweet Liberty* (1986)

62 "A nympho who's an actress couldn't do porno," a young actress states, "because then it wouldn't be acting." – *Rocket Gibraltar* (1988)

63 Struggling New York actor Ted Danson, relegated to television commercials, meets a theatrical director who patronizingly compliments him on his last laxative commercial. "You were hysterical," the director says. "I don't want to sound conceited or anything,

but a lot of people say that when they watched it they believed that I was constipated." – *Three Men and a Little Lady* (1990)

64 Gangster-murderer Bugsy Siegel (Warren Beatty) asks his actor-buddy George Raft (Joe Mantegna): "How would someone go about getting a screen test?" – *Bugsy* (1991)

65 A local villager, coaxed on by some of his neighbors who are trying to impress a visiting surgeon from California, describes his experiences in films. "It was just an army trainin' film," the man says. "It was about V.D. I was the bacterium. I had a big scene with penicillin." – *Doc Hollywood* (1991)

Adultery and Affairs

66 To cheer up a lovesick young man, Al Jolson tells about his brother. "He had a gal and he found out she was untrue to him." "How did he find that out?" the man asks. "He caught her with her husband." – *Big Boy* (1930)

67 Ina Claire reminisces about her divorced husband with her mother. "He was the kind of man who could kiss your hand without looking silly," her mother recalls. "I guess that's what he was doing when I needed him," Claire quips. – *The Royal Family of Broadway* (1930)

68 "I wasn't made to be a housewife," Thelma Todd complains to Groucho Marx. "Some of my best friends are housewives," replies Groucho. – *Monkey Business* (1931)

69 Barrister Ronald Colman, trying to extricate himself from an extramarital affair, asks his longtime friend, Henry Stephenson, if he had any serious love affairs. "As you say, in my time." "And

they came to an end?" Colman asks. "Should I be alive otherwise?" – *Cynara* (1932)

70 Genevieve Tobin, the flirtatious wife of Roland Young, visits Jeanette MacDonald, who is interested in her friend's amorous escapades. "And how's the composer you went with?" "He's gone," Tobin replies, "but he had such a wonderful touch." – *One Hour with You* (1932)

71 "When I married her," Roland Young says of his unfaithful wife, "she was a brunette. Now you can't believe a word she says." – *One Hour with You* (1932)

72 Flirtatious Genevieve Tobin tries to seduce doctor Maurice Chevalier when her husband Roland Young suddenly enters the room. "Madam is in a very serious condition," Chevalier explains as he tries to cover up his presence. "Why shouldn't she be?" Young replies uncaringly, already suspecting his wife of previous affairs. "Conditions are bad everywhere." – *One Hour with You* (1932)

73 As doctor Edmund Lowe receives a telephone call at his office from Jean Harlow, his patient and mistress, his wife, Karen Morley, walks in and instinctively suspects the truth. "You know," he explains lamely to his wife, "women with a lot of time on their hands? I prescribed a sedative, but she doesn't think she needs anything." "How about an apple a day?" his wife suggests. – *Dinner at Eight* (1933)

74 Middle-aged husband Frank Morgan, seeking a last fling, invites a young woman from an escort service to a hotel room. But she is more interested in exploring the psychological ramifications of the affair. "I feel unless one is an artist," she says, "that love's the only release for a man like you." "I wish you wouldn't treat this as though it was a clinic," he complains. – *By Your Leave* (1934)

75 Thelma Todd, the bored wife of a baron, informs visitor Robert Woolsey that her husband will be gone for two weeks on a boar hunt. "Then we'll have four weeks for fun," Woolsey says. "Four weeks? How's that?" "I work twice as fast as anyone else." – *Cockeyed Cavaliers* (1934)

76 The king of a mythical kingdom catches notorious lover Maurice Chevalier in the queen's bedroom. "This must be kept out of history," the king says. "Not a soul must know." "Nobody," the queen quickly agrees, "not a soul." "We were planning not even to tell your majesty," Chevalier adds. – *The Merry Widow* (1934)

77 An attractive young woman enters a talent agent's private office, causing a curious client to question the receptionist. "Who's that dame?" "The wife of a poet," the receptionist returns. "Oh, is

Georgie handling poets now?" "No, just wives." – *Strictly Dynamite* (1934)

78 Egotistical publisher Noel Coward asks a woman with whom he has had an affair if it has wrecked her life. "No," she replies wryly, "decorated it." – *The Scoundrel* (1935)

79 "I'm practically your slave," Mae West's press agent grumbles. "You are not," West counters. "Slaves are generally useful." – *Go West, Young Man* (1936)

80 Jealous husband John Barrymore utilizes chorus girl Claudette Colbert to lure away his wife's lover. Barrymore contentedly informs Colbert that their scheme is working; his wife is becoming deeply affected by her lover's rejection. "She was fighting tears," Barrymore explains. "Who won?" Colbert asks. – *Midnight* (1939)

81 Mae West, married to W. C. Fields, snuggles up to the more handsome Dick Foran. "Are you forgetting you're married?" Foran says. "I'm doing my best," West replies. – *My Little Chickadee* (1940)

82 Stockbroker Charles Ruggles confides to actress Rosalind Russell about his straying wife: "I sent Amanda to a tailor. I haven't seen the tailor since." – *No Time for Comedy* (1940)

83 Lover Fritz Feld arrives at the apartment of Lupe Velez and demands to know the whereabouts of his girlfriend Fifi. "Where is my plum," he cries, "my pigeon, my cooing pigeon?" "I think maybe you got the wrong house by mistake," Velez informs him. "We got no pigeons or plums around here. "What do you think this is – a blue-plate special?" – *Mexican Spitfire's Baby* (1941)

84 Bob Hope, William Bendix and Jerry Colonna appear in a skit in which Bendix suspects his wife of having affairs with other men. But Hope convinces him otherwise. "Can you ever forgive me?" Bendix pleads. "It's not for me to forgive you," Hope says, "but for this little flower whom you have wronged ... You don't know women. But if there's one thing Bob Hope knows, it's women. Goodbye, and remember that little wife of yours is as honest as the day is long." As Hope is about to leave, he opens the closet door by mistake and out steps Colonna. "Short day, wasn't it?" Colonna quips. – *Star Spangled Rhythm* (1942)

85 "How did you lose your money?" an impoverished English duke (Clive Brook) is asked. "Women." "Yes, I know. I mean your big money." "Big women," Brook replies. – *On Approval* (1943)

86 In the famous Manhattan serviceman's center during World War II, Alfred Lunt asks his wife: "Is that the boy who came up to me the other day and said, 'Thank you, Mr. Lunt,' and I said, 'You're welcome, but what for?' and he said, 'I'm having so much fun with your wife'?" – *Stage Door Canteen* (1943)

87 Bandleader Phil Harris, suffering from amnesia, jokes about his condition with his audience: "I tried to find out if I was a doctor, but the guitar player wouldn't let me take out his appendix. So I took out his wife." – *I Love a Bandleader* (1945)

88 Bob Hope makes a play for gangster's moll Lucille Ball. "Big Steve doesn't like me to have other boyfriends," she warns him, "but I could always tell him you're my aunt." – *Sorrowful Jones* (1949)

89 Smalltime English actor Bob Hope, impersonating an earl, tries to impress visiting Americans. "Many an afternoon we had tea, the duchess and I, while her husband the duke was busily engaged in his favorite sport." "Was that cricket?" someone asks. "Perhaps not," he replies, "but she was so irresistible." – *Fancy Pants* (1950)

90 Bob Hope recalls an escapade involving his father: "My mom told me he hid in the broom closet for two weeks. Of course Mom didn't know the maid was in there with him." – *Son of Paleface* (1952)

91 Tailor Bob Hope, posing as Casanova, enters a married woman's boudoir and proceeds to woo her. "Your lips are fire," she says. "I know," Hope replies. "It saves a fortune on matches. Don't turn in the alarm." – *Casanova's Big Night* (1954)

92 Rugged Aldo Ray returns home unexpectedly and finds another man in his bedroom. Ready to smash the interloper, he is suddenly stopped by his wife. "Don't hit him, Sam!" she yells out a warning. "He's the finance man!" – *The Naked and the Dead* (1958)

93 A client hires private detective Jack Palance to recover a priceless gem. "Do you know anything about diamonds?" the client asks. "Yeah," Palance answers. "I know I can't afford them." "Have you ever seen something that became an obsession, something you simply had to possess?" "Uh-huh," the detective responds, "but she ran away with a Texas oil man." – *The Man Inside* (1959)

94 Joan Collins, who has a special place in her heart for equally wedded Paul Newman, pays him a surprise visit in his Washington hotel room. "This is improper," he protests. "Why?" she questions. "We're both married." – *Rally 'Round the Flag, Boys* (1959)

95 Lana Turner asks Rosa, her cleaning woman (Margo), to make some coffee. Rosa thinks her employer's husband (Dean Martin) is having an affair with another woman. "I'm going to make it black, black, black and strong, and then we are going to start thinking about what every red-blooded American woman wants – alimony!" – *Who's Got the Action?* (1962)

96 A not overly discriminating newspaper reporter (Paul Newman) has had an affair with the boss' wife and is about to be transferred to an overseas assignment. "About your wife," Newman says apologetically, "if there's anything I can do—" "You've already done it," the boss replies dryly.—*A New Kind of Love* (1963)

97 Airline pilot Cliff Robertson's girlfriend complains about his erratic flying schedule: "I have all of the disadvantages of an absent lover and none of the benefits. I can't even cheat on you. You might walk in on me."—*Sunday in New York* (1963)

98 Filmmaker Walter Matthau's wife appears suddenly to catch him trying to seduce Debbie Reynolds. "After what you put me through!" she blurts out. "All the screaming and yelling—in five different languages—four of which I couldn't even understand!"—*Goodbye Charlie* (1964)

99 The wife of police inspector Clouseau (Peter Sellers) is having an affair with notorious jewel thief David Niven. As the detective is about to go to bed with his wife, he receives a mysterious call requesting that he report to a distant town. He quickly dresses and prepares to leave. "At times like this," he says to his beautiful wife, "I wish I was a simple peasant." "It's times like this that make me realize how lucky I really am," she replies.—*The Pink Panther* (1964)

100 Distraught husband Dirk Bogarde castigates his sexually restless wife (Julie Christie): "Your idea of fidelity is not having more than one man in bed at the same time."—*Darling* (1965)

101 Jeanne Moreau, the wife of English aristocrat Rex Harrison, is discovered with her lover. "You can divorce me," she proposes. "Divorce is out of the question," Harrison declares. "I know. I realize that." "Then why did you say it?" "Because," Moreau explains, "it *is* out of

the question."—*The Yellow Rolls Royce* (1965)

102 Jane Fonda, as Jason Robards' once-a-week mistress, finally questions his dual loyalty. "How can you possibly sleep with one person while you're supposed to be in love with another?" "Well," Robards rationalizes, "it's for the children." "They like to watch?" a shocked Fonda asks.—*Any Wednesday* (1966)

103 A woman in a small town reacts to a shooting: "Shooting a man for sleeping with someone else's wife? That's silly. Half the town would be wiped out." —*The Chase* (1966)

104 Walter Matthau uses the excuse that he has been to a steam bath whenever he spends evenings away from his wife. His friend Robert Morse suggests that Matthau should tell his wife that he is switching to a Finnish sauna where the customers are struck with tree branches: "Someday you may find yourself with a 'friend' who sort of gets carried away," Morse explains. "The tree branches will explain the scratches on your back."—*A Guide for the Married Man* (1967)

105 Eli Wallach's wife discovers that he is having an affair and comments: "Why is it the only time a wife knows how you feel is when you feel it for another woman?"—*How to Save a Marriage (and Ruin Your Life)* (1968)

106 Unhappy suburbanite Eli Wallach, who is unfaithful to his wife Mary, tries to explain his predicament to Dean Martin. "There's a war going on out there in the suburbs," he cries. "Do you know what it's like in those split level trenches? I'm a casualty. I'm one of the walking wounded." "According to Mary," Martin replies, "you're spending a couple of nights a week at a first-aid station." —*How to Save a Marriage (and Ruin Your Life)* (1968)

107 Just as Jason Robards is about to seduce a young virgin in his hotel room, the girl's father knocks on the door. Robards hides in a closet but is soon exposed by the irate father. "Well, hello," the unruffled Robards announces. "I'm with the hotel. This young lady complained of mice, and I was setting a trap in here when a sudden draft came along and shut the door."–*The Night They Raided Minsky's* (1968)

108 Middle-aged dentist Walter Matthau, dating Goldie Hawn, who is half his age, confides to his nurse Ingrid Bergman about his romantic affair. "I'm the first decent man she met," he says. "Are you quoting her or you?" she asks sardonically.–*Cactus Flower* (1969)

109 Middle-aged businessman Jack Weston, out on a date, meets another of his girlfriends whom he quickly sweeps to one side and offers an explanation. "I'm a member of the C.I.A.," he confides to her. "I thought you were a television actor." "That's my cover," he explains. "If you ever see me in public with another girl, you must pretend you don't know me, or you'll put my life in great danger."–*Cactus Flower* (1969)

110 Pilot Dean Martin becomes sexually charged as a result of the kisses and embraces of mistress Jacqueline Bisset–only to meet stiff resistance. "You get me up to full throttle," Martin grumbles, "and throw me into reverse. You can damage my engine!"–*Airport* (1970)

111 For years Helen Verbit has endured philandering husband Louis Zorich who is apt to leave the house at any moment. "Where are you going in the middle of the night?" she asks her fully dressed spouse. "I'm going to umpire a softball game," he replies.–*Made for Each Other* (1971)

112 "I gave her all the love in the world," Walter Matthau says to an old flame about Carlotta, his third wife, "and she cheated on me with the woman next door." "Are you sure?" "What do you mean, 'Am I sure?' They went to

San Francisco together for three days to go shopping, and all they came back with was the hotel ashtray."–*Plaza Suite* (1971)

113 Tony Roberts discovers that his wife is having an affair with another man. "Why didn't I see it coming?" he wonders. "Me, who had the foresight to buy Polaroid at 8½?"–*Play It Again, Sam* (1972)

114 Overburdened housewife and mother Barbra Streisand suspects her husband, a history professor, of having an affair with one of his colleagues. Streisand daydreams about confronting his lover. "Are you having an affair with my husband?" she asks directly. "Well, as a matter of fact, I am," her rival replies. "A closer relationship is very helpful in our work. I think it's a wonderful way to get rid of superficial inhibitions that exist between colleagues. Don't you agree?"–*Up the Sandbox* (1972)

115 Ryan O'Neal's fiancée charges into his hotel room after hearing a woman's voice there. Meanwhile, O'Neal has hidden Barbra Streisand on the window ledge. "Since when do you take bubble baths?" she asks after inspecting the suite. "It came out of the faucet that way," he quickly explains.–*What's Up, Doc?* (1972)

116 When Shelley Winters' husband runs off with a young woman, she goes to lawyer George Segal's office to file for a divorce. "The girl is a stewardess for some South American airline," she reveals. "I see," Segal says sympathetically. "I hope the plane crashes," she adds.–*Blume in Love* (1973)

117 Forty-year-old Liv Ullmann confides to ex-husband Gene Kelly that she is in love with and intends to marry a 22-year-old. "Do you have to marry him?" Kelly asks. "As opposed to what?" "Couldn't you just adopt him?"–*40 Carats* (1973)

118 "I didn't photograph very well at the last affair," a customer complains to Ernest Borgnine, owner of a hairdresser shop. "That's how I got my divorce," a female worker interjects. "What?" the confused customer asks. "They photographed me at my last affair," the woman hairdresser explains. – *Law and Disorder* (1974)

119 Woody Allen and Diane Keaton realize their romance has come to an end. "A relationship is like a shark," Allen states. "It has to constantly move forward or it dies. And I think what we've got on our hands is a dead shark." – *Annie Hall* (1977)

120 "How did the marriage end?" Jill Clayburgh asks artist Alan Bates. "Not with a whimper, but a bang," he replies. "She wrote poetry for her soul and swam a hundred laps a day for her body... Well, one day I found Matilda in bed with the high diver of the pool...." – *An Unmarried Woman* (1978)

121 Married woman Ellen Burstyn meets annually with long-time lover Alan Alda. "What's your pleasure," she asks, "a walk by the ocean, or a good book, or me?" "You." "Oh," she says, "I thought you would never ask." – *Same Time, Next Year* (1978)

122 George Segal has ex-wife Jacqueline Bisset brought to him from the airport. "They call this kidnapping," she reminds him. "Of course, it goes so well with your other sterling qualities like adultery. Let's not forget adultery." "Come on," Segal protests. "You can't call a roll in the hay with your secretary 'adultery.'" "And what would you call it – shorthand?" – *Who Is Killing the Great Chefs of Europe?* (1978)

123 Valerie Harper, facing a crisis in her life, informs friend Marsha Mason of an assignation. "Don't you understand?" she tries to explain. "If I don't have something like an affair, I'll scream." "Then scream," her friend suggests.

"Well, I thought I'd try this first." – *Chapter Two* (1979)

124 Senior citizen George Burns' married daughter questions his recent behavior, much to the former vaudeville entertainer's dismay. "I'm as sound as I've always been," he insists. "How do you think I've survived all these years? I'm careful." "Then how come you had three paternity suits?" "A man has to ad-lib once in a while." – *Just You and Me, Kid* (1979)

125 George Segal introduces his bride, Glenda Jackson, to his free-spirited mother, Maureen Stapleton, who soon begins to describe her many affairs through the years. Of a one-time lover and critic she recalls: "He was a bastard with a dallying ding-dong." – *Lost and Found* (1979)

126 Anthony Hopkins, who is having an affair with a college student, tries to define his relationship to his distraught wife Shirley MacLaine. "I love you, but I'm smitten by her." "Bitten?" "Smitten," he repeats. "Oh," she quips nervously, "I thought you said 'bitten.' I thought maybe you had rabies." – *A Change of Seasons* (1980)

127 Sensuous socialite Kathleen Turner describes her husband to Florida lawyer William Hurt. "I like him," Hurt says. "He's away most of the time." "I like him even better." – *Body Heat* (1981)

128 When passengers learn that their plane may crash, some begin to confess their transgressions. "I was unfaithful to you – just once," says a middle-aged husband to his wife. "Remember Jo, my first secretary? Forgive me." "I was unfaithful, too," his wife admits. "I understand, darling." "Remember Sue, your last receptionist?" she reminds him. – *Airplane II: The Sequel* (1982)

129 Doctor Tony Roberts is having an affair with one of his married patients in his examination room. "Sweetheart, listen," the woman addresses him.

"We can't go on like this because my husband is beginning to realize there's nothing wrong with me." "It's medically sound to have periodic checkups," he suggests. "Yes, but not so many," she persists. "The president doesn't have this kind of health care." – *A Midsummer Night's Sex Comedy* (1982)

130 Architect Burt Reynolds confides to analyst Julie Andrews that he is having an affair with a married woman and that her husband knows all about it. "He hired a detective to follow us around," Reynolds explains. "He followed us right through a car wash." – *The Man Who Loved Women* (1983)

131 Married man Dudley Moore has fallen in love with Amy Irving, who is carrying his child. He confides to his friend Richard Mulligan that he can't tell Irving, whose father is a professional wrestler, that he is already married. "If you're really worried about breaking her heart," Mulligan replies, "I wonder how she's going to feel when her father kills you." – *Mickie & Maude* (1984)

132 Police officer Raul Julia questions former patient Susan Sarandon about the murder of a local dentist suspected of having affairs with his patients. "You never were intimate with Dr. Fleckstein?" he asks. "No!" she exclaims. "I would never be intimate with – with someone who wore a pinky ring." – *Compromising Positions* (1985)

133 Divorced businessman Rodney Dangerfield tells college instructor Sally Kellerman about his failed marriage. "She played around," he explains. "When she said, 'I do,' I should have said, 'With who?'" – *Back to School* (1986)

134 Philandering Michael Caine, singing the praises of women, particularly likes the "wonderful way they smell." "I told my wife I would never look at another woman if I could cut off my nose." "What did she say!" "She said I was aiming too high." – *Sweet Liberty* (1986)

135 C.I.A. agent James Belushi informs neophyte John Ritter that his wife is having an affair with the local milkman while Ritter is away at work. Ritter goes into a rage, and Belushi is forced to physically restrain him. "I know what you're thinking," Belushi says. "I know what's going through your mind. He's got her in all different kinds of positions. She's telling him about your sexual inadequacies. They're laughing their heads off about it . . . I know. I've been through that." "Your wife did that to you?" Ritter wonders. "No, I'm not married," Belushi replies. "I went through that on the other side. But it's the same thing, right?" – *Real Men* (1987)

136 Police detective Leslie Nielsen shares a romance in his past with his present girlfriend (Priscilla Presley). "I had known her for years," he confides to Presley. "Oh, how I loved her! But she had her music. I think she had her music. She hung out with the Chicago male chorus and symphony. I don't recall her playing an instrument or being able to carry a tune. Yet she was on the road 300 days out of the year. I bought her a harp for Christmas. She asked me what it was." – *The Naked Gun* (1988)

137 Arnetia Walker, the African-American wife of playwright Ed Begley, Jr., learns that her husband has slept with a widow. "A few months ago," she announces vindictively to Begley, "your buddy Howard did some exploration of some parts of my dark continent. Dr. Doolittle here went so deep into areas unexplored by your feeble playwright hands that I got to thinking he was Lewis *and* Clark!" – *Scenes from the Class Struggle in Beverly Hills* (1989)

138 Kirstie Alley, married to a doctor and living a conventional life, criticizes younger sister Jami Gertz for her free-spirited life and her inability to sustain a relationship. "As a matter of fact," the younger sister protests, "I have had quite a few relationships." "No," Alley persists. "To call it a relationship, it has to last more than twenty-four hours." – *Sibling Rivalry* (1990)

139 Playboy millionaire Alec Baldwin on the eve of his wedding has an affair with a nightclub singer. Upon his return, Robert Loggia, his prospective father-in-law, gives him a second chance – with a dire warning: "Next time you go on a honeymoon, you'll go as a eunuch." – *The Marrying Man* (1991)

140 A police detective, assigned to a murder case, meets his old flame Priscilla Presley. "You walk out of my life – no explanation – " "Didn't you get the letters I sent you?" she inquires. "Every one of them. Didn't open them. Tore them up. Threw them in the fire." "Then you didn't get the check for $75,000 that your uncle left you in the will?" – *The Naked Gun 2½: The Smell of Fear* (1991)

141 Pampered television soap opera star Sally Field confides to her writer Whoopi Goldberg that her lover has left her. "He went home to Pittsburgh," she whines, "to Pittsburgh! Does that tell you anything about my appeal?" – *Soapdish* (1991)

Aging

142 "Were you ringing?" an elderly, slow-moving bellhop asks hotel manager Robert Woolsey. "No," Woolsey replies, "I was tolling. I thought you were dead." – *Hook, Line and Sinker* (1930)

143 Middle-aged husband Frank Morgan, trying to impress his wife that he is still young, asks his neighbor's cute seventeen-year-old daughter (Betty Grable) to reserve a dance for him at a local party later that evening. Grable agrees and, before leaving, adds: "I love the way your generation waltzes." "Children certainly can be cruel," Morgan mumbles. – *By Your Leave* (1934)

144 At a private gambling party, one woman watches the roulette wheel and suggests that it is lucky to bet the number of your birthday. "Don't be fanciful, dear," a rival quips. "There are only thirty-six numbers on the board." – *Long Lost Father* (1934)

145 A physician dismisses an aging Don Juan (Douglas Fairbanks, Sr.) who has complained of aches and fatigue. "Aren't you going to give me any prescription?" the disappointed lover asks. "I shall – a very important prescription. Don't climb more than one balcony a day." – *The Private Life of Don Juan* (1934)

146 Myrna Loy tells a reporter that her father is a sexagenarian. "They'll never put that in the paper," he says, shaking his head. – *The Thin Man* (1934)

147 Ginger Rogers confesses that Helen Broderick's husband flirted with her, but her friend takes the news in stride. "My dear," Broderick relates, "when you are as old as I am, you take your men as you find them – that is, if you can find them." – *Top Hat* (1935)

148 A veteran trouper constantly criticizes a group of young actresses. "In my day – " she begins. "Knighthood was in flower," a young actress interjects. – *Stage Door* (1937)

149 Peering at his birthday cake laden with candles, Tully Marshall remarks: "Looks like a forest fire." – *Stand-In* (1937)

150 Stage mother Sophie Tucker brings daughter Judy Garland to a theatrical agent for an audition but has problems getting past a prissy male receptionist. "I am Alice Clayton," she announces. "Surely, you have heard of me." "The name is familiar," the man behind the desk admits. "It should be. It represents eighty years in the American theater." "Really?" the surprised receptionist responds. "I must say, you carry it very well." "You idiot!" Tucker exclaims. "I was speaking of my family!" – *Broadway Melody of 1938* (1938)

151 "You don't have to worry," young Andy Hardy (Mickey Rooney) confides to his father (Lewis Stone). "I'm never going to get married – ever." "That's a momentous decision," his father reminds him. "Not until I'm middle-aged," the son adds, "twenty-five or twenty-six." – *Love Finds Andy Hardy* (1938)

152 Band manager Bob Hope says of an old, money-grubbing landlord: "He's at the stage when a woman gets on his nerves instead of on his lap." – *Some Like It Hot* (1939)

153 The Three Stooges get mixed up with high society, and Moe asks a society matron her age. "How old do I look?" she asks. "You look like a million," Moe compliments her. "Nah," Larry interjects, "she can't be that old." – *No Census, No Feeling* (1940)

154 After several years of success, adventuress and con artist Kay Francis seems to be having a difficult time ensnaring young or old playboys into her net. Faced with a dwindling checkbook and high expenses, she ponders her fate. "What's a woman to do when she's past thirty?" she muses to her companion Margaret Hamilton. "Forget about moonlight and roses, and settle for room and board," Hamilton replies. – *Play Girl* (1940)

155 Everett Sloane, a resident in a home for the aged, muses over the ravages of old age to lifetime crony

Joseph Cotten: "It's the only disease that you don't look forward to being cured of." – *Citizen Kane* (1941)

156 Greta Garbo does not reciprocate the love of Melvyn Douglas, a proper gentleman, who finally asks her whether he is too old. "I like older men," she replies teasingly. "They are so grateful." – *Two-Faced Woman* (1941)

157 An aged gentleman tries to deliver a nugget of wisdom to runaway wife Claudette Colbert. "Cold are the hands of time that creep along relentlessly," he announces. "Alone our memories resist the disintegration . . . That's hard to say with false teeth." – *The Palm Beach Story* (1942)

158 At a social event, slightly inebriated Clive Brook insults a guest by publicly disclosing her age as 41 – causing the embarrassed woman to break into tears. "She's not crying because I said she's forty-one," Brook remarks to a friend. "She's crying because she *is* forty-one." – *On Approval* (1943)

159 "Gosh," says Joan Davis looking at a picture of herself as a young girl, "I was a gainly kid." "How old were you then?" a friend asks. "Well, I'm twenty-seven now –" Davis begins. "But this picture was taken twenty-six years ago." "My, I was big for my age," explains Joan. – *George White's Scandals* (1945)

160 Fred Allen: "Oh, Mr. Benny! I was expecting a much older man." Jack Benny: "You may not believe this, but next year I'll be old enough to vote." – *It's in the Bag* (1945)

161 Retired, elderly adventurer Bob Hope receives a visit from his old crony Bing Crosby, who has a young beauty under each arm. "Take them away!" Hope cries. "The doctor says I can't have them anymore." – *Road to Utopia* (1945)

162 At a formal embassy ball an elderly ambassador gets first crack at dancing with young and pretty Ginger Rogers. "The trouble with seniority," he notes, "is that it's wasted on old men." —*Heartbeat* (1946)

163 When a prominent duke (Patric Knowles) endangers his life by pursuing the woman he loves, French envoy Cecil Kellaway voices his concern to barber Bob Hope. "The man's insane!" exclaims Kellaway. "Risking everything for love!" Can it be that important?" "How old are you?" Hope asks. —*Monsieur Beaucaire* (1946)

164 Teenage Mona Freeman cannot seem to get her boyfriend interested in local politics. "When you're older," she lectures him, "you'll realize that political issues can be much more important than personal relationships between men and women." "I got an uncle who's more interested in women than political issues, and he's forty-eight," the boy counters. —*Dear Wife* (1949)

165 A younger sister disapproves of the relationship between her sister (Linda Darnell) and an older man (Paul Douglas). "It's disgusting!" she exclaims. "He's thirty-five if he's a day!" "I wish I was that disgusting," quips middle-aged Thelma Ritter, a friend of the family. —*A Letter to Three Wives* (1949)

166 "Do you know what I think when I see a pretty girl?" an aged Oliver Wendell Holmes (Louis Calhern) asks. "Oh, to be eighty again!" —*The Magnificent Yankee* (1950)

167 Spencer Tracy is less than happy about the marriage of daughter Elizabeth Taylor and the birth of his grandson. "There's a fly in the ointment," he complains about his son-in-law. "First he steals my daughter; then he makes a grandpa out of me." —*Father's Little Dividend* (1951)

168 "You're a much younger man than I am," Bing Crosby says to Bob Hope. "Who isn't?" Hope quips. —*Road to Bali* (1952)

169 Bing Crosby and Bob Hope are surrounded by a bevy of beautiful natives. "If we can get our speedometers turned back," Hope quips, "we're in business." —*Road to Bali* (1952)

170 Bob Hope, impersonating Casanova, takes to the gondola to serenade his women. "I'm getting to the age where I can only work a canal a day," he sighs. —*Casanova's Big Night* (1954)

171 At a railroad depot in a dusty town somewhere in New Mexico, a retired station master is about to leave for New York. Next to him stands depressed railroad clerk Jerry Lewis, who would like to accompany him. "In fifty-two years you'll be getting *your* pension, and then you'll be on your way to wine, women and song," the man reminds Lewis. "In fifty-two years I wouldn't be able to sing," Lewis returns. —*Living It Up* (1954)

172 "An old man is somebody who can't take yes for an answer," quips Joe E. Lewis (Frank Sinatra) to a nightclub audience. —*The Joker Is Wild* (1957)

173 Play producer Clark Gable, sensitive about his age, is given a surprise birthday party at which he is presented with a birthday cake crowded with 51 candles. The cake particularly attracts the attention of his friend Lee J. Cobb. "It looks like the Chicago fire," Cobb quips. —*But Not for Me* (1959)

174 Aging movie star Victor Mature prides himself on his physical condition and pleads with his agent Martin Balsam to get him youthful romantic roles. "How many people in the world over forty can still say they have their own teeth?" he boasts. "How many people over fifty can still say they're only forty?" Balsam replies. —*After the Fox* (1966)

175 Jane Fonda has just turned 30 and she begins to question her life-style. Although the mistress of middle-aged

Jason Robards, she meets young Dean Jones on her thirtieth birthday and takes a liking to him. "I'm thirty years old!" she confides to him. "You certainly don't look it," he compliments her. "It only happened today."—*Any Wednesday* (1966)

176 Jane Fonda, who has just turned thirty, bemoans this fact to Jason Robards, her middle-aged lover. "I still think of myself as twenty-two," he says. "And you're eighteen. And that's the end of the subject." "What made you pick exactly eighteen for me?" she asks tenderly. "On the advice of my attorney," he explains. "Anything under eighteen is statutory rape."—*Any Wednesday* (1966)

177 Middle-aged English television star Robert Danforth (Peter Sellers) returns home from France with young, attractive Goldie Hawn. Reporters, believing the couple have been secretly married, fire a barrage of questions. "What's the difference in your ages?" one journalist asks. "Minimal," retorts Sellers.—*There's a Girl in My Soup* (1970)

178 Walter Matthau berates his wife Maureen Stapleton for not remembering dates and anniversaries, and especially for forgetting her own age. "How the hell can you make a mistake like that?" he fumes. "Can't you add? The thing that infuriates me about you is you make the mistake the wrong way. Why can't you make yourself younger instead of older, the way other women do?"—*Plaza Suite* (1971)

179 In a small town, con artist James Garner meets an attractive young woman who suddenly disappears. He storms into a barn where an elderly, grizzled caretaker is tidying things up. "Did you see a good-looking woman come in here?" Garner asks excitedly. "I sure did—about fourteen years ago," the man replies. "They've been pretty scarce ever since."—*Skin Game* (1971)

180 A middle-aged client of Liv Ullmann's real estate business admits to her that he is in love with her eighteen-year-old daughter and wants to marry her. He explains that he always wanted a large family, something his former wife failed to give him. "You always wanted children," Ullmann responds indignantly, "so now you're going to marry one."—*40 Carats* (1973)

181 "When you hit fifty," muses Redd Foxx, "clean underwear, color television and stewed prunes are right there in the top ten."—*Norman . . . Is That You?* (1976)

182 "It's comfortable with an old broad like you," middle-aged Walter Matthau says lovingly to Glenda Jackson. "I don't have to explain things all the time—like who Ronald Colman is."—*House Calls* (1978)

183 An elderly customer in a New Orleans whore house is celebrating his 75th birthday. "I haven't had a woman in longer than I care to say," he confides to the madam. "You know, she doesn't have to be beautiful—just patient."—*Pretty Baby* (1978)

184 Alan Alda: "You have to admit it's a bit odd going back to school at your age. Ellen Burstyn: "You think it's easy being the only one in your class with clear skin?"—*Same Time, Next Year* (1978)

185 Valerie Harper confides to friend Marsha Mason that she has been told recently that she has character in her face, but somehow she doesn't feel complimented. "Why is life going by so fast?" she questions. "First I was pretty. Now I'm interesting with character. Soon I'll be handsome, followed by stately; and then, worst of all, finally, remarkable for her age."—*Chapter Two* (1979)

186 Ex-vaudeville comic George Burns meets runaway teenager Brooke Shields and tries to win her confidence by regaling her with tales of his past life—which only fall flat on his young audience.

"You don't make sense," she says. "I'm not supposed to," he replies. "I'm a senior citizen." – *Just You and Me, Kid* (1979)

187 "You know, it's funny," muses senior citizen George Burns, portraying a former vaudeville entertainer. "When I was young I was called a rugged individualist; when I was in my fifties I was considered eccentric; here I am doing and saying the same things I did then and I'm labeled senile." – *Just You and Me, Kid* (1979)

188 College professor George Segal, a widower for several months, marries Glenda Jackson and takes her to meet his peppery mother, Maureen Stapleton. "I guess you're wondering how old I am?" Stapleton remarks. "No, I'm not," Jackson replies. "Good," Stapleton continues, "then I won't wonder how old you are, either." – *Lost and Found* (1979)

189 Rodney Dangerfield, as a rich, obnoxious member of an exclusive country club, saunters through the place insulting other members and their guests. "Oh, what a lovely lady!" he says to a matronly woman enjoying dinner with her friends. "Hey, baby, you're all right. You must have been something before electricity." – *Caddyshack* (1980)

190 When Walter Matthau and girlfriend Glenda Jackson finish playing cards, she reminds him of how much he owes her. "Want to take it out in trade?" he cracks. "What do you have that's worth that much?" she asks. "Like antiques?" Matthau quips. – *Hopscotch* (1980)

191 "Aging does have its compensations," admits Red Buttons. "We found out that all the things we couldn't have when we were young we didn't want anymore. Who could afford it?" – *Off Your Rocker* (1980)

192 "I heard you turned eighty today," a boy says to Henry Fonda. "That's what you heard?" "Man, that's really

old!" "You should meet my father." "Your father is still alive?" "No," Fonda replies, "but you should meet him." – *On Golden Pond* (1981)

193 "How does it feel to turn eighty?" teenager Doug McKeon asks retired professor Henry Fonda. "Twice as bad as when I turned forty," the octogenarian replies. – *On Golden Pond* (1981)

194 Elderly professor Jose Ferrer makes love to young, oversexed nurse Julie Hagerty. "Bite me," she cries. "Harder, harder." "I can't," he concedes. "These are not my teeth." – *A Midsummer Night's Sex Comedy* (1982)

195 Middle-aged Hal Holbrook, dining out with Michael Douglas, scans a restaurant menu. "Sizzling rice soup," Holbrook decides. "I love the sound when they dump the rice in. At my age that's excitement." – *The Star Chamber* (1983)

196 A little old lady enters a local police precinct and forces her way past Robin Williams and other crime victims to the desk sergeant to register her complaint. "I've been accosted!" she exclaims. "In this century?" Williams quips. – *The Survivors* (1983)

197 In a borscht-belt hotel, stand-up comic Woody Allen during a performance asks an elderly woman her age. The guest says she is 81. "You don't look a day over eighty," Allen quips. – *Broadway Danny Rose* (1984)

198 George Burns, as the Devil, appears as an elderly booking agent prepared to make a deal with music publisher Ron Silver. "It's very nice to meet you, sir," Silver shouts, taken aback at Burns' age. "Shall I speak louder?" "Not unless you can't hear what you're saying," Burns quips. – *Oh, God! You Devil* (1984)

199 Ex-convict and senior citizen Kirk Douglas visits a gym. While he is in a prone position and engaged in lifting weights, the young and sexy manager approaches and asks: "You want me to help you get it up?"—*Tough Guys* (1986)

200 Lawyers present a surprise birthday cake bedecked with many candles to a senior partner of the firm. "It looks like the Chicago Fire," she quips.—*From the Hip* (1987)

201 "When you're my age," Alan King says to son Billy Crystal, "you worry about two things—one, you're with a woman and she says: 'Let's do it again right now,' and the other is 'Who's going to come to my funeral?'"—*Memories of Me* (1988)

202 The divorced mother of a teenage daughter who has recently eloped learns that the daughter is pregnant. The suggestion that she is soon to become a grandmother devastates the mother. "I'm too young," she muses. "Grandmothers are old. They bake and they sew ... I was at Woodstock, for Christ sake! I pissed in the fields!"—*Parenthood* (1989)

203 Discussing her unmarried state with her platonic friend Harry (Billy Crystal), Sally (Meg Ryan), now in her thirties, tries to distance herself from time's shadow. "Charlie Chaplin had babies when he was seventy-three," she recalls. "But he was too old to pick them up," Harry adds.—*When Harry Met Sally . . .* (1989)

204 Ninety-one-year-old retired showbusiness star James Caan is reunited on stage with his former partner Bette Midler to receive a special award. "They gave me a big suite upstairs," Caan jokes with Midler. "And I got a big king-size bed." "You ought to lie down," she suggests. "Is that an offer?" "It's a recommendation," Midler replies.—*For the Boys* (1991)

205 Insecure, unhappy Kathy Bates complains to matronly Jessica Tandy: "I'm too young to be old and I'm too old to be young!"—*Fried Green Tomatoes* (1992)

Ambition

206 Cleopatra (Claudette Colbert) to Julius Caesar (Warren William): "Together we could conquer the world." Caesar: "Nice of you to include me." —*Cleopatra* (1934)

207 An impersonator of Don Juan is killed by a jealous husband, and all the women of Seville turn out for the funeral. When the real Don Juan (Douglas Fairbanks, Sr.), who is incognito, asks one of the mourners if she has ever met the great lover, she says no. "Then why are you in mourning?" "Because I've never met him." "But he might have ruined you." "I know," she sighs, "and now it's too late."

—*The Private Life of Don Juan* (1934)

208 Architect Alan Curtis is framed for the murder of his wife and sent to prison. His secretary (Ella Raines) visits him and is shocked at his change. "They've hurt and twisted him so," she cries. "And he had such wonderful plans for model cities."—*Phantom Lady* (1944)

209 Jack Benny, an angel sent to Earth to destroy the planet at 12 midnight, meets Reginald Gardiner, a conductor who envisions himself playing at Carnegie Hall, then in Philadelphia and next month in Chicago. "As Methuselah remarked to me one day," Benny says, "'you should live so long.'" – *The Horn Blows at Midnight* (1945)

210 Baby photographer Bob Hope's next door neighbor is Alan Ladd, a successful private detective. Hope dreams of entering the profession, but Ladd, before he leaves for Chicago, discourages him. "I wanted to be a detective, too," Hope announces in a voice-over. "It only took brains, courage and a gun, and I had the gun." – *My Favorite Brunette* (1947)

211 A spirited Marsha Mason tells husband James Caan what she wants out of life: "I want a home; I want a family and I want a career. I want everything. And there's no harm in wanting it, George, but there isn't a chance in hell we're going to get it all anyway." – *Chapter Two* (1979)

212 It hasn't worked out, and Lynda (Mary Steenburgen) is leaving Melvin (Paul Le Mat). "C'est la vie," she says flippantly. "What's that?" he asks. "French, Melvin. I used to dream of becoming a French interpreter." "You don't speak French." "I told you it was only a dream." – *Melvin and Howard* (1980)

213 Lonely bachelor Tom Hanks has but one pervasive desire: "To meet a woman, fall in love, get married, have a kid, and see him play a tooth in the school play." – *Splash* (1984)

214 A young man ridicules his friend who dreams of traveling into space in the near future. "My dreams are more practical," the realist counters. "I'm going to go to Hollywood, do some modeling and then buy a professional football team." – *Doin' Time on Planet Earth* (1988)

215 A newspaperman, during a speech to his coworkers, reveals one of his goals. "All my life," he announces, "I dreamed of . . . leaving the newspaper business behind and moving to some quiet little town in the country and putting down on paper the novel I know I have inside me." "That's not a novel," someone quips, "that's heartburn." – *Funny Farm* (1988)

216 Dizzy Sally Kirkland laments the loss of lover Keith Carradine, her partner and petty thief who fled with the jewels from their last job. "Every girl has a dream," she confides to another gang member, "and mine has always been to find me a completely dishonest cowboy." – *Cold Feet* (1989)

217 Entering a car race, timid John Candy teams up with Donna Dixon, an aspiring actress and not-too-bright mistress of a racing-car owner. "You know," Candy admits toward the end of the race, "I got a feeling we're gonna win this thing. I'm gonna win the Cannonball. I'm gonna be famous." "We'll both be famous," she adds. "You as a driver and me as an actress on 'Divorce Court.'" – *Speed Zone* (1989)

218 Randy Quaid catches a burglar in the act of looting his apartment. The despondent thief breaks down emotionally and spills out his failed hopes and aspirations to Quaid. "I wanted to be a gentleman burglar," he confesses. "Go to fancy parties, wear a tuxedo, hobnob with all those glamorous women, go upstairs and steal all their jewelry – like Ruffles." "That's 'Raffles,'" Quaid corrects him. "'Ruffles' is a potato chip." – *Martians Go Home* (1990)

Ancestry

219 Southern plantation owner Joe Cawthorn tells Bert Wheeler about one of his ancestors. "They hung her, huh?" Wheeler asks. "I guess so," Cawthorn replies. "She was high strung." – *Dixiana* (1930)

220 "Have any of your ancestors or relatives ever died an unnatural death?" a doctor asks patient Eddie Cantor. "My grandfather," Cantor replies. "He died of throat trouble. They hung him." – *Insurance* (1930)

221 "My ancestors came over on the *Mayflower*," Almira Sessions boasts to Mae West. "You're lucky," West replies. "Now they have immigration laws." – *The Heat's On* (1943)

222 American soldiers are billeted in an old English castle during World War II. One G.I., Robert Young, together with little Margaret O'Brien, meets the local ghost (Charles Laughton), but Young scoffs at the apparition. "Americans, my child," Laughton says to the little girl. "What can people without ancestors know about ghosts?" – *The Canterville Ghost* (1944)

223 Little Margaret O'Brien during World War II welcomes a platoon of American soldiers, stationed in England, to her family castle where she regales her guests with frightening tales of her ancestors. "The dour Duchess of Steffield was found one night on the balcony outside her bedroom stark raving mad," she relates in an ominous tone. "There's the loveliest picture of her gibbering like an idiot." – *The Canterville Ghost* (1944)

224 Lou Costello contends he doesn't have "four fathers" while Bud Abbott insists that he does have "forefathers." "Well, if I did," Costello weakens, "then only one came home nights." – *Comin' Round the Mountain* (1951)

225 A prominent middle-aged couple with a family name dating back many generations wind up at a police station because of a domestic quarrel between their married daughter and son-in-law. "I'm just happy that my forebears of my daddy are not here to witness this disgrace...." the embarrassed mother complains. "Listen, Scarlett O'Hara," her husband (John McGiver) exclaims. "If by your forebears you mean your carpet-baggin' grandpa, jail was no novelty to him!" – *Period of Adjustment* (1962)

Animals and Insects

226 "I was never able to ride a jackass," admits a pompous English jockey to Al Jolson. "You better get on to yourself." – *Big Boy* (1930)

227 "Do you have any wild duck?" a customer asks waiter Robert Woolsey. "No," Woolsey rejoins. "But if you like we'll bring you a tame one and you can aggravate him."–*Half Shot at Sunrise* (1930)

228 "Those moth balls are no good," complains Robert Woolsey after throwing some at moths. "I've never hit a moth yet. Still, I'm glad I didn't because if I hit one, the moth would cry, and I can't stand to see a moth bawl."–*Caught Plastered* (1931)

229 "There are no contented bulls," Robert Young informs his friend Eddie Cantor, who is scheduled to confront a ferocious bull. "Oh, don't be silly," Cantor argues. "There are contented cows." "Yes." "Well," Cantor reasons, "for every contented cow there must be a contented bull."–*The Kid from Spain* (1932)

230 Eddie Cantor, impersonating a famous bullfighter, meets the bull he will subsequently confront in the ring. "He's so tame," someone remarks, "he'll eat off your hand." "Yeah," a reluctant Cantor agrees, "he may eat off your leg, too." –*The Kid from Spain* (1932)

231 A young woman, upon discovering a litter of kittens, muses out loud: "I wonder what their parents were?" "Careless, my cupcake, careless," W. C. Fields replies.–*International House* (1933)

232 "What's that?" Jimmy Durante asks taxidermist Buster Keaton, pointing to a stuffed animal. "A kangaroo," explains Keaton. "A native of Australia." "Oh!" Durante cries in horror. "My sister married one of them!"–*What! No Beer?* (1933)

233 Charlie Chan (Warner Oland) takes on a tough case and remarks: "Hen squats with caution on thin egg."–*Charlie Chan's Courage* (1934)

234 "How are the mosquitoes this summer?" a hotel guest asks manager Harry Ritz. "Oh, they're fine," he replies. "But we're teaching the guests how to bite back."–*Hotel Anchovy* (1934)

235 Eddie Cantor in Egypt is pleasantly surprised when he discovers a young woman he has met is the daughter of a sheik. "A sheik's daughter!" he exclaims. "I thought there was something distinctive about you." "Oh," she replies, "that must be from hanging around with the camels."–*Kid Millions* (1934)

236 Shemp Howard: "Did you ever ride a donkey?" Harry Gribbon: "No." Howard: "Then get on to yourself." –*My Mummy's Arms* (1934)

237 As amateur sleuth William Powell's meek little terrier, Asta, lies passively under a table, the detective warns a miscreant: "Don't make a move or that dog will tear you to pieces." –*The Thin Man* (1934)

238 Gracie Allen scares off a duck, much to the displeasure of George Burns, who informs her that particular species of duck was very rare. "I don't like rare ducks," she replies. "I like my ducks well done."–*We're Not Dressing* (1934)

239 When ranch owner Mae West says she intends to enter one of her horses in an international derby, her lawyer asks: "Are you a good judge of horseflesh?" "I don't know," she replies. "I never ate any."–*Goin' to Town* (1935)

240 Fred Astaire offers to drive Ginger Rogers, dressed for horseback riding, to the stables. "No, thank you," she replies. "I have a hansom cab waiting for me outside." "With a horse in front of it?" he asks. "Yes, the stable people . . . feel the horse is coming back." "Well," Astaire ripostes, "where has he been?"–*Top Hat* (1935)

241 Dancer Fred Astaire and model Ginger Rogers parry about his equestrian skills. "What is this strange power you have over horses?" she asks. "Horsepower," he quips.–*Top Hat* (1935)

242 A woman aboard an ocean liner asks Arthur Treacher where seagulls go at night. "Seagulls?" Treacher muses. "They go to the gullery."–*Anything Goes* (1936)

243 Sailor Buddy Ebsen on shore leave tries to flirt with a waitress. "I'm crossing parrots with carrier pigeons," he says. "What for?" she asks. "So you can send verbal messages."–*Born to Dance* (1936)

244 Joe E. Brown has just ridden a wild horse, barely surviving the episode. After being thrown from the horse at the stable, Brown's servant finds him still grasping a handful of hair from the animal's mane. "Put everything away," Brown orders his servant and, handing him the strands, adds: "Remember the mane."–*Polo Joe* (1936)

245 "I'm like an elephant," police chief Lloyd Nolan boasts. "I never forget." "What's an elephant got to remember?" his assistant wonders.–*Every Day's a Holiday* (1938)

246 Lionel Stander is forced to ride in a cattle car. "Get off my foot!" he yells at a steer. "Get off my foot or I'll cut a steak out of you!"–*Professor Beware* (1938)

247 Shirley Temple, living in an orphan asylum, confronts its stern director who threatens to take away Shirley's pet duck. "My duck does wonderful tricks," the child says, in an effort to save the creature. "My duck can lay an egg." "And what's so wonderful about that?" the matron asks coldly. "Well," Temple replies, "can you lay an egg?"–*Rebecca of Sunnybrook Farm* (1938)

248 Lovely Dorothy Lamour, as a guest of a movie studio, catches film star Bob Hope's eye. "Your face seems very familiar," she says. "You've probably seen it plastered all over the country," he says proudly, "plastered in barnyards, chicken coops and stables." "Well," Lamour responds, "I suppose someone has to keep the cows contented."–*Caught in the Draft* (1941)

249 Edmund O'Brien, posing as a big-game hunter, is forced to lecture before a group of naturalists. "We took a tiger from India to see how he'd like it in Africa," he explains. "How interesting," remarks the leader, Franklin Pangborn. "What were the results?" "He got homesick."–*Obliging Young Lady* (1941)

250 Bing Crosby is trying to persuade Bob Hope to wrestle a live octopus as a carnival attraction, but Hope, after seeing the creature, is reticent. "Why train him to wrestle?" questions Hope. "Why don't you train him to knit? He can work on four sweaters at the same time." –*Road to Zanzibar* (1941)

251 Bob Hope is peeved at his vaudeville partner–a show-stopping penguin. "You keep hogging this act–" Hope threatens, "you and me are going to have a talk with a taxidermist."–*My Favorite Blonde* (1942)

252 Kay Kyser to Mischa Auer: "Maybe we could cross kangaroos with raccoons and raise fur coats with pockets in them."–*Around the World* (1943)

253 "We had a carrier pigeon in the last war," Dr. Watson (Nigel Bruce) regales Sherlock Holmes (Basil Rathbone). "The poor bird kept flying 'round and 'round in circles . . . We found out later it was cross-eyed." –*Sherlock Holmes in Washington* (1943)

254 "Spitz?" someone asks about the species of dog belonging to William Powell. "No, just growls," Powell quips. –*The Thin Man Goes Home* (1944)

255 Bud Abbott: "Did you ever ride a jackass?" Lou Costello: "No." Bud Abbott: "You better get on to yourself." –*Abbott and Costello in Hollywood* (1945)

256 "Those dogs won't bite you," their owner tells Pat O'Brien and George Murphy. "They only bite strangers." "Then how about introducing us?" asks Murphy–*Having Wonderful Crime* (1945)

257 Leon Errol has trouble explaining to Lou Costello that a "horse ate his fodder" and that a racehorse named Lucky George is a mudder. "How can he be a mudder?" asks a befuddled Costello. "Sometimes a 'he' is a better mudder than a 'she,'" Errol explains. "How can you tell?" "By their feet." – *The Noose Hangs High* (1948)

258 Racehorse owner Bing Crosby and his assistant, both broke, ask a stable owner for two cots for themselves. Bing explains that his horse is a winner and shouldn't be left alone. "This horse is a sleeper," he says in an attempt to impress the suspicious stable owner. "You want a cot for the horse, too?" the man asks. – *Riding High* (1950)

259 When young Carleton Carpenter is drafted into the army and takes along his pet lion, he explains to the post commander that he can't bear to be apart from his pet. The colonel asks the soldier's age. "I'm twenty-one, sir." "Oh, if you're going to be in love with a lion, I guess that's the right age for it." – *Fearless Fagan* (1952)

260 Groucho Marx chides his pal, gullible William Bendix, who has been tricked into buying a racehorse with bad ankles. "He's gonna make a million dollars," Bendix insists. "What is he – a counterfeiter as well as a horse?" Groucho asks. – *A Girl in Every Port* (1952)

261 Fred Allen and Oscar Levant find themselves confronting a bear. "He's a cinnamon bear!" Allen exclaims. "I don't care what flavor he is," Levant replies, "he's more apt to taste me!" – *O. Henry's Full House* (1952)

262 Unemployed vaudeville players Bing Crosby and Bob Hope, forced off a train, end up in the midst of a herd of sheep. "You know," quips Crosby, "for a couple of guys on the lam, we're in pretty good company." – *Road to Bali* (1952)

263 Bob Hope and Roy Rogers are captured and tied up by outlaws. "When Trigger sees what a spot we're in," offers Rogers, "he'll get us out. He has horse sense." "If he had any sense," Hope replies, "he wouldn't be a horse." – *Son of Paleface* (1952)

264 "I think your dog ate one of my earrings," guest Doris Day says to a party hostess. "Oh," returns the hostess, "it's so small, I don't think it will do her any harm." – *Please Don't Eat the Daisies* (1960)

265 Jimmy Durante is caught leading an elephant out of a circus. "Where are you going with that elephant?" someone challenges him. "What elephant?" Durante asks, placing his body in front of the pachyderm in a fruitless effort to hide it. – *Billy Rose's Jumbo* (1962)

266 After a flock of gulls dive-bomb a picnic, young Tippi Hedren asks her companion: "Mitch, this isn't usual, is it?" – *The Birds* (1963)

267 At a costume party in which the lights have gone out, police inspector Clouseau (Peter Sellers), dressed in a suit of armor, collides with a female guest masquerading as Cleopatra, who is carrying a live snake. "Take your filthy hands off my asp!" the young woman exclaims. – *The Pink Panther* (1964)

268 Woody Allen, awakened in 2173, nervously questions Diane Keaton about the denizens of the forest: "Are there strange animals I should know about here – anything weird and futuristic like the body of a crab and the head of a social worker?" – *Sleeper* (1973)

269 Police inspector Clouseau (Peter Sellers), checking into a hotel, asks the elderly clerk if his dog bites. When the man answers that it does not, Sellers offers his hand to the creature which proceeds to bite him. "I thought you said your dog does not bite," Sellers remarks. "That is not my dog," the clerk replies. – *The Pink Panther Strikes Again* (1976)

270 Mel Brooks, as the chief psychiatrist of an institute, receives a flashing signal in his office from a patient who thinks he is a cocker spaniel. The doctor has difficulty believing that this disturbed patient can send such an intelligent signal. "Well," his assistant offers, "cockers are very bright." – *High Anxiety* (1977)

271 A scientist urges U.S. officials to consider other means than destruction in dealing with South American killer bees. "You have to listen! You have to listen to what the bees have to say!" "You want us to conduct peace negotiations with bugs?" an army officer questions. – *The Bees* (1978)

272 New York talent agent Woody Allen tries to peddle an act to a prospective client: "What about Eddie Clark's penguin? . . . The penguin skates on the stage dressed as a rabbi." – *Broadway Danny Rose* (1984)

273 Beverly Hills housewife Bette Midler hires a dog psychiatrist to learn why her pet is not eating. "He has other problems," the psychiatrist informs her. "I believe he suffers from nipple anxiety. Probably came from a nine-dog litter." – *Down and Out in Beverly Hills* (1986)

274 Gilda Radner: "Did you hear what the bug said to the windshield?" Gene Wilder: "What?" Radner: "That's me all over." – *Haunted Honeymoon* (1986)

275 Salesman Tom Hanks' pretty hostess takes him on a tour of a ranch where they both observe horses mating. "Afterwards, what do they do," Hanks asks, "go back to the barn for a cigarette?" – *Nothing in Common* (1986)

276 Dom DeLuise, a hospital patient, begins to entertain a group of children in their ward. "First of all, I had this dog – no nose," he says. "How did he smell?" they ask. "Terrible." – *Loose Cannons* (1990)

Appearance

277 Groucho Marx envisions married life with Margaret Dumont: "I could see you now, bending over a stove – only I can't see the stove." – *The Cocoanuts* (1929)

278 "Did anyone ever tell you," Groucho Marx says to Margaret Dumont, "you look just like the Prince of Wales? I don't mean the present Prince of Wales. One of the old Wales. And believe me, when I say Wales, I mean whales. I know a whale when I see one." – *The Cocoanuts* (1929)

279 "I was never so humiliated!" says Trixie Friganza, following a mishap caused by Buster Keaton at a movie preview. "I'm ashamed to show my face!" "I don't blame you," Keaton agrees. – *Free and Easy* (1930)

280 "Say, are you married?" Bert Wheeler's date inquires suspiciously. "No," he replies, "I just naturally look worried." – *Half Shot at Sunrise* (1930)

281 "Last week I looked so terrible," claims hypochondriac Eddie Cantor, "two undertakers left a deposit on me." – *Whoopee!* (1930)

282 A crude delivery boy hands a package to bachelor Lowell Sherman's servant and waits for him to sign the proper form. "Say," the boy remarks, "ain't I seen you someplace before?" "I hardly think so," the servant replies haughtily. "No, I guess not," the boy concludes. "I was mistaken. I thought I seen everythin'." – *Bachelor Apartment* (1931)

283 Ship captain Ben Taggart is searching for stowaway Groucho Marx and describes him to none other than Groucho himself: "He goes around with a mustache." "I go around with a mustache," says Groucho. "Don't you think a mustache can get lonely?" – *Monkey Business* (1931)

284 Bert Wheeler, dressed in drag, invokes a comment from a woman who remarks that Bert looks like a loose woman. "Don't worry," Robert Woolsey responds, "she'll be tight before the evening is over." – *Peach O'Reno* (1931)

285 Student Harpo Marx hangs up a picture of a circus woman wearing tights, and instructor Groucho suspects Chico. "Is this your picture?" Groucho asks. "I don't think so," Chico innocently replies. "It doesn't look like me." – *Horse Feathers* (1932)

286 Former stage actress Marie Dressler, now overweight, recalls her days of fame when she was the toast of Broadway: "They named everything after me – cigars, racehorses, perfume, battleships – they were a little previous on that." – *Dinner at Eight* (1933)

287 "Gentlemen," says the captain of a luxury liner to diplomats Bert Wheeler and Robert Woolsey, "you honor my ship." "After a good look at some of the passengers on this ship," quips Woolsey, "I imagine that anybody would be an honor." – *Diplomaniacs* (1933)

288 Millionairess Margaret Dumont greets the President of Freedonia (Groucho Marx): "Oh, your excellency." "You're not bad yourself," replies Groucho. – *Duck Soup* (1933)

289 "For a woman, you cover quite a bit of ground," Groucho Marx says to Margaret Dumont. "You better beat it.

They're going to build an office on the ground you're standing on." – *Duck Soup* (1933)

290 Ned Sparks, assistant to Broadway producer Warner Baxter, develops a dislike to a music show's cost-conscious investor (Guy Kibbee). "I don't like his face or any other part," Sparks growls. "He looks like a Bulgarian bald eagle mourning its first born." – *42nd Street* (1933)

291 Sailor Jimmy Durante is seen by some British seamen as he is about to dock his dinghy. "Hey, look!" says a British sailor, pointing to Durante's nose. "The Yanks have brought along a bloomin' pelican." – *Hell Below* (1933)

292 Two actresses meet in a theatrical producer's waiting room. "My," says the one leaving, "you're gaining weight." "Yes," replies the one entering, "I'll soon be *your* size." – *Morning Glory* (1933)

293 Admitted kleptomaniac Bert Wheeler and his pal Robert Woolsey overhear one young maid tell another that a countess has had her face lifted. "Don't look at me," Wheeler says, turning to his friend. "I didn't take it." – *Cockeyed Cavaliers* (1934)

294 Eddie Cantor is trapped into marrying the homely daughter of a short-tempered sheik. The sheik orders his men to prepare Cantor for the wedding ceremony. "Take the dog away," the sheik commands. "Take her away," Cantor echoes, directing the guards to the princess. – *Kid Millions* (1934)

295 "If women would only train their stomachs and watch their midriffs," declares eccentric millionaire George Arliss, "the world would be a far better place for a man to live in." – *The Last Gentleman* (1934)

296 British soldier Reginald Denny regales his comrades-in-arms with his amorous experiences with native women in the South Seas. "They're a bit on the dark side," one soldier interjects. "The longer you're there," Denny explains, "the lighter they get." – *The Lost Patrol* (1934)

297 "You're a dangerous woman," wary and distrustful Paul Cavanagh says to Mae West. "Thanks," West rejoins. "You look good to me, too." – *Goin' to Town* (1935)

298 "I notice when you women look at yourselves in the mirror, you always walk up and get a front view of yourselves," observes Bob Burns. "You ought to back up to a mirror once in a while. You don't seem to care how you look in the back." – *The Big Broadcast of 1937* (1936)

299 Radio station manager Jack Benny is trying to rehearse a skit with a motley crew of actors. One extremely overweight actress catches his attention. "Come here, please, both of you," he addresses the woman. – *The Big Broadcast of 1937* (1936)

300 In a frontier town, property owner John Little, standing well over six feet tall, introduces himself to recent arrival Bert Wheeler. "I'm Little." "Well," returns Wheeler, "come around and see me when you're grown up." – *Silly Billies* (1936)

301 Groucho Marx, after examining Margaret Dumont, concludes that she has trouble with her blood pressure. A Viennese specialist objects: "She looks like the healthiest woman I ever met." "You look like you never met a healthy woman," Groucho retorts. – *A Day at the Races* (1937)

302 "She's so stout," quips Robert Woolsey about a woman, "that every time she gets her shoes shined, she has to take the bootblack's word for it." – *High Flyers* (1937)

303 Robin Hood (Errol Flynn) invites the rotund but agile Friar Tuck (Eugene Pallette) to join the men of Sherwood

Forest. "Who's that?" one of the band asks. "He's one of us," Flynn explains. "It seems to be he's three of us," another jests. – *The Adventures of Robin Hood* (1938)

304 Oliver Hardy arrives at a soldier's home prepared to take Stan Laurel home. Hardy hasn't seen his pal for 20 years and, beholding him in a chair designed for an amputee, he assumes the worst. He begins to carry Laurel until he notices his friend has both legs. In exasperation he asks why Laurel didn't tell him he had both legs. "Well, you didn't ask me," Laurel replies. "I've always had them." – *Block-Heads* (1938)

305 When Lucille Ball reports her husband Joe Penner as missing, the police ask her for a detailed description. "He's nondescript," she offers. "That's the best way to describe him." – *Go Chase Yourself* (1938)

306 Jimmy Durante: "I guess I'm not as bad as I look, eh?" Girl: "You couldn't be!" Durante: "That does it! From now on when you talk to me, start the conversation with 'goodbye.'" – *Little Miss Broadway* (1938)

307 Socialites Helen Broderick and her niece, Ann Sothern, find themselves penniless. Victor Moore, one of their meddling creditors, tries to help them. "Suppose you and I put our heads together," he says to the aunt. "You think they'd look well together?" Broderick quips. – *She's Got Everything* (1938)

308 "I look the same – wet or dry," a very proper Margaret Hamilton informs Wallace Beery. – *Stablemates* (1938)

309 "We have a lovely student body," a matronly college official says to Moe Howard. "Yours wouldn't be too bad, either," he retorts, "if you took off about 20 pounds." – *Violent Is the Word for Curly* (1938)

310 Patsy Kelly, a maid at an estate, sees a horrible face staring through one of the windows on a stormy night. "Did you see that face?" she screams. "I'll bet when he gets drunk, snakes see him!" – *The Gorilla* (1939)

311 "I do not like your face," a European aristocrat says to American tourist Bob Hope. "Well," Hope retorts, "if you had a face, I wouldn't like it either." – *Never Say Die* (1939)

312 "He's so big and strong," a divorced woman sighs. "Have you noticed the play in his muscles? Musical! Musical!" "Great Scott!" Marjorie Main interjects. "You don't mean to say his arms squeak?" – *The Women* (1939)

313 "There's been a mistake in my change," a customer sharply says to carnival owner W. C. Fields. "I'm short." "Don't brag about it," Fields replies. "I'm only five-feet-eight myself." – *You Can't Cheat an Honest Man* (1939)

314 Charlie McCarthy to W. C. Fields: "Are you eating a tomato or is that your nose?" – *You Can't Cheat an Honest Man* (1939)

315 Groucho Marx has been previously swindled by Chico. "Say," Groucho inquires, "where did I see your face before?" "Right where it is now," Chico replies. – *Go West* (1940)

316 Rosalind Russell confronts hoodlum Abner Biberman about the emotional state of her future mother-in-law. "What did you pull on Mrs. Baldwin this time – you and that albino of yours?" "You talkin' about Angelina. She ain't no albino. She was born in this country." – *His Girl Friday* (1940)

317 "Clementine," Allyn Joslyn addresses overweight maid Louise Beavers, "are you sitting on my hat?" "So I am," she says apologetically. "I completely covered it. Well, it's a small hat." "A sombrero would have met with the same fate," Joslyn charges. – *No Time for Comedy* (1940)

318 Songwriter Basil Rathbone, unable to create any new tunes, pines for his lost love. "My heart just stopped singing when she died," he sighs. "She didn't die," assistant Oscar Levant reminds him. "She got fat." – *Rhythm on the River* (1940)

319 When English pirates attack and plunder a Spanish ship, the English maid (Una O'Connor) says apologetically to the ambassador's niece (Brenda Marshall): "My lady, they are not typical Englishmen." "You're quite right," interjects a bony-cheeked, toothless, long-nosed pirate. "They ain't all as handsome as we are." – *The Sea Hawk* (1940)

320 "She's the most marvelous girl in the world," James Stewart describes his pen pal to avuncular fellow employee Felix Bressart. "Is she pretty?" "She has such ideals," Stewart continues, "such a point of view on things … She's so far above the girls you meet today. There's simply no comparison." "So she's not very pretty," Bressart concludes. – *The Shop Around the Corner* (1940)

321 "Did anyone ever tell you you look like Deanna Durbin?" Ole Olsen asks Martha Raye. "Why, no." "No wonder!" Olsen and Chic Johnson yell in unison. – *Hellzapoppin* (1941)

322 Eccentric millionaire Charles Laughton has just arisen from his deathbed, surprising his family doctor. He dresses, looks at his profile in the mirror, observes how large his trousers have become, and is piqued by his new shape. "I've been tampered with!" he declares. – *It Started with Eve* (1941)

323 Lou Costello storms into an air force office where a major is berating flier Dick Foran, Lou's friend. "Young man," the major charges, "you're intruding!" "I think so, too," replies Costello, looking at his own paunch. "Maybe I should wear a girdle." – *Keep 'Em Flying* (1941)

324 A domineering nurse attempts to wean defiant Monty Woolley away from sweets. "My great-aunt Jennifer ate a whole box of candy every day of her life," Woolley responds. "She lived to be 102, and when she had been dead three days, she looked better than you do now." – *The Man Who Came to Dinner* (1941)

325 Big-time gambler Humphrey Bogart and sidekick William Demarest search a house which is a front for Nazi spies. Demarest spots a painting of Hitler. "Schickelgruber the house painter," he says to Bogart. "I recognize the face," Bogart replies, "but I don't know where to place it." – *All Through the Night* (1942)

326 "Now," an energetic Jack Carson says, "we'll all go to the Dixie House and have a steak, some French fries and some wine – all on me." "You'd be a pretty sight," Henry Fonda wisecracks. – *The Male Animal* (1942)

327 Lou Costello tells pal Bud Abbott about the only woman he ever loved: "She was a bowlegged cowgirl, but something terrible happened. She couldn't get her calves together." – *Rio Rita* (1942)

328 Hot-tempered island chieftain Anthony Quinn is jealous of Dorothy Lamour's romantic interest in Bing Crosby. "Who is this goat," Quinn inquires, "this moon-faced son of a one-eyed monkey?" "I wouldn't let him call you that," Bob Hope declares, "even if there is a resemblance." – *Road to Morocco* (1942)

329 Eccentric scholar Edward Everett Horton's fortune was derived from toothpaste. Another tycoon, a flabby, rotund man, recognizes him. "You're toothpaste, aren't you?" he asks. "I'm gelatin." "Really?" Horton replies, perusing the portly stranger. "I believe it." – *Springtime in the Rockies* (1942)

330 "You ought to diet," Wally Brown says, pointing to army buddy Alan

Carney's paunch. "No," Carney protests, "I like this color." – *Adventures of a Rookie* (1943)

331 An elderly, straitlaced spinster protests to a producer about her pretty niece appearing in a Broadway musical show. "Do you think I'd let any man see my legs!" she challenges. "Do you think he'd want to?" he asks. – *The Heat's On* (1943)

332 "When I was three months old," prizefighter Leo Gorcey jokes with reporters, "I run away from home. Six months later I come back, my father takes one look at me, and he runs away from home." – *Kid Dynamite* (1943)

333 An American platoon in England during World War II is invited to stay at the de Canterville castle. The men anxiously line up and straighten out their uniforms in anticipation of getting a glimpse of their hostess, Lady de Canterville, a member of royalty. Suddenly, in walks six-year-old Margaret O'Brien. "Holy smoke!" exclaims Rags Ragland. "It's a midget!" – *The Canterville Ghost* (1944)

334 World War II sergeant William Demarest tells dejected Eddie Bracken, discharged after only one month in the Marines, how he fought with Bracken's father in World War I. "He was a fine-looking fellow," Demarest adds. "He didn't look like you at all." – *Hail the Conquering Hero* (1944)

335 Police inspector Richard Lane and his assistant pursue suspected jewel thief Boston Blackie (Chester Morris) into a hotel where the clerk blocks the officers from entering a room. "We're going through!" insists Lane. "Over my dead body!" the woman objects. "Don't be so modest, lady," the other officer says. "There's still plenty of life in you." – *One Mysterious Night* (1944)

336 "A face like mine is hard to forget," Lou Costello says to Bud Abbott. "How do you know?" asks Abbott. "I've been trying for years."—*Abbott and Costello in Hollywood* (1945)

337 Host Clifton Webb venomously characterizes one of his guests: "That's the wife of the Austrian critic. She always looks like she's been out in the rain feeding the poultry."—*The Dark Corner* (1946)

338 Reporter Allyn Joslyn, searching for a missing witness, asks the missing woman's landlady for a description. "She's thin, she's got red hair and I think she's a Republican," the woman replies.—*It Shouldn't Happen to a Dog* (1946)

339 Hotel manager Groucho Marx accuses a distinguished middle-aged couple trying to register at the desk of not being married. "Sir," the husband explodes, "this lady is my wife. You should be ashamed of yourself." "If this lady is your wife," Groucho retorts, "*you* should be ashamed."—*A Night in Casablanca* (1946)

340 "You're looking younger and more beautiful every day," Rex Harrison greets his dour aunt. "How do you do it?" "Simple," the woman replies. "I put it on in the morning and I remove it at night."—*Notorious Gentleman* (1946)

341 Amateur sleuths Leo Gorcey and Huntz Hall investigate phony spiritualist Dan Seymour in his studio where he begins to read their future in his crystal ball: "I see a man—a short man—" "If he's in there," Hall interrupts, "he'd have to be short."—*Hard Boiled Mahoney* (1947)

342 An attractive woman walks into the Three Stooges' (Moe, Larry and Shemp) dry-cleaning store. "Do you dye?" she asks Shemp. "That's his natural expression," replies Moe.—*Sing a Song of Six Pants* (1947)

343 Three somber foreign agents follow radio announcer Bob Hope into an elevator. "Perhaps we should introduce ourselves," one of the trio

says. "You do look familiar," Hope replies, "but I just can't place the graveyard."—*Where There's Life* (1947)

344 Nick Charles (William Powell) joins wife Myrna Loy and little Nick, Jr. (Dean Stockwell) at the breakfast table. "You look like a page out of *Esquire*," his wife comments on his dapper attire. "Not the page I saw," his son interjects.—*Song of the Thin Man* (1947)

345 "Go look in a mirror," Bud Abbott advises Lou Costello. "Why should I hurt my own feelings?" Costello replies.—*Abbott and Costello Meet Frankenstein* (1948)

346 Bob Hope and little Mary Jane Saunders hit it off badly at first, but later when Hope buys her a hearty dinner, her attitude changes. "You're not a monster," the child says. "You only look like a monster."—*Sorrowful Jones* (1949)

347 At a party, theater critic George Sanders points out a producer to aspiring young actress Marilyn Monroe. "Why do they all look like unhappy rabbits?" she questions. "Because that's what they are," he answers. "Now go and make him happy."—*All About Eve* (1950)

348 Andy Devine to his sweetheart Joan Davis: "You're the most beautiful girl in the world, and you've got everything. Of course, some of the things you've got you'd be better off without."—*The Traveling Saleswoman* (1950)

349 Bob Hope, disguised as an elderly spinster, explains that he used to have an hourglass figure. "You still have your hourglass figure, my dear," a woman comments, "but most of the sand has gone to the bottom."—*The Lemon Drop Kid* (1951)

350 When ungainly college student Jerry Lewis appears in his one-piece pajamas, roommate Dean Martin quips: "What are you trying to do—grow up to be a rabbit?"—*That's My Boy* (1951)

351 Bookstore clerk Audrey Hepburn, underestimating her beauty, cannot believe that fashion photographer Fred Astaire can transform her into a model. "When I get through with you," Astaire says confidently, "you'll look like – well, what do you call beautiful? A tree? – you'll look like a tree." – *Funny Face* (1957)

352 Publicity agent Dawn Addams persuades deposed European king Charlie Chaplin to get a facelift for television purposes. He does so, but experiences problems with his upper lip. "It can be lowered by letting a pleat out," she reassures him. "What do you think my face is – a skirt?" he exclaims. – *A King in New York* (1957)

353 Two chorines react to newcomer Frank Sinatra. "He's cute." "You think anybody with pants is cute." "That's a lie. I like lots of people without pants." – *Pal Joey* (1957)

354 Westerner Gary Cooper, seeing a train for the first time, recoils at the leviathan. "That's the ugliest thing I ever saw in my life," he remarks. "You never saw my ex-wife," Arthur O'Connell retorts. – *Man of the West* (1958)

355 A health-obsessed nurse informs submarine captain Cary Grant that proper vitamins will prevent his hair from turning gray. "I like to have gray hair," Grant counters. "That way I can worry and it won't show." – *Operation Petticoat* (1959)

356 "She made me look like a fool," Jack Carson complains about Joanne Woodward. "Don't blame my wife for your looks," returns Paul Newman. – *Rally 'Round the Flag, Boys* (1959)

357 "I'll do it myself if you don't mind," an embarrassed, diminutive patient protests to two nurses who are trying to relieve him of his undergarments. They ignore his objection, remove his underwear and unceremoniously toss him onto his bed. "What a fuss about such a small thing," one of the nurses remarks. – *Carry On Nurse* (1960)

358 Wily, rotund Roman senator Charles Laughton comments to slave trader Peter Ustinov: "Corpulence makes a man reasonable, pleasant and phlegmatic. Have you noticed that the nastiest of talents are invariably thin?" – *Spartacus* (1960)

359 Buddy Hackett, caring for a talking duck that has athletic pretensions, tries to convince it otherwise. "You'd look so stupid," Hackett suggests, "jumping over the net with those short legs." – *Everything's Ducky* (1961)

360 Sheriff James Stewart pokes some good-natured fun at rotund U.S. Cavalry Sergeant Posey (Andy Devine), who is about to mount his horse. "Fetch a ladder," Stewart orders some of the soldiers, "so that Sergeant Posey can get up on that unfortunate animal." – *Two Rode Together* (1961)

361 Intelligence officer Jim Hutton, stationed in Honolulu during World War II, recognizes an attractive nurse (Paula Prentiss) who went to high school with him. She has changed from an awkward, lanky schoolgirl to a beautiful, buxom young woman very much in demand on the base. "From a tall girl I've suddenly developed into a short commodity," she says. – *The Horizontal Lieutenant* (1962)

362 British scientist Terry-Thomas, collecting plant specimens in America's Southwest, gives Milton Berle a ride in his vehicle as he ponders over one of America's obsessions. "In all my time in this wretched, godforsaken country," the visitor says, "the one thing that haunts me most of all is this preposterous preoccupation with bosoms. Don't you realize they've become the dominant theme in American culture? . . . If American women stopped wearing brassieres, your whole national economy would collapse overnight." – *It's a Mad Mad Mad Mad World* (1963)

363 "How about that kid!" exclaims Carol Burnett about a brash young male model. "He's got the body of a Greek god and the mind of Lolita!"—*Who's Been Sleeping in My Bed?* (1963)

364 British agent Harry Palmer (Michael Caine) has just wined and dined an attractive fellow agent. "Do you always wear your glasses?" she asks, after scrutinizing him closely. "Yes," he replies, "except in bed."—*The Ipcress File* (1965)

365 Sheriff Harold Gould doesn't like the answers he's getting from private eye Paul Newman. "I don't care if you take my word or not," Newman angrily explodes, "I'm not working for you!" "If I wanted to be ugly, I—" "You are ugly!" Newman interrupts him.—*Harper* (1966)

366 Intelligence agent Matt Helm (Dean Martin) observes a distraught fellow female agent whom the agency is trying to rehabilitate. "We want her to feel like a beautiful young woman again," someone remarks about the patient who has lost her beauty and youth. "Have you tried prayer?" Martin replies. —*The Ambushers* (1967)

367 Fanny Brice (Barbra Streisand), always sensitive about her looks, makes this quip about her marriage: "To tell the truth, it hurts my pride to know that the groom was prettier than the bride." —*Funny Girl* (1968)

368 Detective George Segal's Jewish mother (Eileen Heckart) is upset that he is dating a gentile woman (Lee Remick), but she cannot refrain from asking about her. "Her name is Katherine," Segal begins. "Short, blonde, beautiful," his mother adds sarcastically. "No," Segal contradicts her. "She's tall and she's got one eye in the middle of her forehead."—*No Way to Treat a Lady* (1968)

369 Goldie Hawn compares middle-aged Peter Sellers to her younger dates: "They all walk around in their tight jeans so you can take a good look and make up your own mind. But you don't put the goods in the store window." —*There's a Girl in My Soup* (1970)

370 Unemployed entertainer Renee Taylor is hired to perform her act in a small club. "I'll bet you thought this was my hair," she tells the audience. "But it's a wig, and it's made of monkey hair. It looks like hair and it feels like hair, it acts like hair—only it smells like a monkey."—*Made for Each Other* (1971)

371 Woody Allen, awakening some time in the future, explains a photograph from his time. "This is some girl burning a brassiere," he says. "You can see it's a very small fire."—*Sleeper* (1973)

372 Young Frankenstein (Gene Wilder), standing in front of his grandfather's castle and carrying buxom fiancée Teri Garr, comments on the two huge metal rings hanging from the door: "What's a pair of knockers!" "Thank you," says Garr.—*Young Frankenstein* (1974)

373 Gene Wilder, as Count Frankenstein's grandson, returns to the ancestral castle and is greeted by the hunchbacked servant Igor (Marty Feldman). "I'm a brilliant surgeon," says Wilder. "Perhaps I can help you with that hump." "What hump?"—*Young Frankenstein* (1974)

374 Obnoxious, sexist ambulance driver Larry Hagman constantly calls buxom Raquel Welch "Jugs," much to her displeasure. "I'm sorry, honey," he says unctuously, "but every time I see those headlights of yours—"—*Mother, Jugs and Speed* (1976)

375 When her husband loses his job, Jane Fonda seeks work as a fashion model. Nervous about appearing in public, Fonda receives encouragement from her employer. "Modeling," the woman asserts, "is nothing more than organized walking."—*Fun with Dick and Jane* (1977)

376 "You have a visitor," announces private eye Peter Falk's secretary as soon as he enters his office. "Pretty?" he inquires. "Prettier than me, but I'm easier." – *The Cheap Detective* (1978)

377 While traveling in Egypt, an elderly Bette Davis introduces her masculine-looking female companion to a fellow tourist: "She did fifteen rounds once with Jack Dempsey. He was never the same man again." – *Death on the Nile* (1978)

378 Excessively overweight food critic Robert Morley rejects his doctor's counsel to cut down on his food intake. "I am what I am precisely because I have eaten my way to the top," he enunciates. "I am a work of art created by the finest chefs in the world. Every fold is a brushstroke, every crease a sonnet, every chin a concerto. In short, doctor, in my present form, I am a masterpiece." – *Who Is Killing the Great Chefs of Europe?* (1978)

379 "Sam could have been tall," a wife says about her husband. "He turned it down." – *A Change of Seasons* (1980)

380 American college student Griffin Dunne, killed by a werewolf in the English moors, returns in a ghoulish state to visit his shocked friend David Naughton. "I realize I don't look so hot," he says, "but I thought you'd be glad to see me." – *An American Werewolf in London* (1981)

381 Goldie Hawn jokingly criticizes the writing style of her boyfriend Burt Reynolds: "Every character you create has breasts too large." "Yes," Reynolds replies, "but I make them suffer for it." – *Best Friends* (1982)

382 Dustin Hoffman in drag is trying out for a female television role. "I'd like to make her a little more attractive," the director says to his cameraman about Hoffman. "How far can you pull back?" "How do you feel about Cleveland?" the cameraman quips. – *Tootsie* (1982)

383 A well-dressed pimp, riding in his chauffeur-driven limousine, is suddenly confronted by two tough, bald-headed hoodlums who drive up next to him and direct him to pull over. "Aren't you boys on your way to a cue-ball convention?" he cracks. – *Doctor Detroit* (1983)

384 Cheech Marin and Tommy Chong are in a restaurant flashing a roll of bills, which quickly attracts a young woman. "He has the mark!" she exclaims. "You have the mark!" "Yeah," Marin replies, "we're the Marks brothers." – *Cheech and Chong's The Corsican Brothers* (1984)

385 A wealthy judge expects the worst when his unpredictable son John Larroquette introduces his pretty bride-to-be to his father. When they are alone, Larroquette asks his father what he thinks about her. "I must admit," the judge replies, "she isn't at all what I thought she'd be." "What did you think she'd be?" "Blind." – *Blind Date* (1987)

386 "Sometimes you can get incredibly powerful vibrations from old brassieres," Shelley Long's kooky sister explains, "but yours just had a slight hum." – *Hello Again* (1987)

387 Space hero Lonestar (Bill Pullman) rescues the daughter of the King of Druidia, but he treats her as just another passenger aboard his spaceship – much to her annoyance. She reminds him that her father is the king of the Druids. "That's all we needed," he says in disgust to copilot John Candy, "a Druish princess." "That's funny," Candy adds, "she doesn't look Druish." – *Spaceballs* (1987)

388 After Harry (Billy Crystal) has seen his ex-wife, he describes her to Sally (Meg Ryan), his girlfriend, saying that "she looked weird. Her legs looked heavy. She must be retaining water." "Harry – " Sally starts to object. "Believe me," he affirms. "The woman saved everything." – *When Harry Met Sally . . .* (1989)

389 In a bookstore, political cartoonist Gene Wilder is busily engaged signing autographs for buyers of his new book. "I always thought that being a cartoonist is the hardest job in the world," a fan remarks. "No," Wilder corrects the man, "I think that job has to go to Noriega's dermatologist." – *Funny About Love* (1990)

390 Aging former film star Shirley MacLaine, recuperating from a traffic accident, confides to film actress daughter Meryl Streep: "You know, I don't mind getting old. I never thought I'd live this long anyway. What I do mind is looking old." – *Postcards from the Edge* (1990)

391 American businessman George Kennedy arrives in a small town in former East Germany and addresses its citizens. "I bring you greetings from the greatest economic power in the world –" he begins. "He doesn't look Japanese," a German woman remarks to a friend. – *Driving Me Crazy* (1991)

392 John Goodman, as the King of England, is briefed by his secretary Peter O'Toole on an upcoming visit by the King of Finland: "The King will be accompanied by his daughter, the Princess Anna, one of the most socially desirable women in the world." "Socially desirable," Goodman ponders. "Does that mean she's ugly?" – *King Ralph* (1991)

393 Ambitious British hospital aide Paul McGann, posing as a doctor, takes home a demonstration skeleton and hides it in his bed. His friend discovers McGann's new "bed partner" and quips: "I don't know what you see in these skinny women." – *Paper Mask* (1992)

Army

394 Stationed in Paris during World War I, doughboys Bert Wheeler and Robert Woolsey pose as officers. "How would you like to be a general?" Woolsey asks jokingly. "Not me," Wheeler replies. "There's no chance for promotion." – *Half Shot at Sunrise* (1930)

395 At the beginning of World War I, Oliver Hardy, in an effort to keep himself and Stan Laurel out of the army, informs a recruiting sergeant that they are incapacitated. "There's a lot of it going around lately," Laurel adds. – *Pack Up Your Troubles* (1932)

396 Lou Costello just passes his army physical by two ounces. "Just for that," he says to his stomach, "you go to bed without any supper." – *Buck Privates* (1941)

397 During maneuvers, shells burst all around Abbott and Costello's unit, making them hit the dirt. "What did I join the army for?" Costello asks. "To defend your native soil," a buddy answers. "Well," Costello says, ejecting a mouthful of dirt, "they don't have to feed it to me." – *Buck Privates* (1941)

398 Drill instructor Bud Abbott orders: "Throw out your chest! Throw it out!" "I'm not through with it yet!" Lou Costello shouts back. – *Buck Privates* (1941)

399 Nella Walker is piqued at the army for the low rank they intend to bestow upon her son. "How can they make a Yale man a private?" she asks an officer. – *Buck Privates* (1941)

400 Gold bricking private Bob Hope, along with buddies Eddie Bracken and Lynne Overman, is sent out of harm's way during army maneuvers. "We're far enough behind the lines to be generals," quips Hope. – *Caught in the Draft* (1941)

401 "My business is shootin', not salutin'!" exclaims crusty old army scout Charles Grapwin to General Custer (Errol Flynn). – *They Died with Their Boots On* (1941)

402 Racketeer tough guy Lucky Jordan (Alan Ladd) joins the army, and noncommissioned officers have now replaced rival mobsters in his life. Ladd is rebuked by his sergeant for shoveling dirt on his feet. "Sorry," Ladd answers. "I thought it was your face." – *Lucky Jordan* (1942)

403 During World War II Jackie Gleason goes for his army examination and is asked to read an eye chart. "I can't," he says. "You mean you can't read that chart?" the doctor asks. "I can't read," Gleason explains. – *Tramp, Tramp, Tramp* (1942)

404 Fresh army recruits exit from a train and board a bus for boot camp. They are soon given a break at a fast-food stop. "Ten-minute rest period," announces a voice. "Make the most of it." "What'll we do with our spare time?" cracks rookie Wally Brown. – *Adventures of a Rookie* (1943)

405 Professional gambler Cary Grant receives his draft notice from Uncle Sam. "They can't do that to me!" he protests. "I'm a civilian!" – *Mr. Lucky* (1943)

406 During World War II, the all-army cast of a musical comedy about army life is ready to give a command performance for President Franklin D. Roosevelt. One G.I., a member of the cast, peeks through the curtain to get a glimpse of his commander-in-chief. "Look, fellas, the President!" he exclaims. "Gosh, I'd like to go out there and thank him for the raise he gave us." – *This Is the Army* (1943)

407 Corporal Leo Gorcey and private Huntz Hall return to their old neighborhood where they meet Mrs. Nussbaum. They inquire about her son Gregory. "Gregory is in the army, too," the woman beams. "He's doing fine. He was promoted to K.P. already." – *Follow the Leader* (1944)

408 During World War II army corporal Leo Gorcey is notified that because of his weak eyesight he is being honorably discharged. His buddy Huntz Hall protests on the grounds that, although the Japanese are small, they are not that small. "I got an idea," Hall finally says. "Tell them you want to fight the Germans. They are much bigger, and you can see them." – *Follow the Leader* (1944)

409 Martha Raye, entertaining World War II troops overseas, asks a G.I. where she is to dine. "You mess with the men," he replies. "I know, but where do we eat?" – *Four Jills in a Jeep* (1944)

410 G.I. Red Buttons at an air force base during World War II describes the facilities to some new cadets: "To the right, gentlemen, is Pneumonia Gulch. That is where we sleep. You fry by day and freeze by night. To the left, just a little ways, about a mile and a half, is Ptomaine Tavern. That is where we eat. The wheat cakes we leave are used by the navy – as depth charges." – *Winged Victory* (1944)

411 Joan of Arc (Ingrid Bergman) gives her orders to the French troops before leading them to victory. "There must be no swearing in this army," she demands. "You want our army to be dumb?" a balking general (Ward Bond) protests. – *Joan of Arc* (1948)

412 A G.I. describes how the brass make certain decisions: "You know, they got a man in the army, a two-star general, who flies around looking for ugly places ... and if it's too hot in summer for human life and too cold in winter ... then he plants an American

flag and proclaims it a U.S. army camp."
—*Battleground* (1949)

413 During an air-raid drill at a German prisoner-of-war camp, an American security officer rushes the last two men out of the barracks. "Must you two always be the last?" he barks. "Oh, yeah?" counters Harvey Lembeck. "You try jumping in these trenches first. Everyone jumps on top of you." "How do you think I got this hernia?" Robert Strauss adds.—*Stalag 17* (1953)

414 Camp commander Paul Ford berates captain Glenn Ford for botching the rehabilitation of an Okinawan village. "All right!" exclaims the exasperated captain. "Shall I kill myself?" "Aw, don't minimize this," the commander replies.—*The Teahouse of the August Moon* (1956)

415 "We're sending *this* to school?" a captain in the Women's Air Force questions after observing hillbilly draftee Andy Griffith. "Yes sir, ma'am," draftee Nick Adams replies. "If he passes the eye test he'll be going to gunnery school." "As what? A target?"—*No Time for Sergeants* (1958)

416 Querulous corporal Tony Curtis, assigned to the mental ward of an air force hospital, meeets his supervisor, captain Gregory Peck. "I believe it is customary for a soldier to address an officer as 'sir,'" Peck announces. "Sir," Curtis says grudgingly, and then continues: "Well, it's customary for a soldier, but it's tough for a civilian." "But you're not a civilian," the captain counters. "But I feel like a civilian," the corporal persists.—*Captain Newman, M.D.* (1964)

417 Cavalry officer Stuart Whitman loses 2,000 rifles in an ambush and later gets himself and adventurer Richard Boone trapped by Apaches. "You're just stupid enough to become a general!" Boone snaps at Whitman.—*Rio Conchos* (1964)

418 After studying 12 U.S. Army prisoners, an army psychiatrist releases his findings to the major in charge (Lee Marvin), who has been assigned to lead the prisoners on a mission behind German lines. "These guys think the U.S. Army is their enemy," the psychiatrist warns. "Well, they know the U.S. Army," Marvin replies. "But the Krauts haven't done anything to them yet."
—*The Dirty Dozen* (1967)

419 The "Dirty Dozen," a group of army criminal misfits, have completed their training for a commando-type operation. Their major (Lee Marvin) rewards them by bringing in a bevy of camp followers, much to the surprise and delight of the team. "Do you think that these guys know tomorrow's Mother's Day?" an officer asks Marvin in a deprecating tone. "Is it?" the major replies.—*The Dirty Dozen* (1967)

420 Army officer Lee Marvin instructs Donald Sutherland, one of his "Dirty Dozen," how to act while impersonating a general inspecting the troops: "Walk slow, act dumb and look stupid."—*The Dirty Dozen* (1967)

421 During World War II, German general Donald Pleasence, thinking to do heroic corporal Tom Courtenay a favor, offers to make him an officer, but Courtenay politely rejects the offer. "I'm shattered," Pleasence says sarcastically. "My world is toppling. What's the point of being a general when corporals prefer to be corporals?"—*Night of the Generals* (1967)

422 A British brigadier and his junior officer are being held prisoner in an Afghan tower when an earthquake shakes the building to its foundations. They both race down the stairs just before it collapses and they experience other dangers before they are out of harm's way. That night, the brigadier reviews the day's events. "By the way, MacKenzie," he rebukes the junior officer, "you came downstairs in front of me this morning."—*Carry On Up the Khyber* (1968)

423 A soldier opens the trunk of a car and finds Paul Newman, an army escape artist, trying to break out of the guardhouse. "Would you close that thing?" Newman asks. "I'll never get these pictures developed." – *The Secret War of Harry Frigg* (1968)

424 Somewhere in France during World War II, an incompetent captain leaves for Paris and orders his sergeant (Telly Savalas) to give his men a few days off – on a deserted, bombed-out farm. "We're ten miles from the nearest town!" Savalas protests. "There's no booze! There's no broads! There's no action!" "Don't fool around with women," the officer continues, ignoring the sergeant's complaints. "Their husbands carry guns. And don't forget: the penalty for looting is death." "Loot what?" Savalas exclaims. "There's nothing here to loot!" – *Kelly's Heroes* (1970)

425 A radio operator is having difficulty reaching an undetermined number of G.I.s reportedly fighting behind German lines. Incompetent but gung-ho general Carroll O'Connor demands that his aide get these reports on the radio. "Yes, sir," the aide replies, "but it's pretty hard to pick them up this time in the morning. It's got something to do with the ionosphere." "Well," orders the general, "get the ionosphere the hell off the air and get them on!" – *Kelly's Heroes* (1970)

426 Uptight nurse Sally Kellerman, exasperated with the antics of surgeon Donald Sutherland, questions "how a degenerated person like that reached a responsible position in the regular army corps." "He was drafted," a doctor replies. – *M*A*S*H* (1970)

427 Black drill sergeant Frank Adu, in the army of Czar Nicholas I, is exasperated with the sloppy soldiering of recruit Woody Allen. "You want a dishonorable discharge?" he threatens. "Yes, sir," Allen replies. "Either that or a furlough." "From now on, you clean the mess hall and the latrine," the

sergeant thunders. "Yes, sir. How will I know the difference?" "Okay," the sergeant continues, "one-two, one-two, one-two!" "Three's next if you're having trouble," Allen offers. – *Love and Death* (1975)

428 Bubble-headed army recruit Goldie Hawn receives her uniform with a measure of disappointment. "Pardon me," she asks. "Is green the only color they come in?" – *Private Benjamin* (1980)

429 Spoiled Goldie Hawn enlists in the army and is shocked by the condition of the barracks. "Look at this place," she says in disgust. "The army couldn't afford drapes?" – *Private Benjamin* (1980)

430 Tough gung-ho paratroop commander Robert Webber alerts his soldiers to ensuing dangers during war games. "There are mine fields up there," he warns. "Most of the mines are inert, some are ert." – *Private Benjamin* (1980)

431 In a documentary on women army recruits in basic training, an instructor begins: "Today's lecture is on the friendly use of nuclear weapons." – *Soldier Girls* (1981)

432 Sergeant Warren Oates immediately suspects new recruit Bill Murray of gold bricking. "You know something, soldier?" Oates says, "I've noticed you're always last." "I'm pacing myself, sergeant," Murray replies. – *Stripes* (1981)

433 Sergeant James Garner arrives at his new army base in Georgia with his personal World War II Sherman tank. "It's hard to shoot yourself while cleaning it," he explains. – *Tank* (1984)

434 Israeli citizen-soldier Amos Kollek is on patrol – no lurking danger, mayhem or women. "I like a little sex with my violence," he cracks. – *Goodbye New York* (1985)

435 "Military intelligence," muses army disc jockey Robin Williams stationed in Saigon. "That's a contradiction in terms." – *Good Morning, Vietnam* (1987)

436 During the Second World War, when army sergeant Christopher Walken directs a group of draftees to answer "Ho!" to roll call, he meets with some resistance. "Do I make myself clear?" Walken sharply questions private Matthew Broderick. "Ho, yes," the recruit answers nervously. "Ho, what?" "Ho, nothing." "Are you having trouble understanding me?" Walken presses.

"No, no," Broderick falters, then tries to correct himself. "I mean no, ho, sergeant – just plain ho." – *Biloxi Blues* (1988)

437 Not-too-bright Anthony LaPaglio tries to enlist in the army but finds himself unprepared for the standard procedures. "I don't really think it's fair that we gotta take a test that we didn't study for," he protests to the sergeant in charge. "This is a damn urine examination, boy!" the sergeant exclaims. – *29th Street* (1991)

Art and Artists

438 "Mm-m, lovely painting," Mae West remarks as she is shown around John Miljan's home. "One of your ancestors?" "This one in particular is an old master," he replies. "Looks more like an old mistress to me," West responds. – *Belle of the Nineties* (1934)

439 Eccentric concert pianist Burgess Meredith invites pretty Merle Oberon to a modern art gallery where she is bewildered by the cubist and surrealist paintings. "Who painted it?" she asks about one art work that he has interpreted for her. "A woman," he announces scornfully. "No man could be so malicious." – *That Uncertain Feeling* (1941)

440 Sophisticated art dealer Clifton Webb quips: "The enjoyment of art is the only remaining ecstasy that is neither illegal nor immoral." – *The Dark Corner* (1946)

441 Walter Pidgeon, who has hired artist Peter Lawford to paint various murals on the walls of his home, criticizes one painting of King Arthur playing poker. "A bit red in the face, isn't he?" Pidgeon jokingly suggests. "That's

what you call a royal flush," Lawford quips. – *Julia Misbehaves* (1948)

442 Aspiring band leader Desi Arnaz berates an auto mechanic who has failed to properly repair the band's bus. "Please," the man objects to Arnaz's harsh words, "I'm an artist. I'm high strung." "They didn't string you high enough!" Arnaz exclaims. – *Holiday in Havana* (1949)

443 Deposed European king Charlie Chaplin settles in New York where he is invited to a party at the home of a wealthy couple. He soon notices the works of art hanging on the walls. "Is that an El Greco?" he asks his host. "Oh, no sir, he's Filipino," the host replies, referring to a guest near the painting. – *A King in New York* (1957)

444 Mame (Rosalind Russell) compliments a sculptor-friend. "A divine man," she extolls. "Such talented fingers. But oh, what he did for my bust!" – *Auntie Mame* (1958)

445 Parisian streetwalker Shirley MacLaine invites former gendarme Jack Lemmon to her small apartment. "It used to be a studio," she explains. "A painter once lived here. Poor guy, he was starving. He tried everything, even cut his ear off." "Who, Van Gogh?" Lemmon inquires excitedly. "No," she replies, "I think his name was Schwartz."—*Irma la Douce* (1963)

446 John Adams (Patrick Daniels) watches a painter preserving Benjamin Franklin (Howard da Silva) for posterity. "He's no Botticelli," Daniels says critically of the artist. "And the subject's no Venus," quips da Silva.—*1776* (1972)

447 "One day," British artist Alan Bates divulges to Jill Clayburgh, "when I was about six, my parents had a row, and my mother—she threw a pickled herring at my dad and missed. It splattered all against the wall. I took one look at that pickled herring, and that's when I decided to become an abstract expressionist."—*An Unmarried Woman* (1978)

448 Billy Crystal's ex-wife informs him that she is about to remarry—this time around to a dentist. Crystal, inwardly hurt, quips: "You're gonna have a lot of clown paintings on your wall."—*Running Scared* (1986)

449 An artist's girlfriend decides she has had enough and walks out on her lover. "You could be the Andrew Wyeth of the '80s," she utters before parting, "but you never once asked to paint me nude."—*Batteries Not Included* (1987)

Assassins and Hit Men

450 Robert Woolsey, the king of a mythical principality, confronts bumbling assassin Bert Wheeler. "You just want to shoot me inadvertently." "I've got to shoot you in the patio," Wheeler corrects him. "You know, this is gonna hurt me more than it does you." "But not in the same place."—*Cracked Nuts* (1931)

451 At a dinner where gangsters during the Roaring Twenties are celebrating a birthday for mob boss George Raft, a huge cake is wheeled in. Suddenly from below the cake, a hit man bursts through and fires a rain of bullets at Raft. "What's going on here?" police detective Pat O'Brien asks after rushing in and seeing Raft on the floor. "Dere was somethin' in de cake dat didn't agree wid him," a party guest blurts out.—*Some Like It Hot* (1959)

452 Gangster Telly Savalas hires a hit man to kill a stranger and destroy the body except for the feet, which the police will think are those of Savalas. "You want everything to burn but his feet," the hit man says, puzzled by the request. "What do you want, bookends?"—*The Man from the Diner's Club* (1963)

453 British agent James Bond (Roger Moore) is informed by his superior that he is the next target of a dangerous, professional assassin who charges one million dollars per assignment. "Who would pay a million dollars to have me killed?" Bond asks. "Jealous husbands, outraged chefs, humiliated tailors—the list is endless."—*The Man with the Golden Gun* (1974)

454 Someone has tried to assassinate Inspector Clouseau (Peter Sellers). "Do you know what kind of a bomb it was?" one of his aides inquires. "The exploding kind," replies Sellers.—*The Pink Panther Strikes Again* (1976)

455 "What line of work are you in?" Jack Lemmon asks hit man Walter Matthau. "Pest control." "Oh, like ants, cockroaches, termites?" "Something like that," Matthau replies. – *Buddy Buddy* (1981)

456 Hired killer Jerry Reed has hidden his occupation from his wife (Marian Hailey) – until she suspects him of infidelity. "I'm not out there committing adultery," he explains. "I'm out there committing murder." "Oh, thank God!" she sighs. – *The Survivors* (1983)

457 "I don't make deals in my business," says thief Jerry Reed, who plans to kill Walter Matthau, a witness to a crime. "I was raised as a very strict Southern Baptist, and I place a high value on human life – $20,000 minimum." – *The Survivors* (1983)

458 Hired killer Kathleen Turner, married to gangster Jack Nicholson, strongly suggests that they both flee the country to escape the wrath of an organized crime family. To persuade him, she begins to describe the huge sum of money she has accumulated. "Listen," she pleads, "I've been doin' three or four hits for the last few years, most of them full pay –" "That many?" her startled husband interjects. "Well, it's not so many if you consider the size of the population." – *Prizzi's Honor* (1985)

459 Slow-witted, smalltime hoodlum and killer Tom Waits confides to fellow gang member Sally Kirkland: "I'm deeper than you realize. Actually, I think of myself as executive material. I don't want to grow old as just another murderer. I'm a professional, but nobody takes me seriously." – *Cold Feet* (1989)

460 Daughter Tracey Ullman is startled not only to hear her mother Joan Plowright suggest the death penalty for Ullman's philandering husband, Kevin Kline, but that she knows some "killers" who can dispatch him. "No, not really killers, no," the mother explains. "They only do it for money." – *I Love You to Death* (1990)

461 Two hit men attempt to bribe law officer Gene Hackman, who is guarding a witness for the prosecution. Hackman begins to poke fun at one of the assassins. "He's very good at what he does," the one in charge warns. "The difference between us is I do it for a living, and he enjoys it." "Well," Hackman adds, "I think that people should have fun at work. It makes the day go by much quicker." – *Narrow Margin* (1990)

Babies

462 "I wonder what the doctor said to your father when you were born," Eddie Cantor says to Eve Sully. "Why bring that up?" she asks. "That's just what I thought," says Cantor. – *Kid Millions* (1934)

463 "I used to be a baby once," reminisces Bert Wheeler. "I had my mother's eyes, my father's nose, my sister's dimples –" "Your appendix is your own," interjects Robert Woolsey. – *Kentucky Kernels* (1935)

464 Scatterbrained Billie Burke, upon seeing a pair of twin babies: "Oh, are they sweet! Twins are so practical. It's always so nice to have a spare." – *Hi Diddle Diddle* (1943)

465 During World War II, a women's auxiliary officer cajoles a charitable donation from Washington bureaucrat Charles Ruggles – the money to go toward the babies of women defense workers. "Fifty dollars will keep my nursery babies in milk for a month," the woman suggests. "They'll get awfully mildewed, won't they?" Ruggles quips. – *The Doughgirls* (1944)

466 Billy De Wolfe and Olga San Juan visit a maternity ward and watch a nurse feed a newborn baby. "Look!" she exclaims ecstatically, "doesn't that sort of make you yearn for something?" "Yeah," De Wolfe returns, "dinner. I'm starving." – *Blue Skies* (1946)

467 Baby photographer Bob Hope has difficulties with one of his subjects. When he places his hand next to the baby in a friendly gesture, the child bites Hope's finger. "Doesn't he get meat at home?" Hope asks the baby's mother. – *My Favorite Brunette* (1947)

468 Bud Abbott and Lou Costello report to a home prepared to work as babysitters. "Have you had any experience with babies," the sister of the children asks Costello. "Yes, sir," he replies. "I've been a baby all of my life." – *Jack and the Beanstalk* (1951)

469 Bob Hope, who works at the U.N., is given an abandoned baby to take care of. "You've got the wrong man," he grumbles. "I didn't even go to the Christmas party." – *A Global Affair* (1964)

470 "We're gonna have a baby," wife Janet Margolin cheerfully informs husband Woody Allen. "That's my Christmas present to you." "All I needed was a tie," Allen grumbles. – *Take the Money and Run* (1969)

471 Broadway comedy star Fanny Brice (Barbra Streisand) complains to songwriter Billy Rose (James Caan) about her many adversities over the years. "Childbirth – was that easy?" he wonders. "Easy!" she echoes. "It was like pushing a piano through a transom!" – *Funny Lady* (1975)

472 Burt Reynolds gives his streetwise housekeeper Juanita Moore a lesson in how a baby's sex is determined. "The sperm carrying the male sex factor is stronger at first than the sperm carrying the female sex factor," he reads aloud. "The only factor I know about," Moore replies, "is when you hold the baby up and there's a factor hanging down, it's a boy; if there isn't, it's a girl." – *Paternity* (1981)

473 A down-and-out pimp, rushing to meet an acquaintance in reference to pulling a job, must first find a place to leave his baby son, who has just communicated with his father. "No, no, not now!" he cries, feeling the wet diaper. "Look, I know this is the only thing you do real good, but there is a time and a place for everything, and this ain't that." – *Crackers* (1984)

474 High-powered business executive Diane Keaton, caring for a baby girl, takes the infant to a business lunch and hands her across the counter to a cloakroom attendant. "You'll get a big, big tip," Keaton promises. – *Baby Boom* (1987)

475 Three socially active bachelors suddenly find themselves caring for a baby. "The book says to feed the baby every two hours," Tom Selleck questions, "but do you count from when you start or when you finish? It takes me two hours to get her to eat, and by the time she's done, it's time to start again, so that I'm feeding her all of the time." – *Three Men and a Baby* (1987)

Bachelorhood

476 An ambitious young woman tries to seduce Bert Wheeler, the king of a mythical land. "Have you never thought seriously of marriage?" she asks. "Certainly," he replies. "That's why I'm single." – *Cracked Nuts* (1931)

477 "Women are like elephants," W. C. Fields proclaims. "I like to watch them, but I wouldn't want to own one." – *Mississippi* (1935)

478 "I've always held that a bachelor is a feller who never made the same mistake once," Texas Ranger Gary Cooper says to Madeleine Carroll. – *North West Mounted Police* (1940)

479 Mrs. Bennet (Mary Boland), always on the prowl for eligible husbands for her five daughters, learns that a wealthy bachelor has settled in the area. "He has 5,000 pounds a year," an acquaintance informs her. "Five thousand pounds a year and unmarried!" Boland sighs. "That's the most heartening piece of news since the Battle of Waterloo." – *Pride and Prejudice* (1940)

480 Film star Bob Hope is trying to avoid being drafted into the army. "Thousands of guys are getting married to avoid the draft," his agent Lynne Overman suggests. "Nothing doing," Hope protests. "That's like cutting your throat to cure laryngitis." – *Caught in the Draft* (1941)

481 At a social gathering a young gentleman confides to an elderly woman seeking a husband. "The love of a good woman is not for me," he says. "Then why don't you try one of the others?" she suggests. – *On Approval* (1943)

482 When happy-go-lucky entertainer Fred Astaire finishes extolling the

glories of bachelorhood, his servant reminds him that married men live longer than bachelors. "If that's true," Astaire responds, "they're only trying to outlive their wives so that they can live like bachelors again." – *Royal Wedding* (1951)

483 Gangster's moll Saturday Knight (Nita Talbot) confides to neighbor Lana Turner: "Tony is the last of the big spenders. He'll buy me anything but a marriage license." – *Who's Got the Action?* (1962)

484 Millionaire John McGiver visits his relatives and shows off his yacht to nephew Barry Gordon. "That baby down there's got all the modern gadgets going," McGiver boasts. "If I could find a woman with as many workable parts, I'd marry her." – *The Spirit Is Willing* (1967)

485 Army sergeant Bob Hope tries to cheer up a young private who has received a "Dear John" letter from home. "What's the hardest thing in the world to find?" asks Hope. "I'll tell you – an unhappy bachelor." – *The Private Navy of Sgt. O'Farrell* (1968)

486 Philadelphia dentist Don Knotts comments on his enduring bachelorhood: "I always thought I was a little too thin for marriage." – *The Shakiest Gun in the West* (1968)

487 "Have you ever been married?" Jack Lemmon asks hired assassin Walter Matthau. "Once," Matthau replies, "but I got rid of her. Now I just lease." – *Buddy Buddy* (1981)

488 "I won't get married again," baseball fan Walter Matthau protests to girlfriend Ann-Margret. "I struck out three times so far. I like sitting on the bench." – *I Ought to Be in Pictures* (1982)

489 Three swinging bachelors are suddenly saddled with fatherhood when one of their girlfriends leaves a baby bundle at their doorstep. "I think it's your turn to change her," says Steve Guttenberg. "I'll give you a thousand dollars if you do it," replies Tom Selleck. – *Three Men and a Baby* (1987)

Battle of the Sexes

490 "I call my girl 'Grapefruit,'" a comic informs his audience, "because every time I squeeze her, she hits me in the eye." – *Glorifying the American Girl* (1929)

491 Mexican bandit Victor Varconi captures a pretty señorita and takes her to his lair where he tries to seduce her. "Oh, come now," he says. "Can't we be friends?" "Would a bird make friends with a snake?" "But I am not a bird," he quips. – *Captain Thunder* (1931)

492 When Gloria Swanson confronts her lover about his current love affairs, he rationalizes them away by saying "a man must live." "I've often wondered why it was necessary in some cases," Swanson muses. – *Indiscreet* (1931)

493 After ceaseless snapping and bickering with wife Norma Shearer, Robert Montgomery tosses sweet reason to the winds. "Certain women," he says, "should be struck regularly – like gongs." – *Private Lives* (1931)

494 "That guy's no good," says Mae West. "His mother should have thrown him away and kept the stork." – *Belle of the Nineties* (1934)

495 "I'm just gettin' even with two guys that are so low, they could walk under that door without taking their hats off," Mae West says to her maid. – *Belle of the Nineties* (1934)

496 "Why do you keep me from having men friends of my own race?" Mae West, tired of her Oriental lover Harold Huber, asks. "Because it is written there are two perfectly good men – one dead, the other unborn." "Which are you?" she questions. – *Klondike Annie* (1936)

497 Eliza (Wendy Hiller) has left Henry Higgins (Leslie Howard) to reside temporarily with his mother. "Get up and go home and don't be a fool," Higgins orders. "Very nicely put indeed, Henry," his mother says. "No one could resist such an invitation." – *Pygmalion* (1938)

498 English magician David Niven performs several tricks on stage, concluding with making a young woman disappear. "And that, ladies and gentlemen," he quips, "is the hardest trick of all – getting rid of a woman." – *Eternally Yours* (1939)

499 "I never knew a dame who wasn't dead from the neck up," private detective James Stewart asserts to poet Claudette Colbert. – *It's a Wonderful World* (1939)

500 Star reporter Rosalind Russell notifies newspaper publisher Cary Grant, her ex-husband, that she is leaving to get married. "He treats me like a woman," she says, describing her fiancé. "What did I treat you like," Grant asks, "a water buffalo?" – *His Girl Friday* (1940)

501 Bartender W. C. Fields and a customer disagree about who knocked out Chicago Nellie years ago. "All right," Fields demurs, "but I started kicking her. Did you ever kick a woman in the midriff when she had a corset on?" "No," the customer replies. "It broke my toe," Fields winces. "Later on, she came back and beat both of us." "Yes, she did," Fields acknowledges, "but she brought another woman with her – elderly little woman with gray hair." – *My Little Chickadee* (1940)

502 "Let's you and me have a heart-to-heart talk," an obnoxious nightclub owner suggests to a pretty patron. "What would *you* use?" she quips as she walks away. – *Slightly Honorable* (1940)

503 When Melvyn Douglas calls Greta Garbo a wicked woman, she retorts: "The good need us for contrast." – *Two-Faced Woman* (1941)

504 "Why do so many marriages go on the rocks?" Dennis O'Keefe asks Edward Everett Horton. "Because women are such lying, scheming, deceitful, mercenary hellcats?" Horton offers. – *Weekend for Three* (1941)

505 "How vulgar!" Leon Errol's wife utters when he suggests attending a prize fight. "How could anyone be so bourgeois as to go somewhere just for a fight!" "I don't have to go anywhere just for a fight," Errol responds. "I could stay home." – *Mexican Spitfire Sees a Ghost* (1942)

506 At a social affair Clive Brook greets a female guest who passes by. The woman who is with Brook is surprised. "I didn't know you knew her," she remarks. "We have a sneering acquaintance," Brook quips. – *On Approval* (1943)

507 Clive Brook and Beatrice Lillie, friendly enemies under normal circumstances, find themselves stranded on her island estate. "Just think what people will say!" she exclaims, annoyed at the awkward situation. "They'll say nothing," he charges. "My reputation will save you from that – my reputation as a man of taste!" "I'm going to bed," she then announces. "Well, you needn't lock your door," he calls out. "Only the rain will want to come in!" – *On Approval* (1943)

508 Excitable fight manager Walter Abel reprimands his secretary, Eve Arden, for not preventing an embarrassing incident while he was out of town. "Remind me to ask you what you were doing with your nights while I was away!" Abel charges. "Same as when you are here – protecting myself," she remarks. – *The Kid from Brooklyn* (1946)

509 "In the battle of the sexes," admits teenage Mona Freeman after an argument with her boyfriend, "nobody ever wins." – *Dear Wife* (1949)

510 French Legionnaire George Tobias, guarding a captured desert princess, observes the fiery daggers in her eyes, which are then translated into curses. "She hates with her tongue as well as her eyes," Tobias says to his fellow soldiers. "She hates with everything; she is a real woman." – *Ten Tall Men* (1951)

511 Anne Baxter tracks down runaway husband Macdonald Carey to an all-male health farm where she is barred from entering. "This secret sanctuary," the attendant announces, "was conceived in liberty and dedicated to the proposition that all men are created henpecked." – *My Wife's Best Friend* (1952)

512 Differences of age, temperament and dance disciplines underlie the disagreements between Fred Astaire and ballerina Cyd Charisse. "We're not quarreling," Astaire asserts. "We're in complete agreement. We hate each other." – *The Band Wagon* (1953)

513 On an ocean voyage Jane Russell resents Elliot Reid's attempts to impress her with his wealth, which ironically he doesn't have. "I'm not that bad all the time," he protests. "I get the picture," she replies. "You're half sweet and half acid." – *Gentlemen Prefer Blondes* (1953)

514 William Holden comments on his failed marriage: "They all start out as Juliets and end up as Lady Macbeths." – *The Country Girl* (1954)

515 Dean Martin, following attractive artist Dorothy Malone out of a publisher's office, says to her: "I never met a lady cartoonist before." "All lady cartoonists are extremely gratified," she retorts sharply. – *Artists and Models* (1955)

516 Portly Raymond Burr publicly denounces his ex–dance-hall girl. "She'll cheat you blind," he says to the townspeople. "I know her like a book." "You never got past the cover, elephant boy," she ripostes. – *Great Day in the Morning* (1956)

517 Prizefighter-sportswriter Gregory Peck is having a fight with wife Lauren Bacall, who is repelled by the blood spilled in the ring. During their battle, she accidentally opens a wound on Peck's nose and draws blood – but not the slightest tremor results on her slender frame. "How is it," Peck acidly asks, "that you can't stand the sight of blood on anyone except me?" – *Designing Women* (1957)

518 Just fired, charming heel Frank Sinatra informs a hostile showgirl that he's leaving for Club El Morocco. "Are you kidding?" she returns. "The only way you'll get to Morocco is if you join the Foreign Legion." – *Pal Joey* (1957)

519 World War II veteran Frank Sinatra, riding home with school teacher Martha Hyer, moves closer and catches a whiff of her perfume. "What do you call that?" he asks. "Bug repellent," she replies. – *Some Came Running* (1958)

520 Fiercely competing advertising account executives Rock Hudson and Doris Day scrap with each other on the tele-

phone. "I don't use sex to land an account," she charges. "When do you use it?" "I don't." "My condolences to your husband." "I'm not married." "It figures," he replies. – *Lover Come Back* (1961)

521 "If you were my husband, I'd give you poison!" shouts angry neighbor Margaret Hamilton at Billy Gilbert. "If I were your husband, I'd take it!" retorts Gilbert. – *Paradise Alley* (1961)

522 A lawyer tries to persuade his well-to-do client to drop her alimony suit against her ex-husband, but she refuses. "It isn't that you win or lose," she explains, "it's how you play the game." – *40 Pounds of Trouble* (1962)

523 Mickey Spillane, portraying his own creation, detective Mike Hammer, says to Shirley Eaton, who cringes in fear: "Hell, I never hit dames . . . I always kick them." – *The Girl Hunters* (1963)

524 Wall Street broker Jim Backus lives in his male-dominated world of high finance. "Women shouldn't be allowed to have lunch clubs," he confides to his colleagues. "We've got to keep them off balance, disorganized – clawing and scratching at each other. Otherwise they might turn on us, like mad dogs." – *The Wheeler Dealers* (1963)

525 Louis Nye, during one of his routine arguments with wife Jill St. John, shouts, "Quiet, or you'll wake up the kids!" "Kids!" she echoes. "You big ape, that's your last marriage! We don't have any kids!" "How lucky can you get!" – *Who's Been Sleeping in My Bed?* (1963)

526 "Last night she was banging on my door for forty-five minutes," Dean Martin says about a showgirl, "but I wouldn't let her out." – *Kiss Me, Stupid* (1964)

527 Eliza Doolittle (Audrey Hepburn) has walked out on Professor Higgins

(Rex Harrison). "What am I to do?" he asks his mother (Gladys Cooper). "Do without, I suppose," she replies. – *My Fair Lady* (1964)

528 "In our family," testy Ruth Gordon informs her prospective daughter-in-law, "we don't divorce our men – we bury them." – *Lord Love a Duck* (1966)

529 Newlyweds Robert Redford and Jane Fonda have a falling out, with Redford leaving their apartment and spending a cold night with a bottle in a Greenwich Village park. Fonda finds him there in the morning. "This is crazy," he says. "It's all wrong for me to run away like this. There's only one right thing to do." "Really?" she asks hopefully. "What?" "You get out." – *Barefoot in the Park* (1967)

530 "What do I look like to you, a dog?" a suburban wife shouts. "You said it, I didn't," her husband fires back. – *Divorce, American Style* (1967)

531 Married couple Dick Van Dyke and Debbie Reynolds visit a marriage counselor. But Dick resists airing his problems and finally storms out with Debbie following close behind. "Please don't go," she pleads. "I know it's hard for you to believe. It's hard for me, too. There's something wrong. We're choking, we're suffocating." "I'll call the fire department!" Dick exclaims. – *Divorce, American Style* (1967)

532 Eleanor of Aquitaine (Katharine Hepburn), after endless quarreling with Henry II (Peter O'Toole), pleads for a little peace. "A little?" O'Toole replies. "Why so modest? I'll give you *eternal* peace." – *The Lion in Winter* (1968)

533 Bob Hope and Jane Wyman, in the throes of a divorce after nineteen years of marriage, duel with each other after Wyman finds Hope with another woman. "Nineteen years!" Wyman cries. "It seems more like ninety!" "Some of us are beginning to show it!" Hope fires back. – *How to Commit Marriage* (1969)

534 The relationship between Woody Allen and Louise Lasser is reaching a dead end. "You're immature," she says. "How am I immature?" "Emotionally, sexually and intellectually," she delineates. "Yeah," Allen accedes, "but what other ways?" – *Bananas* (1971)

535 Ann-Margret, living with Jack Nicholson, sees no prospects of marriage while Nicholson berates her for her fallen state. "This place is a mess," he says. "There's never any food in the house. Half the time you look like you fell out of bed. You're in bed more than any other human past the age of six months." "The reason I sleep all day is I can't stand my life." "What life?" "Sleeping all day," she replies. – *Carnal Knowledge* (1971)

536 Ex-football star Burt Reynolds has a fight with his girlfriend and rides off with her expensive sports car which he ditches into a bay. The police finally catch up to him. "Why did you dump her car in the bay?" an officer asks. "I couldn't find a carwash," Reynolds cracks. – *The Longest Yard* (1974)

537 Redd Foxx, whose wife has run off with his brother, tries to enlighten his son about the opposite sex. "Let me tell you something about women," he begins. "They're selfish, they're conniving, and if you don't care too much for dancing, you don't need them at all." – *Norman . . . Is That You?* (1976)

538 "I don't pick up strange men," a stern Goldie Hawn chides Chevy Chase who tries to flirt with her. "That's your trouble," he says. "So why don't you try it," she ripostes. – *Foul Play* (1978)

539 "I was married for nine years," artist Alan Bates confides to Jill Clayburgh. "The first eight were very passionate. Passion is probably too mild a word for it. It was more like a war." – *An Unmarried Woman* (1978)

540 When Shirley MacLaine discovers that her husband Anthony Hopkins is having an affair, she responds in kind. But Hopkins objects strongly to her young lover. "I have to consider my position," he offers. "Is that 'missionary' or something more imaginative?" she fires back. – *A Change of Seasons* (1980)

541 Husband Quinn Redeker, afraid of granting wife Dyan Cannon a divorce, which might cost him a small fortune, has her institutionalized. She escapes and attacks his property with a truck. He pleads with her to stop. "What is hostility anyway?" he cries out in an attempt to mollify her. "It's just love looking for a home." – *Coast to Coast* (1980)

542 Secretary Dolly Parton has been propositioned, ogled at and chased around her boss' desk numerous times. But when she permits rumors to spread throughout the office that she is sleeping with him, she explodes. "Look!" she exclaims. "I got a gun out there in my purse. And up to now I've been forgivin' and forgettin' because that is the way I was brought up. But I'll tell you one thing! If you ever say another word about me or make another indecent proposal, I'm going to get that gun of mine and I'm going to change you from a rooster to a hen in one shot!" – *Nine to Five* (1980)

543 Prospective Supreme Court justice Jill Clayburgh faces stiff opposition from a panel of Senators at a public hearing. They question her about her ability as a woman to make decisions. "Eggs are not the seeds of insanity," she protests firmly but quietly. "A woman can ovulate and think at the same time." – *First Monday in October* (1981)

544 Married hairdresser Julie Walters signs up for a literature course with disheveled, alcoholic college instructor Michael Caine. "When I come next week I'll bring my scissors and give you a haircut," she announces. "You will not be coming here next week," Caine replies. "Oh, I will be, and you'll be gettin' a haircut." "I will not." "Oh," she says, "I suppose you want to walk around lookin'

like that, do you?" "Like what?" "Like a geriatric hippie." – *Educating Rita* (1983)

545 When Richard Dreyfuss' girlfriend says she has to meet a friend, he jealously asks if she's sleeping with him. "You're sick," she fires back. "You're jealous because you have deep-rooted insecurities about your masculinity." "I do not," he protests. "I have deep-rooted insecurities about her availability." – *The Buddy System* (1984)

546 Smalltime hoodlum Joe Piscopo expounds upon the opposite sex: "Dames are put on this earth to weaken us, drain our energy, laugh at us when they see us naked." – *Johnny Dangerously* (1984)

547 Villainous, sexually charged Tina Turner meets her adversary in leather-clad, ex-cop Mel Gibson. She is a man-eater, eager to chalk up his carcass along with her previous victories. "One day cock-of-the-walk," she sneers, "next day a feather duster." – *Mad Max Beyond Thunderdome* (1985)

548 Rodney Dangerfield's second marriage doesn't seem to be working out. Among other faults, his wife finds him hostile to her party-loving friends. "You have no taste," his wife charges. "You're right," he replies. "I married you, didn't I?" – *Back to School* (1986)

549 "We're the weaker sex!" con artist Steve Martin complains to fellow con man Michael Caine. "We don't live as long as women; we get more heart attacks, more strokes, more prostate trouble. I say, it's time for a change. I say, let them give *us* money! Let's live off them for a while!" – *Dirty Rotten Scoundrels* (1988)

550 As a female soldier is about to go on night patrol at an army base, a fellow soldier suggests that if it gets cold, she should give him a call. "I've got a jacket." "It's not the same as a man." "Neither are you." – *The Presidio* (1988)

551 When Harry (Billy Crystal) confides to platonic friend Sally (Meg Ryan) that his date with another young woman did not work out – although he slept with her anyway and left early – Sally becomes enraged. "Why are you so upset?" Harry asks. "This is not about you." "Yes it is," she protests. "You are an affront to all women, and I am a woman." "Hey, I don't feel great about this, but I don't hear anyone complain." "Of course not," Sally replies. "You're out the door too fast." – *When Harry Met Sally. . .* (1989)

552 Cher rails to a stranger that her husband has absconded with her car and proceeds to describe both. "Are we talking about men or cars?" the confused listener asks. "Both," she replies. "I've been taken for a ride by both." – *Mermaids* (1990)

553 Ambulance-chasing New York lawyer Joe Peschi, out of his element in an Alabama courtroom, grumbles to his fiancée Marisa Tomei that he needs her support and it's not there. "You're gonna go in there and show these people," she says, trying to redress his grievance. "I'm telling you, you're gonna do great!" And then, after a pregnant pause: "If you don't fuck up." – *My Cousin Vinny* (1992)

Body Beautiful

554 Carnival barker William Haines describes a sultry dancer to an inquisitive crowd: "She's too hot to handle with bare hands, and it's against the law for her to sleep in a frame building." – *Way Out West* (1930)

555 W. C. Fields grandly crashes a lavish affair and proceeds to peer down a low-cut dress of a buxom beauty. "Now that I am here," he announces, "I shall dally in the valley – and believe me, I can dally." – *International House* (1933)

556 Hitchhiking with reporter Clark Gable, runaway heiress Claudette Colbert extends her shapely leg sideways onto the road and brings the next car to a screeching halt. "I proved once and for all the limb is mightier than the thumb," she asserts to Gable. – *It Happened One Night* (1934)

557 Fight manager Knobby Walsh (Jimmy Durante) tries to save his fighter Joe Palooka (Stuart Erwin) from the voluptuous and dangerous Lupe Velez by making a play for her himself.

"Let go of me," she protests to Durante. "You're crazy!" "I am crazy – crazy about you! You've got this, you've got that, and boy!" Durante cries, studying her body, "You've got those!" – *Palooka* (1934)

558 At a nightclub, reporters Ann Sothern and Frank Jenks observe a rich, sexy widow whose husband has recently been murdered. "Looks as though the widow Andrews has something on her mind," Sothern says. "I wouldn't know," Jenks replies. "I wasn't looking at her mind." – *There Goes My Girl* (1937)

559 Former magician Hugh Herbert, now assistant to magician David Niven, laments part of his past. "If it hadn't been for a woman, I'd still be playing the Palace," he confesses. "A little blonde thing – a contortionist. I remember how she used to twist her leg around her neck. It was beautiful." – *Eternally Yours* (1939)

560 Scarlett O'Hara (Vivien Leigh) characterizes Rhett Butler (Clark Gable):

"He looks as though he knows what I look like without my shimmy on." – *Gone with the Wind* (1939)

561 On a train, W. C. Fields makes inquiries from straitlaced Margaret Hamilton about Mae West, a fellow passenger. "I'm afraid I can't say anything good about her," she reports. "I can see what's good," Fields utters. "Tell me the rest." – *My Little Chickadee* (1940)

562 Mae West describes her escape from a masked bandit: "I was in a tight spot, but I managed to wriggle out of it." – *My Little Chickadee* (1940)

563 Stockbroker George Sanders has moved into his new Wall Street office where he soon discovers that his window offers a view of a very sexy woman. His girlfriend enters his office and catches him gawking at the beautiful stranger across the way. "Well," Sanders says defensively, "you said to get an office with a view." – *The Gay Falcon* (1941)

564 "Beauty is only skin deep," Bud Abbott explains to Lou Costello. "That's deep enough for me," Costello responds. "I'm no cannibal." – *Rio Rita* (1942)

565 While on leave, sailor Sonny Tufts ogles a chorus line. "That's the kind of flesh I never expected to see in the flesh again," he says to buddy Bing Crosby. "It's just part of the female anatomy," Bing flatly replies, "legs, limbs and, as the poet says, 'gams.'" "Yeah," concurs Tufts, "but where I came from, they were rationed." – *Here Come the Waves* (1944)

566 "You can't save a girl's life and then ignore her," a sexy young woman says to shy Jack Benny. "Oh, yes I can," he insists. "But of course you'll take a lot of ignoring." – *The Horn Blows at Midnight* (1945)

567 Jack Carson leers at Eve Arden fixing her stocking. "Leave something on me," Arden cracks. "I might catch cold." – *Mildred Pierce* (1945)

568 An elderly Bing Crosby, visiting a similarly aging Bob Hope, introduces his two "nieces" to his old-time pal. "Nice family tree," Hope says. "The limbs aren't bad either." – *Road to Utopia* (1945)

569 Groucho Marx, after observing a curvaceous, hip-swinging woman exit from a room: "That reminds me – I must get my watch fixed." – *A Night in Casablanca* (1946)

570 Chased by police, Groucho Marx ducks into a showgirls' dressing room and asks for their protection. "Please don't let them take me," he pleads. "I've got my whole life ahead of me – and I'd like to spend it here." – *Copacabana* (1947)

571 Greer Garson meets strongman Cesar Romero aboard a ship and is attracted to his muscular physique while he, oblivious to her flirting, constantly talks about acrobatics. "In acrobatics, you could say, we changed the whole picture," he boasts. "But you kept the frame," she quips. – *Julia Misbehaves* (1948)

572 Quiz show host Jack Paar asks contestant Red Buttons to identify the following actress: "I'm known for my gorgeous figure, a plunging neckline, long red hair and full red lips. Who am I?" "Who cares?" Buttons answers. "Kiss me!" – *Footlight Varieties* (1951)

573 Landlords William Lundigan and wife June Haver rent an apartment to sexy Marilyn Monroe. When their lawyer-friend Jack Paar comes to visit them, he is aroused by the new tenant who invites him up to help her with the apartment. "He's walking right into a trap," Haver says. "Yeah," her husband agrees, "but look at the bait!" – *Love Nest* (1951)

574 Jane Russell, wearing a low-cut dress, observes Robert Mitchum looking down her cleavage. "Enjoying the view?" she asks. "It's not the Taj Mahal or the

Hanging Gardens of Babylon," he replies, but it's not bad." – *Macao* (1952)

575 Sports promoter Spencer Tracy, upon seeing golf pro Katharine Hepburn for the first time, says appreciatively: "She's nicely packed. Not much meat on her, but what's there is 'cherce'." – *Pat and Mike* (1952)

576 Army draftee Mickey Rooney, meeting fight manager Bob Hope, says that he saw Hope's champion boxer's last fight. "I saw the fight over at my sister-in-law's," Rooney explains. "She has a sixteen-inch screen." "Sounds like a grand girl," Hope returns. – *Off Limits* (1953)

577 Unassuming innocent Marilyn Monroe stands over a subway grating on a hot summer night to receive a refreshing blast of fresh air from an oncoming train. As a gust of wind lifts her dress well above her knees, her married companion Tom Ewell ogles the sensual sight. "It sort of cools the ankles, doesn't it?" he remarks. – *The Seven Year Itch* (1955)

578 "You know," says buxom Jayne Mansfield to Groucho Marx, "you never even tried to kiss me." "I never could get that close," Groucho returns. – *Will Success Spoil Rock Hunter?* (1957)

579 U.S. Navy lieutenant Jerry Lewis is accused of "misplacing" the U.S.S. *Kornblatt*, a destroyer escort. He reports to Ensign Benson (Dina Merrill) of navy intelligence and is surprised to find that Benson is a beautiful, shapely woman. "They let you keep secrets?" he inquires. "Of course," she replies. "Why?" "Oh, nothing. It's just that you look like a girl that has nothing to hide. What I mean to say is that if the *Kornblatt* were built like you, we would never have lost her." – *Don't Give Up the Ship* (1959)

580 Cantinflas, to raise some money in a gambling house, tries his hand at dice. He throws the dice wildly, and they land in the low-cut gown of a buxom beauty. "Did I do good?" he asks Dean Martin. "You sure did," Martin replies. "You just contributed to the Community Chest." – *Pepe* (1961)

581 Ex-vaudeville entertainer takes a close look at stage mother Rosalind Russell's figure and says: "You look like a pioneer woman without a frontier." "Is that good or bad?" a puzzled Russell questions. – *Gypsy* (1962)

582 The Three Stooges are transported back to 900 B.C. by way of a time machine and are invited to a Greek ruler's feast. "You know," one of their friends comments about a wine receptacle, "these old Greek things certainly have lovely curves, haven't they?" "These young Greek things ain't bad either," Moe agrees, referring to his two lovely female companions. – *The Three Stooges Meet Hercules* (1962)

583 Shapely Ann-Margret, dressed in a tight sweater and shorts, stops at a garage and appeals to Elvis Presley to fix her sports car. "I'd like you to check my motor," she asks. "It whistles." "I don't blame it," Presley replies. – *Viva Las Vegas* (1964)

584 Cattleman William Holden, to elude a pursuer, enters a bordello, selects an attractive prostitute and takes her into an upstairs room. As he is about to leave, he hands her several dollars and a book. "I want you to improve your mind," he says. "Your body is already perfect." – *Alvarez Kelly* (1966)

585 At a Roman slave market, prospective buyer Zero Mostel examines luscious twin slaves. "I don't suppose you'd break up a set?" he inquires. – *A Funny Thing Happened on the Way to the Forum* (1966)

586 A well-proportioned female instructor is having trouble keeping the attention of secret agent Matt Helm (Dean Martin) focused on the latest gadgetry and off her figure. "It's a new weapon . . . developed right here in our labs," she explains. "Developed pretty well, too," Martin adds. "May I point out –" "You already do." "– That that's why you're here – to become familiar with our latest equipment." "You're right," Martin agrees. "An agent should always keep abreast of the times." – *The Ambushers* (1967)

587 A suspect who minutes before was sleeping with a svelte bed partner gets the drop on police detectives Richard Widmark and Harry Guardino and makes his getaway. "You bum!" Guardino reproaches Widmark. "You were looking at the broad!" "What were you looking at?" Widmark fires back. – *Madigan* (1968)

588 Buxom Italian beauty Gina Lollobrigida delicately rejects Bob Hope's advances toward her. "You will find a nice American woman who will have much more than I have," she says. "I don't know where she'd put it," Hope quips. – *The Private Navy of Sgt. O'Farrell* (1968)

589 When three very attractive young women cross at a busy intersection, several cars come to a screeching halt. "Hey, girls!" a traffic cop yells out, "on this street *I* stop the traffic!" – *Change of Habit* (1969)

590 "My jokes are stale," court jester Woody Allen ponders, displaying a dash of Hamlet. "I would my life take for a bare bodkin. If I could see the Queen's bare bodkin or anybody's bare bodkin, for that matter, or a bodkin with a little clothes on it even." – *Everything You Always Wanted to Know About Sex (But Were Afraid to Ask)* (1972)

591 Woody Allen watches a curvaceous blonde gyrating across a dance floor. "I'd sell my mother to the Arabs for her," he says. – *Play It Again, Sam* (1972)

592 James Bond (Roger Moore) snatches a secret gold bullet from a seductive café dancer before a brawl erupts in her dressing room. "I've lost my charm!" she cries. "Not from where I'm standing," Moore quips before leaving. – *The Man with the Golden Gun* (1974)

593 Little Tracy's divorced father takes her to a Chinese restaurant to meet his new girlfriend, but Tracy is unimpressed. "She isn't as pretty as Mom." "Well, she has other qualities I find attractive." "Her big boobs?" – *Oh, God! Book II* (1980)

594 Rodney Dangerfield looks across his back yard and sees a sexy young woman, clad only in a bikini, sunbathing. He later meets his new neighbor – the woman's husband. "Wait'll you meet Jessica, my better half," the man says. "I already saw your better half," Dangerfield replies. "In fact, I saw more than half." – *Easy Money* (1983)

595 On a Rio beach, Michael Caine and Joseph Bologna ogle the bare-breasted women. "We can't talk to them," says Caine. "They're practically naked. "Imagine them with clothes on," suggests Bologna. – *Blame It on Rio* (1984)

596 Assistant high-school principal Judd Hirsch mentions a former female student, now a lawyer, to teacher Nick Nolte. "Oh, yes," Nolte recalls. "Bright student, great ass." "Well, nothing has changed." – *Teachers* (1984)

597 To show off the wonders of bosom enhancement surgery, a bikini-clad neighbor at a seaside cottage bares her breasts to a startled John Candy. "What do you think of these?" "Of what?" Candy gasps. "These," she repeats, wiggling her breasts in front of him. "Similar?" he asks. – *Summer Rental* (1985)

598 Police officers Dan Aykroyd and Tom Hanks interview a sexy porno model who, to their surprise, suddenly exposes her breasts to Aykroyd. "Would you say these look like the breasts of a forty-three-year-old woman?" she inquires.

"No, no they don't," the startled officer replies matter-of-factly. "They're quite impressive – bordering on spectacular." – *Dragnet* (1987)

599 Single parent Tony Danza, blessed with two precocious daughters, tries to impress his boy-crazy, fifteen-year-old (Amy Dolenz) with the importance of school. "Let me leave you with one thought," he says awkwardly. "A mind – a good mind – is a terrible thing to waste." "So is a good body," his younger daughter interjects. – *She's Out of Control* (1989)

600 Aging hippie Dennis Hopper comments to F.B.I. agent Kiefer Sutherland about a young woman's breasts: "She looks like she was shot in the back by a pair of Cruise missiles." – *Flashback* (1990)

601 Jeff Bridges brings homeless Robin Williams to his girlfriend Mercedes Ruehl's apartment where she serves him a hot meal. Williams cannot take his eyes off Ruehl's partially exposed breasts as she serves him his food. "You're a wonderful cook," Robin remarks, "and you have a great set of – dishes." – *The Fisher King* (1991)

602 Assigned to investigate a murder case, police officer Leslie Nielsen accidentally meets his former sweetheart who had walked out on him. "There she was – just as I remembered her," he reflects. "That delicately beautiful face, and a body that would melt a cheese sandwich from across the room, and breasts that seemed to say, 'Hey, look at these!' Yeah, she reminded me of my mother, all right." – *The Naked Gun 2½: The Smell of Fear* (1991)

603 Super-sleuth Leslie Nielsen bursts in upon a suspected nest of criminals and confronts a buxom beauty. "Is this some kind of bust!" she asks. "Very impressive," Nielsen mistakenly agrees. – *The Naked Gun 2½: The Smell of Fear* (1991)

604 Madonna, as a tramp on an all-women's baseball team, proposes that to increase attendance she could open a few choice buttons on her uniform. "You think there are men in this country," a teammate remarks, "who ain't seen your bosoms?" – *A League of Their Own* (1992)

Bosses

605 Asleep on his employer's desk, Bobby Clark is awakened by his boss who hits Clark across the bottom of his feet with a cane. "Just because we're working for you," the indignant Clark remarks, "doesn't mean you have to trifle with my soul." – *Love and Hisses* (1934)

606 Reporter Fredric March describes his managing editor (Walter Connolly) to Carole Lombard: "He's sort of a cross between a ferris wheel and a werewolf, but with a lovable streak – if you care to blast for it." – *Nothing Sacred* (1937)

607 When a gruff nightclub owner gives Harry James and his band a difficult time during their five-minute break, they all quit. "That's the first time I ever saw a pair of shoes with three heels," quips one of the musicians. – *Private Buckaroo* (1942)

608 In turn-of-the-century Yonkers, provisions store proprietor Paul Ford tells his only clerk Ambrose (Robert Morse) that he is to be promoted to chief clerk. "What am I now?" asks Ambrose. "Now you're an impertinent fool," Ford replies. "If you behave yourself,

I'll promote you from impertinent fool to chief clerk, and Barnaby may be promoted from idiot apprentice to incompetent clerk." – *The Matchmaker* (1958)

609 During the Cold War, a West Berliner performs a valuable service for overseas soft-drink executive James Cagney. "You're a good man," Cagney says. "How much are we paying you?" "Fifty dollars," the man replies. "That's enough." – *One, Two, Three* (1961)

610 A U.S. embassy clerk in a foreign country complains about his immediate superior to a fellow worker. "I bluffed the old man out of the pot with a pair of deuces," he says. "What is so depressing about that?" his friend asks. "Well, I mean, if I could do it, what are the Russians doing to him?" – *Charade* (1963)

611 Dance-hall hostess Shirley MacLaine leaves her job and returns with her husband-to-be to retrieve some personal articles. "Don't take any hangers," the manager demands. "Every time someone leaves here, they always take the hangers." "He's kind of gruff,"

she explains to her boyfriend, "but inside he's a very rotten person." – *Sweet Charity* (1969)

612 The office spy, an officious supervisor who is distrusted and disliked by her coworkers, hands secretary Lily Tomlin a report on which to work. "Thanks," Lily says, "I know just where to – stick it." – *9 to 5* (1980)

613 Rich, spoiled Goldie Hawn hires carpenter Kurt Russell to build closets aboard her husband's luxurious yacht. As she shows him around the vessel, she treats him with disdain. "Andrew will keep an eye on you," she says, referring to her servant. "Maybe you'd like to take fingerprints before I get started," Russell remarks. – *Overboard* (1987)

614 Insensitive television star Bill Murray scolds his secretary. "A little rough on her, weren't you?" his brother says later. "You know what they say about treating people badly on the way up?" "Yep," replies Murray. "You get to treat them badly on the way down, too." – *Scrooged* (1988)

Bravado

615 African explorer Groucho Marx relates one of his adventures to Margaret Dumont: "One morning I shot an elephant in my pajamas. How he got in my pajamas, I don't know. Then we tried to remove the tusks, but they were embedded in so firmly that we couldn't budge them. Of course in Alabama the Tuscaloosa. But that's entirely irrelephant to what I was talking about." – *Animal Crackers* (1930)

616 "I spent all last summer shooting tigers in Africa," Robert Woolsey boasts, trying to impress a young woman. "But there are no tigers in Africa," she says. "I know," he explains.

"I killed them all." – *Half Shot at Sunrise* (1930)

617 For the woman he loves (Olivia de Havilland), Captain Blood (Errol Flynn) sets sail for Port Royal where the enemy Spanish fleet lies in port. "The gallows are waiting for us at Port Royal," one crew member says portentously, "and no man should be late for his own hanging." – *Captain Blood* (1935)

618 Mississippi riverboat captain W. C. Fields regales his passengers with his earlier battles against hostile Native Americans. "I whipped out my revolver –" "Revolvers weren't invented thirty-five years ago," one skeptical passenger interrupts Fields. "I know that," Fields fires back, "but the Indians didn't know it." – *Mississippi* (1935)

619 "I'm tough, too," W. C. Fields affirms. "I can lick my weight in wildflowers." – *The Big Broadcast of 1938* (1938)

620 Cary Grant, as a British soldier in colonial India, finds himself trapped in the secret temple of the Thuggees – a fanatical sect of stranglers. To stall for time, he saunters casually into their midst. "You're all under arrest," he announces, "the whole bunch of you, and you know why. Her Majesty is very touchy about having her subjects strangled." – *Gunga Din* (1939)

621 The king's soldiers arrive to arrest D'Artagnan and the Three Musketeers, who are spoiling for a fight. "Is the king becoming frugal?" one of the Musketeers asks. "Only nine men?" "There are ninety more outside," the officer replies threateningly. "Flatterer!" Porthos (Alan Hale) thunders. – *The Man in the Iron Mask* (1939)

622 Corrupt land-grabbers steal a deed from Groucho Marx and toss him down a flight of stairs. "I was going to thrash them within an inch of their lives," he announces, "but I didn't have a tape measure." – *Go West* (1940)

623 German Major Strasser (Conrad Veidt), recently arrived in Casablanca, tries to impress café owner Rick Blaine (Humphrey Bogart) with his Nazi thoroughness. He shows Bogart the complete dossier the Germans have on him. "Hm-m," Bogart wonders after scanning the contents. "Are my eyes really blue?" – *Casablanca* (1942)

624 Huntz Hall tells the surrounding crowd that boxing challenger Leo Gorcey is "so tough he told Joe Louis where to get off." However, someone voices incredulity. "Well," Hall backtracks, "they were riding on the

same streetcar together." – *Kid Dynamite* (1943)

625 In a Klondike saloon Bob Hope tries to impress the hardened patrons with his own toughness. "I'll take lemonade – in a dirty glass," he orders from the bartender. – *Road to Utopia* (1945)

626 "Ah, yes," boasts Robin Hood (Cornel Wilde), "a thousand men couldn't take that cursed castle by storm. Yet I – I alone could swim the moat, elude the archers, scale the walls, cut down the guards, make my way to the dungeon, disarm the turnkey and free my father." "Aye," replies Friar Tuck (Edgar Buchanan), "but it might – might be risky, Robin." – *The Bandit of Sherwood Forest* (1946)

627 Embarrassed bodyguard Lionel Stander lies to his boss Walter Abel about how his charge, prizefighter Steve Cochran, got knocked out in a common street brawl. Eve Arden, Abel's secretary, remains skeptical about the description of the "other man." "What a guy!" Stander exclaims. "Shoulders like that! Hands as big as watermelons!" "How does he wind his watch?" Arden quips. – *The Kid from Brooklyn* (1946)

628 Three ominous-looking foreign agents warn Bob Hope that his life is in danger. "Why don't you boys go down to the basement?" Hope suggests. "Tonight's the night they're putting new cheese in the traps." – *Where There's Life* (1947)

629 Roguish soldier-of-fortune Douglas Fairbanks, Jr., returns home to Ireland to uncover a plot involving traitors loyal to Napoleon. They ask Fairbanks to name his price for his silence. "An Irishman silent?" he laughs. – *The Fighting O'Flynn* (1949)

630 Expert swordsman Valvert challenges Cyrano de Bergerac (Jose Ferrer) to a duel and precedes the swordplay with a verbal assault. "Dolt! Bumpkin! Fool!" Valvert fires off. "How do you do?" Cyrano replies. "And I – Cyrano Savinien Hercule de Bergerac." – *Cyrano de Bergerac* (1950)

631 Smalltime actor Bob Hope, impersonating a British earl, regales Lucille Ball and other party guests with one of his imaginary adventures in Africa. "There I was, with a spear through my body – " "Didn't it hurt?" asks Ball. "Only when I laughed," he replies. – *Fancy Pants* (1950)

632 Katharine Hepburn persuades Humphrey Bogart, the captain of a small river launch, the *African Queen,* to try to sink a German gunboat which lies at the end of a virtually unnavigable river. They chug along as crocodiles menacingly approach the launch. "Don't be worried," she shouts encouragingly. "Oh, I ain't worried," Bogart replies. "I gave myself up for dead back where we started." – *The African Queen* (1951)

633 Legionnaire Burt Lancaster is captured by rebellious Arabs and is to be tortured at the same time that the sheik is to be wed. "It's a pity I have to leave for the marriage," the sheik wryly explains to his captive. "Don't stay on my account," Lancaster flippantly fires back. – *Ten Tall Men* (1951)

634 Medicine show huckster Dan Dailey and Scat Man Crothers pick up a boy who has run away from an orphan asylum. Dailey regales the youth with tall tales of his fictitious exploits while Crothers adds to the merriment. "I used to cook for Richard III," Dailey boasts. "And his son, July the Fourth," Crothers quips. – *Meet Me at the Fair* (1952)

635 "That's what I like about you," Leo Gorcey says sarcastically to Huntz Hall. "You're full of bravado." "I never sang for the opera," Hall corrects him. – *The Bowery Boys Meet the Monsters* (1954)

636 Soldier-of-fortune Robert Mitchum, caught by a band of Mexican soldiers, learns that his horse "gave him away." "I told him never to talk to strangers," he wisecracks. – *Bandido* (1956)

637 James Bond (Sean Connery) and innocent Ursula Andress are captured by Dr. No's henchmen and locked up on an island off the coast of Jamaica. A young woman in the villainous doctor's employ tries to make the pair's stay comfortable. "Don't hesitate to ring if there's anything you want – anything at all." "Such as two tickets to London?" Bond suggests. – *Dr. No* (1962)

638 C.I.A. agent Cary Grant becomes enmeshed in a search for $250,000 and meets up with some formidable opposition – including George Kennedy, who has a concealed pistol in his coat. "Do anything funny and I'll kill you," Kennedy warns. "You'll wreck your raincoat," Grant nonchalantly replies. – *Charade* (1963)

639 Horse thief Jack Nicholson catches his nemesis, regulator Marlon Brando, off guard – the latter is taking a bath. Although Nicholson threatens to kill him, Brando remains unruffled. "How am I going to get my nourishment," Brando inquires, "if I spend my dinner hour with you?" – *The Missouri Breaks* (1976)

640 Fire-fighter pilot Richard Dreyfuss finds himself flying over a heavily wooded area with an empty fuel tank. As his twin propellers come to a stop, he notifies his base of his precarious condition. "What do you need? What do you need?" the officer in the control tower asks. "Glider practice," Dreyfuss answers. – *Always* (1989)

641 Private detective Bruce Willis is threatened by a hoodlum holding a knife against his face. "Just once I'd like to hear you scream," the thug taunts. "Play some rap music," Willis quips. – *The Last Boy Scout* (1991)

642 Kathleen Turner, as the tough private investigator V.I. Warshawski, complains to the hoodlum who has just punched her in her pretty face: "You know how hard it is to get blood out of cashmere?" – *V.I. Warshawski* (1991)

Business and Businessmen

643 Stan Laurel and Oliver Hardy discuss going into the fish business. "Well," explains Laurel, "if we caught our own fish, we wouldn't have to pay for it. Then, whoever we sold it to, it would be a clear profit." "Tell me that again," Hardy says, slightly confused. "Well–if you caught a fish–and whoever you sold it to they wouldn't have to pay for it–and the profit goes to–the fish–and–" "I know exactly what you mean," Hardy cheerfully responds. –*Towed in a Hole* (1932)

644 Storekeeper Charles Grapewin stops neighbor Lionel Barrymore to inquire about the price of his son's coat. "Five dollars," Barrymore replies. "You got stung.... Serves you right. I advertise in your paper, you should buy in my store." "Well," replies Barrymore, "as a matter of fact, that's where I did buy it." –*Ah, Wilderness* (1935)

645 Butler William Powell announces that he "sold short" in the stock market, thereby rescuing the funds of the family that has employed him. "I don't understand," Alice Brady, the confused mother of the clan, interjects. "You sold short? You mean gentlemen's underwear?" –*My Man Godfrey* (1936)

646 In a small-town general store, two elderly checker players are busily engaged in combat. One keeps dipping into the cracker barrel until the shopkeeper spots him. "How can I make any money if you keep eating up all the profits?" the owner asks. "They ain't profits," the man answers, "they're crackers." –*Of Human Hearts* (1937)

647 Crooked politicians make a deal with underworld leader Harold Huber. "It's a deal," says the head politician. "And in return, we get fifty percent of the business." "Nothin' doin'!" Huber protests. "I take fifty percent and you get what's left over." –*You Can't Beat Love* (1937)

648 During a stroll in Central Park, unhappy, wealthy manufacturer Walter Connolly meets unemployed worker Ginger Rogers, who disparagingly calls him a capitalist. "I'm not a capitalist!" he exclaims. "I'm a victim of the capitalistic system." –*Fifth Avenue Girl* (1939)

649 Groucho Marx sells a land deed to crooked Robert Barrat who, after getting the deed, welshes on the deal. "We're not gonna pay you nothin'!" Barrat announces. "Well," Groucho replies, "that's one way of reducing your overhead." –*Go West* (1940)

650 Country boy James Stewart, lost in the caverns of New York City, asks cabby Frank Faylen for help. "What subway do I take to get to 72nd Street and Lexington Avenue?" "I ain't giving no information on subways," Faylen replies. "We're competitors." –*No Time for Comedy* (1940)

651 Department store owner Charles Coburn, posing as a salesman to find out the internal problems of the store, reports late for work one morning. "Ah," his section manager says in an icy tone, "we're a little late this morning, aren't we?" "Oh, were you late, too?" Coburn queries. –*The Devil and Miss Jones* (1941)

652 "A wonderful woman," the owner of a fashionable store says to Hal Peary about dizzy Billie Burke. "She overpays on everything. Why don't you marry her?" "Why don't you marry her yourself?" the indignant Peary replies. "What, and lose my best customer?" –*Gildersleeve on Broadway* (1943)

653 Successful radio scriptwriter Dick Powell finds himself in a diner outside of Manhattan without his wallet. "I don't suppose you'd cash a check?" he asks the owner. "We got an agreement with the bank," the man explains. "They don't sell no hamburgers; we don't cash no checks." – *True to Life* (1943)

654 Two gangsters, hired to kill Danny Kaye, chase him through S. K. Sakall's delicatessen shop. To escape, Kaye smashes the front window and leaps through, followed by his pursuers. "Now we are open for business twenty-four hours a day," the flustered Sakall says to his wife. – *Wonder Man* (1945)

655 An executive of an English coffee empire, addressing a group of managers, points out the threat of tea to the coffee business. "The average Englishman has increased his consumption to no less than six cups of tea per day," he states. "What conclusion can we draw from that?" "We're in the wrong business," quips manager Rex Harrison. – *Notorious Gentleman* (1946)

656 Down-and-out Bing Crosby and buddies Raymond Washburn and William Demarest exchange a walking cane for food at a hamburger stand. "Well," the owner balks slightly after examining the cane, "it ain't nearly the size I wanted – " "What do you want for a hamburger," Demarest asks, "a telephone pole?" – *Riding High* (1950)

657 A broadcasting company president hires efficiency expert Spencer Tracy to automate the research department. When he is offered his own office, Tracy refuses. "You don't care whether you impress people or not," the president remarks. "You wait till you get my bill," Tracy responds. "You'll be impressed." – *Desk Set* (1957)

658 A young married couple (Bill Travers, Virginia McKenna), thinking they have inherited a grand-looking movie theater, approach the doorman. "I say," they inquire pleasantly, "how's

business?" "I wouldn't know," the surly man replies. "I mind my own." – *The Smallest Show on Earth* (1957)

659 Military officer Keenan Wynn empties his weapon into a Coca-Cola machine to obtain some desperately needed coins so that English exchange officer Peter Sellers can place a doomsday emergency call. "If you don't get the President on the phone," Wynn warns, "you know what's going to happen to you?" "What?" Sellers asks. "You're going to have to answer to the Coca-Cola Company." – *Dr. Strangelove* (1964)

660 Ambitious Robert Morse has been promoted to advertising manager of a large corporation and assigned to come up with a new campaign. At a meeting, he suggests a treasure-hunt television show. "It can't miss," he announces. "I'm combining greed with sex." – *How to Succeed in Business Without Really Trying* (1967)

661 "When the time comes," boasts successful American tycoon Karl Malden, "I might even put in a bid for all of England." "Aren't you going to wait till it's solvent?" quips Peter Ustinov. – *Hot Millions* (1968)

662 Burlesque comic Norman Wisdom enters a shop to buy a stage-prop snake, but finds the price is too high. "Look at the workmanship," the shop owner points out. "Ten days it took to make such a snake." "Ten days! It only took six days to make the world!" "But look at the way this is made! Is this seam perfect?" "The seam's perfect," Wisdom acknowledges. "And look at the world." – *The Night They Raided Minsky's* (1968)

663 Somewhere in France during World War II, G.I. Clint Eastwood plans to rob several million dollars in gold stored behind German lines and needs the help of Crapgame (Don Rickles), a well-known hustler in charge of army supplies and equipment. "I'm going along to protect my investment," Rickles insists. "I think a firm financial mind should be behind an enterprise such as this. There could be a bonus." – *Kelly's Heroes* (1970)

664 Anthropologist Joan Crawford thaws out an English caveman who has remained frozen and well preserved for centuries. "It's ruining my plans for a housing project," a local businessman grumbles. "No one wants to buy land with an ugly monster running loose." – *Trog* (1970)

665 An Italian resort manager is upset when he discovers that one of the maids has run off after murdering a valet, the father of her unborn child. "It's a tragedy," the manager laments. "If you lose a guest, you can always replace him. But to lose a maid and a valet in the middle of the season–" – *Avanti!* (1972)

666 Housewife Barbra Streisand goes to her insurance company to collect for the theft of her husband's watch and meets stiff resistance. "If you insist," the claims adjuster finally says, "we'll pay. But we'll have to cancel your policy." "Cancel it? For what? Putting in a claim?" "Just think about it," he states. "You may be robbed again, and you won't have any insurance." "What's the use of having insurance if you can't collect?" she asks. "Peace of mind," the adjuster concludes. – *For Pete's Sake* (1974)

667 An unpaid contractor removes his equipment and supplies from the property of married couple George Segal and Jane Fonda. Fonda protests loudly. "Your mother may have carried you for nine months," the contractor says to her, "but we're only going to carry you for two." – *Fun with Dick and Jane* (1977)

668 George Hamilton asks a bartender if it's all right to pay by check. "I would prefer cash," the bartender says. "Oh, Uncle Sam?" "No," the man replies, "Uncle Irving. He owns the joint." – *The Happy Hooker Goes to Washington* (1977)

669 Photographer Keith Carradine enters a house of prostitution to sell his pictures. "You're in the wrong place, monsieur," the madam quickly informs him. "We are not in the business of buying." – *Pretty Baby* (1978)

670 An adult-bookstore owner with a wry sense of humor has a Beethoven Birthday Sale. "Did you ever see so many men in raincoats looking for a bargain?" he asks. – *Soup for One* (1982)

671 Struggling family man Rodney Dangerfield comes into big money when his wealthy mother-in-law is killed in a plane crash. "Silver is down?" he says to a broker on the telephone. "Well, call the Lone Ranger. He'll cheer him up." – *Easy Money* (1983)

672 Young Tom Cruise befriends a teenage hooker who decides to leave Guido, her "manager." Guido finds Cruise and engages him in a mock business conference. "In a sluggish economy," Guido warns, "never fool with another man's livelihood." – *Risky Business* (1983)

673 Two millionaire brothers (Ralph Bellamy and Don Ameche) who own the brokerage firm of Duke & Duke explain their business to streetwise Eddie Murphy. "No matter whether our clients make or lose money, Duke & Duke gets the commissions," says Bellamy. "Well," Ameche asks Murphy, "what do you think?" "It sounds to me like you guys are a couple of bookies," replies Murphy. – *Trading Places* (1983)

674 Wealthy businessman Jonathan Winters suddenly has a heart attack at his desk while discussing family matters with grandson Art Hindle. "Get me my lawyer," Winters gasps. "You mean a doctor?" Hindle asks. "No, my lawyer," Winters persists. "I want to change my will." – *Say Yes* (1986)

675 "I don't understand these bankers," says African ranch owner Joss Ackland. "When the sun's shining, they can't wait to lend you an umbrella. The minute it starts to rain, they want it back." – *White Mischief* (1987)

676 Teenager River Phoenix, who needs another eighty dollars to get to Hawaii, approaches his enterprising kid sister who wants his record player for "collateral." "It's not mine," he explains, watching her get up to leave. "Okay, it's yours." "Twenty dollars," she offers. "Twenty dollars?" "What do you expect for stolen property?" – *A Night in the Life of Jimmy Reardon* (1988)

677 Ambitious Wall Street secretary Melanie Griffith comments to her superiors about the eventual success of large companies who create food products: "No one ever got rich overestimating what the American public wants to taste." – *Working Girl* (1988)

678 Wall Street employees Melanie Griffith and Harrison Ford, desperate to put over a big merger, plan to crash the wedding of a tycoon's daughter so that they can interest him in their proposal. Ford, however, has second thoughts about the scheme. "This is a perfect opportunity," she reassures him. "He's happy, he's had a little champagne, we look for an opening – trust me." "What are we supposed to do," he questions, "jump out of the wedding cake?" – *Working Girl* (1988)

Captivity

679 In ancient Rome, slave Eddie Cantor is placed on the auction block for various citizens to examine. "Lady," Cantor reproaches a potential customer, "please don't touch unless you intend to buy." – *Roman Scandals* (1933)

680 Slave Rex Ingram confides to Mickey Rooney as Huck Finn: "I'm savin' enough money to buy myself." – *The Adventures of Huckleberry Finn* (1939)

681 On board a plane, spoiled heiress Bette Davis wants to know what exorbitant fee her hired kidnapper-pilot James Cagney is being paid. "Just the carrying charges," Cagney retorts. – *The Bride Came C.O.D.* (1941)

682 Bob Hope and Bing Crosby are captured by cannibals and are being prepared for dinner. One native suddenly belches. "It must have been somebody he ate," Hope figures. – *Road to Zanzibar* (1941)

683 Amateur sleuth Boston Blackie (Chester Morris) and his assistant (George E. Stone) are captured by diamond thieves, bound hand and foot and hung upside down in a closet. "The blood is rushing to my head," Stone utters, "and my feet are falling asleep." "Most of the time it's just the reverse," quips Morris. – *One Mysterious Night* (1944)

684 Bob Hope and Dorothy Lamour become the captives of a gang of international spies. Locked in a room together, they realize their predicament. "We're caught like rats in a trap," Hope wails. "Well, at least we're a boy rat and a girl rat." – *My Favorite Brunette* (1947)

685 Bud Abbott and Lou Costello have been captured by a tribe of cannibals, tied up and prepared for cooking in a large vat of boiling water. "Now I know what they mean when they say, 'Boy, are you in hot water!'" Costello says. – *Africa Screams* (1949)

686 A blustering American general, a prisoner-of-war in a mythical European country, cautions one of his captors, a buxom duchess (Peter Sellers). "I warn you," he says, "I know the Geneva Convention by heart." "Oh, how nice," the duchess responds. "You must recite it for me sometime." – *The Mouse That Roared* (1959)

687 The Three Stooges, transported back in time to 900 B.C., become captives of a Greek tyrant. "I condemn them to the galleys!" the ruler decrees. "Galleys?" echoes Curly Joe. "We're gonna do some cooking?" – *The Three Stooges Meet Hercules* (1962)

688 British agent Cliff Robertson finds himself captive of a circus troupe. Locked in a wagon with a dark-eyed beauty, he learns that they have a long ride to the mountains. "Whatever will we do to pass the time?" he asks, embracing his riding companion. – *Masquerade* (1965)

689 During the reign of Louis XIV of France, French soldiers arrive at a farm to arrest the owner's pretty daughter. "Come along quietly or we'll burn down your farm," the officer charges. "I will go quietly because it's best for everyone – for the people, for France," the prisoner announces, raising her voice. "As quickly as we shall treat each

other with human kindness, with love! I will go quietly, not for myself, for my personal safety, but for the good of mankind, the good of my countrymen, my village, my family, for France!" "You said you'd go quietly," the officer cuts in and, turning to his troops, adds: "Burn down the farm!" – *Start the Revolution Without Me* (1970)

690 In ancient Egypt, idol maker Dudley Moore is captured by bandits. "They'll ransom you," says the bandit chief. "I'll send them a nose or an ear – send them to your family as proof of your capture." "They'll probably think it was only junk mail," counters Moore. – *Wholly Moses* (1980)

691 Woody Allen and Mia Farrow, kidnapped and bound by gangsters, are guarded by a hoodlum. "The two of us can take him, almost," she says. "The man has an axe," Allen points out. "Two of us'll be four of us." – *Broadway Danny Rose* (1984)

692 Catwoman (Michelle Pfeiffer), in a fierce battle with Batman (Michael Keaton) on a roof top, uses her bullwhip to suspend him from a weather vane. "I'm not to be taken for granted," she hisses. "Are you listening? You, Batman, you!" "Hanging on your every word," he replies. – *Batman Returns* (1992)

Children

693 "I've known my son since infantry!" insists Southern plantation owner Joe Cawthorn. – *Dixiana* (1930)

694 Real estate agent Cliff Edwards reports to an East Side tenement to collect rent and sees a large group of children who seem to belong to one mother. "Are all these kids yours or is this a picnic?" "They're mine, thank

you." "Don't thank *me*," Edwards says. – *Sidewalks of New York* (1931)

695 Dean Groucho Marx of Huxley College makes a request of a young woman sitting on his son's lap: "Young lady, would you mind getting up so I could see the son rise?" – *Horse Feathers* (1932)

696 "I married your mother because I wanted children," Groucho Marx grumbles to his son Zeppo. "Imagine my disappointment when you arrived." – *Horse Feathers* (1932)

697 "Do you like children?" Alison Skipworth asks W. C. Fields. "I do – if they are properly cooked," he replies. – *Tillie and Gus* (1933)

698 Eighteen-year-old orphan Loretta Young runs away from her group while visiting a zoo and becomes the object of an intense search, much to the annoyance of the attendants. "Why do they let orphans in the zoo!" grumbles one guard. "Why do people have orphans anyway?" – *Zoo in Budapest* (1933)

699 Broadway bookie Sorrowful Jones (Adolphe Menjou), owner of a betting parlor, accepts a customer's little daughter (Shirley Temple) as security for a bet. "A little doll like that's worth twenty bucks any way you look at it," Menjou concludes. "Yeah," his cashier, Lynne Overman, agrees, "she ought to melt down for that much." – *Little Miss Marker* (1934)

700 May Robson, as the hard-working mother of three failing sons and one daughter, tries to instill hope in her children. "You talk like Horatio Alger!" one son blurts out. "Why don't you write a novel?" "I don't have to," she is quick to reply. "I have four children. That's a serial." – *Strangers All* (1935)

701 W. C. Fields wants to dispose of jinxed daughter Martha Raye, whose gaze, for example, turns mirrors into shards of glass. "You can't throw your own daughter overboard," the captain says. "Why not?" replies Fields. "Let the sharks protect themselves." – *The Big Broadcast of 1938* (1938)

702 Circus manager W. C. Fields lambastes a child: "You disgust me – reeking of popcorn and lollipops." – *You Can't Cheat an Honest Man* (1939)

703 Mrs. Bennet (Mary Boland) is overly concerned that her five eligible daughters will never find husbands. "Look at them!" she cries to her husband Edmund Gwenn. "Five of them without dowries. What's to become of them?" "Yes, what's to become of the wretched creatures?" Gwenn returns lightly. "Perhaps we should have drowned some of them at birth." – *Pride and Prejudice* (1940)

704 Bob Hope wants to marry Dorothy Lamour to escape the draft, while she, at cross purposes, envisions Hope looking splendid in an army uniform. "Maybe we can raise our son to be a soldier," Hope suggests. "Our son?" "Sorry," Hope cracks, "I forgot about the preliminaries." – *Caught in the Draft* (1941)

705 During World War II, American businessman Leon Errol asks an English lord to send him a French war orphan for Errol's married nephew and his wife to raise. The orphan arrives – not the expected child, but Fifi, a buxom French beauty. "There's some mistake here someplace," Errol apologizes to his nephew. "I cabled Lord Epping to send over a war orphan." "He did," the bewildered nephew replies, "but you didn't specify which war. Fifi's an orphan of the last war!" – *Mexican Spitfire's Baby* (1941)

706 Worldly Mary Astor encourages her wealthy, eccentric brother Rudy Vallee to propose to Claudette Colbert, whom he has recently met, but he prefers to be cautious. He wants to know more about her, how she is with children, for example. "What are you going to do, rent some?" Astor wisecracks. "Perhaps we could borrow some," he suggests. – *The Palm Beach Story* (1942)

707 William Demarest complains about daughters to his children Betty Hutton and Diana Lynn. "They're a mess no matter how you look at 'em," he expounds; "a headache till they get married – if they get married – and, after that, they get worse. Either they leave their husbands and come back with four children and move into your guest room, or their husband loses his job and the whole *caboodle* comes back. Or else they're so homely you can't get rid of them at all and they hang around the house like Spanish moss and shame you into an early grave." – *The Miracle of Morgan's Creek* (1944)

708 A precocious eight-year-old boy explains to his older sister why he doesn't like the idea of babysitters: "It's a psychological stumbling block. The juvenile mind resents the restraint of adult authority." – *Jack and the Beanstalk* (1951)

709 Bob Hope reports to a lawyer's office in a western town to claim his father's inheritance. "The reason I leave all my money to my son, Junior," Hope reads aloud, "is that being of sound mind I can't never leave my money to my wife because I ain't never forgiven her since the day she presented me with an idiot for a son." – *Son of Paleface* (1952)

710 Peggy Lee as a gangster's moll takes a hard look at her childless future: "Well, there won't ever be no patter of little feet in my house – unless I was to rent some mice." – *Pete Kelly's Blues* (1955)

711 At a dinner to honor showman Eddie Foy (Bob Hope), Hope banters with another Broadway legend, George M. Cohan (James Cagney). "Do you know what I'd give to have your seven kids?" Cagney remarks. "Do you know what I'd give you to take them?" Hope retorts. "I've met your kids. You couldn't afford it." – *The Seven Little Foys* (1955)

712 A suburban father aboard a commuter train shows a porno magazine to his companions. "I know you won't believe this," he announces, "but I confiscated this from my son's lunch box." "I believe it," fellow suburbanite Tony Randall interjects. "Some kids will eat anything." – *Boys' Night Out* (1962)

713 Tony Curtis, babysitting a five-year-old girl, is trying to avoid taking her to Disneyland. "Why don't you take off now and let me get dressed, and we'll talk about Disneyland later." "All right," the child says. "That's what grownups say when they really mean no." – *40 Pounds of Trouble* (1962)

714 Good-natured but irresponsible family man Jackie Gleason has his best relationship with his six-year-old daughter (Linda Bruhl), in whom he occasionally tries to instill a little history – often with unexpected results. "What is today, July the eighth, famous for?" he asks. "Your going to church." – *Papa's Delicate Condition* (1963)

715 United Nations employee Bob Hope tries to avoid taking possession of an abandoned baby handed to him by a fellow worker. "They don't allow children in my apartment – only dogs," he explains. – *A Global Affair* (1964)

716 British secret agent Tom Adams chases a suspect to a sewer and drops a pellet down the opening. Suddenly a burst of white smoke emerges from the sewer. "What's that?" a child, who happens to be walking by, asks. "Laughing gas," the agent replies. "Oh, you mean nitrous oxide," the boy says, casually strolling away. – *Where the Bullets Fly* (1966)

717 Audrey Hepburn, married to Albert Finney, wants to begin a family. "We agreed before we were married," he reminds her, "we weren't going to have any children." "And before we were married we didn't have any," she riposte. – *Two for the Road* (1967)

718 "I don't know," widow Ellen Burstyn complains to 12-year-old son Alfred Lutter. "I'm an okay sort of person. How did I get such a smart-ass kid?" "You got pregnant," Alfred replies. – *Alice Doesn't Live Here Anymore* (1975)

719 In a Southern swamp, police raid a local still and arrest an elderly man and his nine-year-old granddaughter. The child bites the hand of one of the detectives who cries out in pain. "Don't you hit that child!" the man blurts out. "I'm not going to hit her," the officer replies. "I just don't want to feed her."—*Gator* (1976)

720 During a squash game, George Segal's opponent vehemently asserts that he doesn't "care who wins a lousy squash game," that he plays to work out so that when he goes home, he doesn't take a swing at his kids. "I've seen your kids," Segal cuts in. "You're making a big mistake."—*Lost and Found* (1979)

721 Martin Mull and Tuesday Weld visit their teenage daughter who has joined a religious cult whose members all wear purple and gush forth love phrases. "I think we lost her," Weld says after she and her husband leave. "No," Mull disagrees. "Maybe for a little while. She's a smart girl. Besides, she hates purple."—*Serial* (1980)

722 A floozie relates a sad childhood tale to a drunken Dudley Moore. "My mother died when I was six," she begins. "My father raped me when I was twelve." "So you had six relatively good years," Dudley says.—*Arthur* (1981)

723 Little Adam Rich tries to match up his widowed mother, Susan Anspach, with bachelor Elliott Gould. "You know what you are?" Anspach rebukes the boy. "You are the only eleven-year-old procurer in the business."—*The Devil and Max Devlin* (1981)

724 Tycoon Jackie Gleason hires unemployed Richard Pryor as a companion for his seven-year-old spoiled son (Scott Schwartz), but the boy's outlandish behavior causes him to quit. "I only have the boy for one week a year—" Gleason pleads. "Well," Pryor returns, "you ought to get better lawyers. You shouldn't have to have him that long." —*The Toy* (1982)

725 Photographer Rodney Dangerfield is taking a picture of a fat, homely boy

whose features are being admired by his parents. Mother: "He's got my eyes." Father: "And my nose." Dangerfield: "And my sympathy."—*Easy Money* (1983)

726 Single parent Susan Sarandon drives her precocious young son to a school outside their district, explaining she wants the best education for him. "You never got to college," the child acknowledges her concern, "because you got knocked up."—*The Buddy System* (1984)

727 Precocious eleven-year-old Fred Savage steps out of a limousine and speaks rudely to the chauffeur while a doorman looks on. "Is he famous?" the doorman asks after the child leaves. "He will be," the chauffeur replies. "I'm gonna kill him."—*Vice Versa* (1988)

728 A tough little street urchin who runs errands for Harlem gambling house owner Richard Pryor has just shot a troublesome gambler. When Pryor offers to return the child to his parents, the boy says they are both dead. "Did you kill them?" Pryor asks.—*Harlem Nights* (1989)

729 At a party, the youngest child of Steve Martin and his wife displays an idiosyncrasy that disturbs other guests. "He likes to butt things with his head," the child's mother says nonchalantly. "How proud you must be!" a relative replies sarcastically.—*Parenthood* (1989)

730 "You have much more hair in your nose than my dad," preadolescent Macaulay Culkin is quick to point out to his uncle John Candy. "Nice of you to notice," Candy sarcastically acknowledges. "I'm a kid," Culkin returns, "that's my job."—*Uncle Buck* (1989)

731 In one of his cartoons, controversial cartoonist Gene Wilder portrays an officer of the National Rifle Association saying: "Guns don't kill children; children kill children." – *Funny About Love* (1990)

732 Television reporter Kirstie Alley roams around Los Angeles sampling public opinion on various questions. She targets a harried mother in a supermarket who is trying to prevent her unruly brood from destroying the store. "What's your secret summer fantasy?" the roving reporter asks the woman. "Chloroform," comes the reply. – *Madhouse* (1990)

733 Impish seven-year-old orphan Michael Oliver explains why he is living in an institution: "You see, no one really accepted me. Who would be that caring?

Who'd be that loving? Who'd be that – dumb?" – *Problem Child* (1990)

734 A grown-up Peter Pan (Robin Williams), now a father, rebukes his young son (Charlie Korsmo). "When are you going to stop acting like a child?" he barks. "I am a child!" the boy counters. – *Hook* (1991)

735 Police lieutenant Leslie Nielsen meets his ex-lover Priscilla Presley, who walked out on him. "How are the children?" he inquires solicitously. "We didn't have any children," she replies. – *The Naked Gun 2½: The Smell of Fear* (1991)

Cleanliness

736 "How much would you want to run into an open manhole?" Groucho Marx asks Chico. "Just-a the cover charge," Chico replies. "Well, drop in some time." "Sewer." "Well," Groucho concludes, "I guess we cleaned that up." – *Animal Crackers* (1930)

737 Two English acquaintances of the swarthy charlatan Svengali (John Barrymore) ask him when he last took a bath. "Not since I tripped and fell in the sewer." – *Svengali* (1931)

738 An aggressive vacuum-cleaner salesman nudges his way into Shemp Howard's apartment and throws a bagful of dirt on the floor to demonstrate his product. But the machine fails, and the salesman says he will have to take the cleaner back to the factory. "How about taking this dirt back with you!" an irate Howard demands. "Don't worry," the salesman says, "I've got plenty more dirt outside in a suitcase." – *While the Cat's Away* (1935)

739 "Imagine a man drowning his wife in a bathtub," Alice Brady says to com-

panion Mischa Auer, referring to a newspaper story. "Maybe that was the only way he could get her to take a bath," Auer offers. – *My Man Godfrey* (1936)

740 When Blondie (Penny Singleton) and Dagwood (Arthur Lake) arrive at their vacation lodge, she takes one look at Baby Dumpling's dirty and disheveled appearance and cries: "Oh, look at your child!" "Whenever he looks like that," Dagwood complains, "he's *my* child!" – *Blondie Takes a Vacation* (1939)

741 When cowboy Tim Holt, busy polishing his boots, puts down his boot brush for a moment, a fellow ranch hand borrows it to use on his hair. "Hey," Holt cautions, "don't use that on your hair!" "Why not? I ain't got dandruff." – *Along the Rio Grande* (1941)

742 Marlene Dietrich is about to visit captain Bruce Cabot's ship, and Cabot is dissatisfied with the condition of the vessel. "This boat looks like a pig pen!" he barks at seaman Andy Devine. "You want her to think we live like this?" "Well," Devine fires back, "don't we?" – *The Flame of New Orleans* (1941)

743 Larry, one of the Three Stooges, learns that Curly is heir to a fortune. "We're filthy with dough!" he exclaims. "You're filthy without it!" Moe replies. – *If a Body Meets a Body* (1945)

744 The owner of a laundry is murdered, and amateur sleuth Boston Blackie (Chester Morris) meets his old adversary, Inspector Farraday (Richard Lane), at the scene of the crime. "Well, inspector, what are you doing here," Blackie asks, "airing some dirty laundry?" – *Boston Blackie's Chinese Adventure* (1949)

745 Spencer Tracy removes his favorite silk scarf from the mouth of his baby grandson – to the wails of the child's displeasure. "Honey," his wife Joan Bennett demands, "what are you doing?" "He was eating my scarf," Tracy says defensively. "That's all right," she replies. "It's clean." – *Father's Little Dividend* (1951)

746 Social worker Barbara Harris falls in love with anti-establishment dropout Jason Robards, Jr., and surprises him by cleaning his untidy apartment. "I've been attacked by the *Ladies' Home Journal!*" he exclaims. – *A Thousand Clowns* (1965)

747 First comic: "Hey, did you take a bath today!" Second comic: "Why, is there one missing?" – *The Night They Raided Minsky's* (1968)

748 Walter Matthau, complaining about roommate Jack Lemmon's obsession with cleanliness: "Two single men should not have a cleaner house than my mother." – *The Odd Couple* (1968)

749 Felix (Jack Lemmon), who has moved in with Oscar (Walter Matthau) and whose sanitary eccentricities have almost unhinged his roommate, has attempted suicide. "He'll kill himself just to spite me," Matthau frets. "Then his ghost will come back to haunt me – haunting and cleaning, haunting and cleaning, haunting and cleaning." – *The Odd Couple* (1968)

750 In London's Hyde Park a shabbily dressed speaker gets up on a box and addresses a crowd. "What is the most powerful thing in the world today?" he asks gravely. "B.O.!" someone calls out. – *Number One of the Secret Service* (1977)

751 Sid Caesar's wife Shelley Winters won't permit her dripping-wet nephew to sit in the living room of her suburban home. "What are you worried about?" Caesar asks. "Everything's covered with plastic! A battleship couldn't do any damage in here!" – *Over the Brooklyn Bridge* (1984)

752 Susan Sarandon calls the police after discovering someone has broken into her home. One officer, after searching all the rooms for the intruder, returns empty-handed. "The house is clean," he reports. "You obviously haven't seen my closet," Sarandon quips. – *Compromising Positions* (1985)

753 A group of World War II draftees are making their way by train from the Northeast to their training camp in Biloxi, Mississippi. Narrator Matthew Broderick, one of the soldiers, points out that nobody has washed for days. "We were getting ready to fight Germany and Japan," he says, "but instead we were stinking up America." – *Biloxi Blues* (1988)

754 "Let me tell you how bad the water pollution is," Burt Lancaster says. "Half the scuba equipment being sold is being sold to the fishes." – *Rocket Gibralter* (1988)

Clothing

755 Clothing-store owner Eddie Cantor and his partner try to sell a customer an incomplete tuxedo. "Here's a fine hunting suit." "Why do you call it a hunting suit?" "We've been hunting the pants for two years." – *Glorifying the American Girl* (1929)

756 Eddie Cantor and his clothing-store partner fit a jacket on a customer. "The buttons don't meet," the partner notices. "I don't think they were introduced," the customer adds. – *Glorifying the American Girl* (1929)

757 Oliver Hardy searches for his hat, which happens to be where he placed it – on his head. "You must have put it somewhere," his wife chides him. "Hats don't walk!" "Why not? They feel, don't they? You've heard of felt hats, haven't you?" – *Hog Wild* (1930)

758 "That fellow is a human dynamo," observes house detective Hugh Herbert about Bert Wheeler. "Everything he has on is charged," quips Robert Woolsey. – *Hook, Line and Sinker* (1930)

759 "My brother had a good job," Gracie Allen confides to George Burns. "He was a pocket maker. He made pockets for men's pants. But he's not working now. They just got an order from Scotland." – *Once Over, Light* (1931)

760 George Burns challenges Gracie Allen with the following riddle: "A fellow is in a restaurant. He orders spinach, sliced tomatoes and ice cream. How did I know he was a soldier?" "Oh," Gracie replies, "he wore a uniform." – *Once Over, Light* (1931)

761 Charles Ruggles learns by way of a telephone call that a dinner party he has been invited to is not a costume affair.

Foolishly dressed as Romeo, he rebukes his servant. "Marcel," he says sharply, "why did you tell me it was a costume party?" "Ah, monsieur," his servant replies, "I did so want to see you in tights." – *One Hour with You* (1932)

762 Jean Harlow, seeking to impress and win over her young handsome boss, tries on a new dress. "Can you see through this?" she asks a matronly saleswoman. "I'm afraid you can, dear." "I'll wear it." – *Red-Headed Woman* (1932)

763 Unemployed showgirl Aline McMahon learns that her former Broadway producer Barney Hopkins (Ned Sparks) is planning a new show, but she doesn't have anything decent to wear to the tryouts. "If Barney could see me in clothes –" she begins. "He wouldn't recognize you," quips one of her roommates. – *Gold Diggers of 1933* (1933)

764 Two old maids, strolling in a park, are startled by a man running around with only a loin cloth. "Officer," one exclaims, "there's a man in the park!" "And he's – he's in the – altogether!" the second old maid adds. – *King of the Jungle* (1933)

765 Radio singer Ginger Rogers' wedding to Norman Foster inspires prissy dressmaker Franklin Pangborn: "I'll dress her in white. But of course the honeymoon clothes must be in pastel shades. I'll have the loveliest trousseau in all New York." – *Professional Sweetheart* (1933)

766 A short-tempered governess takes her charge, an alert young boy, to the local zoo where they feed fish to the seals. She enlightens the child about seals, pointing out that the boy's grandfather once had a coat made of seal. "Did he feed it fish?" the child questions. —*Zoo in Budapest* (1933)

767 Robert Woolsey, a guest at an English estate, compliments hostess Thelma Todd on her low-cut dress. "My dressmaker says it's the coming thing," she says. "It must be coming," he adds, "because there's a lot that hasn't arrived yet." —*Cockeyed Cavaliers* (1934)

768 Warren Hymer and another Broadway tough dress in stolen suits of armor for a masquerade party. "How are we gonna get this hardware back to the museum?" his pal asks. "We'll throw these suits in the river," Hymer replies, "but we gotta remember one thing." "What's that?" "First we gotta get out of the suits." —*Little Miss Marker* (1934)

769 The police are searching the apartment of Nick and Nora Charles (William Powell and Myrna Loy). "What's that man doing in my drawers?" Loy remonstrates. —*The Thin Man* (1934)

770 "Young man, I'll tell you a secret—just between men," a hotel executive confides to bellhop Francis Lederer. "All women's hats are monstrosities. That's a secret we men must carry to our graves." —*The Gay Deception* (1935)

771 "They tell me in Paris if you don't buy your gown from Roberta, you're not dressed at all," Randolph Scott advises Fred Astaire about the fashion designer's revealing styles. "I see," Astaire responds. "Nude if you don't and nude if you do." —*Roberta* (1935)

772 "She wore a blue cocktail dress," writer Jean Arthur informs amateur sleuth William Powell. "What's a cocktail dress?" "Something to spill cocktails on," she quips. —*The Ex-Mrs. Bradford* (1936)

773 "I only had one fur coat in my life," Joan Davis confesses. "I think it was unborn mule." —*Josette* (1938)

774 "Get a move on, kid," gangster Alan Baxter, who is in a rush, orders his gun moll Lyda Roberti. "Pack all your clothes in a trunk." "And go out with nothin'?" the bemused blonde questions. "It's too cold." —*Wide Open Faces* (1938)

775 During a gun battle between Canada's Mounted Police and rebel settlers, Scotsman Lynne Overman shoots the belt off the pants of foe Akim Tamiroff, one of the rebellious leaders, who struggles to keep his britches from falling. "Yon goes the seat of the government," Overman quips. —*North West Mounted Police* (1940)

776 Mrs. Smith (Carole Lombard) wishes to wear the same bridal dress she wore the first time she had married—but it's too tight. "Inhale, Mrs. Smith, inhale," her maid suggests. "I can't understand anything hanging in the closet shrinking so much," Lombard remarks. —*Mr. and Mrs. Smith* (1941)

777 Bing Crosby wants Bob Hope to hide part of a map in a safe place. "What do you think of my underwear?" Hope suggests. "Not much," answers Crosby, "but hide it there anyway." —*Road to Zanzibar* (1941)

778 Olivia De Havilland returns from France and announces to her husband Jack Carson: "I felt like buying every dress in Paris." "I thought you did," he quips after perusing the bills. —*Strawberry Blonde* (1941)

779 "How do you like the suit?" asks Victor McGlaglen about his garish new outfit. "First time I ever saw a horseblanket with lapels," comments Edmund Lowe. —*Call Out the Marines* (1942)

780 Mischa Auer: "How would you like to be wearing a royal robe of beautiful feathers?" Kay Kyser: "I'd be tickled to death." —*Around the World* (1943)

781 Nobleman Walter Slezak complains to a tailor measuring him for a new suit of clothes: "You were supposed to fit me, not fondle me!" – *The Spanish Main* (1945)

782 Charlie Chan (Sidney Toler), his son (Benson Fong) and their chauffeur (Mantan Moreland) visit a jail in search of information. "You'd better get out of here before they put you in garments to fit your personality," says Toler. "What garment is that?" asks Moreland. "Straitjacket." – *Dark Alibi* (1946)

783 Bob Hope comments on Dorothy Lamour's snug attire: "How did you get into that dress – with a spray gun?" – *Road to Rio* (1947)

784 In postwar Berlin, American congresswoman Jean Arthur and army captain John Lund study films of German nightclub entertainer Marlene Dietrich, suspected of high-level Nazi connections. "I wonder what holds up that dress," Arthur questions. "It must be that German will power," replies Lund. – *A Foreign Affair* (1948)

785 William Powell tries to purchase a woman's sweater as a gift. "It comes in a gay spectrum of springtime hues," an enthusiastic salesperson announces, holding up a particular model. "Pistachio, purple almond, banana, marshmallow, peach and licorice." "Would you be good enough to tell me something?" Powell inquires. "Whatever became of blue?" – *Mr. Peabody and the Mermaid* (1948)

786 "This dress came from Paris," Joan Davis boasts. "It was created by Madam Celeste. The madam is still in here with me." – *The Traveling Saleswoman* (1950)

787 "That's quite a dress you almost have on," Gene Kelly teases Nina Foch. – *An American in Paris* (1951)

788 Diminutive army draftee and aspiring boxer Mickey Rooney tries to impress fight manager Bob Hope by emphasizing his physique. "I'll admit the uniform's a little deceiving," Rooney confesses. "Deceiving?" repeats Hope. "It's perjury." – *Off Limits* (1953)

789 Huntz Hall explains that his expensive suit came with two pairs of pants. "But I have a lot of trouble getting into two pairs of pants," he grouses, "very bulky, very bulky." – *The Bowery Boys Meet the Monsters* (1954)

790 A U.S. Navy officer on a Pacific island during World War II cannot find proper substitutes for loin cloths for the natives. "You'd be surprised at the variance in loins." "Well," officer Glenn Ford declares, "live and loin, man." – *Don't Go Near the Water* (1957)

791 "This lady comes out with a gown," explains comic Joe E. Lewis (Frank Sinatra) to his audience. "It's backless, it's frontless and it's strapless. Come to think of it, it's a belt." – *The Joker Is Wild* (1957)

792 An admiral investigates a disturbance and learns that the captain in charge (Dennis O'Keefe) had been fishing at the time. "Catch anything, captain?" the admiral asks sarcastically. "Nothing very much, sir," O'Keefe answers nervously. "Just an old tire, a soggy lamp shade and a brassiere. The brassiere gave me a pretty tough fight." "They usually do," the admiral acknowledges. – *All Hands on Deck* (1961)

793 At a wedding reception sculpture instructor Elizabeth Montgomery is surprised and shocked at the amorous advances of her male model. "Sitting around the art class flexing his muscles, he looked so simple and sweet." "Well," confidante Carol Burnett adds, "I always say you never get to know a person till they put their clothes on." – *Who's Been Sleeping in My Bed?* (1963)

794 Freelance writer George Segal enters a porno theater and is immediately approached by a vendor. "Overcoat?" the man asks. "I don't have one," Segal replies. "You want to rent one?" – *The Owl and the Pussycat* (1970)

795 Jack Carter, portraying a broken-down comic and striptease-club emcee, tries to distract police lieutenant Burt Reynolds from questioning him about a murder. "A guy walks into an elevator and there's a naked broad in there, see," Carter nervously begins. "And he says to her, 'Hey, my wife's got the same outfit.'" – *Hustle* (1975)

796 Ryan O'Neal accidentally discovers a new rave in fashion jeans, thereby saving the failing clothing business of his father (Jack Warden). The new jeans consist of two clear plastic windows that are built into the rear of the jeans and expose the wearer's buttocks. "We changed the face of America," O'Neal says proudly. "The face?" questions Warden. – *So Fine* (1981)

797 A gay Zorro (George Hamilton) dresses outlandishly as he rides throughout old California protecting the peons against tyrant Ron Leibman. "Remember, people," the masked hero addresses a group of peasants, "there is no shame in being poor – only dressing poorly." – *Zorro, the Gay Blade* (1981)

798 For insurance purposes, Bette Midler schemes to make her husband's suicide look like an accident. Physically abused by him throughout their marriage, Bette discovers a way to exact a small degree of revenge. "Remember that outfit you said you wouldn't be caught dead in?" she says to the corpse while dressing it. "Well, guess what? This is it." – *Jinxed!* (1982)

799 Undercover cop Ryan O'Neal, who is "straight," is assigned to set up housekeeping with gay cop John Hurt to trap a serial killer, but Hurt goes beyond the call of duty. "Stop ironing my underwear," O'Neal pleads. "Guys don't iron other guys' clothes." – *Partners* (1982)

800 Mermaid Daryl Hannah dresses herself in men's clothes and enters Bloomingdale's to find more suitable attire. "Do yourself a favor and stop in the lingerie department," a saleswoman outfitting her with a dress advises. "A girl as pretty as you are shouldn't be wearing boxer shorts." – *Splash* (1984)

801 Rodney Dangerfield notices a society matron wearing a green evening gown and can't resist saying: "If that dress had pockets, you'd look like a pool table." – *Back to School* (1986)

802 Yuppie stockbroker Jon Cryer, hiding out from the mob, wants to trade his expensive suit jacket for a tramp's coat, but the tramp refuses to trade. "Are you crazy?" Cryer exclaims. "This is a five-hundred-dollar Italian-made coat. I bought this in Milan." "You paid five Cs for that and you're asking me if I'm crazy?" – *Hiding Out* (1987)

803 Tough corporate executive Bette Midler arrives at her office headquarters and is taken aback by a woman employee who is wearing a red dress. "This is how you dress for the office?" Midler blurts out. "You look like a blood clot." – *Big Business* (1988)

804 At a business party, Wall Street department head Harrison Ford is attracted to secretary Melanie Griffith. "You're the first woman I've seen at one of these damn things that dresses like a woman," he remarks, "not how a woman thinks a man would dress if he were a woman." – *Working Girl* (1988)

805 Wall Street secretary Melanie Griffith's live-in boyfriend Alec Baldwin gives her another sensual undergarment for her birthday. "You know," she says, "just once I could go for a sweater or some earrings – a present that I could actually wear outside this apartment." – *Working Girl* (1988)

806 At a wedding, matronly Olympia Dukakis compliments young Daryl Hannah on her dress. "The thing that separates us from the animals," she adds, "is our ability to accessorize." – *Steel Magnolias* (1989)

807 American entertainer John Goodman, by some fluke, is the next heir to the throne of England. He reluctantly accepts the title and is fitted for a royal wardrobe. "Would this be to your liking, your majesty?" asks a tailor. "I kind of like that," Goodman says, pointing to some cloth draped over a couch. "That's an upholstery fabric, your majesty." "The English people," interjects the King's secretary Peter O'Toole, "don't generally like their monarch to look like a sofa." – *King Ralph* (1991)

808 An animal-rights activist accosts a wealthy woman who is about to enter her chauffeur-driven limousine. "Do you know how many poor animals they had to kill to make that coat?" "Do you know how many rich animals I had to fuck to get this coat?" the woman retorts. – *Switch* (1991)

809 Unhappy, insecure wife Kathy Bates joins a support group. "Tonight," the group leader announces, "we are going to begin to explore our own femaleness by examining the source of our strength and our separateness – our vaginas," after which she notices Kathy fidgeting in her seat. "Do you find it threatening?" she asks Kathy. "Do you have a problem with your sexuality?" "I do have a problem with my girdle," Kathy innocently explains. – *Fried Green Tomatoes* (1992)

Communication

810 The hotel desk phone rings and owner Groucho Marx answers. "You want to know where to get hold of Mrs. Potter?" Groucho asks. "I don't know, she's awfully ticklish." – *The Cocoanuts* (1929)

811 Helen Twelvetrees is asked if she always lisps. "No," she replies, "only when I speak." – *The Ghost Talks* (1929)

812 "I don't mind telling you things," Oliver Hardy says to Stan Laurel. "It's the *explaining* that wears me down." – *Another Fine Mess* (1930)

813 Charlie McCarthy visits eye doctor Edgar Bergen, who asks McCarthy if he sees spots. "Yes." "That's too bad," Bergen says. "That is, I see spots when I look at spots," McCarthy explains. – *The Eyes Have It* (1931)

814 During an ocean voyage Chico Marx asks to see the captain's bridge. "I'm sorry," says Groucho Marx. "He always keeps it in a glass of water while he's eating." – *Monkey Business* (1931)

815 Joe E. Brown, invited by the president of a company to demonstrate his invention, arrives at the building too late. "Hey!" a policeman calls out to Brown, who is hammering at the door. "What are you doing around here?" "I was looking for the president," Brown says innocently. "You're in the wrong town, buddy," the officer replies. "Try Washington, D.C." – *Fireman, Save My Child* (1932)

816 College president Groucho Marx's secretary announces: "The dean is furious. He's waxing Roth." "Is Roth out there, too?" asks Marx. "Tell Roth to wax the dean for a while." – *Horse Feathers* (1932)

817 Bert Wheeler: "What's a secret?" Robert Woolsey: "A secret's something you tell practically everybody confidentially." – *Diplomaniacs* (1933)

818 Smalltime Broadway hoodlum Ned Sparks, with his disreputable English, continually ridicules Warren William's servant. "If I had a choice of weapons with you, sir," the servant calmly responds, "I'd choose grammar." – *Lady for a Day* (1933)

819 Two attractive young women stow away in Charles Ruggles' cabin aboard a luxury liner. "Suppose my wife should hear about it?" he nervously says. "We'll tell her it was only a platonic friendship," one replies. "We'll do nothing of the kind," her friend protests. "I won't go to jail for any man." – *Melody Cruise* (1933)

820 Stan Laurel and Oliver Hardy try to comfort Bo-Peep (Charlotte Henry), who is compelled to marry the treacherous Barnaby. "Why, Stan is so upset he's not even going to the wedding, are you, Stan?" Hardy says. "Upset?" Laurel reacts. "Why, I'm housebroken." – *Babes in Toyland* (1934)

821 Alice Brady visits a Venice vacation spot and sits at a table in a hotel café. "What have you?" she asks waiter Eric Blore. "Crumpets," he suggests. "That's too bad," she quips. "Does it run in the family?" – *The Gay Divorcee* (1934)

822 "Where can I get hold of your father?" Eddie Cantor asks Eve Sully. "I don't know," she replies hesitantly. "He's awfully ticklish." – *Kid Millions* (1934)

823 "We don't like the ocean," Oliver Hardy says to a sea captain. "It's infatuated with sharks." "He means 'infuriated,'" Stan Laurel explains. – *The Live Ghost* (1934)

824 Dapper butler Monty Collins answers the door to trickster Bobby Clark, who then surreptitiously pins the "Welcome" doormat on the seat of the butler's uniform. "Don't sit down," Clark says, "or you'll wear out your welcome." – *Love and Hisses* (1934)

825 W. C. Fields as Mr. Macawber announces his arrival: "I have quartered the malevolent machinations of our scurrilous enemies. In short, I am here." – *David Copperfield* (1935)

826 "I always say it with flowers," announces Robert Woolsey as he hands a rose to secretary Margaret Dumont. "What, only one rose?" she asks. "You know me, I don't talk much." – *Kentucky Kernels* (1935)

827 About to read a contract, Groucho asks Chico if he can hear. "I haven't heard anything yet." "Well," Groucho explains, "I haven't said anything worth hearing." "That's a-why I didn't hear anything." "That's why I didn't say anything." – *A Night at the Opera* (1935)

828 Two waitresses aboard a ship bring a food order to a stateroom. "Are they my hard-boiled eggs?" Chico Marx asks. "I can't tell till they get into the room," Groucho replies. – *A Night at the Opera* (1935)

829 "I say," Moe Howard addresses Larry Fine, "what comes after seventy-five?" "Seventy-six," Larry answers. "That's the spirit." – *Disorder in the Court* (1936)

830 During a murder trial a frustrated prosecutor begs witness Curley Howard to "kindly speak English and drop the vernacular." "Vernacular?" a confused Curly echoes, looking at his hat. "That's a 'doiby'!" – *Disorder in the Court* (1936)

831 Stable boy Willie Best helps amateur sleuth Helen Broderick investigate a murder. "I think you'll go far," she compliments Best. "Yes ma'm," he replies. "How far should I go?" – *Murder on a Bridal Path* (1936)

832 A policeman investigating a jewel theft at a wealthy Fifth Avenue home notices the housekeeper leaving the room. "Just a minute, sister," he calls out. "If I thought that were true," she retorts, "I'd disown my parents." – *My Man Godfrey* (1936)

833 Dentist Bert Wheeler and assistant Robert Woolsey are kidnapped off their stagecoach to care for an outlaw leader. Wheeler examines the bandit's swollen mouth and bad tooth. "I've got to extract," Wheeler decides. "No, you don't!" the outlaw protests. "You're gonna pull it." – *Silly Billies* (1936)

834 "Give me a sentence with the word 'formaldehyde,'" a gag writer asks the Singing Kid (Al Jolson). "I don't know," Jolson says. "From all de hiding places come the Indians." – *The Singing Kid* (1936)

835 Parkyakarkus, carrying a letter of reference, seeks a job from amusement park manager Eddie Cantor. "I have a letter for you from Butch," the stranger announces. "It says I been a brother to him and I gonna be a brother to you." "'Dear Eddie,'" Cantor begins to read, "'this fellow has been a bother to me and he'll be a bother to you....'" – *Strike Me Pink* (1936)

836 Scottish inventor Franchot Tone asks American showgirl Jean Harlow if she knows what a stabilizer is. "Well," she surmises, "it has something to do with horses, hasn't it?" – *Suzy* (1936)

837 On an English road David Niven and his servant Jeeves (Arthur Treacher) pick up hitchhiker Willie Best, who is seeking to rejoin his band. Suddenly two thieves, posing as police, stop Niven's car. "You'd better search him first," one man says, referring to Best. "He may be an accomplice." "I ain't no accomplice," Best counters. "I'm an American." – *Thank You, Jeeves!* (1936)

838 Two con artists trick the Three Stooges into thinking a house contains treasure buried by Captain Kidd's son. "It'll cost you two hundred dollars for the privilege of digging it up," explains the first crook. "Two hundred dollars?" questions Curly. "Two hundred or nothin'," repeats the second crook. "Well," Curly says, "we'll take it for nothin'." – *Cash and Carry* (1937)

839 Secretary Gracie Allen answers the telephone for her boss, George Burns. "It's a Hawaiian," she announces.

"A Hawaiian?" George questions. "Well, he must be," Gracie affirms. "He said he's Brown from the *Morning Sun*." – *A Damsel in Distress* (1937)

840 To buy meat for a pet leopard named Baby, Cary Grant enters a butcher shop and orders thirty pounds of sirloin steak. "How will you have it cut?" asks the startled butcher. "Just in one piece." "Are you going to roast it or broil it?" "Neither," Grant says. "It's going to be eaten raw." "Say, do you grind this up before you eat it?" the storekeeper asks. "This isn't for me," Grant explains. "It's for Baby." – *Bringing Up Baby* (1938)

841 "Are you a real crook?" a woman asks burglar and safecracker Olin Howland. "Well," he explains, "the last lawyer what defended me said I was antisocial. I kind of like that better than 'crook,' don't you?" – *The Mad Miss Manton* (1938)

842 When a nagging landlord badgers young, unemployed Danielle Darrieux for her rent, fellow lodger Helen Broderick intercedes. "I have to live, too, you know!" the landlady persists. "Why?" Broderick wisecracks. "Don't talk to me like that!" "I'll do better than that," Broderick continues. "I won't even talk to you at all." – *The Rage of Paris* (1938)

843 Charles Coburn shouts at son James Stewart: "Don't shout! Shouting is the effort of a limited mind to express itself!" – *Vivacious Lady* (1938)

844 Bob Hope is forced to fight a duel, but Martha Raye, who loves Hope, bribes the man who loads the pistols. "All you got to do is tell him this," the man begins to explain. "There's a cross on the muzzle of the pistol with the bullet, and a nick on the handle of the pistol with the blank." "Oh, I see," Raye says, and then adds: "Give me that again." – *Never Say Die* (1939)

845 Russian emissary Felix Bressart enters a posh Parisian hotel with his

Russian colleagues. "I'm afraid our rates are too high," the manager warns the three Bolsheviks. "Why should you be afraid?" Bressart asks. – *Ninotchka* (1939)

846 "Is Lord Epping in?" Mexican spitfire Lupe Velez asks the clerk at a hotel desk. "Who should I say is calling?" the clerk inquires. "Me," she answers. – *Mexican Spitfire* (1940)

847 Rosalind Russell accuses husband James Stewart of having an affair with a married woman. Meanwhile their maid Louise Beavers enters the room. "Now just what's behind that dark innuendo?" Stewart charges. "There ain't nothin' behind me, boss," Beavers interjects. – *No Time for Comedy* (1940)

848 When a dangerous killer boards Laurel and Hardy's boat and threatens the pair, Laurel enlightens his pal Hardy: "Self-reservation is the last law of – average." – *Saps at Sea* (1940)

849 A young refugee woman, riding in farmer John Wayne's car, asks: "What kind of car is this?" "A jalopy," Wayne replies. "Oh," she says delightedly, "an Italian car!" – *Three Faces West* (1940)

850 "If there is such a word as 'weasel,'" muses bandleader Kay Kyser to his radio audience, "it's the singular of 'measles.' Is tht right or am I too rash?" – *You'll Find Out* (1940)

851 Chico Marx serves as bodyguard to Tony Martin and is determined to keep his charge out of harm's way. "From now on," Chico vows, "you and me are going to be insufferable." – *The Big Store* (1941)

852 Film actor Jackie Cooper, rehearsing with a precocious youngster, turns to the boy's ruffled guardian William Demarest: "Don't let him split any infinitives while I'm gone," Cooper orders. "Don't worry," Demarest replies, "I won't let him lay a finger on nothin'!" – *Glamour Boy* (1941)

853 Bud Abbott and Lou Costello have been hired as waiters at a posh restaurant, and Abbott reviews a waiter's routine to Costello. "When you get your order you should show the checker your slip." "What?" Costello asks. "You show the checker your slip." "I can't," Costello confesses. "Why not?" "I'm not wearing one." – *Hold That Ghost* (1941)

854 Lupe Velez's mother-in-law, who falsely believes Lupe has a secret lover, tries to warn her son. "Dennis," the woman announces, "we're living in a fool's paradise." "Well, let's move," Lupe interjects. "We don't have to live here." – *Mexican Spitfire's Baby* (1941)

855 Broadway tough guy Humphrey Bogart enters a high-class auction which he suspects is a front for Nazi spies. To gain entrance to the rear, he bids in his own jargon – to the bewilderment of the other patrons. "One grand!" he calls out, then, "Two Gs!" and finally, "I'll see the lady and raise five!" – *All Through the Night* (1942)

856 Smalltime mobster Billy Gilbert takes his boss's gal to a fancy restaurant but has problems interpreting the sophisticated menu. "Give me some of this," he says to the waiter. "You no can have this," the waiter says. "I don't see why not," Gilbert persists. "This," the waiter explains, referring to Gilbert's choice, "is the proprietor." – *Mr. Wise Guy* (1942)

857 Bud Abbott and Lou Costello, fleeing from the law, reach a closed door. "Why don't you knock on the door?" Abbott asks. "I don't know," Costello replies. "I just don't give a rap anymore." – *Pardon My Sarong* (1942)

858 Jack Buchanan gets struck on the head and is transferred back to the Middle Ages. "What's afoot?" someone asks him. "Twelve inches, I think," he replies. – *When Knights Were Bold* (1942)

859 Rags Ragland describes to Red Skelton the effects of a knockout powder upon an unwary victim: "He goes into a coma for a fortnight–maybe longer–maybe five days."–*DuBarry Was a Lady* (1943)

860 Revolutionists Gene Kelly and Zero Mostel are captured and sentenced to death by France's Louis XV. "Be brave, my friend," Kelly comforts his friend. "You're dying for your country." "But I was born in the city," Mostel counters.–*DuBarry Was a Lady* (1943)

861 Unpretentious Gracie Fields studies the esoteric menu of an exclusive French restaurant. Finally, she asks the waiter to describe an item on the menu. "That, madam," he answers scornfully, "is the name of the selection the orchestra is playing." "Well," the spirited Gracie parries, "there's not much nourishment in that."–*Holy Matrimony* (1943)

862 Eve Arden proposes to soldier Bob Hope that he serve as a companion to lonely, married servicewomen. "I'm not going to carry on an *affaire de coeur*," he protests. "Why not?" "I don't know what it is."–*Let's Face It* (1943)

863 Red Skelton is all packed and about to leave to be married when Miss Pringle, a reporter, intrudes. To avoid an interview, Skelton orders his chauffeur (Rags Ragland): "Put that bag in the car." "You can't talk about Miss Pringle like that!" Ragland protests. –*Whistling in Brooklyn* (1943)

864 A buddy and fellow club member criticizes Leo Gorcey, leader of the East Side Kids. "There's even limitations to what I say," Gorcey acknowledges. "None of us is inflammable."–*Block Busters* (1944)

865 Muggs (Leo Gorcey) enlightens Glimpy (Huntz Hall) on the meaning of "No Cover Charge" printed on a sign: "That means you don't pay nothin' for the table cloth."–*Million Dollar Kid* (1944)

866 Burlesque show owner Dennis O'Keefe asks a soda jerk how to go about attaining culture. "Culture?" the clerk ponders. "Ain't that what they put on flowers to make them grow?"–*Doll Face* (1945)

867 A tough doorman-bouncer sasses amateur private eye Boston Blackie (Chester Morris), when Morris questions him about a female employee. "If she took a powder on you," the man rasps, "just charge it to 'love is a racket.'" "Oh, a philosopher?" Morris cracks. "Watch your language, chum," the bouncer warns. "I don't like mysterious words."–*Boston Blackie's Rendezvous* (1945)

868 The villainous pirate Captain Kidd (Charles Laughton) has killed off another of his rivals and begins his usual eulogy to his victim. "Though me heart bleeds–" "'My heart,' sir," his servant Shadwell corrects him. "Though my heart bleeds–confound you, Shadwell, you drove the thought right out of my head. And it was an uncommon pretty one."–*Captain Kidd* (1945)

869 Fred Allen calls on Minerva Pious, but she does not let him enter her apartment. "Outside I am speaking," she announces, "inside I am having company–the telephone company. They're taking out my telephone." "If I can call later–" "You could call later," she interjects, "without a telephone I couldn't answer." "All I want is some information." "To get information, you are needing a telephone," she concludes.–*It's in the Bag* (1945)

870 Yukon gold prospectors Bob Hope and Bing Crosby hide from two killers beneath a mountain of snow. Hope, hiccuping in the direction of the slope, brings down some menacing slides. "The other way," Crosby orders, trying to stave off an avalanche. "I don't know any other way!" Hope replies.–*Road to Utopia* (1945)

871 Private sleuth Nick Charles (William Powell) enlists the aid of jazz musician

Keenan Wynn, who volunteers to take Powell and his wife Myrna Loy to jazz joints to find a murder suspect. "The first place we hit is Mitch Talbin's," Wynn announces. "Boy, they really flick the whiskers at his base. I brought along the old licorice stick. Of course, if the reed man's already ridin', I'm nowheres." – *Song of the Thin Man* (1947)

872 "Just think," says Bud Abbott about some Mexican jewelry he admires, "when it comes out of the ground, it is nothing but crude hunks of silver ore." "Silver or what?" questions Lou Costello. "Silver ore! . . . It's been lying in the ground for thousands of years. When they dig it up, they smelt it." "If it's a thousand years old, *no wonder* they smelt it," Costello says. – *Mexican Hayride* (1948)

873 During the Civil War, a Union officer selects bungling hotel bellhop Red Skelton for a dual mission – to turn over a false map to a Confederate officer and give a secret paper to a fellow agent. "The paper's in the pocket of the boot with the buckle," the officer explains to a befuddled Skelton, "and the map is in the packet in the pocket of the jacket." – *A Southern Yankee* (1948)

874 Bud Abbott finds a gun in hotel bellhop Lou Costello's room and asks Costello where he got it. "I don't know." "For the last time – where did you get that gun?" "I don't know." "Where did you get that gun?" Abbott persists. "That's not fair," returns Costello. "You said, 'For the last time.' I answered it." – *Abbott and Costello Meet the Killer* (1949)

875 In Morocco, Lou Costello cries to Bud Abbott: "Three men chased me with large knives – and little ones, too." "You mean dirks," Abbott explains. "Yeah," Costello agrees, "all three of them were dirks." – *Abbott and Costello in the Foreign Legion* (1950)

876 Judy Holliday, dominated mistress to corrupt junk dealer Broderick Craw-

ford, finally stands up to him. "This country and its institutions," she proudly announces, "belong to the people who inhibit it." – *Born Yesterday* (1950)

877 "As usual, I have to do everything myself," grumbles a frustrated Oliver Hardy to Stan Laurel. "Get up on deck and stand by." "Stand by for what?" bemused Laurel asks. – *Atoll K* (1951)

878 "See if the barometer has fallen," Captain Kidd (Charles Laughton) orders sailor Lou Costello. "It's still hanging on the wall," replies Costello. – *Abbott and Costello Meet Captain Kidd* (1952)

879 A butler of a spooky mansion informs Bowery Boys Leo Gorcey and Huntz Hall: "This old house goes back to colonial times. Take this chair, for instance – 1775." "Seventeen seventy-five?" questions Gorcey. "Anybody who paid over three bucks for it got rooked!" – *The Bowery Boys Meet the Monsters* (1954)

880 Bud Abbott and Lou Costello are required to dig a ditch, and Costello says to his pal, "Take your pick." When Abbott selects a shovel, Costello is upset because Abbott did not select a pick as requested. Confusion then reigns. "The shovel is your pick and your pick is the shovel and the pick is my pick," Costello says cautiously. "Now you've got it!" Abbott beams. "Now I've got it!" Costello blurts out. "I don't even know what I'm talking about!" – *Abbott and Costello Meet the Mummy* (1955)

881 Danny Kaye, as a member of a band of dissidents seeking to overthrow a malevolent king, disguises himself as an elderly deaf peasant. The king's troops stop his wagon. "Who are you?" a captain demands. "Fine, thank you," Kaye replies. – *The Court Jester* (1956)

882 Just as Danny Kaye manages to memorize that "the pellet with the poison is in the vessel with the pestle, and the chalice from the palace is the brew that is true," Glynis Johns informs him that "they broke the chalice from the palace." "The pellet with the poison is in the flagon with the dragon; the vessel with the pestle is the brew that is true," she explains to the befuddled Kaye. – *The Court Jester* (1956)

883 A famous movie queen is interviewed as she is about to board a plane. "I'm just going to New York with my secretary for rest and seclusion," she announces, and then turns to her companion and adds: "'Seclusion'– is that right?" "That's right," her secretary whispers. "It means you want to be alone." "'Seclusion' sounds so dirty," the star persists. "Well, it isn't," the secretary reassures her. – *Will Success Spoil Rock Hunter?* (1957)

884 Cary Grant is perturbed by the numerous phone calls made by Ingrid Bergman's sister. "What would she have done a hundred years ago?" he asks himself. "Probably send carrier pigeons. The sky would have been blackened with them." – *Indiscreet* (1958)

885 Draftee Nick Adams helps simpleminded country boy Andy Griffith fill out an army form. "Ever broke any bone?" Adams asks. "Broke a leg once," Griffith replies, "the right – no, it was the left." He then adds: "He still limps a mite." "Who does?" "That feller whose leg bone I broke." – *No Time for Sergeants* (1958)

886 Spanish nobleman Arthur O'Connell, sponsoring a reception in New York, impatiently awaits the arrival of the guests. "What time do the guests arrive?" he asks butler Edward Everett Horton. "Oh," says Horton, "no one arrives first, sir. They all arrive last." – *Pocketful of Miracles* (1961)

887 Long-winded Bing Crosby enters the hangout of Chicago gang leader Frank Sinatra to ask for a secretarial job. "This unheralded intrusion," Crosby begins, "this unseemly advance into your august presence is not, not for the purpose of soliciting pecuniary oblations. I beseech you, do not so misconstrue." "I

t'ink dere's something wrong wit' his t'roat," one hoodlum suggests. – *Robin and the Seven Hoods* (1964)

888 A British agent gets into a taxi and says to the driver: "Waterloo." "What, the station, sir?" the driver asks. "It's a bit late for the battle," the agent replies. – *Where the Bullets Fly* (1966)

889 "We all have days like that," says a stranger casually making small talk in a western town. "You can say that again," affirms sheriff Allyn Joslyn. "I said, 'we all have days like that.'" – *The Brothers O'Toole* (1973)

890 Jewish mother Shelley Winters crashes her son's party and meets a black reveler named Bernstein. "Are you Jewish?" she asks. "No, I'm gay," he replies and promptly whirls her around the floor. "I don't care how you feel," she joyfully responds. "You can dance!" – *Next Stop, Greenwich Village* (1976)

891 San Francisco nightclub owner James Coco introduces his star singer, who has just returned "from the islands," to a German attaché. "Caribbean or Virgin?" the German asks. "Let's just say I came back." – *The Cheap Detective* (1978)

892 "Just take me home," Glenda Jackson says to overly talkative cabby Paul Sorvino. "And silently." "Very well," the disappointed Sorvino replies, "but I think you're depriving yourself of a very sympathetic ear." "It's not the ear that worries me," she replies. "It's the mouth." – *Lost and Found* (1979)

893 Martin Mull has just broken up a wild teenage party at his house, angering his daughter who storms out of the room. "You know what you have just done to her peer group dynamic?" his wife Tuesday Weld charges. "Her socialization? Her individuation? Not to mention the father-daughter interface?" "What are you talking about?" he blurts out. "What's interface? A new word for oral sex? Can't you just speak English?" – *Serial* (1980)

894 George Hamilton dons the black cape and mask of the once famous Zorro to help the peasantry of his community. After rescuing one farmer, he proudly carves a large "Z" on the man's door. "Do you recognize this famous sign?" he asks the man. "Yes, señor. It is a number 2." – *Zorro, the Gay Blade* (1981)

895 "Here's your drink, sir," a butler attends upon guest Steve Martin. "Can I get you anything else? I'm about to retire." "Really?" questions Martin. "You seem so young." – *The Man with Two Brains* (1983)

896 Russian musician Robin Williams, visiting the U.S. with his ensemble, decides to defect in a New York department store, where his Russian agents pursue him. He grabs hold of a guard by his uniform and tries to explain his dilemma. "I defected," he barely whispers to the store guard. "You're not going to do that here," the security guard protests. "I told you where the men's room was." – *Moscow on the Hudson* (1984)

897 Political cartoonist Gene Wilder meets an attractive, outspoken college graduate and is surprised at her foul language. "I'm just curious," he interrupts her. "Were you abandoned at birth and raised by a gang of longshoremen?" – *Funny About Love* (1990)

898 Villainous gang leader Dom DeLuise points a gun at innocent Thomas Gottschalk. "Don't make me make a mess, mister," DeLuise threatens, and then, surprised, adds: "That's alliteration." – *Driving Me Crazy* (1991)

899 A fellow pilot tries to instill in top-gun hot-shot pilot Charlie Sheen the importance of team spirit – to no avail. "I got the sky, the smell of jet exhaust, my bike – " Sheen begins to explain. "A loner," the pilot remarks. "No," Sheen returns, "I own it." – *Hot Shots!* (1991)

900 When mobster Sylvester Stallone learns that his daughter is pregant, he tries to marry her off to his elocution tutor Tim Curry. "Listen, doc," Stallone tries to explain, "I'd like to talk to you about a little difficulty my daughter is having." "Really?" Curry interjects. "She seems to have such nicely rounded diphthongs." "That's what got her into this jam!" Stallone exclaims. – *Oscar* (1991)

Con Artists

901 A sexy con artist targets popular but naive baseball pitcher Joe E. Brown for her next victim. "When a feller knows he's a big shot," Brown begins to boast, "he doesn't have to tell nobody. Take me, for instance – " "Just give me time," the woman cracks. – *Fireman, Save My Child* (1932)

902 Jean Harlow portrays a film star whose public and private life is exploited and manipulated by her studio and ruthless agent Lee Tracy. When she protests against a series of scandalous stories, Tracy justifies them by enlightening her about her importance. "Strong men take one look at your picture," he asserts, "and go home and kiss their wives for the first time in ten years. You're an international tonic. You're a boon to repopulation in a world thinned out by war and famine!" – *Bombshell* (1933)

903 To get a discount on her train ticket, former saloon owner and gambler Alison Skipworth poses as a missionary who has just returned from China. "How did you conduct your work?" the curious ticket agent inquires. "Through kindness, of course," Skipworth replies. "My object was to bring them in out of the darkness, put more spirits into them, as it were, and relieve them of their material wealth." – *Tillie and Gus* (1933)

904 W. C. Fields and Alison Skipworth, as the uncle and aunt of a young woman who has inherited an estate, plot to cheat her out of half the money. Their niece, who hasn't seen them for years, thinks they have come to help her. "You two are angels straight from heaven," she says. "We detoured slightly on the way," Fields retorts. – *Tillie and Gus* (1933)

905 Con artist Ethel Merman, to get her hands on a seventy-seven million dollar inheritance left to simpleton Eddie Cantor, poses as his long-lost mother. "How old are you?" Cantor asks. "I'm nineteen." "I'm twenty-five," Cantor says, then calculates: "twenty-five – nineteen – say, maybe I'm *your* mother!" – *Kid Millions* (1934)

906 Con man Charlie Ruggles, hiding out aboard an ocean liner, shares a cabin with Bing Crosby. "I'm a crook," Ruggles confesses to Crosby. "I'm wanted in America." "What would they want with another crook in America?" Crosby quips. – *Anything Goes* (1936)

907 Jewel thief Marlene Dietrich is about to swindle a Parisian jeweler out of a valuable pearl necklace. The merchant, delighted with the alleged sale, guarantees to take the necklace back within the next two years if she is dissatisfied with it. "You don't know me," she explains. "If I take these pearls, you will never see them again. You can depend on that." – *Desire* (1936)

908 Bogus French count Fritz Feld tries to pass off Lucille Ball as his relative. "She's my cousin, she's my cousin," Feld insists under heavy questioning. "You said it twice," someone remarks. "She's my second cousin." – *Go Chase Yourself* (1938)

909 Lloyd Nolan, in a Latin American country, hires actor Akim Tamiroff to impersonate the president of that country to help pull off a multi-million-dollar deal. But the actor sees a ray of goodness in Nolan. "You're not a very good crook," Tamiroff says. "The fact is, you're quite a decent fellow." "That's right," Nolan replies indignantly, "insult me." – *The Magnificent Fraud* (1939)

910 Groucho Marx enters into negotiations with Chico and Harpo. "Now, let's see," figures Groucho, "that's twenty plus one, that's twenty-one." "We meet you half way," Chico says. "We'll give you one." "You must have come the short way," quips Groucho. – *Go West* (1940)

911 Con men Chico and Harpo Marx, while exchanging money with Groucho, keep stealing the same bill from him. "Say," Groucho, now suspicious, remarks, "did you see something flying across here?" "Might have been a pigeon," Chico suggests. "No, it wasn't a pigeon. It was green." "Must've been a frog." "It had numbers on it," Groucho adds. "Those were the license plates." – *Go West* (1940)

912 Gold digger Kay Francis and her nineteen-year-old protégé scheme to bilk middle-aged businessman Nigel Bruce, who has come to take both of them out on the town. "I'm dying to see some of your nightclubs," the young woman says. "Before you're through," Bruce replies, "I'll show you the whole town. Take it from me." "Don't worry," Francis mutters, "we will." – *Play Girl* (1940)

913 Con artist Frank Morgan has returned to his daugther, Mary Howard, after an absence of fifteen years. Following several weeks of his boasting about gaining and losing fortunes, she questions their financial status. "Oh," she explains, "I was just wondering about darning those holes in your socks." "Those are not holes," her penniless father replies. "It's a system of ventilation I picked up in India." – *The Wild Man of Borneo* (1941)

914 Con artist Bing Crosby tricks his vaudeville pal Bob Hope into accompanying him on a boat to the Alaskan gold fields, but Hope takes charge of their money. "We've got to be careful," Crosby warns. "This is a strange boat. There's a lot of crooks around." "Yeah," Hope replies, "you won't be lonesome." –*Road to Utopia* (1945)

915 Charlatan Walter Slezak: "If I'm not telling the truth, may I be a wandering gypsy." Danny Kaye: "But you are a wandering gypsy." Slezak: "That just proves my point." –*The Inspector General* (1949)

916 Sailor and con man Groucho Marx is confronted by some of his victims–his fellow sailors: "A certain island in the South Pacific which we bought." One sailor reminds him: "only later it turns out that this island has sunk to the bottom of the ocean in 1809." "We were a little late, that's all," Groucho explains. "Lucky thing we weren't on it." –*A Girl in Every Port* (1952)

917 Con man James Garner meets fellow con artist Susan Clark who has robbed him once and whom he catches trying to rob him a second time while he is bathing. "You've been through my pockets more times today than I have!" he complains. –*Skin Game* (1971)

918 Two suspicious police officers nab con artist Eddie Murphy, dressed as a legless, sightless beggar. They remove his sunglasses and lift him bodily off his little cart as his legs, previously hidden from view, suddenly drop down. But quick-thinking Murphy attributes his prompt recovery to miraculous healing powers. "I can see! I can see!" Murphy shouts with joy. "I can walk! I can walk!" –*Trading Places* (1983)

919 Bungling con artists Dana Carvey and Tedd Graff, who are facing hard times, have recently escaped with their lives from one of their jobs. Graff next suggests they burglarize a nearby wealthy home that seems abandoned. "We are not break-in men!" Carvey protests. "We are con artists!" –*Opportunity Knocks* (1990)

Courage

920 Charlie Chan (Warner Oland): "Only a very brave mouse will make nest in cat's ear." –*Charlie Chan Carries On* (1931)

921 At a private gym, lawyer John Barrymore observes that a notorious gangster, who is about to exercise, has a hand gun in his back pocket. "You better take that 'courage' out of your back pocket," Barrymore reminds him, "before you blow your brains out." –*State's Attorney* (1932)

922 Ginger Rogers at the last moment of her wedding ceremony decides to say

"no" as a French magistrate asks if she will take Melville Cooper for her husband. "I congratulate you!" the elderly magistrate announces. "For thirty years now I have had a monotonous job. I've been marrying couple after couple. Just when I've been bored to death, you come along and have the courage to say no. Bravo! mademoiselle!" –*Heartbeat* (1946)

923 In the early days of Nazi-occupied Poland, theatrical producer and actor Mel Brooks courageously permits a small family of Jews to hide out in his theater. The number of escapees soon expands into a fair-sized group. "We started out with three," Brooks recalls. "What are they, Jews or rabbits?" – *To Be or Not to Be* (1983)

924 A grave narrator introduces the plot of this World War II farce by ex-plaining how a group of determined Americans have volunteered to stop an embittered Nazi officer from capturing a fuel dump in North Africa. "Five brave Americans against one sour Kraut," he concludes. – *A Man Called Sarge* (1990)

Courtroom

925 Courtroom witness Buster Keaton, who cannot understand the fast-talking officer administering the oath, turns to the judge. "I can't understand what he's saying." "He's asking you if you swear–" "No," Keaton interrupts, "but I know all the words." – *Sidewalks of New York* (1931)

926 In a courtroom an exasperated judge raises his voice to witness Buster Keaton: "Were you or were you not attacked by this boy before me?" "Before you?" Keaton repeats. "When did he attack you?" – *Sidewalks of New York* (1931)

927 Wealthy landlord Buster Keaton's secretary, Cliff Edwards, pays a court fine for his boss, but complains: "You mean we don't get ten percent off for cash? This is the last time we do business in this court!" – *Sidewalks of New York* (1931)

928 Eccentric spinster Edna May Oliver shows up late at court where she has been called as a juror in a murder case. She offers her apologies to the judge, whom she recognizes as a neighbor. "You must be examined," the judge says coolly. "Why Judge Fish!" she exclaims. – *Ladies of the Jury* (1932)

929 Stan Laurel and Oliver Hardy are up before a judge on a vagrancy charge, and he asks them "on what grounds" do they plead "not guilty." "We weren't on the grounds," replies Laurel. "We were sleeping on a park bench." – *Scram* (1932)

930 Chico Marx is being tried as a spy, and Groucho, as his defense attorney, calls him an abject figure. "I abject," Chico shouts. – *Duck Soup* (1933)

931 Chico Marx is found guilty of spying, and Groucho, addressing the court, recommends the following sentence: "Ten years in Leavenworth or eleven years in Twelveworth." "I take five and ten in Woolworth's," Chico proposes. – *Duck Soup* (1933)

932 In a divorce case, lawyer Bobby Clark learns from questioning a witness that she has been married to the defendant for two years. "During that time did he ever beat you?" Clark asks. "Why, no." "Why?" "Because I never did anything wrong," the witness returns. "Aha!" Clark exclaims. "Married two years and never did anything! A slacker!" – *Odor in the Court* (1934)

933 During a murder trial, scatter-brained witness Curly Howard cannot comprehend the oath that he must take before he testifies. "He's asking if you swear–" the judge tries to assist. "No," Curly interrupts, "but I know all the words." – *Disorder in the Court* (1936)

934 "Take the stand!" an exasperated judge orders confused murder-trial witness Curly Howard. "I got it," Curly says, lifting up the chair. "What do I do with it?" – *Disorder in the Court* (1936)

935 Deputy sheriff James Stewart tells sheriff Charles Winninger about a boy who killed his parents with a crowbar. At the trial, Stewart continues, the judge asked the boy if he had anything to say for himself. "The kid said, 'Well, I just hope that you have some regard for the feelin's of a poor orphan.'" – *Destry Rides Again* (1939)

936 When Mae West wisecracks her way through her trial, the judge becomes impatient. "Are you trying to show contempt for this court?" "No," she retorts, "I'm doing my best to hide it." – *My Little Chickadee* (1940)

937 As Dorothy Lamour, posing as a streetwalker, testifies at a trial, the judge's attention is drawn to her exposed legs. "I hate these short skirts, too," she says to the judge. "I always say, 'Give me a medium-long skirt and let the trade winds do the rest.'" – *The Fleet's In* (1942)

938 A buxom beauty takes the stand before a judge. "Were you ever up before me?" "I don't know," she answers. "What time do you get up?" – *Lady of Burlesque* (1943)

939 Leo Gorcey, arrested for disturbing the peace, disrupts the courtroom at his trial. "Order! Order!" bellows the judge. "Yeah," Gorcey responds, "a hot dog and a bottle of pop." – *Block Busters* (1944)

940 In a Parisian courtroom a judge observes that witness Jane Russell doesn't understand the swearing-in procedures. "You will please swear," he says to her in English. "Oh, judge," she demurs, "I never swear." – *Gentlemen Prefer Blondes* (1953)

941 "South Sea woman" Virginia Mayo testifies at the court martial of sergeant Burt Lancaster, affirming that he is every inch a marine. "Why," she states, "he thinks when you go to heaven, you end up in the Halls of Montezuma." – *South Sea Woman* (1953)

942 "Where the hell did Cain's wife come from?" defense attorney Spencer Tracy asks witness Fredric March. "The Bible satisfies me," March affirms. "It's enough." "It frightens me to think of the state of learning in the world if everyone had your driving curiosity," Tracy fires back. – *Inherit the Wind* (1960)

943 Judge: "When you were sitting there in the dark and you felt that man's hand on your knee and again on top of your stocking, why didn't you scream for help?" Woman: "How did I know he was after my money?" – *The Night They Raided Minsky's* (1968)

944 "Weren't you up before me two weeks ago?" a judge asks a sexy defendant. "I don't know, your honor," the woman replies. "What time do you get up?" – *The Night They Raided Minsky's* (1968)

945 Failing Broadway producer Zero Mostel and accountant Gene Wilder are caught bilking investors in their show and are brought to trial. The jury announces its sentence: "We find the defendants *incredibly* guilty." – *The Producers* (1968)

946 A policeman testifies at the trial of Fielding Mellish (Woody Allen). "He's a bad apple, a Commie, a New York Jewish intellectual Communist," the officer states, and then adds, "I don't want to cast any aspersions." – *Bananas* (1971)

947 John Alton, falsely accused of a string of crimes, tries to appeal to the emotions of the judge and jury of the western town. "My mother was a lady," he cries. "And his father was a bachelor," interjects the town mayor. – *The Brothers O'Toole* (1973)

948 Judge John Forsythe comments on the previous convictions of a young defendant facing him in court: "One for assault, one for arson, one for grand larceny, and now we have indecent exposure. What's the matter? Can't you decide what you want to be when you grow up?" – *...And Justice for All* (1979)

949 Pals Gene Wilder and Richard Pryor, in a case of mistaken identity, are persuaded to plead guilty to the charge of robbing a bank in exchange for a light sentence. The judge then gives them 125 years. "One hundred and twenty-five years!" Pryor explodes. "I'll be one hundred sixty-nine when I get out!"—*Stir Crazy* (1980)

950 A young, inept defense lawyer tries to plea-bargain a suspended sentence for his client, a vicious armed robber, rapist and killer. Both the lawyer and prosecuting attorney are negotiating in front of the judge. "The police found rugs in his apartment made of human hair," the prosecutor announces in an effort to describe the depravity of the defendant. "Well," the lawyer responds, "bad taste is not a crime, your honor."—*Armed and Dangerous* (1986)

951 Kooky lawyer John Larroquette makes a deal with the judge, who happens to be his father, promising never to practice in his jurisdiction again if he dismisses the case against his client. "I

swear on my mother's grave," the son promises. "Your mother is playing the back nine at Bel Air," the judge reminds him. "I was speaking in the future tense."—*Blind Date* (1987)

952 Rich, idle Shelley Long, who has turned troop leader for a group of young campers, takes the girls to a courtroom to experience a divorce case—her own. "Never go to Reno, girls," she counsels her troop. "The California community property laws cannot be beat."—*Troop Beverly Hills* (1989)

953 Eccentric small-town judge Dan Aykroyd offers his own interpretation of the speeding laws to defendants driving a hearse: "If it's in an ambulance, you've got a chance; if it's in a hearse, it's got to be worse."—*Nothing But Trouble* (1991)

954 Brooklyn trial lawyer Joe Pesci, defending two young clients in an Alabama courtroom, refers to them as "these two yoots," an expression which compels judge Fred Gwynne to interrupt Pesci. "What are 'yoots'?"—*My Cousin Vinny* (1992)

Cowardice

955 Bert Wheeler and Robert Woolsey observe a mob beating up a young lad, and Wheeler decides to help the victim. "We're men of iron," he suggests to his pal. "Yeah," Woolsey retorts, "but I'm a little rusty today."—*Cockeyed Cavaliers* (1934)

956 Fight manager Adolphe Menjou is perturbed to learn that his middleweight champ has just gotten into trouble. "Every time I leave town something happens," Menjou says to reporters. "That *is* news!" remarks one journalist. "As a rule, something happens, and then you leave town!"—*The Milky Way* (1936)

957 When Joe E. Brown's fear of horses keeps him from playing polo, his servant warns him of the consequences: "Do you want Miss Hilton to think that you're a coward?" "You mean do I want her to *find out* that I'm a coward," Brown corrects him.—*Polo Joe* (1936)

958 Bob Hope, forced into a pistol duel with aristocrat Alan Mowbray, procrastinates. "Are you going to go through with this or do you wish to be branded a coward?" one of the judges asks. "Yes," Hope replies.—*Never Say Die* (1939)

959 The East Side Kids, inside a spooky house, elect Sunshine Sammy Morrison to stay in a room with another member of the gang who has been hurt. Sammy, the only black member of the gang, objects. "You're yellow," someone suggests. "If I's yellow, you's colorblind," Sammy returns. – *Spooks Run Wild* (1941)

960 Bob Hope and Bing Crosby plan to rescue Dorothy Lamour from the hands of Arab chieftain Anthony Quinn. "We have to storm the place," Crosby explains. "You storm," Hope retorts. "I'll stay here and drizzle." – *Road to Morocco* (1942)

961 On board a vessel, entertainer Bob Hope has disguised himself in women's clothes to avoid being captured or killed by pirates. "You ought to be ashamed of yourself in that disguise," princess Virginia Mayo says scornfully. "Why don't you die like a man?" "Because I'd rather live like a woman." – *The Princess and the Pirate* (1944)

962 French barber Bob Hope is being encouraged to fight off some attackers. "Go on, help him," someone suggests. "You're a man. You've got blood in your veins." "Yeah," says Hope, "and I want to keep it there." – *Monsieur Beaucaire* (1946)

963 Bing Crosby pleads with Bob Hope to save desperate Dorothy Lamour. "This girl's in trouble," Crosby explains. "You gotta help her – like any guy would with red blood in his veins." "Well, I got news for you," replies Hope. "I'm anemic." – *Road to Rio* (1947)

964 Lou Costello balks when the police want to use him as a decoy to catch a serial killer. "Would you rather die like a hero or live like a rat?" his pal Bud Abbott asks. "Get the cheese ready," Costello returns. – *Abbott and Costello Meet the Killer* (1949)

965 When a jealous suitor goes after Bob Hope for fooling around with his girlfriend, Hope tries to stave him off: "Only a coward would hit a coward." – *Fancy Pants* (1950)

966 Lou Costello, posing as a formidable prizefighter, is with a gambler's pretty girlfriend when he is brazenly insulted. "If you weren't here," Costello says to his companion, "I'd sock him." "That's all right," she replies. "I'm leaving now." "I'll go with you," Costello rejoins. – *Abbott and Costello Meet the Invisible Man* (1951)

967 Vaudeville performer Bob Hope, who happens to resemble a notorious spy, is pressured by government agents into accepting a dangerous assignment. "What are you, a sniveling coward, a yellow belly?" an agent fires at Hope. "I'm in there somewhere," Hope replies. – *My Favorite Spy* (1951)

968 After much coaxing, vaudeville comic Bob Hope reluctantly volunteers as a secret agent and is sent on a dangerous mission. "Don't you want to be a hero?" a fellow agent asks Hope, who is on the verge of quitting. "What for?" Hope replies. "I've been happy all my life as a coward." – *My Favorite Spy* (1951)

969 David Niven confides to ingenue Maggie McNamara that he once hit his ex-wife in the behind with a muffin pan. "You struck a woman?" she asks in disbelief. "Why certainly," he replies. "In fact, I hardly strike anyone but a woman. Oh, I'm not the belligerent type. I'm also a coward." – *The Moon Is Blue* (1953)

970 In North Africa during World War II, a villainous, saber-rattling sultan threatens Huntz Hall, but this time Hall stands his ground. "Come on," he responds. "They don't call me the Fighting Coward for nothin'." – *Looking for Danger* (1957)

971 The mayor of a town about to be raided by a gang of hired killers pleads with the citizens to remain and defend their homes. All know that the local villain is behind the scheme. "Can't you see that's the last act of a desperate man?" he explains. "We don't care if it's the first act of *Henry V*," a voice calls out, "we're leaving!" – *Blazing Saddles* (1974)

972 The narrator of this western satire wonders what the old B westerns would look like if they were made today: "In the first place, the bad guys wouldn't all be such cowards." – *Rustlers' Rhapsody* (1985)

973 A vigilante assails Woody Allen for fearing a maniacal killer stalking an East European city. "Are you a coward or a worm or a yellow-belly?" the man asks. "No," replies Allen, "but keep going." – *Shadows and Fog* (1992)

Crime and Criminals

974 Hotel owner Groucho Marx notices that two of his new guests, Chico and Harpo, have checked in with an empty suitcase. "I know," Chico acknowledges. "We fill it up before we leave." – *The Cocoanuts* (1929)

975 College student Zeppo Marx proposes to his father, dean Groucho Marx, that the school can build a winning team by illegally buying gridiron stars at a local speakeasy. "How dare you suggest that I, a college dean, look for football players in a speakeasy," the indignant Groucho protests, "without even telling me where it is?" – *Horse Feathers* (1932)

976 Con man Warren Hymer and Ethel Merman plot to murder Eddie Cantor, a millionaire's son, and steal his fortune. She poses as Cantor's long-lost mother and introduces Hymer as Cantor's uncle. "Gee," Cantor wonders, "isn't that Uncle Louie a funny duck?" "Oh, wait'll you get to know him," Merman replies. "He'll kill you." – *Kid Millions* (1934)

977 Aboard a luxury liner, con artist Warren Hymer decides to get rid of heir Eddie Cantor by throwing him overboard. To accomplish this, he persuades Cantor to sit in a wheel chair. "Oh, are we going for a ride?" Cantor asks. "You

took the words right out of my mouth." – *Kid Millions* (1934)

978 Ranch owner Mae West is warned to look out for crooks. "Let the crooks look out for themselves," she replies. – *Goin' to Town* (1935)

979 During an ocean voyage a blackmailer tries to shake down passenger Fred MacMurray. "Shall I throw him to the sharks?" MacMurray's friend asks. "What's the matter?" MacMurray replies wryly. "Don't you like sharks?" – *The Princess Comes Across* (1936)

980 In the Casbah, the forbidden quarters of Algiers, Alan Hale, as the purchaser of stolen goods, has his shop raided by the police. As he escapes through a secret panel, he complains: "Every few weeks I have to get new doors." – *Algiers* (1938)

981 When ex-convict Paul Guilfoyle tries to get a job as script consultant for a crime movie, his wife Lee Patrick adds her support. "My husband is an authority on crime," she says to Hollywood screenwriter Lee Tracy. "He's been in – he's studied in every prison in the country." – *Crashing Hollywood* (1938)

982 Racketeer Akim Tamiroff sends strong-arm hoodlum Brian Donlevy to collect some old debts. "You start with Madam La Hoya," he orders. "You tell that old battle-ax it's two hundred fifty dollars or Madam La Hoya doesn't Hoya anymore." – *The Great McGinty* (1940)

983 Wall Street broker Edward Arnold, sentenced to five years for embezzlement and about to leave for prison, is interviewed by reporters. Suddenly another criminal standing nearby objects. "Hey, how about me?" he yells at the reporters. "I steal an empty slot machine and get ten years, and this guy steals a million and gets five. Figure that out, will you?" "That's why you got the ten," a reporter quips, "to figure it out." – *Johnny Apollo* (1940)

984 Proud pickpocket Mischa Auer takes umbrage when he is associated with members of the underworld. "I'm not a thief," he protests, "I'm an artist." – *Seven Sinners* (1940)

985 Racketeer Lloyd Nolan explains to his hoodlum pal why he donated an $8,000 fire engine to a town instead of a $2,000 sewer: "A fire engine is big, it's red, it's shiny. It socks 'em between the eyes. What fun could they get out of a sewer?" – *Buy Me That Town* (1941)

986 A mean-looking gangster walks into a small nightclub and peruses the customers. "Looking for someone?" owner Fritz Feld asks. "Yeah." "Pleasure or business?" "A little of both," the gangster replies. "It would be a pleasure to give him the business." – *Four Jacks and a Jill* (1941)

987 Lou Costello describes to detectives a corpse he has discovered. "He was tied with a lot of string, and he had something across his mouth." "He had a gag in his mouth," Bud Abbott offers. "If he did," Costello adds, "he never had a chance to tell it." – *Hold That Ghost* (1941)

988 "It's just my luck," mutters hotel detective and ex-hoodlum Paul Guilfoyle to amateur sleuth George Sanders. "I spend all my time looking for lost kids and old ladies' glasses, and the first time there's a real crime, there ain't no corpus delicious." – *The Saint in Palm Springs* (1941)

989 Big-time gambler Humphrey Bogart describes to pal Frank McHugh how a murder victim had his hand raised just before he was killed. "He was trying to tell me something," Bogart figures. "Maybe he wanted to leave the room," McHugh suggests. – *All Through the Night* (1942)

990 A nightclub owner is murdered and reporters ask amateur sleuth George Sanders, one of the patrons, if he is going to work on the case. He says that the police will be on their own. "What a break for crime!" quips his chauffeur Allen Jenkins. – *The Falcon Takes Over* (1942)

991 Mobster Edward G. Robinson, recently released from prison, learns that in his absence the police have destroyed his slot machines. "Why, that's criminal!" Robinson rages. "Not the machines, but the wanton destruction of private property." – *Larceny, Inc.* (1942)

992 Would-be bank robber Edward G. Robinson buys a luggage store next to a bank and orders one of his gang to get two pickaxes for the digging. "Wouldn't that look suspicious?" his sidekick queries. "Tell them we're building good will," replies Robinson. – *Larceny, Inc.* (1942)

993 Mobster Edward G. Robinson, planning a bank robbery, reminds his cohorts: "This job's gotta be handled with finesse." "Who's that?" one of the gang asks. – *Larceny, Inc.* (1942)

994 The East Side Kids capture smalltime mobster Billy Gilbert and try to get him to confess to a murder. "You're gonna hang by the neck until dead," one gang member threatens. "I don't hang around no place," Gilbert fires back. – *Mr. Wise Guy* (1942)

995 Shemp Howard asks Olsen and Johnson: "Want to buy an oven? It's hot." – *Crazy House* (1943)

996 Held captive by a gang of murderers, radio actor Red Skelton tries to bribe his guard Sam Levene. "With that kind of dough you can live the life of Riley," Skelton says. "You'll have nothing to worry about – unless Riley comes home, of course." – *Whistling in Brooklyn* (1943)

997 A murder is committed and light-headed Carole Landis becomes involved. When a suspect is found unconscious, she calls in a local doctor. "What's his occupation?" the physician inquires. "I think he's a murderer," she replies. – *Having Wonderful Crime* (1945)

998 Not too impressed when his pal Leo Gorcey introduces him to a local hoodlum, Huntz Hall remarks: "He's been 'up the river' so manny times they call him 'Showboat.'" – *Hard Boiled Mahoney* (1947)

999 Bob Hope, hired as a detective, investigates a home where Peter Lorre lunges at him with a knife. Hope escapes and returns with the police who question Lorre. "Have you got a knife?" "Sure I have a knife," Lorre answers. "I'm the gardener." "What do you think I was last night," Hope interjects, "a chrysanthemum?" – *My Favorite Brunette* (1947)

1000 Amateur sleuth Boston Blackie (Chester Morris) and Runt, his sidekick, posing as diamond thieves, call on Louie, an ex-convict out on parole. After they leave, Louie addresses his female accomplice. "You know," he says about the visitors, "when I was in stir I heard they were going straight. Isn't it terrible the vicious gossip you hear about people?" – *Trapped by Boston Blackie* (1948)

1001 A captive locked in a trunk complains to psychopathic gangster James

Cagney that he can't breathe. Cagney pulls out his gun and, before shooting holes into the trunk, rasps: "I'll give you some air." – *White Heat* (1949)

1002 Hotel bellhop Lou Costello discovers the body of a guest in one of the rooms. "Mr. Strickland has been murdered!" Costello exclaims, reporting it to manager Alan Mowbray. "We don't permit murders in this hotel," Mowbray declares. – *Abbott and Costello Meet the Killer* (1949)

1003 Gangster Cesar Romero, who has murdered dozens of his competitors, takes another rival gang leader for a ride and then splurges on a big funeral for his victim. "How much did the casket set you back?" a reporter asks. "Three thousand and forty dollars," Romero replies. "Really?" quips the reporter. "I thought you got a wholesale rate." – *Love That Brute* (1950)

1004 Several members of the French Foreign Legion stumble across an unopened, abandoned safe in the middle of a Moroccan desert. Knowing that it contains a huge military payroll, they plead with one of their comrades – a former safecracker – to open it. "I'll try," the man reluctantly agrees. "Watch out for the police." – *Ten Tall Men* (1951)

1005 "My own cousin involved with gangsters!" Jerry Lewis exclaims, referring to Dean Martin. "I just can't believe it! I'm nonplused! My plus has never been so non!" – *Money from Home* (1953)

1006 Elegant heiress Grace Kelly helps retired French Riviera cat burglar Cary Grant maintain his new respectability. "I've never caught a jewel thief before," she beams. "It's stimulating." – *To Catch a Thief* (1955)

1007 Ex-army officer Jack Hawkins, while planning a bank robbery, gives instructions to his men: "This is our battlefield. And I promise you this will be our finest hour. What price glory? One million pounds." – *The League of Gentlemen* (1960)

1008 When Chicago mobster Peter Falk asks his gang for ideas about how to get rid of his partner – a corrupt local sheriff – one hood suggests making the victim part of the cornerstone of the new police station. "The sheriff is over six feet and the cornerstone is only three feet," another reminds the group. "How about if we fold him once?" a third offers. "That'll do it." – *Robin and the Seven Hoods* (1964)

1009 Peter Sellers, as a master criminal now "residing" in a European prison, worries about his adolescent sister who seems to be going astray. "Nobody will marry the sister of a thief," he broods, "except another thief. Ah, if I could only steal enough to be an honest man." – *After the Fox* (1966)

1010 When Dustin Hoffman barges into the home of Mrs. Robinson (Anne Bancroft) seeking the girl he loves (Katharine Ross), Bancroft telephones the police. "Will you send a patrol car?" she suggests. "We have a burglar here. Just a moment, I'll see ... Are you armed?" – *The Graduate* (1967)

1011 The mistress of arch-criminal Karl Malden, trying to alleviate his frustration resulting from a bungled assassination attempt, wryly proposes: "Maybe we can find somebody to run over on the way home." – *Murderers' Row* (1967)

1012 U.S. Treasury clerk Robert Hutton hires hard-of-hearing safecracker Jack Gilford to steal the plates used for printing money. Meanwhile Gilford has lost his hearing aid and can't hear the safe tumblers. "Try to think," Hutton says frantically. "Where did you lose your hearing aid?" "You'll have to talk louder," replies Gilford. "I lost my hearing aid." – *Who's Minding the Mint?* (1967)

1013 Broadway producer Zero Mostel, deeply in the red, appeals to his accountant, Gene Wilder, to rescue his sinking theater enterprise. "Do me a favor," he pleads. "Move a few decimal points around. You can do it. You're an accountant. You're in a noble profession. The word 'count' is part of your title." – *The Producers* (1968)

1014 "Gentlemen, gentlemen," con artist and bank robber Zero Mostel says as he gathers his gang together for a briefing, "kindly be seated. Time is a thief." "You can't trust anyone these days," a gang member blurts out. – *The Great Bank Robbery* (1969)

1015 Bank employee Warren Beatty and dizzy hooker Goldie Hawn have pulled off a successful million-dollar bank heist. Hawn ecstatically handles some of the bills. "Do you think there's any connection between crime and sex?" she beams. – *$ (Dollars)* (1971)

1016 Al Pacino relates to girlfriend Diane Keaton how his father (Marlon Brando) and one of his henchmen paid a visit to a stubborn bandleader who quickly agreed to their terms. "Why did he do that?" Keaton asks. "My father made him an offer he couldn't refuse." – *The Godfather* (1972)

1017 Moses Gunn, an African delegate to the U.N., hires a team of inept thieves to recover a priceless jewel belonging to his country. After several blundering escapades, the gang fails. "I've heard of the habitual criminal, of course," Gunn says, "but I never dreamed I'd become involved with the habitual crime." – *The Hot Rock* (1972)

1018 A young man is accused of biting off a dog's left nipple, and small-town police chief James Garner is in charge of the case. "What are you going to charge him with," laughs a fellow officer, "grand theft? Or maybe it was tit for tat?" – *They Only Kill Their Masters* (1972)

1019 Jack Nicholson, who has just confessed to murdering his wife for her inheritance, adds the following thought: "I've been wrestling with my conscience in regard to this two hundred thousand dollars, which now due to this tragic state of affairs, I'm not sure I'm in line to get it or not."–*The Fortune* (1975)

1020 "We've been robbed," Anne Bancroft informs husband Jack Lemmon. "You mean someone walked in here and robbed us?" Lemmon repeats in disbelief. "What do you think–they called up and made an appointment?" –*The Prisoner of Second Avenue* (1975)

1021 Publisher Gene Wilder, falsely accused of murder, escapes from the police in a patrol car. In the back seat, unknown to Wilder, is handcuffed prisoner Richard Pryor. Once the two fugitives are in the clear, Pryor introduces himself. "What do they want you for anyway, man?" he asks. "Murder," Wilder casually replies. "Drop me off anywhere along here, okay? I don't want to mess with the big 'M.'"–*Silver Streak* (1976)

1022 Goldie Hawn discovers a body in her apartment and calls the police. But by the time detective Chevy Chase arrives, the body mysteriously disappears. "The dead body!" she exclaims. "It's gone! It vanished!" "Maybe it was embarrassed," Chase offers.–*Foul Play* (1978)

1023 Sean Connery pulls off the greatest train robbery in England's history, but at the last moment he gets caught and is brought to trial. "On the matter of motive," the judge asks, "why did you conceive, plan and execute this dastardly and scandalous crime?" "I wanted the money," Connery replies. –*The Great Train Robbery* (1979)

1024 A petty thief presents his newest acquisition to a smalltime fence. "Another typewriter," the fence grumbles. "It's not even electric." "It's a collector's item," the crook proclaims. "It's worth a lot of money–antique. The Magna Carta was typed on it."–*Hot Stuff* (1979)

1025 Smalltime racketeer Burt Lancaster, now retired, reminisces about the Atlantic City of the Prohibition era. "Rackets, whoring, guns," he says wistfully. "It used to be beautiful."–*Atlantic City* (1980)

1026 Tough former gangster's moll Gena Rowlands packs a 44 Magnum as she protects a young Puerto Rican boy marked for murder. At one point, she gets the drop on the pursuers. "Okay, you bananas," she orders, "up against the wall!"–*Gloria* (1980)

1027 A servant informs detectives Don Knotts and Tim Conway about a fellow servant's experiences in India: "His tongue was cut out when he was caught trying to steal a ruby from his commanding sergeant's wife." "That's a tough penalty for trying to steal a ruby," Conway remarks. "It was in her navel at the time," the servant explains.–*The Private Eyes* (1980)

1028 Falsely accused of bank robbery, Chevy Chase has sought refuge with his ex-wife Goldie Hawn. "I can't stand being a fugitive any more," he admits to her. "The hardest part is finding a bathroom."–*Seems Like Old Times* (1980)

1029 Unemployed New York City wine salesman Paul Bartel and his wife, nutritionist Mary Woronov, murder weirdoes for their money by hitting their victims on the head with a frying pan. "Can you buy another frying pan?" Woronov asks her husband who is about to go shopping. "I'm just a little squeamish about cooking in the one we're using to kill people."–*Eating Raoul* (1982)

1030 Masked robber Jerry Reed holds up a drug store and orders all the customers and workers to line up. He then scoops out the contents of the cash register. "Look at here! You ain't got no money!" He then complains to the owner: "What do they pay you with– food stamps? You ought to be robbing me!"–*The Survivors* (1983)

1031 Donald Sutherland and his gang of social misfits plan to crack a safe. The only problem is they don't know how. They ask former safecracker and two-time loser Professor Irwin Corey, who is currently out on parole, to help them. "They'll look for any excuse to revoke parole!" the eccentric Corey says. "The cops don't like short people." – *Crackers* (1984)

1032 In this satire an idealistic, crime-fighting assistant district attorney brings a bulging portfolio of evidence against a notorious gangster to the home of his boss, district attorney Danny De Vito. "I got enough evidence here to put Johnny Dangerously where he belongs. I have got conclusive evidence, notarized depositions, tire prints, blood samples, eye-witness accounts, murder weapons, recordings – " "Hold it!" De Vito interrupts him. "It's flimsy, it's not enough. It'll never hold up – not in a courtroom." – *Johnny Dangerously* (1984)

1033 Police officer Raul Julia questions Susan Sarandon as to where she has last seen her dentist, who has been murdered. "At his office," she answers. "Just at his office?" the lawman persists. "Well," she responds, "he wasn't the kind to perform gum surgery at Pizza Hut." – *Compromising Positions* (1985)

1034 Organized crime member Jack Nicholson confides to his former girlfriend Anjelica Huston that the woman he loves is a criminal and a hired killer. "Do I 'ice' her? Do I marry her?" he asks. "Marry her!" Huston replies. "Just because she's a thief and a hitter doesn't mean she's not a good woman in all the other departments ... You and she is in the same line of business." – *Prizzi's Honor* (1985)

1035 Smalltime hoodlum Moe Dickstein (Joe Piscopo) tries to rationalize his profession to his critical mother. "Did you ever stop to think that maybe I'm a trailblazer," he explains, "that maybe I'm opening up new areas here in Newark for the Jews – that Moe Dickstein is the Jackie Robinson of organized crime in New Jersey?" – *Wise Guys* (1986)

1036 "What line of work are you in?" someone asks Whoopi Goldberg. "I'm a cat burglar," Whoopi replies. "What do you do with them?" "What?" the burglar questions quizzically. "The cats." – *Burglar* (1987)

1037 Tough hoodlum Harvey Keitel issues his typical warning to a defiant, young Robert Downey: "Get lost, cupcake, unless you want your neck separated from your face." – *The Pick-Up Artist* (1987)

1038 "I have a theory criminals want to get caught," suggests a nightclub comic at a Lake Tahoe resort. "Reports say that eighteen of every twenty suspects arrested have organized crime ties. If you don't want to get caught, don't wear the ties." – *Things Change* (1988)

1039 Smalltime crook and family patriarch (Sean Connery), currently in prison, expresses his pride in grandson Matthew Broderick's educational achievements and his ingenuity in planning a million-dollar heist. "That's America," Broderick comments. "Every generation does a little better." – *Family Business* (1989)

1040 Police officer Nick Nolte and carefree thief Eddie Murphy argue about the nature and roots of crime and criminals. "I just arrest crooks," Nolte says. "I don't make them steal." "You make it sound like everybody went down to the guidance counselor, took a test and the results came back: 'Crook was the only job you are qualified for.'" – *Another 48 Hours* (1990)

1041 When Mel Gibson, under a witness-protection program, learns that mobsters have discovered his new identity, he and his girlfriend, Goldie Hawn, hide out in the control room of a zoo. "You stay in here," he cautions her as he prepares to confront his pursuers, "because it's a zoo out there." – *Bird on a Wire* (1990)

1042 Underworld kingpin Al Pacino, as Big Boy, says to his cronies: "'All's fair in love and business'–Benjamin Franklin."–*Dick Tracy* (1990)

1043 Cynical detective Fred Ward is on the trail of a dangerous, crazed psychopath called Junior. "I'd hate to meet Senior," Ward says.–*Miami Blues* (1990)

1044 When smalltime hoodlum Steve Martin is arrested with a variety of stolen goods in the trunk of his car, he offers an excuse for each item. Assistant district attorney Joan Cusack finally asks him why he needs twenty-five copies of the same book. "In case I want to read it more than once," he explains. –*My Blue Heaven* (1990)

1045 "Do you ever do any fencing?" the King of Finland asks the King of England (John Goodman), a former American lounge entertainer. "Just a little, when I was a kid," replies Goodman. "A couple of watches here and there." –*King Ralph* (1991)

1046 Arriving late at the scene of a mass murder, detective Leslie Nielsen studies the situation and asks a fellow officer: "Any other victims?" "You're standing on one right now."–*The Naked Gun 2½: The Smell of Fear* (1991)

1047 Slow-witted hoodlum Chazz Palminteri, bodyguard to gang leader Sylvester Stallone, can't keep up with the complexities of his boss's personal and business affairs. Stallone, about to interview a visitor, orders his bodyguard to leave. "Can't I stay, boss?" Palminteri pleads. "Every time I leave I fall behind."–*Oscar* (1991)

Cultures

1048 Little Shirley Temple, left by her father in a betting parlor, notices the black porter (Willie Best) sweeping up. "I know you," she addresses him. "You're the Black Knight." "Go on, child," he protests. "I'm black day and night."–*Little Miss Marker* (1934)

1049 When the son of impoverished Mexican-American fisherman J. Carrol Naish becomes a World War II hero, local businessmen of a southern California village attempt to exploit the news. Expecting visits by important dignitaries, they move the elderly father from his squalid surroundings to a new, temporary home complete with breathtaking vistas. "See all that country?" one man says in an effort to impress Naish. "Try to imagine that your ancestors owned it." "They did," the old fisherman says.–*A Medal for Benny* (1945)

1050 In a scheme to con a racist Southern landowner, self-appointed black reverend Ossie Davis seeks to enlist the aid of kitchen worker Ruby Dee. "Where is your racial pride?" Davis challenges her. "I got racial pride," she bristles. "I just don't need it in my line of work."–*Gone Are the Days* (1963)

1051 New York City detective Godfrey Cambridge, coming across bales of cotton during his investigation, sighs to fellow black officer Raymond St. Jacques: "It's been a long time since I saw raw cotton." "Man," his partner replies, shaking his head, "you ain't never seen raw cotton. You was born in New York City just like me."–*Cotton Comes to Harlem* (1970)

1052 Former political activist Elliott Gould turns down his friend, a young

African-American activist, who wants Gould to join a protest rally. "I don't want to marry your sister!" the young man half-sarcastically calls out to the departing Gould. "You marry my sister!" Gould fires back. "I will arrange it for you! Man, with the analyst and the astrologist and the two neurotic kids and the payments on the pool and the bill for the hysterectomy – you can be husband number four she wipes out!" – *Getting Straight* (1970)

1053 Elderly Cheyenne Chief Old Lodge Skins (Chief Dan George), wishing to enter the Happy Hunting Grounds, tries a mystical array of Indian rites to evoke the spirits of Death. Nothing happens. "Well," the chief says with resignation, "sometimes the magic works and sometimes it doesn't." – *Little Big Man* (1970)

1054 A twist of fate lands criminal Eddie Murphy on the right side of the law. Relishing his newfound power, he enters a redneck bar and begins to rile the patrons. "I'm your worst nightmare," Murphy yells, "a nigger with a badge!" – *48 Hours* (1982)

1055 "Jews know two things," comedy writer Mark Linn-Baker quips to secretary Jessica Harper, "suffering and where to find great Chinese food." – *My Favorite Year* (1982)

1056 Unemployed Richard Pryor is hired to babysit tycoon Jackie Gleason's spoiled seven-year-old son Scott Schwartz. "Were you ever a thief?" the boy asks Pryor. "Don't you know it's part of the black cultural imperative?" Pryor quips. – *The Toy* (1982)

1057 Woody Allen's Jewish mother haunts every aspect of his life. "Don't get married," she advises. "After all, where do you come to a blonde with three children? What are you – an astronaut?" – *New York Stories* (1989)

1058 Father-of-the-bride Steve Martin is forced by his wife and daughter into selecting a catering service owned by "Franco," a barely understood heavily accented foreigner. "Right away I realized this was a mistake of gargantuan proportions," he muses. "This guy was going to coordinate our wedding? How? With subtitles?" – *Father of the Bride* (1991)

1059 To find a murderer, attractive police detective Melanie Griffith dresses modestly and goes undercover in a Hasidic rabbi's house – where scholarship is all and sex is only a gender. She then shows the rabbi's son, Eric Thal, her new chaste outfit. "On the Hasidic scale of sexiness," she asks, "how do I rate?" – *A Stranger Among Us* (1992)

Dance

1060 "Do you dance?" Robert Young asks his unemotional servant. "Not as a rule, sir," the man replies, "but on one occasion, with the aid of six very old cocktails, I executed, if you will pardon me, sir, a 'Shuffle Off to Buffalo.'" – *It's Love Again* (1936)

1061 "If it weren't for two things," Gracie Allen says to George Burns,

"you'd be a terrific dancer." "What's that?" he asks. "Your feet." – *A Damsel in Distress* (1937)

1062 Lecherous Broadway producer Adolphe Menjou approaches hoofers Ann Miller and Ginger Rogers while they are rehearsing a dance routine. "Are you practicing a new number?" he asks. "No," Rogers snaps, "we're just getting over the D.T.s." – *Stage Door* (1937)

1063 Theatrical producer Robert Taylor reveals to his publicity agent (Robert Benchley) that he has found a leading lady for his next musical. He had met her aboard a train in a boxcar, traveling with a horse. "Let me get this straight now," Benchley says. "You found a girl and a horse in a boxcar." "Right!" "And she's a great dancer?" Benchley queries. "Right!" "You mean the girl?" "Yes, the girl," Taylor reaffirms. "That's a relief," Benchley quips. – *Broadway Melody of 1938* (1938)

1064 Mary Todd (Marjorie Weaver) meets Abe Lincoln (Henry Fonda) at a ball and is anything but impressed with his grace. "Why, Mr. Lincoln," she says, "at least you're a man of honor. You said you wanted to dance with me in the worst way, and I must say you kept your word. This is the worst way I've ever seen." – *Young Mr. Lincoln* (1939)

1065 Sexy dancer Lucille Ball is about to go out on stage at a burlesque theater and do her number when the manager approaches. "Give them all you got, baby," he says. "They couldn't take it." – *Dance, Girl, Dance* (1940)

1066 Bob Hope boasts to Paulette Goddard: "The girls call me Pilgrim because every time I dance with one, I make a little progress." – *The Ghost Breakers* (1940)

1067 At an English ball an elderly gentleman comments to Laurence Olivier that "dancing is one of the first refinements of a polished society." "It has the added advantage, sir," Olivier notes, "of being one of the refinements of savages. Every Hottentot can dance." – *Pride and Prejudice* (1940)

1068 Lonely hayseed Grady Sutton is mesmerized by the sensual body gestures of a shapely dancer doing her specialty number in a small nightclub. "That's the most wonderful music I ever

saw," he sighs. – *Four Jacks and a Jill* (1941)

1069 "Don't you like dancing?" Martha Raye asks Lou Costello. "No," he replies, "it's just a whole lot of hugging set to music." "What don't you like about that?" "The music," Costello says. – *Keep 'Em Flying* (1941)

1070 When Broadway producer Cary Grant discovers a dancing caterpillar, the story makes the headlines across the country. "A dancing caterpillar?" a female cabby questions. "Well, why not?" replies another. "He can't be any worse than some of the worms that's dragged me around the dance floor." – *Once Upon a Time* (1944)

1071 Leo Gorcey and his East Side gang visit a dance studio where several young men are on stage rehearsing a ballet. "Let's get out of here," Billy Benedict says. "This may be catching." "What's the matter with you?" Gorcey questions him. "Ain't you got no integrity for art?" "Yeah," Benedict replies, "but they ain't paintin'!" – *Come Out Fighting* (1945)

1072 Leo Gorcey leads his East Side gang in dancing lessons, but can't seem to get the boys to keep in step. "I want to get this in unison," he announces. "*Western* Unison?" Huntz Hall asks. – *Come Out Fighting* (1945)

1073 Jack Benny, as an angel recently arrived on Earth, is puzzled by couples dancing in a hotel ballroom. "Pardon me, sir," he asks a waiter. "What are they supposed to be doing?" "I don't know, sir. They call it dancing." "I must tell St. Vitus about this," Benny muses. – *The Horn Blows at Midnight* (1945)

1074 When Fred Astaire's partner leaves him, he takes on novice Judy Garland. At their first session, she is nervous and awkward. "What idiot ever told you you were a dancer?" a frustrated Astaire asks. "You did," she replies. – *Easter Parade* (1948)

1075 Federal agent Burt Lancaster shares a limerick with his girlfriend Maggie McNamara: "There was once a fella named Lancelot,/ Whose girlfriend insisted he dance a lot./ But his armor had riveting,/ So bad that when pivoting,/ The poor guy kept losing his pants a lot."–*Mister 880* (1950)

1076 The upstanding parents of Tony Randall's fiancée (Barbara Eden) are shocked at the after-dinner entertainment he has provided, including a sensual, exotic belly dancer. "Actually," Randall explains, "she does this to support an invalid aunt."–*The Brass Bottle* (1964)

1077 After the dancing partner of James Bond (Sean Connery) is murdered in his arms, he glides over to a nearby table, seats the victim and nonchalantly addresses the patrons. "Do you mind if my friend sits this one out?" he asks. "She's just dead."–*Thunderball* (1965)

1078 In a complex scam, Broadway producer Zero Mostel approaches Nazi-obsessed playwright Kenneth Mars about staging his play *Springtime for Hitler*. Mars thrills at the suggestion that he can "show the real world the true Hitler." "Not many people knew it," he says, "but the Fuhrer was a terrific dancer."–*The Producers* (1968)

1079 A narrator describes Woody Allen's descent into the underworld: "He was wanted by federal authorities for dancing with a mailman."–*Take the Money and Run* (1969)

1080 Undercover cop Serpico (Al Pacino) tells a fellow detective that he is taking ballet lessons and begins to describe some of the techniques of ballet. "There are five positions," Pacino states. "You're being shortchanged," the detective quips. –*Serpico* (1973)

Dating

1081 Robert Woolsey asks Bert Wheeler where he was last night. "I had a date with one of the Siamese twins, but she couldn't get away."–*Caught Plastered* (1931)

1082 Struggling dancer Ginger Rogers criticizes a haughty actress for dating wealthy Broadway producer Anthony Powell (Adolphe Menjou), known for seducing his dates. "You know," the actress retorts, "I think I can fix you up with Mr. Powell's chauffeur. He has a very nice car, too." "Yes," Rogers comes back, "but I understand Mr. Powell's chauffeur doesn't go as far in his car as Mr. Powell does." "Even a chauffeur has to have an incentive."–*Stage Door* (1937)

1083 "How about you and I putting on the nosebag?" a fresh dispatcher asks pretty pilot Alice Faye. "No, thanks," she retorts. "I never eat with horses." –*Tail Spin* (1939)

1084 Desperate Roland Young asks beautiful Greta Garbo to have dinner with him. "I've only just met you," she demurs. "Tomorrow night?" he persists. "I'll have forgotten you," Garbo replies. –*Two-Faced Woman* (1941)

1085 After a soldier rejects her, Joan Davis boasts that she has plenty of men–seventy, eighty, ninety. "Why don't you go out with them?" Kay Kyser asks. "Who wants to go out with men seventy, eighty or ninety?"–*Around the World* (1943)

1086 Second-rate burlesque comic Michael O'Shea tries to date singer Barbara Stanwyck. "The only date I make with a comic is with the Sunday funnies," she replies. – *Lady of Burlesque* (1943)

1087 "Some beautiful women in Tunis," Groucho Marx suggests to a nobleman who is planning a trip to that city. "I'm not interested in beautiful women," the man replies. "Then you ought to look up some of the girls I've taken out," Groucho quips. – *A Night in Casablanca* (1946)

1088 New York cop William Bendix, suspicious of his sister's boyfriend, questions her about his actions during their dates. "I don't know what you're talking about," she innocently replies. "When I went out with Michael, it was no different than when you go out with a girl." "I'll kill him!" Bendix explodes. – *Where There's Life* (1947)

1089 Lou Costello complains about his half of a double date: "Mine had so much bridgework, every time I kissed her I had to pay a toll." – *Abbott and Costello Meet Frankenstein* (1948)

1090 Neighbor David Wayne confesses tongue-in-cheek to Katharine Hepburn. "You're the only one I know why I love," he says, "and you want to know why? Because you live right across the hall from me . . . It's so convenient. Is there anything worse than that awful taking the girl home and that long trek back alone?" – *Adam's Rib* (1949)

1091 Inhibited masseur Red Skelton laments his inexperience with women. "You mean your mother wouldn't let you go out with members of the opposite sex?" asks Ricardo Montalban. "Yeah," Skelton replies, "but she wouldn't tell me which ones were the opposite sex." – *Neptune's Daughter* (1949)

1092 A very buxom matron at a women's prison tells some of the inmates about her upcoming date with a boyfriend, vaunting that her man got a car just for her. "It must be a truck," one of the inmates cracks. – *Caged* (1950)

1093 Vaudeville comic Bob Hope reluctantly agrees to impersonate an international agent whom he resembles. Hope is flown to North Africa where he is about to embark on a dangerous mission. "You have a date with destiny," his contact says. "I'll book my own dates," Hope responds, "but hang on to her phone number." – *My Favorite Spy* (1951)

1094 Sailors Groucho Marx and William Bendix both show up to take out Marie Wilson, much to their bewilderment. "I thought I'd kill two birds with one stone," she explains, "so I made a date with both of you." "What's the matter," asks Groucho, "is there a shortage of stones?" – *A Girl in Every Port* (1952)

1095 American diplomat Cary Grant, who has just met European actress Ingrid Bergman, tries to entice her into attending a dinner with him. "I wish you'd come," he says. "I'm an extra man. You'd make the dinner come out even." "How many people will be there?" "Six hundred." "Yes, five hundred and ninety-nine people," she replies. "It does look untidy." – *Indiscreet* (1958)

1096 After an all-night romp on the town, advertising executive Rock Hudson is driven straight to work by his date and he plants a fleeting, mechanical kiss on her lips. "Wait a minute!" she exclaims. "What kind of a good-night kiss is that? We're not married!" – *Lover Come Back* (1961)

1097 Meddling mother Eileen Heckart asks detective-son George Segal, who has been tirelessly working on a case involving a serial strangler, where he's taking girlfriend Lee Remick. "We're gonna have dinner at her own place," he says. "You mean her own apartment?" his mother exclaims. "The two of you alone?" "Well, we were going to invite the strangler, but he couldn't make it." – *No Way to Treat a Lady* (1968)

1098 A mean-spirited chain-gang guard, after barking his orders at the prisoners, asks, "Are there any questions?" "Do you think a girl should pet on her first date?" Woody Allen pipes up. – *Take the Money and Run* (1969)

1099 Jack Nicholson asks roommate Arthur Garfunkel's girlfriend Candice Bergen for a date. "He won't mind," Nicholson says. "How do you know?" "I won't tell him," he explains. – *Carnal Knowledge* (1971)

1100 Struggling entertainer Renee Taylor has strayed from the Jewish fold, dating men of varied backgrounds, including Chinese and gays. "And none of them Jewish," her mother (Helen Verbit) notes. "But I thought I'd never see the day when you'd go with a Capricorn." – *Made for Each Other* (1971)

1101 Woody Allen's friend wants to arrange a date for him, but Woody demurs. "I haven't looked at a girl in two years," he explains. "I'm out of practice. Even when I was in practice, I was out of practice." – *Play It Again, Sam* (1972)

1102 Standing in front of a painting in a museum, Woody Allen becomes aware of an intense young woman alongside him. "What are you doing Saturday night?" he inquires. "Committing suicide." "What are you doing Friday night?" he asks. – *Play It Again, Sam* (1972)

1103 During a carriage ride in New York's Central Park, Woody Allen tells his teenage girlfriend Mariel Hemingway: "Geez, on my prom night I went around this park five times, six times. If I had been with a girl, this would've been an incredible experience." – *Manhattan* (1979)

1104 Schoolteacher Marsha Mason, a widow and mother of a teenage boy, gives refuge to her father who has returned from his wanderings with a large sum of stolen money. Meanwhile police officer Donald Sutherland, whom she had recently met when her car was stolen, takes her out on a date. But her thoughts are elsewhere. "I've got a lot on my mind – I don't know – maybe we shouldn't be seeing so much of each other." "This is our first date," he replies. – *Max Dugan Returns* (1983)

1105 Former astronaut and ladies' man Jack Nicholson, specializing in very young women, eventually asks widowed neighbor Shirley MacLaine for a date. "Imagine you having a date with someone where it wasn't necessarily a felony," she remarks. – *Terms of Endearment* (1983)

1106 "I think I'm attracted to teachers," Rodney Dangerfield confesses to college instructor Sally Kellerman. "I took out an English teacher. That didn't work at all. I wrote her a love letter. She corrected it." – *Back to School* (1986)

1107 Vivacious Sally Field lays down her courtship rules to an experienced Michael Caine: "I make it a policy never to have sex before the first date." – *Surrender* (1987)

1108 Harry (Billy Crystal) describes to Sally (Meg Ryan) the highlight of his date with a very young woman: "When I asked her where she was when Kennedy was shot, she said, 'Ted Kennedy was shot?'" – *When Harry Met Sally . . .* (1989)

1109 "I've been dating longer than I've been driving," confesses video store owner Mercedes Ruehl. "I can't believe that." – *The Fisher King* (1991)

Death

1110 Hotel owner Groucho Marx, frustrated by the antics of guest Chico, who is ruining Groucho's outdoor real estate auction, utters, "Get away from that tree before it dies." – *The Cocoanuts* (1929)

1111 Devil's Island convict Louis Wolheim has a tattoo of a dotted line around his neck. A guard asks the significance of the unusual markings. "When you are ready," Wolheim explains, "just cut on the dotted line." – *Condemned* (1929)

1112 Buster Keaton has trouble with his girlfriend's mother (Trixie Friganza), who continually belittles him. "You ought to be with your grandfather!" she exclaims. "He's dead." "I know that!" – *Free and Easy* (1930)

1113 When Stan Laurel mentions that his uncle plunged through a trap door and broke his neck, his pal Oliver Hardy inquires whether the man had been building a home. "No," Laurel replies, "they were hanging him." – *The Laurel-Hardy Murder Case* (1930)

1114 From the press room of a county jailhouse, the ominous sound of a gallows trap door can be heard below. "What was that?" an edgy Mary Brian asks. "They're fixing up a pain in the neck for your boyfriend," a reporter answers. – *The Front Page* (1931)

1115 Controversial newspaper columnist Ricardo Cortez receives a package which he promptly hands to his secretary. "Take this out in the hall and open it," he orders. "It might be a bomb. And if it is, I'll write you a nice epitaph: 'Here lies Bea; she was a good girl, but she went to pieces.'" – *Is My Face Red?* (1932)

1116 W. C. Fields' wife arrives at his grocery store to announce that his ailing uncle in California has died. "It seems he was getting better," she explains, "but he attended a picnic and he choked to death eating an orange. His heart couldn't stand it." "I didn't know oranges were bad for the heart," Fields concludes. – *It's a Gift* (1934)

1117 A sheik's guards prepare to kill Eddie Cantor, who appears only in a diaper. "What's this?" the angry sheik exclaims. "This is the way I came into the world, and this is the way I'm going out," Cantor replies. – *Kid Millions* (1934)

1118 Bert Wheeler and Robert Woolsey are tied to a tree by a rival clan in preparation for a firing squad and are asked if they have any last requests. "I'd like to say goodbye to my mother," Woolsey says. "Where is your mother?" "In Australia." – *Kentucky Kernels* (1935)

1119 "An heir is when somebody dies, you get the rest," servant Eric Blore enunciates. – *To Beat the Band* (1935)

1120 Elderly but sprightly Aunt Olga (Zeffie Tilbury), who enjoys a little nip now and then, muses: "You know," people wouldn't be so afraid of dying if they could take a little brandy with them." – *Desire* (1936)

1121 Hazel Flagg (Carole Lombard), a young woman purportedly dying of radium poisoning, is wined and dined in New York by reporter Fredric March, who is seeking to exploit her condition in a series of articles. However, he soon becomes nauseated at the insincere sentimentality heaped upon her by the public. "For good clean fun," he comments sardonically, "there's nothing like a wake." "Oh, please, please," she pleads, "let's not talk shop." – *Nothing Sacred* (1937)

1122 Stan Laurel informs a young woman that her father is dead. "Is my poor daddy really dead?" she asks, seeking confirmation. "I hope so," Laurel replies. "They buried him." – *Way Out West* (1937)

1123 Poet-rogue François Villon, thrown into prison with several friends, is busily engaged in writing a poem. "Now here is our epitaph," he announces. "Epitaph?" a fellow prisoner questions. "What's that?" "Usually something good about somebody bad – after they're dead." – *If I Were King* (1938)

1124 Poet François Villon (Ronald Colman) faces the hangman with the following couplet: "Here goes François, child of France,/ To swing into his final dance." – *If I Were King* (1938)

1125 Constance Moore, as the daughter of circus manager W. C. Fields, appreciates the talents of Edgar Bergen and Charlie McCarthy, although the team nettles her father. "You were fortunate to acquire their services," she says. "They'll be fortunate if I don't attend their services," Fields replies. – *You Can't Cheat an Honest Man* (1939)

1126 "Squawk Mulligan tells me you buried your wife last year," a customer says to bartender W. C. Fields. "Yes, I had to," Fields replies. "She died." – *My Little Chickadee* (1940)

1127 When three pals (Fred MacMurray, Gilbert Roland, Albert Dekker) are placed in front of a Mexican firing squad and offered their last smoke, they all accept the offer except Dekker. "No three on a match," he says. "That's bad luck." – *Rangers of Fortune* (1940)

1128 Idealistic lawyer Pat O'Brien acts as a pallbearer at the funeral of Clarence Buckman, a corrupt politician. "This is the first time Clarence has ever been on the level," O'Brien quips. – *Slightly Honorable* (1940)

1129 Local rebel leader George Tobias, who is to be shot by the authorities of a Latin American country, gives Ann Sheridan his medallion. "Where I'm going I won't need it," he says. "Afraid it'll melt, eh?" she replies. – *Torrid Zone* (1940)

1130 Cranky, intractable Monty Woolley reserves one of his most caustic barbs for his doctor (George Barbier): "Dr. Bradley is the greatest living argument for mercy killings." – *The Man Who Came to Dinner* (1941)

1131 "Drown in a vat of whiskey," W. C. Fields ponders. "Death, where is thy sting?" – *Never Give a Sucker an Even Break* (1941)

1132 "If I'm the one who gets killed," Lou Costello says to pal Bud Abbott, "get twenty-five beautiful girls to walk around me." "Why?" Abbott asks. "If I don't get up, then you'll know I'm dead." – *Rio Rita* (1942)

1133 Soldiers of Louis XV (Red Skelton) capture revolutionists Gene Kelly and Zero Mostel and take them before the French king. "For fighting without a license, you get thirty days," Skelton decrees. "For trying to knock me off, you get the guillotine. I've decided to give you a break. I'll cancel the thirty days." – *DuBarry Was a Lady* (1943)

1134 Ten strangers are invited to a remote island where, one by one, they fall victim to the macabre scheme of their unknown host. Those remaining are approached by butler Richard Haydn who routinely inquires: "How many of you will be for dinner tonight?" – *And Then There Were None* (1945)

1135 George Murphy and Carole Landis, while on their honeymoon at a country inn, open a strange trunk and discover a man's body. They quickly inform amateur detective Pat O'Brien. "Who was it?" the sleuth inquires. "I don't know," responds Murphy. "He was too dead to tell me." – *Having Wonderful Crime* (1945)

1136 The Three Stooges, who are down but not out, peruse the want ads of a newspaper. "Say," Larry suggests, "how about this: 'Wanted: grave digger, good salary–'" "No," Moe cuts in. "Too, too morbid." "The morbid, the merrier," quips Curly.–*If a Body Meets a Body* (1945)

1137 Following a battle between a nobleman and some highwaymen, Bob Hope brushes against one of the slain brigands. "One of them is still kicking," Hope says. "Oh," the nobleman assures him, "he's dead." "Then I don't blame him for kicking."–*Monsieur Beaucaire* (1946)

1138 French barber Bob Hope, who earlier had tried to hang himself because of unrequited love, is imprisoned by the king and sentenced to face the guillotine the next morning. "Be brave, my friend," a fellow inmate suggests. "You wanted to go anyway." "But like a man," Hope replies, "not a salami."–*Monsieur Beaucaire* (1946)

1139 Bud Abbott and Lou Costello, who have lost $50,000 belonging to gangster Joseph Calleia, are given only a few hours to recover the money or they will be "rubbed out." "Well," says Abbott, "it's been a short and happy life." "Goodbye, pal," Costello adds. "The time allotted me has expired." "Where did you get that from?" the startled Abbott inquires. "I got it off my insurance policy."–*The Noose Hangs High* (1948)

1140 Sinister swami Boris Karloff plots to have Lou Costello kill himself by having Lou select the method of his own demise. "How do you wish to die?" Karloff drawls. "Of old age," Costello returns.–*Abbott and Costello Meet the Killer, Boris Karloff* (1949)

1141 A vexed Arthur Kennedy complains to mother Gertrude Lawrence: "Every morning you come in yelling, 'Rise and shine! Rise and shine!' I think, 'How lucky dead people are.'"–*The Glass Menagerie* (1950)

1142 Bob Hope asks a fortune teller what the future holds for him. When

each card he picks signifies death, he remarks: "Do you have a permit to carry those cards?"–*My Favorite Spy* (1951)

1143 Captain Kidd (Charles Laughton) relates that if he had a son, he would not raise him to be a pirate. "Any son of yours," adds cutthroat Hillary Brooke, "would rise to great heights–aided by the hangman's noose."–*Abbott and Costello Meet Captain Kidd* (1952)

1144 Huntz Hall and Leo Gorcey are in an airplane spinning wildly out of control. Hall grabs the flying manual and turns to a page entitled, "How to Face Death in the Air." "Keep turning," Gorcey says. "'How to Face Death in the Air,'" Hall keeps repeating as he turns the pages–until he reaches the last chapter: "Now That You're Dead." –*Clipped Wings* (1953)

1145 Ham entertainer Bob Hope, who thinks he is going to die, makes a final request: "Can I have my name in lights on my tombstone?"–*Here Come the Girls* (1953)

1146 Railroad clerk Jerry Lewis allegedly had radiation poisoning, and the public grieves for him–for various reasons. "How long do you think he'll last?" a hotel bellhop asks Lewis' doctor (Dean Martin). "Sixteen days? Fifteen days?" "That's hard to tell," Martin replies. "Well, if you get a hint," the bellhop persists, "tip me off because I got the fourteenth day in the pool." –*Living It Up* (1954)

1147 Waterfront mobsters eliminate an informer by having him thrown off a roof. "A canary," one thug sneers. "Maybe he could sing," another adds, "but he couldn't fly."–*On the Waterfront* (1954)

1148 In England, the Bowery Boys get mixed up with diamond smugglers, and Huntz Hall thinks he is a candidate for the guillotine. "They don't guillotine you here," one of his pals says. "No?" Hall sighs in relief. "No," his friend explains, "they hang you."–*In the Money* (1958)

1149 A wealthy woman with little appreciation for art or culture enters an exclusive decorating shop and touches various expensive art objects. "Be careful," the shop owner cries in frustration. "This is priceless." "What is it?" "A fourteenth century crematory urn." "Is anybody in it?" she inquires. "Not at the moment," he replies sarcastically. – *Pillow Talk* (1959)

1150 At a party a guest questions undertaker Ernie Kovacs: "Haven't I seen you before somewhere?" "Quite possibly," Kovacs replies. "I meet everybody – sooner or later." – *Five Golden Hours* (1961)

1151 A car trailing James Bond (Sean Connery) swerves out of control and rolls over a cliff, bursting into flames. "How did it happen?" a passerby asks. "I think they were going to a funeral," Bond replies. – *Dr. No* (1962)

1152 Tony Curtis is invited to say a few words at the service for Charlie, his departed friend shot by an irate husband who caught him in bed with his wife. Curtis concludes his eulogy: "Anyway, he's gone, and he went – to paraphrase Mr. Eliot – not with a whimper, but a bang." – *Goodbye Charlie* (1964)

1153 "I've got some bad news," Rock Hudson says to friend and neighbor Tony Randall. "Nothing that's going to affect property values, I hope." "It's my ticker," Hudson explains. "It's curtains." "Holy cow, that's terrible! Are you going to tell your wife? You remember how she was when the dog died. This could be worse." – *Send Me No Flowers* (1964)

1154 Paul Lynde informs would-be burial-plot purchaser Rock Hudson of an attractive feature. "All the monuments are four feet tall," he points out. "As you see, it gives a wonderful impression of uniformity." "Sort of a Levittown of the hereafter," ripostes Hudson. – *Send Me No Flowers* (1964)

1155 Jane Fonda, recuperating from hepatitis in a hospital, receives a visit from suitor Jason Robards, who has ordered flowers for her room. "I don't like flowers – real ones anyway," she confesses. "I don't like to watch them die. I have plastic ones at home." – *Any Wednesday* (1966)

1156 Ladies' man Tony Curtis jokes about death to a beautiful Italian widow who rebukes him: "In Italy, death is a very serious business." "For the living, perhaps," he counters, "but for the dead – it can be an awful drag." – *Arrivederci, Baby* (1966)

1157 Lady killer (literally) Tony Curtis kills his women for their money. Fox huntress Fenella Fielding, one of his victims, gallops off a cliff crying: "Tally ho!" – *Arrivederci, Baby* (1966)

1158 Woody Allen objects to facing a firing squad: "I have a low threshold of death." – *Casino Royale* (1967)

1159 Felix (Jack Lemmon) has taken a whole bottle of pills. "Get an ambulance!" a panicky friend screams. "What for?" Oscar (Walter Matthau) questions. "Maybe they were vitamins. He could be the healthiest one in the room." – *The Odd Couple* (1968)

1160 Max, an elderly elevator operator, gives his passengers his usual bumpy ride. "Well," says one shaken rider as he leaves, "we cheated death again, Max." – *How to Frame a Figg* (1971)

1161 "I shall walk through the valley of death," ponders Woody Allen. "In fact, now that I think of it, I shall *run* through the valley of death." – *Love and Death* (1975)

1162 Private eye Peter Falk has a niggardly habit of never tipping cabbies, and in each case offers a different excuse. "No tip," he says to a cabby as he leaves the vehicle. "A death in the family." "I wish it was you!" the cabby calls out. – *The Cheap Detective* (1978)

1163 Private detective Peter Falk's partner is killed, and the deceased man's wife shows up at his apartment with an urn filled with her husband's ashes. "I had him cremated," she explains. "This is all that's left of him. Look. I always thought of him as a bigger man." – *The Cheap Detective* (1978)

1164 A famous Swiss chef is killed by being baked in a large oven. Renowned food critic Robert Morley emphatically denies he is the murderer. "It certainly wasn't I," he states. "Only an amateur would bake anything Swiss in a four hundred fifty degree oven." – *Who Is Killing the Great Chefs of Europe?* (1978)

1165 Country-club member Rodney Dangerfield eyes an elderly gentleman and informs him: "The graveyard is two blocks to the left." – *Caddyshack* (1980)

1166 Broadway gambler Sorrowful Jones (Walter Matthau), seeking to hire a chef, gets a recommendation from crony Bob Newhart. "He learned it up in Sing Sing," Newhart reassures Jones. "He was the one who cooked the pot roast with the arsenic in it that knocked off Billy the Squealer. Billy's last words were 'Delicious, just like my mother's.'" – *Little Miss Marker* (1980)

1167 When Luke Fuchs (Jack Warden), owner of a used car lot, succumbs to a heart attack, his loyal friend and top salesman Kurt Russell buries him secretly in a used car right on the lot. "Luke Fuchs," Russell eulogizes, "you're about to drive over the curb for the last time . . . We can't carve your name on a granite tombstone, but we can keep it flying high above this lot . . . You'll be surrounded by a constantly revolving inventory of the finest quality, low-mileage, discount cars. Ford, General Motors, Chrysler will be your headstone; high volume, high visibility will be your epitaph. Rest in peace, Luke." – *Used Cars* (1980)

1168 Mel Brooks, as the waiter at the Last Supper, inquires: "Separate checks?" – *History of the World – Part 1* (1981)

1169 Famous sculptor Richard Dreyfuss, paralyzed from the neck down as the result of an auto accident, wants his life-support system to be disconnected. "This hospital will kill no quadriplegic before his time," he taunts his doctors. – *Whose Life Is It Anyway?* (1981)

1170 Rodney Dangerfield notifies his wife about her mother's sudden death: "There was a plane crash. Your mother earned her wings." – *Easy Money* (1983)

1171 Marsha Mason's roving father (Jason Robards) returns after a fifteen-year absence and announces he has only a few months to live. "How do I know you have only six months to live?" "We can sit here and wait," he suggests. – *Max Dugan Returns* (1983)

1172 Nazi spy José Ferrer informs Colonel Ehrhard (Mel Brooks) that the colonel is known outside of Poland as "Concentration Camp Ehrhard." "I do the concentrating," Brooks laughs, "the Poles do the camping." – *To Be or Not to Be* (1983)

1173 Mia Farrow tells Woody Allen that her gangster husband got shot in the eyes. "Is he blind?" "He's dead." "That's right," Allen ponders. "Bullets go right through." – *Broadway Danny Rose* (1984)

1174 To escape from two hoodlums, Ted Danson steals a car, picks up his friend Howie Mandel, a waiter at a fast-food restaurant, and speeds away to avoid the police who are in hot pursuit. "We're gonna die! We're gonna die!" cries Mandel. "I still got orders!" – *A Fine Mess* (1986)

1175 Policeman Billy Crystal has just had a brush with death, an incident that drives home his vulnerability. "If there's anything worse than dying young," he confesses to his partner, Gregory Hines, "it's dying young with money in the bank." – *Running Scared* (1986)

1176 Charlie Callas stares at a corpse and concludes: "If Harvey were alive today, he'd be a very sick man." – *Amazon Women of the Moon* (1987)

1177 Shelley Long describes to her husband how her friend Kim's third husband died in bed: "According to Kim, he came and went." – *Hello Again* (1987)

1178 Two untalented singer-songwriters (Warren Beatty and Dustin Hoffman), searching for the mythical kingdom of Ishtar, end up in a North African desert with buzzards hovering overhead. "We're not dead," they both yell in unison, "we're just resting." – *Ishtar* (1987)

1179 "When I buy a new book," Harry (Billy Crystal) explains to Sally (Meg Ryan), "I always read the last page first. That way in case I die before I finish it, I always know how it ends. That, my friend, is a dark side." – *When Harry Met Sally...* (1989)

1180 While recovering from a car accident, Shirley MacLaine, portraying a former movie queen, confides to daughter Meryl Streep: "You know, it's in my will that they don't bury me without my eyebrows. I do not go in the ground without them." – *Postcards from the Edge* (1990)

1181 Ebullient Jamie Lee Curtis is interviewed by undertaker Dan Aykroyd. "I have a wonderful disposition," she says. "I put people right at ease." "Well," says Aykroyd, "these people are already at ease. This isn't a beauty parlor; this is a funeral parlor." – *My Girl* (1991)

1182 In a funeral parlor John Candy meets a young woman who touches up faces of corpses to resemble famous personalities. "Did you mean him to look like Clark Gable?" he asks about her latest accomplishment. "Yes," she replies. "He's a dead ringer," Candy quips. – *Only the Lonely* (1991)

1183 Peter Riegert warns mobster Sylvester Stallone's crooked accountant about stealing from their boss. He relates how another in a similar situation met with an untimely death. "Somebody stepped on his fingers," Riegert says. "And that killed him?" the accountant questions. "He was hanging from the roof of the Edison Hotel at the time." – *Oscar* (1991)

1184 Funeral director Louis Mustillo perceives his mortuary business as a staging area for the great beyond. When Jack Warden, the patriarch of a large family, passes away, Mustillo is especially attentive. "Well," he gushes, "let's get the great man a great casket." – *Passed Away* (1992)

Detectives

1185 Charlie Chan (Warner Oland), who does not believe that the police have an open-and-shut case, remarks: "Perfect case like perfect donut – has hole." – *Charlie Chan in Paris* (1935)

1186 Amateur detective Nick Charles (William Powell) appears bewildered when he finds his wife (Myrna Loy) knitting a tiny article of clothing. "And you call yourself a detective," she says teasingly. – *After the Thin Man* (1936)

1187 After Charlie Chan (Warner Oland) solves a complex case, his eager son dashes in with fresh evidence. "Excellent clue," Oland notes, "but like the last rose of summer, bloom too late." – *Charlie Chan at the Opera* (1936)

1188 Charlie Chan (Warner Oland) has already cracked a tough case when his inept but enthusiastic son (Keye Luke) excitedly presents a new clue. "Too late," Chan indulgently intones. "Save for next case, please." – *Charlie Chan at the Race Track* (1936)

1189 When police detective James Gleason falsely arrests amateur sleuth George Sanders, Wendy Barrie, Sanders' fiancée, fumes at the officer: "What makes you think you're a detective? Just because your arches are broken down?" – *A Date with the Falcon* (1941)

1190 A murder suspect about to be booked by police detective Sam Levene protests that his gun has not been fired. "So it hasn't been fired," Levene remarks, sniffing the barrel of the weapon. "It must be using a new perfume – black powder." – *Shadow of the Thin Man* (1941)

1191 Philip Marlowe (Humphrey Bogart) asks gangster and casino owner John Ridgely how he entered an apartment. "Is it any of your business?" "I could make it my business." "I could make your business mine." "You woulnd't like it," Bogart replies. "The pay's too small." – *The Big Sleep* (1946)

1192 Chief of detectives Lee J. Cobb has broken a suspect after an all-night grilling and obtained a confession. Everything fits into place like a jigsaw puzzle – the suspect's criminal record, motive, opportunity, weak alibi, witnesses and fingerprints. "Then what's bothering you?" the district attorney asks. "I don't know," Cobb says. "It's just too pat – too perfect." – *Boomerang* (1947)

1193 Private eye Groucho Marx relates how he single-handedly unraveled the famous uranium-scandal case: "Scotland Yard was baffled. They sent for me, and the case was solved immediately. I confessed." – *Love Happy* (1949)

1194 Bud Abbott and Lou Costello, having graduated from a detective school and being assigned to work as detective's assistants, receive a prospective client. "You boys interested in a case?" the stranger inquires. "A case of what?" Costello asks. – *Abbott and Costello Meet the Invisible Man* (1951)

1195 A detective is hired to find Dudley Moore who in turn is searching for his girlfriend. "Question:" the sleuth ponders, "What am I doing in a place like this looking for some palooka who's looking for his girl? Answer: For twenty-five a day plus expenses, you don't ask questions." – *30 Is a Dangerous Age, Cynthia* (1968)

1196 Robert Stephens, as Sherlock Holmes, scolds his maid for tidying up his room despite his orders to the contrary. "I made sure I didn't disturb anything," she says defensively. "Dust is an essential part of my filing system," he explains. "By the thickness of it, I can calculate the date of any document immediately." "Some of the dust was two inches thick," she protests. "That would be March 1883." – *The Private Life of Sherlock Holmes* (1970)

1197 A crooked hotel desk clerk, in collusion with the house detective, plots to steal a guest's jewels, but the detective fails to uphold his end of the mission. "What kind of house detective are you?" the clerk chides him. "You cannot commit a simple burglary!" "I'm ashamed." – *What's Up, Doc?* (1972)

1198 Moving in a tangled web of murder and city corruption, Los Angeles private eye Jack Nicholson makes a crucial observation: "He passed away two weeks ago and he bought the land a week ago ... that's unusual." – *Chinatown* (1974)

1199 Outlaw Jack Nicholson, reporting back to his gang after returning from town, says he spotted a detective. "How did you know he was a detective?" "A rancher's wife kept wanting to go to bed with him," Nicholson explains, "and he kept giving her a 'no.'" – *The Missouri Breaks* (1976)

1200 Detective Charlie Chan (Peter Sellers) examines a lifeless body. "No pulse, no heartbeat," he observes. "If condition does not change, this man is dead." – *Murder by Death* (1976)

1201 Aging private sleuth Art Carney's eccentric client, Lily Tomlin, is exhilarated by the danger and excitement of his work. "I'm going to get a private detective's license," she announces. "If we teamed up, we'd be great together." "That's just what this town has been waiting for," he replies. "A broken-down old private eye with a bum leg and a hearing aid and a fruitcake like you." – *The Late Show* (1977)

1202 Narcotics detective Sharkey (Burt Reynolds), demoted to the vice squad after mishandling a crucial case, is physically threatened by Vittorio Gassman, a violent underworld leader seeking revenge upon Reynolds. "I'm not good at this," Reynolds grumbles. "Even when I was good at this I was not good at this." – *Sharkey's Machine* (1981)

1203 Police detective Nick Nolte springs convict Eddie Murphy from prison to help capture Ganz, a murderous gang leader. "Now get this," Nolte charges, hammering out their relationship. "We're not partners, we're not brothers, we're not friends! I'm puttin' you down and keepin' you down until Ganz is locked up or dead, and if Ganz gets away, you're going to be sorry you ever met me!" "I'm sorry already," Murphy says. – *48 Hours* (1982)

1204 Cool-headed, even-tempered Los Angeles detective and family man Danny Glover is confounded by his new partner and polar opposite – wild-eyed and hot-headed Mel Gibson. "Did you ever meet anybody you didn't kill?" Glover asks, wryly paraphrasing Will Rogers. – *Lethal Weapon* (1987)

Diplomacy

1205 Matronly English duchess Violet Kemble-Cooper asks her friend Lady George (Constance Bennett) to find work for her young lover, who has no gift for languages, no head for figures and no office skills. "The only thing I could see he'll do for," suggests Bennett, "is the diplomatic service." – *Our Betters* (1933)

1206 Nazi officer Conrad Veidt, during an official visit to Casablanca, contemptuously dismisses the Americans as blunderers. "But we mustn't underestimate American blundering," says Vichy police chief Claude Rains. "I was with them when they blundered into Berlin in 1918." – *Casablanca* (1942)

1207 At a lecture, young Hedy Lamarr asks the speaker, a member of the French Foreign Office (William Powell), what would happen if an ambassador were attracted to a woman he couldn't resist. "Well, he would probably be very brave and put duty before pleasure," Powell replies. "I thought the brave deserve the fair," she parries. "Unfortunately, diplomats very seldom get what they deserve," he concludes. – *Crossroads* (1942)

1208 "In international diplomacy," malevolent Nazi operative Sydney Greenstreet states, "the shortest distance between two points is never a straight line." — *Background to Danger* (1943)

1209 During the Cold War, American doctor Douglas Fairbanks, Jr., is detained in a totalitarian Eastern country by Jack Hawkins, the head of the secret police, who inquires: "May I ask you a question?" "It's a free country," Fairbanks replies, then continues, "Sorry, that slipped out." — *State Secret* (1951)

1210 After a Las Vegas hotel is robbed, its manager approaches a television crew busily engaged in interviewing witnesses. "Say, do me a favor," he asks. "If you're going to interview people, pick elderly couples. Some of the others don't always belong together." — *Ocean's Eleven* (1960)

1211 "The important thing in diplomacy," explains Peter Ustinov, "is to have a door that will lock — even if there is nothing behind it." — *Romanoff and Juliet* (1961)

1212 U.S. President Peter Sellers reprimands a general and the Soviet ambassador as they wrestle with each other at an emergency meeting. "Please, gentlemen, you can't fight here! This is the War Room!" — *Dr. Strangelove* (1964)

1213 A U.S. State Department official tries to get the Notre Dame football team to lose a game to the team from a mythical Arab kingdom. The school representative complains that it would not be ethical. "What do ethics have to do with diplomacy?" the government man comments. — *John Goldfarb, Please Come Home* (1964)

1214 Claudia Cardinale, visiting New York on personal business, gets a guided tour of the city from a friendly cab driver. "That's the United Nations building," he points out. "Yeah?" she responds. "Even from here I could see nothing is happening." — *A Fine Pair* (1969)

1215 Chicago detective James Belushi and his partner greet Russian cop Arnold Schwarzenegger, on temporary assignment in the U.S., at the airport. Belushi's partner offers his Russian counterpart a warm welcome and begins engaging in small talk. "I hate to break up this romance," Belushi cuts in, "but I'm parked in a red zone." He then turns to Schwarzenegger and adds: "No offense." — *Red Heat* (1988)

Disguise

1216 Eddie Cantor, marked for death by a sheik, hides in an Egyptian tomb of mummies and disguises his voice as that of the spirit of the sheik's uncle. "Your voice sounds so young," the sheik remarks. "Ben Hamid died when he was 76. Are you his spirit?" "Yes," Cantor's eerie voice responds, "I'm the spirit of '76." — *Kid Millions* (1934)

1217 Brian Aherne tells a mustached Katharine Hepburn in drag: "I don't know what it is that gives me a queer feeling when I look at you." — *Sylvia Scarlett* (1935)

1218 Southerner Robert Cummings, for whom the Civil War has never ended, is about to enter into a secret plot. "There's a new organization springing up all over the South," he explains to girlfriend Joan Bennett. "It's called the Ku Klux Klan. We meet at night . . . and wear masks. . . ." "How childish," she responds. — *The Texans* (1938)

1219 Song writer Red Skelton, trapped in an apartment by a Great Dane, dresses in drag to trick the canine. Later, when he meets his manager, Skelton explains his peculiar attire: "I'm dressed like a dame to escape a Dane." — *Bathing Beauty* (1944)

1220 Bob Hope, playing an actor with a repertoire of seven disguises, is interrupted in his rehearsal by the entrance of a cat. "I already have seven faces," he says to the feline. "I don't need another puss." — *The Princess and the Pirate* (1944)

1221 Smalltime racketeer Keenan Wynn, on the lam from a rival gang, and posing as a dentist, refuses to help someone in pain. "They burned my bridges," he claims. — *Love That Brute* (1950)

1222 The Doge of Venice and his entourage storm into the quarters of Bob Hope, who is posing as Casanova. "We're here to unmask an impostor," one of the Doge's advisers announces. "You mean he really isn't the Doge?" Hope questions. — *Casanova's Big Night* (1954)

1223 At a cocktail party, security guard Paul Lynde, working for a space project, disguises himself as a woman in hopes of exposing Doris Day, whom he suspects is a spy. "What the devil are you made up for?" C.I.A. agent Eric Fleming asks Lynde. "No man's land," he explains. "The powder room – in case she goes there again." — *The Glass Bottom Boat* (1966)

1224 Midget Michael Dunn confesses to detective George Segal that he is the much-sought-after serial killer. The detective patiently informs him that several witnesses said that the murderer was a much taller man. "You see how I fooled them?" Dunn explains. "I'm a master of disguise." — *No Way to Treat a Lady* (1968)

1225 Woody Allen, once rejected by Louise Lasser, returns in a bearded disguise as the President of San Marcos, whom she hero-worships. He, of course, reminds her of someone she once knew. "No, he was really nothing like you," she says to Allen. "You're terrific. He was just a stupid clown. I don't know why I even mention it. He was an idiot – a real idiot." — *Bananas* (1971)

1226 To penetrate a castle of terrorists led by Herbert Lom, Inspector Clouseau (Peter Sellers) disguises himself as a dentist and is brought before Lom. "I don't usually make castle calls in the middle of the day," Sellers announces. — *The Pink Panther Strikes Again* (1976)

1227 George Hamilton assumes the disguise of Zorro to protect the peasantry of a community in old California. After assisting one peon, Zorro has trouble expressing his mission: "To help the helpless, befriend the friendless and to defeat the – defeatless!" — *Zorro, the Gay Blade* (1981)

1228 In a complex show business scam, Robert Preston persuades Julie Andrews to impersonate a young man imitating a woman. "Oh, God," she cries on opening night, "I'll never make it!" "Now listen to me," he says. "From the beginning we've had two major obstacles to overcome –" "My bosoms," she interjects. — *Victor/Victoria* (1982)

Divorce

1229 Alice Brady, Ginger Rogers' aunt, helps her niece get a divorce by arranging for a corespondent. "A corespondent must be something of an artist," the aunt reflects. "He has to have a sense of balance – something like a mountain goat." – *The Gay Divorcee* (1934)

1230 Divorce lawyer Edward Everett Horton hires Italian gigolo Erik Rhodes to act as corespondent, but warns him not to try anything. "With me, strictly business," Rhodes promises. "My slogan: Your wife is safe with Tonetti – he prefers spaghetti." – *The Gay Divorcee* (1934)

1231 Eddie Cantor explains the American system of divorce to a sheik. "In America," Cantor says, "when you get rid of a wife, you still got to keep paying her money." "Oh," the sheik questions, "but isn't that like buying oats for a dead horse?" – *Kid Millions* (1934)

1232 Little Virginia Weidler finds one consolation in her socialite parents' parting. "That's the only good thing about divorce," she pipes. "You get to sleep with your mother." – *The Women* (1939)

1233 Marjorie Main, a housekeeper at a Reno hotel, complains to one of the guests about how badly her husband treats her. "But you live in Reno!" the guest exclaims. "You could get a divorce overnight!" "Great Scott!" Main returns. "A woman can't get herself worked up over a thing like that overnight!" – *The Women* (1939)

1234 At a racetrack, divorced horse owner Randall (Joel McCrea) extols the virtues of a horse based on the animal's past record. His lawyer-friend, Roland Young, however, differs. "They don't pay off on looks and past performances, you know," Young reminds him. "Oh, don't they?" McCrea challenges. "Then just what am I paying Mrs. Randall for?" – *He Married His Wife* (1940)

1235 Cary Grant tries to dissuade ex-wife Rosalind Russell from remarrying by disparaging their own divorce. "You got an old-fashioned idea that a divorce is something that lasts forever," he says, "till death do us part." – *His Girl Friday* (1940)

1236 "I don't want to lose Amanda," cuckolded Charles Ruggles says sadly. "I don't want to have my tombstone cluttered up with the names of my formerly beloved wives. It would leave no room for the more important data." – *No Time for Comedy* (1940)

1237 Bob Hope watches as chieftain Anthony Quinn, who is after the hand of princess Dorothy Lamour, thunders into town with his band, all firing their rifles in wild celebration. "I'd hate to be around for the divorce," comments Hope. – *Road to Singapore* (1940)

1238 "I don't believe in divorces," Lou Costello relates to Bud Abbott. "I believe in a fight to the finish." – *Rio Rita* (1942)

1239 Divorcee Lauren Bacall explains to Betty Grable that she did not do well financially in the final settlement. "It was one of those divorces where I finished second," she explains. "That's against the law, isn't it?" Grable asks. – *How to Marry a Millionaire* (1953)

1240 Thelma Ritter prompts friend Marilyn Monroe to claim deprivation of personal rights and physical violence at a divorce hearing. "Must I say that?"

Monroe asks. "Why can't I say he wasn't there. I mean, you could touch him, but he wasn't there." "If that were grounds for divorce," her friend explains, "there wouldn't be a marriage left." – *The Misfits* (1961)

1241 "I'm going to get the best divorce lawyer in town," says an angry wife who has just learned about her husband's dalliance. "Won't that be terribly expensive?" a friend warns. "I don't care, as long as he's vicious." – *Boys' Night Out* (1962)

1242 "Did you know we have the lowest divorce rate in the world?" a French beauty, boasting about her country, informs Bob Hope. "Is that because nobody bothers to get married?" he returns. – *A Global Affair* (1964)

1243 Vixenish Elizabeth Taylor taunts her resigned, weak-willed husband Richard Burton: "I swear – if you existed, I'd divorce you." – *Who's Afraid of Virginia Woolf?* (1966)

1244 In a divorce proceeding, suburban housewife Debbie Reynolds – fighting none too cleanly – gets the house, the car and the custody of the two children. "The uranium mine to her," husband Dick Van Dyke grumbles, "and the shaft to me." – *Divorce, American Style* (1967)

1245 "Is it a crime for a husband to see his wife?" asks George Segal, forcing his attention upon former wife Jacqueline Bisset. "Ex-husband, ex-wife, and ex-cuse me, but I have a very important appointment," she fires back. – *Who Is Killing the Great Chefs of Europe?* (1978)

1246 "You don't look any different," says Valerie Harper to divorce-seeking Marsha Mason. "Your features don't actually change until your final papers come through," Mason replies. – *Chapter Two* (1979)

1247 Kathryn Walker is fed up with husband John Lithgow and their strained marriage. "I want a divorce!" she blares out. "I want a nice, intelligent, angry divorce just like everybody else I know." – *Rich Kids* (1979)

1248 During a party, divorce lawyer Bob Dishy, himself divorced, states: "Divorce is one of America's biggest growth industries." – *The Last Married Couple in America* (1980)

1249 Billy Crystal's elderly Aunt Sophie thinks he has gotten together again with his ex-wife, but soon learns that the couple are still divorced. "Italians don't get divorced," Aunt Sophie declares. "It's a sin. They're just not together. That's all." – *Running Scared* (1986)

1250 An attorney informs Chevy Chase that he owes $4,387 in back alimony and, if he doesn't pay, he will end up in jail. "You're right," Chase says sarcastically. "I've been foolishly squandering my salary on food and heat." – *Fletch Lives* (1989)

1251 "How do you pay your alimony?" detective Wings Hauser asks his partner. "Once a month I give her a check signed in my own blood – then I pray the bitch chokes on it." – *Blood Money* (1991)

Doctors

1252 Princess Jeanette MacDonald has fainted, and a lady in waiting rushes into the vestibule where lovelorn Myrna Loy is sitting alone. "Could you go for a doctor?" she asks. "Why, certainly," Loy replies. "Bring him right in." – *Love Me Tonight* (1932)

1253 When doctor William Powell enters his office, he finds a new secretary behind the desk who informs him that his regular secretary is ill. Powell, concerned about her health, offers to help. "Oh, no," the substitute says. "She has her own doctor." "My head is bloodied but unbowed," Powell quips. – *The Ex-Mrs. Bradford* (1936)

1254 Horse doctor Groucho Marx, posing as an eminent neurologist, examines a patient and issues his diagnosis: "Either this man is dead or my watch has stopped." – *A Day at the Races* (1937)

1255 Veterinarian Groucho Marx, posing as a physician, wants to examine Margaret Dumont, but her doctor objects. "Her X-rays show nothing wrong with her." "Who are you going to believe," Groucho asks, "me or those crooked X-rays?" – *A Day at the Races* (1937)

1256 Emcee Bob Hope to his audience: "Then there's this fellow that went to the dentist. He only had a dollar so they gave him buck teeth." – *The Big Broadcast of 1938* (1938)

1257 "I have a very pleasant surprise for you," a solicitous family doctor says to recovering patient Charles Laughton. "How long will you be gone?" Laughton asks. – *It Started with Eve* (1941)

1258 A doctor, arriving late at the French court of Louis XV (Red Skelton) to treat the king, offers his apologies. "I saved a man's life this morning," the physician boasts. "He sent for me, but I didn't go." – *DuBarry Was a Lady* (1943)

1259 Frank Morgan, as a doctor during World War II, examines pretty Lucille Ball, who wants to enlist in the WAVES. "Just taking your pulse," he explains, grabbing her hand. "Very irregular; rapid, too." "You have your

fingers on my wrist watch," she informs him. – *Thousands Cheer* (1943)

1260 During World War II, barber Frank Morgan poses as a doctor at a WAVE recruiting station where he interviews prospective young women. "Waist?" he asks pretty Marsha Hunt. "Twenty-three," she replies. "Hips?" "Thirty-three." "Neck?" "Sometimes." – *Thousands Cheer* (1943)

1261 Unless Doc Holliday (Victor Mature) operates immediately, saloon entertainer Linda Darnell will die. But Doc is too far gone. He's been boozing; he demonstrates how his hands shake; he hasn't operated in five years; he knows nothing about the latest surgical techniques; and the bullet is lodged near a major artery too close for even the best surgeons. Linda overhears the conversation and asks him to her bedside. "Doc," she utters, "you worry too much." – *My Darling Clementine* (1946)

1262 At an Indian campsite, Calamity Jane (Jane Russell) and dentist Bob Hope observe the tribe preparing to burn someone at the stake. "Who are they going to burn?" Hope asks. "The medicine man," Russell replies. "Serves him right for practicing without a license." – *The Paleface* (1948)

1263 Hooker Barbra Streisand visits her neighbor, part-time writer George Segal, only to discover that he has been observing her through a pair of powerful binoculars. "It's part of my work," Segal explains. "It's part of my studies, you might say." "What are you studying to be, a gynecologist?" she shouts. – *The Owl and the Pussycat* (1970)

1264 In a vaudeville skit, doctor Walter Matthau asks patient George Burns to stick out his tongue. "You have a white coat," the doctor observes. "What did you expect?" Burns asks. "A gray sports jacket?" – *The Sunshine Boys* (1975)

1265 Obese, irascible food critic Robert Morley is shortening his life by overeating. "How long have I got to live?" he asks his doctor. "That will depend on you." "I'm relieved to know," Morley returns, "it will not depend on you." – *Who Is Killing the Great Chefs of Europe?* (1978)

1266 Undercover cop Dom DeLuise tells the following story to a fellow officer: "The lady said, 'Doctor it's a very serious operation; I'd like a second opinion.' 'All right, you're also very ugly.'" – *Hot Stuff* (1979)

1267 Crackpot inventor Woody Allen and his wife Mary Steenburgen invite Allen's friend, doctor Tony Roberts, to their country home for a summer weekend. He invariably brings a different female companion each time. "I don't know where he comes up with some of these women," she wonders. "He's a doctor," Allen explains, "so these poor women are in a tubercular ward – they show him gratitude." – *A Midsummer Night's Sex Comedy* (1982)

1268 At Woody Allen's country home, doctor Tony Roberts argues with pompous professor José Ferrer about spiritual matters. "I'm a doctor," Roberts declares, "and I believe in the spirit world." "You have to," Allen interjects. "That's where all your patients wind up." – *A Midsummer Night's Sex Comedy* (1982)

1269 Brain surgeon Steve Martin, facing a difficult operation, says to hospital director: "There's only one other person I'd trust to perform this operation – Brickman. Not only is he dead, he's six thousand miles away." – *The Man with Two Brains* (1983)

1270 "The only time we doctors should accept death," Steve Martin argues with crazed physician David Warner, "is when it's caused by our own incompetence." "Nonsense," protests Warner. "If the murder of twelve innocent people can help save one human life, it would be worth it." – *The Man with Two Brains* (1983)

1271 Doctor Billy Crystal, who has just recovered from a heart attack, says to girlfriend JoBeth Williams: "I'm a heart surgeon. I should have seen it coming. Even the Indians warned Custer: 'Don't come over here.'" – *Memories of Me* (1988)

1272 "A wonderful doctor gave this guy six months to live," comic Henny Youngman regales his audience. "When he couldn't pay his bills, he gave him another six months." – *GoodFellas* (1990)

Domestics

1273 Newly arrived prisoner Bert Wheeler is assigned to domestic chores in the warden's home, in which also lives the warden's spinster sister Edna May Oliver and his daughter Barbara (Betty Grable). "From now on," Oliver announces, "you're a houseboy. Barbara will break you in." "I'm already housebroken," Wheeler returns. – *Hold 'Em Jail* (1932)

1274 Edward Everett Horton's manservant Eric Blore introduces himself to his employer's acquaintance Fred Astaire. "Allow us to introduce ourselves, sir," he announces. "We are Bates." – *Top Hat* (1935)

1275 Wealthy, camera-shy Henry Kolker learns that a photographer is hiding in one of the bedrooms of his mansion. "Go in and shoo him out," he orders his servant E. E. Clive. "I'm afraid, sir," the hesitant Clive replies, "I should be a colossal failure as a 'shooer.'" – *They Wanted to Marry* (1937)

1276 Wealthy Melville Cooper and his wife have problems hiring proper servants. "They're a vanishing race," she remarks. "The only ones I've seen during the week are either escaped convicts or congenital idiots." "If you see any escaped convicts, hire them," Cooper suggests. – *Tovarich* (1937)

1277 Walter Connolly, a wealthy but unhappy manufacturer, asks his servant (Franklin Pangborn) if he is happy. "I find my work here very pleasant," Pangborn states. "Why?" "Do you want me to be frank, sir?" "By all means," Connolly insists. "We servants enjoy the luxuries of the rich and have none of the responsibilities." – *Fifth Avenue Girl* (1939)

1278 When a serial killer makes a brief appearance at maid Patsy Kelly's window, it's enough to force her to confront her employer Lionel Atwill. "I know it's customary to give notice –" she begins. "Why, Kitty, you're not trying to tell me you're going to leave me?" "Oh, no, sir, I am trying to tell you that I've left you." – *The Gorilla* (1939)

1279 Willie Best introduces himself to Paulette Goddard: "I'm the old family detainer." – *The Ghost Breakers* (1940)

1280 Playboy Raffles (David Niven), having just proposed to Olivia De Havilland, tells his servant E. E. Clive the good news. "Did I remember to tell

you that she's the most wonderful girl in all the world?" Niven asks, as Clive retires to his room. "I had hoped, sir, that you were going to spare me that." – *Raffles* (1940)

1281 "It wouldn't surprise me if she turned out to be a foreign agent," Jack Benny says about his maid Hattie McDaniel. "All she does around here anyway is come in and rearrange the dust." – *George Washington Slept Here* (1942)

1282 After a night of heavy imbibing, college professor Henry Fonda answers the telephone himself instead of allowing maid Hattie McDaniel to fulfill her role. "You didn't think you was me, did you?" she asks, looking askew at Fonda. – *The Male Animal* (1942)

1283 Overburdened housewife Barbra Streisand answers her apartment door when a voice on the other side calls out, "The colored woman." "It's a terrible thing to call yourself," Streisand says sympathetically to her housekeeper whom she lets in. "That's what I am," the woman replies. "The colored woman who comes to clean up for the white woman who's too lazy to clean up for herself. I clean so Mrs. White Folk won't chip any nail polish off her lily-white hands." – *For Pete's Sake* (1974)

1284 A guest arrives at an isolated, spooky mansion and comments to blind servant Alec Guinness: "Very large house. Any other servants?" "I'm not sure. I haven't seen anyone." – *Murder by Death* (1976)

Drink

1285 "You know," says crocked Robert Woolsey, "this stuff makes you see

double and feel single." – *Hook, Line and Sinker* (1930)

1286 Bert Wheeler and Robert Woolsey discover a liquor cellar in an old castle. "As good old Caesar said," quotes Woolsey, "'All roads lead to rum.'" – *Cracked Nuts* (1931)

1287 Groucho Marx is trying to gain entrance to a speakeasy, but Chico won't allow him to enter without the password "swordfish." Chico gives a hint that it's a fish, and Groucho guesses, "Mary." "That's-a no fish," Chico replies. "She isn't?" Groucho queries. "But she sure drinks like one." – *Horse Feathers* (1932)

1288 "Will you join me in a glass of wine?" Peggy H. Joyce hospitably asks W. C. Fields. "You get in first," Fields wisecracks, "and if there's room enough, I'll join you." – *International House* (1933)

1289 Aboard a luxury liner, steward Chic Chandler tries to flirt with two pretty stowaways by offering them champagne. "Is it good stuff?" one asks. "Good? I'd say – 1875!" "Eighteen seventy-five? What – a case?" – *Melody Cruise* (1933)

1290 Barber Jimmy Durante, while shaving Buster Keaton, is ecstatic to hear on the radio that Alabama voted two to one to repeal Prohibition. "Two to one!" he shouts. "Two to one!" "Why, that's only three votes," Keaton figures. – *What! No Beer?* (1933)

1291 Thelma Todd informs Robert Woolsey, posing as a doctor, that her uncle is suffering from insomnia. "I'm going to prescribe a glass of whiskey every 15 minutes," Woolsey states. "For Uncle?" "No," he replies, "for me." – *Cockeyed Cavaliers* (1934)

1292 A real estate agent who is trying to swindle W. C. Fields out of his land meets with stiff resistance. "You're drunk!" the frustrated agent charges. "Yeah, and you're crazy," retorts Fields. "I'll be sober tomorrow, but you'll be crazy the rest of your life." – *It's a Gift* (1934)

1293 "Stay away from that cider," Beulah Bondi cautions Ralph Remley. "Remember the strawberry festival when you were flitting about telling everyone you were a butterfly?" – *Ready for Love* (1934)

1294 Myrna Loy tells a reporter that her amateur-sleuthing husband is working on a case. "What case is that?" "A case of scotch." – *The Thin Man* (1934)

1295 Amateur detective Nick Charles (William Powell), who considers himself a connoisseur of drink, instructs a bartender: "The important thing is the rhythm. The dry martini you always shake up to waltz time." – *The Thin Man* (1934)

1296 Two gossips aboard a train recognize that their neighbor W. C. Fields is slightly tipsy. "Is he a hard drinker?" one asks. "Hard?" comes the reply. "It is the easiest thing he does." – *You're Telling Me* (1934)

1297 With the start of a new job, bibulous Wallace Beery is cautioned by his brother's family to "stay away from the you-know-what." "If anyone ever offers me a drink," Beery assures them, "I'll kill him – that is, if they change their minds." – *Ah, Wilderness* (1935)

1298 Aboard a luxury liner, perpetually inebriated author Robert Benchley pulls through a typhoon and a pirate attack without a scratch. But after the ship docks at Singapore, he stumbles off the gang plank and falls into the water. "These streets are in deplorable condition," he remarks. – *China Seas* (1935)

1299 Constantly inebriated doctor Charles Winninger is carried from his New York hotel room and placed aboard a cruise ship by his patient Carole Lombard. When he awakens several days later, he peers out of the porthole and sees nothing but ocean. "Run for your life!" he cries out. "The hotel is flooded!" – *Nothing Sacred* (1937)

1300 Army captain Pat O'Brien tries to impress nightclub singer Ann Sheridan with his captain's rank, but she continues to address him as "Sergeant." "You know what these two bars mean?" he demands, pointing to the two brass strips on his shoulder. "Sure," she replies, "twice as many drunks as one bar." – *San Quentin* (1937)

1301 Film studio executive Lionel Stander relates to boss Adolphe Menjou the latest drinking spree of matinee idol Fredric March: "Mr. Norman Maine, America's Prince Charming, was apprehended driving an ambulance down Wilshire Boulevard with the sirens going full blast. He explained that he was a tree surgeon on a maternity case." – *A Star Is Born* (1937)

1302 "Don't mind him," someone comments about a souse. "He's just plain drunk." "Your friend just insulted me," says the intoxicated man. "I'll admit to some of the fanciest binges on record, but plain drunk? Never!" – *You Can't Beat Love* (1937)

1303 Joe E. Brown, bent on committing suicide, drinks from a jug labeled 'ant poison' which someone has replaced with liquor. Totally intoxicated, he remarks: "Boy, ants certainly have a beautiful death." – *Flirting with Fate* (1938)

1304 "I've been drinking for over 40 years," jovial Guy Kibbee boasts to Alice Brady, "and I haven't acquired the habit yet." – *Joy of Living* (1938)

1305 Bob Hope, as the potential heir to an eccentric uncle's estate, journeys to the eerie family mansion for the reading of the will. "There are spirits all around you," someone ominously warns Hope. "Can you put some in a glass with a little ice?" Hope asks. – *The Cat and the Canary* (1939)

1306 In the midst of mysterious doings at a spooky mansion, Bob Hope suggests: "Let's drink Scotch and make wry faces." – *The Cat and the Canary* (1939)

1307 Widower John Barrymore's two small children tell their grandparents they got into a fight with a bully who called their father a drunk. When the grandparents ask them if their father is an alcoholic, the children become indignant. "Of course not," they protest. "He only drinks a quart a day." – *The Great Man Votes* (1939)

1308 "Some weasel took the cork out of my lunch," complains imbiber W. C. Fields. – *You Can't Cheat an Honest Man* (1939)

1309 Bank guard W. C. Fields, taking no chances, overpowers an eight-year-old boy outfitted with a cowboy suit and a cap pistol. "Is that gun loaded?" Fields queries. "No," the irate mother replies, "but you are." – *The Bank Dick* (1940)

1310 "Was I in here last night and did I spend a twenty-dollar bill?" W. C. Fields queries a bartender. "Yeah," comes the reply. "Oh, boy!" Fields sighs. "What a load that is off my mind! I thought I'd lost it." – *The Bank Dick* (1940)

1311 In a western saloon Groucho Marx comments on a drunkard sitting at his table: "He's so full of alcohol that if you put a lighted stick in his mouth he'd burn for three days." – *Go West* (1940)

1312 Leon Errol, locked in a hotel room for a week because his clothes have not arrived, complains to a window washer he has just met outside his window. "I've been incarcerated for a week," he explains. "What! And no hangover?" the window washer questions. – *Mexican Spitfire Out West* (1940)

1313 "You know how you can sell more beer around here?" Wallace Beery says to a bartender. "How?" "Don't put so much foam in the glasses." – *20 Mule Team* (1940)

1314 "I feel like getting drunk," says Lou Costello. "No, you don't want a drink," replies Bud Abbott. "Remember, every time you go into a barroom the devil goes in with you." "If he does," counters Costello, "he buys his own drink."—*Keep 'Em Flying* (1941)

1315 On an airplane W. C. Fields awakens with an awesome hangover. "Are you sick, sir?" the flight attendant asks. "No, dear," Fields grumbles. "Somebody put too many olives in my martini last night." "Could I get you a bromo?" "No," he mutters, "I couldn't stand the noise."—*Never Give a Sucker an Even Break* (1941)

1316 W. C. Fields talks to niece Gloria Jean about his one great love. "She drove me to drink," he recalls. "That's the one thing I was indebted to her for." —*Never Give a Sucker an Even Break* (1941)

1317 "Suffering sciatica!" exclaims W. C. Fields upon meeting a gorilla. "Last time it was pink elephants!" —*Never Give a Sucker an Even Break* (1941)

1318 "Ethel," a drunk calls his house, "get all the kids off the street. I'm driving home."—*Obliging Young Lady* (1941)

1319 Actor John Barrymore has tripped during rehearsals and hurt his leg. "Have you tried rubbing alcohol?" a fellow passenger suggests. "Not since Prohibition," Barrymore quips.—*Playmates* (1941)

1320 Mrs. Charles (Myrna Loy) remarks that their child is getting to be more like his father, Nick (William Powell), each day. "That's true," maid Louise Beavers interjects. "This morning I found him playing with the corkscrew."—*Shadow of the Thin Man* (1941)

1321 George E. Stone, suffering from a cold, tells Chester Morris that Florida rainwater will help his condition. "Is rainwater good for colds?" Morris asks with a note of skepticism. "Oh, sure," Stone replies. "You take two drops of

rainwater and put it in a glass, and you fill the glass with whiskey."—*Boston Blackie Goes Hollywood* (1942)

1322 Monty Woolley, portraying a former actor who works as a department-store Santa Claus, arrives one day three sheets to the wind. He appears on his assigned platform hiccuping—shocking the customers. "And what did you expect, madam," he addresses one woman, "chimes?"—*Life Begins at Eight-Thirty* (1942)

1323 Good-hearted lush Mabel Paige befriends and adopts A.W.O.L. soldier Alan Ladd as her son and shields him from the F.B.I. and gangsters. In gratitude, Ladd buys her a quart of gin. "Gee," she cries, "that's the sweetest thing a kid ever gave his mother." —*Lucky Jordan* (1942)

1324 Robert Benchley offers Ginger Rogers a drink: "No matter what the weather, I always say, 'Why don't you get out of your wet clothes and into a dry martini?'"—*The Major and the Minor* (1942)

1325 "I'm one of those nip 'n' tuck drinkers," Stan Laurel says to a stranger. "What's that?" the stranger asks. "One nip and they tuck me away for the night."—*Jitterbugs* (1943)

1326 England's Lord Epping (Leon Errol) orders a few drinks before lunch, saying to acquaintance Hugh Beaumont: "Never eat on an empty stomach." —*Mexican Spitfire's Blessed Event* (1943)

1327 Curly tells Moe the title of a certain song: "'Don't Chop the Wood, Mother—Father's Coming Home with a Load.'"—*Booby Dupes* (1945)

1328 "Champagne!" Joan Davis beams. "I love it. It tastes like your foot's asleep."—*George White's Scandals* (1945)

1329 Fred Allen visits Robert Benchley's hotel room where they both imbibe in champagne. "Oh, what big bubbles,"

Benchley comments as he lifts the glass. "Yes," Allen acknowledges, "they had big grapes that year."—*It's in the Bag* (1945)

1330 "I envy people who drink," admits Oscar Levant. "At least they know what to blame their troubles on." —*Humoresque* (1946)

1331 Bartender Edgar Kennedy to customer Harold Lloyd: "It always appeared to me that the cocktail should approach us on tiptoe like a young girl whose first appeal is innocence."—*The Sin of Harold Diddlebock* (1947)

1332 Penniless racetrack tout Bob Hope is sentenced to ten days for panhandling for a private charity—himself. "That judge didn't look honest to me," Hope complains to a policeman. "For eighteen years he's been a member of the bar," the officer replies. "That's what I mean," Hope says. "Drinking on duty."—*The Lemon Drop Kid* (1951)

1333 Bob Hope: "Have you heard the latest about McTavish? He's living on the roof." Bing Crosby: "Why's he living on the roof?" Hope: "He heard someone say the drinks are on the house."—*Road to Bali* (1952)

1334 Kenneth More virtually lives for the annual Brighton-London vintage car race while his wife Kay Kendall cannot comprehend what all the fuss is about. "Never mind," he says. "When that car gets started, you'll be intoxicated by the exuberance of your own velocity. Get that?" "I said I'm not drinking anything today—nothing at all!" she replies. —*Genevieve* (1953)

1335 Entertainer Bob Hope proposes a toast with a glass of champagne to theatrical producer Fred Clark. "Hm-m, domestic and terribly flat," Hope evaluates his drink. "That's the water," Clark explains.—*Here Come the Girls* (1953)

1336 Financially hard-pressed, aging film star Bette Davis is further put upon by her greedy sister and brother-in-law, both of whom she had once lavished money upon. She throws the ingrates out and turns to her faithful Academy Award statuette. "Come on, Oscar," she cries, "let's you and me get drunk." —*The Star* (1953)

1337 "There's no great achievement in getting drunk," John Wayne concludes. "Even a dog can do it."—*Trouble Along the Way* (1953)

1338 Nightclub comedian Joe E. Lewis (Frank Sinatra) jokes about a racehorse he bet on: "The horse drove me to drink. But I was going in that direction anyway."—*The Joker Is Wild* (1957)

1339 "I only drink to steady my nerves," says comic Joe E. Lewis (Frank Sinatra) to a nightclub audience. "And sometimes I get so steady I can't move." —*The Joker Is Wild* (1957)

1340 Two friends of lush Kay Kendall are concerned about her imbibing. "Why does she drink?" asks Taina Elg. "There must be a reason." "There is," Mitzi Gaynor replies. "She likes it."—*Les Girls* (1957)

1341 At a street rally, soused Lee Marvin vows to take a temperance pledge. "I'll take the pledge right now," he yells. "We want men to take the pledge only when they're sober," a woman leader retorts. "If they're sober," Marvin questions, "what's the sense of them taking the pledge?"—*Raintree County* (1957)

1342 In Paris, Russian investigator Cyd Charisse surrenders to the "decadence" of the West. "I have made a discovery," she confesses. "Champagne is more fun to drink than goat's milk." —*Silk Stockings* (1957)

1343 "Was it in the Rose Bowl he made his famous run?" Jack Carson asks his wife about heavy-drinking, ex-football star Paul Newman. "It was the punch bowl, honey."—*Cat on a Hot Tin Roof* (1958)

1344 Yves Montand: "You don't hold your liquor very well." Tony Randall: "I don't seem to be leaking out anything." – *Let's Make Love* (1960)

1345 Executive-playboy Rock Hudson sends word to an advertising council meeting that he cannot attend because he is at the Red Cross donating blood. "They wouldn't take his blood!" fierce rival Doris Day exclaims. "It's eighty-six proof." – *Lover Come Back* (1961)

1346 Teenage Bobby Rydell is evicted from a nightclub. "I'm way over twenty-one," he protests. "I only look young from too much drinking." – *Bye Bye Birdie* (1963)

1347 Nobel Prize winner Paul Newman, in Sweden for the ceremonies, is interviewed by a battery of reporters. "What was your first reaction when you received the news of your Nobel Prize?" a journalist asks. "No reaction at all," Newman replies. "I was dead drunk at the time." – *The Prize* (1963)

1348 At a traffic mishap a policeman chastises a foursome for drinking. "Drinking and gasoline don't mix," he reminds them. "We ain't been drinking gasoline," offers Tuesday Weld. – *Soldier in the Rain* (1963)

1349 Dean Martin comments on his own image as a whiskey-imbibing womanizer: "If I skip one night, I wake up with such a headache." – *Kiss Me, Stupid* (1964)

1350 "My doctor said, 'Stop drinking,'" singer-comic Dean Martin tells his audience, "so I'm not going to drink anymore. I'm going to freeze it now and eat it like a popsicle." – *Kiss Me, Stupid* (1964)

1351 In ancient Rome, Zero Mostel examines a jug of wine with the air of a connoisseur. "Was one a good year?" he inquires. – *A Funny Thing Happened on the Way to the Forum* (1966)

1352 Dean Martin and a brewery guide are suddenly pushed into a large vat of beer. The guide cries out that he can't swim. "Drink your way to the bottom," advises Martin. – *The Ambushers* (1967)

1353 U.S. intelligence agency chief tries to explain to agent Matt Helm (Dean Martin) his next mission. "Have you ever seen a flying saucer?" "Is that your way of offering me a drink?" Martin asks. – *The Ambushers* (1967)

1354 U.S. soldiers and sailors, isolated on a Pacific island during World War II, are dejected when a ship carrying a cargo of beer is sunk by the Japanese. "Not being a drinking man myself," a navy officer comments, "I don't understand the importance of liquor." "That would be like a cannibal ordering a baked potato," Bob Hope quips. – *The Private Navy of Sgt. O'Farrell* (1968)

1355 A U.S. Navy officer is amazed at the background of nurse Phyllis Diller, whose father and mother were bootleggers. "You mean to say your parents made liquor themselves?" "Of course," she answers, "in a bathtub." "Where'd you bathe?" the astonished officer inquires. "In the bathtub, silly," she says. "Till this day when I see a martini, I start taking my clothes off." – *The Private Navy of Sgt. O'Farrell* (1968)

1356 Jackie Gleason's girlfriend notices that he has been drinking heavily from a flask. "Honey," she pleads, "will you put that away?" "I am putting it away," Gleason replies. – *How to Commit Marriage* (1969)

1357 Outside a liquor store, underaged adolescent Charlie Smith asks a disheveled drunk to purchase a bottle of Old Harper for him – explaining that he lost his I.D. in a flood. "Why, certainly," the drunk says. "I lost my wife, too. Her name wasn't Idy though, and it wasn't in a flood." – *American Graffiti* (1973)

1358 Mame (Lucille Ball) asks best friend Beatrice Arthur: "Could you be persuaded to have a drink, dear?" "Well," her friend replies, "maybe just a tiny triple."—*Mame* (1974)

1359 "You know what they say about martinis?" a bar girl asks Warren Beatty. "They say they're like a woman's breast," Beatty replies. "Three are too many and one is not enough."—*The Parallax View* (1974)

1360 Englishman Michael Caine meets his drinking actress-wife Maggie Smith in a posh hotel bar. "How many gin and tonics have you had?" he asks. "Three gins, one tonic," she replies.—*California Suite* (1978)

1361 College student Peter Riegart places his loyalty to his fraternity, which has the worst reputation on campus, above his love for Karen Allen. "Is this really what you're going to do the rest of your life?" she asks in frustration. "What do you mean?" "I mean hanging around with a bunch of animals getting drunk every weekend?" "No," he replies. "After I graduate, I'm going to get drunk every night."—*National Lampoon's Animal House* (1978)

1362 Superman (Christopher Reeve) flies onto Lois Lane's (Margot Kidder) apartment terrace. "Would you like some wine?" she asks graciously. "No, thanks," he replies. "I never drink when I fly."—*Superman* (1978)

1363 "Every time I worked Pittsburgh," ex-vaudeville comic George Burns reminisces, "I played with a band that was so high, Gabriel played first trumpet."—*Just You and Me, Kid* (1979)

1364 Bumbling detective Don Knotts questions the domestic staff of a mansion whose owners have been murdered. Meanwhile he has nonchalantly helped himself to a drink. "What is this stuff?" he asks a housekeeper. "I believe it's ink," she replies.—*The Private Eyes* (1980)

1365 Hollywood movie star Alan Swann (Peter O'Toole) shows up quite drunk in a New York television studio where he was scheduled to rehearse a forthcoming comedy show. "He's plastered!" the head comedy writer exclaims. "So are some of the finest erections in Europe," O'Toole counters. —*My Favorite Year* (1982)

1366 An inebriated popular movie star (Peter O'Toole), after a night on the town in New York, is picked up by the police. "What were you doing naked in Central Park in the Bethesda Fountain at three o'clock in the morning?" they ask him. "The backstroke," he replies. —*My Favorite Year* (1982)

1367 At a fancy Paris restaurant Robert Preston questions the quality of the house wine. "The last time I saw a specimen like this they had to shoot the horse," he declares to the waiter. —*Victor/Victoria* (1982)

1368 Bored with his job as college instructor and troubled by his private life, Michael Caine finds solace in the bottle. "There's been a bit of a complaint," a colleague confides to him. "Apparently, you were a little drunk at your tutorial today." "No," Caine replies. "No?" "No," Caine repeats, "I was a lot drunk." —*Educating Rita* (1983)

1369 Neophyte comic Robert De Niro, on television for the first time, relates stories about his alcoholic mother: "We used to drink milk together after school. Mine was homogenized, hers was loaded." —*The King of Comedy* (1983)

1370 As James Bond (Sean Connery) is nursing a drink on a wharf, a shapely water skier bumps into him. "I've made you all wet," she apologizes. "Ah, yes," Bond returns, "but my martini is still dry."—*Never Say Never Again* (1983)

1371 Mickey Rourke approaches attractive barfly Faye Dunaway. "I'm gonna ask you the same damn thing people keep asking me," he announces. "What?"

"What do you do?" "I drink," she replies. – *Barfly* (1987)

1372 To rid Chicago of gambling, prostitution and bootlegging, federal agent Elliot Ness (Kevin Costner) takes on the crime syndicate and destroys it. In the last scenes a reporter asks Ness: "They say they're going to repeal Prohibition. What will you do then?" "I think I'll have a drink," he grins. – *The Untouchables* (1987)

Eccentrics

1373 Stan Laurel admonishes Oliver Hardy for threatening their rambunctious sons. "Don't talk to them like that," Laurel explains. "Treat them with kindness. Remember the old adage: you can lead a horse to water, but a pencil must be lead." – *Brats* (1930)

1374 Stan Laurel telephones Oliver Hardy and informs him that he has two tickets for the Cement Workers' Bazaar. "We might win a prize," Laurel adds. "They're going to give away a steam shovel." – *Their First Mistake* (1932)

1375 "Have you seen my stethoscope?" physician George Burns asks. "Not now, doctor," nurse Gracie Allen replies. "I'll look at it later." – *International House* (1933)

1376 "I've got a good mind to get a different nurse," George Burns confides to Franklin Pangborn about Gracie Allen. "No, no, doctor," Pangborn replies, "don't do that. This one is different enough." – *International House* (1933)

1377 An upset Ginger Rogers, arriving in England, searches for her aunt after Fred Astaire has accidentally torn her dress while attempting to release it from a trunk. "Oh, here you are," Rogers says. "I've just had the most embarrassing experience. A man tore my dress off." "My goodness!" the shocked aunt exclaims. "Anyone we know?" – *The Gay Divorcee* (1934)

1378 Scatterbrained Alice Brady, going through customs, hands an attendant a fruit basket which is later returned to her. "Oh, for me?" she remarks delightedly. "And I do adore fruit baskets. But you shouldn't have been so extravagant. We've just met, you know." – *The Gay Divorcee* (1934)

1379 "Your niece has three feet?" George Burns suspiciously questions Gracie Allen. Reading a letter from her sister, Gracie explains: "'You wouldn't know little Jean. Since you last saw her, she's grown another foot.'" – *Six of a Kind* (1934)

1380 Quirky Hugh Herbert quips to Glenda Farrell: "Snuff is not to be sneezed at." – *Gold Diggers of 1935* (1935)

1381 Whimsical radio sponsor Gracie Allen asks broadcasting executive Jack Benny whatever happened to him. "I became vice-president," he announces. "I heard of vice," she admits, "but I never knew they had a president for it." – *The Big Broadcast of 1937* (1936)

1382 Little Darla Hood begins her nightly prayers. "Now I lay me down to sleep, I pray the Lord my soul to keep, if – what's next?" she asks Stan Laurel and Oliver Hardy. "Laurel whispers into his pal's ear and Hardy finishes it for her: "If at first you don't succeed, try, try again." – *The Bohemian Girl* (1936)

1383 "We must hurry," Donald Meek says to Clark Gable. "You see, at twelve o'clock I turn into a pumpkin."—*Love on the Run* (1936)

1384 Longfellow Deeds (Gary Cooper) is forced into court on a sanity hearing when he decides to give away twenty million dollars during the Depression. Two staid sisters from his home town give damaging testimony that he is "pixilated"—until one of them (Margaret Seddon) blurts out: "Why, everybody in Mandrake Falls is pixilated—except us."—*Mr. Deeds Goes to Town* (1936)

1385 "Did you say you can tear a telephone book in half?" Eddie Cantor asks Parkyarkus. "Yes, sir," he affirms and proceeds to tear out one page at a time. "Wait a minute, wait a minute!" Cantor protests. "You're tearing out one page at a time!" "I ain't in a hurry."—*Strike Me Pink* (1936)

1386 Gracie Allen answers the phone as George Burns says, "I'm not in." "He's not here," Gracie says. "I tell you he's not here. Oh, you don't? Well, you can ask him yourself if you don't believe it. George, will you tell him you're not here. He doesn't believe me."—*A Damsel in Distress* (1937)

1387 Hazel Flagg (Carole Lombard), supposedly suffering from deadly radium exposure, admits to some visitors that the medical reports were a mistake. One disappointed woman finds the news difficult to bear. "Miss Flagg," the woman protests, "the Girlfriends of the Forest has just organized a Hazel Flagg unit with me as chief ranger. Already we have four thousand members. If you persist in flaunting your recovery in this flagrant manner, the trees of America will be without girlfriends."—*Nothing Sacred* (1937)

1388 Daffy mother Mary Boland, seeking a wealthy prospect for one of her daughters, learns that Burgess Meredith has struck it rich in Alaska. "It turned out to be a bonanza!" he announces about his gold mine before he leaves Boland's home. "Isn't it funny?" she later

muses. "He called it a bonanza. I always thought it came in bunches."—*There Goes the Groom* (1937)

1389 Stan Laurel and Oliver Hardy try to cheer up the daughter of a dead prospector before they tell her of her father's fate. "Every cloud has a silver lining," Hardy begins. "That's right," Laurel agrees. "Any bird can build a nest, but it isn't everyone can lay an egg, is it, Ollie?"—*Way Out West* (1937)

1390 Jockey Buddy Ebsen goes to a gym to lose weight and is interrogated by a kooky receptionist. "How do you eat?" she asks. "Like a horse," Ebsen answers. "Frankly, you'll have to cut that out," the woman orders. "From now on you'll sit up at the table like everyone else."—*Broadway Melody of 1938* (1938)

1391 Eccentric gymnast college instructor Ben Blue embraces a startled woman gym teacher in front of her students. "Haven't you forgotten yourself?" she reminds him. "Oh," Blue replies, "I'll go get him."—*College Swing* (1938)

1392 "You never signed the contract," Bob Hope complains to Gracie Allen. "How do you know I didn't sign it?" "There's no signature on it." "If there's no signature on it, how do you know *I* didn't sign it?" Allen asks. "Maybe somebody else didn't sign it."—*College Swing* (1938)

1393 Moe and Larry of the Three Stooges scheme to collect insurance by claiming Curly is crazy. They take him to a doctor's office where he poses as a dog. "Which one is the crazy one?" the doctor inquires after meeting all three.—*From Nurse to Worse* (1940)

1394 A young woman is impressed with Cesar Romero's equestrian expertise and says to dizzy Mary Boland: "The way a horse responds to him you'd think they were man and wife." "Oh," replies Boland, "nobody ever marries a horse."—*He Married His Wife* (1940)

1395 "My," Topper's wife (Billie Burke) reflects, "isn't it strange how it's cold in the winter and warm in summer, isn't it?" – *Topper Returns* (1941)

1396 Throckmorton P. Gildersleeve (Hal Peary) introduces himself to screwball Billie Burke. "Oh, what an odd name," she says, spraying him with cologne. "That's not the only odd thing around here, madam," he cracks. – *Gildersleeve on Broadway* (1943)

1397 At a nightclub, Martha Scott and her scatterbrained mother, Billie Burke, prepare to give the waiter their orders. "Tom Collins," Scott says. "How do you do, Mr. Collins," her mother addresses the waiter. – *Hi Diddle Diddle* (1943)

1398 "You irk me," daffy Huntz Hall says to fellow teenager Bobby Jordan. "The only thing I can't stand is an irk." – *Kid Dynamite* (1943)

1399 When the Three Stooges report to a spooky mansion to collect Curly's inheritance, a detective investigating the murder of Curly's rich uncle asks Curly to identify himself. "I'm Curly Q. Link." "Oh," the police officer says. "You're the missing link." "No," Curly returns, "I'm the foundlink." – *If a Body Meets a Body* (1945)

1400 Servant Edward Everett Horton confesses: "The siphon bottle and the banana peel always convulse me." – *The Ghost Goes Wild* (1947)

1401 "I was walking down along and I heard this voice saying 'Good evening, Mr. Dowd,'" Elwood P. Dowd (James Stewart) explains. "Well, I turned around and here was this big six-foot rabbit leaning against a lamp post. I thought nothing of that because when you've lived in this town as long as I have, you get used to the fact that everyone knows your name." – *Harvey* (1950)

1402 Kooky Irma (Marie Wilson) tells roommate Diana Lynn that their tele-

vision set is on the blink. "I don't know," explains Irma, "ever since I took the insides out and washed them, it's acting crazy." – *My Friend Irma Goes West* (1950)

1403 "When you kiss me, I like it," says hypochondriac sailor Jerry Lewis to his girlfriend. "The other girls inflame my uvula." – *Sailor Beware* (1951)

1404 Jerry Lewis' fairy godfather Ed Wynn, who earlier has been shunned by Lewis, suddenly appears in drag. "If you can no longer believe in your fairy godfather, maybe it will be easier for you to believe in your fairy godmother. I'm up on all this Oedipus nonsense, you know." – *Cinderfella* (1960)

1405 An aggressive buyer of David Niven's apartment barges in and begins measuring and planning. When Niven protests, she declares: "I'm tired. I don't like being awake in the daytime. I know you're in a spot, but it's *your* spot." "What does she mean – she doesn't like being awake in the daytime?" Niven asks the accompanying real estate manager. "What is she – a vampire bat?" – *Please Don't Eat the Daisies* (1960)

1406 West Berlin soft-drink executive James Cagney lambastes harebrained Southerner Pamela Tiffin for floating balloons with the logo "Yankee, Go Home!" from East Berlin to West Berlin. "It's not anti-American," she protests. "It's anti-Yankee. We're all against the Yankees." – *One, Two, Three* (1961)

1407 Spirited Manhattanite Jason Robards yells into his alley, expressing dissatisfaction with the "second-rate garbage" of his neighbors. "By next week I want to see a better class of garbage ... Champagne bottles and caviar cans ... So let's snap it up and get on the ball!" – *A Thousand Clowns* (1965)

1408 With his wife suing for divorce, a perturbed Jerry Lewis retreats to a bar. "What do they want from us?" Lewis demands from the bartender. "What do women want from men?" "It's this fluoride they're dumping in our drinking water," replies the bartender. – *Don't Raise the Bridge, Lower the River* (1968)

1409 A Broadway director interviews hippy Dick Shawn, whose mind has been blown by drugs. He is asked his name, which he struggles to remember. "Lorenzo St. Dubois," he finally says. "My friends call me L.S.D." "And what have you done?" "About six months." "What do you do best?" "I can't do that here," Shawn explains. "That's why they put me away, babe." – *The Producers* (1968)

1410 Believing he is Sherlock Holmes in pursuit of Professor Moriarty, George C. Scott intends to enter the New York headquarters of the telephone company. "You can't go barging in!" his psychiatrist and confidante (Joanne Woodward) objects. "I never barge," he parries. "I infiltrate – I filter." – *They Might Be Giants* (1971)

1411 Kooky Barbra Streisand intrudes upon musicologist Ryan O'Neal's very quiet life and creates havoc. "I know you don't mean any harm," he says. "You're just – different." "I know I'm different," she acknowledges, "but from now on I'm going to try to be the same." "The same as what?" he asks. "The same as people who aren't different." – *What's Up, Doc?* (1972)

1412 Woody Allen apologizes to his date (Diane Keaton) for refusing to enter a movie theater once the picture has begun – though only the credits were being shown. "I'm sorry, I'm anal," Woody explains. "That's a polite word for what you are," Diane retorts. – *Annie Hall* (1977)

1413 Madeline Kahn meets Mel Brooks, her father's psychiatrist, and suddenly makes a play for him – beginning with a compelling kiss. "What's your sign?" the surprised Brooks asks. "It's unlisted." – *High Anxiety* (1977)

1414 When Bill Murray loses his girlfriend, job, apartment and car, he and his best friend Harold Ramis decide to join the army. "Are you guys homosexuals?" the recruiting sergeant asks. "No," Ramis replies optimistically, "we're not homosexuals, but we're willing to learn." – *Stripes* (1981)

1415 Inebriated Hollywood movie star Alan Swann (Peter O'Toole) explains to his pretty bed partner why he doesn't wear a watch: "I don't trust them. One hand is shorter than the other." – *My Favorite Year* (1982)

1416 Heroic Robin Williams, shot while helping to prevent a holdup, is visited by his flaky girlfriend. "I never thought I'd be engaged to a man with a bullet wound," she cries. "It's very eighties – it's very sexy – in a way." – *The Survivors* (1983)

1417 Lonely guy Steve Martin finally meets Iris, the young woman of his dreams. Iris falls for him and suggests they return to his apartment where, after some lovemaking, she has second thoughts. "It's not going to work," she says, as she prepares to leave. "You're wrong for me." "Why?" Martin asks. "Because you're so right for me," she replies. – *The Lonely Guy* (1984)

1418 "You're not playing with a full deck, are you?" a police lieutenant asks his slow-witted assistant. "Oh," answers the subordinate, "I don't play cards." – *Police Academy 2: Their First Assignment* (1985)

1419 Library clerk Judge Reinhold each morning greets a fellow clerk who is plotting to mail bombs disguised as books to the major television networks for taking his favorite program off the air. "There are two things in this world that I love," the plotter reveals, "the Dewey Decimal System and demolition pyrotechnics." – *Off Beat* (1986)

1420 Former train robbers Burt Lancaster and Kirk Douglas, unable to face their lives as senior citizens, return to their former profession and hold up a train. Assisted by kooky hit man Eli Wallach, they are soon surrounded by a small army of police. "I'm gonna get a hundred of those coppers!" Wallach exclaims while aiming his shotgun. "There's only fifty of them," Lancaster explains. "So I'll shoot them twice!" – *Tough Guys* (1986)

1421 A disheveled panhandler loitering in front of New York's famous Plaza Hotel informs an out-of-towner: "If you stand here long enough you see yourself come out." – *Big Business* (1988)

1422 Eccentric widow Shirley MacLaine complains to her next door neighbor who is busy shooting off his pistol in an attempt to chase blackbirds out of a tree. "I don't know if I'm comin' or goin'!" she exclaims. "Yeah," the neighbor agrees, "I heard you got so screwed up you cut your dog out of your will and had an ungrateful nephew put to sleep." – *Steel Magnolias* (1989)

1423 Elaine May, having run out of patience with her capricious and disorganized neighbor, Marlo Thomas, exclaims: "Your mind is like my apartment. It's just a lot of junky things in it,

and I don't know what any of it is for!" – *In the Spirit* (1990)

1424 In this farce about hot-shot pilots, air force general Lloyd Bridges says to a fellow officer: "I want to thank you for having us over for dinner the other night. Cheryl and I thought the strogonoff was marvelous." "Sir," the officer replies, "we didn't have dinner the other night." "Really? Then where the hell was I? And who's this Cheryl?" – *Hot Shots!* (1991)

1425 Flaky cosmetologist Jamie Lee Curtis applies as assistant to mortician Dan Aykroyd. "I promise I'll take good care of the people," she assures him. "They deserve it – they're dead. All they've got left is their looks." – *My Girl* (1991)

1426 Leslie Nielsen, introduced to an oil company executive, says excitedly: "I believe I've used some of your restrooms." – *The Naked Gun 2 1/2: The Smell of Fear* (1991)

1427 At a 1967 drag contest in New York's Town Hall, a roomful of "queen" hopefuls sit around in their bouffants and high heels and exchange makeup secrets. One wit remarks: "Wouldn't it be great for the draft board to call us right now?" – *The Queen* (1993)

Education

1428 "I had to leave school on account of pneumonia," Al Jolson says. "How come?" "I couldn't spell it." – *Big Boy* (1930)

1429 "Why did you leave school?" Robert Woolsey asks Bert Wheeler. "On account of dyspepsia." "On account of dyspepsia?" "Yes," Wheeler explains, "I couldn't spell it." – *Caught Plastered* (1931)

1430 Professor Groucho Marx asks his not overly bright students Chico and Harpo: "Now then, baboons, what is a corpuscle?" "That's easy," Chico answers. "First there's a captain, then there's a lieutenant, then there's a corpuscle." "That's fine," Groucho responds. "Why don't you bore a hole in yourself and let the sap run out?" – *Horse Feathers* (1932)

1431 College dean Groucho Marx inquires of his faculty: "Do we have a university? Do we have a football stadium? Well, we can't afford both. Tomorrow we start tearing down the university." "But professor," a colleague objects, "where will the students sleep?" "Where they always slept," replies Groucho, "in the classroom." – *Horse Feathers* (1932)

1432 Student Harpo Marx disrupts professor Groucho Marx's class on anatomy. Groucho threatens punishment and turns to a pretty young thing sitting in the front row. "Just for that, you stay after school." "I didn't do anything," the girl protests. "I know," Groucho replies, "but it's no fun keeping him after school." – *Horse Feathers* (1932)

1433 "I bet you never got past the fifth grade," George Burns challenges Gracie Allen. "Oh, don't be silly," Gracie replies. "I spent three of the happiest years of my life in the sixth grade." – *Six of a Kind* (1934)

1434 When her wealthy father fails to confront a bohemian artist living in Greenwich Village, Miriam Hopkins decides to take charge. "You don't have enough experience," her father warns her. "You forget that I was a senior at Vassar," she retorts. – *Wise Girl* (1937)

1435 Student Gracie Allen is having trouble graduating from school. Principal Edward Everett Horton explains that she is continually puzzled by the questions. "It's not the questions," she corrects him, "it's the answers that puzzle me." – *College Swing* (1938)

1436 Widower John Barrymore answers a knock at the door with a loud "Enter!" "I beg your pardon," he apologizes to a pretty stranger. "I thought it was my children returning from their alleged school of learning." "I am your children's alleged teacher," the stranger introduces herself. – *The Great Man Votes* (1939)

1437 Mae West, taking over an unruly class of adolescents, scans the blackboard on which is written: "I am a good boy." "I am a good man." "I am a good girl." "What is this – propaganda?" West quips. – *My Little Chickadee* (1940)

1438 Lou Costello tries to explain a mathematics problem to Bud Abbott. "Did you ever go to school, stupid?" Abbott asks. "Yeah," Costello replies, "and I came out the same way." – *In the Navy* (1941)

1439 "How can you read in the dark?" one of the East Side Kids asks Huntz Hall. "I went to night school," Hall replies. – *Spooks Run Wild* (1941)

1440 Former college football star Jack Carson visits his alma mater, and his old English professor recalls Carson as his student. "I remember you not only from the gridiron, but from my Shakespeare class. You slept very quietly." – *The Male Animal* (1942)

1441 Bud Abbott has a difficult time explaining something to Lou Costello and finally gives up in frustration. "Did you ever go to school, stupid?" he asks Costello. "Yes sir," comes the reply. "And I came out the same way." – *Rio Rita* (1942)

1442 "Good old Bessie," Charlie McCarthy recalls one of his classmates. "She sat in front of me in history class." "Did you learn much about history?" Edgar Bergen asks. "Not as much as I learned about Bessie," replies McCarthy. – *Stage Door Canteen* (1943)

1443 At a racetrack school for jockeys, teacher Gail Russell clashes with newly admitted, impudent Stanley Clements. After he addresses her as "Toots," she asks him to leave. "Aw, don't get sore, baby," he pleads. "Can't you be like me – broadminded?" "Get out!" she exclaims. "You're expelled!" "A new record!" Clements declares jubilantly. "In and out of school in three minutes!" – *Salty O'Rourke* (1945)

1444 In Paris, Basil Rathbone runs a strict school for beginning pickpockets of all ages. He is quick to remind a student about the high standards of decorum at his establishment: "How many times do I have to tell you that I will not tolerate slang in my classroom?" –*Heartbeat* (1946)

1445 Myrna Loy complains about teenage daughter Shirley Temple's poor work in geometry. "I don't consider geometry a part of life," Temple replies. "Mr. Roberts does," Loy counters. "He says you're the first student he has ever had who defines a triangle as two women crazy about one man." –*The Bachelor and the Bobby-Soxer* (1947)

1446 Joan Davis confides to Jean Peters that her hoodlum-husband was killed by other gangsters. "How did it happen?" Peters asks. "I heard they dropped him in the cement mixer when they were building the new Wilson Avenue school," Davis explains. "Poor Biff, he finally got educated – the hard way." –*Love That Brute* (1950)

1447 Good-natured racketeer Paul Douglas places a street-wise, unmanageable, ten-year-old orphan in a military academy where students are marching on the parade grounds. After Douglas leaves, the boy announces to the officer-in-charge: "Let's get this, Napoleon. I don't mind working the machine-gun, but sweating out there with them monkeys – out!!!" –*Love That Brute* (1950)

1448 Red Buttons recalls his days in public school: "I was an honor student – 'yes, your honor; no, your honor...'" –*Footlight Varieties* (1951)

1449 The finance committee of a small college balks at extending the library, reminding dean Charles Coburn that they built an extension several years earlier. "There have been two or three volumes written since then," Coburn pointedly remarks, "or would you have the college subscribe to the Book-of-the-Month Club and call it quits?" –*Trouble Along the Way* (1953)

1450 Leo Gorcey: "How can you read in the dark?" Huntz Hall: "I went to night school." –*The Bowery Boys Meet the Monsters* (1954)

1451 Dock worker Marlon Brando to Eva Marie Saint: "The nuns tried to beat an education into me, but I outfoxed them." –*On the Waterfront* (1954)

1452 Big-time gambler Big Louie gives Nathan Detroit (Frank Sinatra) an I.O.U. "'I owe you one thousand dollars – signed X,'" Sinatra reads aloud. "How come you can write 'one thousand,' but you cannot write your name?" "Oh," Louie replies, "I was good in arithmetic, but I stunk in English." –*Guys and Dolls* (1955)

1453 During the occupation of Okinawa after World War II, army officer Paul Ford expresses his unbounded determination to Americanize his charges: "My job is to teach these natives the meaning of democracy, and they're going to learn democracy if I have to shoot every one of them!" –*The Teahouse of the August Moon* (1956)

1454 College student Jane Fonda is hired as babysitter for a professor's children, and she brings her boyfriend Ray (Anthony Perkins) along for company. "You'll be glad to know that Ray has promised to help me with my chemistry tonight," she announces to the professor. "Just as a guide to Ray and his tutoring, where would you suggest I was weakest?" "I'd say on page one." –*Tall Story* (1960)

1455 Itinerant handyman Sidney Poitier, in an impish mood, teaches English to a group of immigrant nuns and asks them to repeat after him: "Ah stands up, you all." –*Lilies of the Field* (1963)

1456 A gentleman at an inn belittles Tom Jones (Albert Finney) for his lack of learning. "Sir," Jones retorts, "it is as easy for a man not to have been at school and know nothing as it is for a man to have been at school and know nothing." – *Tom Jones* (1963)

1457 During the campus riots of the late sixties, Bob Hope and his wife Jane Wyman are surprised to see their daughter return from college before the end of the semester. "Maybe the faculty locked the students out," Hope quips. – *How to Commit Marriage* (1969)

1458 "Why did I quit college?" Woody Allen regretfully questions himself. "I could have been something today." "What would you have been if you finished school?" a fellow employee asks. "I don't know," Allen answers. "I was in the black studies program. By now I could have been black." – *Bananas* (1971)

1459 Professional thief Robert Redford hires explosives expert Paul Sand, who demonstrates several home-made bombs. "I never saw one like that before," Redford remarks. "I learned it when I was at the Sorbonne," Sand replies, who then demonstrates another and says: "I picked that up at Berkeley." "You studied a lot, I guess." "I love school." – *The Hot Rock* (1972)

1460 "We had a saying," recalls Woody Allen about his childhood, "that 'those who can't do, teach, and those who can't teach, teach gym, and those who can't do anything, were assigned to our school.'" – *Annie Hall* (1977)

1461 John Belushi, the chief slob and roisterer of "Animal House," the worst fraternity house at Faber College, has just been expelled from school after the dean examines Belushi's grade average of zero. "Seven years of college down the drain," he moans, lying on the floor. – *National Lampoon's Animal House* (1978)

1462 Young woman: "I'm getting a degree in sociology. I don't know what to do with it." Henry Winkler: "Open up a sociology store." – *The One and Only* (1978)

1463 Prim, strict principal Mary Woronov is struck by rebellious student P. J. Soles. "You have detention for life!" she cries. – *Rock 'n' Roll High School* (1979)

1464 Student Dey Young presents to matronly principal Mary Woronov a written excuse covering each of the three days of her absence – the death of her mother, her father and her goldfish. Later, the principal is shown the supposedly dead goldfish swimming merrily in their bowl. "I'm sure her parents are alive, too," she concludes. – *Rock 'n' Roll High School* (1979)

1465 Tightfisted Walter Matthau, as Broadway bookie Sorrowful Jones, considers Mrs. Clancy as a teacher for a little orphan. "Mrs. Clancy ain't no teacher," his friend Bob Newhart says. "She's a cleaning woman." "But where does she clean, dummy?" Matthau insists. "In a classroom. In school." "Thirty years in a classroom," Matthau adds. "You don't think she picked up a few tips?" – *Little Miss Marker* (1980)

1466 George Burns, as God, gives little Tracy a week to come up with an advertising slogan to help promote the Lord. "Just a week?" the child questions. "That's long enough. Look how much I accomplished in a week. And I did it without computers." "Yeah," Tracy replies, "but You didn't have a math test coming up." – *Oh, God! Book II* (1980)

1467 "Have you studied filmmaking in school?" someone asks director-screenwriter Woody Allen at one of his screenings. "No, no, I didn't study anything in school," Allen replies. "They studied me." – *Stardust Memories* (1980)

1468 Bored college instructor Michael Caine, who has failed as a poet, has been coming to class quite drunk. Sitting in his classroom, he stares out the window, oblivious to his students' comments about literature. One young man complains that Caine is not listening. "Doctor," the student calls out, "are you drunk?" "Drunk?" Caine echoes. "Of course I'm drunk. You don't really expect me to teach this when I'm sober." –*Educating Rita* (1983)

1469 Amateur comic Robert De Niro informs a television audience that when he was young, others used to pick on him. "They used to beat me up once a week," he says, "and after a while the school worked it into the curriculum. And, if you knocked me out, you got extra credit." –*The King of Comedy* (1983)

1470 In a Florida town, Bible-thumping evangelist Bill Wiley organizes the Righteous Flock – a group of self-appointed moral overseers – to stop a high school from presenting "An Evening of Shakespeare." Meeting with the school principal, they argue the case for Shakespeare's lewdness and degeneracy. "Get the flock out of here!" the exasperated principal finally yells. –*Porky's II: The Next Day* (1983)

1471 In suburban Connecticut, Scottish poet Tom Conti, living a shabby life, whimsically says to his blonde girlfriend Kelly McGillis: "I did something much better than go to Oxford. I was expelled from Oxford." –*Reuben, Reuben* (1984)

1472 "In the high school I went to," says Rodney Dangerfield, "they asked a kid to prove the law of gravity, and he threw the teacher out of the window." –*Back to School* (1986)

1473 Teenage River Phoenix quotes his eccentric inventor-father Harrison Ford: "He said he dropped out of Harvard to get an education." –*The Mosquito Coast* (1986)

1474 Chicago cops Billy Crystal and Gregory Hines, about to pursue two street hoodlums, pause to inspect their weapons. "You know," Crystal says, referring to the young thugs, "this kind of thing starts in the home." "It's the education system," Hines disagrees. "The new math drives them nuts," Crystal adds. –*Running Scared* (1986)

1475 At a medical college an instructor invites his freshman students into his classroom where gross human anatomy is to be taught. "Come in, come in," he entreats them. "Your cadavers will wait patiently for you. I promise." –*Gross Anatomy* (1989)

1476 Movie mogul Robert Loggia is suspicious about his future son-in-law, millionaire playboy Alec Baldwin, and intends to learn more about him in a private meeting. "Exactly how much schooling have you had?" "I went to a few Harvard-Yale football games," Baldwin cracks. –*The Marrying Man* (1991)

1477 When a young woman mocks retired slumlord Vincent Gardenia for his insensitive attitude toward the minority poor, he asks her how far she went in school. "When I was in high school," she begins after a long pause, "I wouldn't let a guy touch me, but when I got to community college I turned pretty wild." –*The Super* (1991)

1478 Feisty blonde television reporter Ally Walker tries to read some top-secret documents. "You know," she acknowledges, "I feel like I'm back in high school or something. I can't make heads or tails out of any of this stuff." –*Universal Soldier* (1992)

Ethics and Morality

1479 Douglas Fairbanks, Jr., in love with a fellow officer's mistress, breathes a sigh of relief when he learns from her that she does not really care for her lover. "I'm glad," Fairbanks says. "Morals have never bothered me too much, but taste is *so* important." — *Scarlet Dawn* (1932)

1480 At an English ball aristocrat Nigel Bruce engages in light conversation with beautiful Becky Sharp (Miriam Hopkins). "It was Father who shipped me off to India to hunt the blasted pachyderm," he says. "What were you doing in India?" she questions and, observing an African serving boy waiting on Bruce, adds: "Your son?" "Becky!" he protests. "You blacken my character!" — *Becky Sharp* (1935)

1481 Mae West: "Yes, for a long time I was ashamed of the way I lived." Man: "You mean to say you reformed?" West: "No. I got over being ashamed." — *Goin' to Town* (1935)

1482 "Well, I'll say one thing," Bert Wheeler asserts, flirting with a young and pretty teacher. "You got some class. You know, I was stuck on a schoolteacher once. She had a lot of class but no principle." — *Silly Billies* (1936)

1483 In Moscow during the late 1930s, reporter Clark Gable is prepared to share his former hotel room, but its present occupant, a stern German correspondent, demands it all. "That's a fine way to talk," Gable responds. "I get the room, I fix it up, I pay for it in advance, and I live in it. And you march in and try to throw me out. Now is that a nice way for a Nazi to act — I ask you?" — *Comrade X* (1940)

1484 Mae West derides a deceitful Broadway producer: "Why, if he had been with Washington, he'd have double-crossed the Delaware." — *The Heat's On* (1943)

1485 Mark Twain (Fredric March): "Man is the only animal that blushes — or needs to." — *The Adventures of Mark Twain* (1944)

1486 Landlords William Lundigan and wife June Haver know that con artist Frank Fay, their otherwise charming tenant, has duped rich widows out of thousands of dollars, so they are surprised to learn that he is broke. "I had nothing left after I paid my taxes," he explains. "You paid your taxes on that money?" Lundigan questions. "Why, my boy, I have my ethics." — *Love Nest* (1951)

1487 Reporter Janet Leigh tries to convince editor Fred Clark to exploit a story about a young man supposedly dying of radiation poisoning as a publicity stunt. "Think of the headlines," she says enticingly. "'Humanitarian Editor Saves Hero's Life' . . . There's always politics. Think what it means to be a senator. Your mail goes free." — *Living It Up* (1954)

1488 When one of James Garner's married friends considers taking on a mistress, Garner warns him that he will have to spend a fortune on her wardrobe. "Nothing doing," the husband protests. "I'm not dressing her better than my wife." "Why not?" "My conscience would bother me." — *Boys' Night Out* (1962)

1489 A group of daring thieves plot a heist aboard the *Queen Mary* but need a mechanic. When one thief recommends such a person, another questions if the mechanic will go along with the scheme. "His morality is as flexible as ours," the friend says. — *Assault on a Queen* (1966)

1490 Zero Mostel in ancient Rome chides an innocent young man for falling in love with a courtesan. "Is that shameful?" the youth asks. "It's hardly an achievement," Mostel replies. — *A Funny Thing Happened on the Way to the Forum* (1966)

1491 Fellow prisoner Jim Hampton explains to Burt Reynolds, former football star suspected of throwing a game, why the other convicts dislike him. "You could have robbed banks, sold dope . . . none of us would've minded," Hampton says. "But shaving points off a football game — man, that's un–American." — *The Longest Yard* (1974)

1492 Happy hooker Xaviera Hollander (Joey Heatherton) has been subpoenaed to appear before a U.S. Senate committee investigating the decline of morality in the country. Reporters surround her and ask about the effects of sex on the nation. "What's good for general intercourse is good for the country," she quips. – *The Happy Hooker Goes to Washington* (1977)

1493 Career criminal Sean Connery, possessing his own particular code of honor, is repulsed by a scam involving the purchase of apartments belonging to terminally ill cancer patients. "You're mucking around in other people's misery," he rails at the woman schemer. "When you rob someone without risk, without sticking your neck out, that's immoral." – *Family Business* (1989)

1494 Slumlord Louis Kritski (Joe Pesci) is sentenced to spend one hundred twenty days in a rat-infested building which had been advertised as a "furnished fifth-floor charmer with a view." Kritski denies that there are any rats present. "Maybe they're avoiding your floor out of professional courtesy," one tenant suggests. – *The Super* (1991)

1495 Following his natural instincts, a sprightly Huck Finn (Elijah Wood) runs off with an escaped slave. "What's the use you learning to do right," he reckons, "when it's troublesome to do right and ain't no trouble to do wrong?" – *The Adventures of Huck Finn* (1993)

Etiquette and Manners

1496 An irate husband charges into bachelor Lowell Sherman's apartment asking his friend to help find the man having an affair with his wife Agatha. The intruder believes it is one of their friends. "Suppose it isn't any of the people in our set?" Sherman points out. "You don't think it would be an ordinary man – the grocer's clerk or a vacuum cleaner salesman?" the shocked husband questions. "No, no," Sherman reassures his visitor. "Agatha might commit a sin, but she'd never commit a *faux pas*." – *Bachelor Apartment* (1931)

1497 Hostess Billie Burke panics when she finds herself short one male guest at a formal dinner she has arranged. "I never could understand why it has to be just even – male and female," her cousin wonders. "They're invited for dinner, not for mating." – *Dinner at Eight* (1933)

1498 At the dinner table, W. C. Fields corrects the bad manners of his small son who then questions his father's love. Fields raises his arm as if to crack the little nipper. "Don't you strike that child!" his shrewish wife cries out. "He's not going to tell me I don't love him," Fields mutters in an offended tone. – *It's a Gift* (1934)

1499 W. C. Fields' erratic manners shock a snobbish matron who exclaims: "Your naive gaucheries are amazing!" "Thanks," the puzzled Fields acknowledges. "Thanks very much. Nice of you to mention it." – *You're Telling Me* (1934)

1500 Bert Wheeler and Robert Woolsey, wards of young Spanky McFarland, suspect a crooked lawyer of trying to cheat the child out of his inheritance. Woolsey calls the attorney a "weasel." "Weasel!" the offended lawyer sputters. "Why, I was never so insulted in my life!" "That's your fault," adds Wheeler. "You don't get around much." –*Kentucky Kernels* (1935)

1501 A waiter hands the check to Groucho Marx, who in turn flings it over to Margaret Dumont. "Nine-forty!" he exclaims. "This is an outrage! If I were you, I wouldn't pay it." –*A Night at the Opera* (1935)

1502 Sultry blonde Esther Muir tries to frame Groucho Marx but is foiled by the zany antics of Harpo and Chico. "I've never been so insulted in my life," she cries in frustration. "It's still early in the evening," Groucho warns. –*A Day at the Races* (1937)

1503 At breakfast, banker Cosmo Topper (Roland Young) greets his wife Clara (Billie Burke), who directs him to stop running to catch the morning train. "Besides," she says, "you know how you puff when you run." "Of course I puff. Everybody puffs. You puff yourself, Clara. I remember that day –" "Cosmo, please," she interjects. "Don't be vulgar." –*Topper* (1937)

1504 "I'm afraid I've sat on your hat," Helen Broderick says apologetically to Victor Moore. "Don't be afraid," Moore responds, "you just did." –*We're on the Jury* (1937)

1505 Playboy Preston Foster returns home after a night on the town, still wearing his tuxedo. Servant Herbert Mundin awakes and notices his employer and his attire. "I can understand buying the *Saturday Evening Post* on Wednesday or having a little nightcap in the early hours of the morning," Mundin comments, "but dress clothes at this time of day –" –*You Can't Beat Love* (1937)

1506 Two western bandits, son and father, are disputing a particular plan. "Aw, that's crazy," the son says. "Careful, son," the elder warns. "You're talking to your dad, you know." –*Lawless Valley* (1938)

1507 A maid cautions Higgins (Leslie Howard) not to use the word "bloody" in the presence of Eliza (Wendy Hiller). He promptly denies the charge. "Only this morning, sir," she reminds him, "you applied it to the boots, to the butter and to the brown bread." "Oh, that!" he exclaims. "Mere alliteration, Mrs. Pierce, natural to a poet." –*Pygmalion* (1938)

1508 Tim Holt, son of wealthy manufacturer Walter Connolly, mistreats unemployed Ginger Rogers, who he thinks is a gold digger after his father's money. "I understand you play polo," she says. "Yes," he replies. "What's that got to do with it?" "Nothing," she says. "Just that I'm amazed to discover that horses have better breeding than the people who ride them." –*Fifth Avenue Girl* (1939)

1509 Crooked political boss Akim Tamiroff, riding in his limousine, tries to relate to ambitious low-life McGinty (Brian Donlevy) the story of his rise to power. But McGinty, more interested in the car, constantly interrupts him. "What makes this bus so quiet?" "It's armored," replies Tamiroff as he tries to continue. "Armored for what?" McGinty interjects. "So I shouldn't be interrupted!" Tamiroff explodes. –*The Great McGinty* (1940)

1510 "To me," states snobbish Miss Bingley (Frieda Inescort), "there's something unrefined about excessive laughter." "Oh," counters Elizabeth Bennet (Greer Garson), "if you want to be really refined, you have to be dead. There's no one as dignified as a mummy." –*Pride and Prejudice* (1940)

1511 "How do you do?" an executive greets Groucho Marx. "That's a rather personal question, isn't it, old man?" Groucho counters. "What I do and how I do it is my concern." –*The Big Store* (1941)

1512 Bud Abbott is critical of the table manners of Lou Costello, who grabs at the food. "Don't reach," Abbott instructs.

"If you want something, ask for it. You have a tongue, haven't you?" "I can reach further with my hands," replies Costello. – *Hold That Ghost* (1941)

1513 Mary Martin, posing as a Southern belle, asks Broadway director Don Ameche about the statue of a lady in front of General Sherman on a horse. "Who is that lady in front?" "That's Victory." "Isn't it just like a Yankee," she concludes, "to let a lady walk?" – *Kiss the Boys Goodbye* (1941)

1514 "Confound it, June!" irascible Sheridan Whiteside (Monty Woolley) exclaims to his secretary. "When will you learn that I am always kind and courteous! Bring that idiot in!" – *The Man Who Came to Dinner* (1941)

1515 Entertainer Mae West invites wealthy, insular Victor Moore to her apartment for a few drinks. "Do you have any lemon squash?" wealthy Victor Moore asks hostess Mae West. "Not if I can help it," West replies. "How about a little Napoleon brandy?" "Oh, no," Moore replies. "I wouldn't like to take anything that belongs to somebody else." – *The Heat's On* (1943)

1516 Radio scriptwriter Dick Powell, having trouble coming up with ideas for his show, addresses a middle-aged man sitting next to him in a subway car. "What do you think the average – just the simple average – person wants out of life?" "Not to be pestered with stupid questions by strangers," the man fires back. – *True to Life* (1943)

1517 East Side gang member Huntz Hall interjects himself into a conversation between two matrons of society. "Tell me something, Mrs. Retread –" he begins. "Treadwell is my name," says the woman in an annoyed tone. "I wonder what the poor people are doing," Hall continues. "Aren't you being a trifle forward?" "I could move back." – *Block Busters* (1944)

1518 Police detective Dana Andrews, investigating a murder, unceremoniously enters Gene Tierney's apartment. She is entertaining newspaper columnist Clifton Webb. "Haven't you heard of science's newest triumph – the doorbell?" Webb inquires. – *Laura* (1944)

1519 At a nightclub, show producer George White sends an inscribed cake to the table of some of his former showgirls celebrating their twenty-sixth reunion. "Don't you think we should send him an answer?" one young woman suggests. "Of course," Joan Davis agrees. "Waiter, get me a blank cake." – *George White's Scandals* (1945)

1520 As Bud Abbott and Lou Costello, dressed in tuxedos, enter a plush nightclub, Costello puts a stick of gum in his mouth. "It don't look nice chewing gum in that suit," Abbott suggests. "I'm chewing in my mouth," Costello corrects him. – *The Naughty Nineties* (1945)

1521 Gruff junk dealer Broderick Crawford hires a tutor to educate and dignify his brassy girlfriend, ex-showgirl Judy Holliday, but his plan goes awry. "You eat terrible," she rails at him, "you got no manners! That's another thing – picking your teeth. You're just not couth!" – *Born Yesterday* (1950)

1522 As Bob Hope is about to spend the night with lovely Arlene Dahl, his gentleman's gentleman (William Demarest) reminds him: "A gentleman is never alone with a lady, sir." "You're now working for a cad," Hope replies. – *Here Come the Girls* (1953)

1523 "You should never say 'my feet hurt,'" David Niven cautions ingenue Maggie McNamara. "'My foot – singular – hurts' is an intriguing statement; 'my feet – plural – hurt' is a rather sordid admission." – *The Moon Is Blue* (1953)

1524 On board a train, attractive Marilyn Maxwell enters a car of G.I.s destined for boot camp. Soldier Bob Hope approaches her: "If you're from the U.S.O., honey, you're just in time. My morale is dragging." "So are your manners," she fires back. – *Off Limits* (1953)

1525 During the Korean War, Soviet colonel Oscar Homolka interrogates American prisoners captured by North Korean troops. His Soviet aide and yes-man, eager to please, keeps interjecting with "Yes, indeed," until Homolka finally rebukes him: "At least wait till I finish my sentence." – *Prisoner of War* (1954)

1526 At an elegant Mexican ball, rough-hewn, unshaven American adventurer Burt Lancaster stuffs his mouth and eats with both hands from the buffet table. An officer approaches and says sarcastically: "Your acquaintance with etiquette amazes me, monsieur. I had no idea you knew which hand to use." – *Vera Cruz* (1954)

1527 "Be nice," scheming rancher Burl Ives suggests to his raffish son (Chuck Connors), who is courting the owner of a neighboring ranch. "Treat her right. Take a bath sometime." – *The Big Country* (1958)

1528 "I like that butler," says gangster Glenn Ford's bodyguard-chauffeur Mickey Shaughnessy. "He calls me 'sir,' then he bows to me. Makes me feel like a broad." – *Pocketful of Miracles* (1961)

1529 At a pretentious social event a boorish woman has dominated the conversation. "That diamond ring took my breath away," she comments at one point. "Not completely," quips Mary Tyler Moore. – *Thoroughly Modern Millie* (1967)

1530 Fagin (Ron Moody) instructs his little street urchins on more than picking a pocket or two: "While you're in class, boys, take your hats off." – *Oliver!* (1968)

1531 Jenny (Ali McGraw) uses an off-color word while awaiting the arrival of boyfriend Ryan O'Neal. "Don't use profanity in this house," her father (John Marley) orders. "What the hell's he gonna think?" – *Love Story* (1970)

1532 Outspoken Judge Roy Bean (Paul Newman) has insulted his marshals' wives, all former prostitutes, by calling them whores, and when his men beg him to apologize to the women, he agrees. "I ask you to note," he says calmly, "that I did not call you callous-assed strumpets, fornicatresses or low-born gutter sluts, but I did say 'whores.' And for that slip of the tongue, I apologize." – *The Life and Times of Judge Roy Bean* (1972)

1533 Joseph Bologna and Renee Taylor have just finished making love on the floor when her mother (Helen Verbit) walks in. Taylor introduces her mother to the naked Bologna, who is only partially covered with a throw rug. "Don't get up," the mother politely insists. "I always say, 'Why be formal when you can be relaxing?'" – *Made for Each Other* (1973)

1534 From his car seat, oriental detective Wang (Peter Sellers) says to a fellow sleuth standing at the curb: "Treacherous road like fresh mushroom. Must always–" But before he can complete his aphorism, his driver-son takes off, causing Wang to flare up at his son: "not finish mushroom story, you idiot!" – *Murder by Death* (1976)

1535 "Don't you ever take your hat off?" runaway bride Sally Field asks bootlegger Burt Reynolds. "I take my hat off for one thing and one thing only," he replies. – *Smokey and the Bandit* (1977)

1536 Chevy Chase and Dan Aykroyd, as U.S. undercover agents-in-training, grow discouraged with the rigorous drills and decide to call it quits. "We'd like to go home now," Chase informs their tough superior officer. "Thanks for the bruises, and you can keep the stool samples." – *Spies Like Us* (1985)

1537 At the dinner table, little Wednesday (Christina Ricci) requests the salt. "What do we say?" Morticia (Anjelica Huston), always the instructive mother, asks. "Now!" the child yells. – *The Addams Family* (1991)

Family

1538 Doughboy Robert Woolsey, stationed in Paris, meets an attractive Russian woman. "My father was born in Moscow," she says, "my mother was born in Vladivostok, and I was born in St. Petersburg." "Is that so?" Woolsey responds. "Funny how you all got together." – *Half Shot at Sunrise* (1930)

1539 Groucho Marx: "The picnic is off. We don't have any red ants." Chico Marx: "I know an Indian with some red aunts." – *Monkey Business* (1931)

1540 Wealthy uncle C. Aubrey Smith threatens to cut off wastrel nephew Charlie Ruggles without a cent, addressing him as an impertinent jackanapes, liar and cheat. "You'll be insulting me in a minute," Ruggles parries. – *Love Me Tonight* (1932)

1541 Irascible millionaire-patriarch George Arliss has assembled his greedy, fortune-hunting family who are about to have dinner. "I doubt if it will do this graceless and disgraceful gathering any good," he announces, "but nevertheless I will say grace." – *The Last Gentleman* (1934)

1542 "I'm an aristocrat and the backbone of my family," a haughty Ivan Lebedeff announces to Mae West. "Then your family'd better see a chiropractor," quips West. – *Goin' to Town* (1935)

1543 "I got an aunt who's got a complexion like a peach – yellow and fuzzy," says Bob Burns to a radio audience. – *The Big Broadcast of 1937* (1936)

1544 Edward G. Robinson visits England and meets with stodgy relatives who want to know about Robinson's grandfather – the only member of the family to settle in the States. "He

certainly had a great career in the U.S.A.," Robinson explains. "He investigated jails – that is, as an inmate. It was his ambition to serve time in every state of the union, but he died before he got to South Dakota." – *Thunder in the City* (1937)

1545 Bob Hope looks at a portrait of his rich uncle and quips: "He was so crooked that when he died they had to screw him into the ground." – *The Cat and the Canary* (1939)

1546 Drama critic Sheridan Whiteside (Monty Woolley) boasts of his precociousness: "I left home at the age of four, and I haven't been back since. They can hear me on the radio, and that's good enough for them." – *The Man Who Came to Dinner* (1941)

1547 Pompous Hal Peary, guardian to his little nephew and teenage niece, is endlessly entangled in their problems. When the boy confides that his sister has romantic problems, Peary decides to take charge. "You leave this to an older and wiser head," Peary says confidently. "Who've you got in mind?" his nephew asks. – *Gildersleeve on Broadway* (1943)

1548 Elderly Don Ameche, having lived a full life, dies peacefully in his sleep. His spirit reports to the Devil and relates his last moments: "There were all my relatives, speaking in low tones and saying nothing but the kindest things about me. Then I knew that I was dead." – *Heaven Can Wait* (1943)

1549 "Insanity doesn't run in my family," theater critic Cary Grant confesses to fiancée Priscilla Lane, "it gallops." – *Arsenic and Old Lace* (1944)

1550 "I had an uncle who was a diver," a bartender informs a customer. "He stayed under water for three weeks. He hit a rock." – *Having Wonderful Crime* (1945)

1551 Rex Harrison, ne'er-do-well son of an English statesman, has failed at another position and once again faces his father and a tough aunt who try to plan his future. "Dad and I will have a private talk later," Harrison suggests. "Do you think you can get rid of me as easily as that?" the aunt asks. "No," Harrison replies glibly, "it's hard work." – *Notorious Gentleman* (1946)

1552 An updated Parisian Bluebeard (Charlie Chaplin), having dispatched many an unwary wife to an early grave, notices his small son pulling a cat's tail. "There's a cruel streak in you," Chaplin observes. "I wonder where you get it." – *Monsieur Verdoux* (1947)

1553 Out on the town investigating a murder in a jazz club, Nick and Nora Charles (William Powell and Myrna Loy) return home to find Nick, Jr. (Dean Stockwell), waiting up for them. "Look what time it is!" the boy disapprovingly exclaims. – *Song of the Thin Man* (1947)

1554 Former playboy Fred Astaire's dowager aunt (Marjorie Main) warns his fiancée (Vera-Ellen) about him. "Charles has one trait," she says, "a characteristic inherited from his uncle's side of the family." "What's that?" Vera-Ellen asks. "He's no good." – *The Belle of New York* (1952)

1555 "You really look a mess," a teenage girl chides her six-year-old sister (Linda Bruhl). "When are you going to grow up?" "Never," the child replies. "I've seen what it's done to you." – *Papa's Delicate Condition* (1963)

1556 "It's a free country," sulking teenager Barry Gordon says to his parents (Sid Caesar and Vera Miles). "Don't I have the right to be miserable?" "No, not yet," his father asserts. "Not while I'm still paying the bills." – *The Spirit Is Willing* (1967)

1557 Embroiled in court intrigue and beset by disloyal sons, Eleanor of Aquitaine (Katharine Hepburn) argues and fights with Henry II (Peter O'Toole) over the succession to the throne and the fate of England. "Well," Hepburn casually remarks after an emotionally drenched battle involving the entire clan, "what family doesn't have its ups and downs?" – *The Lion in Winter* (1968)

1558 Retired navy officer and widower Henry Fonda responds to the smoldering resentment of his ten children that he had neglected their mother through the years: "It seemed to me there was enough physical evidence that I hadn't neglected her completely." – *Yours, Mine and Ours* (1968)

1559 A doctor is summoned to examine one of eighteen children belonging to parents Henry Fonda and Lucille Ball. "What's the name of this organization?" the puzzled doctor asks. "We were just married today," Fonda explains. "Congratulations," the visitor offers. "The next twenty years ought to be a lulu." – *Yours, Mine and Ours* (1968)

1560 Bob Hope and Jane Wyman are shocked when they learn that their daughter has quit college. She returns with her boyfriend David, whom she intends to marry. "David comes from a broken home," she explains to her parents. "I was the only child in kindergarten who could spell dirty words correctly," David quips. "I'm amazed you didn't write a best seller," Hope retorts. – *How to Commit Marriage* (1969)

1561 Liv Ullmann parries thrusts from both her mother and daughter about her parasitic ex-husband. "Every man has a time in his life when he is broke," she says to her daughter, "and your father is no exception." "Oh, he certainly isn't," adds Liv's mother. "He's the rule!" – *40 Carats* (1973)

1562 Parents Bob Crane and Barbara Rush learn from their teenage daughter that an oddball artist has forced her into an engagement and has given her a painting in place of a ring. "He says the painting is mine and I'm his," the terrified girl explains, "and if anything ever comes between us, he'll do something awful – like kill himself!" "That's not all bad," Crane ponders. – *Superdad* (1974)

1563 "My granny never gave gifts," Woody Allen remarks to Diane Keaton. "She was too busy being raped by Cossacks." – *Annie Hall* (1977)

1564 Steve Martin, a white orphan raised by a poor black family in the South, finally comes of age and learns the truth from his black guardians. "It's your birthday," his black mother reminds him, "and it's time you knew the truth. You're not our natural-born child." – *The Jerk* (1979)

1565 "We don't see eye to eye," George Burns says about his strained association with his married daughter. "It's more of a mouth to mouth relationship." – *Just You and Me, Kid* (1979)

1566 Aspiring young actor Donny Most is packed and ready to leave for Los Angeles. "Dad," he says, "I don't believe it. I'm moving three thousand miles and you're not even going to say goodbye? At least say goodbye, that's all. Just goodbye." "Goodbye," his father says grudgingly. "That's all you're going to say is goodbye?" – *Leo and Loree* (1980)

1567 Unemployed circus clown Jerry Lewis, living with his married sister, does not get along with brother-in-law Robert. "Robert has something good to tell you," Lewis' sister says. "Oh," Lewis utters, "he's leaving home?" – *Hardly Working* (1981)

1568 Hollywood writer Walter Matthau's daughter Dinah Manoff, who has not seen her father for years, shows up at his home early one morning. "What a surprise!" he exclaims. "Do you feel like that?" "No," she replies, "I knew I was

coming." – *I Ought to Be in Pictures* (1982)

1569 In a Jewish delicatessen, Hollywood writer Walter Matthau promises his long-absent daughter Dinah Manoff that she can stay with him temporarily. "There, it's official," he declares. "I swore before a Jewish waiter. That's more binding than a lawyer's contract." – *I Ought to Be in Pictures* (1982)

1570 At the wedding of Julie Walters' sister, her father expresses disappointment in Julie – married four years and no offspring. "Here your sister is married two minutes," he says, beaming, "and she's already four months' pregnant." – *Educating Rita* (1983)

1571 John Candy sees his bikini-clad teenage daughter with a handsome lifeguard in a remote beach tower. "What's Jennifer doing up there?" he asks his wife. "Just talking." "That's how *she* got here, remember?" he reminds his wife. – *Summer Rental* (1985)

1572 Family patriarch and career criminal Sean Connery chides son Dustin Hoffman, who has long given up his own life of crime and has gone legitimate. "When the hell did you get it into your head that it was so terrible to be a thief?" Connery asks. – *Family Business* (1989)

1573 A grandmother and her granddaughter accidentally see several moments of a pornographic videotape before they are whisked away by the latter's mother. "One of those men reminded me of your grandpa, God bless him," the grandmother remarks. – *Parenthood* (1989)

1574 Bride-to-be Julia Roberts objects to several pretentious distant relatives having been invited to her wedding and reminds her mother (Sally Field): "Daddy always says, 'An ounce of pretension is worth a pound of manure.'" – *Steel Magnolias* (1989)

1575 Eight-year-old Macaulay Culkin's family, in its haste to catch its plane to Paris, has inadvertently left him at home–alone. When he awakens and discovers everyone is gone, he declares: "I made my family disappear!"–*Home Alone* (1990)

1576 Morticia (Anjelica Huston) intercepts her daughter Wednesday (Christina Ricci) who is going after young Pugsley with a carving knife. "I don't think so," she says thoughtfully, handing her daughter a more efficient meat-ax.–*The Addams Family* (1991)

1577 When mobster Sylvester Stallone learns that his daughter is pregnant, he immediately orders that she marry the father of the child. "After you're married," he says, "you're going to move into a nice ground floor apartment." "Why a ground floor apartment?" "Because after I break his legs, he's not going to make it up any steps."–*Oscar* (1991)

1578 "My grandmother," relates stand-up comedienne Ellen DeGeneres, "she started walking five miles a day when she was 60. She's 97 today–and we don't know where the hell she is." –*Wisecracks* (1992)

Fear

1579 Although the Civil War has ended, a visiting Southern plantation owner threatens to horsewhip Gus the jockey (Al Jolson in blackface). "Don't be scared," a fellow black man later reassures Jolson. "Remember what our parson said: that someday the lion and the lamb is going to lay down together." "Yeah," Jolson says, "but the lion will be the one to get up."–*Big Boy* (1930)

1580 Bullfighters, including a reluctant Eddie Cantor, wait to show their prowess in the ring. "Boy, do you hear that band?" Cantor's friend Robert Young exclaims. "Listen to those castanets!" "Castanets, my eye," Cantor replies. "Those are my knees shaking."–*The Kid from Spain* (1932)

1581 Jimmy Durante and Buster Keaton enter a dark and abandoned warehouse where they suddenly hear scuffling. "We're not alone in this place," says Durante. "You soon will be," replies Keaton, who heads for the exit.–*What! No Beer?* (1933)

1582 Fight manager Adolphe Menjou tries to persuade milkman Harold Lloyd to fight a professional boxer, stating that eighty thousand people will be at the arena. "Not quite eighty thousand," Lloyd corrects him. "What do you mean?" "Because I won't be there." –*The Milky Way* (1936)

1583 Joe E. Brown, who is allergic to horses, refuses to play in a polo game. "You can't back down now," his servant pleads. "Everyone will think you're frightened." "But I'm not frightened," Brown replies. "I'm scared to death." –*Polo Joe* (1936)

1584 Newsreel cameraman Clark Gable and sidekick Leo Carrillo enter an African jungle to the tune of ominous drums. "What are you shivering about?" Gable asks. "I was just thinking how cold I'm going to be when they take off my skin and I have to sit around in my bones," Carrillo replies.–*Too Hot to Handle* (1938)

1585 "I'm so scared," admits Bob Hope in a haunted house, "even my goose pimple got goose pimples."–*The Cat and the Canary* (1939)

1586 The Wizard of Oz (Frank Morgan) expounds upon the way he arrived at Oz. "While performing spectacular stratospheric feats never before attempted by civilized man," he explains, "an unfortunate phenomenon occurred – the balloon failed to return to earth." "Weren't you frightened?" the cowardly lion (Bert Lahr) queries. "Frightened?" Morgan echoes. "You're talking to a man who laughed at the face of death, sneered at doom, chuckled at catastrophe – I was petrified!" – *The Wizard of Oz* (1939)

1587 After Dorothy (Judy Garland) is captured by the Wicked Witch, the Cowardly Lion (Bert Lahr) screws up all his courage to enter the witch's castle to save Dorothy. "There's only one thing I want you fellers to do," he says to Tin Man Jack Haley and Scarecrow Ray Bolger. "What's that?" they ask. "Talk me out of it." – *The Wizard of Oz* (1939)

1588 Bob Hope is investigating a spooky Cuban mansion. "I'm going upstairs to look around," he says to valet Willie Best. "If two fellows come running down, let the first one go – that'll be me!" – *The Ghost Breakers* (1940)

1589 Bob Hope and Bing Crosby, down and out in Singapore and desperate, order a hearty meal. They are soon faced with impending danger. "These guys got knives," Hope observes. "They don't monkey around. They may want to get the food back the hard way." – *Road to Singapore* (1940)

1590 Bing Crosby tries to persuade circus performer Bob Hope into wrestling with an octopus. "Those things are murderous," Hope complains. "That's not spaghetti he's waving. Besides, those things are poisonous. They spit ink." "That's even better," Crosby says. "You can wrestle him and write home at the same time." – *Road to Zanzibar* (1941)

1591 Topper (Roland Young) informs his frightened chauffeur Eddie "Roches-ter" Anderson that they're looking for a body. "Better look for me too," Rochester requests, "'cause the one I'm using is numb." – *Topper Returns* (1941)

1592 During a murder investigation, chauffeur Eddie "Rochester" Anderson tells his boss Topper (Roland Young) that he's returning to Jack Benny where life was serene. "Come, come," says Young, "darkness never hurt anybody." "It ain't the darkness," Rochester grumbles, "it's what's in it." – *Topper Returns* (1941)

1593 "Aren't you afraid?" someone questions struggling songwriter Bert Lahr, who volunteers to confront a gang of crooks. "Have you ever heard my courage questioned?" Lahr challenges. "I've never even heard it mentioned," his girlfriend Patsy Kelly quips. – *Sing Your Worries Away* (1942)

1594 In a restaurant, Mischa Auer is challenged to a duel. To avoid the fight, he tries to leave the premises with these words: "Pardon me, I've got to see a man about a hearse." – *Around the World* (1943)

1595 Ole Olsen and Chic Johnson are in a supposedly haunted house where they hear strange sounds. "Now don't get the idea that I'm afraid," Chic announces, "because I don't believe in ghosts. But, then, I didn't believe in radio either." – *Ghost Catchers* (1944)

1596 Several murders have occurred at an isolated mansion where a will is to be read. The lawyer for the deceased, who is investigating the deaths, asks insurance salesman Jack Haley to act scared as a means of distracting the suspects. "Pretend I'm scared?" Haley repeats. "What do you think I'm shaking from – enthusiasm?" – *One Body Too Many* (1944)

1597 Detective Charlie Chan's chauffeur Mantan Moreland would rather not join Benson Fong, the sleuth's son, in investigating a murder.

"Why do you always have to hurry to a murder case?" Moreland asks. "Why can't you just ooze on down to one?"
—*Dark Alibi* (1946)

1598 Bud Abbott and Lou Costello are in a chamber of horrors where they are delivering two crates containing the dormant bodies of Frankenstein and Dracula. "I've got just two words to say to you," Costello utters. "What's that?" "Hurry back."—*Abbott and Costello Meet Frankenstein* (1948)

1599 Bud Abbott: "I can't understand why you have this terrible fear of animals. What is it?" Lou Costello: "When I was a little baby I was scared by my piggy bank."—*Africa Screams* (1949)

1600 Lou Costello has just had a narrow escape from the clutches of Moroccan cutthroats. "Let's go back to America," he says to Bud Abbott. "There's something I want to take home." "What?" "Me!"—*Abbott and Costello in the Foreign Legion* (1950)

1601 Advertising executives Dennis Morgan and Zachary Scott fear a meeting with their cantankerous client Edmund Gwenn. "Are we late?" Morgan worriedly asks Gwenn's secretary. "I stopped to make my will," Scott quips. —*Pretty Baby* (1950)

1602 Waiter Lou Costello mistakenly gains possession of a valuable map belonging to the notorious pirate Captain Kidd and turns it over to his pal Bud Abbott. "This map is worth a fortune to us," Abbott concludes. "All we have to do is go to Skull Island, search around and find where they buried the treasure." "And if we're caught," Costello adds, "who's going to find where they buried us?"—*Abbott and Costello Meet Captain Kidd* (1952)

1603 A gaunt-looking butler of a spooky mansion answers the door to Leo Gorcey and Huntz Hall, who appear fearful. "In the library, if you please,

gentlemen," the butler directs them. "I haven't got my library card with me," a reluctant Hall blurts out.—*The Bowery Boys Meet the Monsters* (1954)

1604 Jerry Lewis joins a circus and reluctantly signs up as a lion tamer so that he may eventually get a crack at performing as a clown. "Don't be frightened," chief lion tamer Sig Rumann says. "They're only cats." "The only cats I like," Lewis offers, "is my uncle Harry Katz."—*Three Ring Circus* (1954)

1605 Bud Abbott and Lou Costello, visiting the home of a murdered man, witness strange, mysterious sounds. "There's somebody in this house who doesn't belong here," Abbott remarks. "I know who it is," Costello says. "Who?" "Me," Costello replies.—*Abbott and Costello Meet the Mummy* (1955)

1606 Servant Edward Everett Horton, working temporarily for gangster Glenn Ford and his henchmen, all of whom are involved in a scam, stealthily tries to quit when the scheme seems to be unraveling. "Where do you think you're going?" Ford asks. "I'm fleeing from Armageddon, sir," Horton confesses. "With my cardiac condition, I cannot take unhappy endings."—*Pocketful of Miracles* (1961)

1607 When Bing Crosby proposes that Bob Hope pilot a spaceship to the moon, Hope begins to exit the room. "If you leave now," Crosby declares, "you'll be running out on your fellow man." "That still leaves my fellow women," Hope replies.—*The Road to Hong Kong* (1962)

1608 The Three Stooges are stranded on a Greek island. "You go up on the rocks and reconnoiter," Moe directs Curly-Joe, "and if you see any cyclopses, you know what steps to take." "Yeah, fast ones," says Curly-Joe.—*The Three Stooges Meet Hercules* (1962)

1609 U.S. agents are pressuring a reluctant Bob Hope into taking on an assignment in Africa. "There's a plane standing by," an agent informs him. "A plane!" Hope protests. "I get dizzy wearing elevator shoes." – *Call Me Bwana* (1963)

1610 Captain Newman (Gregory Peck) tries to allay the fears of Tony Curtis, a corporal assigned to a mental ward: "Patients are not allowed to have matches or razors or sharp objects of any kind." "But teeth they've got," Curtis counters. – *Captain Newman, M.D.* (1964)

1611 When his fiancée knocks at his door, Ryan O'Neal tries to hide Barbra Streisand outside his hotel window. "I can't," she says. "I'm terrified of heights. I have height-a-phobia." "It's only a ledge," he insists. "I have ledge-a-phobia." – *What's Up, Doc?* (1972)

1612 Harry (James Caan) sees a way to cheat a notorious and quite dangerous safecracker. "Those plans are worth a million bucks!" he says to his pal Walter (Elliott Gould). "Oh, great!" Gould replies. "We could buy a couple of expensive suits to get buried in!" – *Harry and Walter Go to New York* (1976)

Fighting

1613 Chico Marx gets into an altercation with lemonade vendor Edgar Kennedy. "I'll teach you to kick me!" Kennedy rages. "You don't have to teach me," Marx returns. "I know how." – *Duck Soup* (1933)

1614 Stan Laurel tries to prevent a duel between an irate husband and innocent Oliver Hardy. "If you had a face like mine," Laurel explains to the man, "you'd punch me right in the nose – and I'm just the feller that can do it!" – *The Fixer-Uppers* (1935)

1615 Groucho Marx gets into an argument with a competitor bidding for a deed. "If you weren't smaller than me," Groucho snaps, "I'd beat the daylights out of you." "I'm bigger than you are," the man says, rising from his seat. "Well," Groucho parries, "that's another reason." – *Go West* (1940)

1616 W. C. Fields, caught cheating an Indian during a poker game, defends himself against his fellow player who has reached for his bow and arrow. Fields cracks a bottle over the Indian's head. "All they can get me for," he slyly mutters, "is splitting a bottle of whiskey with an Indian." – *My Little Chickadee* (1940)

1617 Servant Eddie "Rochester" Anderson has a swollen eye, resulting from a brawl. Appearing before his employer who asks about his condition, Anderson tries to make light of the incident. "I got into an altercation with an Ethiopian," he explains. – *Birth of the Blues* (1941)

1618 In a dance hall Bud Abbott prods Lou Costello to confront some men who insist on charging Costello an additional fee for listening to the music. "I ain't gonna fight these guys here," Costello explains. "I'll fight them on the field of honor." "They have no honor," Abbott declares. "That's okay," Costello replies. "I got no field." – *In the Navy* (1941)

1619 Bob Hope, locked in a cage, is battling a gorilla, while Bing Crosby shouts glib words of encouragement. "Pour it on him!" Crosby blurts out. "Pour what on him," Hope cries, "my blood?" – *Road to Zanzibar* (1941)

1620 Wealthy Rudy Vallee, who is misled by Claudette Colbert into thinking her husband is a brute, promises to "thrash him within an inch of his life." But he has second thoughts when he discovers the size of her husband. "That's one of the tragedies of this life," he muses. "The men that are most in need of a beating up are always enormous." – *The Palm Beach Story* (1942)

1621 Leader of the East Side Kids Leo Gorcey, who wants to stir up a rival gang, orders one of his boys to throw a tomato into the enemy camp. "That we shall do with relish." "What are you going to do," asks Huntz Hall, "give them a whole meal?" – *Block Busters* (1944)

1622 Challenged to a duel, dashing pianist Louis Jourdan has no intention of keeping the appointment. "I don't mind so much being killed," he quips, "but you know how hard it is for me to get up in the morning." – *Letter from an Unknown Woman* (1948)

1623 "Can't we have some peace here on New Year's Eve?" a mother pleads with her noisy, arguing daughters. "You're confusing New Year's Eve with Christmas," Thelma Ritter corrects her. "This is when we go back to killing each other." – *A Letter to Three Wives* (1949)

1624 "Sir," Montfleury bellows, "I will not allow you to insult me in this manner." "Really?" Cyrano (José Ferrer) questions his romantic rival. "In what manner would you prefer?" – *Cyrano de Bergerac* (1950)

1625 Bob Hope relates the story of how his father fought a Native American with one hand tied behind his back. "Of course," Hope adds, "it might have been a different story if that redskin didn't have one hand tied behind his back." – *Son of Paleface* (1952)

1626 King Arthur (Graham Chapman) does battle with the Black Knight (John Cleese), who continues to fight fiercely even as Arthur is slicing off his arms and legs. "All right," the knight finally relents, "we'll call it a draw." – *Monty Python and the Holy Grail* (1975)

Flirtation

1627 In a Southern gambling house Robert Woolsey cajoles a pretty ingenue: "Come hither and rest on the vest of the chest of the guest who loves you best." – *Dixiana* (1930)

1628 Doughboy Robert Woolsey tries to pick up a French woman in the streets of Paris. "You're making a bad mistake," she warns him. "You may be bad," Woolsey replies, "but you're no mistake." – *Half Shot at Sunrise* (1930)

1629 Sailor Lloyd Hughes, while flirting with saloon entertainer Bebe Daniels, wastes no time. "How'd you like to see where I'm tattooed?" he asks. – *Love Comes Along* (1930)

1630 Nurse: "Let me hold your hand." Eddie Cantor: "I can hold it, it's not heavy." – *Whoopee!* (1930)

1631 A pretty passenger whose taxi has become involved in an auto accident accepts a ride in a limousine from man-about-town Lowell Sherman, who then orders his chauffeur to ride around Central Park. "Now, now," he says, putting his hand on hers as he tries to allay her fears, "be reasonable." "I knew I should have taken a taxi," she says, pulling her hand away. "I'd act the same way in a taxi," he quips. – *Bachelor Apartment* (1931)

1632 Charles Ruggles is in love with longtime friend Jeanette MacDonald, who is happily married to Maurice Chevalier, but this doesn't stop Ruggles from flirting with her. "I tell you," he confesses, "if I didn't have a splendid education, I'd yield to the animal in me." – *One Hour with You* (1932)

1633 "Sing to me," a sexy blonde entreats Bert Wheeler. "How about 'One Hour with You'?" he suggests. "Sure," she replies, "but first sing to me." – *Diplomaniacs* (1933)

1634 Sensual dancer Mae West parades along her runway titillating the male audience. "Penny for your thoughts," she quips. "Am I makin' myself clear, boys?" – *I'm No Angel* (1933)

1635 Sailor Randolph Scott comes on to Lucille Ball with a winsome line and smile: "Hello, how was heaven when you left?" "Tell me, little boy," she indignantly replies, "did you get a whistle or a baseball bat with that suit?" – *Follow the Fleet* (1936)

1636 Mae West's limousine breaks down, and local mechanic Randolph Scott is called in to make the repairs. "I'm sorry," he says. "I don't carry spare parts." "Of course not," she replies, noticing his well-built frame. "I wouldn't expect you to." – *Go West, Young Man* (1936)

1637 Stranger Bob Hope and Shirley Ross sit next to each other in a producer's waiting room. Hope comes on strong with a barrage of chatter. "Do you mind being quiet?" she requests. "I'm trying to concentrate on ignoring you." – *Some Like It Hot* (1939)

1638 In a doctor's office Curley of the Three Stooges, who is impersonating a dog, flirts with another patient and asks

her for a date. The woman slaps him in the face. "Oh, hit a dumb animal, will you?" he mutters. – *From Nurse to Worse* (1940)

1639 Groucho Marx joins several stagecoach passengers journeying to the West. The bumpy ride causes one woman to go spinning around in the coach. "Madam," he addresses the ruffled passenger, "It's none of my business, but are you wearing a revolving door? If you are, I'd like to go around with you sometime." – *Go West* (1940)

1640 "I wonder what kind of a woman you are," masked bandit Joseph Calleia challenges flirtatious Flower Belle (Mae West). "Too bad I don't give out samples," she returns. – *My Little Chickadee* (1940)

1641 Texas Ranger Gary Cooper, only in Canada a few days, has been romancing nurse Madeleine Carroll. Lynne Overman, a scout for the Royal Mounted Police, has been noticing Cooper's progress. "Do you have fast horses in Texas?" asks Overman. "Yes," Cooper replies, puzzled by the question. "I'm bettin' they can't keep up with the men." – *North West Mounted Police* (1940)

1642 Cowboy Franchot Tone and flirtatious seventeen-year-old Peggy Moran are heading back to the ranch. "Walk behind me," he orders. "Why?" she asks. "Because that's where you put temptation." – *Trail of the Vigilantes* (1940)

1643 Aboard an ocean liner, gullible scientist Henry Fonda, more knowledgeable about reptiles than women, wishes to spend more time with con artist Barbara Stanwyck. "Don't you think we ought to go right to bed?" she suggests innocently. – *The Lady Eve* (1941)

1644 "Don't be so free with your hands," a waitress warns W. C. Fields. "Listen, honey," Fields replies, "I was only trying to guess your weight."

–Never Give a Sucker an Even Break (1941)

1645 Ladies' man Edmund Lowe approaches attractive Binnie Barnes at a racetrack. "Pardon me, may I look at your form," he announces, then quickly adds "–your racing form?"*–Call Out the Marines* (1942)

1646 Pretty reporter Lynn Bari charms slow-witted policeman Ed Gargan into giving her some information she needs and then thanks him for his help. "Always glad to help a good-looking babe," he says. "Aren't you cute?" "Cuter than you think, sister," he adds. "Want to see my baby pictures?" "Not at night. I scare too easy."*–The Falcon Takes Over* (1942)

1647 Underworld figure Edward G. Robinson acquires a leather goods store next to a bank he intends to rob and inadvertently attracts a widow who owns a lingerie shop across the street. "I wish you'd drop in and look over my lingerie sometime," she offers. "Yes," Robinson returns, "and you drop in and look over my trunks."*–Larceny, Inc.* (1942)

1648 British agent Madeleine Carroll feigns an interest in Bob Hope so that she can retrieve a broach she had earlier planted on him. "Kiss me," she demands. "I've given up kissing strange women," he declares. "What made you stop?" "Strange women."*–My Favorite Blonde* (1942)

1649 Photographer and ladies' man Philip Terry comes on too strong to Audrey Long. "Please play hard to get," she informs him. "I hate pushovers." *–Pan-Americana* (1945)

1650 Humphrey Bogart likens Lauren Bacall to a thoroughbred. "You've got a touch of class, but I don't know how—how far you can go." "Depends who is in the saddle," Bacall teases.*–The Big Sleep* (1946)

1651 Allyn Joslyn, interested in Carole

Landis, who is walking her dog, tries an indirect approach. "Does he do tricks– retrieve, things like that?" he asks nonchalantly. "Yes," she answers politely, "but he doesn't pick up."*–It Shouldn't Happen to a Dog* (1946)

1652 A voluptuous guest sidles over to Cornblow, the new hotel manager (Groucho Marx). "I'm Beatrice Rheiner. I stop at the hotel." "I'm Ronald Cornblow. I stop at nothing."*–A Night in Casablanca* (1946)

1653 "High polish or dull finish?" an attractive manicurist in a barbershop asks customer Frank Fay. "My dear," he retorts, "I don't think anything you start could have a dull finish."*–Love Nest* (1951)

1654 Jewel thief Peter Lawford sees voluptuous Dawn Addams for the first time. "I think if a jewel thief looked at you," he remarks, "he'd never know what jewelry you were wearing."*–The Hour of 13* (1952)

1655 "In college," Bob Hope says to Jane Russell, "I majored in geology and anthropology and running out of gas on Bunker Hill. What's your name, honey?" *–Son of Paleface* (1952)

1656 "You're the most attractive girl in the room," Elliot Reid says to Jane Russell. "So I came over to tell you." "I might as well warn you," Russell replies. "Flattery will get you anywhere."*–Gentlemen Prefer Blondes* (1953)

1657 Picnicking on the scenic French Riviera, elegant Grace Kelly extends to suave Cary Grant a basket of chicken. "Would you like a leg?" she asks. "I think I'd prefer a breast, actually," he says after a slight deliberation.*–To Catch a Thief* (1955)

1658 Flirtatious Janis Paige, failing to entice happily married David Niven, suggests that he is cold. "I'm not cold," he objects. "I'm just not available." "Don't be silly, sweetie," she counters.

"Everyone's available who isn't dead." –
Please Don't Eat the Daisies (1960)

1659 On a Swiss hotel terrace, debonair C.I.A. undercover agent Cary Grant meets modish, detached Audrey Hepburn and begins to flirt with her. "I already know a great many people," she says. "Until one of them dies, I couldn't possibly meet anyone else." – *Charade* (1963)

1660 Swedish foreign ministry liaison employee Elke Sommer meets womanizer and Nobel Prize winner Paul Newman at the Stockholm airport. Following some verbal parrying, he asks: "Will you marry me?" "We have a saying in Sweden," she replies. "'Why settle for one dish when there is smorgasbord?'" – *The Prize* (1963)

1661 "I'm not sticking to any one girl," boasts eligible bachelor Dean Martin. "My life's going to be one big happy smorgasbord." "Well," says available Carol Burnett, "if you ever need a piece of herring, you know where to find me." – *Who's Been Sleeping in My Bed?* (1963)

1662 James Bond (Sean Connery) pursues a pretty suspect, forces her car into a ditch, and makes the incident seem like an accident. "You don't look like the sort of girl who should be ditched," he remarks before offering her a ride. – *Goldfinger* (1964)

1663 Pretty secretary Michele Lee, who likes new employee Robert Morse, volunteers to help him with any problems. "I'm always available," she offers. "One of these days I hope I could show my appreciation –" "Lunch," she interjects. "Huh?" "I said lunch." "What about lunch?" he asks, a little slow on the uptake. "I'd love to," she quickly replies. "I thought you'd never ask me." – *How to Succeed in Business Without Really Trying* (1967)

1664 Foreign ambassador Vito Scotti relentlessly pursues nurse Ingrid Bergman for a date. "The members of my family are very persistent," he remarks, pressing his point. "For two hundred years after Columbus, we persisted in thinking the world was flat." – *Cactus Flower* (1969)

1665 British agent James Bond (Roger Moore) is briefed on his next assignment, but before leaving headquarters he obtains further information from Miss Moneypenny, his superior's secretary. "Moneypenny," Bond says, "you're better than a computer." "In all sorts of ways," she adds, "but you never take advantage of them." – *The Man with the Golden Gun* (1974)

1666 "You know," Bill Cosby says to shapely Raquel Welch, "if I was only twenty years younger –" "I'd only be three," she interjects. – *Mother, Jugs and Speed* (1976)

1667 "You've got a nice profile," hitchhiker Sally Field says to truck driver Burt Reynolds, "especially from the side." – *Smokey and the Bandit* (1977)

1668 C.I.A. operative Walter Matthau cautiously eyes Glenda Jackson's sleek Doberman. "Does he bite?" he asks. "Only people he doesn't like." "I only bite people I like," says Matthau leeringly. – *Hopscotch* (1980)

1669 Womanizing doctor Tony Roberts, wishing to have a female companion for his trip to the country, approaches a young, shapely nurse (Julie Hagerty). "Did you not know that I've had my eye on you these last two weeks?" he says sweetly. "Well," she replies, "I've only been working here for five days." – *A Midsummer Night's Sex Comedy* (1982)

1670 Minor league baseball pitcher Richard Pryor and his carefree pal John Candy come before a tough judge on charges of fighting over a woman in a bar. "So you were making advances to a woman who was involved with another man," the judge states. "If you don't make calls, you don't make any sales,"

Candy jokingly replies to the judge.
— *Brewster's Millions* (1985)

1671 A young Mexican beauty finds Chevy Chase sexually attractive. "We could take a walk and you could kiss me on the veranda," she suggests. "Lips will be fine," he replies. — *Three Amigos!* (1986)

1672 Infatuated with pretty Molly Ringwald, pick-up artist Robert Downey tries one of his standard lines on her. "Did anyone ever tell you you're too good to be true?" "Only that I'm too truthful to be good," she fires back. — *The Pick-Up Artist* (1987)

1673 Across a spacious, crowded movie set, visitor Bugsy Siegel (Warren Beatty) zeros in on obscure actress Annette Bening standing with an unlit cigarette. He moves quickly to her side. "May I?" he asks. "If you want a simple yes or no," she replies teasingly, "you're going to have to finish the question." — *Bugsy* (1991)

1674 A backstage technician who is attracted to a script girl asks: "What do I have to give you for one little kiss?" "Chloroform," she replies. — *For the Boys* (1991)

1675 "Anybody ever tell you you've got a cute butt?" man-crazed waitress Cora (Kate Nelligan) says to Johnny (Al Pacino), recently released from prison where he worked in the kitchen. "Yeah," he replies, "on my last job." — *Frankie and Johnny* (1991)

1676 Two hapless buddies at a Harlem dance try to pick up a sexy young woman who seems to be alone. "Excuse me," one says, "do we know you?" "Not in this lifetime," she retorts. — *A Rage in Harlem* (1991)

Food

1677 "We want to double up," hotel guest Chico Marx, accompanied by Harpo, says to hotel owner Groucho. "Eat some green apples," Groucho advises. — *The Cocoanuts* (1929)

1678 "I can't eat this duck," a customer complains to waiter Robert Woolsey. "Send for the manager." "It's no use," Woolsey replies. "He won't eat it either." — *Half Shot at Sunrise* (1930)

1679 Convicts Spencer Tracy and Warren Hymer escape from prison. "I hate these country prisons," Tracy remarks. "I hate all prisons," Hymer adds. "The food is bad." — *Up the River* (1930)

1680 Hypochondriac Eddie Cantor brings a small calf to his nurse. "What's that?" she asks. "Condensed milk," he quips. — *Whoopee!* (1930)

1681 Mexican bandit Victor Varconi checks out the captive women his lieutenant has rounded up. "Aren't you afraid of me?" Varconi says to one particularly brazen señorita. "No," she replies. "I know — what you call — my onions." "I guess you know all the vegetables," he quips. — *Captain Thunder* (1931)

1682 "Will you join me in a bowl of soup?" Robert Woolsey asks Robert Wheeler. "I'd love to. Will there be room for both of us?" — *Caught Plastered* (1931)

1683 "Poached eggs on toast, please," a woman orders at a drug store counter. "Adam and Eve on a raft!" Bert Wheeler shouts to the cook. "No," the customer says, "scramble them, please." "Break the raft!" Wheeler calls out. — *Caught Plastered* (1931)

1684 "How about my order of liver?" a woman asks counterman Bert Wheeler. "Your order of liver?" he echoes. "Why, lady, there are three orders ahead of you. Surely, you don't want your liver out of order."—*Caught Plastered* (1931)

1685 Charlie Chan (Warner Oland): "This is unexpected as squirt from aggressive grapefruit."—*Charlie Chan's Chance* (1932)

1686 Eugene Pallette, a worker with a failing carnival, informs barker Lee Tracy that several other members have quit the show, including the snake charmer. "Too bad," comments Tracy. "We could have eaten that python." —*The Half Naked Truth* (1932)

1687 The twelve jurors of a murder case are confined to the jury room where they argue the fine points of the case. Later, food is delivered, and juror Ken Murray distributes the platters. "I ordered pork chops and wanted them lean," demands a finicky juror. "You want them to lean to the right or to the left?" Murray quips.—*Ladies of the Jury* (1932)

1688 Jimmy Durante, as a cook aboard a submarine, is indignant when sailor Eugene Pallette complains about the food. "What's the matter with the ham? It's imported from the United States." "They must have towed it all the way over," Pallette growls. "It's salty." "That's the way you cure ham," Durante explains. "If that ham was cured," Pallette ripostes, "it had a relapse." —*Hell Below* (1933)

1689 "Beulah," Mae West orders her maid, "peel me a grape."—*I'm No Angel* (1933)

1690 "What have you got in the way of steaks?" a customer asks grocery-store owner W. C. Fields. "Nothing's in the way of steaks," he quips. "You can get right to them."—*It's a Gift* (1934)

1691 W. C. Fields enters a boarding-house dining room to find a full table of house guests noisily slurping away. "The soup sounds good," he says.—*The Old Fashioned Way* (1934)

1692 Gracie Allen to George Burns: "Your breakfast will be ready in six minutes. I'll just put on two three-minute eggs."—*Six of a Kind* (1934)

1693 "How about a nice plate of beans and a pot of steaming hot coffee?" Oliver Hardy suggests. "Swell," Stan Laurel replies. "You sure know how to plan a meal!"—*Them Thar Hills* (1934)

1694 William Powell and Myrna Loy, as Nick and Nora Charles, host a dinner for criminals and police in an attempt to solve a murder case. "Waiter, will you serve the nuts," Nora orders, and then corrects herself. "I mean, will you serve the guests the nuts."—*The Thin Man* (1934)

1695 Wallace Beery, who knows that his brother Lionel Barrymore harbors a peculiar notion that a certain oil in bluefish is poisonous, teases him about the fish he is eating. "I suspect a plot," Beery suggests. "This fish looks blue to me. Very blue. In fact, it looks despondent."—*Ah, Wilderness* (1935)

1696 "Have you got any stewed prunes?" Groucho Marx asks a waiter. "Sure." "Well," Groucho advises, "give them some coffee. That'll sober them up."—*A Night at the Opera* (1935)

1697 "Take a hamburger, for instance," Allen Jenkins questions self-proclaimed chef Eric Rhodes. "Did you ever toss one together, maestro?" "Please," Rhodes says, "never mention that disgusting word in my presence again." "What word? 'Maestro'?"—*A Night at the Ritz* (1935)

1698 Mae West, having put sugar in her coffee, hands the spoon to Victor McLaglen. "Here, you do it," she requests. "Stirring gets on my nerves." —*Klondike Annie* (1936)

1699 "Judge Teller will sit on my right hand and you will sit on my left hand," Margaret Dumont announces to Groucho Marx." "How will you eat?" Groucho asks. "Through a tube?"–*At the Circus* (1939)

1700 Groucho Marx introduces socialite Margaret Dumont to a formal gathering. Each time she tries to speak, the sound of an elephant is heard from the circus outside. "You should cut out starches," Groucho mutters to Dumont. –*At the Circus* (1939)

1701 A foppish guest at a French estate is in a quandary over his breakfast selection. Should he dine on kidneys, chicken livers or an omelet? "Wasn't there some animal," he asks, "who starved between two haystacks because he couldn't decide?" "Yes," confirms host John Barrymore. "Jackass."–*Midnight* (1939)

1702 Band leader Kay Kyser questions a contestant during one of his radio quiz shows: "If I take the yellow of four eggs, a quart of milk, three cups of flour, a whole hunk of lard, a pinch of butter and mix them all up, what would you have?" "Indigestion."–*That's Right, You're Wrong* (1939)

1703 "Haven't you come to the wrong college?" a student prankster asks Stan Laurel and Oliver Hardy. "You're dressed for Eton." "That's swell," Stan answers. "We haven't eaten since breakfast."–*A Chump at Oxford* (1940)

1704 Texas Ranger Gary Cooper, hunting for an outlaw in Canada, is invited to spend the night at the barracks of the Royal Mounties. "Reveille is at six o'clock," sergeant Preston Foster announces. "Say, you fellas are pretty fancy," remarks Cooper, "having Italian food for breakfast."–*North West Mounted Police* (1940)

1705 "I don't care what you say about the soup," waitress Ginger Rogers jokes with one of her customers, "but don't

pick on the coffee–it's too weak to fight back."–*Primrose Path* (1940)

1706 Sailor Lou Costello examines a blackened piece of toast on the way to the captain's quarters. "What's this," he asks, "a burnt offering?"–*In the Navy* (1941)

1707 "Now I know why drug stores have lunch counters," drug store employee Deanna Durbin remarks. "They lose a lot of money on food and make a big profit on bicarbonate of soda."–*It Started with Eve* (1941)

1708 Lou Costello's soup contains a grunting frog while Bud Abbott is enjoying every mouthful from his plate. "The soup speaks for itself," Abbott reassures his critical pal. "You can say that again," replies Costello.–*Keep 'Em Flying* (1941)

1709 Song plugger Red Skelton, amazed by his girlfriend Virginia O'Brien's ravenous appetite, watches her consume everything and anything within her reach. "You know," he cautions her, "you're going to ruin your appetite if you don't stop eating between bites." –*Lady Be Good* (1941)

1710 Elderly U.S. Senator Victor Moore enters an exclusive French restaurant in New Orleans and, unable to decipher the exotic dishes, orders a ham sandwich. "We don't serve ham sandwiches!" the indignant owner states emphatically. "Oh, I understand," Moore replies. "This is a kosher restaurant." –*Louisiana Purchase* (1941)

1711 New Orleans restaurant owner Vera Zorina joins U.S. Senator Victor Moore for lunch. Moore, who drinks only hot water with his meals, offers some to his guest. "Hot water?" he asks. "No, thank you," she replies. "I've just had a bath."–*Louisiana Purchase* (1941)

1712 "I didn't make disparaging remarks about your steak," W. C. Fields explains to plump waitress Jody Gilbert. "I merely said that I hadn't seen that old horse that you used to keep outside around here lately." – *Never Give a Sucker an Even Break* (1941)

1713 A disagreeable chef at a country inn watches as a group of annual guests enter the premises. "Now *they'll* want lunch," he grumbles to the owner. "Well, they had lunch last year." "And they're able to come back again?" a maid quips. – *Obliging Young Lady* (1941)

1714 Bob Hope and Bing Crosby are surrounded by hostile African natives, and Hope prepares to do battle. "What do you want to be," Crosby questions, "the man who came to dinner?" – *Road to Zanzibar* (1941)

1715 In an expensive nightclub, innocent Buddy Ebsen questions the high cost of a plain hamburger. "That includes the cover charge," a friendly cigarette girl explains. "What do they cover it with?" he questions. – *Sing Your Worries Away* (1942)

1716 The guests at a wedding are ushered into another room for the ceremony. Adolphe Menjou, the father of the groom, observes a mother breast feeding her baby. "Wedding breakfast *after* the ceremony, please," he quips. – *Hi Diddle Diddle* (1943)

1717 "Did you ever see an exciting photograph of an egg?" photographer Claudette Colbert asks her sister Ilka Chase. "The only time an egg ever excites me," Chase replies, "is when I'm hungry." – *No Time for Love* (1943)

1718 Googie Withers, waiting upon the self-centered Clive Brook, acknowledges that her rice pudding leaves something to be desired. "I'm afraid I haven't put enough milk in it," she confesses. "I agree," he says. "But what it lacks in milk it makes up for in rice." – *On Approval* (1943)

1719 Entertainer Bob Hope, traveling on a galleon, sees the crew scurrying to and fro after they discern a pirate ship

in the distance. Hope, however, is oblivious to the impending danger. "What is it," he asks, "lunch hour?" – *The Princess and the Pirate* (1944)

1720 Hypochondriac Danny Kaye and pal Dana Andrews take their dates to an expensive restaurant where Danny questions the kind of milk he is served. "Cow's milk," the waiter says. "Haven't you got any goat's milk?" Danny asks. "No," the waiter replies, "the goat is out shooting pool with his friends." – *Up in Arms* (1944)

1721 Wealthy American Lea Penman informs English butler Bob Hope: "I want to chew the fat." "So soon after dinner?" asks Hope. – *Fancy Pants* (1950)

1722 The local giant captures Jack (Lou Costello) and the village butcher (Bud Abbott) and takes them to his fortress where his cook asks if he wants any supper. "Just a midnight snack," says the giant. "Anyone we know?" she inquires. – *Jack and the Beanstalk* (1951)

1723 Bud Abbott tells Lou Costello to study a treasure map of Skull Island and swallow it so that only he will know its secret. Costello chews, swallows and hiccups. "It must have been one of the rocks on the island," he figures. – *Abbott and Costello Meet Captain Kidd* (1952)

1724 Groucho Marx at a drive-in food stand: "I'll take the full-course dinner for eighty-five cents. On second thought, cancel the dinner and give me the eighty-five cents." – *A Girl in Every Port* (1952)

1725 Pals Victor Mature and Jesse White visit Esther Williams in her apartment where she invites them to stay for dinner. "I'm making Australian stew," she announces. "What's that?" White asks. "The same as Irish stew, except the meat's down under." – *Million Dollar Mermaid* (1952)

1726 A native mother rebukes her two cannibal sons for roughing up white captives Bob Hope and Bing Crosby. "How many times have I told you," she shouts, "don't play with the food!" – *Road to Bali* (1952)

1727 "Why don't you eat something?" U.S. Marine Mort Saul suggests to a buddy during World War II. "I keep throwing up," the fellow Marine replies. "It's all part of nature's plan," Saul explains. "It's protection against C rations." – *In Love and War* (1958)

1728 The Three Stooges are transported to a Greek battlefield, circa 900 B.C., where their presence helps a tyrant win the way. As a reward, he invites them for wine and food. "Sounds good to me," says Curly-Joe. "I haven't eaten in three thousand years." – *The Three Stooges Meet Hercules* (1962)

1729 When teenager Barry Gordon urges his society-dropout uncle Jason Robards to look for work, Robards claims he can't – it's a "holiday." "Irving R. Feldman's birthday is my personal national holiday," Robards explains. "...He is the proprietor of perhaps the most distinguished kosher delicatessen in our neighborhood, and as such, I hold the day of his birth in reverence." – *A Thousand Clowns* (1965)

1730 Ina Mela, the wife of an exterminator, wants to prove to her husband that she is interested in his work. She bakes him a cake in the shape of a termite. "What is that?" he cries. "A termite cake," she answers. "I exterminate them!" he exclaims. "I don't eat them!" – *Crazy Quilt* (1966)

1731 At a cocktail party, amateur spy Dom DeLuise has planted a tiny radio transmitter in an hors d'oeuvre – to the consternation of one of the guests. "I thought I saw one of the hors d'oeuvres move!" the guest exclaims. "Oh, sure," a skeptical Paul Lynde remarks, "probably a shrimp trying to get back to sea." – *The Glass Bottom Boat* (1966)

1732 Elliott Gould rushes into his favorite delicatessen and shouts to a waiter: "Let me have a double on an onion roll – half brisket, half pastrami, pickles, sour tomatoes, no sauerkraut. My stomach's acting up." – *The Night They Raided Minsky's* (1968)

1733 Waiter: "Who ordered a herring? We're out." Customer: "Oh." Waiter: "For you I'll stretch a sardine." – *The Night They Raided Minsky's* (1968)

1734 Oscar (Walter Matthau) prepares to share his apartment with Felix (Jack Lemmon), who mentions that he can cook. "You don't have to cook," Matthau explains. "I have enough potato chips to last me a year." – *The Odd Couple* (1968)

1735 The friendship between roommates Walter Matthau, a confirmed slob, and Jack Lemmon, obsessed with neatness, has deteriorated. Matthau finally explodes and throws a plate of what he thinks is spaghetti against the wall. "It's linguine," the fastidious Lemmon corrects him. "Now it's garbage," Matthau counters. – *The Odd Couple* (1968)

1736 Former chain gang convict Virgil Starkwell (Woody Allen) describes the meals given to his fellow prisoners: "The men got only one hot meal a day – a bowl of steam." – *Take the Money and Run* (1969)

1737 At a diner which adheres to a set of strict rules, Jack Nicholson can't substitute tomatoes for potatoes or get a side order of toast. Determined to get his order, he asks for a chicken-salad sandwich on wheat toast. "Now all you have to do," he instructs the reluctant waitress, "is hold the chicken, bring me the toast, give me a check for the chicken-salad sandwich, and you haven't broken any rules." – *Five Easy Pieces* (1970)

1738 Charles Grodin, who is pursuing blonde midwesterner Cybill Shepherd, is having dinner in her parents' home. "It's simple food," she says to Grodin. "I imagine that you tried just about every exotic dish in New York." "Exactly," Grodin responds. "It's exotic, but it's not honest. It's fancy but it's not real. But this is honest food. There's no lying in that beef. There's no insincerity in those potatoes. There's no deceit in the cauliflower. This is a totally honest meal. You don't know what a pleasure it is in this day and age to eat food that you can believe in." – *The Heartbreak Kid* (1972)

1739 "There's an old joke," Woody Allen narrates at the beginning of the film. "Two elderly women are at a Catskill Mountain resort, and one of them says, 'Boy, the food at this place is really terrible.' The other one says, 'Yeah, I know, and such small portions.'" – *Annie Hall* (1977)

1740 Condo developer Rodney Dangerfield at a country-club dinner comments on the meat he is served: "This steak still has the mark of the jockey's whip on it." – *Caddyshack* (1980)

1741 Woody Allen's car breaks down on a country road at dusk. With no other vehicles or houses in sight, girlfriend Jessica Harper tries to cheer him up. "You know," she says, "there's got to be something around here." "I don't know," Allen replies. "They're going to find us wandering in the woods six months from now living on locusts and wild honey." – *Stardust Memories* (1980)

1742 Los Angeles detectives Tommy Chong and Cheech Marin are sniping at each other over lunch. "Man, I like you fat," Chong confesses. "It makes me look skinnier. I don't have to go on a diet. I just let my partner eat like a pig." – *Cheech and Chong's Nice Dreams* (1981)

1743 Raoul (Robert Beltran), a smalltime criminal, is eating in a fast food restaurant when a stranger (Susan Saiger), dressed as a nun, accosts him. "You have been very wicked and are in terrible danger," she warns him. "So is everybody who eats here," he quips. – *Eating Raoul* (1982)

1744 In this black comedy, unemployed wine salesman Paul Bartel and his wife

Mary Woronov, who hope to open a gourmet restaurant, kill weirdoes for their money. They murder Raoul, their Hispanic partner, and serve him as the main dinner course to their guest, a real-estate broker. "I hope you make this a permanent item on your menu," the guest suggests. "It's French?" "No," Woronov replies. "Actually, it's more Spanish." – *Eating Raoul* (1982)

1745 Down-and-out singer Julie Andrews plans not to pay the check at a Paris restaurant, so she orders double portions of each course. At one point she complains to the waiter about one dish, mentioning that the meat was slightly tough. "Maybe the way you are eating," the waiter ripostes, "your jaws are getting tired." – *Victor/Victoria* (1982)

1746 Robert De Niro is riding in a crowded elevator contentedly eating a hot dog. "You shouldn't be eating here," an angry woman sharply rebukes him. "People have clothes on." – *Falling in Love* (1984)

1747 While having dinner at a lavish Long Island residence, Richard Crenna, one of Brooklyn's nouveau riche, rejects the tomato aspic: "I don't want anything on my plate that moves." – *The Flamingo Kid* (1984)

1748 Big-time gangster Johnny Dangerously (Michael Keaton) visits his impoverished mother (Maureen Stapleton) and kid brother. "Whatcha cookin', Ma?" "Beer," she replies. – *Johnny Dangerously* (1984)

1749 Nightclub owner and gangster Johnny Dangerously (Michael Keaton), serving time in the "big house," receives a visit from his girlfriend who informs him that one of his underlings is ruining his club. "He's turning the place into a dive," she explains. "He's attracting the worst element. And Johnny–" "Don't tell me!" he interjects. "He put in a salad bar!" – *Johnny Dangerously* (1984)

1750 Popular radio actors Gene Wilder and Gilda Radner announce to reporters that they will be married within the week. "How's her cooking?" a reporter asks. "Have you tasted it yet?" "Sure, sure," Wilder replies, "but we're getting married anyway." – *Haunted Honeymoon* (1986)

1751 A lawyer approaches assistant district attorney Robert Redford to thank him for his help. "You were right about the landlady," the attorney affirms. "I got her on the stand and she cracked like an egg. I crushed her like a walnut. She blubbered like bleu cheese." "He ought to run a restaurant," Redford quips about his poetic colleague. – *Legal Eagles* (1986)

1752 In a Saigon open-air market a Vietnamese youth urges U.S. army disc jockey Robin Williams to taste a native delicacy. Williams stares suspiciously at the dish and says: "I don't like to eat anything that's still paddling." – *Good Morning, Vietnam* (1987)

1753 "Thin's my middle name," police sergeant Danny Glover says to his partner Mel Gibson. "With your wife's cookin'," jokes Gibson, "I'm not surprised." "Remarks like that will not get you invited to Christmas dinner." "My luck's changing for the better every day." – *Lethal Weapon* (1987)

1754 One draftee at an army base during World War II comments on the mess hall food: "If they ever dropped this stuff over Germany, the entire country would come out with their hands up." – *Biloxi Blues* (1988)

1755 "I don't know if she's Irish," Burt Lancaster says about his wife, "but every time I eat a cookie, I turn green." – *Rocket Gibraltar* (1988)

1756 On a small apple orchard, struggling farmer Sam Elliot may have to sell his tractor. "Will there be enough to eat?" asks nine-year-old Rebecca Harrell. "Sure," Elliot answers. "We'll have apple sauce, apple juice, stewed apples, apple pie, baked apples . . . ." – *Prancer* (1989)

1757 Harry (Billy Crystal) tries to entertain a dull date who has taken him to an Ethiopian restaurant. "Hey," he says, "I didn't know they had food in Ethiopia. This will be a quick meal. I'll order two empty plates and we can leave." – *When Harry Met Sally . . .* (1989)

1758 Granny (Judith Malina) dishes out one of her concoctions to her brood. "Eat the eyes first," she lovingly suggests. – *The Addams Family* (1991)

1759 American businessman George Kennedy, seeking investments in the former East Germany, visits a small town and, addressing its citizens, promises them "all the things you ever dreamed of." "Take-out Chinese food?" asks an excited German. – *Driving Me Crazy* (1991)

1760 At a pretentious party, down-to-earth Dutch (Ed O'Neill) tries to make conversation with some of the other guests: "I never cared for caviar. I make it a rule never to eat anything a fish deposits on a riverbed." – *Dutch* (1991)

1761 Italian-American Danny Aiello and his ne'er-do-well son Anthony LaPaglia sit down to eat a pizza which Aiello has just made. "You made this?" the son asks. "Yeah, and it cost me one dollar to make – one dollar." "Pop," LaPaglia confesses after taking one bite, "you get better pizza in Korea. Who the hell made that, Michelin? You could put this in the trunk and use it as a spare." – *29th Street* (1991)

1762 Brooklyn attorney Joe Pesci takes his long-term fiancée Marisa Tomei to a quiet little Alabama town where he is defending his cousin on a murder charge. She steps out of his car and takes in the somnolent atmosphere. "I bet the Chinese food in this town is terrible," she remarks. – *My Cousin Vinny* (1992)

Friendship

1763 Stan Laurel and Oliver Hardy are captured by bandits whose chieftain (Dennis King) orders Laurel to hang Hardy. Despondent Laurel reluctantly places the noose around his pal's neck. "Before you go," says Laurel, "there's just one more thing I want to ask you. After you're gone, do you want to be buried or shall I have you stuffed?" "What do you mean 'stuffed'?" Hardy demands to know. "Well, I thought it would be nice to keep you in the living room." – *The Devil's Brother* (1933)

1764 Jack Benny, manager of a penniless troupe of entertainers, wishes to register in a Paris hotel. "We must collect in advance," the clerk announces. "You're strangers." "We're not strangers," Benny protests. "I've known these boys for years, haven't I, fellers?" – *Artists and Models Abroad* (1938)

1765 Oliver Hardy is reunited with his old army buddy Stan Laurel after twenty years and brings him home to his apartment where Hardy's wife complains that he constantly brings his "tramp friends" home. "But I haven't seen Stan in twenty years!" he pleads. "I couldn't see him in a hundred years!" she retorts. – *Block-Heads* (1938)

1766 Two old-time desert rats join a sheriff's posse who are hunting a killer. Once out in the blistering desert, one pal runs out of water. But the other, Francis Ford, refuses to share his canteen. "You wouldn't do that to an ornery horn toad," his friend protests. "No, I wouldn't," replies Ford. "But you haven't advanced that far." – *Bad Lands* (1939)

1767 Circus owner Kenny Baker admits to worker-friend Chico Marx that he has financial problems. "You can always count on me," Chico reassures his pal. "I ain't got nothin', but you can always have half." – *At the Circus* (1939)

1768 "Are you still on speaking terms with your last husband?" Linda Darnell asks acquaintance Binnie Barnes. "Oh, sure," Barnes replies. "I never let a divorce break up a friendship." – *Day-Time Wife* (1939)

1769 Rejected by the woman he loves, Oliver Hardy plans to commit suicide and expects Stan Laurel to join him, but Laurel objects. "Why," Hardy then patiently explains, "people would stare at you and wonder what you are – and I wouldn't be there to tell them." – *The Flying Deuces* (1939)

1770 Pilot Ray Milland, thought to have been killed in the Spanish Civil War, escapes to France where he meets buddies Walter Abel and Dennis O'Keefe. "Hey, you're wearing my suits!" he exclaims. "We wanted something to remember you by," explains Abel, "something that had been very close to you." "How about a couple of pairs of shorts?" Milland suggests jokingly. "We're wearing those too," they laugh. – *Arise, My Love* (1940)

1771 "White man red man's friend!" pronounces Groucho Marx. "White man want to make friends with red brother!" "And sister too," adds Chico Marx. – *Go West* (1940)

1772 "I'll lend you the money on one condition," George Tobias says to friend James Cagney. "If you can't pay me back, you won't get mad at me." – *Strawberry Blonde* (1941)

1773 Charles Coburn, the patriarch of a New York family, welcomes to his home Kansas meat packer Eugene

Pallette and his wife Marjorie Main. "I hope this will be the beginning of a life-long friendship," Coburn announces. "May you lie as solidly anchored in our hearts as you do in our stomachs." *–Heaven Can Wait* (1943)

1774 At a bar, married couple George Murphy and Carole Landis tease their best friend Pat O'Brien, who is trying to avoid them at the moment. "Who are they?" someone asks O'Brien. "A couple of bar flies in the ointment," he quips. *–Having Wonderful Crime* (1945)

1775 Amateur detective Nick Charles (William Powell) has a bottle of his favorite brandy shot out of his hand by a sniper. "Was anyone hurt?" a neighbor inquires. "Yes," Powell quips, "an old friend of mine went completely to pieces." *–Song of the Thin Man* (1947)

1776 Private Jerry Lewis cannot understand why he is being ordered about and hassled by sergeant Dean Martin–who happens to be his old pal. "You were the best man in my wedding," Lewis reminds Martin. "You're not kidding," Martin replies. *–At War with the Army* (1950)

1777 Anne Baxter, who is experiencing marital problems, blames best friend Catherine McLeod for part of the trouble. "I hate you!" Baxter explodes. "I've always hated you! And you've always hated me!" "But that doesn't mean we can't be the best of friends," McLeod replies. *–My Wife's Best Friend* (1952)

1778 Reporter Gene Kelly characterizes prosecuting attorney Fredric March: "He hasn't an enemy in the world. Only his friends hate him." *–Inherit the Wind* (1960)

1779 Quack doctor Peter Sellers awakens a cobra with his flute-playing, and patient Bob Hope begins to panic. Sellers reassures him that if he is bitten, all he need do is suck out the venom and spit it out. "But suppose it bites me in a place I can't reach?" Hope questions.

"That's when you find out who your true friends are," Sellers replies. *–The Road to Hong Kong* (1962)

1780 "I can't take it anymore, Felix," Walter Matthau complains to roommate Jack Lemmon. "I told you one hundred fifty-eight times I cannot stand little notes on my pillow: 'We are all out of corn flakes, F.U.' It took me three hours to figure out F.U. was Felix Unger." *–The Odd Couple* (1968)

1781 The problems of two incompatible friends, Oscar (Walter Matthau) and Felix (Jack Lemmon), have boiled over, and Oscar orders Felix to leave. "In other words, you're throwing me out," Lemmon cries. "Not 'in other words'!" Matthau retorts. "Those are the perfect words!" *–The Odd Couple* (1968)

1782 Three suburban husbands (Ben Gazarra, John Cassavetes, Peter Falk) find in their friendship an embracing, unparalleled camaraderie. "Except for sex–and my wife's very good at sex," Gazarra acknowledges, "I like you guys better." *–Husbands* (1971)

1783 Quirky idealist Bronco Billy (Clint Eastwood) confides to a lady friend how he found his ex-wife in bed with his best friend. "What did you do?" the woman asks. "I shot her." "What?" she exclaims. "What about him?" "He was my best friend." *–Bronco Billy* (1980)

1784 When Steve Martin begins to set up his own apartment, fellow bachelor and friend Charles Grodin is there to assist: "Have you got your towels yet?" "I forgot all about that." "I can get them for you wholesale," Grodin suggests, "if you don't mind other people's initials. I get them from divorced couples." *–The Lonely Guy* (1984)

1785 "In England," quips the eighty-three-year-old gay Englishman Quentin Crisp, "nobody is your friend–you have to make friends. It's very tiring, and when you've made them, you get stuck with them, which is even more tiring. But in America you never get stuck with anybody. Three weeks is a meaningful relationship." – *Resident Alien* (1991)

Gambling

1786 W. C. Fields, on trial for shooting "High Card," a fellow poker player, addresses the jury about the nine aces that showed up in one game. "What is my astonishment," he explains, "when 'High Card' there lays down five aces against my four. I'm a broadminded man, gents. I don't object to nine aces in one deck, but when a man lays down five aces in one hand – and, besides, I know what I dealt him." – *Tillie and Gus* (1933)

1787 "Say, what are you – a bookie?" Helen Broderick asks Victor Moore. "I prefer to be called a horse broker." "It's all right with me if the horses don't mind," she returns. – *She's Got Everything* (1938)

1788 Fuzzy Knight is enticed into a card game by W. C. Fields. "Is this a game of chance?" Fuzzy asks. "Not the way I play it," replies Fields. – *My Little Chickadee* (1940)

1789 Servant Mantan Moreland has heard that by snapping your fingers and saying a few magic words you can disappear. "You can't make anything disappear by snapping your fingers," says a nearby police officer who has been watching him practice the ritual. "No?" questions Moreland. "Then how come every time I snap my fingers and say, 'Come seven,' all my money disappears?" – *Black Magic* (1944)

1790 Broadway producer Cary Grant is about to lose his theater, but crony James Gleason intends to come through in the pinch. "I got a hot poker game tonight," Gleason says. "I better go home and mark some cards. One of us has got to make a living." – *Once Upon a Time* (1944)

1791 Victims of a crooked roulette wheel, Bud Abbott and Lou Costello watch as the ball hops off their winning number to another. "What kind of ball is that?" Abbott complains. "It's got the hiccups," Costello adds. – *The Naughty Nineties* (1945)

1792 "I've had my ups and downs," racetrack gambler Raymond Washburn admits, "but today I can finally say my system is infallible." "It certain is," fellow bettor William Demarest replies. "Fifteen straight losers." – *Riding High* (1950)

1793 Racetrack tout Bob Hope owes a large sum of money to gangsters who inform him that it's serious business. "I always wanted to be a man about town," Hope wisecracks, "but never in chunks." – *The Lemon Drop Kid* (1951)

1794 An oil magnate tells reporters that he struck it rich during a crooked poker game. "How did you know it was crooked?" a reporter asks. "Because I was dealing." – *The French Line* (1954)

1795 Big-time gambler Big Julie comes to New York to shoot craps, but during the game he insists on using his own dice. Nathan Detroit (Frank Sinatra) looks them over and smells a rat – there are no spots on the dice. "I had the spots removed for luck," Julie says reassuringly. "But I remember where the spots formerly were." – *Guys and Dolls* (1955)

1796 Nightclub comic Joe E. Lewis (Frank Sinatra) to his audience: "I only come to Las Vegas for sentimental reasons – I come to visit my money." – *The Joker Is Wild* (1957)

1797 Wealthy executive Yves Montand regales several acquaintances at his club with a story about a man who has taught his dog to play poker. "But the poor dog was a terrible gambler," Montand explains, "because every time he got a good hand he would wag his tail." – *Let's Make Love* (1960)

1798 Steve McQueen and Jim Hutton have developed a system to beat the roulette table at a Venice casino. Hutton, engaged to millionairess Paula Prentiss, introduces her to McQueen. Thinking she is trying to muscle in on his racket, McQueen tries to bribe her. "She's got sixty million dollars of her own," Hutton explains. "What system do you use?" McQueen asks her. – *The Honeymoon Machine* (1961)

1799 Judge John McGiver berates gambling boss Walter Matthau for his involvement in off-track betting. Matthau then accuses the judge of betting on the races. "That's different," McGiver replies. "I play for a specific reason. I don't expect to win." "Then why do you bet?" inquires Matthau. "It annoys my wife." – *Who's Got the Action?* (1962)

1800 Jackie Gleason is stopped on his way to church by a little boy. "Would you buy a raffle for the church for fifty cents?" the lad asks. "Now what would I do with a church if I won one?" Gleason jokes. – *Papa's Delicate Condition* (1963)

1801 The air is heavy with cigarette smoke and tension during a poker game in a Western saloon. "You haven't lost a single hand since you got the deal," a suspicious card player remarks to the Sundance Kid (Robert Redford). "What's the secret to your success?" "Prayer," replies Redford. – *Butch Cassidy and the Sundance Kid* (1969)

1802 "The last horse he bet on was so slow," says Red Buttons about an inveterate gambler, "he kept a diary of the trip." – *Off Your Rocker* (1980)

Gender

1803 Buster Keaton castigates movie actor Robert Montgomery for trying to take advantage of ingénue Anita Page. "You know," Montgomery apologetically begins to explain, "summer night, moonlight, propinquity – " "Huh?" says Keaton. "I don't believe it. If it was, it was all on your side." – *Free and Easy* (1930)

1804 Ace reporter Hildy Johnson (Pat O'Brien), preparing to leave with his fiancée for the East, stumbles upon an escaped convict and, smelling a possible scoop, hides him in the local city hall press room. His sweetheart enters and demands to know what's going on. "Tell her nothing!" exclaims his hardboiled managing editor Walter Burns (Adolphe Menjou). "She's a woman, you fool!" – *The Front Page* (1930)

1805 "I'd love to kiss you," says Bette Davis, warding off being kissed, "but I just washed my hair." – *Cabin in the Cotton* (1932)

1806 Happily married Ronald Colman is dining out with his elderly confidant Henry Stephenson, who befriends two young women at an adjacent booth. "Shall I ask them to join us?" Stephenson asks. "Good heavens, no," Colman replies. "They're respectable girls." "Call no woman respectable until she's dead," his friend quips. – *Cynara* (1932)

1807 "You know," Bobby Clark says to a young beauty, "it's women like you who make men like me make women like you make men like me." – *The Iceman's Ball* (1932)

1808 Jeanette MacDonald admits to friend Charles Ruggles that she was wrong in accusing her husband Maurice Chevalier of having an affair. "You have a right to be wrong," Ruggles says in her defense. "You're a woman. Women are born to be wrong. I like my women wrong." – *One Hour with You* (1932)

1809 Mae West's female acquaintance asks: "Who'd want me after what I've done?" "When women go wrong, men go right after them," West replies. – *I'm No Angel* (1933)

1810 Outside a courtroom a reporter asks Mae West why she admitted to knowing so many men. "It's not the men in my life," she explains, "but the life in my men." – *I'm No Angel* (1933)

1811 Showgirl Aline McMahon meets rich, middle-aged Guy Kibbee and sees a future in the relationship. "He's the kind of man I was looking for," she says to her roommates. "Lots of money and no resistance." – *Gold Diggers of 1933* (1933)

1812 Marlene Dietrich on men: "They're the only animals who have money and buy champagne." – *Song of Songs* (1933)

1813 Maid (Libby Taylor): "Mr. Brooks sure been good to you. Weren't you a little nervous when he gave you those jewels?" Mae West: "No, I was calm and collected." – *Belle of the Nineties* (1934)

1814 Mae West announces to several men at a bar: "It's better to be looked over than overlooked." – *Belle of the Nineties* (1934)

1815 "Gay divorcee" Ginger Rogers does not know how to react to exuberant Fred Astaire. "How shall I treat him?" she asks her aunt. "Be feminine and sweet," her aunt suggests, "if you can blend the two." – *The Gay Divorcee* (1934)

1816 When a garrulous, matronly innkeeper asks Don Juan's man-servant Melville Cooper to describe his favorite dish, he replies: "My favorite dish is a middle-aged woman's tongue cut out by its roots, chopped very small and eaten raw!" – *The Private Life of Don Juan* (1934)

1817 "Why don't you take your wife home a present?" a friend advises W. C. Fields. "A little pet of some kind. Women are crazy about pets." "They're just crazy," Fields retorts. "Pets haven't a thing to do with it." – *You're Telling Me* (1934)

1818 French entertainer Ann Sothern at first rejects baron Maurice Chevalier's romantic overtures but later shows up at his estate. "I know I said I wouldn't come," she reminds him coyly, "but women always mean yes when they say no." – *Folies Bergere* (1935)

1819 Helen Broderick comforts man-troubled Ginger Rogers: "The only difference between men is the color of their tie." – *Top Hat* (1935)

1820 "Get my topcoat and a revolver," a Scotland Yard inspector orders his butler after receiving a phone call. "I'm going out after vampires." "I always thought you went after them with checkbooks, sir," the valet questions. "Don't be facetious," the inspector replies. – *Dracula's Daughter* (1936)

1821 Key Luke, as Charlie Chan's number one son, quotes his famous father: "When woman plays with fire, man gets burned." – *Charlie Chan at the Olympics* (1937)

1822 "What does a brokenhearted dame do first?" a reporter asks a bartender. "Well, generally, they go out and buy themselves a new hat."–*There Goes My Girl* (1937)

1823 "All women pursue–all of them!" Edward Everett Horton warns. "They're like cats in the jungle. They sniff out their man and they stalk after them. They prowl and they sharpen their claws and they pounce!"–*College Swing* (1938)

1824 "What do you got against gals anyway?" Fuzzy Knight asks cowboy pal Gary Cooper. "Oh, they chew your ears off." "Well, maybe you'll get a break and get a dumb one." "That kind ain't been born yet," Cooper complains.–*The Cowboy and the Lady* (1938)

1825 "The way to a man's heart is through his eyes–that's the modern version," remarks Helen Broderick.–*The Rage of Paris* (1938)

1826 "There's only one way to handle a woman," Warner Baxter says to his troubled father-in-law, "be kind but firm!" "I was firm, but she was firmer." –*Wife, Husband and Friend* (1939)

1827 "I've trusted men all my life," admits kooky hostess Mary Boland to her house guests, "and I've never been deceived yet–except by my husbands–and they don't count."–*He Married His Wife* (1940)

1828 Secretary Rosalind Russell regretfully informs confidant John Carroll that her boss Brian Aherne only notices her in the coming of spring. "I put him in his place," she declares. "A good opening move," Carroll adds. "No," she corrects him, "he stayed there." –*Hired Wife* (1940)

1829 When a wealthy house guest displays concern about her valuable jewels, fellow guest Peter Lorre points out that one particular brooch is worthless. "Oh, well," she says philosophically, "so was the man who gave it to me."–*I Was an Adventuress* (1940)

1830 College football player and ladies' man Eddie Bracken surrounds himself with a bevy of pretty Western co-eds who question him about girls from the East. "I went out with a senior at Wellesley," he says. "They're all air-conditioned." "What do you mean 'air-conditioned'?" someone asks. "Forty degrees cooler in the house than on the street," he explains.–*Too Many Girls* (1940)

1831 Ophelia the spinster reveals to Edgar Bergen that she found a burglar under her bed. "Did you call the police?" asks Bergen. "What for?" she replies. "I found him–he's mine!"–*Look Who's Laughing* (1941)

1832 Rooming-house cook Marjorie Main discovers Mary Howard in Dan Dailey's room. "He just wanted to show me his moving pictures," the young woman tries to explain. "Men have been thrown in jail for less," Main replies. –*The Wild Man of Borneo* (1941)

1833 Gardener Edgar Buchanan offers an earthly analogy to a disheartened jealous Henry Fonda: "The earth is a woman–loves one man today, another tomorrow. You'd think she appreciates these flowers as decorations. But no. Again she proves she's a woman at heart by showing a preference for weeds."–*You Belong to Me* (1941)

1834 "Imagination is a wonderful thing," ponders gardener Edgar Buchanan. "Without it, women would wither like prunes."–*You Belong to Me* (1941)

1835 Helen O'Connell to a group of sailors: "I once asked a sailor, 'Would you help a girl in trouble?' and he said, 'Depends on what kind of trouble she wants to get into.'"–*The Fleet's In* (1942)

1836 Englishman Walter Pidgeon, returning from the military-civilian rescue operation at Dunkirk during World War II, is unaware that, during his absence, his wife Greer Garson has heroically captured a downed German pilot. "Oh, darling," he says patronizingly, "I'm almost sorry for you, having such a nice quiet peaceful time when things were really happening. But that's what men are for, isn't it – to go out and do things while you womenfolk look after the house?" – *Mrs. Miniver* (1942)

1837 Claudette Colbert to husband Joel McCrea: "Men don't get smarter as they grow older. They just lose their hair." – *The Palm Beach Story* (1942)

1838 Journalists Roscoe Karns and Spencer Tracy are nettled when fellow writer, political analyst Katharine Hepburn, writes disparaging remarks about baseball. "We men have got only ourselves to blame," Karns confesses. "It's our own fault. Women should be kept illiterate and clean – like canaries." – *Woman of the Year* (1942)

1839 "I love little boys," sexy Lupe Velez boasts, "and big ones, too." – *Mexican Spitfire's Blessed Event* (1943)

1840 After months at sea, several members of the merchant marine recall the girlfriends they left behind and how badly they miss their women. "I don't even have a girl," admits one sailor, "and she's driving me crazy." – *Seven Days Ashore* (1944)

1841 Burlesque theater owner Dennis O'Keefe offers some advice to singer Perry Como, who is suffering from unrequited love: "Women and carpets – they're much better when you beat them regularly." – *Doll Face* (1945)

1842 "A man doesn't chase a fox because he wants a fox," Audrey Long informs Eve Arden, "it's the chase that's fun." – *Pan-Americana* (1945)

1843 Lord Henry (George Sanders) advises the vain Dorian Gray (Hurd Hatfield): "Being adored is a nuisance. You'll discover, Dorian, that women treat us just as humanity treats its gods:

they worship us but keep bothering us to do something for them." – *The Picture of Dorian Gray* (1945)

1844 "I'm analyzing women at present," announces the imperious Lord Henry (George Sanders). "The subject is less difficult than I was led to believe. Women represent the triumph of matter over mind, just as men represent the triumph of the mind over morals." – *The Picture of Dorian Gray* (1945)

1845 A plumber arrives at Reginald Gardiner's apartment, but he and his guest Charles Boyer are surprised that the plumber is a woman (Jennifer Jones). "She's not dressed for plumbing," Boyer comments, "but what woman is?" – *Cluny Brown* (1946)

1846 Society snob Clifton Webb, while giving some information to a detective investigating a murder case, makes this wry observation about a suspect's hatred for a woman: "He loathed her intimately." – *The Dark Corner* (1946)

1847 Franchot Tone's fiancée suspects him of having an affair with another woman. "Call it intuition, if you like," she explains. "Intuition!" he exclaims. "That's a woman's infallible way of arriving at wrong conclusions!" – *Honeymoon* (1947)

1848 William Powell tells his wife (Myrna Loy) he is ready to return home where he can be alone with her. "Give me my pipe, my slippers and a beautiful woman, and you can have my pipe and slippers," he jokes. – *Song of the Thin Man* (1947)

1849 "There are only two kinds of men," says womanizer Nigel Bruce to Walter Pidgeon, "those who admit they like women and the liars." – *Julia Misbehaves* (1948)

1850 "Why did you say I run after everything in skirts?" French captain Cary Grant asks WAC Ann Sheridan. "I didn't," she protests. "You did." "I said

'anything.'" "Oh, that's different, then."
– I Was a Male War Bride (1949)

1851 Lawyer Brian Donlevy, infatuated with nightclub singer Dorothy Lamour, says to the club manager: "A beautiful person adds to the outer graces – the charm and spiritual loveliness. Do I make myself clear?" "Yeah," the manager replies, "you got a yen for the dame." *– The Lucky Stiff* (1949)

1852 A pretty woman rushes into the Three Stooges' detective agency and begs them to help her. "I'm in desperate trouble," she cries. "Strange men are following me." "They'd be strange if they didn't," Shemp quips. *– Dopey Dicks* (1950)

1853 In a restaurant, Paul Douglas notices Ginger Rogers laughing at playwright William Holden's every line. "A woman's laugh," Douglas comments, "is often her mating call." *– Forever Female* (1953)

1854 "I wonder why it is," muses David Niven, "that young men are always cautioned against bad girls; anyone can handle a bad girl. It's the good girls men should be warned against." *– The Moon Is Blue* (1953)

1855 "Women are like oranges," concludes Bob Hope, posing as the great lover Casanova. "When you've squeezed one, you've squeezed them all." *– Casanova's Big Night* (1954)

1856 Sky Masterson (Marlon Brando) spells out his attitude toward the opposite sex to Nathan Detroit (Frank Sinatra): "I am not putting the knock on dolls. It's just that they're something to have around only when they come in handy – like cough drops." *– Guys and Dolls* (1955)

1857 Arthur O'Connell, as friend and guardian of Bo (Don Murray), tells Marilyn Monroe that she was the first girl Bo ever kissed. "He sure didn't kiss

like it was the first time," she says. "Well," O'Connell explains, "Bo picks up things real fast." *– Bus Stop* (1956)

1858 Joan Blondell relates to friend Katharine Hepburn how a handsome, gray-haired gentleman was driving his car around the block with the prospect of making her acquaintance. "It has been my experience," Hepburn, slightly intoxicated, explains, "when a car cruises around the block slowly . . . that they are mostly looking for a place to park." *– Desk Set* (1957)

1859 "What kind of a girl are you looking for?" Jayne Mansfield asks Cary Grant. "One that doesn't smoke or drink or has no bad habits." "What for?" she questions. *– Kiss Them for Me* (1957)

1860 Successful actor Dan Dailey has problems with wife Ginger Rogers and tries to resolve them by drinking heavily. "The way things are," he enunciates to friends, "men and women will never really get together, you know. And for a very good reason. They each want something completely different. Man wants a woman, woman wants a man – impossible!" *– Oh, Men! Oh, Women!* (1957)

1861 Ingrid Bergman is with her sister and brother-in-law when she receives a call from Cary Grant inquiring whether she is alone. "Certainly, I'm alone," she answers. "There is no sincerity like a woman telling a lie," her brother-in-law notes. *– Indiscreet* (1958)

1862 Five army nurses aboard a submarine are hanging their clothes to dry in the engine room. "They're like snakes," crusty chief machinist Arthur O'Connell complains to captain Cary Grant. "When they shed their skins, they're the most dangerous." *– Operation Petticoat* (1959)

1863 Jack Lemmon, dressed in drag to escape gangsters, is pinched in an elevator. "I'm not even pretty," he complains to friend Tony Curtis. "They don't care," Curtis explains. "It's like waving a red flag in front of a bull." – *Some Like It Hot* (1959)

1864 Meeting Marilyn Monroe on the beach, musician Tony Curtis poses as a millionaire with a yacht offshore. "Tell me," she asks, "who runs up that flag – your wife?" "No. My flag steward." "And who mixes the cocktails – your wife?" "No," Curtis answers, "my cocktail steward. Look, if you're interested in whether I'm married or not – " "I'm not interested at all," Marilyn says. "Well, I'm not," Curtis admits. "That's very interesting." – *Some Like It Hot* (1959)

1865 "I'm the one who's going into politics," says Dean Martin to a group of ex–World War II buddies. "What's going to be your platform?" Sammy Davis, Jr., asks. "Repeal of the fourteenth and twentieth amendments, take the vote away from women, make slaves out of them." – *Ocean's Eleven* (1960)

1866 "Darling," Zsa Zsa Gabor, the latest mistress of a New York executive, informs her meal ticket, "a girl can't make a success on instincts alone. To understand a man takes a lifetime of study." – *Boys' Night Out* (1962)

1867 Airline pilot Cliff Robertson can't seem to coordinate his flying schedule with his social life, resulting in an angry girlfriend. She hangs up the telephone when he tries to explain another in a long line of broken dates. "What's the matter with you women?" he asks a stewardess standing next to him. "Men," she retorts. – *Sunday in New York* (1963)

1868 "What's so special about oriental women?" remarks Jack Soo to his poker-playing pals. "Once you get over the novelty of their bringing peace and dignity into the home, and their all-consuming, self-sacrificing compassion for their mates, they're just like any other woman." – *Who's Been Sleeping in My Bed?* (1963)

1869 "Give a woman an acorn and the next thing you know you're up to your rump in oak trees," Burt Lancaster warns. – *The Hallelujah Trail* (1965)

1870 Anne Bancroft is a newly arrived and outspoken doctor at a Chinese mission inhabited by women and one male teacher (Eddie Albert). "Well," she addresses Albert at the dinner table, "how does it feel to be the only rooster in this hen house?" – *Seven Women* (1965)

1871 Eli Wallach tries to describe his mistress to his bachelor-friend Dean Martin. "How do you describe a saint?" he says. "Usually, they're dead," Martin replies. "Saint she ain't. So throw me some of her mortal qualities." "Honest, loyal, selfless, devoted, dedicated, understanding. You never met anyone like this." "I don't think you have either," Martin rejoins. – *How to Save a Marriage (and Ruin Your Life)* (1968)

1872 Sherlock Holmes (Robert Stephens) complains about how he is being portrayed in the writings of his friend Dr. Watson (Colin Blakely): "You've given the reader the distinct impression that I'm a misogynist. Actually, I don't dislike women, I merely distrust them – the twinkle in the eye, the arsenic in the soup." – *The Private Life of Sherlock Holmes* (1970)

1873 Failing with women, klutzy Woody Allen invokes the spirit of his hero, Humphrey Bogart (Jerry Lacy), for assistance. "Dames are simple," Bogie expounds. "I never knew one that didn't understand a slap in the mouth or a slug from a .45." – *Play It Again, Sam* (1972)

1874 Divorced couple Alan Alda and Jane Fonda spar for custody of their daughter. "Are you going to call Jenny or shall I?" Fonda asks. "No," Alda replies. "No, what?" "No, sir!" he returns. – *California Suite* (1978)

1875 College instructor Anthony Hopkins tries to rationalize to his wife his having an affair with one of his students: "Men are different, you know.

Our needs are more – baroque." – *A Change of Seasons* (1980)

1876 "You seem like a nice feller," a pretty woman pilot says affectionately to middle-aged Walter Matthau. "You remind me of my father." "That's always been my trouble," Matthau adds. – *Hopscotch* (1980)

1877 Siren Kathleen Turner is favorably impressed with smalltime lawyer William Hurt. "You're not too smart," she says. "I like that in a man." – *Body Heat* (1981)

1878 A Supreme Court justice tries to placate fellow justice Walter Matthau, who is angry about the President's decision to nominate a woman (Jill Clayburgh) to the court. "I hear she plays tennis," the colleague offers. "Hitler played the harmonica," Matthau returns. – *First Monday in October* (1981)

1879 "Pretty girl," executive Paul Dooley comments about an attractive young woman who has just passed him and his friend Norman Fell on the street. "'Pretty,'" Fell echoes. "We don't say 'pretty' anymore. That's sexist. Now we say 'she's got good bone structure.'" – *Paternity* (1981)

1880 Television news reporters Albert Brooks and Holly Hunter, covering the civil war in Nicaragua, are about to follow some troops into battle. "If anything happens to me," says Brooks, "you tell every woman I've ever gone out with that I was talking about her at the end. That way they would have to reevaluate me." – *Broadcast News* (1987)

1881 "I like older men," ambitious, sexy Greta Scacchi remarks. "They have more money." – *White Mischief* (1987)

1882 "All the men I'm attracted to either turn out to be gay or want to take over," divorced Mary Woronov confides to widow Jacqueline Bisset. "I don't think you're setting your sights low enough," her friend quips. – *Scenes from the Class Struggle in Beverly Hills* (1989)

1883 Smalltime gangster Steve Martin, trying to prove to uptight assistant district attorney Joan Cusack that she has no sense of humor, offers her this riddle: "What's the difference between a light bulb and a pregnant woman?" "What?" she asks. "You can unscrew a light bulb." – *My Blue Heaven* (1990)

1884 Snappy, man-obsessed waitress Kate Nelligan is disparagingly told by a coworker: "You see something cute in every guy." "I know," Nelligan agrees, her eyes shining. "I'm lucky like that." – *Frankie and Johnny* (1991)

1885 College professor Woody Allen describes his attraction to self-destructive femmes fatales: "I've always had a penchant for what I call Kamikaze women.... They crash their plane into you, and you die with them." – *Husbands and Wives* (1992)

1886 "Every time I go to the mechanic," says comedienne Emily Levine, "they always look at me like I'm stupid. And they say: "It's a gasket, honey...' Like I know what a gasket is. A gasket is one hundred fifty dollars, but a 'gasket, honey,' is two hundred dollars." – *Wisecracks* (1992)

Generation Gap

1887 A police officer in his patrol car is berated by his superiors for listening to a popular detective show on the radio. "I got to," the cop explains, "so I can talk to my kids." – *Whistling in Brooklyn* (1943)

1888 During the Civil War a young Southern soldier berates his middle-aged colleague William Demarest: "How did a decrepit old man like you ever get in the war?" "Because all the smart young men like you was losing it," Demarest quips. – *Escape from Fort Bravo* (1953)

1889 A Swedish-born father asks his daughter to come with him into the next room. "In a minute," she says. "In the old country a child didn't say 'in a minute' to a father." "That's why I like America," she replies. – *Run for Cover* (1955)

1890 Guardian James Cagney informs Pamela Tiffin, a Coca-Cola tycoon's daughter, of the consequences of her marrying an East German Communist: "Your father is going to cut you off without a red cent – pardon the expression." "That's true," the young woman confirms. "Daddy gets mad when I order Russian dressing." – *One, Two, Three* (1961)

1891 Navy officer Henry Fonda, a widower with ten children, is about to retire from the service. "In a few short hours I was going into combat – against my own children," he narrates. "Anybody who has a child knows what I'm talking about. That's the real war – our generation against theirs." – *Yours, Mine and Ours* (1968)

1892 Beau Bridges, as a young liberal Harlem landlord, says to his wealthy, ultra-conservative mother: "Mother, you're just another castrated, liberated butch American broad, but I love you anyway." – *The Landlord* (1970)

1893 Destitute tailor Leonard Frey asks Tevye (Topol) for the hand of his oldest daughter. "Either you're crazy or you're out of your mind," the stunned father responds. – *Fiddler on the Roof* (1971)

1894 "I just had an orgasm with the man I love," Renee Taylor casually remarks to her mother, Helen Verbit. "That's a nice thing to tell a mother." "Did you ever have one?" Renee asks. "In my days," her mother declares, "there was no such thing." – *Made for Each Other* (1971)

1895 Hard-working and responsible Paul Dooley is bewildered by son Dennis Christopher's free-wheeling life-style. "He's never tired," Dooley complains to his wife. "He's never miserable." "He's young," she explains. "When I was young, I was tired and miserable." – *Breaking Away* (1979)

1896 Forty-two-year-old Dudley Moore chastises young, pot-smoking Bo Derek, recently married, for sleeping around just to satisfy her sexual whims. "I don't know what your problem is," she retorts, "but I don't think you're going to solve it by solving mine. I don't think I have a problem." "That's your problem," he returns. – *10* (1979)

1897 Drug-addicted actress Meryl Streep speaks for her sensation-hungry generation when she comments: "Instant gratification takes too long." – *Postcards from the Edge* (1990)

1898 While family head Danny Aiello is struggling to find a way to move to a better neighborhood, his ne'er-do-well son (Anthony La Paglia) has starry-eyed visions of being a spaceman. "I could be the first Italian on the moon," he says to his father. – *29th Street* (1991)

Government

1899 Jimmy Durante substitutes for the President during a radio speech about the economy. "Depression!" Durante begins. "What's a depression? The dictionary says a depression is a dent. And what's a dent? Everybody knows a dent is a hole. And what's a hole? You tell me what's a hole! And I'll tell you that a hole is nothin'! Just nothin'! And if you think that I'm gonna stand here and talk about nothin', you're crazy!" – *The Phantom President* (1932)

1900 Crooked businessman Wallace Beery, growing tired of seeing his wife Jean Harlow lounging in her bed all day, urges that she "get out and do things." "You know why I'm going to Washington tonight?" he says proudly. "Because the President wants to consult me about the affairs of the nation. That's why." "What's the matter with them?" she questions. – *Dinner at Eight* (1933)

1901 A member of the Freedonia cabinet becomes increasingly irritated at the shenanigans of Groucho Marx, the country's president. "You are trying my patience," the minister protests. "I don't mind if I do," Groucho retorts. "You must come over and try mine some time." – *Duck Soup* (1933)

1902 Una Merkel tells her three-year-old daughter that her father works for Uncle Sam. "What does Uncle Sam do for a living?" the child asks. "He's a collector," Merkel quips. – *Born to Dance* (1936)

1903 A politician hears his candidate for the U.S. Senate suggest a shady vote-getting scheme involving a football game. "Americans will put up with bad government," the politician says, "but they won't stand for poor sportsmanship." – *Hold That Coed* (1938)

1904 Plantation owner Cary Grant, in early Ohio, is elected to the House of Burgesses. "The most important requisite for a back-country member," a fellow member informs him, "is that he learns to sleep without snoring." – *The Howards of Virginia* (1940)

1905 Presidential hopeful Victor Moore explains to Bob Hope the advantages of the office: "You get your name in the history books with the other Presidents." "You mean there was somebody before Roosevelt?" Hope queries. – *Louisiana Purchase* (1941)

1906 Draftee Alan Ladd castigates his lawyer (Lloyd Corrigan) for not making the right connections to keep him out of the army. "You can't fix Washington," the lawyer explains. "For one thing, you can't find out who's in charge." – *Lucky Jordan* (1942)

1907 "In Washington, D.C.," Ed Wynn informs a group of soldiers, "they have canteens where the Congressmen wait on the boys. These boys'll starve to death down there. You mark my words." "Why, Mr. Wynn?" a soldier asks. "Well, you know how long it takes for a Congressman to pass anything." – *Stage Door Canteen* (1943)

1908 "I'm changing my will," Charles Ruggles announces. "I found a new way

to beat the inheritance tax. I'm leaving everything to the federal government."
— The Doughgirls (1944)

1909 During World War II perplexed storekeeper Wallace Beery reports to a local bureaucrat for help in filling out forms related to food-rationing stamps. He meets a fellow businessman with the same problem. "What's the matter with you, Hank?" Beery inquires. "You look like you lost twenty pounds. You been ailin'?" "Nope," Hank replies, "just fillin' out forms." *— Rationing* (1944)

1910 In heaven, angel Maureen O'Hara tells her superior that there is a shortage of angel power and that she has drawn up a new questionnaire. "What!" he exclaims. "Another questionnaire? Red tape, red tape and more red tape! Next thing you know they'll be forming a new bureau to handle the new questionnaire!" *— The Horn Blows at Midnight* (1945)

1911 "I apologize for the intelligence of my remarks, Sir Thomas," says Lord Henry (George Sanders). "I had forgotten that you were a member of Parliament."
— The Picture of Dorian Gray (1945)

1912 "If you're a veteran, you have no housing problem," Jack Paar explains to an audience. "The government has taken care of that. They have something new, and it's absolutely free. It's called reenlistment." *— Variety Time* (1948)

1913 A corrupt official excitedly reports to his cohorts about an inspector general's investigation in a neighboring town—where heads have rolled: "He uncovered such corruption that even I was shocked." *— The Inspector General* (1949)

1914 "As chairman of the city council," announces Hans Conried at a public hearing, "my main function is to obstruct the due process of the law."
— Rock-a-Bye Baby (1958)

1915 Reporters swarm around Peter Ustinov, president of a small European country, as he leaves the United Nations headquarters. "Are you in favor of German rearmament?" one journalist asks. "German rearmament?" Ustinov replies. "My government was opposed to German armament since the beginning of the First Crusade." *— Romanoff and Juliet* (1961)

1916 Polly Bergen, as the first woman President, hesitates to continue foreign aid to Latin American dictator Eli Wallach. "We have elections in my country," Wallach assures the President. "When was the last one?" "The last one," Wallach mutters, "preceded the one we will have immediately in the future."
— Kisses for My President (1964)

1917 Fred MacMurray, as the husband of the country's first woman President, finds himself in an unusual role. "Please tell me what the family would like for dinner and where you wish it served," inquires the chief servant of the White House. "Joseph," replies the perplexed MacMurray, "that's a little out of my line. Who usually plans the menus?" "The First Lady, sir." *— Kisses for My President* (1964)

1918 Woody Allen objects to being made president of San Marcos. "Let me be vice-president," he suggests. "That's a real idiot's job." *— Bananas* (1971)

1919 "I have come to the conclusion," announces John Adams (William Daniels), "that one useless man is called a disgrace, that two are called a law firm and that three or more become a congress." *— 1776* (1972)

1920 Scheming, tightfisted Allen Garfield, who owns a shady ambulance business, berates his lawyer for not paying off local politicians. "You can't bribe city officials with I.O.U.s," the attorney fires back. *— Mother, Jugs and Speed* (1976)

1921 "I'm just going to talk to a congressional committee," says corporate president Ed McMahon at a party. "They think Charlie's been paying off some people besides them," quips his wife. –*Fun with Dick and Jane* (1977)

1922 Supreme Court justice nominee Jill Clayburgh tells a Senate confirmation committee that she "disposed of anything that might possibly raise a question of conflict of interest." "But you were still married to a very active and successful corporation lawyer," a senator inquires. "Was I expected to dispose of him?" she questions. –*First Monday in October* (1981)

1923 Teenager Michael J. Fox meets crazed inventor Christopher Lloyd, whose DeLorean car has the power to transport Fox back to the past. He meets Lloyd of 1955, who refuses to believe that Fox is of another era. "If you're from 1985," Lloyd demands, "then

who's President then?" "Ronald Reagan," Fox replies. "Ha!" Lloyd exclaims, now assured of Fox's derangement. "That cowboy in television! And who's Vice-President, Jerry Lewis?" –*Back to the Future* (1985)

1924 President of the planet Spaceballs Mel Brooks and crew are trapped aboard a spaceship about to self-destruct. "You've got to help me!" Brooks cries to the captain. "I don't know what to do! I can't make decisions! I'm a President!" –*Spaceballs* (1987)

1925 "Now the Fourth of July," Burt Lancaster says, "there's an interesting holiday. You try explaining to your kids why they can't buy firecrackers while the government is buying H-bombs." –*Rocket Gibraltar* (1988)

Happiness

1926 "Marriage is the road to happiness," Edgar Bergen informs Charlie McCarthy. "Yes," McCarthy agrees, "but you can have a lot more fun on the detours." –*At the Races* (1934)

1927 Jean Harlow, as a lowbrow, tough-talking woman of the world, tries to put on a brave facade to maid Hattie McDaniel following her breakup with Clark Gable. "I'm happy!" she declares. "Do you hear? Happy!" "I know you are," her maid replies, "but you'll soon get over it." –*China Seas* (1935)

1928 Baroness Merle Oberon suggests to an overbearing French casanova that he find his own wife. "If I can't be happy with another man's wife," he claims, "how can I be happy with my own?" –*Folies Bergere* (1935)

1929 "I was never so happy since I kissed my mother-in-law with a cigar in

my mouth," exclaims nightclub owner Bert Lahr. –*Josette* (1938)

1930 A Nazi in occupied Poland tries to explain the purpose of Hitler's New Order to citizen Carole Lombard. "We are only trying to create a happy world," he states. "People who don't want to be happy have no place in this happy world," she says, feigning agreement. –*To Be or Not to Be* (1942)

1931 Birmingham (Mantan Moreland) takes a job as servant in a spooky house where seances are held. "You said something about seances?" he asks the servant he is replacing. "Oh," the man explains, "men and women sit around a table in the dark and hold hands." "Does that make them happy, holding hands?" Moreland asks. "It sort of raises their spirits though," the man replies. –*Black Magic* (1944)

1932 Father Fitzgibbon (Barry Fitzgerald) confides to Bing Crosby: "The joy of giving is indeed a pleasure – especially when you get rid of something you don't want." – *Going My Way* (1944)

1933 Retired businessman Charles Coburn, who believes the key to success is to marry a rich woman, confides to son-in-law Paul Douglas: "When I was a young man, I fell desperately in love with an extremely poor girl – not a buck in the family. Then one day she made me the happiest man in the world – she left town." – *Everybody Does It* (1949)

1934 Comic Joe E. Lewis (Frank Sinatra) regales his nightclub audience: "A man doesn't know what happiness is until he gets married – and then it's too late." – *The Joker Is Wild* (1957)

1935 Tony Randall, as a neurotic head of an advertising firm, looks pathetically at his office workers and remarks: "Those poor people, they go through life convinced they're happy. They never realize how sick they are." – *Lover Come Back* (1961)

1936 Utilizing a judo allegory for rough sex, motel guest Peter Sellers perplexes the desk clerk. "She's a yellow belt, I'm a green belt," he explains. "That's the way nature made us. What happens is she throws me all over the place." "She throws *you* all over the place?" the incredulous clerk asks. "Yes," Sellers replies. "She gets me in . . . a sweeping ankle throw. She sweeps my ankles away from me. I go down in one hell of a bang. I sort of lay there in pain, but I love it." – *Lolita* (1962)

1937 Dick Van Dyke, after fighting with his girlfriend, decides to get drunk. Acquaintance Paul Lynde drives him to a bar. "I'd go in there with you," Lynde explains, "but I'm a happy family man and not allowed to enjoy myself." – *Bye Bye Birdie* (1963)

1938 Middle-aged Maureen O'Sullivan and Paul Ford react to impending parenthood. "I thought everyone would be so happy," she says. "There's all kinds of happiness," he explains. "This is the happiness that everybody isn't too happy about." – *Never Too Late* (1965)

1939 Joseph Hindy informs his parents (Richard Castellano and Beatrice Arthur) that his marriage is on the rocks. "These kids today!" says Castellano. "All they're looking for is happiness!" "Don't look for happiness," Arthur adds. "It'll only make you miserable." – *Lovers and Other Strangers* (1970)

1940 Diane Keaton muses on the uncomplicated, happy life of the village idiot. "It's easy to be happy," husband Woody Allen explains, "if your one concern in life is to figure how much saliva to dribble." – *Love and Death* (1975)

1941 Publisher Gene Wilder, a fugitive from the law, gets a ride in an eccentric spinster's two-seater airplane. "It ain't like the joy of sex," she says from her cockpit, "but it don't last like the fun of flying." – *Silver Streak* (1976)

1942 Taxi driver: "I can't change ten dollars." George C. Scott: "I don't want to change it. I want you to enjoy it." – *Movie Movie* (1978)

1943 Wealthy Richard Dreyfuss, dissatisfied with his money-oriented lifestyle, befriends likable bum Nick Nolte, who introduces him to poverty – the one thing he cannot buy. Following a night of carousing, Dreyfuss returns to his wife Bette Midler. "I ate garbage last night," he announces, "and I loved it." – *Down and Out in Beverly Hills* (1986)

1944 The wooden-like Morticia (Anjelica Huston) and the urbane Gomez (Raul Julia) exchange sado-masochistic marital pleasantries. "Unhappy, darling?" "Oh, yes, completely." – *The Addams Family* (1991)

1945 "I'm gonna teach you to play football," a determined Nick Nolte promises teenage Jason Gould. "I'm gonna teach you well. I'm gonna run your butt off every day." "Wait a second," Jason interjects. "My violin lessons–" "And after I run you till you drop," Nolte continues, "make you tackle till your arms crack, something's gonna happen to you that's never happened in your miserable little life!" "What's that, sir?" "You're gonna be happy, kid."–*The Prince of Tides* (1991)

Health

1946 "Didn't you tell me you gave your horse turpentine when he was sick?" a neighboring jockey angrily confronts Gus (Al Jolson). "Yeah," Jolson replies. "What about it?" "I gave my horse turpentine and he died," the neighbor complains. "So did mine."–*Big Boy* (1930)

1947 "Here are your oysters," announces waiter Al Jolson to a customer. "They're not so healthy, but you're lucky. They're not so large."–*Big Boy* (1930)

1948 Life insurance salesman Robert Woolsey, after convincing a traffic cop that he looks pale, asks the officer to stick out his tongue. "Has it got a coat on it?" the worried officer asks. "Not only a coat," Woolsey replies, "but a vest and a pair of pants."–*Hook, Line and Sinker* (1930)

1949 Eddie Cantor, seeking an insurance policy, enters a doctor's office for the necessary examination. "Young man," the physician announces, "I don't think you could pass." "You give me a pair of dice," Cantor replies. "I'll show you if I could pass or not."–*Insurance* (1930)

1950 Two hypochondriacs compare their illnesses. "I had pneumonia four times," one boasts. "I'm even with you," says Eddie Cantor. "I had double pneumonia twice."–*Whoopee!* (1930)

1951 Hypochondriac Eddie Cantor quips: "The doctor said if I have one more operation, he's going to put in a zipper."–*Whoopee!* (1930)

1952 Someone asks Eddie Cantor's nurse about her patient's health. "He's so full of pills," she replies, "they can't operate on him. He keeps rolling off the table."–*Whoopee!* (1930)

1953 Groucho Marx introduces a celebrated singer: "Her father was the first to serve spaghetti with bicarbonate of soda, thus causing and curing indigestion at the same time."–*A Night at the Opera* (1935)

1954 "You should take care of that cold," a sympathetic young woman says to a sneezing Joe E. Brown. "I don't want to take care of it," he replies, "I want to get rid of it."–*Polo Joe* (1936)

1955 When a thermometer is stuck in patient Harpo Marx's mouth, he playfully chews it up and swallows the instrument. "That temperature sure went down fast," Groucho Marx quips.–*A Day at the Races* (1937)

1956 Racetrack tout Chico Marx tries to sell unwary Groucho a book of racing tips for one dollar, promising: "One dollar and you remember me the rest of your life." "That's the most nauseating proposition I ever heard," Groucho remarks.–*A Day at the Races* (1937)

1957 Linda Darnell reports for her first day's work as secretary and meets receptionist Joan Davis. "I'm Miss

Applegate," Davis introduces herself. "You know, an applegate a day keeps the doctor away." – *Day-Time Wife* (1939)

1958 W. C. Fields offers his sure-fire cure to an insomniac: "Get plenty of sleep." – *Never Give a Sucker an Even Break* (1941)

1959 Agent Patsy Kelly tries to interest a radio advertiser in one of her clients. "He'll sell more of your Vitamin L tablets – " "Not Vitamin L," the man corrects her, "Vitamin A." "Well, they taste like 'L' to me," Patsy replies. – *Playmates* (1941)

1960 "What in heaven's name brought you to Casablanca?" Vichy police chief Claude Rains asks the enigmatic adventurer and café owner Rick Blaine (Humphrey Bogart). "My health," Bogart answers directly. "I came to Casablanca for the waters." "What waters?" asks Rains. "We're in the desert." "I was misinformed," replies Bogart. – *Casablanca* (1942)

1961 Elderly Don Ameche, who has died in his sleep, reports to the Devil (Laird Cregar) and describes his last evening. "I'd finished my dinner – " "A good one, I hope?" Cregar asks courteously. "Excellent, excellent," Ameche replies. "I ate everything the doctor forbade." – *Heaven Can Wait* (1943)

1962 Little morbid Margaret O'Brien, growing up in turn-of-the-century St. Louis, presents her doll's prognosis: "I bet she won't live through the night. She has four fatal diseases." – *Meet Me in St. Louis* (1944)

1963 Hypochondriac Danny Kaye, now in the army, appears healthy to his buddy Dana Andrews, but Kaye persists he is ill. "You never looked better in your life," Andrews says. "The army agrees with you. You ate two steaks." "That's the worst symptom," counters Kaye, "overhunger." – *Up in Arms* (1944)

1964 On board a train Edward Brophy finds a little girl's lost dog. "You've got Diogenes," the child says in relief, seeing him with her pet. "What, me?" he questions. "I ain't never been sick a day in my life." – *The Falcon in San Francisco* (1945)

1965 "I hate cold showers," Oscar Levant complains. "They stimulate me; then I don't know what to do." – *Humoresque* (1946)

1966 Tough, cynical fight manager Walter Abel, who is suffering from nerves and on the verge of a breakdown, is given some pills. "I can't swallow pills," he pleads. "I got a tiny throat." – *The Kid from Brooklyn* (1946)

1967 After treating most of Clifton Webb's twelve children for the whooping cough, a doctor comments: "I'll say one thing for you. Your children don't get sick very often. But when they do, they certainly mess up the statistics of the state of New Jersey." – *Cheaper by the Dozen* (1950)

1968 Good-natured racketeer Paul Douglas takes Harry, a young streetwise orphan, into his home. "Harry frightens me a little," admits his governess Jean Peters. "He's definitely over-precocious." "Yeah?" questions Douglas. "He doesn't seem sickly to me." – *Love That Brute* (1950)

1969 "I wonder if Stevie is photogenic," Diana Lynn says to roommate Irma (Marie Wilson). "Of course not," Irma objects. "He's as healthy as a horse." – *My Friend Irma Goes West* (1950)

1970 Nymphomaniac Jill St. John wants her husband Louis Nye to make love to her, but her passions only invoke memories of past heart attacks he has undergone while trying to satisfy her desires. He decides to play cards with his buddies. "I need this night to rest up between cardiograms," he explains. – *Who's Been Sleeping in My Bed?* (1963)

1971 "In Japan," an oriental beauty says to Bob Hope while giving him a bath, "fewer people die of ulcers or heart condition than in any place in the world." "They probably all drown in bathtubs," he quips.–*A Global Affair* (1964)

1972 "Do you believe that kissing is unhealthy?" a girl on a beach asks her companion. "I don't know," the boy replies. "I've never been–" "You've never been kissed?" "No, I've never been sick."–*The Horror of Party Beach* (1964)

1973 Although nurse Phyllis Diller is the only woman on a Pacific island with thousands of soldiers and sailors, she is unable to attract a man. She decides to make a play for army sergeant Bob Hope. "Remember, I'm a nurse," she says, cuddling up to Hope. "I got the cure for what ails you." "Nobody's that sick," he cracks.–*The Private Navy of Sgt. O'Farrell* (1968)

1974 Psychoanalyst Rip Torn explains to a young hippie why he won't make love to her: "Your chromosomes must look like the inside of a twenty-four-hour cold capsule. Because if I knocked you up we'd probably get a giraffe."–*Coming Apart* (1969)

1975 An aide asks Woody Allen, the new President of San Marcos, what the chief export of his country is. "Dysentery," replies Allen.–*Bananas* (1971)

1976 "T.B. or not T.B.," says Woody Allen. "That is the congestion. Consumption be done about it?"–*Everything You Always Wanted to Know About Sex (But Were Afraid to Ask)* (1972)

1977 "Where are all my friends?" Woody Allen, awakening in 2173, asks. "You must understand," a scientist explains, "that everyone you knew in the past has been dead nearly two hundred years." "But they all ate organic rice," Allen says in disbelief.–*Sleeper* (1973)

1978 Woody Allen is challenged to fight a duel to the death. "I can't do anything to the death," Woody declares. "I have an ulcer condition, and dying is one of the worst things for it."–*Love and Death* (1975)

1979 "I can take anything from you," no-nonsense nurse Rosetta Le Noire says to crotchety Walter Matthau, who is recovering from a heart attack. "I have a sense of humor." "If you nurse as good as your sense of humor," Matthau returns, "I won't make it till Thursday." –*The Sunshine Boys* (1975)

1980 Jill Clayburgh, suddenly thrust into the single world when her husband walks out on her, meets with her friends. "You know," one confidante begins, "since I started taking Lithium, I feel more sensible than this month's *Good Housekeeping*."–*An Unmarried Woman* (1978)

1981 Corporation president Jonathan Winters has just suffered a heart attack. A doctor and nurse are rushed to his side. "Don't touch me!" he shouts to a nurse holding a hypodermic needle. "That needle or you yourself! Understand, nurse? I don't know where either of you have been."–*Say Yes* (1986)

1982 Private investigator Robert De Niro picks up bail jumper Charles Grodin in New York and prepares to take him back to California by airplane, but Grodin complains that he can't fly. "I also suffer from acrophobia and claustrophobia," Grodin explains. "Well, I'll tell you what," replies De Niro. "If you don't cooperate, you're going to suffer from fistophobia."–*Midnight Run* (1988)

1983 "You don't eat standing up," Harrison Ford says to his little son. "Sit down." "The food goes down easier if it has the help of gravity," the boy explains.–*Presumed Innocent* (1990)

1984 A fellow pilot who has trouble with his eyes explains to top-gun pilot Charlie Sheen why he is being grounded: "In order to keep from damaging the eye sockets, they've got to go through the rectum. Ain't no man gonna take that route with me!" – *Hot Shots!* (1991)

1985 A dental accident causes patient John Goodman to mutate into half-man,

half-ant. Later, the dentist, offering some good news, announces: "I did get your X-rays back. I don't suppose it makes much difference to you now, but you didn't have a single cavity." – *Matinee* (1993)

High Society and Socialites

1986 At a posh social gathering Groucho Marx introduces Margaret Dumont to one of the guests: "I now take great pleasure in presenting to you the well-preserved and partially pickled Mr. Potter." – *The Cocoanuts* (1929)

1987 Lady George (Constance Bennett), a noted London socialite, has problems getting a certain lord to attend her social functions. "I'll get him here somehow," she confides to a friend. "If he comes once because I force him, he'll come again because he likes it. This house is like heaven: I have to compel them to come in." – *Our Betters* (1933)

1988 Entrepreneur Groucho Marx has promising prospects for millionairess Margaret Dumont – he will invest two hundred thousand dollars of her money in the opera. "Don't you see?" he asks. "You'll get into society. Then you can marry me and they'll kick you out of society, and all you've lost is two hundred thousand dollars." – *A Night at the Opera* (1935)

1989 After a night on the town, socialite Constance Bennett awakens in the morning in her convertible roadster parked in front of a bank. As dozens of startled passersby stop to stare at her in her evening dress, she nonchalantly opens the door and hands a string extending from the car to one of the male onlookers. "Just hold the car, please," she requests. "I'll be back in a couple of days." – *Topper* (1937)

1990 Socialite Barbara Stanwyck and her friends become involved in the investigation of a murder. As they search an empty house, Stanwyck asks one young sleuth to cover the upstairs. "I'm not much of an individualist," she replies. "We'll search it together." "Why, that's communism!" another socialite asserts. – *The Mad Miss Manton* (1938)

1991 Opera singer Linda Darnell persuades her reluctant escort John Hoyt to attend a chic social event, a type of affair he abhors. "Would you like to meet some of our guests?" the hostess suggests. "I'd rather be shot from a cannon," he replies. – *Everybody Does It* (1949)

Honesty and Dishonesty

1992 "Truth like football," announces Charlie Chan (Warner Oland), "receives many kicks before reaching goal." – *Charlie Chan at the Olympics* (1937)

1993 Police captain Edmund Lowe presents con artist Mae West with twenty-five warrants for her arrest. "This reflects on my honesty," West protests. "Have you ever heard it questioned?" Lowe asks. "I never heard it mentioned," she snickers. – *Every Day's a Holiday* (1938)

1994 Danielle Darrieux confides to Helen Broderick that she has regrets about misleading a desirable bachelor. "All women are dishonest," Broderick reassures her. "If they weren't, the world would be divided into two classes of people – old maids and bachelors." – *The Rage of Paris* (1938)

1995 "How would you like to make a few honest dollars for yourself?" a con artist approaches W. C. Fields. "Do they have to be honest?" Fields replies. – *You Can't Cheat an Honest Man* (1939)

1996 Cliff Edwards is fed up with buddy Guinn Williams' tall tales. "You're gonna make a valuable man on a cattle ranch," Edwards says, "– the way you can throw the bull." – *American Empire* (1942)

1997 A laborer comments on the character of the ruthless executive "Pittsburgh" (John Wayne): "He's so crooked he could hide behind a corkscrew." – *Pittsburgh* (1942)

1998 A bartender, wanting to send some flowers to an opera singer, hands his porter some money. "Spend five bucks and spend it all," he says suspiciously. "What do you mean?" the porter questions. "I'm as honest as you are." "That's what I mean," the bartender replies. – *Hi Diddle Diddle* (1943)

1999 Bob Hope catches Bing Crosby trying to swindle him. "Way down underneath I'm honest," Crosby declares. "Yeah," Hope agrees, "but on the surface you're a rat." – *Road to Utopia* (1945)

2000 When William Bendix purchases a racehorse – which he later learns has bad ankles – his pal Benny (Groucho Marx) devises a scheme to resell the horse to its owner. "Benny and me just want to get even, that's all," Bendix explains to those involved in the sale. "We don't want to do anything crooked, do we, Benny?" "Well," replies cautious Groucho, "let's not go overboard." – *A Girl in Every Port* (1952)

2001 Shady sports promoter Spencer Tracy is duly impressed with golf pro Katharine Hepburn – except for one drawback. "You see her face?" he asks his assistant. "A real honest face. Only thing disgusting about her." – *Pat and Mike* (1952)

2002 Wealthy Parisian Louis Jourdan ends his flowering romance with American Maggie McNamara when she admits that she had designs on him all along. His friend Clifton Webb tries to explain the breakup: "These girls in love never realize they should be honestly dishonest instead of being dishonestly honest." – *Three Coins in the Fountain* (1954)

2003 Edward G. Robinson, familiar with his brother Frank Sinatra's ploys, balks on the telephone at lending him any money, even after Sinatra hints that his 12-year-old son is ill. After Sinatra hangs up, Robinson's wife, Thelma Ritter, inquires about the call. "What's the difference what he said," Robinson replies. "Even when he's lying, he's lying." – *A Hole in the Head* (1959)

2004 Advertising agency president Tony Randall rejects the choice of a particular chemist. "Money can't buy him – he's incorruptible!" Randall explains. "As Dad always said: 'A man that can't be bribed can't be trusted.'" – *Lover Come Back* (1961)

2005 Akim Tamiroff, who has pulled off one of the largest gold heists, keeps tabs on his partner, master thief Peter Sellers, in charge of smuggling the gold into Italy. "What's the matter, don't you trust me?" Sellers asks. "Do you trust me?" Tamiroff returns. "Absolutely!" "Neither do I." – *After the Fox* (1966)

2006 Marsha Mason and her daughter go backstage to see actor-friend Richard Dreyfuss who has just bombed in *Richard III.* "Be tactful," Mason cautions. "What's tactful?" her daughter asks. "Lie." – *The Goodbye Girl* (1977)

2007 Slow-witted Chazz Palminteri says of his boss, retired mobster Sylvester Stallone: "Even in the old days he was known as an honest crook." "That's an oxymoron," speech tutor Tim Curry points out. "Gee, doc," Palminteri mumbles, "you shouldn't oughta said that." – *Oscar* (1991)

Honeymooners

2008 W. C. Fields, just married to Mae West by a fake preacher, finds himself locked out of the bridal suite. "Come, my phlox, my flower," he pleads. "I have some very definite pear-shaped ideas I'd like to discuss with thee." – *My Little Chickadee* (1940)

2009 Honeymooners Jack Carson and Jane Wyman plan their first evening as man and wife in their Washington hotel room. "We'll have a wonderful dinner up here," he explains, "just the two of us. Then I'll have them send up a nightcap – " "You're not going to sleep in one of those old-fashioned things, are you?" Wyman interjects. – *The Dough-girls* (1944)

2010 Lawyer Pat O'Brien, to avoid the police, forces himself upon friends George Murphy and Carole Landis, who are about to embark upon their honeymoon. "You miss the whole idea," Murphy protests. "We are on our honeymoon." "So what?" O'Brien persists. "I'm broadminded." – *Having Wonderful Crime* (1945)

2011 Playboy George Peppard: "What would you like to see on your honeymoon?" Fiancée Elizabeth Ashley: "Lots and lots of lovely ceilings." – *The Carpetbaggers* (1964)

2012 Newlyweds Jane Fonda and Robert Redford arrive at the New York Plaza Hotel in a horse-drawn carriage. "If the honeymoon doesn't work out," says Fonda, "let's not get divorced; let's kill each other." "Let's have one of the maids do it," Redford adds. "I hear the service here is wonderful." – *Barefoot in the Park* (1967)

2013 Navy officer Henry Fonda, widower with ten children, marries widow Lucille Ball, who has her own brood of eight. After the wedding ceremonies, the couple prepare to leave on their honeymoon, but not before they say goodbye to each of their children. "By the time they say goodbye," wedding guest Van Johnson remarks, "the honeymoon will be over." – *Yours, Mine and Ours* (1968)

2014 Beatrice Arthur, recalling her wedding night to daughter-in-law Diane Keaton, describes how shocked she was to discover that her husband Richard Castellano could suddenly change from a "clean" to a "physical" person. "I was so nauseous," she concludes, "I locked myself in the bathroom and stayed there all night. I didn't want to make a scene." – *Lovers and Other Strangers* (1970)

2015 Driving to Florida on their honeymoon, Charles Grodin already finds his new bride Jeannie Berlin tiresome as she envisions their future together. "Why do you keep saying forty or fifty years?" he carps. "We're not even out of Georgia yet."—*The Heartbreak Kid* (1972)

2016 Woody Allen explains to friend Tony Roberts how his marriage began: "We went to Mexico on our honeymoon. I spent the entire two weeks in bed—I had dysentery."—*Play It Again, Sam* (1972)

2017 "Conversation like television set on honeymoon—unnecessary," says oriental sleuth Mr. Wang (Peter Sellers) à la Charlie Chan.—*Murder by Death* (1976)

2018 Joseph Bologna sends off his just-married brother with the following advice: "Here's your plane ticket and com-plete honeymoon instructions. Come out of your room at least once a week. Food is very important."—*Chapter Two* (1979)

2019 Outspoken bookstore owner Maureen Stapleton is happy to give advice to son George Segal and his new bride, Glenda Jackson: "The best thing lovers could do is get into bed and revel in it."—*Lost and Found* (1979)

2020 Rodney Dangerfield's not-too-bright daughter has just married a Latino, but she is unprepared for the honeymoon. "I don't know what to do," she confesses. "I bought a book, *The Joy of Sex*," her young husabnd announces, handing it to her on the bed. "In Spanish," she says, disappointed. "I'm going to translate it for you," he explains. "It has a happy ending."—*Easy Money* (1983)

Husbands and Wives

2021 Southern plantation owner Joe Cawthorn is suddenly awakened from a deep sleep by his overbearing wife (Jobyna Howland). "Oh," he exclaims, "I just had the most wonderful dream." "Tell me, darling, what was it?" "I dreamed I was once again a widower." —*Dixiana* (1930)

2022 "Where is your husband?" Groucho Marx asks Margaret Dumont. "Why, he's dead." "I bet he's just using that as an excuse." "I was with him to the very end," she avows. "No wonder he passed away." "I held him in my arms and kissed him," she recalls. "Oh, I see," Groucho concludes. "So it was murder." —*Duck Soup* (1933)

2023 Despotic, gluttonous Henry VIII (Charles Laughton) wryly sums up the angst of his numerous marriages. "Six wives," muses the monarch, "and the best of them was the worst."—*The Private Life of Henry VIII* (1933)

2024 The niece of W. C. Fields and his wife Alison Skipworth plans to enter her broken-down riverboat in a race, the outcome to determine who wins a river franchise. An inspector is leery of the age and condition of the boat. "This boat was launched in 1881," the inspector points out. "So was my wife," Fields counters, "but she's still seaworthy." —*Tillie and Gus* (1933)

2025 The game-plan of con artists Bert Wheeler and Robert Woolsey is to telephone an executive and send him on a wild goose chase. "Tell him some bad news," Wheeler explains. "I'll tell him his wife ran away." "That's not bad news," Wheeler replies.—*Hips, Hips, Hooray* (1934)

2026 "My husband left me," an hysterical woman cries to hotel employee Al Ritz. "He found out I have a glass eye." "Is this your engagement ring?" Ritz asks as he examines it. "Don't worry, lady. It's glass, too." –*Hotel Anchovy* (1934)

2027 "These are my wives," a sheik boasts to Eddie Cantor. "I have not so many now – a mere one hundred twenty-five." "I know," Cantor empathizes. "Everybody cut down during the Depression." –*Kid Millions* (1934)

2028 Henry Stephenson counsels Miriam Hopkins: "As the fiancée is bent, the husband will grow." –*The Richest Girl in the World* (1934)

2029 Jimmy Durante, as the star of a radio show, regales his audience: "My wife said to me: 'Are you going out tonight?' And I said: 'No, not completely.'" –*Strictly Dynamite* (1934)

2030 Married couple William Powell and Myrna Loy are sitting across from each other in a restaurant. "It was spring in Venice and I was so young, I didn't know what I was doing," he reminisces. "We're all that way on my father's side." "By the way," she asks, "how is your father's side?" "It's much better, thanks," Powell replies. "And yours?" –*The Thin Man* (1934)

2031 Off to investigate a crime, Nick Charles (William Powell) introduces his wife Nora (Myrna Loy) to an acquaintance. "This is my dog and this is my wife." "You might have introduced me first," she complains. –*The Thin Man* (1934)

2032 W. C. Fields succeeds in selling his invention of a puncture-proof tire. His wife, who considers him a failure, has not learned about his success when a stranger congratulates her. "I think you're the luckiest woman in the world," the stranger says. "Is my husband dead?" Fields' wife asks. –*You're Telling Me* (1934)

2033 "A betrayed husband," professes baron Maurice Chevalier, "under certain conditions, can remain a tragic figure, but a husband who is laughed at is a fool. It's an old Chinese proverb; if it's not, it should be." –*Folies Bergere* (1935)

2034 "Would you have any objections if I scared your husband so that he'll never *look* at another woman?" Ginger Rogers asks Helen Broderick. "My dear," her friend quips, "no man is ever too scared to look." –*Top Hat* (1935)

2035 Sailor Sid Silvers returns to wife Una Merkel after a four-year absence. Having known each other for only a few short days before they were married, she hardly recognizes him. "Aren't you glad to see me?" he asks. "I don't know yet." "But I'm your husband!" "Don't remind me of it!" she exclaims. –*Born to Dance* (1936)

2036 Fashion designer Warner Baxter and model Joan Bennett, both separated from their mates, are out on the town, but Baxter's heart is not in it. "My wife's favorite song," he says to Bennett in a nightclub. "My wife's favorite dance," he then remarks. But, determined to salvage the evening, he suggests: "Come on, let's rumba." "No," she responds, "let's go home and read your wife's favorite book." –*Vogues* (1937)

2037 Blondie (Penny Singleton) to husband Dagwood (Arthur Lake): "Sometimes I think it's harder to raise a husband than a baby." –*Blondie* (1938)

2038 Gale Sondergaard, whose husbands have met mysterious deaths, becomes interested in marrying millionaire Bob Hope. "Poor Pierre," she confesses to Hope about her most recent spouse. "He fell off the Matterhorn. He was never found." "Did they look?" Hope asks. –*Never Say Die* (1939)

2039 After witnessing the problems that his business partner Warner Baxter has with his wife who is pursuing a singing career, Craig (Eugene Pallette) confides to Baxter: "This afternoon Mrs. Craig started to hum, and I smacked her right across her mouth." – *Wife, Husband and Friend* (1939)

2040 Devious newspaper editor Walter Burns (Cary Grant) tries to win back ex-wife Hildy (Rosalind Russell), who is planning to marry dull insurance salesman Ralph Bellamy. "I sort of like him," Bellamy says naively of Grant. "He's got a lot of charm." "He comes by it naturally," explains Russell. "His grandfather was a snake." – *His Girl Friday* (1940)

2041 Lupe Velez laments to Uncle Leon Errol that his wife doesn't like her. "What are you kicking about?" Errol replies. "I've been married to her for twenty years and she still doesn't like me." – *Mexican Spitfire* (1940)

2042 Leon Errol's wife, who dislikes their nephew's bride, Lupe Velez, grumbles: "I'd give her a piece of my mind." "You'd better hang on to what you got left, honey," Errol remarks. – *Mexican Spitfire* (1940)

2043 "Nobody is going to follow in my footsteps," boasts Leon Errol. "Not if he wants to stay in decent company," adds wife Elisabeth Risdon. – *Mexican Spitfire Out West* (1940)

2044 Shipwrecked on an island for seven days and declared legally dead, Irene Dunne returns to husband Cary Grant on his wedding day. "Are you sure you don't love her?" she asks him about his bride. "The moment I saw you I knew –" Grant answers. "Oh, go on!" his wife interjects. "I bet you say that to all your wives." – *My Favorite Wife* (1940)

2045 "Wives are funny, aren't they?" a bellhop muses to John Barrymore. "Definitely," Barrymore replies. "Ask the man who owns one." – *Playmates* (1941)

2046 Dennis O'Keefe discusses the uniqueness of wives to Edward Everett

Horton. "My first wife was different – for a while," Horton recalls. "Then she became indifferent." – *Weekend for Three* (1941)

2047 Fibber Magee's eccentric, mild-mannered neighbor explains that his suit is too large because his wife buys his clothes for him. "Why doesn't she get them to your size?" Magee asks. "She says I'm not the man she thought I was," the neighbor explains. "She still keeps buying clothes for the other man." – *Here We Go Again* (1942)

2048 Robert Benchley quips about his wife's joining a national defense program: "My only regret is that I have but one wife to give to my country." – *The Major and the Minor* (1942)

2049 Henry Fonda is going up to bed while his wife (Olivia de Havilland) is going dancing with an old college boyfriend (Jack Carson) who has come to visit. "You'd better take a hot water bottle to bed with you," she advises. "Nice of you to arrange a substitute," Fonda acidly replies. – *The Male Animal* (1942)

2050 Leon Errol faces the wrath of his wife's sharp tongue. "I've stayed awake enough nights waiting for you to come home," she complains. "I'm sorry," he murmurs. "That's better." "From now on," he adds, "I'll stay out all night." – *Mexican Spitfire Sees a Ghost* (1942)

2051 "Somehow you look so incomplete," Lady Epping says to eccentric Lord Epping (Leon Errol). "Have you ever found me wanting in anything?" he questions. "Frankly," she replies, "I have." – *Mexican Spitfire's Blessed Event* (1943)

2052 Wealthy, unloved Mr. Skeffington (Claude Rains) says to his vain, carping wife (Bette Davis): "You mustn't think so harshly of my secretaries. They were kind and understanding when I came to the office after a hard day at home." – *Mr. Skeffington* (1944)

2053 "How I dislike those French names!" matronly Alice Cooper remarks to a servant. "My husband always used to call me by them." "I thought they meant lovely things in French, madam," the servant says. "They do," she affirms. "He was a supreme hypocrite." –*Mrs. Parkington* (1944)

2054 Distraught Dorothy Lamour, mistaking Bob Hope for a detective, shows him a picture of her invalid husband as she begins to unfold her dilemma. "I'm in trouble, deep trouble." "What's the wheelchair for?" Hope asks. "My husband is an invalid," she explains. "He hasn't been out of the wheelchair in seven years." "You're in trouble," Hope concurs. –*My Favorite Brunette* (1947)

2055 Cary Grant has become jealous of family friend Melvyn Douglas and complains to wife Myrna Loy: "Every time he goes out of the house he shakes my hand and kisses you." "Do you prefer it the other way?" his wife asks. –*Mr. Blandings Builds His Dream House* (1948)

2056 William Powell is worried about turning fifty years old. His wife, Irene Hervey, takes his birthday in stride. "A wife doesn't feel safe," she explains, "until her husband turns the 'fifty' corner." –*Mr. Peabody and the Mermaid* (1948)

2057 "A husband is what's left of a sweetheart after the nerve has been killed," Lou Costello remarks to Bud Abbott. –*The Noose Hangs High* (1948)

2058 Calamity Jane (Jane Russell) marries dentist Bob Hope as a ploy to capture some deperadoes. "Remember," Jane reminds Hope, "you promised to love, honor and protect me." "Yeah," Hope concurs, "let's do it in the order named." –*The Paleface* (1948)

2059 Presidential candidate Spencer Tracy rediscovers his wife (Katharine Hepburn) on the campaign trail. "You know," Tracy says, "I think this trip has agreed with you. You have no right to look this pretty – a woman of your age." –*State of the Union* (1948)

2060 Feather-brained blonde Judy Holliday is accused of shooting her husband. "When did you suspect you were losing your husband's affections?" her attorney Katharine Hepburn asks her. "When he stopped batting me around," Holliday replies. –*Adam's Rib* (1949)

2061 Paul Douglas' marriage is suffering since his wife decided to take singing lessons. His business partner, Craig (Millard Mitchell), has learned from Douglas' experience. "This afternoon Mrs. Craig started to hum," Mitchell says to his partner. "I smacked her right across the kisser." –*Everybody Does It* (1949)

2062 Anne Baxter, who is having marital problems with husband Macdonald Carey, locks herself in her room. She refuses to talk to her mother, but requests that her father (Cecil Kellaway), a soft-spoken reverend, come up. "Your daughter must have something on her conscience, something she's ashamed to tell me," Kellaway's wife pronounces formally. "She knows your standards are lower." –*My Wife's Best Friend* (1952)

2063 Popular radio couple Fred Allen and Ginger Rogers are not on speaking terms in their private life and carry their spats to the studio during rehearsals. "If you've got to fight," the producer interjects, "fight at home, not here!" "We can't fight at home," Allen explains. "We don't speak there." – *We're Not Married* (1952)

2064 Jet pilot Gregory Walcott, on his way to meet invaders from outer space, tells wife Mona McKinnon to lock the doors after he leaves the house. "I'll be in bed before half an hour's gone – with your pillow beside me." "My pillow?" "Well, I have to have something to keep me company while you're away." –*Plan 9 from Outer Space* (1959)

2065 Neglected Arlene Francis complains about her husband, James Cagney, a Coca-Cola executive, that to him their "marriage has gone flat like a glass of stale beer." "Why do you have to bring in a competing beverage?" he retorts. –*One, Two, Three* (1961)

2066 After Bob Hope, as critic Parker Ballantine, pans his wife's play, she almost leaves him. But they mend their differences, and the next morning he leaves a note on his pillow: "A memorable evening – Ballantine." –*Critic's Choice* (1963)

2067 After Polly Bergen wins the Presidency of the U.S., she and husband Fred MacMurray finally get a chance to be alone. As he is about to kiss her, the telephone rings. "Which one is it? she asks. "The red one or the white one?" "I have no idea," he replies, "but isn't it nice to be interrupted in a choice of decorator colors?" –*Kisses for My President* (1964)

2068 At a resort, international jewel thief David Niven is carrying on an affair with the wife of police inspector Clouseau (Peter Sellers). Niven ridicules her husband, but she insists that Clouseau has some redeeming qualities. "Name one," Niven challenges her. "He's kind, loyal, faithful, obedient." "You're either married to a boy scout or a dachshund," Niven quips. –*The Pink Panther* (1964)

2069 The head of a wealthy French family wishes to keep a minor crime private and asks the French police inspector for his discretion. "You can rely on me," the inspector pledges. "And your superior?" "My wife will say nothing," the policeman replies. –*Wild and Wonderful* (1964)

2070 Wealthy socialite Lauren Bacall hires private detective Harper (Paul Newman) to investigate the disappearance of her husband and enlightens Newman on their relationship. "I have no intention of gathering material for divorce proceedings," she explains. "I only want to outlive him – and see him in

his grave. It's a terrible thing to say." "People in love will say anything," replies Newman. –*Harper* (1966)

2071 At a small gathering, Richard Burton offers his wife Martha (Elizabeth Taylor) a drink: "Martha – rubbing alcohol for you?" –*Who's Afraid of Virginia Woolf?* (1966)

2072 Jane Fonda: "You cannot go to sleep now, Paul. We're having a fight!" Robert Redford: "You have the fight. When you're through, would you turn off these lights, please." –*Barefoot in the Park* (1967)

2073 "Did you miss me today?" newlywed Jane Fonda inquires. "No," lawyer-spouse Robert Redford responds. "Why not?" "Because you called me eight times. I don't talk to you that much when I'm home." –*Barefoot in the Park* (1967)

2074 At the advice of wife Debbie Reynolds, Dick Van Dyke reluctantly visits her marriage counselor (Martin Gabel), who targets Dick's sex life as part of his marital problems. "When was the last time you had relations?" Gabel asks. "You should know," Van Dyke replies. "You see her twice a week." "I wanted your answer." "Well," Van Dyke says, "it will be about the same as hers." –*Divorce, American Style* (1967)

2075 Philandering husband Joey Bishop, caught with a young woman in his bed, denies everything. "What bed? What girl?" he questions. He promptly whisks the stranger out, straightens out the bedroom, enters the living room and settles down to read. "What do you want for dinner?" his wife asks. –*A Guide for the Married Man* (1967)

2076 Anthony Quinn is kidnapped, but when the ransom is demanded from his wife, she says: "For two hundred thousand dollars you can keep the son of a bitch." –*The Happening* (1967)

2077 "How dear of you to let me out of jail," remarks wife Eleanor of

Aquitaine (Katharine Hepburn). "It's only for the holidays," explains Henry II (Peter O'Toole). – *The Lion in Winter* (1968)

2078 Christmas Eve brings no respite in the intense battle between Henry II (Peter O'Toole) and his wife (Katharine Hepburn) for dominance, power and possessions. "Well, what shall we hang," he asks spiritedly, "the holly or each other?" – *The Lion in Winter* (1968)

2079 Just-separated Felix Unger (Jack Lemmon) receives a telephone call from his wife who, intending to redecorate his room, wants to know when he will pick up his clothes. "I was ready to kill myself," Lemmon laments, "and she's picking out colors." – *The Odd Couple* (1968)

2080 One of the townspeople of Santa Vittoria gossips about the marital life of Anthony Quinn and Anna Magnani: "It is a sad house where the cock is silent and the hen makes all the noise." – *The Secret of Santa Vittoria* (1969)

2081 "I'm trying to sound like a wife," Dick Van Dyke's girlfriend says. "Don't," he chides her. "The big-hit wives – the ones that get held over year after year – are the ones that make their husbands forget they're a wife." – *Some Kind of a Nut* (1969)

2082 Indian Chief Dan George asks newlywed Dustin Hoffman how he's getting on with his Indian wife: "Does she show a pleasant enthusiasm when you mount her?" – *Little Big Man* (1970)

2083 "I know why married men live longer," declares Peter Sellers to a friend. "They're half dead already." – *There's a Girl in My Soup* (1970)

2084 Busy husband Walter Matthau wants his wife Maureen Stapleton to go to the movies by herself. "What if I get picked up?" she asks. "Call me," Matthau replies. "I won't wait up for you." – *Plaza Suite* (1971)

2085 Married couple Walter Matthau and Lee Grant learn that their daughter is afraid to get married, fearing she and her husband will end up like her parents. "I don't think we're so bad, do you?" Grant asks Matthau. "So we yell and scream a little. So we fight, curse, aggravate each other. So you blame me for being a lousy mother, and I accuse you of being a rotten husband. That doesn't mean we're unhappy, does it?" – *Plaza Suite* (1971)

2086 The wife of recently revealed transvestite Lou Jacobi complains to him: "You could have come to me and said: 'Tess, I have a diseased mind; I'm a sick individual; I need help; I need treatment; I'm perverted; I'm unfit to function with normal people.' I would have understood." – *Everything You Always Wanted to Know About Sex (But Were Afraid to Ask)* (1972)

2087 In bed at night, Woody Allen reaches out for his wife (Diane Keaton). "No," she says, "not here." – *Love and Death* (1975)

2088 Jane Fonda, married to Marine Bruce Dern, stoically shares with him the military. "You know what they tell them?" a girlfriend informs her. "If the Marine Corps had wanted you to have a wife, they would have issued you one." – *Coming Home* (1978)

2089 Ellen Burstyn tells her once-a-year lover Alan Alda she thought she had a good marriage until one day her husband said that the best years of his life were spent in the army. "What's wrong with that?" Alda asks. "A lot of guys feel that way about the service." "Harry was in the army four years," Burstyn explains. "Three of them were in a Japanese prison camp." – *Same Time, Next Year* (1978)

2090 C.I.A. chief Ned Beatty, nettled by his feather-brained wife, comments to an acquaintance: "I should have terminated her twenty years ago." – *Hopscotch* (1980)

2091 A wife whose husband has run off with his secretary receives encouraging words from a friend: "He'll be back. As soon as they run out of clean socks and underwear, they always come back." —*How to Beat the High Cost of Living* (1980)

2092 An abandoned wife who has lost her husband to his secretary confides to a bartender: "Nine years I loved him. I loved him when I married him. Lately, it's like trying to put toothpaste back into the tube...." —*How to Beat the High Cost of Living* (1980)

2093 Philadelphian Donny Most, recently arrived in Los Angeles, is invited to a party where the host is entertaining his guests. "It's boring," Most overhears the comments of a woman. "He's boring." "You shouldn't talk about him like that," he interjects. "He's the host." "I'm the hostess," the woman returns. "I'm his wife; believe me, he's boring." —*Leo and Loree* (1980)

2094 "Sweetheart," a senior citizen addresses his wife, "we've been together for sixty years. There's only one thing I want to know. Was I the only one you ever slept with?" —*Off Your Rocker* (1980)

2095 Goldie Hawn, married to Charles Grodin, has a soft spot for taking in stray dogs, and several of them follow her directly to bed. "Why am I always the last one in the neighborhood to get into bed with you?" Grodin grumbles. —*Seems Like Old Times* (1980)

2096 Goldie Hawn's marriage is going from bad to worse, and she is buckling under the strain. "Once upon a time you had a sense of humor," husband Charles Grodin reminds her. "I remember it," she recalls. "The day I married you." —*Seems Like Old Times* (1980)

2097 Martin Mull, trying to patch things up with estranged wife Tuesday Weld, says: "I think we have some important stuff going for us." "Yeah," she

says, "anger, mistrust, alienation, lack of communciation—" "Right, and I'm not going to give that stuff up without a fight." —*Serial* (1980)

2098 Husband Jack Weston faults wife Rita Moreno: "Do you have to say everything on your mind? Do you think your thoughts should just fall down on your tongue like a gum ball machine?" —*The Four Seasons* (1981)

2099 Clothing manufacturer Jack Warden asks a long-time acquaintance and salesman about his wife, only to learn the man has lost two spouses. "I consider myself a fortunate man," the salesman contends. "I found myself a third, wonderful wife." "How is she?" Warden asks. "A little under the weather." —*So Fine* (1981)

2100 "There is a little tiny seed sprouting in my mind," Jack Nicholson's wife says before she presents her idea. "I married a banana," Nicholson blurts out. —*The Border* (1982)

2101 Rob (Dudley Moore) and his wife have split up, and his friend Richard Mulligan tries to bring them together again. "Look," he pleads with Rob's wife, "I'm not saying he didn't make some major mistakes. When it comes to value judgments, Rob's right up there with Custer and Nixon." —*Micki & Maude* (1984)

2102 Suburbanite Sid Caesar grumbles about his wife's covering all the living room furniture with plastic. "I haven't sat in that room since my son was born," he says. "I keep sliding off everything." —*Over the Brooklyn Bridge* (1984)

2103 "All you do is drink and play dice," Mia Farrow protests to her unemployed husband Danny Aiello, "and I wind up getting smacked." "I always warn you first," he replies. —*The Purple Rose of Cairo* (1985)

2104 "Do I think you're extravagant?" Rodney Dangerfield says to his avaricious wife. "Of course not. Everybody goes to Switzerland to have their watches fixed." – *Back to School* (1986)

2105 Businessman Rodney Dangerfield complains about his second wife to his chauffeur and confidant, Burt Young: "She gives great headache. I can't believe I'm married five years. It seems like yesterday. And you know what a lousy day yesterday was." – *Back to School* (1986)

2106 At a Beverly Hills Thanksgiving dinner, a bored wife infatuated with her yogi announces to her husband she would like to walk on hot coals. "Is that a tax deduction, yogi?" the husband asks. "Yes." "It is? Then walk on hot coals." – *Down and Out in Beverly Hills* (1986)

2107 Shelley Long berates her husband: "I don't want someone who puts off foreplay until he can find a padded hanger for his cashmere blazer." – *Hello Again* (1987)

2108 Alan King, estranged from his wife for many years, learns from his son Billy Crystal that she has moved to Vermont. "Vermont?" King remarks. "A woman her age is supposed to move to Florida. Who moves to Vermont?" "She likes the cold," Crystal explains. "She should. She invented it." – *Memories of Me* (1988)

2109 "My husband and I fell in love at first sight," divorced Mia Farrow admits to Woody Allen. "Maybe I should have taken a second look." – *Crimes and Misdemeanors* (1989)

2110 Comic Henny Youngman jokes about his wife: "I said, 'Where do you want to go for your anniversary?' She said, 'I want to go somewhere I've never been before.' I said, 'Try the kitchen.'" – *GoodFellas* (1990)

2111 John Larroquette and his wife Kirstie Alley discuss a friend who has left his wife. "What did you tell him?" Alley asks. "All I said was that he should try standing up for himself once in a while," Larroquette admits. "You saw what a wreck he was." "But he was her wreck," she explains. "She liked him like that. She craved human sacrifice and he was it." – *Madhouse* (1990)

2112 Slinky Morticia Addams (Anjelica Huston) sympathetically gazes at her agonizing husband Gomez (Raul Julia). "Don't torture yourself," she says. "That's my job." – *The Addams Family* (1991)

2113 "Oh, congratulations," police detective Leslie Nielsen says to fellow officer George Kennedy. "I understand that Edna's pregnant again." "Yes, and if I catch the guy who did it –" – *The Naked Gun 2 1/2: The Smell of Fear* (1991)

Ideals and Convictions

2114 Hungry circus entertainer Robert Woolsey is torn between adhering to his pride and accepting charity when a gentleman invites him to spend a few days on a Southern plantation. "Home cooking and three meals a day," he muses. "The old hat says: 'Wear me high,' but the stomach whispers: 'Chicken and hot cakes.'" – *Dixiana* (1930)

2115 When war breaks out between Freedonia and Sylvania, Groucho Marx looks at Margaret Dumont and says to his brothers: "Remember, we're fighting for this woman's honor, which is probably more than she ever did." – *Duck Soup* (1933)

2116 Socialite Barbara Stanwyck has been threatened by a killer, and Henry Fonda comes to her rescue. "Hilda," he addresses Stanwyck's maid (Hattie McDaniel), "can you handle a gun?" "No, sir," she replies sharply, "I's a pacifist." – *The Mad Miss Manton* (1938)

2117 Avowed anti–Communist Felix Bressart escapes from Russia and joins his daughter Hedy Lamarr and son-in-law Clark Gable in the U.S. They take him to his first baseball game where he is awakened suddenly by a cheering crowd. "What happened?" he asks. "The Dodgers are murdering the Reds!" Lamarr shouts with joy. "Aha!" proclaims Bressart. "The counter-revolution!" – *Comrade X* (1940)

2118 Courtesan Isabel Jeans, retired from active service, trains Gigi (Leslie Caron) to carry on the class-tradition of their profession: "It doesn't matter who gives them, as long as you never wear anything second-rate. Gigi, hold on to your ideals." – *Gigi* (1958)

2119 Good-natured Jerry Lewis shops for his neighbor, an elderly woman constantly glued to her TV set. "I'm sorry I interrupted you during the commercial," he says. "I believe in loyalty to the sponsor," she explains. "That's what's wrong with the world today – not enough loyalty." – *Rock-a-Bye Baby* (1958)

2120 A fervent cockney Marxist tells her equally eccentric son Morgan (David Warner) about his dead father: "He wanted to shoot the royal family and put everyone who had been to public school in a chain gang. He was an idealist, your dad was." – *Morgan* (1966)

2121 Glenda Jackson, as a young woman who believes in the doctrine of Chairman Mao, says: "I believe in China's violent revolution, but I couldn't kick a nun." – *Tell Me Lies* (1968)

2122 Smalltime private eye Richard Dreyfuss tracks down a former sixties revolutionary who is now an advertising executive living a plush life in a Los Angeles suburb. "You know why nobody lasts as a revolutionary in this country?" the former radical remarks. "Because it's like being a spoilsport at an orgy – all those goodies spread out in front of you...." – *The Big Fix* (1978)

2123 As the nine Supreme Court justices assemble for a photograph, they casually comment upon their principles. "My convictions don't move," declares a conservative justice. "Neither did the dinosaurs," quips justice Walter Matthau." – *First Monday in October* (1981)

2124 In an old California town ruled by Mexico, landowner George Hamilton is attracted to a young woman activist who is busily engaged in handing out fliers to the peasantry encouraging them to fight against oppression. "A new wind is blowing across the land," she declares to Hamilton, "the wind of independence. And it carries aloft the bird of freedom which will drop the egg of democracy on your head." – *Zorro, the Gay Blade* (1981)

2125 An F.B.I. agent identifies former hippies Eric Roberts and Cheech Marin in a photograph. "I know these men," the first agent says. "Are they terrorists?" "Much worse. They're idealists!" – *Rude Awakening* (1989)

Incarceration

2126 Upon the release of former bootleggers Stan Laurel and Oliver Hardy from prison, warden Wilfred Lucas tells them to forget their incarceration, to start life anew and then asks if he can be of any help. "Can we take your order for a couple of cases?" Laurel asks. – *Pardon Us* (1931)

2127 "My brother goes to San Quentin," Gracie Allen informs George Burns. "He *goes* to San Quentin?" Burns questions. "He's working his way through." – *The Big Broadcast* (1932)

2128 During a football game between two rival prisons, the announcer (Robert Armstrong) gets carried away with the excitement of the moment: "It's first down and ten years to do – I mean ten yards to go!" – *Hold 'Em Jail* (1932)

2129 In a Hollywood restaurant a meddlesome publicity hound forces himself on popular film director Lowell Sherman, who holds a rather low opinion of his uninvited guest. "Every hour you're out of jail, you're away from home," Sherman quips. – *What Price Hollywood?* (1932)

2130 During a visit to a prison to see her convicted lover, Mae West recognizes an old acquaintance. "He's one of the fastest guys in the business," she remarks, "but he's taking his time now." – *She Done Him Wrong* (1933)

2131 "What's that?" Roman prisoner Eddie Cantor asks his cell-mate after hearing frightening roars. "Hungry lions in the next cell." "Oh," innocent Cantor remarks, "I'd like to feed them." "You will," his fellow prisoner says ominously. – *Roman Scandals* (1933)

2132 When a fellow prisoner tries to get newspaper cameraman Gordon Jones into a card game, another inmate intrudes. "What ill wind brought this gentleman here, I do not know," the man announces. "But that he will deign to consort in a game of chance with ruffians of our caliber is out of the question." – *They Wanted to Marry* (1937)

2133 Socialite Betty Furness ends up in jail for the second time in a few days, and a guard recognizes her. "I shall always remember this place for its excellent service," she jokes, "and recommend it to my friends." "There's nothing too good for our regular patrons," the guard returns. – *They Wanted to Marry* (1937)

2134 Convict Warren Hymer bids farewell to freed cell-mate Henry Fonda: "Gee, Eddie, the old cell won't seem the same without you." – *You Only Live Once* (1937)

2135 Wallace Ford and two fellow ex-cons discuss their attitudes about police, with Ford concluding that cops "do the best they can." "I wish you wouldn't use that word 'can,'" says Stuart Erwin. "Why not?" questions the third. "'Can' is a 'voib.'" "It may be a 'voib' to you," Erwin argues, "but to me it's a joint where you do six months." – *Back Door to Heaven* (1939)

2136 British sergeant Cary Grant in colonial India lands in the guardhouse and asks water boy Gunga Din (Sam Jaffe) to bring him a tool to help him break out. Din faithfully responds by returning to the barred window with – a fork. "What do you think I want to break out of," Grant storms, "a bloomin' pudding?" – *Gunga Din* (1939)

2137 During the Spanish Civil War, a monk visits condemned American pilot

Ray Milland in his last hours. "This is my first execution," the monk confesses. "It's mine, too," Milland rejoins. – *Arise, My Love* (1940)

2138 Convict Guinn "Big Boy" Williams informs John Garfield of at least one prison-escape hazard: "I knew a guy who spent six months diggin' his way out of here and came up in the warden's office." – *Castle on the Hudson* (1940)

2139 Locked up for starting a donnybrook, sailor Lou Costello is visited by his chief. "Hello, boss," Costello greets him. "What are you in for?" – *In the Navy* (1941)

2140 Convict James Cagney, a former dentist, seizes on the opportunity of working on the warden's teeth. Although out of practice, Cagney hopes to confirm the pardon promised by the warden. "You fool!" the warden shouts. "You drilled right through the bridge!" "This won't spoil the pardon, will it, warden?" Cagney asks as he is dragged away. – *Strawberry Blonde* (1941)

2141 "Your stay at the prison camp can be made most intolerable," the German commander threatens. "It's okay to visit," pilot Ronald Reagan cracks, "but we wouldn't want to live there." – *Desperate Journey* (1942)

2142 Rookies Wally Brown and Alan Carney are A.W.O.L. and worry that their plan might backfire. "Instead of getting out of the guardhouse in fifty years," Brown muses, "we'll get out in seventy years. What's the difference?" "Twenty years," Carney replies. – *Adventures of a Rookie* (1943)

2143 Amateur sleuth Red Skelton, in a police station, remarks to his chauffeur Rags Ragland: "It's so crowded here I feel like a sardine." "Well," replies Ragland, "you're in a can, ain't you?" – *Whistling in Brooklyn* (1943)

2144 Joan Davis questions Jack Haley about a photo in his family album. "That's

an uncle of mine involved in a counterfeit mess." "My, he's tall," she remarks. "That's because he was up the river for a stretch." – *George White's Scandals* (1945)

2145 Detective Charlie Chan's chauffeur, Mantan Moreland, discovers friend Willie Best in a jail cell. "Maybe I can get you out," Moreland says. "I got an 'in' around here." "I don't need no 'in,'" Best replies. "I'm already in. I want to get out." "What are you in for?" "Oh," explains Best, "just loitering." "Where?" "In a bank." "When?" Moreland asks. "Around midnight." – *The Shanghai Chest* (1948)

2146 Bob Hope, posing as Casanova, is thrown into a Venetian dungeon and sentenced to death. However, his half-mad cell-mate (Lon Chaney) offers him an escape route through a secret tunnel he has dug in exchange for Hope's fine clothing. "If you've been here all this time," Hope questions, "how come you've never used this tunnel to escape?" "Me, escape?" Chaney laughs. "Good sir, it took me seventeen years to dig that tunnel. I make my living renting it to my cell-mates. It is my only source of income." "The world will always remember you as the man who invented the toll tunnel," Hope concludes. – *Casanova's Big Night* (1954)

2147 While in Paris, Bob Hope is mistakenly arrested and placed in jail overnight. U.S. embassy employee Martha Hyer arrives the next morning to bail him out. "Have you seen the morning paper?" she asks, referring to the gravity of the charges. "I wanted to go down to the corner for one," Hope quips from his cell, "but they're terribly square around here." – *Paris Holiday* (1958)

2148 Among the prisoners of a small-town jail in the Southwest is a garrulous preacher. "Ah, the temptations of the flesh," he reflects. "I fought them my whole life long." "Then how come you're in here?" a fellow prisoner asks. "I said I fought them," the preacher replies. "I didn't say I fought them off." – *Lonely Are the Brave* (1962)

2149 In a World War II Japanese prison camp chiefly for British soldiers, officer Tom Courtenay, in charge of camp discipline, accuses American hustler George Segal of buying and selling stolen goods, particularly an officer's gold ring. "Did he ever show you the ring?" Courtenay charges. "No," Segal replies flippantly. "As far as I remember, he never discussed marriage." – *King Rat* (1965)

2150 Convict Woody Allen gets mixed up with a prison break and is asked to steal the guards' underwear as part of the plan. "If you've got their uniforms," Woody asks two fellow plotters, "why do you need their underwear?" "We want to do this as realistically as possible," one explains. "I'm known for my detailed work," the other replies. – *Take the Money and Run* (1969)

2151 The Duke De Sisi, a French aristocrat, intends to strike fear into the heart of a peasant held captive in a dungeon. "Do you know who I am?" the Duke imperiously demands. "The scrounge of Corsica?" the humble prisoner asks. "That's 'scourge'!" the Duke blares. – *Start the Revolution Without Me* (1970)

2152 Television star Bob Hope is arrested on suspicion of murder in a small Southwestern town and taken into custody. "I'm entitled to one phone call," he reminds sheriff Keenan Wynn. "If somebody phones you, I'll let you know," the lawman replies. – *Cancel My Reservation* (1972)

2153 When a fellow inmate asks Donald Sutherland what he's in jail for, he says that he held up several liquor stores. "Did you ever kill anyone?" his cell-mate asks. "No," Sutherland replies, "but in the last one the clerk fainted." – *Steelyard Blues* (1973)

2154 Ex-football star Burt Reynolds is asked by fellow chain-gang convict Jim

Hampton why he had shaved points during a game. "It's a long story," Reynolds says. "I got eight years," Hampton replies. – *The Longest Yard* (1974)

2155 Convict Michael Caine, a sophisticated bank robber who is living the "good life" in his prison cell, explodes at the clumsiness of his two inept servants, fellow prisoners James Caan and Elliott Gould. "I want these two clods assigned to the nitro detail as soon as possible!" he orders the intimidated warden (Burt Young). "You mean permanently?" "Not permanently! Just until they die!" – *Harry and Walter Go to New York* (1976)

2156 A jail guard, before placing a gay prisoner into a cell, begins to search under the man's dress. "You got any concealed weapons?" the guard asks. "You got something concealed?" "But it ain't no weapon," a fellow prisoner blurts out. – *...And Justice for All* (1979)

2157 Convicts Gene Wilder and Richard Pryor have been falsely accused of robbing a bank and have been sentenced to one hundred and thirty years. "The fact is you were railroaded," their lawyer's assistant asserts. "Just another example of a repressive criminal system coming down on the bottom layer of society." "I don't know about the bottom part," Wilder timidly demurs, "but I couldn't agree with you more on the rest." – *Stir Crazy* (1980)

2158 Convicts Gene Wilder and Richard Pryor, recent inmates at a tough prison, observe an oversized, mean-looking fellow inmate in another section of the mess hall and inquire about his background. "The biggest mass murderer in the history of the Southwest," another convict relates. "He killed his entire family and all his relatives in one weekend. And then he killed some more people who reminded him of his family." "Is he here for rehabilitation?" Wilder asks. – *Stir Crazy* (1980)

2159 Richard Pryor and his buddy John Candy, the only two arrested for brawling in a saloon, are in jail awaiting their trial. "Why is it when there's trouble, we're the ones that get into it?" Pryor wonders aloud. "There's a bar full of people and we're the only ones in jail." "I don't think it's racial, you know," Candy replies, "because I'm in here with you." – *Brewster's Millions* (1985)

2160 "Your time's just been doubled," announces a voice of authority to a young reform-school inmate. "Yeah," the young woman retorts, "and so's your chin." – *Reform School Girls* (1986)

2161 Spoiled, rich Beverly Hills daughter Ally Sheedy is arrested for speeding and possession of drugs and placed in a cell with a local hooker. "My poor father," Sheedy muses aloud. "When this hits the papers – he's a philanthropist." "Is he serving time, too?" her cell-mate asks. – *Maid to Order* (1987)

2162 Californian Chevy Chase, in the South on business, is arrested and falsely accused of murder. "You feel like making a statement?" a sheriff asks him. "A statement?" Chase repeats. "'Ask not what your country can do for you; ask what you can do for your country.'" – *Fletch Lives* (1989)

Incompetence

2163 A bungling mayor of a Mexican village tries to make a speech in the square but has trouble staying on his horse. "Why don't you get a bicycle?" someone shouts from the crowd. "What do you mean?" the offended mayor barks. "I know how to ride a horse. I be part of a horse." "Yeah," the voice continues, "and I know what part." – *Captain Thunder* (1931)

2164 Inept movie studio supervisor Jack Oakie over-orders the number of airplanes necessary for a film. "Did you order four hundred sixty airplanes?" his boss shouts. "Well," Oakie falters, "don't you believe in aviation?" – *Once in a Lifetime* (1932)

2165 Inept American pilots Spencer Tracy and George Cooper are stationed in France during World War I. "I bring down one more of our planes," one of the pair cracks, "and I'll be a German ace." – *Sky Devils* (1932)

2166 Louis Calhern hires Chico and Harpo Marx to follow Groucho. "Well," Chico reports, "you remember you gave us a picture of this man and said 'Follow him'? Well, we get on-a the job right away and in one hour – even less than an hour – " "Yes?" Calhern asks anxiously. "We lose-a the picture," Chico announces victoriously. "That's pretty good, eh?" – *Duck Soup* (1933)

2167 Manicurist Carole Lombard twice draws blood from Fred MacMurray's cuticles. "If you think I should have ether," he says wryly, "don't be afraid to say so." – *Hands Across the Table* (1935)

2168 Parkyakarkus applies for the position of bodyguard to amusement park manager Eddie Cantor. "You say you've been a bodyguard to one man for six years?" Cantor asks. "Sure," the stranger replies, "and I could still even have that job today." "But what?" "But he was killed." "You must have been a fine bodyguard." "You bet. They don't get me." – *Strike Me Pink* (1936)

2169 Wealthy Miriam Hopkins takes a taxi to Greenwich Village and grudgingly pays the driver. "You can keep the change," she announces. "Gee, thanks." "It's for driving lessons," she adds. — *Wise Girl* (1937)

2170 Bob Hope's scheme to defame a U.S. senator backfires, and he tries to abate the anger of his coconspirators. "I admit on the surface it looks bad," he admits, "but if you think about it a little while – it gets worse, doesn't it?" — *Louisiana Purchase* (1941)

2171 Bungling detective Donald MacBride is summoned to investigate a murder. "Where's your taxi?" he shouts at cabby Dennis O'Keefe. "Where do you think?" replies O'Keefe. "I'm not paid to think!" MacBride bellows. "I'm from City Hall!" – *Topper Returns* (1941)

2172 George Jessel, on the phone with his sister, tries to convince her that her boyfriend is unemployable. "Any fellow who gets fired from a five-and-ten-cent store because he can't remember the prices...." – *Stage Door Canteen* (1943)

2173 International correspondent Bob Hope bungles several major assignments such as the Rothstein murder, the Munich bombing and Hitler's invasion of Russia. His news agency boss restrains himself from committing mayhem on the returning incompetent. "You've wrecked my nervous system, ruined my reputation, you've cost me money, customers and good will!" he cries. "Does that mean you're dissatisfied with my work, chief?" Hope asks. – *They Got Me Covered* (1943)

2174 Reporter Bob Hope provides a defense for his complete incompetence to girlfriend Dorothy Lamour. "Everyone makes mistakes," he explains. "Is it my fault I'm good at it?" – *They Got Me Covered* (1943)

2175 Feather-brained Jane Wyman pleads with Washington bureaucrat Charles Ruggles for a job in his office. "I could file things, and generally I could find them," she boasts. "And if she can't," her friend Ann Sheridan adds, "you could always offer a reward." – *The Doughgirls* (1944)

2176 Four bands are welcoming home World War II hero Eddie Bracken, and prissy master of ceremonies Franklin Pangborn despairs. He is unable to sort out which band is to play what and when. "O Death," he cries, "where is thy sting?" – *Hail the Conquering Hero* (1944)

2177 Newly appointed airline stewardess Jane Wyman makes her debut by forgetting to have the passengers' meals brought onto the plane, which has to return to the airfield. Following the completion of the flight, she is summoned to the airline chief's office. "Come in, Miss Lewis." "You know who I am?" she asks, surprised. "The whole airline knows who you are," he announces. "Aviation stocks are tumbling." – *Three Guys Named Mike* (1951)

2178 Employer Charles Coburn orders his secretary (Marilyn Monroe): "Get someone to type this." – *Monkey Business* (1952)

2179 A masseur, ordered to massage comic Phil Silvers' bald head, proceeds to pound the comedian's backside. "You're a lousy judge of distance," Silvers cracks. – *Top Banana* (1954)

2180 Jerry Lewis, as bumbling Lieutenant John Paul Steckler of the U.S. Navy, is accused of "misplacing" a destroyer escort, a ship he cannot account for. Branded a possible spy and traitor by his superiors, he objects strongly. "The navy is my whole life," he confesses. "Before I was in the navy I was just John Paul Steckler – the meatball. Now, Lieutenant John Paul Steckler – the meatball." – *Don't Give Up the Ship* (1959)

2181 "I just thought of something," a bungling American government employee in a foreign delegation states. "Should we slip this to the United Press or give this to Billy Graham?" his superior asks sarcastically. "Miracles don't come easy." – *John Goldfarb, Please Come Home* (1964)

2182 In Paris, Commissioner of Police Herbert Lom is furious with the inept Inspector Clouseau (Peter Sellers) for bungling a multiple murder case. "Give me ten men like Clouseau," Lom says to an assistant, "and I could destroy the world." – *A Shot in the Dark* (1964)

2183 Jason Robards, married to Rosemary Murphy, has set up a "love nest" for him and Jane Fonda under the guise of an executive suite. But his blundering secretary, who was his wife's roommate at college, has almost exposed his sweet setup several times. "I can't fire her," Robards exclaims, "but I could kill her!" – *Any Wednesday* (1966)

2184 Clumsy electrician Dom DeLuise is tricked into spying for foreign agents but is found out by Doris Day. "I never wanted to be a spy," he breaks down and weeps. "I never spied on anything. And listen, I would defect, but I don't know where to defect to." – *The Glass Bottom Boat* (1966)

2185 The police arrive at the scene of a crime. "Thirty-five minutes," private detective Marlowe (Robert Mitchum) remarks. "Not bad for a killing. Luckily it wasn't anything serious." – *Farewell, My Lovely* (1975)

2186 French chief of police Dreyfuss (Herbert Lom) cannot fathom the mayhem and destruction caused by officer Clouseau (Peter Sellers). "Compared to Clouseau," Lom acknowledges, "Attila the Hun was a Red Cross worker!" – *The Return of the Pink Panther* (1975)

2187 Detectives Don Knotts and Tim Conway, investigating the murder of a society couple, question one of the domestics. "We will have to know where you were during the entire incident," Knotts asks the woman. "I was in Parker's Restaurant," Conway answers. "I was in the little booth – " "Not you, blockhead!" Knotts interrupts. – *The Private Eyes* (1980)

2188 At a restaurant, executive Bruce Willis screws up a major deal between his boss and a Japanese businessman, embarrassing both parties. "Do I have to say the words?" his employer asks calmly. "I'm fired?" Willis asks. "Fired?" his boss responds. "I only wish we were in the army – so I could have you shot – twice!" – *Blind Date* (1987)

2189 Inexperienced troop leader Shelley Long wants to take her girls into the wilderness, but her assistant leader objects. "I can't let you take the girls out there alone." "Why?" Long inquires. "Because you get lost in your walk-in closet," one of her campers replies. – *Troop Beverly Hills* (1989)

2190 "You know," groggy general Lloyd Bridges addresses his navy pilots, "I personally have flown one hundred ninety-four missions and was shot down during every one. Come to think of it, I've never landed a plane in my life." – *Hot Shots!* (1991)

In-Laws

2191 Jimmy Durante can't seem to please his future mother-in-law (Trixie Friganza), who abuses him each time they meet. When he tries to visit his girlfriend, his nemesis appears at the door. "Oh, it's you, is it?" she grumbles. "I always did say a bad penny has no sense." – *Free and Easy* (1930)

2192 To attend an afternoon wrestling match, W. C. Fields tells his employer that he has to go to the funeral of his mother-in-law. "It must be hard to lose your mother-in-law," his boss commiserates. "Yes, it is," Fields mumbles. "Very hard, almost impossible." – *The Man on the Flying Trapeze* (1935)

2193 Vaudeville performer Eddie Foy (Bob Hope) marries an Italian dancer and inherits her older, meddlesome sister who lives with them for years. At one point Hope raises his voice to the sister, and his wife warns him that she is their guest. "After fourteen years," Hope remarks, "the word is 'tenant.'" – *The Seven Little Foys* (1955)

2194 Milton Berle stops for a few minutes to see if he can help a driver who has driven off a cliff. He then returns to his wife and his shrewish mother-in-law (Ethel Merman) waiting in the car. "Take it easy, honey," he says to his wife. "These things happen." "Now what kind of an attitude is that?" Merman bellows. "'These things happen.' They only happen because the whole country is full of people who, when these things happen, they just say, 'These things happen.' And that's why

these things happen!" – *It's a Mad Mad Mad Mad World* (1963)

2195 In ancient Egypt Dudley Moore's wife has turned into a pillar of salt when she dared to look back at the wicked city of New Sodom. A saddened Moore takes the statue home to his father, James Coco. "Maybe you ought to cover her with a cloth," Coco suggests. "I would never forgive myself if a daughter-in-law of mine got chipped." – *Wholly Moses* (1980)

2196 Struggling baby photographer Rodney Dangerfield is assailed by his wealthy mother-in-law Geraldine Fitzgerald. "Walk out on him, dear," she says to her daughter. "His entire body is bloodshot." – *Easy Money* (1983)

2197 Struggling baby photographer Rodney Dangerfield takes a battery of verbal abuse from his wealthy mother-in-law. "You're an inspiration for twin beds," he retorts during one of their battles. – *Easy Money* (1983)

2198 "You hate my parents," Patricia Wettig charges husband Billy Crystal. "I don't hate your parents," he insists. "You know my father since you're eighteen years old and you've never called him by name." "What *is* his name?" Billy asks after a slight pause. – *City Slickers* (1991)

Innocence

2199 Oliver Hardy angrily asks Stan Laurel why he drank the whole soda they were supposed to share. "I couldn't help it," Laurel apologizes. "My half was on the bottom." – *Men o' War* (1929)

2200 Police officers Stan Laurel and Oliver Hardy witness a burglary in

progress. "We're just in the nick of time," says Hardy. "What time is it?" asks the bemused Laurel. – *The Midnight Patrol* (1933)

2201 Oliver Hardy, hiding in an attic, boasts to pal Stan Laurel: "To catch a Hardy, they've got to get up very early in the morning." "What time?" asks Laurel. – *Sons of the Desert* (1933)

2202 To weigh down the corpse of a man Oliver Hardy concludes will never get to heaven, he asks Stan Laurel to find a large piece of coal. "Do you have to take your own coal with you when you go to 'the other place'?" Laurel asks. – *The Live Ghost* (1934)

2203 "Every day you learn more and more about less and less," George Burns says to Gracie Allen, "until the day will arrive when you'll know everything about nothing." "Oh, George," an impressed Gracie replies, "why don't you say things like that when we're out with company?" – *Six of a Kind* (1934)

2204 Country girl Frances Dee, in New York for a fling, dines at a fancy restaurant where she has trouble ordering from the menu of foreign-named dishes. When she points to a dish which the waiter refuses to bring her, she demands to know why. "Because that's the proprietor!" – *The Gay Deception* (1935)

2205 Naive smalltown playwright Jack Haley wants visiting Broadway producer Roger Pryor to read his long script, but Pryor prefers a synopsis. "A synopsis?" Haley ponders. "I don't think we have any synopsis, but I can get you some home-made wine." – *The Girl Friend* (1935)

2206 "Do you think a woman can be innocent?" publisher Noel Coward asks a woman of the world. "Hm-m, yes," she replies, "unless you would care to call it arrested development." – *The Scoundrel* (1935)

2207 Anthony Adverse (Fredric March), an orphan raised as a rich man's son, falls in love with the cook's daughter (Olivia de Havilland). Riding in a rustic wagon, he tries to kiss her. "You mustn't," she says. "Not out on a road like this. Let's sing." – *Anthony Adverse* (1936)

2208 At a restaurant, Stan Laurel and Oliver Hardy cannot pay their bill. Their waiter (Alan Hale) is furious. "Either you give me that dough," Hale threatens, "or I'll beat you both up, or I'll have you pinched, or maybe I'll beat you both up and have you pinched, too." "Can't you make up your mind?" Stan inquires innocently. – *Our Relations* (1936)

2209 The Three Stooges unknowingly dig into a U.S. government vault while searching for buried treasure. They are brought before the President of the U.S., who exonerates them when he learns they innocently wanted to help a crippled child raise money for an operation. "In view of the extenuating circumstances," the President announces, "I find it possible to extend executive clemency." "No, please, not that!" pleads Curly. – *Cash and Carry* (1937)

2210 Scatterbrained socialite Katharine Hepburn misplaces a rare bone paleontologist Cary Grant has brought back from an expedition. "It took three expeditions and five years to find that one!" he shouts. "Now that they know where to find them," she suggests, "couldn't you send them back to get another?" – *Bringing Up Baby* (1938)

2211 "How are the acoustics here? a singer at a hotel asks little Shirley Temple. "Oh," Shirley replies, "we don't have any. We use Flit." – *Little Miss Broadway* (1938)

2212 French Foreign Legionnaires Stan Laurel and Oliver Hardy are sentenced to face a firing squad as deserters. "That's a nice pickle we're in–shot at sunrise," Ollie muses. "I hope it's cloudy tomorrow," Stan says. – *The Flying Deuces* (1939)

2213 Hostess Mary Boland sees a man creeping past her window at night and awakens house guest Nancy Kelly. "I want to know why–I mean I want to know why he's creeping–*past* my window." – *He Married His Wife* (1940)

2214 Englishman John Sutton and his two Canadian fur-trading companions, dressed in buckskins and coonskin caps, have just arrived in England and appear at the King of England's ball. "What odd costumes!" the King exclaims to his dancing partner. "They look like aborigines." "Where's that?" the young woman asks. – *Hudson's Bay* (1940)

2215 "If the world was run right," suggests Bing Crosby, "only women would get married." "Hey," Bob Hope questions, "can they do that?" – *Road to Singapore* (1940)

2216 Eddie Bracken and two other college football players are ordered not to play in the following day's big game. "We're turning in our suits," Bracken sadly informs his girlfriend of the bad news. "You mean you're going to play in the nude?" she asks. – *Too Many Girls* (1940)

2217 As war clouds gather across America, film actor Bob Hope tries to warn his foreign-born housekeeper to register with the proper authorities. "You're an alien," he explains, "and you're supposed to register." "They got enough aliens," the woman replies. "They don't need me." – *Caught in the Draft* (1941)

2218 Art collector Lloyd Corrigan, helping to investigate a warehouse containing stolen art treasures, is accused by a policeman of planning a burglary. The innocent man pleads his case in vain. "If you have anything to say, you can tell it to the sergeant," the officer announces. "You have a little Gestapo in you," Corrigan grumbles as he is marched off. – *Confessions of Boston Blackie* (1941)

2219 In 1933 President Roosevelt declared a five-day nationwide bank holiday. Several years later, Bob Hope is close to winning a ten thousand dollar wager that he could tell nothing but the truth for twenty-four hours. "In six more hours," he informs his servant Willie Best, "it'll be Christmas." "Is Roosevelt moving the holidays around again?" Best asks. – *Nothing But the Truth* (1941)

2220 Charming, scatterbrained American Ginger Rogers is in Austria during the Nazi Anschluss. "Hitler is here!" shouts correspondent Cary Grant as the German army rolls into Vienna. "Well, I can't see him now," Rogers replies, poking her head through the door. "I'm dressing." – *Once Upon a Honeymoon* (1942)

2221 Two crooked nightclub owners who are trying to frame gullible songwriter Bert Lahr on a murder charge invite him on the telephone to join them at their office. "I think they're going to give me part of the business," Lahr says to girlfriend Patsy Kelly. "I think they're trying to give you *all* of the business," she quips. – *Sing Your Worries Away* (1942)

2222 Tarzan (Johnny Weissmuller), in a Manhattan apartment, walks into a shower fully clothed. "Rain!" he exclaims. "Rain feel good!" – *Tarzan's New York Adventure* (1942)

2223 Cigarette girl Virginia O'Brien, desperate for any man, is out to ensnare fellow nightclub worker Red Skelton. "Can't you see I love you and want you for the father of my children?" she entreats him. "I didn't know you had any," he replies. – *DuBarry Was a Lady* (1943)

2224 Huntz Hall's sister, who is about to be married, plans to move with her husband to the suburbs. "What is it with those suburbs?" Huntz Hall asks his pal Leo Gorcey. "What are they?" "Well," Gorcey explains, "that's a place where you got no running water, you got no trolley cars, you got nothin'." "Oh, poor people, huh?" "That's right." – *Ghosts on the Loose* (1943)

2225 "You know, Ollie," says Stan Laurel, "I was just thinking." "About what?" "Nothing. I was just thinking." – *Jitterbugs* (1943)

2226 Nancy Kelly and George Murphy inform show-business pal Eddie Cantor about their marriage plans and tell him that they are "going to have something that brings people closer together." "You're buying a double bed?" Cantor queries. – *Show Business* (1944)

2227 The male star of a forthcoming romantic movie invites his leading lady, a young starlet, to his beach house, but her friend Lou Costello objects. "Oh, no you don't!" Costello exclaims. "You're not going to take her down to your beach house and get her all sunburned." – *Abbott and Costello in Hollywood* (1945)

2228 "Don't you ever do anything on time?" someone asks chauffeur Mantan Moreland. "Sure I do," he replies. "I bought a car once." "How?" "On time," Moreland replies. – *Dark Alibi* (1946)

2229 Alan Ladd, as a foppish, wastrel son of a shipping tycoon, is shanghaied onto one of his father's ships and suddenly finds himself in the midst of a harsh seaman's life. "You must be glad to help sail your father's ship," a young stowaway says to him. "I'm practically in convulsions," Ladd returns. – *Two Years Before the Mast* (1946)

2230 Theater critic Addison DeWitt (George Sanders) brings blonde companion Marilyn Monroe to a party where she confuses the guests with the service staff. "That's not the writer," he corrects her at one point. "That's the butler." "Well," she explains, "I can't very well shout out, 'Butler!' That may be someone's name." "That's a point," DeWitt says icily, "an idiotic one, but a point." – *All About Eve* (1950)

2231 A U.S. Congressman and his wife visit businessman Broderick Crawford and his uncultured girlfriend, ex-chorus girl Judy Holliday, in their Washington hotel suite. "Too bad the Supreme Court is not in session," the Congressman's wife says in an effort to strike up a conversation with Judy. "You'd love that."

"So what is it?" Judy asks. – *Born Yesterday* (1950)

2232 Big-time reporter Kirk Douglas, exiled to a small-town paper far from New York, complains to his fellow workers about the things he misses, such as Lindy's, Madison Square Garden and Yogi Berra. "What do you know about Yogi Berra?" he asks an employee. "Yogi," she replies. "It's a sort of religion, isn't it?" – *Ace in the Hole* (1951)

2233 Vaudeville comic Bob Hope is mistaken for an international spy and arrested in an alley by police. "Put your hands up higher!" they order. "I can't," Hope counters. "They're attached to my wrists." – *My Favorite Spy* (1951)

2234 Civilian Jerry Lewis lines up with other young men prepared to join the U.S. Navy. Once inside the recruiting station, a sailor approaches the shy recruit. "Would you mind going over in the corner and disrobing?" "I don't even know you!" a shocked Lewis replies. – *Sailor Beware* (1951)

2235 Namby-pamby sailor Jerry Lewis gets duped into a boxing match and enters the ring with a no-nonsense prizefighter. Lewis begins prancing about. "Let's go!" the referee orders. "Where're we going?" Lewis asks. – *Sailor Beware* (1951)

2236 In Rome, runaway princess Audrey Hepburn is befriended and given lodging by reporter Gregory Peck. "This is very unusual," she murmurs. "I've never been alone with a man before – even with my dress on. With my dress off – it's most unusual." – *Roman Holiday* (1953)

2237 Sailors aboard a U.S. Navy vessel discover the nurses' quarters on a nearby island. Using binoculars, they happily while away the hours. One young seaman, distracted by another view, exclaims: "Look, there goes a sea gull!" – *Mister Roberts* (1955)

2238 During World War II sexy reporter Eva Gabor arrives on a Pacific island and asks naval officer Glenn Ford to introduce her to an admiral. "I can't introduce you to an admiral," Ford says. "Why not?" she inquires. "You're both in the same war."—*Don't Go Near the Water* (1957)

2239 Navy officer Cary Grant is dancing with Jayne Mansfield. "I'll say this," he admits. "You have beautiful hair." "And it's natural, except for the color." "Hm-m," Grant responds.—*Kiss Them for Me* (1957)

2240 To get simple-minded private Andy Griffith out of harm's way, sergeant Myron McCormick assigns the backwoods draftee to permanent latrine duty—a job that delights Griffith. "Well," Griffith concludes, "It just goes to show you how good things happen to you when you least expect them."—*No Time for Sergeants* (1958)

2241 "Ain't you ever heard of the Women's Air Force?" draftee Nick Adams asks hillbilly buddy Andy Griffith. "You mean they got one too?" Griffith says in disbelief. "Sure." "Against ours?" Griffith asks.—*No Time for Sergeants* (1958)

2242 "Do you play the market?" Tony Curtis asks Marilyn Monroe. "No," she replies, "the ukulele."—*Some Like It Hot* (1959)

2243 Jerry Lewis is chosen by his fairy godfather Ed Wynn to represent the ordinary people of the world. "There were those who were against you," Wynn informs him. "They thought that the one chosen should be tall, handsome and clever. But I fought for you." "Thank you, godfather, for taking my part."—*Cinderfella* (1960)

2244 Several college students celebrating their spring rites in Fort Lauderdale visit a swank nightclub replete with a giant water tank inhabited by buxom "Lola, the Sea Nymph." Jim Hutton stares wide-eyed at her curvaceous figure. "What lungs!" he gasps.—*Where the Boys Are* (1960)

2245 Off the coast of Jamaica, British agent James Bond (Sean Connery) meets an island-innocent (Ursula Andress) who tells him how a man raped her when she was younger. "And what happened after that?" Connery asks sympathetically. "I put a black widow spider under his mosquito net—a female, and they're the worst. It took him a whole week to die."—*Dr. No* (1962)

2246 In Paris, C.I.A. agent Walter Matthau has widow Audrey Hepburn report to his office. "Do you know what the C.I.A. is?" he asks her. "I don't suppose it's an airline, is it?" she replies. —*Charade* (1963)

2247 An attractive young Greek woman is in love with returning American veteran Robert Preston who knew her only as a little girl. They haven't seen each other for fifteen years. "How shall I tell him?" she cries to her mother. "He thinks I'm six years old." "Kiss him," the mother advises. "You'll see how quickly you age."—*Island of Love* (1963)

2248 "All men are vain," Jackie Gleason, as a protecting, savvy sergeant, says to his innocent army buddy Steve McQueen. "I happen to be a narcissist." "Really?" McQueen exclaims. "I thought you were nuts about girls like everybody else."—*Soldier in the Rain* (1963)

2249 Jane Fonda has made an agreement with her brother (Cliff Robertson) that neither would have sex with anyone until each is married. One day Jane discovers that Cliff has been having an active sex life. "How could you lie to me!" she exclaims. "You swore you didn't sleep with girls!" "That's a loophole—'sleeping,'" Cliff argues.—*Sunday in New York* (1963)

2250 A plain, ingenuous Manchester man visits a prostitute to win a bet and, looking for something interesting to do, asks: "Have you got a dartboard?" "You're not only old-fashioned, darling," the woman concludes, "you're unbelievable."—*Rattle of a Simple Man* (1964)

2251 An orphaned ten-year-old boy (Fergus McClelland) traveling across Africa describes the home he left: "We had lots of servants in baggy silk trousers. One was an ex-eunuch."—*A Boy Ten Feet Tall* (1965)

2252 Halfback Luther "Boom Boom" Jackson (Ron Rich), who accidentally injured television cameraman Jack Lemmon during a football game, visits him in the hospital and finds Lemmon in the wheelchair which Jackson purchased for him. "Use it in good health," Jackson utters awkwardly.—*The Fortune Cookie* (1966)

2253 In ancient Rome, house-of-pleasure owner Phil Silvers informs callow youth Michael Crawford that a beautiful virgin-courtesan has just arrived from Crete. "Is that good?" Crawford asks.—*A Funny Thing Happened on the Way to the Forum* (1966)

2254 Wealthy husband James Mason makes a handsome proposal to his butler's daughter (Lynn Redgrave). "I want you to be my mistress," he says as he hands her a contract. "Will we have shareholders and things?" she asks, wide-eyed.—*Georgy Girl* (1966)

2255 Anne Bancroft, as a married woman with a grown daughter, attempts to seduce recent college graduate Dustin Hoffman. "Do you find me desirable?" she asks. "Oh, no, Mrs. Robinson," he replies. "I think you're the most attractive of all my parents' friends."—*The Graduate* (1967)

2256 A naive farm boy, recently introduced to some of the gamier sides of city life, awakens in a brothel. He finds his woman-of-the-night next to him and, with a contrite heart, laments: "I've ruined you!"—*Gaily, Gaily* (1969)

2257 Town ne'er-do-well Mickey Rooney recommends his sister as a prospective bride for the local blacksmith, but other citizens object. "Your sister's so bucktoothed she eats squash through a picket fence," Noah Beery says. "Yeah, what do you know?" Rooney corrects him. "She doesn't even like squash."—*Cockeyed Cowboys of Calico County* (1970)

2258 Alan Arkin portrays an innocent involved with three women. "Aren't you appalled at the promiscuity you find everywhere?" one of the objects of his desires comments. "I haven't found it anywhere," the disappointed Arkin replies.—*Last of the Red Hot Lovers* (1972)

2259 Pompous, sadistic prison warden Eddie Albert boasts about the power he sways over the inmates. "Why is it, do you suppose, that I can walk through this yard—surrounded by hate—and in total command?" he asks one of his guards. "Because you got fifteen gun hands all around you that say you can."—*The Longest Yard* (1974)

2260 Guileless Steve Martin meets Bernadette Peters and immediately falls in love with her. She tells him she's a cosmetologist. "A cosmetologist! he exclaims. "That's unbelievable! Impressive! It must be tough to handle weightlessness."—*The Jerk* (1979)

2261 Drunken millionaire playboy Dudley Moore reminisces with his servant John Gielgud about their many years together. "Remember how we would play hide-and-seek and you couldn't find me?" Moore recalls. "I couldn't find you," Gielgud confesses, "because I didn't look for you."—*Arthur* (1981)

2262 A passenger plane on the way to the moon is on a collision course with the sun. Lloyd Bridges, in charge of the airport control tower, is called in to prevent the impending disaster. "I want to know absolutely everything that's happened up to now," he commands his assistant. "Well, let's see," the man ponders. "First, the earth cooled, and then the dinosaurs came...."–*Airplane II: The Sequel* (1982)

2263 Harried executive Kevin McCarthy discovers a report is missing from his desk and believes the janitor knows where it is. "I assume you know why I called you," McCarthy bellows. "Because you're lonely?" the janitor responds. –*UHF* (1989)

2264 Con artist Dana Carvey, impersonating a successful corporate executive, has problems ordering from an esoteric menu in an exclusive restaurant. "Excuse me," a discreet waiter whispers to him, "but that is the address of the wine distributor."–*Opportunity Knocks* (1990)

2265 When helpful video rental store owner Mercedes Ruehl observes a customer unobtrusively skulking toward the pornography section, she asks: "You want a plot?"–*The Fisher King* (1991)

2266 Two little children sit on a dock by the lake on a warm summer day. "Have you ever kissed anyone?" the little girl asks. "Like they do on TV?" the boy asks. "No." "Maybe we should try it," she suggests. "Close your eyes." "Then I won't be able to see anything."–*My Girl* (1991)

2267 Young Danny LaPaglia receives a letter about his military status which his father Danny Aiello has opened. "You see this letter?" Aiello says. "You know what it says? It says the United States government thinks you're a calculated risk!" "Is that good or bad?" LaPaglia asks.–*29th Street* (1991)

2268 At the time of the Cuban Missile Crisis, politically conscious Lisa Jakub tells a new student (Simon Fenton) at her high school that she was given detention for protesting an air raid drill. "Gandhi was put away for a year," she beams. "I don't know that many people," he replies after a long pause.–*Matinee* (1993)

Intelligence

2269 Store owner Eddie Cantor calls his partner a fool in front of a customer and is later rebuked. "Don't you tell anyone I'm a damn fool!" his partner exclaims. "I didn't know it was a secret," Cantor retorts.–*Glorifying the American Girl* (1929)

2270 "How long can a man live without brains?" a doctor wonders out loud after trying to elicit information from giddy patient Eddie Cantor. "I don't know," Cantor replies. "How old are you?" "Forty-two," the doctor volunteers.–*Insurance* (1930)

2271 Convict Warren Hymer tries to comprehend the results of his intelligence test. "What does M-O-R-O-N spell?" asks the bemused Hymer, exiting from the test. "Why, that spells 'moron,'" replies a fellow inmate. "I passed one hundred percent!" Hymer proudly exclaims.–*Up the River* (1930)

2272 Escaped convict Warren Hymer, while visiting a wealthy home, sees a photograph on a mantel. "Is that your father?" he asks the pretty hostess. "No," she replies. "That's Abraham Lincoln."–*Up the River* (1930)

2273 Robert Woolsey: "Some people call me a wit." Bert Wheeler: "And they're half right."–*Caught Plastered* (1931)

2274 Jean Harlow, having schemed to personally deliver the office mail to her worried boss' home, is walking with her level-headed friend Una Merkel toward his residence. "I'm beginning to get nervous," Harlow says, pausing. "I'd be nervous too if I didn't have any more brains than you've got." – *Red-Headed Woman* (1932)

2275 Freedonia's leader Groucho Marx at a cabinet meeting is presented with a document for his consideration. "Is it clear?" a member asks. "Clear?" echoes Groucho. "Why, a four-year-old child could understand this report. Turning to his secretary, he orders: "Go out and get a four-year-old child. I can't make heads or tails of it." – *Duck Soup* (1933)

2276 "You know," Franklin Pangborn says to nurse Gracie Allen, "you're very smart. To what do you attribute your smartness?" "Three things," Gracie answers proudly. "First, my good memory, and the other two things, I forgot." – *International House* (1933)

2277 Stan Laurel proposes that a baby would bring the Hardys closer together, and Ollie thinks he is right. "You bet I'm right," Laurel declares. "You know I'm not so dumb as you look." – *Sons of the Desert* (1933)

2278 Fight manager Knobby Walsh (Jimmy Durante) is knocked down by a crooked fighter. "Are you gonna give me that money?" the fighter demands. "I'm givin' you a slight curl of my lip," Durante replies after rising up. But he is knocked down again. "What's brawn against brains? Mentally, I got you licked!" – *Palooka* (1934)

2279 Charlie Chan (Warner Oland): "Hasty conclusion easy to make – like hole in water." – *Charlie Chan in Egypt* (1935)

2280 "I've got an idea!" lawyer Aline McMahon's not-too-bright partner exclaims. "Beginner's luck," she scoffs. – *To Beat the Band* (1935)

2281 Jack Oakie, portraying a ham actor who thinks he is an amateur sleuth, receives threats on his life. Publicity agent Ann Sothern, concerned for his safety, suggests: "Let me get you a bodyguard." "Did Sherlock Holmes have a bodyguard?" Oakie asks. "No," she replies, "but he had brains." – *Super-Sleuth* (1937)

2282 A local Algerian police officer explains to a cynical police inspector, recently arrived from Paris, why it is difficult to arrest someone in the Casbah, with its labyrinthian streets. "When one can't use guns," the officer concludes, "one must use brains." "I prefer guns," the inspector counters. "In your case, honest sir, such a preference is unavoidable." – *Algiers* (1938)

2283 Scarecrow Jack Haley thinks he has a brain, but his neurons are hopelessly crossed. "The sum of the squares of any two sides of an isosceles triangle is equal to the square root of the remaining sides. Oh, joy! Rapture! I got a brain!" He turns to the Wizard of Oz (Frank Morgan) and says: "How can I ever thank you enough?" "Well," the Wizard replies, "you can't." – *The Wizard of Oz* (1939)

2284 Street-smart burlesque dancer Sugarpuss O'Shea (Barbara Stanwyck) decides to help professor Gary Cooper write a lexicon on slang. Fingering a book on Greek philosophy, she remarks: "I got a set like this with a radio inside." – *Ball of Fire* (1941)

2285 Police chief Arthur Shields grills innocent suspect Allen Jenkins about a murder. "You know me," Shields says affably, "I have a heart." "Yeah," Jenkins retorts, "and I only wish you had a brain to go with it." – *The Gay Falcon* (1941)

2286 Correspondent Cary Grant tells girlfriend Ginger Rogers of his impressions when he first met her: "If a gnat had dived into your pool of knowledge, it would have broken its neck." – *Once Upon a Honeymoon* (1942)

2287 Pet shop employee Lou Costello brings down the wrath of his boss who has warned him repeatedly not to take a particular dog out without a muzzle. "I put a muzzle on," Costello insists, "but I couldn't breathe." – *Rio Rita* (1942)

2288 Bob Hope and Bing Crosby are adrift on a raft in the Mediterranean after their ship has sunk. "I took one look at that crate, and I knew it would blow up in our faces," Hope says. "Wait till they find out who was smoking in the powder room," Crosby replies. – *Road to Morocco* (1942)

2289 During World War II, store owner Wallace Beery is accused of selling illegal meat to his customers. "You don't think I'm mixed up in that black market thing, do you?" he asks neighbor Marjorie Main. "Certainly not," she replies. "You don't have brains enough to be a crook." "Gee," a grateful Beery says, "them's the kindest words you spoke to me in twenty years." – *Rationing* (1944)

2290 Robert Benchley visits flea-circus owner Fred Allen to protest a developing relationship between their children. "If my daughter has been out with your half-witted son," replies Allen, "it's only that she's been taught to be kind to dumb animals." – *It's in the Bag* (1945)

2291 "You don't have the brains of a two-year-old child!" hotel owner George Tobias berates bellhop Ben Blue. "I know," Ben returns. "Look at the difference in our ages." – *My Wild Irish Rose* (1947)

2292 "A man's only as smart as the people he surrounds himself with," police inspector Farraday (Richard Lane) enlightens his slow-witted assistant. Then, after studying his companion, he adds: "In the dull, blank expanse of your face, I could read the dismal promise of the years to come." – *Trapped by Boston Blackie* (1948)

2293 In the Three Stooges' first case as private eyes, their young and beauti-

ful client disappears. "How are you going to handle the case?" Moe questions Shemp. "Easy. I'll use my wits." "Now she's really in trouble." – *Dopey Dicks* (1950)

2294 A fearless publisher in the Yukon delivers his papers personally to patrons and employees of a local saloon. "Paper, Miss?" he offers one of the bar girls. "What for?" she replies sharply. "Maybe you can get someone to read it to you," he cracks. – *Those Redheads from Seattle* (1953)

2295 Sugar (Marilyn Monroe) relates to Tony Curtis, impersonating a female saxophone player, her mysterious attraction to sax players – although they have all betrayed her. "See what I mean?" she says, tapping her head. "Not very bright." "Brains aren't everything," Curtis replies after scanning her figure. – *Some Like It Hot* (1959)

2296 The staid Edith Evans exasperatingly says to hearty squire Hugh Griffith: "Your ignorance, brother, as the great Milton says, almost subdues my patience." – *Tom Jones* (1963)

2297 Brooklyn youth John Travolta becomes enamored of English dancer Finola Hughes. "I just respect her dancing, that's all," he says to girlfriend Cynthia Rhodes. "Did you hear the way she talks? It's so intelligent, like." "An accent doesn't make someone intelligent," Cynthia retorts. "If it did, you'd be Einstein." – *Staying Alive* (1984)

2298 College student Paul Reiser has gone into the trucking business and has had classy business cards printed. "Let me show you something," he says to his slow-witted friend Rick Overton, handing him a card. "Feast your eyes on these." "Little white cards – very clever," Overton comments, looking at the blank side. – *Odd Jobs* (1985)

2299 Dan Aykroyd studies a special aluminum case which a pretty American doctor is carrying and describes it to

buddy Chevy Chase: "It's a highly intelligent piece of hardware." "So she's a
high-class intelligent piece," Chase
replies. – *Spies Like Us* (1985)

2300 A bungling antiques smuggler is
forced to have his wife correct his
mistake. "Credit me with some intelligence," the husband says. "On what basis?"
his wife ripostes. – *Vice Versa* (1988)

Journalists

2301 Reporter Frank McHugh
telephones a woman from the city hall
press room as other newspapermen
listen in. "Is it true, madam," McHugh
inquires, "that you are the victim of a
peeping Tom?" "Ask her if she's worth
peeping at," one colleague blurts out.
"Tell her to come over here," suggests
another. "We'd like to reenact the
crime." – *The Front Page* (1930)

2302 A prying gossip columnist interviews Hollywood's favorite married couple, movie star Constance Bennett and
millionaire Neil Hamilton, and, following
several intimate questions, asks
Hamilton: "Have you a photograph
showing your marvelous physique?" "No,
but I have my appendix in the other
room in a bottle," Hamilton replies sarcastically. "Perhaps you'd like to
photograph that?" – *What Price
Hollywood?* (1932)

2303 Reporter ZaSu Pitts, who wants
an exclusive interview with radio singer
Ginger Rogers, boasts about all her contacts among the movie stars. "I know
them all – I eat with them, I sleep with
them – " "You sleep with them?" questions Rogers. – *Professional Sweetheart*
(1933)

2304 Big city newspaper editor
Spencer Tracy tries to stop a libel suit
brought on by wealthy Myrna Loy. "If
you go through with this case," he
pleads, "it's going to throw five hundred
people out of employment. Men and
women – jobless – walking the streets –

women like yourself, tired, cold and
hungry, driven to drink, ruined." "You
write the editorials, don't you?" Loy
quietly replies. – *Libeled Lady* (1936)

2305 Newspaper manager Spencer
Tracy, intending to use a phony story
planted in his paper as a ploy, hands the
bogus page to copy boy Billy Benedict.
"Tell Douglas to print up one copy of the
evening edition," Tracy orders. "One
copy?" Benedict questions. "That's what
I said." "Gosh," the bewildered copy boy
mumbles, "our circulation is certainly
falling off." – *Libeled Lady* (1936)

2306 Doctor Charles Winninger confides to newspaperman Fredric March
what he thinks of reporters: "The hand
of God reaching down into a mine
couldn't elevate one of them to the
depths of degradation." – *Nothing Sacred*
(1937)

2307 Hardboiled newspaper editor
Walter Connolly witnesses the fainting
of a young woman in a nightclub. Suspecting her collapse may be fatal, he
says to the doctor: "I want to know the
worst. I don't want you to spare our
feelings. We go to press in fifteen
minutes." – *Nothing Sacred* (1937)

2308 Movie studio boss Adolphe Menjou says to starlet Janet Gaynor before
she meets caustic Lionel Stander: "And
now I'm going to turn you over to our
demon press agent. Don't let him
frighten you. He has a heart of gold –
only harder." – *A Star Is Born* (1937)

2309 Managing editor Cary Grant and his paper have defended a man now sentenced to death. Grant intends to have the sentence commuted. "Get the governor on the phone!" he orders his city editor. "I can't locate him. He's out fishing." "How many places to fish are there?" Grant asks. "Oh, at least two," the city editor offers. "The Atlantic and the Pacific." "Well, that simplifies it, doesn't it?" – *His Girl Friday* (1940)

2310 A newspaper editor awaiting the imminent death of a wealthy social celebrity holds the front page in his hands when his publisher calls and orders the presses to roll without the story. "He's gonna die for me!" the editor insists. "Exclusive – he's mine! He dies for me – not the *Herald!*" – *It Started with Eve* (1941)

2311 "I got a brother who works on a newspaper," Rags Ragland boasts to a reporter. "Life job." "Life job?" "Yeah, the *San Quentin Evening Bugle.*" – *Whistling in Brooklyn* (1943)

2312 A reporter phones in her scoop to her editor – an exclusive in which she identifies the "Constant Reader," a serial killer terrorizing New York City. "Constant Reader?" her editor questions. "This paper has never had a constant reader." – *Whistling in Brooklyn* (1943)

2313 An unscrupulous fiction magazine publisher gives orders to proofreader Danny Kaye: "Tell Joe to doctor up that story. Lord Cecil was only stabbed once. We've always given our readers their money's worth. Have him stabbed in the front, the back and the side – and save the heart for last. Why should we stint on things like that?" – *The Secret Life of Walter Mitty* (1947)

2314 Reporter Janet Leigh, envisioning a long-running human-interest series about obscure railroad clerk Jerry Lewis, who allegedly is dying of radiation poisoning, tries to interest her New York editor Fred Clark in the story. "'The Morning Chronicle Pays Its Debt

to Humanity!'" she suggests as a headline. "It wouldn't hurt circulation either," Clark adds. "I knew your better instincts would triumph," she says sarcastically. – *Living It Up* (1954)

2315 New York newspaper editor Fred Clark is persuaded by manipulative reporter Janet Leigh to bring to the city a patient suffering from radiation poisoning and given only a few weeks to live. Although he envisions a long-running human-interest series, he harbors at least one major drawback. "What if this kid doesn't die in three weeks?" he asks Leigh. – *Living It Up* (1954)

2316 "There's a sex maniac loose in the city," an editor reminds aspiring young reporter Beau Bridges. "Do you know what a sex maniac does?" "I think so," Bridges replies hesitatingly. "I'll tell you what a sex maniac does!" the editor blares out. "A sex maniac sells newspapers!" – *Gaily, Gaily* (1969)

2317 A member of the Supreme Court has died, and the President has nominated a woman to fill the empty seat. Columnist Jack Anderson has written about this decision before some justices become aware of it. "How does a newspaperman like Jack Anderson find out what happens in the oval office so fast?" one justice wonders. "Simple," quips justice Walter Matthau. "He's got a friend in the Soviet embassy." – *First Monday in October* (1981)

2318 "I have to fly to Dallas tonight," reporter Jeff Goldblum remarks. "I'm interviewing a fourteen-year-old blind baton twirler." "Where do you get those stories?" a college friend asks. "It's just good investigative journalism," Goldblum replies. – *The Big Chill* (1983)

2319 Reporter Chevy Chase is trying to uncover corruption in a city administration. "What's your occupation?" a police chief snaps at him. "I'm a shepherd," Chase replies. – *Fletch* (1985)

2320 "Those that can't do, teach," expounds film critic Craig Gilmore, "and those that can't teach get twenty-five cents a word to rip other people's work to shreds." – *The Living End* (1992)

Languages

2321 "I can speak French," Sid Silvers boasts to Jack Benny, and proceeds to utter: "Si, si, señor." "That's Spanish." "Gee," the astonished Silvers utters, "I can speak Spanish, too." – *Broadway Melody of 1936* (1935)

2322 A provincial American ranching couple have won Ruggles, an English butler (Charles Laughton), in a poker game. Social-climbing wife Mary Boland tingles with delight when Ruggles says "indubitably." "What beautiful French you speak, Ruggles," she remarks. – *Ruggles of Red Gap* (1935)

2323 New York police inspector Harold Huber greets famous Hawaiian detective Charlie Chan at the dock. "The bigwigs expect you to tear a duck apart with them tonight," Huber says. "So sorry," Chan replies. "Come again, please?" "You'll have to excuse the inspector's broken English, Mr. Chan," reporter Donald Woods interjects. "He's a Brooklyn immigrant." – *Charlie Chan on Broadway* (1937)

2324 Annabella: "You talk like an American." David Niven: "Only when I get excited. My mother was three times removed – from the Statue of Liberty." – *Dinner at the Ritz* (1937)

2325 Housekeeper Lupe Velez asks guest Robert Woolsey if he speaks Spanish. "Sure, sure," he acknowledges. "Oui, oui, mademoiselle." "This is not Spanish," she says disappointedly, "this is French." "Oh, what do you know about that! I speak French, too, and didn't even know it." – *High Flyers* (1937)

2326 Dim-witted wrestler Nat Pendleton cannot comprehend the normal speech of his promoter, Humphrey Bogart. "Aw, gee," he pleads, "talk United States, will ya?" – *Swing Your Lady* (1938)

2327 American correspondent Joel McCrea becomes entangled in an assassination plot and is arrested in Holland. "I hope the chief of police speaks English," he says. "We all speak English," the Dutch officer replies. "That's more than I could say for my country," McCrea quips. – *Foreign Correspondent* (1940)

2328 In a French restaurant in New Orleans, feisty old Victor Moore complains to the waiter about the high price of ninety cents for a sandwich and coffee. "Here's a dollar," Moore grumbles. "Ten cents for you." "Merci, monsieur," the waiter replies and leaves. "He didn't even say 'thank you,'" Moore observes. – *Louisiana Purchase* (1941)

2329 A Nazi officer, working on the assumption that all good things originated in Germany, informs Englishman Leslie Howard that Shakespeare wrote all his plays in German. "You must admit that the English translation is most remarkable," Howard ripostes. – *Pimpernel Smith* (1941)

2330 A German couple leaving Casablanca for America make a decision to speak only English. While sitting in Rick's Café, they begin to practice. "What is the watch?" the middle-aged husband asks. "Ten watch," his wife replies. "You'll get along beautifully in America," remarks friendly waiter S. Z. Sakall. – *Casablanca* (1942)

2331 Ginger Rogers poses as a twelve-year-old so she can ride on a train for half fare, telling two skeptical conductors that she is Swedish and tall for her age. "If you're Swedish," one conductor challenges, "suppose you say something in Swedish." "I vant to be alone," she replies. – *The Major and the Minor* (1942)

2332 Baseball pitcher Eddie Albert, receiving a phone call from his Spanish-born wife, cannot understand her. "I'll tell you in English when I see you in Spanish," she concludes. – *Ladies' Day* (1943)

2333 Charles Laughton, as a friendly sixteenth-century ghost condemned to haunt an English castle, cannot comprehend the American jargon of G.I. Robert Young, who has been stationed there during World War II. "Nowadays," Laughton observes, "England and America have everything in common except, of course, the language." – *The Canterville Ghost* (1944)

2334 Servant Edward Everett Horton does not know where his employer is and replies to one caller: "He's incommunicado – that's Spanish for 'you've got me.'" – *The Ghost Goes Wild* (1947)

2335 Artist Gene Kelly explains why he's in France instead of in the United States: "Back home everyone said I didn't have any talent. They might be saying the same thing over here, but it sounds better in French." – *An American in Paris* (1951)

2336 Marjorie Main, staid aunt of playboy Fred Astaire, observes his dancing with a voluptuous showgirl. "Who is

that unclad creature, and what are those obscene remarks she's making?" "It's not obscene," Astaire explains, "it's French." "French is obscene!" his aunt bellows. – *The Belle of New York* (1952)

2337 When down-and-out gambler Dean Martin fails to pay off a local gangster-bookie, the hoodlum sends strong-arm man Maxie Rosenbloom to collect. "I'll have more than three Gs in collateral tonight," Martin promises. "Collateral?" echoes Rosenbloom. "Talk English." – *Hollywood or Bust* (1956)

2338 Reporters aboard a cruise ship interview American entertainer Bob Hope about his trip to Paris. "Do you speak French?" one journalist asks. "Just enough to get my face slapped." – *Paris Holiday* (1958)

2339 Recently divorced James Mason is interested in renting a room for the summer from widowed Shelley Winters, who tells him about her late husband. "You know," she says, "I believe it's only in the Romance languages one is able to really relate in the mature fashion. When we were on our honeymoon abroad, I knew I never felt myself married until I heard myself addressed as 'señora.'" "You were in Spain?" Mason asks. "No," she replies. "Mexico." – *Lolita* (1962)

2340 College instructor George Segal quotes Oscar Wilde: "The Americans and the English are divided by the barrier of a common language." – *Lost and Found* (1979)

2341 American disc jockey Robin Williams, stationed in Saigon, befriends a Vietnamese teenager who says, "Come, we go." "Sounds like you learned English from Tonto," Williams wisecracks. – *Good Morning, Vietnam* (1987)

Law and Lawyers

2342 When a brutal Southerner threatens to horsewhip the jockey Gus (Al Jolson in blackface), a fellow African-American whispers to him: "You're any man's equal now. The Constitution says so." "When a man's got a pistol in your abdomen," counters Jolson, "boy, you ain't got no Constitution." – *Big Boy* (1930)

2343 A traffic cop stops Bert Wheeler and Robert Woolsey. "You broke the law!" the officer exclaims. "Well, couldn't you get another one?" Woolsey quips. – *Hook, Line, and Sinker* (1930)

2344 Vagabonds Bert Wheeler and Robert Woolsey, in merry old England, are pilloried for theft. "Do you think we should send for a lawyer?" Bert suggests. "Certainly not," his pal replies. "We're in enough trouble." – *Cockeyed Cavaliers* (1934)

2345 Norman Foster and Lupe Velez, out joyriding, are stopped by a traffic cop. "Do you know anything about traffic regulations?" the tough officer announces. "Sure," Foster cracks. "What is it you want to know?" – *Strictly Dynamite* (1934)

2346 Police inspector Nat Pendleton, visiting Nick and Nora Charles (William Powell, Myrna Loy), finds a revolver in their bureau. "You got a pistol permit?" he asks. "No," Powell replies. "Ever hear of the Sullivan Act?" "That's all right," Loy returns, "we're married." – *The Thin Man* (1934)

2347 Crooked landowner Berton Churchill is infuriated with Robert Woolsey who is about to ruin Churchill's scheme to fleece the local farmers. "It's only the law that makes me keep my hands off you!" Churchill blares out. "It's only the law that makes you keep your hands off a lot of things," Woolsey retorts. – *The Rainmakers* (1935)

2348 While studying a contract, Chico Marx questions a clause. "That's what they call a sanity clause," Groucho Marx explains. "You can't fool me," Chico smiles knowingly. "There ain't no Santy Claus." – *A Night at the Opera* (1935)

2349 Circus owner Kenny Baker pours out his financial troubles to sympathetic Chico Marx, who offers the following advice: "Whenever you got business trouble, the best thing to do is get a lawyer. You got more trouble, but at least you got a lawyer." – *At the Circus* (1939)

2350 Circus acrobat Eve Arden invites lawyer Groucho Marx to walk on the ceiling with her. "I'd rather not," a reluctant Groucho says. "I have an agreement with the horseflies. The flies don't practice law, and I don't walk on the ceiling." – *At the Circus* (1939)

2351 Lawyer Groucho Marx observes circus entertainer Eve Arden, who is in league with crooks, hiding ten thousand dollars of stolen money in her cleavage. "The thing I like about you is that money doesn't go to your head," Marx cracks. "Right now I could use the long arm of the law." – *At the Circus* (1939)

2352 "I'm going to a shower for a girlfriend," divorcee Nancy Kelly informs lawyer-friend Roland Young. "She's getting married." "Give her my office address," Young says. – *He Married His Wife* (1940)

2353 New York City prosecuting attorney Paul Guilfoyle sees problems ahead in convicting his latest criminal suspect. "A first offender at Christmas

time is tougher than tiger meat."
—*Remember the Night* (1940)

2354 The police threaten chauffeur Allen Jenkins with arrest but, believing he is innocent, he refuses to change his alibi. "You can't scare me," he fires back. "I know the law. You ain't got nothin' on me until you prove corpus delicious."
—*The Falcon Takes Over* (1942)

2355 Chauffeur Rags Ragland explains to his boss Red Skelton that although he once cut a main elevator cable, the car did not plunge to the bottom of the shaft. "That's against the law of gravity," Skelton remarks. "That was before the law was passed," explains Ragland.
—*Whistling in Brooklyn* (1943)

2356 Charlie Chan's son Benson Fong berates chauffeur Mantan Moreland during a criminal investigation. "You don't even know what a lawsuit is," Fong challenges. "Sure I do," Moreland insists. "It's something that a police wears."—*Dark Alibi* (1946)

2357 "Lawyers should not marry other lawyers," says David Wayne. "This is called inbreeding from which comes idiot children and other lawyers."—*Adam's Rib* (1949)

2358 Zsa Zsa Gabor confides to her friend Toulouse-Lautrec (José Ferrer) about her latest romance with a lawyer: "I wasn't the vision of his dreams; I was the party of the first part. He didn't declare his love; he merely acknowledged that a state of affection existed."
—*Moulin Rouge* (1952)

2359 Football coach John Wayne agrees to work for a small Catholic college run by Charles Coburn, but Wayne's eleven-year-old daughter is more pragmatic. "Shouldn't we get it on paper?" she suggests. "I'll draw up a contract," Coburn replies and, turning toward the child, asks: "I presume you are a notary public?"—*Trouble Along the Way* (1953)

2360 Candy store owner Bernard Gorcey, searching for Leo Gorcey and Huntz Hall, falls into the hands of mad scientist John Dehner. "Sorry," Dehner announces. "You just signed your death warrant." "I won't sign nothin' without my lawyer," the storekeeper protests.
—*The Bowery Boys Meet the Monsters* (1954)

2361 Little orphan George "Foghorn" Winslow, visiting Spring Byington's home, is directed upstairs to take a bath. "Saturday night," he mumbles, "gotta take a bath. I ain't gonna argue with a judge. She's got the law on her side."—*The Rocket Man* (1954)

2362 In a burlesque routine, Phil Silvers, carrying a ladder and a wooden case, announces: "I'm taking my case to a higher court." He then returns with an empty coat hanger and says: "I lost my suit."—*Top Banana* (1954)

2363 Shyster lawyer Walter Matthau involves reluctant brother-in-law Jack Lemmon in a fraudulent lawsuit. After ordering food from a Chinese restaurant, they break open a fortune cookie which alludes to Abraham Lincoln's comments about not being able to fool all the people all the time. "Those Chinese!" Matthau exclaims. "What do they know!"—*The Fortune Cookie* (1966)

2364 "We were awarded six cents," lawyer Robert Redford admits to wife Jane Fonda about his last case. "How much of that do we get?" she asks.
—*Barefoot in the Park* (1967)

2365 Shady laywer Zero Mostel learns that his son has been arrested and charged with illegal entry and theft of a valuable jewel. "My client is innocent," Mostel proclaims. "No court could convince me otherwise. Unfortunately, the fact that my client was captured the night of the robbery traipsing around the museum in a guard's uniform might seem to an uninformed juror slightly more than circumstantial evidence."
—*The Hot Rock* (1972)

2366 Divorce lawyer George Segal: "It isn't very difficult to do well as a divorce lawyer in Beverly Hills, California. Our waiting room was like a doctor's office." –*Blume in Love* (1973)

2367 In a Harvard lecture hall, crusty law professor John Houseman, while inwardly appreciating the intelligence of his best student (Timothy Bottoms), calls him forward theatrically and hands him a dime. "Call your mother," Houseman suggests, "and tell her you will never be a lawyer." –*The Paper Chase* (1973)

2368 Woody Allen speaks of the sexual inclinations of the male animal: "Some men are heterosexual; some men are bisexual; some men don't think about sex at all–they become lawyers." –*Love and Death* (1975)

2369 Boris (Woody Allen) is to be executed at six o'clock in the morning. "I was supposed to go five o'clock," he explains, "but I have a smart lawyer." –*Love and Death* (1975)

2370 In judge Jack Warden's chambers, lawyer Al Pacino notices that Warden carries a gun in a shoulder holster. "Do you always carry that thing with you?" he asks. "There's law and there's order," Warden explains. "And that's order." –*...And Justice for All* (1979)

2371 Lawyer Al Pacino's client, whose car has been severely damaged, explodes with rage against the other driver. "You get every nickel and have him put away!" he orders Pacino. "I'll see that he gets the death penalty," Pacino replies. "Death is okay, too!" –*...And Justice for All* (1979)

2372 At a diner a group of gamblers are disappointed in young Mickey Rourke, who is always heavily in debt as a result of betting. "Nobody wants to make an honest buck anymore," says one gambler. "I heard he's going to law school," says another. "That's what I mean," concludes the first. "Nobody wants to make an honest buck." –*Diner* (1982)

2373 Lawyer Robert Redford tells fellow attorney Debra Winger he believes their attractive client Daryl Hannah, whom he has slept with, is innocent. "Based on what?" "A hunch–instinct," Redford offers. "Let's hope it's coming from above the waist." –*Legal Eagles* (1986)

2374 Assistant district attorney Robert Redford is caught sleeping with murder suspect Daryl Hannah, and the press has splashed the story on its front pages. The furious district attorney summons Redford to his office where he lambastes him. "I had one more year," the D.A. grumbles. "Now what do you think they're going to remember–the sixty-seven thousand convictions I got? No, they're going to remember the one horny bastard who made my office the laughing stock of the city. Damn it! When we service this community, we do it with our pants on!" –*Legal Eagles* (1986)

2375 Divorce attorney Danny DeVito: "What do you call five hundred lawyers lying on the bottom of the ocean? A good start." –*The War of the Roses* (1989)

2376 A hit man tries to buy off deputy district attorney Gene Hackman. "Tell me," the assassin asks, "how much does a deputy district attorney make in a year?" "Enough," Hackman replies. "I doubt that." "Are you thinking of becoming a lawyer?" Hackman sarcastically inquires. –*Narrow Margin* (1990)

Lawmen (Western)

2377 W. C. Fields pronounces: "I always talk loud – I'm a sheriff!" – *Six of a Kind* (1934)

2378 "Are you busy?" a hotel owner asks sheriff W. C. Fields. "I'm about as busy as a pickpocket in a nudist colony," ripostes Fields. – *Six of a Kind* (1934)

2379 Tex Ritter, relentlessly chasing after a villain across the plains, a desert and through countless gulches, overtakes the culprit. "Tryin' to make a getaway, huh?" Ritter utters. – *Tex Rides with the Boy Scouts* (1937)

2380 An officer in the Mounties asks visiting Texas Ranger Gary Cooper why he wears two guns. "One doesn't shoot far enough," Cooper quips. – *North West Mounted Police* (1940)

2381 Easterner Joe E. Brown is mistaken for a fast-shootin' tough hombre by the citizens of a frontier town whose former marshals were murdered by an outlaw gang. The townspeople quickly make the reluctant Brown their peace officer. "I'm sure you're gonna make a fine, upstanding marshal," the mayor assures him. "They don't upstand very long, do they?" Brown quips. – *Shut My Big Mouth* (1942)

2382 Bewhiskered old-timer George "Gabby" Hayes enlightens newcomer John Wayne that the town has no sheriff. "Don't you believe in law and order?" Wayne inquires. "It depends on who's dishing it out," replies Hayes. – *Tall in the Saddle* (1944)

2383 Lawman Bat Masterson (Randolph Scott) and his sidekick George Gabby Hayes finally bring law and order to a frontier town. "Larkin," Hayes says, addressing the chief outlaw, "you're gonna get thirty days for that killin'. Then we're gonna hang you." – *Trail Street* (1947)

2384 Texas Rangers John Wayne and Stuart Whitman discover the hideout of a dangerous band of outlaws but are captured and left dangling by their wrists over a deep chasm. Whitman begins to growl at their predicament. "We found their hideout, didn't we?" Wayne offers as a consolation. "I wonder if they know how much trouble they're in," Whitman replies sarcastically. – *The Comancheros* (1961)

2385 Local sheriff Walter Matthau is exasperated at his assistant's turning every order into a question. "When I say 'machine,'" Matthau complains, "you say 'machine? Right,' when I say 'McNeil,' you say 'McNeil? Right.' There's something about the way you make a question out of it that gets on my nerves." "Nerves?" the assistant repeats. "Right." – *Lonely Are the Brave* (1962)

2386 Former lawman Joel McCrea, now broke, semiretired and shabbily dressed, still has his pride intact. An old friend (Randolph Scott) notices a hole in his pal's boot. "Juan Fernandez made those boots for me in San Anton' – special order," McCrea explains. "I had a hell of a time getting him to put that hole there. A fine craftsman, Juan, but he never did understand the principle of ventilation." – *Ride the High Country* (1962)

2387 Sheriff Sonny Bono enters a saloon and is immediately challenged by a tough hombre. "I got a six-gun here that says you're yeller," the man snarls. "Where does it say that?" Bono asks, leaning over to study the man's holster. – *Good Times* (1967)

2388 Con man John Alton tries to persuade the citizens of a western town to accept a fancy gambling establishment in the midst of their community: "The proceeds rebounding in civic assets, including a downtown park, a circulating library and a lyceum, of course." "Don't talk vulgar," sheriff Allyn Joslyn orders. — *The Brothers O'Toole* (1973)

2389 The townspeople are horrified that their new sheriff (Cleavon Little) stepping up to the podium is black. As he reaches into his belt for his acceptance speech, he announces, followed by shrill screams of alarm: "Excuse me while I whip this out." — *Blazing Saddles* (1974)

2390 Marshal Rooster Cogburn (John Wayne) has no problems with lawbreakers, but he has his hands full when he tangles with strong-willed Katharine Hepburn, who is searching for her father's murderers. "Any varmint that crosses this lady's path," Wayne says, "has met his match." — *Rooster Cogburn* (1975)

2391 Bumptious, feisty sheriff Jackie Gleason cannot believe that his passive, namby-pamby son could possibly come from his genes. "First thing I'm going to do when I get home," the fuming sheriff yells, "is punch your mama in the mouth." — *Smokey and the Bandit* (1977)

Life and Living

2392 Bachelor-playboy Lowell Sherman, whose life has become complicated with his friends' wives and other women chasing after him, confides to his servant: "I'm sick of the parties, the women, the champagne as flat as the women." — *Bachelor Apartment* (1931)

2393 John Barrymore to a flirtatious brunette: "Ambrose Bierce said: 'A sweetheart is like a bottle of wine; a wife is like a wine bottle.'" — *Long Lost Father* (1934)

2394 A patient says to medical student Leslie Howard: "Here I am in a charity hospital because my father loves fast women and slow horses." — *Of Human Bondage* (1934)

2395 "What excuse has a gal like you for running around single?" a suitor asks Mae West. "I was born that way." — *Goin' to Town* (1935)

2396 Cargo ship captain Victor McLaglen returns to Mae West's cabin and finds her strumming a guitar. "I didn't know you played," he says. "I've been playing all my life," West replies. "This is work." — *Klondike Annie* (1936)

2397 Bored English playboy David Niven announces to his servant Jeeves (Arthur Treacher) that they are about to embark on the "great adventure." "But I'm not ready for the great adventure, sir," Treacher replies. "I want to live a little longer, sir." — *Thank You, Jeeves!* (1936)

2398 Elderly college instructor Harry Davenport, who has just returned from taking his pretty niece Merle Oberon to a nightclub that was raided by the police, bubbles over with exhilaration. "Oh, when I think of the years I wasted teaching political economy," Davenport says to Henry Kolker, his stuffy brother. "Sometimes I think you're in your second childhood!" Kolker exclaims. "Well, come on in, the water's fine," Davenport retorts. — *The Cowboy and the Lady* (1938)

2399 When a wealthy banker hears that his future son-in-law (Cary Grant) is interested neither in finance nor in making money, he declares in a disapproving tone: "I consider his attitude un–American."–*Holiday* (1938)

2400 Commissar Greta Garbo, assigned temporarily to Paris, questions playboy Melvin Douglas about his frivolous life. "What do you do for mankind?" "For mankind, not much," he confesses. "But for womankind, my record is not so bleak."–*Ninotchka* (1939)

2401 Pilot James Cagney has kidnapped Bette Davis and taken her in his plane. "Don't you get lonesome up here?" she asks. "No," Cagney replies. "I like people. Not seeing any of them keeps me liking them."–*The Bride Came C.O.D.* (1941)

2402 Gentleman con artist Charles Coburn tells his assistant and daughter Barbara Stanwyck that they must maintain the standards of their profession: "Let us be crooked, but never common." –*The Lady Eve* (1941)

2403 Held captive by a gang of murderers, radio actor Red Skelton tries to bribe his guard Sam Levene: "With that kind of dough you can live the life of Riley; you'll have nothing to worry about–unless Riley comes home, of course."–*Whistling in Brooklyn* (1943)

2404 The U.S. Cavalry arrives to take hard-drinking, rowdy Victor McLaglen into custody. He is asked to come along peacefully. "Laddie," he responds, "I've never gone anyplace peacefully in my life."–*She Wore a Yellow Ribbon* (1949)

2405 Humphrey Bogart, the dissolute skipper of a river launch, announces: "Never do today what you can put off till tomorrow."–*The African Queen* (1951)

2406 Rancher Clark Gable is rebuked for taking time out to review a young woman's appealing features. "I just

believe in living a balanced life," Gable parries, "a little of this, a little of that." –*Lone Star* (1951)

2407 Toulouse-Lautrec (José Ferrer) at a party with friends: "Love is a state of confusion in which the victim cannot distinguish between spiritual aspiration, carnal desire and pride of ownership. A wise man satisfies different thirsts at different fountains."–*Moulin Rouge* (1952)

2408 "Going to a man's apartment," explains outspoken ingenue Maggie McNamara to William Holden, "almost always ends up in one of two ways– either the girl is willing to lose her virtue or she fights for it. I don't want to lose mine, and I think it's vulgar to fight for it. So I always put my cards on the table."–*The Moon Is Blue* (1953)

2409 "When I was born," admits fight manager Bob Hope, "the doctor said, 'Boil some hot water,' and I've been in it ever since."–*Off Limits* (1953)

2410 A troubled industrialist summons playboy son William Holden, who has involved himself with gold-digging women. "The old man would like to see you," brother Humphrey Bogart says. "What about?" Holden asks. "Guess." "Animal, vegetable or mineral?" "Definitely animal," Bogart replies.–*Sabrina* (1954)

2411 Lady-in-waiting Marita Hunt grumbles about her tedious position with the grand duchess (Helen Hayes): "With Her Majesty, life is one eternal glass of milk."–*Anastasia* (1956)

2412 Auntie Mame (Rosalind Russell) reveals the meaning of her book to her secretary: "Life is a banquet, and most poor suckers are starving to death." –*Auntie Mame* (1958)

2413 Free-wheeling junior officer Tony Curtis informs submarine captain Cary Grant that he joined the navy to boost his social position with a wealthy heiress he was pursuing–and caught. "When the preacher says, 'Do you *take* this woman,'" Grant comments, "he won't be kidding, will he?" – *Operation Petticoat* (1959)

2414 Executive Doris Day criticizes ladies' man Rock Hudson for his loose life-style. "So I have sown a few wild oats," he admits. "A few!" she echoes. "You could qualify for a farm loan!" – *Pillow Talk* (1959)

2415 "If there's anything worse than a woman living alone, it's a woman saying she likes it," Thelma Ritter remarks. – *Pillow Talk* (1959)

2416 Career woman Doris Day parades her life-style before her maid Thelma Ritter. "I have a good job, a lovely apartment, I go out with very nice men to the very best places. What am I missing?" "When you have to ask," Ritter ripostes, "believe me, you're missing it." – *Pillow Talk* (1959)

2417 "When a man stands on the assembly line of death day in and day out," explains undertaker Ernie Kovacs to a client, "life becomes really glamorous." – *Five Golden Hours* (1961)

2418 At a party in France during the 1920s an American businessman asks a European nobleman: "What's your place in the economy of life?" "I shoot buffalo in Africa, tigers in India, Bolsheviks in Europe," the aristocrat answers. "Don't you ever get the urge to do anything?" "Yes. I would like to restore the Holy Roman Empire." – *Tender Is the Night* (1962)

2419 "Life is a total war," Parisian bistro owner Lou Jacobi says to former gendarme Jack Lemmon. "No one has the right to be a conscientious objector." – *Irma la Douce* (1963)

2420 "There are worse things than chastity," Deborah Kerr reminds Richard Burton. "Yes," he replies, "lunacy and death." – *The Night of the Iguana* (1964)

2421 At a dinner party, a guest contrasts the romantic escapades of fellow guest Sir Charles (David Niven), an international playboy, with those of the famous Don Juan. The guest emphasizes that the latter was forced to climb balconies, fight duels and keep his women apart. "Charles, on the other hand," he points out, "drives a Ferrari, enters with a key and resorts to collective bargaining." – *The Pink Panther* (1964)

2422 Soldier-of-fortune and dynamite expert Burt Lancaster is hired for an assignment in Mexico. "So what else is on your mind," a friend asks, "besides one hundred–proof women, ninety-proof whiskey and fourteen-karat gold?" "Amigo," Lancaster replies, "you just wrote my epitaph." – *The Professionals* (1966)

2423 Broadway producer Zero Mostel prods neurotic accountant Gene Wilder towards risk, wealth and adventure. "You miserable, cowardly, wretched little caterpillar!" he exclaims. "Don't you ever want to become a butterfly? Don't you want to spread your wings and flap your way to glory?" – *The Producers* (1968)

2424 "If God ever made two better inventions than a pretty woman and a bottle of whiskey," declares fur trapper Burt Lancaster, "I ain't heard of it." – *The Scalphunters* (1968)

2425 An alleged boyfriend of dance-hall hostess Shirley MacLaine has stolen her purse, and her coworkers try to help her. "If he stole your purse," one proposes, "why don't you call the cops? They can always pick him up." "Oh, girls," another counters, "do you know how many guys are running around the city carrying pocketbooks?" – *Sweet Charity* (1969)

2426 Woody Allen explains why he turned to a life of crime: "You're your own boss, the hours are good and you travel a lot." – *Take the Money and Run* (1969)

2427 A married friend criticizes middle-aged television star Peter Sellers for his promiscuity: "You treat your sex life like a continuous wine-tasting – roll them around and spit them out."
– *There's a Girl in My Soup* (1970)

2428 Blume (George Segal), divorced from his wife, meets a sexy young woman who is enmeshed in the "swinging couples" scene during the Vietnam War. "Our entire society is screwed up sexually," she explains to Segal while they are in bed. "But one of these days everybody will be swinging and everybody will be happy." "Do you think swinging will end the war?" Segal asks.
– *Blume in Love* (1973)

2429 Eccentric Mame (Lucille Ball) zestfully rattles off her daily schedule: "Every day, up at the crack of noon."
– *Mame* (1974)

2430 "Human beings are divided into mind and body," Woody Allen enlightens the audience. "The mind embraces all the nobler aspirations like poetry and philosophy, but the body has all the fun."
– *Love and Death* (1975)

2431 Aggressive, single-minded television programming executive Faye Dunaway seduces TV news producer William Holden, whose news show she wants to control. "My husband ran off with his boyfriend," she reveals, "and I had an affair with my analyst who told me I was the worst lay he ever had. I can't tell you how many men told me what a lousy lay I am. I arouse quickly, consummate prematurely, and I can't wait to get dressed and get out of the bedroom . . . All I want out of life is a twenty share and a thirty rating."
– *Network* (1976)

2432 Redd Foxx cannot accept the idea that his twenty-three-year-old son is gay and argues: "Listen, if I had done what you're doin', you wouldn't be here doin' what you're doin'!" -- *Norman . . . Is That You?* (1976)

2433 Robert Preston, owner of a football team, chastises Jill Clayburgh, his free-spirited daughter. "It don't look right my daughter living with two of my players," he begins. "I'm not sleeping with them, Daddy." "That's what I mean," he explains. "It ain't normal."
– *Semi-Tough* (1977)

2434 Fiercely independent bookstore owner Maureen Stapleton boasts about her past trysts with several famous authors to her son's betrothed and concludes: "I don't believe in marriage . . . A bed is the only place that offers a man and a woman equal opportunity." – *Lost and Found* (1979)

2435 Eddie Albert shows up unexpectedly at his divorced daughter's home to tell her that her mother has found someone else. "What's his name?" the shocked daughter asks. "His name?" Albert echoes. "His name is Shirley Levine! That's right! Your mother – age sixty-four – has joined the Sun City Gay Liberation Movement!" – *How to Beat the High Cost of Living* (1980)

2436 "Can you imagine how many gays China must have?" a gay man says to his lover. "Figure ten percent of the population – that's eighty million. Fantastic!" – *The Last Married Couple in America* (1980)

2437 Martin Mull, who has left his wife, cannot understand why his attractive and seductive secretary is breaking off with him – especially now that he is single again. "Married guys make clean deals," she explains. "Single ones want to get into your life as well as your pants. It's just a hassle, that's all." – *Serial* (1980)

2438 Convict Eddie Murphy belittles police detective Nick Nolte's battered convertible as having no class. "Class isn't something you buy," Nolte fires back. "Look at you. You have a five hundred dollar suit on. You're still a lowlife." "Yeah," says Murphy, "but I look good." – *48 Hours* (1982)

2439 "Nietzsche," hypochondriac Woody Allen ponders, "said that the life we live, we're going to live over and over again the exact same way for eternity. Great. That means I'll have to sit through the Ice Capades again." – *Hannah and Her Sisters* (1986)

2440 Baseball catcher Kevin Costner criticizes groupie Susan Sarandon for dressing very scantily. "'The road of excess leads to the palace of wisdom' – William Blake," she counters. – *Bull Durham* (1988)

2441 Beauty-parlor owner Dolly Parton is intrigued by her mysterious new young employee whom she thinks has a secret past. "She can't be more than eighteen," customer Olympia Dukakis corrects her. "She hasn't had time to have a past." "Oh, get with it," Parton replies. "This is the eighties. If you could achieve puberty, you could achieve a past." – *Steel Magnolias* (1989)

2442 A police officer teases her superior, uptight, lonely assistant district attorney Joan Cusack, who is interested only in meeting college graduates. "That probably seems quite comical to you," Cusack replies. "It's your life, suit yourself." "I did," Cusack admits, "and look where it got me." – *My Blue Heaven* (1990)

2443 Millionaire playboy Alec Baldwin is engaged to the daughter of wealthy movie mogul Robert Loggia, who is determined to find out more about his future son-in-law. "How would you characterize yourself – as a playboy?" "I would prefer the word 'sportsman,'" Baldwin replies. – *The Marrying Man* (1991)

2444 Ne'er-do-well Anthony LaPaglia and his buddies are riding in a car when one of his young pals announces that he has "just developed a theory on life." "Listen," he expounds, "it's very complicated. First you're born and you're like a baby – a child. Then you start to mature a little until you hit adolescence. And then you grow old, and then you grow older, and then you die. And that's it." – *29th Street* (1991)

Literature

2445 A matronly woman, trying to seduce Robert Woolsey, asks him to suggest a racy book for her to read. "How about *The Four Horsemen?*" he suggests. – *Caught Plastered* (1931)

2446 High-school student Eric Linden recites Swinburne to girlfriend Cecilia Parker: "Oh, that I durst crush thee out of life and love and die. Die of thy pain and my delight." "You mean you want to kill me?" she asks. – *Ah, Wilderness* (1935)

2447 As part of their circus act, Edgar Bergen saws Charlie McCarthy in half. "'Parting is such sweet sorrow' – Shakespeare," quotes McCarthy. – *You Can't Cheat an Honest Man* (1939)

2448 Allan Jones, portraying a Roman nobleman in a musical comedy of errors, threatens an underling: "Will you get out of here before I make a Greek sonnet out of you!" – *The Boys from Syracuse* (1940)

2449 "All's well that end's well," someone quotes from Shakespeare. "Shakespeare, eh?" replies John Wayne. "Well, he must've come from Texas. We've been saying that down there for years." – *Dark Command* (1940)

2450 Singer Dorothy Lamour trips over some books strewn on the office floor of lawyer Charles Grapewin. "Don't let that worry you," he remarks. "We must all stumble over Shakespeare once in our lives." – *Johnny Apollo* (1940)

2451 For brawling at a dance, sailors Bud Abbott, Lou Costello and Dick Powell are thrown into jail. "'Stone walls do not a prison make, nor iron bars a cage,'" Powell quotes. "If they don't, they got us hypnotized," Costello the realist responds. – *In the Navy* (1941)

2452 Slow-witted soda jerk Sterling Holloway and Charlie McCarthy are suffering from unrequited love. "Oh, what fools we morons must be," Holloway sighs. – *Look Who's Laughing* (1941)

2453 Talent agent Patsy Kelly tries to impress a radio advertiser with one of her clients: "You should have seen him in Shakespeare's *Thirteenth Night!*" she exclaims. "*Twelfth Night,*" the advertiser corrects her. "Well, he was so good, they held him over." – *Playmates* (1941)

2454 Danny Kaye, to learn who murdered his twin brother, impersonates him in a nightclub act. The killers are in the audience. "Oh, what a tangled web we weave, when we first practice to deceive," he quotes. "Sir Walter Scott, *Marion,* Canto six, Stanza seventeen. How beautiful," an anonymous stagehand responds. – *Wonder Man* (1945)

2455 A dimwitted young woman, searching for a sergeant (Dean Martin), is distracted by his buddy, a corporal. "'Ours not to reason why. Ours but to do or die,'" the corporal recites dramatically. "That's cute," the woman says. – *At War with the Army* (1950)

2456 Smalltime hoodlum James Whitmore, who has a philosophical bent, tries to cheer up romantically troubled Howard Keel: "Just remember what the bard once said – 'All the world's a stage,

and all the men and women merely players.'" – *Kiss Me Kate* (1953)

2457 At a railroad station, fashion photographer Fred Astaire attempts to elicit the emotion of despair from model Audrey Hepburn. "You're a creature of tragedy, heartache, suffering," he explains. "You're Anna Karenina." "Shall I throw myself under a train?" – *Funny Face* (1957)

2458 "You're out of vodka," Tony Curtis says to his friend. "Try the bookcase. I used to hide stuff there from the maid." "Where in the bookcase?" Curtis asks. "Behind *War and Peace.* Where else would you hide vodka?" – *Goodbye Charlie* (1964)

2459 Anti-establishment dropout Jason Robards, Jr., raising his teenage nephew, is visited by social worker Barbara Harris, who paints a bleak picture of the boy's future. "Who writes your material for you, Charles Dickens?" Robards asks. – *A Thousand Clowns* (1965)

2460 "Good gardeners are so hard to come by," Rosemary Murphy informs a visitor to her palatial home. "I think no woman really had any luck with gardeners since Lady Chatterley." – *Any Wednesday* (1966)

2461 A Chinese assistant to sheriff Clint Walker quotes: "Any man more right than all his neighbors makes a majority of one." "Confucius say?" Walker asks. "Henry David Thoreau." – *The Great Bank Robbery* (1969)

2462 "It was Henry James, wasn't it?" Woody Allen questions, trying to identify an author. "*My Sexual Problem* by Henry James – sequel to *The Turn of the Screw*"? – *Annie Hall* (1977)

2463 When Martin Mull complains to wife Tuesday Weld that her therapist, Leonard, is too costly, she says she'll pay for the sessions herself. "With what?" he asks. "I'll get a job." "Doing what? You got a B.A. in literature. You're going to go door-to-door explaining the hidden meaning of *Huckleberry Finn?"* – *Serial* (1980)

2464 College instructor Ryan O'Neal during a conference is tested by his superior about the origin of a quotation. O'Neal identifies the lines. "My father is in the dress business," O'Neal later explains to a confidant. "I always liked *The Merchant of Venice."* – *So Fine* (1981)

2465 Hairdresser Julie Walters, taking an evening course in literature, is asked by one of her customers the title of the book she is carrying. *"Of Human Bondage,"* she replies. "Yeah?" the woman acknowledges. "My husband's got a lot of books like that." "Somerset Maugham books?" "No, bondage books." – *Educating Rita* (1983)

2466 Business tycoon Rodney Dangerfield invites several well-shaped college coeds into his jacuzzi. "What's your subject?" he asks a pretty blonde. "Poetry." "Really?" he replies. "Well, maybe you could help me straighten out my Longfellow." – *Back to School* (1986)

2467 The mayor of Los Angeles, expecting a visit from the Queen of England, warns police detective Leslie Nielsen: "I don't want any more trouble like you had last year on the South Side, understand? That's my policy." "Yes," Nielsen responds, "well, when I see five weirdoes dressed in togas stabbing a man in the middle of a park in full view of one hundred people, I shoot the weirdoes. That's my policy." "That was a Shakespeare-in-the-park production of *Julius Caesar,* you moron! You killed five actors!" – *The Naked Gun* (1988)

2468 When television executive Bill Murray develops a commercial for an upcoming Christmas show which instills fear in the viewers, his assistant points out that he may be going too far. "We don't want to scare the Dickens out of them," Murray agrees. – *Scrooged* (1988)

2469 Unconventional English teacher Robin Williams at a New England prep school informs his students: "I was the intellectual equivalent of a ninety-eight-pound weakling. I would go to the beach and people would kick copies of Byron in my face." – *Dead Poets Society* (1989)

2470 A grown Peter Pan (Robin Williams), visiting Lost Boys Camp in an attempt to recapture his lost childhood, meets a motley group of unruly orphans. "What is this?" he questions. "Some *Lord of the Flies* preschool?" – *Hook* (1991)

Love

2471 "Love is peace, quiet and tranquility," sighs Bert Wheeler. "That isn't love," challenges Robert Woolsey, "that's sleep." – *Half Shot at Sunrise* (1930)

2472 Artist Gary Cooper and playwright Fredric March and their girlfriend Miriam Hopkins have all agreed that there are to be no entangling intimacies between them. But one evening, alone with Cooper, Hopkins confesses that she loves him and stretches out provocatively on the couch. "I know we have a gentleman's agreement," she murmurs, "but unfortunately I am no gentleman." – *Design for Living* (1933)

2473 "Do you love me?" bridegroom Edward Everett Horton asks wife Miriam

Hopkins. "People should not ask that question on their wedding night," she replies. "It's either too late or too early." *– Design for Living* (1933)

2474 Fred Astaire has met Ginger Rogers, the love of his life – and she has rejected him. As he pines over his unrequited love, his lawyer-friend Edward Everett Horton reminds him that there are other young women. "I know," Astaire acknowledges, "but not like her. She's the buzzing of the bees in clover; she's the rustle of the leaves in trees; she's the lapping on the shore." "She sounds like a series of strange noises to me," Horton quips. *– The Gay Divorcee* (1934)

2475 Wealthy socialite Claudette Colbert walks out on Clark Gable thinking he dislikes her. "He despises me," she confides to her father. "He despises everything about me. He says that I'm spoiled and selfish and pampered and thoroughly insincere. He doesn't think so much of you either. And he blames you for everything that's wrong with me. He says that you raised me stupidly. Oh, he's marvelous!" *– It Happened One Night* (1934)

2476 "Were you ever in love?" Hugh Herbert asks his servant Eric Blore. "Oh, no sir, but I've been married." *– To Beat the Band* (1935)

2477 Groucho Marx expresses his love to Margaret Dumont: "It's the old story: 'Boy meets girl – Romeo and Juliet, Minne-Apolis and St. Paul.'" *– A Day at the Races* (1937)

2478 Photographer Gordon Jones ends up in the local jail with an eccentric cellmate who tries to cheer him up: "Let not the lashing tongue of parental anger obstruct the path of romance. Love marches on." *– They Wanted to Marry* (1937)

2479 "You know what the psychiatrists say," a young socialite articulates to her friend. "Hate is just a step away

from love." "Yes, but it's the lull in between that drives you crazy." *– The Mad Miss Manton* (1938)

2480 An officer in the French Foreign Legion tries to prevent Oliver Hardy, who has been rejected by the woman he loves, from committing suicide. "After all, there are plenty more fish in the sea," the soldier reminds him. "He's not in love with a fish," Stan Laurel explains. "It's the girl he loves." *– The Flying Deuces* (1939)

2481 "My dear," John Barrymore counsels Claudette Colbert on marriage, "it's amazing how little one has to explain to a man in love." "And when he stops being in love?" she asks. "Well," he replies cheerfully, "that's when the alimony begins." *– Midnight* (1939)

2482 Martha Raye, vacationing in Europe, tells Bob Hope about her boyfriend back home and the extent of his love. "He'd do anything for me," she boasts. "When we were kids he ate a beetle just 'cause I asked him to." "Sounds like a handy guy to have around the garden." *– Never Say Die* (1939)

2483 "Ninotchka," Melvyn Douglas confides to Greta Garbo, "let me confess something. Never did I dream that I could feel this way toward a sergeant." *– Ninotchka* (1939)

2484 "Love burns up energy, you know," hostess Mary Boland says to Lyle Talbot and Nancy Kelly, who have been out in the moonlight. "Yes, I know," acknowledges Kelly. "I always know I'm in love when I'm so hungry, and I'm always so hungry when I'm in love." *– He Married His Wife* (1940)

2485 "Do you believe in love at first sight?" asks George Raft. "Well," responds Ann Sheridan, "it saves a lot of time." *– They Drive by Night* (1940)

2486 "Love can make your timing wrong, all right," college football player

Eddie Bracken informs his pals about another player he had known. "We had a third string quarter at Harvard . . . He was killed in a movie. He reached for an usherette, missed and fell over the balcony." – *Too Many Girls* (1940)

2487 Edgar Bergen is an ardent butterfly chaser – until he meets a young woman and falls in love. "Well, that's the way it goes," comments Charlie McCarthy. "Love comes in the door, butterflies out the window." – *Here We Go Again* (1942)

2488 Mary Wickes describes to Anne Shirley how she fell in love with her boyfriend Millard Mitchell. "I've been crazy about him since the first day I met him," Wickes begins. "We were sitting next to one another. He squeezed a piece of lemon into a glass of tea and it squirted in my eye and I loved him ever since." – *The Mayor of 44th Street* (1942)

2489 Canadian Mountie Errol Flynn assures his bride Julie Bishop that he has known many girls, but she is the only one he has ever loved. Then, turning and confiding to the audience, he blurts out: "What am I saying?" – *Northern Pursuit* (1943)

2490 College instructor Gary Cooper confides to a colleague back home that he has met a young woman on a trip to New York. "What was she like?" "Did you ever see a sunset come up?" Cooper replies. "I have," the colleague admits. "It's nauseating." – *Casanova Brown* (1944)

2491 Trying to unravel his feelings for Clementine (Cathy Downs), Wyatt Earp (Henry Fonda) consults bartender J. Farrell MacDonald. "Mac, you ever been in love?" "No," MacDonald says. "I've been a bartender all my life." – *My Darling Clementine* (1946)

2492 "You only find the girl you love once." "That many times?" Oscar Levant questions. – *An American in Paris* (1951)

2493 José Ferrer, as a cynical Toulouse-Lautrec, says to a female dinner companion: "A wise woman patterns her life on the theories and practices of modern banking. She never gives her love, but only lends it on the best security and the highest rate of interest." – *Moulin Rouge* (1952)

2494 Defense lawyer Spencer Tracy questions cynical reporter Gene Kelly: "Have you ever been in love?" "Only with the sound of my own words, thank God." – *Inherit the Wind* (1960)

2495 Poet Sean Connery addresses a dignified, matronly audience. "Women, have you had love?" he asks. "How was it told? With diamonds and brocades? Did he ever say he loved your moments of glad grace? Did he ever say: 'My love is like a red, red rose that's newly sprung in June'? Women, you're red, red roses, you are. Blossom! Unfold! Open your corsets and bloom!" – *A Fine Madness* (1966)

2496 Elizabeth Taylor relates to a small gathering how she once fell in love with Richard Burton. "Yeah, she did," Burton chimes in. "You should have seen it. She'd sit outside my room and howl and claw at the turf. I couldn't work so I married her." – *Who's Afraid of Virginia Woolf?* (1966)

2497 Newlywed Jane Fonda discovers her husband (Robert Redford) is always "proper and dignified," much to her displeasure. "You always dress right," she says critically. "You always look right. You always say the right thing. You're very nearly perfect!" "That's a rotten thing to say," Redford fires back. – *Barefoot in the Park* (1967)

2498 Newlywed Jane Fonda greets spouse Robert Redford at a bus stop. "I decided to meet you here every day," she explains. "It takes you so long to climb the stairs, and I can't wait for you." "You will not meet me here every day!" Redford orders. "The bus driver will think you're my mother." – *Barefoot in the Park* (1967)

2499 "I knew I was in love," Woody Allen says. "First of all, I was very nauseous." – *Take the Money and Run* (1969)

2500 Blume (George Segal), a divorced lawyer, muses: "To be in love with a woman who scorns you is a problem; to be in love with a man who scorns you is a dilemma; but to be in love with your ex-wife is a tragedy." – *Blume in Love* (1973)

2501 Dry-cleaning store-owner Redd Foxx, whose wife has run off with his own brother, reports the bad news to his son Dennis Dugan. Dugan, trying to figure out what has happened, asks his father if he loved his wife who worked in the family store. "Of course I loved her!" Foxx insists. "If I didn't love her, would I let her put her hands in my cash register?" – *Norman . . . Is That You?* (1976)

2502 Television comedy writer Mark Linn-Baker is in love with fellow employee Jessica Harper, who constantly tries to avoid him. He finally catches up to her. "We have an understanding," he insists. "An understanding?" she questions quizzically. "That I am hopelessly in love with you, and you couldn't care less about me." – *My Favorite Year* (1982)

2503 Tom Hanks, discovering that Daryl Hannah is a mermaid, expresses his sorrow to brother John Candy. "All my life I've been waiting for someone, and when I find her, she's a fish."

"Nobody has said love is perfect," replies Candy. – *Splash* (1984)

2504 One college student asks another if he has called his girlfriend. "I haven't spoken to her for two – for about five months." "That's love," sighs the first. – *Odd Jobs* (1985)

2505 Underworld hit man Jack Nicholson falls in love with fellow assassin Kathleen Turner. "I look at you," he coos, "I see what I want to see. That's what love is." – *Prizzi's Honor* (1985)

2506 Cher tells her mother (Olympia Dukakis) she is going to get married. "Do you love him?" Dukakis asks. "No." "Good," her mother remarks. "When you love them, they drive you crazy because they know they can." – *Moonstruck* (1987)

2507 Homeless Robin Williams, a former Columbia University professor, falls in love – from a distance – with socially backward office worker Amanda Plummer, whom he stalks through New York's streets. "If anybody ever told me I'd be in love with a girl who chews jawbreakers," he remarks, "I'd say they were nuts." – *The Fisher King* (1991)

2508 Private eye Bruce Willis has been scarred by his secret service work and by his two-timing wife. "I believe in love, I believe in cancer," he says to his sidekick Damon Wayans. "What, they're both diseases?" Wayans questions. – *The Last Boy Scout* (1991)

Marriage

2509 Stepin Fetchit complains to his wife about the way she treats him. "You don't feed a fish after catchin' him," she retorts. – *Hearts in Dixie* (1929)

2510 Groucho Marx expounds on the subject of marriage: "Yeah, but the trouble is you can't enforce it. It was put over on the American people while our boys were over there and our girls were over here." – *Animal Crackers* (1930)

2511 "Love is an intoxication," a young woman says to Bert Wheeler. "And marriage is the hangover," he adds. – *Cracked Nuts* (1931)

2512 Thelma Todd complains about her miserable married life. "Four years of neglect, four years of battling, four years of heartbreak," she confides to Groucho Marx. "That makes twelve years," Groucho figures. "You must have been married in Rompers. Mighty pretty country there." – *Monkey Business* (1931)

2513 Oliver Hardy invites Stan Laurel to be a witness at his wedding ceremony, an affair conducted by cross-eyed reverend Ben Turpin. "Do you take this woman to be your lawful wedded wife?" Turpin pronounces. "Who, me?" the befuddled Laurel asks. "Not you," Hardy corrects him. "He means me." "Well, he's looking at me." – *Our Wife* (1931)

2514 Rosco Ates on marriage: "It's a lot of foolishness, but it's like the measles: It's better to have it young and get it over with." – *Too Many Cooks* (1931)

2515 "That's the trouble with marriage," comments venerable Henry Stephenson to his young friend Ronald Colman. "Women always hope it's going to change the husbands; men always hope it won't change the wives. And both are disappointed." – *Cynara* (1932)

2516 "It's no crime being married," Fred Astaire acknowledges. "It's just a weakness that men have that women take advantage of." – *The Gay Divorcee* (1934)

2517 "A wedding is a funeral where you smell your own flowers," quips Eddie Cantor. – *Kid Millions* (1934)

2518 "The ability to fool one another," notes John Barrymore, "is the secret of all happy marriages." – *Long Lost Father* (1934)

2519 "Marriage is like a beleaguered city," observes Don Juan (Douglas Fairbanks, Sr.). "Those who are out want to get in; those who are in want to get out." – *The Private Life of Don Juan* (1934)

2520 Douglas Fairbanks, Sr., as an aging Don Juan, has just left the balcony of one of his conquests. It is late at night and he can't seem to get a ride home. "Marriage may have its disadvantages," he muses, "but it saves a lot of walking." – *The Private Life of Don Juan* (1934)

2521 "Don't you think marriage is wonderful?" a young woman asks W. C. Fields. "It's all right – for women," Fields replies. – *Mississippi* (1935)

2522 Sailor Sid Silvers is in a rush to get ashore to see his wife. "Who'd marry you?" someone asks. "A minister," he quips. – *Born to Dance* (1936)

2523 To help inspector James Gleason solve a murder, amateur sleuth Helen Broderick searches the pants pockets of a suspect while he is asleep. "Are you sure you've never been married?" Gleason asks. – *Murder on a Bridal Path* (1936)

2524 Impoverished mother Mary Boland, desperate for her daughter to marry a millionaire, learns that a prospective son-in-law may have mental problems. "A man doesn't have to be in his right mind to get married, does he?" she asks. "He usually ain't," chuckles old-timer Roger Imhoff. – *There Goes the Groom* (1937)

2525 Detective Harold Huber, in a relaxed moment, confesses to Japanese sleuth Peter Lorre: "Yes, sir, I'd still be single if I hadn't gone to the policemen's ball one year in a tiger skin." – *Mr. Moto's Gamble* (1938)

2526 To spread the Marxist doctrine, icy Russian streetcar conductor Hedy Lamarr marries American reporter Clark Gable. On their wedding night she espouses the antithesis of the ideal American match. "It is like going into partnership with somebody," she says flatly. "It's like opening a store. If business is bad, you close the store." – *Comrade X* (1940)

2527 Mary Boland, who has been married several times, searches for her favorite recording. "Here it is!" she exclaims, showing the record to her servant. "'The Wedding March.' I was afraid I'd lost it." "I was afraid you'd worn it out, madam," the servant adds. – *He Married His Wife* (1940)

2528 Rosalind Russell describes suitor Ralph Bellamy to ex-husband Cary Grant: "He's kind and he's sweeet and he's considerate. He wants a home and children." "He sounds more like a guy I ought to marry," Grant quips. – *His Girl Friday* (1940)

2529 A landlady admonishes her young daughter for wrongfully accusing a young couple living on the premises of not being married. "They didn't look married–" the child explains, "kissing each other all the time." – *I'm Still Alive* (1940)

2530 The mother of Zorro (Tyrone Power) relates that his father is dismayed and angry that his son intends to marry the niece of a hated tyrant. "I had no say in my father's marriage," Zorro responds, "so why should he in mine?" – *The Mark of Zorro* (1940)

2531 At a party Genevieve Tobin boasts about her long-term marriage to Philo (Charlie Ruggles). "Philo and I have been married for–how long is it now, dear?" "They know at City Hall," Philo replies evasively. – *No Time for Comedy* (1940)

2532 Pilot James Cagney is hired by Bette Davis' tycoon father to kidnap her

to prevent her upcoming marriage. Cagney takes her to a cabin belonging to kindly old recluse Harry Davenport. "Ain't much difference between kidnapping and marriage," the old man philosophizes. "You get snatched from your parents. But in marriage, nobody offers a reward." – *The Bride Came C.O.D.* (1941)

2533 Bud Abbott asks Lou Costello about his relationship with Joan Davis. "She and I had a runaway marriage," Costello answers. "A runaway marriage?" "Yeah, she got the marriage license and I run away." – *Hold That Ghost* (1941)

2534 "Marriage is like an institution," Lucille Ball reminds cynical Charlie McCarthy. "So is Alcatraz," McCarthy ripostes. "But I wouldn't want to live in it." – *Look Who's Laughing* (1941)

2535 Secretary Bette Davis teases newspaperman Richard Travis, who has dreams of marriage. "I suppose some poor girl could fall for you," she says, "–if you came with a set of dishes." – *The Man Who Came to Dinner* (1941)

2536 "Every married man ought to be a bachelor," announces Edward Everett Horton. "Marriage is strictly for women." – *Weekend for Three* (1941)

2537 Cecil Kellaway, as the warlock-father of early American witch Veronica Lake, enlightens her: "Every man who marries, marries the wrong woman." – *I Married a Witch* (1942)

2538 Anne Shirley is amazed at how often her friend Mary Wickes argues with her boyfriend. "You know," Shirley suggests, "you two could save money by getting married and quarreling under the same roof." – *The Mayor of 44th Street* (1942)

2539 Sportswriter Spencer Tracy is on the telephone telling his mother that he is getting married to a wonderful young woman (Katharine Hepburn). "Ma, you don't ask a girl that," Tracy says. "I know it's important. All right, I'll ask her if she can cook." – *Woman of the Year* (1942)

2540 Cynical Ralph Morgan offers these few words to Gary Cooper, who is about to be married: "Under a democracy, every individual enjoys the right and privilege of being as much of an imbecile as he pleases." – *Casanova Brown* (1944)

2541 "It's bad luck to postpone a wedding," a woman comments. "Not if you postpone it long enough," quips Donald Meek. – *Rationing* (1944)

2542 Joan Davis' marriage to Jack Haley is being held up by his spinster aunt (Margaret Hamilton). "Jack promised our dear departed mother," Hamilton explains, "that since I'm all alone in the world, that he wouldn't marry before I did." "Well," says Joan, "how do you know he'll live that long?" – *George White's Scandals* (1945)

2543 French barber Bob Hope and royal maid Joan Caulfield fall in love and envision their future. "I can see it all now," she whispers. "Just you and I alone in a little cottage." "And perhaps in a year or two –" he begins. "There will be a little wail in the nursery." "Personally, I'd rather have children," Hope says. – *Monsieur Beaucaire* (1946)

2544 Lou Costello considers marriage so he can legally adopt French war orphan Beverly Simmons. "Well," he muses, "if you marry a pretty girl, she's liable to run away." "Uncle Herbie," the little orphan responds, "isn't a homely girl liable to run away too?" "Yeah," he replies, "but who cares?" – *Buck Privates Come Home* (1947)

2545 Bob Hope hears about the forthcoming wedding of Dorothy Lamour. "The whole countryside will be there," a villager announces. "How about people?" Hope queries. – *Road to Rio* (1947)

2546 Radio announcer Bob Hope, about to be married, is followed by three foreign agents who mistake him for the heir to the kingdom. "I wish I could make you understand that your life is in great danger," one agent warns. "Oh," Hope replies, "it's not as bad as that. Guys have gotten married before." – *Where There's Life* (1947)

2547 Jane Russell as Calamity Jane marries dentist Bob Hope as a cover for her government work. At the wedding ceremony the parson goes through all the rites. When he announces: "And now for the kiss," Hope kisses the clergyman. "Not me, you fool – her!" the parson exclaims. – *The Paleface* (1948)

2548 French captain Cary Grant questions why he and WAC Ann Sheridan are required to complete a battery of forms before they can get the army's permission to marry. "It's the army's way of finding out if you really want to get married," she explains. "I know a much better way," Grant beams. – *I Was a Male War Bride* (1949)

2549 Bank clerk Frank Sinatra earns a meager $42.50 per week, but sweetheart Jane Russell is anxious to marry. "Oh, I'm sure something will come along," she says encouragingly. "Yeah," Sinatra groans, "and we'll have to feed it, too." – *Double Dynamite* (1951)

2550 A young native orderly encourges Burt Lancaster, a sergeant in the French Foreign Legion, to settle down and marry. "If I settle down," Lancaster explains, "you'll be out of a job. Orderlies are for fighting men." "Married men *are* fighting men," the boy states. – *Ten Tall Men* (1951)

2551 "Marriage is like a dull meal with the dessert at the beginning," observes José Ferrer as Toulouse-Lautrec. – *Moulin Rouge* (1952)

2552 Bride-to-be Jane Russell snaps "Shut up!" to Bob Hope. "Shut up?" Hope indignantly questions. "You can't talk like that to me until after we're married!"—*Son of Paleface* (1952)

2553 To learn why he has romantic problems, entertainer Danny Kaye goes to a psychiatrist who sedates him and questions him about his childhood. "My mommy and daddy are always fighting and yelling and screaming and throwing things at each other," he reveals while unconscious. "Why do they do that?" the psychiatrist asks. "Because they have to," he replies. "They're married." —*Knock on Wood* (1954)

2554 "No matter who you marry," remarks Marlon Brando to Frank Sinatra, "you wake up married to someone else."—*Guys and Dolls* (1955)

2555 A childlike, innocent Marilyn Monroe discovers that her flirtatious neighbor Tom Ewell has a wife on vacation. She is not in the least displeased, for she harbors a distinct appreciation for a married man's limitations. "No matter what happens," she explains to Ewell, "he can't ask you to marry him." —*The Seven Year Itch* (1955)

2556 The stormy marriage of sportswriter Gregory Peck and successful dress-designer Lauren Bacall has settled into a kind of calm. "Mike and I are still together," of course," Bacall says. "We never argue anymore. And when we do, it never lasts more than a week or two. We're really very happily married." —*Designing Woman* (1957)

2557 Courtesan Isabel Jeans informs Gigi (Leslie Caron) of her marital possibilities. "Marriage is not forbidden to us," she explains. "But instead of getting married at once, it sometimes happens we get married at last."—*Gigi* (1958)

2558 While sharing a telephone party line, Doris Day overhears Rock Hudson expound upon the perils of marriage. "Before a man gets married," Hudson states, "he's like a tree in the forest. He stands there, independent, an entity

unto himself. And then he's chopped down. His branches are cut off—he's stripped of his bark—and he's thrown into the river with the rest of the logs." —*Pillow Talk* (1959)

2559 Sophia Loren, as one of the wealthiest women in the world, has an imaginary conversation with her deceased father about her ill-fated marriage to an athlete. Her father wonders why she ever married him. "He looked exciting," she replies, "and he had a wonderful backhand."—*The Millionairess* (1960)

2560 Peter Lawford, spoiled son of a wealthy woman who is about to marry for the sixth time, arrives for his periodic allowance and announces he is going on vacation. "You won't miss the wedding?" his mother asks. "Mother, have I ever missed one of your weddings?" "Yes, the first one."—*Ocean's Eleven* (1960)

2561 Reporter Barbara Eden receives alliterative counsel: "Don't hurry, give yourself time. It's better to be single and sad than married and miserable."—*All Hands on Deck* (1961)

2562 "A man your age needs a wife," James Garner's mother nags. "As a famous philosopher once wrote," Garner retorts, "if you could get milk for a penny a quart, you wouldn't keep a cow." "No," his mother adds, "not if all you wanted was milk."—*Boys' Night Out* (1962)

2563 Nita Talbot, after living with gangster Walter Matthau, suggests they get married. "Listen, honey," Matthau explains, "I'm a guy who deals in numbers and averages. My whole life I spent trying to beat the price. The day that marriage becomes a good bet, I'll get in touch with you."—*Who's Got the Action?* (1962)

2564 Con man Robert Preston and sidekick Tony Randall meet up with two young Greek women. "I just don't like aggressive women," Randall comments. "I know," Preston replies. "One wrong word and you're picking rice out of your ears."–*Island of Love* (1963)

2565 A group of married friends watch their bachelor buddy Dean Martin, contemplating marriage, walk off in a daze. "One of the great swingers of our generation is about to get married," laments one pal. "Maybe we should try and talk him out of it," suggests another. "Why should we?" says a third. "No one talked *us* out of it."–*Who's Been Sleeping in My Bed?* (1963)

2566 "Are you married?" writer Alan Bates asks Zorba (Anthony Quinn). "Am I not a man," Zorba replies, "and is not a man stupid? I'm married."–*Zorba the Greek* (1964)

2567 "Marriage is compromise," explains Rosemary Murphy to Jane Fonda. "For instance, I love bright colors. John can't bear them. I don't wear them." "That's compromise?" the surprised Fonda asks. "Well, according to John it is."–*Any Wednesday* (1966)

2568 "Funny thing about marriage," muses Jack Lemmon. "It's like being in the army. Everybody knocks it, but you'd be surprised how many guys reenlist."–*The Fortune Cookie* (1966)

2569 Albert Finney to Audrey Hepburn: "Marriage is when a woman asks a man to remove his pajamas because she wants to send them to the laundry." –*Two for the Road* (1967)

2570 Bea Arthur comments on a floundering marriage: "I can understand her wanting to leave, but I can't understand her leaving."–*Lovers and Other Strangers* (1970)

2571 Nurse Trish Van Devere informs prospective employer George Segal that she was once married for thirty-two hours. "That's not very long," he notes. "It was an eternity," she replies. –*Where's Poppa?* (1970)

2572 Walter Matthau is an unhappy man on the day of his daughter's wedding. She has decided to lock herself in the bathroom of their hotel room moments before the ceremony, and Matthau is furious. "Will you please lower your voice," his wife suggests. "Everybody will hear us." "Well, how long do you think we can keep this a secret? As soon as that boy down there says, 'I do,' and there's nobody standing next to him, they're going to suspect something!"–*Plaza Suite* (1971)

2573 Distraught New York City housewife and mother Barbra Streisand collapses from exhaustion only to find her overbearing suburban mother at her bedside. "Remember," the mother asserts, "marriage is a seventy-five–twenty-five proposition. The woman gives seventy-five."–*Up the Sandbox* (1972)

2574 "It's hard to believe you haven't had sex for two hundred years," Diane Keaton says to Woody Allen, who has awakened in the year 2173. "Two hundred and four if you count my marriage," Allen corrects her.–*Sleeper* (1973)

2575 "Some Jews are smart," Woody Allen muses, "but I hear their wives don't believe in sex after marriage." –*Love and Death* (1975)

2576 Richard Dreyfuss meets an old flame from his radical college days. "Why didn't I ever see you again?" he asks. "At that time I thought monogamy was a male conspiracy," she explains. –*The Big Fix* (1978)

2577 When judge Jack Warden insists that lawyer Al Pacino go flying with him, Pacino asks why the judge doesn't take his wife. "The last thing we did together," replies Warden, "was get married."–*...And Justice for All* (1979)

2578 "The trouble with marriage is that it's relentless," grumbles Joseph Bologna. "Every morning when you

wake up, it's still there. If I could only get a leave of absence once in a while— like the army. I always came back."
—*Chapter Two* (1979)

2579 While jogging, college professor George Segal meets Riley, the town's garrulous taxi driver (Paul Sorvino). "I was very sorry to hear about your good lady's passing," Sorvino says. "Thank you, Riley." "God bless you, professor." "I remarried," Segal informs the cabby. "God forgive you, professor."—*Lost and Found* (1979)

2580 "People should mate for life," Woody Allen remarks to girlfriend Mariel Hemingway, "like pigeons or Catholics."—*Manhattan* (1979)

2581 Unemployed actor Dom DeLuise meets his old pal George Segal at a skating rink. "I'm divorced—third time," Dom confesses. "But I just got married again, though. I need to be in love. I can't live without the aggravation."
—*The Last Married Couple in America* (1980)

2582 Jack Lemmon's wife Paula Prentiss has run off with a crazed doctor who runs a sex clinic. Lemmon finally tracks her down and pleads with her to return to their married life. "What's happened to us?" he cries. "Where has all the magic gone? We've been together for twelve years." "That long?" she questions.—*Buddy Buddy* (1981)

2583 "When I married her," Len Cariou says of his wife, Sandy Dennis, "I wanted someone stable. She's stable, all right—she's inert."—*The Four Seasons* (1981)

2584 Lois Lane (Margot Kidder) describes to a reporter what life would be like married to Superman. "I guess," she says, "it's sort of like being married to a doctor."—*Superman II* (1981)

2585 Karen Black, as the wife of town tyrant Ron Leibman, visits George Hamilton, her former suitor, in his

bedroom and tries to seduce him. "Why didn't I marry you instead of him?" she wonders. "Perhaps because he asked you and I did not," Hamilton offers.—*Zorro, the Gay Blade* (1981)

2586 Married Daniel Stern discusses his own premarital experiences with his friend Steve Guttenberg, who is about to wed. "When we were dating," Stern confides, "we spent most of our time talking about sex—why I couldn't do it, where could we do it, were her parents going to be out so we could do it . . . Then, when you're married . . . we've just got nothing to talk about."—*Diner* (1982)

2587 A changed Rita (Julie Walters), who has recently discovered the joys of literature, is asked by her husband to accompany him to the local pub. He excitedly explains the bar is now offering "eight different beers to choose from." "Who would have thought," Rita responds, "that we have paradise at the end of our street?"—*Educating Rita* (1983)

2588 Already married Dudley Moore has blundered into a second love affair and has decided to take on a second wife. As he leaves the service, a happy bridesmaid reflects upon her own marital prospects and says: "I guess I'm next." "Oh," Moore's friend, Richard Mulligan, comments, "I don't think he has the time."—*Micki & Maude* (1984)

2589 Cher, whose husband was killed years earlier by a bus after only two years of marriage, tells her father (Vincent Gardenia) that she plans to remarry. Gardenia objects, claiming that her first marriage didn't work out. "And what killed him?" her father asks. "He got hit by a bus." "No," Gardenia replies. "Bad luck. Your mother and I were married fifty-two years. Nobody died."
—*Moonstruck* (1987)

2590 Valley girl manicurist Geena Davis whines that her unimpassioned beau Charles Rocket hasn't made love to her for two weeks. "At the rate we're having sex," she adds, "we may as well be married already." – *Earth Girls Are Easy* (1989)

2591 Mystery writer Tom Selleck, whose career is floundering, discusses his dilemma with his editor, explaining: "I'm researching all the time. I just can't come up with any new crimes." "Get married again," his editor suggests. "You'll think of crimes you never knew existed." – *Her Alibi* (1989)

2592 Husband Craig T. Nelson is suing Shelley Long for divorce because of her wild spending sprees. "Did it ever occur to you that marriage is a partnership?" she parries, trying to change his mind. "Yeah, that's right," he replies. "I earn the money and my partner spends it." – *Troop Beverly Hills* (1989)

2593 Sally (Meg Ryan) meets two girlfriends for lunch, and the conversation inevitably turns to finding a mate and getting married. "Don't wait too long," one warns Sally. "Remember what happened with David Warsaw? His

wife left him and everyone said, 'Give him some time, don't move in too fast.' Six months later he was dead." "What are you saying?" Sally protests. "I should get married to someone right away in case he is about to die?" "At least you could say you were married," suggests the second friend. – *When Harry Met Sally...* (1989)

2594 "I was married for three years," Christine Lahti admits to Gene Wilder. "What happened?" "It was all my fault," she explains. "I just couldn't get along with the other woman." – *Funny About Love* (1990)

2595 Widow Marlo Thomas reflects upon the loss of her husband: "Sometimes I loved him so much that I didn't think I could live on this planet without him. Sometimes he was a real pain in the ass that I could have killed him. It was a perfect marriage." – *In the Spirit* (1990)

2596 Frustrated wife: "Why did I marry you?" Husband: "Because I said 'yes.'" – *The Addams Family* (1991)

Marriage Proposals

2597 "Please marry me," Eddie Cantor's nurse pleads. "Why, I'd take such good care of you – I'd keep you comfy and warm." "It would be much cheaper for me to get a hot water bottle," Cantor replies. – *Whoopee!* (1930)

2598 When Gloria Swanson learns that her lover has been having several affairs behind her back, she breaks off with him. As a last resort, he proposes marriage. "I really mean it this time," he pleads. "Mean what?" she asks. "Marriage and all that." "No," she persists. "I'm afraid it would be too little marriage and too much 'all that.'" – *Indiscreet* (1931)

2599 A matronly English duchess (Violet Kemble-Cooper) confides to a friend: "When Gaston proposed to me, he went down on his knees and took my hand and said he couldn't live without me. Of course I knew that – because he hadn't a cent." – *Our Betters* (1933)

2600 Suitor John Miljan: "I must have your golden hair, fascinating eyes, alluring smile, your lovely arms, your form divine." Mae West: "Wait a minute. Is this a proposal or are you taking inventory?" – *Belle of the Nineties* (1934)

2601 The homely daughter of a sheik wants to marry Eddie Cantor and tries to prove she is desirable. "I'll have you know I was asked a thousand times to get married," she boasts to Cantor. "Who asked you?" he inquires. "My father." – *Kid Millions* (1934)

2602 "Any other dame, and I wouldn't give a hoot," Fred Kohler says in his proposal to Mae West. "But with you I'm dynamite." "Yeah," West agrees, "and I'm your match." – *Goin' to Town* (1935)

2603 Groucho Marx woos Margaret Dumont. "Will you be truly mine or truly yours or yours truly?" – *A Night at the Opera* (1935)

2604 It's anniversary day – for twenty years suitor Charlie Ruggles has faithfully called on his sweetheart – and for twenty years she has desperately hoped that he would pop the question. "You know, Tessie," Ruggles coos, "you haven't changed one little bit." "No, I haven't," she says unhappily. "I was single then and I'm still single." – *Early to Bed* (1936)

2605 Racetrack enthusiast Groucho Marx asks for the hand of Margaret Dumont: "Marry me and I'll never look at another horse." – *A Day at the Races* (1937)

2606 Rodeo cowboy Gary Cooper confides to pal Walter Brennan that he is about to propose to Merle Oberon. "If it's for keeps," Brennan explains, "you gotta get down on your knees and spout poetry." "You tried it?" "I tried it once," Brennan says, "but I got a crimp in my knee, so I gave it up." – *The Cowboy and the Lady* (1938)

2607 Henry Fonda proposes to socialite Barbara Stanwyck and suggests honeymooning in South America. "Can you afford it?" she asks. "No, but you can." "Isn't there a drop of red blood in your veins?" she inquires. "I wanted to live on your income." "That's foolish,"

he returns. "Who's going to live on yours?" – *The Mad Miss Manton* (1938)

2608 W. C. Fields meets Mae West aboard a train and proposes to her. His traveling bag, bursting with money, has not gone unnoticed by West. "I will be all things to you," Fields continues, "father, mother, husband, counselor, Japanese bartender." "You're offering quite a bundle, honey," she replies. "My heart is a bargain today," he confesses. "Will you take me?" "I'll take you – and how?" she says. – *My Little Chickadee* (1940)

2609 Groucho Marx's marriage proposal to wealthy Margaret Dumont only arouses her suspicion. "I'm afraid after we've been married a while," she remarks, "a beautiful young girl will come along and you'll forget all about me." "Don't be silly," Groucho replies. "I'll write you twice a week." – *The Big Store* (1941)

2610 Down-and-out private detective Groucho Marx to department-store owner Margaret Dumont: "If you marry me, your concern will be my concern." – *The Big Store* (1941)

2611 Groucho Marx woos Margaret Dumont – with his usual ulterior motives. "There are many bonds that will hold us together through eternity," he says. "Really? What are they?" "Your government bonds, your savings bonds, your liberty bonds, and maybe a little baby bond." – *The Big Store* (1941)

2612 Wealthy middle-aged Sara Allgood, who has loved the now broken-down and alcoholic actor Monty Woolley since her youth, asks him to marry her. "Would you like a direct answer?" he enunciates. "Rather than marry you, I would dive naked into a barrel of rattlesnakes." "That's final, I take it?" "Does it sound like equivocation?" he asks. – *Life Begins at Eight-Thirty* (1942)

2613 Edward Brophy, looking for a wife to lower his income tax, proposes to a widowed hotel cleaning woman who has been married three times. "I remember at the funeral of the last one," she replies to Brophy's proposal, "lookin' down at his coffin sayin' my last goodbye to him. He looked better then than you do right now." – *The Falcon in San Francisco* (1945)

2614 Ray Bolger, a fastidious and petty Washington bureaucrat, turns down a taxi driver's request for a tip. "I believe your rates are set by the Interstate Commerce Commission," Bolger remarks, "and I'm sure you receive a living wage." "Would you like to marry me for my money?" the driver asks. – *April in Paris* (1953)

2615 Raffish millionaire Joe E. Brown, falling for Jack Lemmon in drag, proposes marriage. "I'm terrible," Lemmon responds, trying to dissuade him. "For three years I lived with a saxophone player." "I forgive you." "We can never have children." "We can adopt some," Brown persists. "You don't understand," Lemmon finally declares, whipping off his wig. "I'm a man!" "Well, nobody's perfect." – *Some Like It Hot* (1959)

2616 Mobster Jack Nicholson has just slept with hired killer Kathleen Turner, with whom he has fallen in love. "With everything being equal," he whispers slowly to her, "will you marry me?" – *Prizzi's Honor* (1985)

2617 Cold, efficient and ambitious Wall Street executive Sigourney Weaver confides to her secretary Melanie Griffith that her boyfriend will probably propose to her over the weekend. "I think he's going to pop the question," Weaver says. "We're in the same city now. I've indicated that I'm receptive to an offer. I've cleared the month of June. I am, after all, me." "What if he doesn't 'pop the question'?" Griffith asks. "I really don't think that's a variable." – *Working Girl* (1988)

2618 To win Dana Delaney, the woman he has always loved, architect Steve Martin has built a dream house in a picturesque New England town. Showing her the "House Beautiful" off a circular driveway and wrapped in a huge red ribbon, he pops the question. "So, will you?" "No," she says. – *Housesitter* (1992)

Media

2619 "Haven't I seen your photograph in all the periodicals?" a woman says to popular baseball pitcher Joe E. Brown. "Well, I don't know about that," the embarrassed Brown replies, "but I've had my picture in newspapers and magazines a lot." – *Fireman, Save My Child* (1932)

2620 "A marvelous invention, the radio," a town banker asserts. "In a few minutes we'll be talking to everybody in the county." "I don't like that," Robert Woolsey replies. "There's a few people I'm not speaking to." – *The Rainmakers* (1935)

2621 Judge Hardy (Lewis Stone) explains to his son Andy (Mickey Rooney) that he is about to expose a group of corrupt Washington businessmen. "You'll hear all about it when I talk on the radio tomorrow night." "You mean you're going to talk on the radio?" Rooney exclaims in delight and astonishment. "You mean broadcast – like you were toothpaste or cold cream?" – *Judge Hardy's Children* (1938)

2622 Groucho Marx describes a scene for playwright Frank Albertson, conjuring up an image of a crying mother waiting by a fireside. "But we have no fireside," the young writer objects. "You have no fireside?" Groucho asks. "How do you listen to the President's speeches?" – *Room Service* (1938)

2623 Joan Blondell and Carole Landis arrive at an eerie old mansion to claim the latter's inheritance. An ancient housekeeper shows them to their bedroom and opens the windows, letting in the sounds of ocean waves. Landis inquires about the cause of the ominous sounds. "It's the waves, angry waves," the woman explains. "Day after day, night after night, they beat with savage fury against the black rocks below. For twenty years they've been calling, calling, calling someone who never answers." "Just like the 'Pot of Gold' program," Blondell quips. – *Topper Returns* (1941)

2624 Judge Lewis Stone pontificates to daughter Cecilia Parker: "I think a newspaper article should be about as long as a lady's skirt – long enough to cover the subject, but short enough to be interesting." – *The Courtship of Andy Hardy* (1942)

2625 During World War II political columnist Katharine Hepburn is surprised to learn that the newspaper she writes for has two reporters covering a baseball game. "We only have one man at Vichy," she grumbles to sports writer Spencer Tracy. "Vichy?" Tracy quips. "Are they still in the league?" – *Woman of the Year* (1942)

2626 A woman accosts radio personality Fred Allen, who hosts a morning radio show with his wife. The stranger explains how his program has helped her and her husband to overcome several problems in their own marriage. Allen stares at the woman in disbelief and then blurts out: "Are you insane?" – *We're Not Married* (1952)

2627 Radio personality Fred Allen reprimands his producer who gloats over signing up several additional sponsors. "When the revolution comes," cries

Allen, "the first blow struck will be against radio programs that mention more than twenty-five sponsors during the first ten minutes!" – *We're Not Married* (1952)

2628 Comic book artist Dorothy Malone invites neophyte writer Jerry Lewis to appear on a television panel to discuss the effects of comics. "Are you nervous?" she asks him. "No," he replies, facing the T.V. cameras, "just my knees are nervous. They've never been on television before." – *Artists and Models* (1955)

2629 Aspiring actress Marilyn Monroe, who does a live laundry commercial on television, is awed by the size of her audience. "Every time I wash a shirt on T.V.," she explains to neighbor Tom Ewell, "I'm appearing before more people than Sarah Bernhardt appeared before in her whole career. It's something to think about." – *The Seven Year Itch* (1955)

2630 Gene Kelly, as the reporter H. L. Mencken, pungently remarks: "It is the duty of a newspaper to comfort the afflicted and to flick the comfortable." – *Inherit the Wind* (1960)

2631 It is the beginning of radio – 1925 – and Clarence Darrow (Spencer Tracy) is being interviewed. "Radio! God, this is going to break down a lot of walls." "You're not supposed to say 'God' on the radio," the announcer warns. "Why the hell not?" "You're not supposed to say 'hell' either." "This is going to be a barren source of entertainment," Tracy concludes. – *Inherit the Wind* (1960)

2632 At a U.S. Senate hearing about the disintegration of morality in America, a television censor complains about television fare. "I don't know what they're doing!" he rants about the network leaders. "Each one trying to outdo the other. Prostitution, abortion, homosexuality – and that's only in the commercials!" – *The Happy Hooker Goes to Washington* (1977)

2633 A sleazy publisher wants football player Burt Reynolds to write about the sex, drugs and scandals that have infiltrated the sport. "My great grandfather," the executive boasts in an effort to impress Reynolds, "started the firm right after the Civil War with the help of Oliver Wendell Holmes." "Who did he play for?" Reynolds quips. — *Semi-Tough* (1977)

2634 "In an insane society, a sane man must appear insane," explains a ten-year-old boy to Martin Mull. "Where did you get that?" *"Star Trek."* — *Serial* (1980)

2635 Millionaire idler Dudley Moore: "I think I'll take a bath." Valet John Gielgud: "I'll alert the media." — *Arthur* (1981)

2636 Unintelligent but handsome television announcer John Hurt is quickly moved up to anchor a late-breaking news story. Bright, ambitious and clever Holly Hunter, the news producer in the control room, guides him through the story by whispering instructions into his ear phone. "What a feeling having you inside my head!" he later confesses to her. "Indescribable! You knew just when to feed me the next line. There was — like — rhythm we got into. It was like great sex!" — *Broadcast News* (1987)

2637 The wealthy publisher of *Bait*, a porno magazine, is quick to defend his publication. "The intelligent subscriber," he explains, "regards it as a politically oriented socially impacting monthly." — *Dragnet* (1987)

2638 Abrasive talk-show host Eric Bogosian gives us his motto to explain the barbs and insults he hurls at his audience: "Sticks and stones may break my bones, but words cause permanent damage." — *Talk Radio* (1989)

Miserliness

2639 Lynne Overman is cynical about his boss, the miserly bookie Sorrowful Jones (Adolphe Menjou), who has just lost twenty dollars on a bettor he trusted. "Every time I get big-hearted —" Menjou begins. "When was the other time?" Overman interjects. — *Little Miss Marker* (1934)

2640 "Listen," insists miserly bookie Sorrowful Jones (Adolphe Menjou), "I've always been generous in a quiet way." "Practically silent," cracks his cashier Lynne Overman. — *Little Miss Marker* (1934)

2641 At a railway depot in Scotland, passenger Donald Crisp finds ample reason not to tip village porter Brian Aherne. "I do not intend to encourage the spirit of Communism in this community by offering you a gratuity." "I'm not a Communist," protests Aherne. "I'm an individual collectivist." "Well," concludes Crisp, "you'll not be collecting from me." — *What Every Woman Knows* (1934)

2642 Groucho Marx explains how to develop a film negative. "You can use the potassium or the silver nitrate," he says. "Use the night rate," suggests Chico. "It's cheaper." — *The Big Store* (1941)

2643 Fred Allen, attempting to locate a particular chair, learns that its new owner is Jack Benny. "If Jack Benny ever finds out there's three hundred thousand dollars in that chair," Allen exclaims, "he'll divorce Mary Livingston and marry the chair!" – *It's in the Bag* (1945)

2644 As Bob Hope stamps his foot on a penny rolling down the street, a small boy claims that it is his. "Identify it!" Hope demands. "It's got Abe Lincoln's picture on it," comes the reply. "You kids with a college education!" Hope grumbles. – *Sorrowful Jones* (1949)

2645 Fiscally conservative store owner Edward G. Robinson presents a cab driver with a ten-cent tip. "Oh, pardon me, sir," the driver says. "Do you happen to have a snapshot of yourself?" "What?" Robinson asks, surprised. "You know, sir, I haven't gotten a dime tip since 1932. I'd just love to frame it along with the picture of the sport who gave it to me." – *A Hole in the Head* (1959)

2646 On Christmas Eve, with the air sprinkled with the joys of the holiday, Bob Cratchit, the good-spirited clerk, approaches his employer, the miser Scrooge (Albert Finney), for his wages. Scrooge's face contorts as if in pain. "The trouble with you, Cratchit," he cackles, "is that all you think of is pleasure." – *Scrooge* (1970)

2647 "If I could only see a miracle," Boris (Woody Allen), searching for faith, says. "A burning bush, or the seas part, or my uncle Sasha pick up a check." – *Love and Death* (1975)

2648 A nationally famous television comedy star makes a play for one of his pretty assistants. "Did you like the shoes I sent you?" "Yeah," she replies coldly. "Then why did you send them back?" "They were the wrong size and they were used." – *My Favorite Year* (1982)

2649 Miserly millionaire brothers Ralph Bellamy and Don Ameche are waited upon by their faithful elderly servant. "I'll bet you thought I forgot your Christmas bonus," Bellamy announces, handing the man a bill. "Five dollars," the servant says gratefully. "Maybe I'll go to the movies – by myself." "Half of it is from me," Ameche adds. – *Trading Places* (1983)

2650 Vincent Gardenia, upon hearing that his daughter Cher is going to marry, refuses to pay for the wedding. "He didn't used to be cheap," his wife Olympia Dukakis explains to Cher. "He thinks that if he holds on to his money, he'll never die." – *Moonstruck* (1987)

2651 Greedy, uncaring slumlord Joe Pesci refuses every request from his long-suffering tenants who complain about lack of heat, hot water, electricity, etc. "If you want your electricity fixed," he yells at a mother, "move to the Plaza!" "Look at my boy," the distraught woman cries, "how's he to do his homework – by candlelight?" "Lincoln did," he replies. "If he's got anything on the ball, maybe *he'll* grow up to be President." – *The Super* (1991)

Money

2652 "When are you going to pay me my money you owe me?" one comic asks. "When you're alone," says the second comic. "I'm alone now." "No you ain't. I'm here." – *Up the River* (1930)

2653 In a dice game Robert Woolsey has won the crown from the king of a mythical kingdom. As the new king, he is told that within a week he will get his face on all the coins of the realm. "Never mind getting my face on them," he remarks. "What I want to do is get my hands on them." – *Cracked Nuts* (1931)

2654 Opera singer Maxine Castle receives some dubious advice from Groucho Marx: "That's what I always say. Love flies out the door when money comes innuendo." – *Monkey Business* (1931)

2655 A corrupt safari guide tells his cohort that Tarzan knows the location of gold worth ten thousand pounds. "Hey listen," the friend replies, "if Tarzan knows where there's that much gold, why doesn't he buy himself a pair of pants?" – *Tarzan the Fearless* (1933)

2656 In England, George Burns and Gracie Allen join a tour of a famous castle. "His lordship paid five thousand pounds for that portrait," announces the guide. "Five thousand pounds of what?" asks Gracie. – *A Damsel in Distress* (1937)

2657 Doris Nolan is hesitant about breaking the news of her engagement to her suspicious millionaire father. "It'll be the same old story, of course – I'm being married for my money," she says to her sister Katharine Hepburn. "That's always flattering, isn't it?" Hepburn asks. "Well, what's the use of all this jack we've got unless it's to get a superior-type man?" – *Holiday* (1938)

2658 Chico Marx's friend and boss, Kenny Baker, has been robbed of ten thousand dollars, and Chico asks lawyer Groucho Marx for advice on how to retrieve the money. "Very easy," Groucho replies. "Just offer a reward of fifteen thousand dollars." – *At the Circus* (1939)

2659 High-spirited band singer Una Merkel offers manager Bob Hope a joke designed to put some pizzazz into their act: "You say, 'I swallowed a quarter.' I say, 'Did you feel anything?' You say, 'No change yet.'" – *Some Like It Hot* (1939)

2660 The Three Stooges decide to take out an insurance policy, but they need money. Moe turns to Curly. "Where's that dollar?" he asks. "Oh, no," Curly falters. "My favorite dollar. I raised it from a cent." – *From Nurse to Worse* (1940)

2661 Shady street-corner vendor Bud Abbott asks his shill Lou Costello how much money he has. "I have in the vicinity of twenty-eight dollars," Costello replies, "but in the neighborhood of two dollars." – *Buck Privates* (1941)

2662 "I'm not so obsessed with money as you seem to be," Mary Astor says to Humphrey Bogart. "Stick around with me and you'll get plenty of practice," he quips. – *Across the Pacific* (1942)

2663 The East Side Kids accuse a local gambler of passing counterfeit money. "The last time you gave me a five," charges Huntz Hall, "Lincoln was winkin'." – *Kid Dynamite* (1943)

2664 "Why is it rich people have all the money?" hat-check boy Red Skelton muses. – *DuBarry Was a Lady* (1943)

2665 A young man of modest means explains to his friend Clive Brook that he has fallen in love with a much older woman. "My income is three hundred a year," the young man adds. "Hers is twenty-five thousand." "You've given me a reason why you are right to love her," Brook remarks. "Are you suggesting that I love her for her money?" "I'm suggesting a reason why you should." – *On Approval* (1943)

2666 Cockney Cary Grant mocks his precarious existence: "Money talks, they say. All it ever said to me was 'Goodbye.'" – *None But the Lonely Heart* (1944)

2667 Bob Hope is on Death Row in San Quentin. A group of reporters anxiously await his story. He begins by explaining how he got started in a sweet racket. "Was it legitimate?" a reporter asks. "Better than legitimate," Hope retorts. "It was profitable." – *My Favorite Brunette* (1947)

2668 A down-and-out gambler accosts Harold Lloyd, asking him for a loan. "A fool and his money are soon parted," Lloyd quotes. "Yeah, but think what beautiful memories he lays up." – *The Sin of Harold Diddlebock* (1947)

2669 Show business couple Eddie Cantor and Joan Davis learn that the government owes them a large sum of money – the interest alone amounts to five thousand dollars an hour. "Do you realize we made forty-five thousand dollars last night while we were in bed?" Joan figures. Cantor responds by pulling her by the hand. "Where are we going?" she asks. "Back to bed," he replies. – *If You Knew Susie* (1948)

2670 "Suppose you had five dollars in one pants pocket and five dollars in the other pants pocket," Bud Abbott suggests to Lou Costello. "What would you have?" "Somebody else's pants on," Costello returns. – *The Noose Hangs High* (1948)

2671 "This is Sorrowful Jones, who fell in love with money at the age of six," a voice-over announces, "and they've been going steady ever since." – *Sorrowful Jones* (1949)

2672 With the wedding expenses for their daughter's marriage piling up, Spencer Tracy grumbles to his wife Joan Bennett: "It's only two syllables from bank to bankruptcy." – *Father of the Bride* (1950)

2673 Joan Davis pleads with a banker for a loan for her father' soap factory. "This bank," the owner insists, "is not in the habit of lending money to people who are broke." "Who else needs it?" Davis asks. – *The Traveling Saleswoman* (1950)

2674 Money-crazed Marilyn Monroe explains to friend Jane Russell how the

lack of money can lead to a loveless marriage: "If a girl has to worry about all the money she doesn't have, how is she going to have time for love?" "That baffles me," replies her befuddled friend. – *Gentlemen Prefer Blondes* (1953)

2675 Golddigger Marilyn Monroe tells her millionaire future father-in-law Charles Coburn that she is not marrying his son for his money. "No," she replies. "I'm marrying him for *your* money." – *Gentlemen Prefer Blondes* (1953)

2676 Seeing Frank Sinatra's lavish apartment for the first time, David Wayne is overwhelmingly impressed. "Do all theatrical agents live like this?" he asks. "How much money are you making?" "Almost as much as I'm spending," Sinatra replies. – *The Tender Trap* (1955)

2677 "Lend me ten," Burt Lancaster asks an acquaintance. "I'll pay you back tomorrow." "I may be dead tomorrow," the man says. "I'll put the money in your grave," Lancaster replies. – *Trapeze* (1956)

2678 "Money isn't everything, believe me," comic Joe E. Lewis (Frank Sinatra) informs an audience. "It can't buy poverty." – *The Joker Is Wild* (1957)

2679 "Can I buy you a drink?" someone offers Huntz Hall. "No, thank you," Hall replies, "I don't drink, but I'll take the money instead." – *In the Money* (1958)

2680 "I'm aware of my debt to the Indians," a venal Hollywood producer remarks glibly, "and I get very sentimental when I book cowboys where they're shooting Indians in cold blood. I always look the other way." "Toward the ticket booth," writer Lee J. Cobb says scathingly. – *But Not for Me* (1959)

2681 Conniving navy lieutenant Tony Curtis' ambition – to marry into money – has been temporarily suspended during World War II. "When I was growing up," he explains to his captain (Cary Grant), "people were always telling me money isn't everything. Then I realized that the people that were saying it had all the money."—*Operation Petticoat* (1959)

2682 Comic Milton Berle, playing himself, is offered a lucrative contract to teach a wealthy executive how to be a comedian. "This is a very fantastic figure," Berle declares, referring to the contract. "You know, the first time I read it I didn't know if this was what you were going to pay me or my social security number."—*Let's Make Love* (1960)

2683 Ladies' man and young stud Tony Curtis, looking for wealthy, single women in a gambling casino, says: "The last way to make money in the casinos is at the tables."—*Arrivederci, Baby* (1966)

2684 Ambulance-chasing lawyer Walter Matthau tries to convince brother-in-law Jack Lemmon, who has been hurt by a football player, to sue. "What's wrong?" Matthau asks. "Insurance companies have so much money they have to microfilm it!"—*The Fortune Cookie* (1966)

2685 Harper (Paul Newman) orders a beer at a swank bar and pays a surly bartender accustomed to hard drinks and large tips. "Keep the change," Newman says. "There isn't any." "Keep it anyway."—*Harper* (1966)

2686 A gang of thieves prepares for a major heist. "Money breeds money," one gang member remarks. "Mine must be on the pill," another returns.—*Robbery* (1967)

2687 "Money is like manure," Barbra Streisand remarks to miserly Walter Matthau. "It's no good unless you spread it around."—*Hello, Dolly!* (1969)

2688 At a gathering somewhere in the Ukraine of 1905, a villager declares that money is the world's curse. "May the Lord smite me with it," Tevye (Topol)

responds, "and I should never recover."—*Fiddler on the Roof* (1971)

2689 "Have you got thirty-five cents?" a New York panhandler asks Art Carney. "Why thirty-five?" the curious Carney inquires. "I want to buy a mink coat."—*Harry and Tonto* (1974)

2690 Unemployed aerospace executive George Segal turns to crime to maintain his life-style. "It's not the money," he rationalizes to his wife (Jane Fonda), "it's the principle of the thing." "Principle?" she questions. "What principle is there in robbing a drugstore?" "That's right, it's the money—that's the 'prinicipal,'" he chatters on. "That's the principal of the thing. You wouldn't understand."—*Fun with Dick and Jane* (1977)

2691 Eccentric Steve Martin has become a millionaire by a fluke, and a host of representatives from various charities clamor at his mansion door seeking large donations. "There are some charity people here to see you, sir," announces his servant. "No, send them away," Martin orders. "There's a lot of people more deserving than me."—*The Jerk* (1979)

2692 Financially strapped veterinarian Richard Benjamin has to turn down his wife's request for another ten thousand dollars to pour into her failing antiques business. "I love sleeping with you," his wife admits. "Sometimes I think it might be the only thing we have in common." "We have something else in common—money," he replies. "My ability to make it and yours to spend it."—*How to Beat the High Cost of Living* (1980)

2693 Blind nun Susan Saiger, carrying a cup for donations, approaches smalltime thief Robert Beltran, who makes a contribution. "Do you believe in the sixth sense?" she asks. "I think I gave you over a dollar," he replies.—*Eating Raoul* (1982)

2694 Entertainer Julie Andrews' agent brings news that a nightclub owner has offered her a "fortune" to appear at his club. "Would you be more specific with your nouns?" Robert Preston, Andrews' assistant, asks anxiously. "Ten thousand dollars a week." "That's not a noun," Preston replies. "That's a fortune." —*Victor/Victoria* (1982)

2695 Two miserly millionaire brothers (Ralph Bellamy and Don Ameche) discuss and argue the nuances of their favorite subject—money. "Money isn't everything," Bellamy insists. "Oh," Ameche responds, "grow up." "Mother always said you were greedy." "She meant it as a compliment." —*Trading Places* (1983)

2696 "What do you get married for?" Shelley Long's friend muses. "Love? Love is for six to eight months tops. Money is forever!" —*Hello Again* (1987)

2697 A counterfeiter, turning out millions of bogus dollars of high quality, looks at a sample bill and cracks: "And they say there's no money in printing." —*Blood Money* (1991)

2698 People say money talks," dedicated New York City cop Michael Keaton muses, "but between you and me, money keeps a better secret than anyone I know." —*One Good Cop* (1991)

2699 Larry Garfield (Danny DeVito), also known as Larry the Liquidator because of his voracious appetite of taking over companies, is driven not so much by greed as by the "game" itself. "Make as much as you can for as long as you can," he expounds. "Whoever has the most when he dies, wins." —*Other People's Money* (1991)

2700 Deadbeat Danny DeVito, upon discovering twin brother Arnold Schwarzenegger's strength, suggests that they go into the fight racket. "I don't think I could fight for money," Schwarzenegger confesses. "No problem," DeVito parries. "You do all the fighting, and I'll keep all the money." —*Twins* (1991)

Movies

2701 Two fading vaudeville performers, planning to open a speech school in Hollywood for silent screen stars, approach a foreign-born movie mogul who has a heavy accent. "We'll not only teach your people to talk," they promise, "but we'll have them talking as well as you do." "Vell," the flattered producer replies, "I don' esk you fer miracles." —*Once in a Lifetime* (1931)

2702 Hollywood studio mogul Gregory Ratoff complains to his staff that a good plot summary should take only fifty words. "The whole story of creation was written in three hundred fifty words in the Book of Genesis," he cites as an

example. "Genesis," director Lowell Sherman echoes. "That's a guy you should sign up." —*What Price Hollywood?* (1932)

2703 Louise Closser Hale grouses about being a part-time wife: "Ed hates anything that keeps him from going to the movies every night. I guess I'm what you call a Garbo widow." —*Dinner at Eight* (1933)

2704 Egomaniacal Broadway producer John Barrymore histrionically tries to shake straying star Carole Lombard back to her senses: "Those movies you were in—it's sacrilege! . . . I felt some magnificent ruby had been thrown into a platter of lard." – *Twentieth Century* (1934)

2705 Movie star Lucille Ball notifies her boss that she is quitting pictures. After much begging and cajoling, the studio producer finally explodes. "All right," he shouts, "you think you're going to walk out on me? I'll make your life miserable!" "What're you going to do," asks secretary Ruth Donnelly, "make her sit through her own pictures?" – *Annabel Takes a Tour* (1938)

2706 Movie star Lucille Ball falls in love with a novelist and announces to her producer that she is retiring from the screen. "Why didn't you fall in love with one of the writers at the studio," a top executive utters, "get yourself a good picture?" – *Annabel Takes a Tour* (1938)

2707 Soda jerk Joe E. Brown, desiring to emulate the screen's popular fictional detective the Thin Man, asks: "What does William Powell have that I don't have?" "Myrna Loy," replies his boss. – *Wide Open Faces* (1938)

2708 Muggs (Leo Gorcey), searching in a mansion and feeling more like a detective every moment, asks, "Hey, what's the Thin Man got that I haven't got?" "Myrna Loy," pal Bobby Jordan answers. – *Boys of the City* (1940)

2709 After an engineer is bound and gagged on a train, Groucho Marx informs the audience: "This is the best gag in the picture." – *Go West* (1940)

2710 A father and two burly friends prepare for the shotgun wedding of his daughter – with Bob Hope as the reluctant bridegroom. "All I did was take her to a movie," Hope protests. "You were out all night with her," the father asserts. "Could I help it if it was a double feature?" – *Road to Singapore* (1940)

2711 Ghost-town hermit Harry Davenport, a recluse for forty years, admits to

gruff sheriff William Frawley that he "ain't never seen a movie!" "Never seen a movie!" Frawley echoes in disbelief. "Well, it sounds un–American to me!" – *The Bride Came C.O.D.* (1941)

2712 Bob Hope says he is looking forward to his date with film star Veronica Lake, whose peekaboo hair style became her trademark. "She's going to show me her other eye." – *Star Spangled Rhythm* (1942)

2713 U.S. Marine Lionel Stander on Guadalcanal during World War II asks a fellow leatherneck about a book he is reading. "Gettysburg," the soldier replies. "Gettysburg?" a puzzled Stander repeats. "Yeah," says another, "the Civil War. Remember?" "Oh, you mean the war they had in *Gone with the Wind!*" he recalls. "Boy, that was a war!" – *Guadalcanal Diary* (1943)

2714 In the last scene, after Bob Hope rescues princess Virginia Mayo from the clutches of pirates, she falls into the arms of guest-appearing Bing Crosby. "How do you like that?" Hope fumes. "I knock myself out for nine reels, and some bit player from Paramount comes over and gets the girl! Boy, that's the last picture I do for Goldwyn!" – *The Princess and the Pirate* (1944)

2715 Fred Allen, posing as the president of the Jack Benny Fan Club, informs the honored star that he can't get people into the theater to see Benny's movies. "Have they tried to give away dishes?" Benny inquires. "Yes," Allen replies, "and the people threw them at the screen." "Have they tried not giving away dishes?" "Yes, but the people bring their own dishes and throw them at the screen." – *It's in the Bag* (1945)

2716 Retired millionaire Bob Hope and his wife (Dorothy Lamour) are suddenly visited by his rival, Bing Crosby. "And I thought this was going to be an 'A' picture," Hope grumbles. – *Road to Utopia* (1945)

2717 William Powell and Myrna Loy, as Nick and Nora Charles, wait in a taxi outside a suspect's home. When their party appears and drives away, the taxi driver springs into action. "Follow that cab?" he asks dutifully. "Hmm," Nora mutters, "a movie fan." – *Song of the Thin Man* (1947)

2718 Bud Abbott and Lou Costello, lost in a desert, see a mirage of East Side Kid Leo Gorcey selling newspapers. "Can I help it if they gave me a bad corner?" he explains. – *Abbott and Costello in the Foreign Legion* (1950)

2719 College instructor Clifton Webb, a former silent screen idol who is surprised to see his old films on television, comments: "It's like exhuming a man from his grave." – *Dreamboat* (1952)

2720 During World War II lieutenant Jack Palance moves his company through a field to a French village crawling with Germans. "In the cowboy movies," he mutters to himself, "there's always one joker that says, 'it's quiet out there – too quiet.'" – *Attack!* (1956)

2721 Movie lover Jerry Lewis describes the latest role of Anita Ekberg, his favorite actress, to gambler Dean Martin: "She played the part of a girl who was searching, searching, searching–" "What was she searching for?" Martin asks. "She didn't know," Lewis answers. "That's why she was always searching, searching." – *Hollywood or Bust* (1956)

2722 Army sergeant Jackie Gleason saves a young woman (Tuesday Weld) from being manhandled. "You were just like Randolph Scott on the late, late movie," she joyfully thanks him, then adds: "a fat Randolph Scott." – *Soldier in the Rain* (1963)

2723 After necking with Robert Taylor, virginal Jane Fonda quips: "In movies, this is where the screen usually goes dark." – *Sunday in New York* (1963)

2724 Woody Allen, as a criminal, plans to show a film on the site of a proposed heist, and precedes it with *Trout Fishing in Quebec*. "Aah," one robber grumbles, "there's always a boring short." – *Take the Money and Run* (1969)

2725 "I love the movies," confesses hooker Barbra Streisand to neighbor George Segal. "I used to go every night to Forty-Second Street. The only trouble was there was always somebody sitting next to me trying something weird." "Did you ever try reading?" Segal asks. "That wouldn't stop them." – *The Owl and the Pussycat* (1970)

2726 "Honey," says a parched sunbather, "will you get me a Tab? My mouth is so dry they could shoot *Lawrence of Arabia* in it." – *The Last of Sheila* (1973)

2727 At a movie drive-in, ladies' man Burt Reynolds, enthralled with Errol Flynn, tells his date that he loves the actor. "Are you queer or somethin'?" she asks. "I don't know, but if I turn queer, that's the guy I'm gonna turn queer for." – *W.W. and the Dixie Dancekings* (1975)

2728 Mel Brooks, as Dr. Thorndyke, a psychiatrist, meets Madeline Kahn, the daughter of one of his patients. "Richard H. Thorndyke," she ponders. "What does the 'H' stand for?" "Harpo," he replies. "My mother loved the Marx brothers. She saw all their movies." – *High Anxiety* (1977)

2729 In a steam bath a twice-divorced friend of George Segal and Bob Dishy confides: "Now I know what I'm looking for – a real, old-fashioned romance, just like in *Love Story*. Did you guys see that? That's what I'm looking for." "What are you talking about?" demands Segal. "The girl in that died. "Oh," the friend moans, "maybe that's what I'm really looking for." – *The Last Married Couple in America* (1980)

2730 Aspiring young actor Donny Most has been having trouble getting past studio gates to get an audition. "You know something?" he says to his girlfriend. "Hitler isn't dead. They didn't get him. He's a guard at Universal Studios." – *Leo and Loree* (1980)

2731 After the screening of a film featuring Woody Allen and Tony Roberts, the two actors appear on stage to answer questions. "Was the scene between you and Sandy Bates in the wax museum an homage to Vincent Price's horror movie *The House of Wax?*" someone asks. "An homage?" Roberts echoes. "Not exactly. We just stole the idea outright." – *Stardust Memories* (1980)

2732 Tom Hanks introduces himself to his fiancée's dull ex-boyfriend: "The name is Bond – James Bond." – *Bachelor Party* (1984)

2733 Young police detective Judge Reinhold and his partner are pinned down by bursts of gunfire from a gang of smugglers. "You remember *Butch Cassidy and the Sundance Kid* when Redford and Newman are surrounded by the Bolivian army?" Reinhold says excitedly. – *Beverly Hills Cop* (1984)

2734 A movie character (Jeff Daniels) literally steps out of the screen and into the life of childless, unloved housewife and waitress Mia Farrow. "I'm so confused," she cries. "I'm married; I just met a wonderful man. He's fictional, but you can't have everything." – *The Purple Rose of Cairo* (1985)

2735 During the 1940 London blitz two English children watch a war scene in a newsreel. "Can't we just see the end?" "They've got the real thing outside." "It's not the same." – *Hope and Glory* (1987)

2736 Movie extra Alan King describes to his son Billy Crystal the unsung role of his fellow extras: "You won't see our names in the credits – not above the title or below the title. We like to think of ourselves as behind the title." – *Memories of Me* (1988)

2737 One of Burt Lancaster's daughters describes a script she has written for a Hollywood studio: "Eddie Murphy plays an agent who stumbles upon a murder case in South Africa." "Black comedy, huh?" Lancaster cracks. – *Rocket Gibraltar* (1988)

2738 Beauty-parlor owner Dolly Parton informs her new employee Daryl Hannah about the owner of a local boarding house. "Her whole life has been an experience in terror," Parton says. "Her husband got killed in World War II. Then her son got killed in Vietnam. I have to tell you – when it comes to suffering, she is right up there with Elizabeth Taylor." – *Steel Magnolias* (1989)

2739 College freshman Matthew Broderick in New York innocently gets involved with a gang of smugglers who deal in endangered species. Unable to disentangle himself from the gang, he reveals all to his film studies teacher and adviser. "It has a real film noir quality, don't you think?" the instructor muses, completely ignoring Broderick's personal dilemma. "If it was done right – black and white, grainy, sort of a 'Kiss Me Deadly' feeling." – *The Freshman* (1990)

2740 Jeff Bridges and Robin Williams find a bleeding, abandoned over-the-hill gay "queen" lying in New York's Central Park and take him to a hospital. In the waiting room the raving, wounded man, nestled helplessly in Bridges' arms, says he wants to go somewhere. "Where do you want to go?" Bridges asks. "Venice – like Katharine Hepburn in *Summertime*," the delirious man cries. "Why can't I be Katharine Hepburn?" – *The Fisher King* (1991)

2741 "Did I tell you clowns," an aspiring songwriter informs his buddies, "Esther Williams likes one of my songs? MGM wants her to sing it in her next picture." "Where," a friend asks, "under water?" – *The Marrying Man* (1991)

2742 Inebriated coach of a women's baseball team Tom Hanks unwittingly kisses its demure chaperone and then recoils in revulsion. "By the way," he

snipes, "I loved you in *The Wizard of Oz*." – *A League of Their Own* (1992)

Music

2743 Rudy Vallee arrives late for band rehearsal, using his new saxophone as an excuse. He then plays a few notes. "That bird reminds me of Fritz Kreisler," says a musician. "Fritz Kreisler is no saxophone player," another comments. "Neither is he," cracks the first. – *The Vagaband Lover* (1929)

2744 "I don't care for grand opera," announces matronly Marie Dressler to Rudy Vallee and his band. "I'm too American. Jazz – I just adore jazz! It kind of does something to me. I'm just an Indian!" – *The Vagaband Lover* (1929)

2745 Intrepid African explorer Groucho Marx introduces the festivities to the guests at a wedding: "Signor Ravelli's first selection will be 'Somewhere My Love Lies Sleeping' with a male chorus." – *Animal Crackers* (1930)

2746 Chico Marx, at the piano, begins to repeat the same note over and over. "I can't think of the end," he says. "Funny," returns Groucho, "I can't think of anything else." – *Animal Crackers* (1930)

2747 A woman calls out from her window to street vendors Stan Laurel and Oliver Hardy, who are playing the organ and bass violin. "How much money do you boys average a street?" she asks. "Fifty cents," says Hardy. "There's a dollar," she says, tossing down a bill. "Move down a couple of streets." – *Below Zero* (1930)

2748 Woman: "My father gave me five thousand dollars to cultivate my voice."

Bert Wheeler (after hearing her sing a few notes): "I bet he wondered what you did with the money." – *Caught Plastered* (1931)

2749 Groucho Marx, as master of ceremonies at a posh coming-out party, announces: "The buffet will be served in the next room in five minutes. To get you in that room quickly, Mrs. Shnahauser will sing the next aria." – *Monkey Business* (1931)

2750 Bert Wheeler complains about one of his girlfriend's idiosyncrasies to pal Robert Woolsey. "You know," Wheeler says, "she always makes me sing to her, and then she chokes me." "Yeah?" Woolsey wisecracks. "Maybe she's a music lover." – *Diplomaniacs* (1933)

2751 Groucho Marx, in Margaret Dumont's bedroom, speculates on the source of a Sousa march heard on the downstairs level. "It sounds to me like mice," he concludes. "Mice?" Dumont questions. "Mice don't play music." "Oh, yeah?" Groucho counters. "What about the old maestro?" – *Duck Soup* (1933)

2752 At an audition a contralto resents being rejected. "I've sung before crowned heads," the singer protests to stage director James Cagney. "You've laid yourself wide open for a crack," Cagney begins, "but we'll let it go." – *Footlight Parade* (1933)

2753 "Ever since I sang that song, it's been haunting me," confesses a singer in a run-down saloon. "It should," snips piano player Fuzzy Knight. "you murdered it." – *She Done Him Wrong* (1933)

2754 W. C. Fields is awakened by his wife (Kathleen Howard) with shocking news. "There are some burglars singing in the cellar," she cries. "What are they singing?" Fields questions. "What difference does it make what they're singing!" she shouts.—*The Man on the Flying Trapeze* (1935)

2755 Groucho Marx, dressed appropriately in a tuxedo and top hat, arrives at the opera house in a carriage and reprimands the driver: "Hey you! I told you to slow down. Because of you, I almost heard the opera."—*A Night at the Opera* (1935)

2756 A very demanding stage actor, rehearsing a musical, is dissatisfied with his cast, especially his leading female singer whom he reproaches. "But I'm doing my best!" she pleads. "Yes, I know," he says. "That's what makes it so pitiful."—*It's Love Again* (1936)

2757 Concertina player Fred MacMurray courts Carole Lombard aboard a luxury liner by serenading her in the next cabin. Alison Skipworth, her chaperone, is considerably less impressed. "A concertina—and very vulgar," she remarks in a deprecating tone. "A definite symbol of the lower classes. Put the thing on the floor and it crawls."—*The Princess Comes Across* (1936)

2758 Patricia Wilder admits to emcee Bob Hope that she wants to sing, but that she cries during her singing. "Why do you cry?" he asks. "Because I can't sing," she replies.—*The Big Broadcast of 1938* (1938)

2759 "Grand Opera is no worse than a slight case of influenza," remarks Warner Baxter. "It just seems worse, that's all." —*Wife, Husband and Friend* (1939)

2760 "You know what the chocolate sody said to the lemon sody when they heard a knock on the door?" Millard Mitchell asks his girlfriend Mary Wickes. "I hear a rhapsody."—*The Mayor of 44th Street* (1942)

2761 A cab driver turns on his radio, tunes in to the symphony hour and relaxes. "Every time I hear this," he remarks ecstatically, "it sends me!" —*Boston Blackie's Rendezvous* (1945)

2762 Patron of the arts Joan Crawford provides financial and physical sustenance to violinist John Garfield—and she expects a strong return. "I'm tired of playing second fiddle to the ghost of Beethoven," she cries.—*Humoresque* (1946)

2763 Private detective Edgar Kennedy is in awe of symphony conductor Rex Harrison. "Nobody handles Handel like you handle Handel!" the detective exclaims. "And your Delius! Delirious!" —*Unfaithfully Yours* (1948)

2764 The sheriff is searching for conman rainmaker Burt Lancaster, who has succeeded in instilling in an otherwise plain Katharine Hepburn a touch of beauty. Lancaster is singing as he rounds a bend, where the lawman is waiting. Hepburn tries to warn him, but it is too late. "If you hadn't been singing, you'd have heard me," she says. "I never regret singing," Lancaster replies.—*The Rainmaker* (1956)

2765 "As you know," advertising executive Henry Jones proudly addresses a board meeting composed of his colleagues, "this agency had the foresight to pioneer in the singing commercial, and in so doing, raised the level of musical culture in the American home." —*Will Success Spoil Rock Hunter?* (1957)

2766 Ray Walston, as a professor of ethics and music lover at a small college: "Well, I always feel that, when moving into a new home, the first person you ask in is Beethoven."—*Tall Story* (1960)

2767 Rock group promoter Jackie Gleason checks up on one of his rock bands and hurls out a string of criticism: "Wait a minute! Number one: it sounds like music; number two: you're singing and I can understand what you're saying. Now come on, get with it." – *How to Commit Marriage* (1969)

2768 A former cello teacher recalls the musical ineptness of former pupil Woody Allen. "Virgil had no conception of the instrument," the instructor explains, referring to the cello. "He would try to blow into it." – *Take the Money and Run* (1969)

2769 At a mineralogists' convention musicologist Ryan O'Neal explains his theory that prehistoric man may have made music from rocks. When someone scoffs at the theory, Barbra Streisand, posing as O'Neal's girlfriend, adds a helping hand. "It so happens that Howard has had discussions with Leonard Bernstein about the possibility of conducting an avalanche – in E flat." – *What's Up, Doc?* (1972)

2770 Dudley Moore's sexual fantasy turns into reality when he finds himself alone with Bo Derek, who describes to him her own sexual turn-on: "Uncle Fred said the 'Bolero' was the most descriptive sex music ever written – and he proved it." – *10* (1979)

2771 "I don't know much about classical music," Woody Allen acknowledges. "For years I thought that the Goldberg Variations were something Mr. and Mrs. Goldberg tried on their wedding night." – *Stardust Memories* (1980)

2772 At a railroad station in a small Nebraska town, citizens turn out to welcome home the remains of a Vietnam war hero. A gay bandleader enthusiastically strikes up the band. "What's he playing?" mayor Brian Dennehy asks an aide. "'Mad About the Boy.' What else?" – *Finders Keepers* (1984)

2773 There's a saying that country music speaks to the heart," says a college student. "The only trouble is that it has to go through the ears to get there." – *Odd Jobs* (1985)

2774 "I hate the opera," a gangster's moll complains. "Why do we have to go to the opera anyway? They don't even sing in English. At least they could sing in English." – *Death Wish 4: The Crackdown* (1987)

Names

2775 Bert Wheeler introduces his buddy Robert Woolsey to Mary Marsh (Dorothy Lee). "I love the name of Marsh," Woolsey comments. "It's so mellow." – *Hook, Line and Sinker* (1930)

2776 Bert Wheeler and Robert Woolsey examine a map which lists towns with such odd names as What and Which. "The town of Which is where General Diddy died," says Wheeler. "Diddy?" "Yes, he did. Now we come to the river, but it's impossible to ford the river here." "Why?" Woolsey inquires.

"For divers reasons." – *Cracked Nuts* (1931)

2777 "Why do they call Luke the Hermit 'Luke'?" Bert Wheeler asks Robert Woolsey. "Because he's not so hot," comes the reply. – *Diplomaniacs* (1933)

2778 Aspiring young actress Katharine Hepburn confides to veteran thespian C. Aubrey Smith why she has chosen a stage name. "I don't want to use my family name," she says, "because I shall probably have several scandals while I live and I don't want to cause them any trouble until I'm famous. Then nobody will mind."—*Morning Glory* (1933)

2779 Tough carnival con man Fredric March starts to fall for new chorus girl Sylvia Sidney, but catching himself in time, he begins to explain that he's not the marrying kind: "Now listen, baby—" "Stop calling me 'baby,'" she protests. "I don't like it." "I call all dames 'baby.'" —*Good Dame* (1934)

2780 "My name is Grace," Gracie Allen introduces herself, "but everyone calls me Gracie for short."—*Six of a Kind* (1934)

2781 Gambler Joe E. Brown is arrested for brawling and later released. "Did you ever hear of habeas corpus?" a detective explains. "You mean the Italian who runs the pool room over at 51st Street and Eighth Avenue?" Brown asks.—*A Very Honorable Guy* (1934)

2782 Destitute Margaret Sullavan, posing as a socialite at a ball, does not want to reveal her name. "You're incognito," one gentleman offers. "No," she replies, "that's not it."—*The Good Fairy* (1935)

2783 "You may call me Tanka," Ginger Rogers says, introducing herself to Fred Astaire. "Tanka?" questions Astaire. "You're welcome," she replies.—*Roberta* (1935)

2784 Curly of the Three Stooges collapses after being kissed by a Hollywood starlet. Moe tries to revive him. "Tell me your name so I could tell your mother," Moe pleads. "My mother knows my name," Curly responds.—*Movie Maniacs* (1936)

2785 Homeless tramp William Powell is hired as a butler at a ritzy Fifth Avenue home. He arrives at the kitchen entrance well attired where he meets a wise-cracking housekeeper. "May I be frank?" he asks politely. "Is that your name?" "No, my name is Godfrey." "All right, be frank."—*My Man Godfrey* (1936)

2786 Rainmaker Ben Blue, attracted to Judy Canova whom he has been following, finally introduces himself: "I'm Jupiter Plubius the Second." "Don't tell me there are two of you!"—*Artists and Models* (1937)

2787 Russian immigrants Charles Boyer and Claudette Colbert, in post–World War I France on July 14, learn that the French are celebrating a holiday that has something to do with the "Bastille." "It's the name of a subway station," Colbert says. "Isn't that sweet of them to celebrate a subway?" —*Tovarich* (1937)

2788 Native American Chief Dog-in-the-Manger (Paul Guilfoyle) threatens mild-mannered Joe Penner with a knife, demanding that he hand over a love letter. "Yes, Mangy Dog," Penner acquiesces. "Not Mangy Dog!" Guilfoyle exclaims. "Chief Dog-in-the-Manger!" —*I'm from the City* (1938)

2789 "This is my top hand," rancher Bob Steele introduces his pal to a settler's daughter. "His name is Happy because he never is."—*Feud of the Range* (1939)

2790 When asked for his opinion about the influential Todd family, Abraham Lincoln (Raymond Massey) remarks: "The Todd family are mighty high-class people. They spell their names with two 'd's,' which is pretty impressive when you consider one was enough for God." —*Abe Lincoln in Illinois* (1940)

2791 Young, precocious Virginia Weidler does not approve of her sister Katharine Hepburn's fiancé John Howard. At the local stable, he has trouble controlling his horse. "What's the matter, Betsy?" he says to the animal, trying to calm it down. "You act worried." "Maybe because his name is Jack," Virginia explains.—*The Philadelphia Story* (1940)

2792 Police inspector Richard Lane boards a luxury liner that has just docked in New York and confronts alleged jewel thief Boston Blackie (Chester Morris), one of the passengers. "No," Morris replies, "I'm using my maiden name."—*Meet Boston Blackie* (1941)

2793 Warren William, as a secret agent in London during World War II, tries to retrace his steps to the hideout of Nazi spies which he had earlier visited when he was blindfolded. Depending only on certain sounds he had heard earlier, he asks a local resident about running water. "Who's he, a blinking Indian?" the man quips.—*Counter-Espionage* (1942)

2794 At a bar an attractive woman insists she knows the eccentric Lord Epping (Leon Errol). "I can't think of what your name is," he admits. "Diana, silly." "Diana?" he echoes. "I like that. But I don't think much of the last part—Silly."—*Mexican Spitfire's Elephant* (1942)

2795 Bud Abbott: "Call me a cab." Lou Costello: "All right, you're a cab."—*Abbott and Costello in Hollywood* (1945)

2796 Painter Phil Harris, after receiving a bump on the head, ends up in a hospital suffering from amnesia. "For the time being," a doctor says, "you're registered as John Doe." "Dough?" Harris echoes happily. "That ain't hay!"—*I Love a Bandleader* (1945)

2797 "My name is Curly Q. Link," explains Curly of the Three Stooges. "What does the 'Q' stand for?" Larry asks. "Cuff." "Oh," Larry figures, "Cuff Link."—*If a Body Meets a Body* (1945)

2798 English nobleman Reginald Owen is unable to remember the name of his foreign house guest. "I say," Owen asks his wife, "what's the fellow's name again?" "It's so hard to remember," she replies. "So many foreigners do have foreign names, don't they?"—*Cluny Brown* (1946)

2799 Voluptuous hotel guest Lisette Verea receives roses from manager Groucho Marx and cries, "Oh, Mr. Cornblow!" "Call me Montgomery," he croons. "Is that your name?" "No, I'm just breaking it in for a friend."—*A Night in Casablanca* (1946)

2800 Reporter Allyn Joslyn rents a single room from landlady Mrs. James, who he thinks is overcharging him. But he finally agrees to pay. "Okay, Mrs. James," he says, then adds: "Hear from Jesse lately?"—*It Shouldn't Happen to a Dog* (1946)

2801 Bob Hope gets mixed up with a group of spies seeking to control a mine which produces a rare ore. He gives the map to government agent Reginald Denny who informs Hope that the important mineral is Cryolite. "Cryolite, huh?" Hope muses. "Well, we can't let them get it. What's Cryolite?" "Cryolite is an ore containing Criptobar," Denny explains. "Criptobar?" Hope echoes. "Oh, we can't let them get that. What's Criptobar?"—*My Favorite Brunette* (1947)

2802 Bud Abbott explains to Lou Costello how jewelry is made. "It's melted down—it's made into these ornaments by a smith." "Couldn't it be made by a Jones?" Costello questions. "Certainly," Abbott concludes, "and Jones would have to be a smith."—*Mexican Hayride* (1948)

2803 "You're the most beautiful plank in your husband's platform," party boss Adolphe Menjou compliments his candidate's wife (Katharine Hepburn). "That's a heck of a thing to call a woman," she returns.—*State of the Union* (1948)

2804 Bud Abbott and Lou Costello, employees at a hotel, decide to investigate the room of a murder suspect. When Abbott's keys fail to open the lock, Costello lends him his key. "Where did you get that?" Abbott inquires. "Fred." "Fred who?" "Fred Skeleton," Costello says. "It's a Skeleton key. It opens up any door." – *Abbott and Costello Meet the Killer* (1949)

2805 Judy Holliday has just insulted her lover, wealthy junk man Broderick Crawford, and left the room in triumph. "You know what she called me before?" Crawford says to his lawyer. "A Fascist! I was born in Plainfield, New Jersey. She knows that." – *Born Yesterday* (1950)

2806 Gangster David Brian finds Joan Crawford a "cheap dame" but is willing to "educate" her. "Lesson number one:" he says, "An Etruscan vase is not a flower pot." – *The Damned Don't Cry* (1950)

2807 Swashbuckler Torin Thatcher enlightens his captain, Burt Lancaster: "If you'll forgive my pointing it out, skipper, you can't leave a pretty woman unmolested aboard ship. It'll give piracy a bad name." – *The Crimson Pirate* (1952)

2808 Hollywood star James Mason learns that a young aspiring actress's name is Esther Blodgett (Judy Garland). "You must have been born with that name," he says. "You couldn't have made it up." – *A Star Is Born* (1954)

2809 "Johnny," says a teenager embraced by a boy, "I never let anyone kiss me like this before!" "My name's not Johnny!" "Well, what is it?" "Irving." "Irving!" she utters, and then purrs, "What's in a name?" – *The Horror of Party Beach* (1964)

2810 "I remember my first visit to your country," Latin American dictator Eli Wallach recalls in a conversation with Fred MacMurray. "I was introduced to a woman – a lovely woman – but she had the name 'Sammy.' Now I ask you – man to man – how it is possible to hold the hand and say nice things to a woman with the name 'Sammy'? On my first date I didn't know whether to bring her flowers or shaving soap." – *Kisses for My President* (1964)

2811 Eccentric Jason Robards explains to social worker Barbara Harris that he has permitted his nephew to use any name until his thirteenth birthday. "He went through a long period of dogs' names when he was very little, King and Rover having a real vogue for a while ... He received his library card in the name of Rafael Sabatini." – *A Thousand Clowns* (1965)

2812 Language expert Gregory Peck, who becomes entangled in the intrigues of a Middle East country, at one point is forced to seek refuge in the bathroom of a local beauty (Sophia Loren). "Call me Yasmin," she nonchalantly calls, "at least while you're in my bathroom." – *Arabesque* (1966)

2813 Quint (Oliver Reed) at a school reunion meets his old headmaster who mistakes Quint for someone else. "Ah, Eldridge," the headmaster announces, "you don't look too well. You should get out and play some games, Eldridge." "Quint," Reed corrects him. "Quint?" the headmaster ponders. "I don't think I know the game." – *I'll Never Forget What's 'is Name* (1967)

2814 Ryan O'Neal proposes to an incredulous Ali McGraw that their baby be named Bozo – after a popular superjock tackle. "You would actually call our soon-to-be conceived offspring 'Bozo'?" she questions. "Only if he's a boy," rejoins O'Neal. – *Love Story* (1970)

2815 Impoverished playboy Walter Matthau is introduced at a party to Mr. and Mrs. Darryl Hitler. "Are you related to the Boston Hitlers?" he asks. – *A New Leaf* (1971)

2816 Government agent Jack Weston, sent from his New York office to help clean up corruption in a Southern town, works with local character Gator (Burt Reynolds). "Look at this," Weston assesses. "I'm riding with a nut named Gator loking for a putz named Bama. Don't you people have regular names?" "Oh," retorts Reynolds, "you mean those intelligent names like you got up in New York City like Yogi?" – *Gator* (1976)

2817 "Speed" (Harvey Keitel) romances hard-to-get "Jugs" (Raquel Welch), who slowly falls for him. "We both know I'm not the type to roll over on the first date," she reminds him. "Well," he replies, "they don't call me Speed for nothing." "Well, let's hope they don't call you Speed for everything." – *Mother, Jugs and Speed* (1976)

2818 Private eye Peter Falk receives a phone call late at night from his partner's wife. "Lou?" the voice says. "It's Georgia." "Oh, hello, Georgia," Falk replies. "I just had you on my mind." – *The Cheap Detective* (1978)

2819 Pilot Peter Graves, in charge of a passenger plane, receives an emergency telephone call from the Mayo Clinic, which is then interrupted by a second important call from a Mr. Ham. "All right," Graves says to the operator, "give me Ham on five and hold the Mayo." – *Airplane!* (1980)

2820 During a passenger airplane flight, ex-pilot Robert Hays pleads with passenger-doctor Leslie Nielsen about the passengers and crew members who have been poisoned. "Surely, there's something you can do!" Hays exclaims. "I'm doing everything I can," Nielsen replies, "and stop calling me Shirley." – *Airplane!* (1980)

2821 "Call me Fred," the evil Dr. Fu Manchu (Peter Sellers) introduces himself. "That's what they called me at Eton." – *The Fiendish Plot of Dr. Fu Manchu* (1980)

2822 Neighbor Dan Aykroyd informs John Belushi about a new Italian restaurant that has just opened in the area: "It's got a cute name," Aykroyd says. "Caesar's Garlic Wars." – *Neighbors* (1981)

2823 As Burt Reynolds mulls over various names for his future son, his housekeeper Juanita Moore listens in.

"Erasmus," he considers out loud. "I wonder what that means." "It means your son won't have any friends," Moore chimes in. "That's what it means." – *Paternity* (1981)

2824 Captain Over (Peter Graves), in charge of a passenger flight to the moon, is introduced to his fellow crew members, including officers Dunn and Under, all of whom seem to know each other from previous assignments. "Both Dunn and I were over Under even though I was under Dunn," Over's copilot announces. "Dunn was over Under and I was over Dunn," Over replies. – *Airplane II: The Sequel* (1982)

2825 A reporter, interviewing an internationally famous brain surgeon (Steve Martin), mispronounces his name and apologizes. "A lot of people mispronounce it," Martin acknowledges. "But it sounds just the way it's spelled: H-F-U-H-R-U-H-U-R-R – "Hfuhruhurr." – *The Man with Two Brains* (1983)

2826 Steve Martin's girlfriend, Danielle, a ballet dancer, has left him for Raoul, another dancer. Martin later meets a divorced woman whose husband has had an affair with a ballet dancer. "Was her name Danielle?" Steve inquires. "No," the woman replies, "Raoul." – *The Lonely Guy* (1984)

2827 East German hoyden Lucy Gutteridge meets rock-star-turned-agent Val Kilmer and apprises him of her given name's significance. "Hillary," she beams, "means she whose bosoms defy gravity." – *Top Secret!* (1984)

2828 Gene Wilder and Gilda Radner arrive at Wilder's family estate where the family servant, who has known Wilder all his life, greets him. "May I have your name, please?" "Is he kidding?" Radner says to Wilder. "Come in, Mr. Kidding," the servant acknowledges. – *Haunted Honeymoon* (1986)

2829 While making love to a young pitcher of a minor league team, Susan

Sarandon calls out the name of the catcher on the same team – to the displeasure of her bed partner. "Honey," she coos while explaining, "would you rather I was making love to him using your name or making love to you using his name?" – *Bull Durham* (1988)

2830 A father describes to his young daughter and son the origins of some names, such as baker, explaining that what people did for a living often determined what they were called. "So what did John Hancock do?" the son asks. – *Repossessed* (1990)

2831 Socially awkward Amanda Plummer enters a video rental store where Jeff Bridges introduces her to Robin Williams, who secretly loves her. "This is our coworker, Perry – Perry –" "Perry Perry?" Plummer repeats. "No," Williams nervously corrects her, "just Perry." "Oh, like Moses," she concludes. – *The Fisher King* (1991)

2832 In Manhattan a young Yo Yo (Giancarlo Esposito) hails a taxi driven by an East German called Helmut, who cannot properly handle the language or the car. Yo Yo soon ends up in the front and, upon learning the cabby's name, is convulsed with laughter. "Helmut! Helmut!" he guffaws. "It's like calling your child 'Lampshade.'" – *Night on Earth* (1991)

2833 A floozie (Madonna) on a women's baseball team introduces herself: "Hi, my name's Mae, and that's more than a name. It's an attitude." – *A League of Their Own* (1992)

2834 Police officers Mel Gibson and Danny Glover are repeatedly in hot water with their superior who charges: "The only thing they do contribute is mayhem and chaos!" "I'm Chaos," Gibson quips and, pointing to Glover, adds: "and he's Mayhem." – *Lethal Weapon 3* (1992)

Nationalities

2835 Svengali (John Barrymore) wonders why his English acquaintances, visiting his native Poland, take daily baths. "The Englanders get dirty very quickly," he concludes. – *Svengali* (1931)

2836 Jimmy Durante and Lupe Velez are costars of a radio show. In a short sketch they portray a captain and a passenger aboard a ship ravaged by a storm. "Oh," she asks fearfully, "will this storm ever spend itself?" "Spend itself?" Durante repeats. "No, it's off the coast of Scotland." – *Strictly Dynamite* (1934)

2837 Stranger Parkyakarkus visits amusement park manager Eddie Cantor and announces that he is a G-Man. "You mean a Government man?" Cantor asks. "No, a Greek." – *Strike Me Pink* (1936)

2838 When Charlie Chan (Sidney Toler) hears that Chamberlain will confer with Hitler in Germany, he comments: "When spider send invitation to house, fly better beware." – *Charlie Chan in City in Darkness* (1939)

2839 Petty pickpocket Peter Lorre, posing as a house guest and Russian emigré at a formal party, is questioned by other curious guests. "Are you a white Russian?" someone asks. "No." "Then you must be Red," another concludes. "No," Lorre replies. "Then what are you?" "Pink," he utters nervously. – *I Was an Adventuress* (1940)

2840 English privateer Errol Flynn attacks and plunders a rich Spanish ship. When first mate Alan Hale labels Spain a heathen country, an English lady-in-waiting protests. "Spain is an old country with a very rich history," she explains. "In fact, there is much in Spain that we English can profit by." "Well," Hale replies laughingly, "we're certainly doing the best we can." – *The Sea Hawk* (1940)

2841 Privateer Errol Flynn has taken the jewels of Spanish beauty Brenda Marshall as part of the booty he and his fellow pirates have captured. She castigates him for stealing her jewels, calling him a thief. "I wonder how the Aztec Indians were persuaded to part with them," he replies bitingly. – *The Sea Hawk* (1940)

2842 Major Strasser (Conrad Veidt) has just arrived in Casablanca from Nazi Germany and visits Rick's Café, where he meets its American owner, Humphrey Bogart. "What is your nationality?" the major asks him. "I'm a drunkard," Bogart remarks casually. – *Casablanca* (1942)

2843 When servant Mantan Moreland offers Leon Errol, who is impersonating an English lord, a stiff drink, the latter protests. "What do you think I am – an inebriate?" "No, sir," Moreland replies thoughtfully, "you're English." – *Mexican Spitfire Sees a Ghost* (1942)

2844 Correspondent Cary Grant, in Vichy, France, during World War II, agrees to collaborate with a Nazi propagandist by "explaining the German view to America" via short-wave radio. Grant makes certain that his message gets across. "Germany has no designs on us," he announces into the microphone. "Tell all the armed forces . . . especially, tell it to the Marines!" – *Once Upon a Honeymoon* (1942)

2845 Nazi spies clash with two escaped convicts who assert their one-upmanship over the Germans: "We're hoodlums – but we're American hoodlums!" – *Seven Miles from Alcatraz* (1942)

2846 During World War II in North Africa, Nazi officers treat with scorn their ally, a genial Italian general. But he dismisses their insults. "Can a nation that belches understand a nation that sings?" he quips. – *Five Graves to Cairo* (1943)

2847 Seventeen-year-old Shirley Temple, stranded in a Mexican airline terminal when her prospective husband doesn't show up, approaches a local policeman for help. "Where do people go when they get into trouble?" she asks. "Same as United States, miss," the officer replies. "They go to jail." – *Honeymoon* (1947)

2848 "How are our American women compared to your English women?" a gentleman asks English actor Bob Hope. "Oh, I think your American women are much prettier." "How about your horses?" another American inquires. "Oh," Hope responds, "I think your American women are even prettier than our horses." – *Fancy Pants* (1950)

2849 In post–World War II Vienna, American Harry Lime (Orson Welles), trafficking in diluted penicillin, defends his noxious racket to his friend (Joseph Cotten): "In Italy for thirty years under the Borgias they had warfare, terror, murder, bloodshed. They produced Michelangelo, Leonardo da Vinci and the Renaissance. In Switzerland they had brotherly love, five hundred years of democracy and peace. And what did they produce? The cuckoo clock." – *The Third Man* (1950)

2850 Arthur Hunnicutt persuades his boss, Texas millionairess Jane Russell, who has been jilted by her fiancé, to take a trip to Paris. "We'll see new faces, meet new people," he suggests. "I hear they got a lot of foreigners over there." – *The French Line* (1954)

2851 American widow Eva Marie Saint, helping Jewish refugees on Cyprus, shows particular interest in one teenager. "She works and thinks and acts just like an American," she proudly says to British general Ralph Richardson. "I can think of no higher praise," the officer intones sarcastically. – *Exodus* (1960)

2852 Nobel Prize winner and womanizer Paul Newman is met at the Stockholm airport – to his surprise – by attractive Swedish foreign ministry representative Elke Sommer. "Oh, you mean your reputation with women?" she asks. "Something like that." "I hope you'll forgive me," she explains, "but in matters of sex, compared to the average Scandinavian, you would be considered a mere amateur." – *The Prize* (1963)

2853 When British secret agent Jack Hawkins asks his headquarters to enlist the aid of his American friend, one official balks at the suggestion. "I grant you he didn't go to Eton," Hawkins argues, "but try to find it in your heart to forgive him. Like the American economy, he's fundamentally sound." – *Masquerade* (1965)

2854 "Everyone in America is rich," Fred Astaire announces to his daughter. "Are there no ill-housed and ill-clad?" she asks. "Yes," he answers, "but they're the best ill-housed and the best ill-clad in all the world." – *Finian's Rainbow* (1968)

2855 American businessman Jack Lemmon journeys to Italy to claim the body of his father, who has died in a car accident. He meets a resort manager who enlightens him about one of Italy's customs – the extended lunch hour. "Here we take our time," the man explains. "Here we cook our pasta . . . we drink our wine, we make love –" "What do you do in the evening?" Lemmon interjects. "In the evening we go home to our wives." – *Avanti!* (1972)

2856 A Loyalist reminds Benjamin Franklin (Howard da Silva) that the English don't mind Americans being called Englishmen. "Nor would I," retorts da Silva, "if I were given the full rights of an Englishman. But to call me

one without those rights is like calling an ox a bull. He's thankful for the honor, but he'd much rather have restored what's rightfully his." – *1776* (1972)

2857 John Houseman, as a mysterious international figure, tells private eye Peter Falk about a little-known fact that had occurred in 1853: "Twelve Albanian fishermen conquered China, Tibet and Mongolia." "My goodness!" Falk exclaims. "I didn't know that." "That's because you didn't take history in Albania." – *The Cheap Detective* (1978)

2858 "I was married to two Americans and one Israeli," Dom DeLuise says to his friend George Segal. "The Israeli – please! Now I know why they won the Six-Day War." – *The Last Married Couple in America* (1980)

2859 Soviet citizen Robin Williams, who has come to New York as part of a band, decides to defect. He breaks away from K.G.B. agents while shopping in Bloomingdale's where black store guard Cleavant Derricks protects him from the Soviet agents. "You're in my jurisdiction," Derricks proudly announces to the Russians. – *Moscow on the Hudson* (1984)

2860 An explosive mix of Japanese businessmen, Arabs, a motorcycle gang and a bevy of merrymaking gays soon ignites into a fracas at a classy nightclub, and the police are summoned. "I guess it's one of those gay-Arab-biker-sushi bars," surmises one officer in his description of the club. – *Protocol* (1984)

2861 Con artist Steve Martin finds himself in a French jail after a former sweetheart, seeing him with another woman, reports him for theft. "She caught me with another woman!" Martin pleads with the police chief. "Come on, you're French. You understand that!" "To be with another woman – that's French," the officer admits. "To be caught – that's American." – *Dirty Rotten Scoundrels* (1988)

2862 Chicago police captain Peter Boyle greets Russian policeman Arnold Schwarzenegger, on temporary assignment in the U.S. "Look," Boyle asks, "just out of curiosity – since I figure cops are cops the world over – how do you Soviets deal with all the tension and stress?" "Vodka," the Russian replies. – *Red Heat* (1988)

2863 Tracey Ullman discovers husband Kevin Kline is cheating on her, and her European-born mother, Joan Plowright, thinks nothing of hiring someone to kill him. "In America people kill each other left and right," Plowright explains. "It's like a national pastime." – *I Love You to Death* (1990)

2864 At an English estate an anxious bridegroom and his nervous mother-in-law wonder why the local vicar who is to perform the ceremony, as well as a second clergyman they have sent for, has not arrived. "You can't swing a dead cat around these English countrysides without hitting a vicar," the mother-in-law says. – *Three Men and a Little Lady* (1990)

Nature

2865 "What causes the water in watermelon?" Bobby Clark wonders out loud. "They plant the seeds in the spring," buddy Paul McCullough replies. – *Love and Hisses* (1934)

2866 "Fryer-less cookers!" Elizabeth Patterson voices her suspicions about another example of modern technology. "Seems like it's goin' against nature somehow." – *Men Without Names* (1935)

2867 During a violent dust storm a bartender questions John Wayne. "You ain't aimin' to drive back to your farm tonight, mister?" "Why not?" Wayne asks. "Save time by stayin' put. Let the wind blow the farm to you." – *Three Faces West* (1940)

2868 Businessman Leon Errol gets the best of a conniving salesman who was trying to steal Errol's account. "You sure made a monkey out of him," says Lupe Velez, Errol's niece. "Well, I can't take credit for that. Nature gave him a head start." – *Mexican Spitfire's Blessed Event* (1943)

2869 "How I detest the dawn!" remarks Clifton Webb. "The grass looks like it's been left out all night." – *The Dark Corner* (1946)

2870 Husband Robert Young inquires of wife Maureen O'Hara what their neighbor Richard Haydn is doing in their flower bed. "It seems we have a very healthy male iris," she explains, "and he asked if he could have some pollen so he could feed it to one of his." "We ought to charge him a stud fee." – *Sitting Pretty* (1948)

2871 Television star Phil Silvers and his cohorts work on their one-liners: "It was so hot, people were walking in their shadows... It was so hot, everyone was reading fan magazines... It was so hot, the ferry took off its slip." – *Top Banana* (1954)

2872 Deadly giant plants crawl ominously everywhere on earth. A scientist, battling this menace, says to his wife: "Stay behind me. There's no sense in getting killed by a plant." – *The Day of the Triffids* (1963)

2873 Woody Allen rejects an outing to the beach: "I hate the sun. I'm pale and I'm redheaded. I don't tan – I stroke." – *Play It Again, Sam* (1972)

2874 Teenage prostitute Brooke Shields, hiding from her pimp, takes refuge in the home of ex-vaudeville comic George Burns. "It's a big place," she says, admiring his well-furnished house. "I carved it out of the wilderness," he quips. – *Just You and Me, Kid* (1979)

2875 Hollywood writer Walter Matthau says of the sun: "I hate it. It tries to get at me through the cracks in the door. I have to hide." – *I Ought to Be in Pictures* (1982)

2876 "See that?" Hollywood writer Walter Matthau says proudly to visiting daughter Dinah Manoff. "That's my orange tree. I grew that, I planted it, I fed it, I grew it. That's my tree." "I thought only God could make a tree," she wonders. "That's back East," he explains. "Out here anyone can do it." – *I Ought to Be in Pictures* (1982)

2877 Sexually free nurse Julie Hagerty and her lover Tony Roberts, on a group walk in the woods, linger in the rear. "There's another sapsucker!" she cries. "How come everything you say sounds dirty?" Roberts asks. – *A Midsummer Night's Sex Comedy* (1982)

2878 Rich and pampered troop leader Shelley Long, instead of camping overnight in the great outdoors with her girls, takes her troop to a hotel and leaves her superior the following message: "Will you tell her ... her recommendation for a campsite was totally unsuitable. There were no outlets, and there was dirt and bugs and – and it rained there." – *Troop Beverly Hills* (1989)

Navy

2879 Raymond Walburn, as the captain of a U.S. warship, invites families of his crew aboard. "Can I visit the crow's nest?" a young woman asks him. "Certainly not," Walburn replies. "This is the mating season." – *Born to Dance* (1936)

2880 "Why do you want to join the navy?" Frank Morgan asks Ann Sothern. "I have a sister ... who's a WAC and a cousin who takes care of a lighthouse." "What is she, a wick?" quips Morgan. – *Thousands Cheer* (1943)

2881 "The best thing you three can do," an officer warns a trio of sailors due for shore leave, "is to go ashore and act like gentlemen." "What's the next best thing?" asks one sailor. – *Seven Days Ashore* (1944)

2882 On a twenty-four-hour shore leave, sailor Frank Sinatra is obsessed with sightseeing and expresses his excitement to buddies Gene Kelly and Jules Munshin. "I want to take in the beauties of New York!" he exclaims. "And I want to take them out," Munshin adds. – *On the Town* (1949)

2883 Captain Queeg (Humphrey Bogart) takes over command of a slack ship and explains to his exec officers that he "goes by the book." He then orders shaves and haircuts for the men and says: "Woe betides the man that has another shirt tail flapping." "He's certainly navy," one officer remarks after Queeg leaves. "So was Captain Bligh," officer Fred MacMurray wisecracks. – *The Caine Mutiny* (1954)

2884 During World War II a bellicose admiral accuses navy public relations officer Glenn Ford of having something to do with sexy reporter Eva Gabor being aboard his fighting ship. "Do you realize how long this ship has been in the Pacific?" the admiral exclaims. "Thirty-one months and thirteen days, sir," Ford replies. "And do you have any notion what the sight of a woman, any woman – but especially that woman – can do to men who haven't even seen a woman in all that time?" – *Don't Go Near the Water* (1957)

2885 On a Pacific island during World War II, a U.S. Navy officer one evening tries to lure pretty nurse Anne Francis onto an abandoned beach. "During this time of the year," he explains about a particular species, "these slippery little creatures come up on the beach, stop, spawn and then go out to sea again." "Sounds like some naval officers I know," she quips. – *Don't Go Near the Water* (1957)

2886 U.S. Marine Mort Saul, aboard a troop transport during World War II, reads aloud from a handbook entitled *Know Your Enemy:* "'The most fanatical of the enemy can be encouraged to surrender by offering him clean clothes, a bed and a warm meal.'" "Are they kidding?" a fellow marine remarks. "No," Saul replies. "That's how I got in." – *In Love and War* (1958)

2887 Jerry Lewis, a U.S. Navy lieutenant, is accidentally placed in command of a destroyer escort, which he promptly grounds on a reef. He refuses to send for help. "We'll sit right here and wait for the tide to come back in," he says to a subordinate. "That's it – wait

for the tide. It couldn't have gone very far." – *Don't Give Up the Ship* (1959)

2888 During World War II a submarine is seriously damaged, and a scheming junior officer (Tony Curtis) and his band of raiders pilfer every island supply depot within range. "To paraphrase Churchill," Captain Cary Grant writes in his log, "never have so few stolen so much from so many." – *Operation Petticoat* (1959)

2889 During World War II, a U.S. submarine with a broken radio is depth-charged by an American destroyer. Captain Cary Grant decides to jettison some underclothes belonging to nurses aboard the sub, hoping the garments will be recognized as American. "The Japanese have nothing like this!" exclaims the destroyer's captain as he zeros in on the floating objects. "Cease fire!" – *Operation Petticoat* (1959)

2890 Captain Dennis O'Keefe is ordered back to his ship only to discover a strange turkey, the crew's mascot, wandering around. "What's that?" he asks. "It's a turkey, sir," an officer replies meekly. "How did he get aboard?" O'Keefe questions. "Did he enlist?" – *All Hands on Deck* (1961)

2891 Zorro (George Hamilton) receives a visit from his former gay roommate who says his father shipped him to sea to make him more manly. "They say the navy makes men," the visitor comments. "Well, I'm living proof they made me." – *Zorro, the Gay Blade* (1981)

Old West

2892 A judge in a Western town closes a case involving two outlaws who were gunned down: "I find that these worthless skunks come to their untimely

ends through their own willful negligence – just a little slow on the trigger." – *The Texas Rangers* (1936)

2893 A U.S. Senator, journeying to the West by stagecoach, complains that he has arrived before a letter he had written. "That's nothing," comments army sergeant Edgar Buchanan. "Private Mulligan didn't get the letter with his reprieve till after they hung him. Come to think about it, he never did get it." – *Buffalo Bill* (1944)

2894 Daring, audacious cowboy Errol Flynn joins a group of stagecoach passengers and ensconces himself next to pretty dance-hall entertainer Alexis Smith. "Is it a western custom to push yourself in where you're not wanted?" she asks. "Yes, ma'am," Flynn retorts. "That's the way the West was won." – *San Antonio* (1945)

2895 Bungling dentist Painless Potter (Bob Hope) is mistakenly hailed as the hero who has just saved a group of women and children from a hostile band of ravaging Indians. As the tumult and the shouting subside, Hope is prepared to make a speech. "Ladies and gentlemen. At this time I'd like to say a few words–" he begins. "Let's get out of here before the Redskins come back!" the wagon master interjects. "Those are the words!" Hope adds. – *The Paleface* (1948)

2896 Bob Hope, who doesn't like the looks of a ghost-town hotel, says to Jane Russell: "You can get a room here with an adjoining hole in the head." – *Son of Paleface* (1952)

2897 Clark Gable and his brother Cameron Mitchell are riding to a town when they come upon a man hanging from a tree. "It looks like we're getting close to civilization," Gable remarks. – *The Tall Men* (1955)

2898 When the fiery head of a women's temperance movement (Lee Remick) plans to lead her followers from the safety of a frontier army fort to intercept a shipment of whiskey to Denver, a worried sergeant voices his concern to fort commander Burt Lancaster. "A march to Denver through

country like this – without escort, without protection," the sergeant warns. "What if they come upon a bunch of bloodthirsty Indians, sir?" "I suggest that we pray for the Indians," Lancaster returns. – *The Hallelujah Trail* (1965)

2899 Doc Holliday (Jason Robards) and Wyatt Earp (James Garner) corner the Clanton gang leader (Robert Ryan) in Mexico, after which Robards asks: "You got some kind of plan?" "Yep," Earp replies. "You want to tell me about it?" "We take whoever gets in our way." "You call that a plan?" "You got a better one?" "Nope." – *Hour of the Gun* (1967)

2900 Rivals John Wayne and gunfighter Kirk Douglas team up to carry out a revenge holdup. At one point they are challenged by two gunslingers who are quickly dispatched. "Mine hit the ground first," boasts Douglas. "Mine was taller," counters Wayne. – *The War Wagon* (1967)

2901 Judge Roy Bean (Paul Newman), who runs the Texas frontier town of Vinegaroon including the only saloon and gambling parlor, is losing heavily at poker. To raise fifty dollars, he charges twenty-five dollars for a glass of beer to the winning players. "What's a man supposed to do?" questions a thirsty winner. "Start losing or quit drinking," suggests Newman. – *The Life and Times of Judge Roy Bean* (1972)

2902 "Do you know what Sheridan said about Arizona?" the commander of a Southwestern army post asks lieutenant Bruce Davison. "No, sir." "He said that if he had a choice between Hell and Arizona, he'd live in Hell and rent out Arizona." "I think he said that about Texas, sir." "But he meant Arizona." – *Ulzana's Raid* (1972)

2903 A western town is about to hang John Alton, who they think is a notorious bandit. The local undertaker, in charge of preparing the prisoner for the event, is busily engaged in giving Alton a haircut. "You know," he admits, "this is a new experience for me. I never barbered anyone sitting up before." – *The Brothers O'Toole* (1973)

2904 A proud, elderly Indian (Chief Dan George) says to Josey Wales (Clint Eastwood): "I myself never surrendered. But they got my horse, and it surrendered." – *The Outlaw Josey Wales* (1976)

2905 Cowboy hero Tom Berenger confronts the town villain in a saloon – both poised for a shootout. "Go home, Blackie," Berenger warns. "Go home?" "Yeah, that's right." "Go home?" Blackie repeats in disbelief. "Yeah, and see someone about your hearing." – *Rustlers' Rhapsody* (1985)

2906 In this western satire, hero Tom Berenger, dressed in white, enters a saloon and orders a glass of milk which the bartender refuses to serve him. "Is this one of those really tough bars? Then let me have a large glass of warm gin with a human hair in it." – *Rustlers' Rhapsody* (1985)

2907 Cowboy hero Steve Martin, as Lucky Day, saves a squalid, dusty Mexican village from the ravages of a local bandit. As he and his two pals are about to leave, he turns to say goodbye to a young Mexican woman. "I'll come back one day," he promises. "Why?" she inquires. – *Three Amigos!* (1986)

Outlaws (Western)

2908 A U.S. Marshal catches up with outlaw Wallace Beery, who has been hiding out in a little town near Death Valley for eight years and who has gone straight. "I'm here to tell you you're getting amnesty," the lawman announces. "Amnesty?" the defensive Beery protests. "I stand on my constitutional rights for a straight hangin'!" – *20 Mule Team* (1940)

2909 A town judge, while busy testing a special trap door of the gallows, asks outlaw Guinn Williams, who is to be hanged, if he has any final request. "I got one," Williams says. "Keep your trap shut." – *The Desperadoes* (1943)

2910 An outlaw, after reading a poster, reports to marshal Randolph Scott and explains: "It was a week before we found out what 'amnesty' meant." – *Ride Lonesome* (1959)

2911 Butch and Sundance (Paul Newman and Robert Redford) have robbed E. H. Harriman's trains one time too often. There is a hunt for them –

dead or alive. "That crazy Harriman!" Newman grumbles. "If he'd just give me what he's spending to make me stop robbing him, I'd stop robbing him!" – *Butch Cassidy and the Sundance Kid* (1969)

2912 Train robbers Butch Cassidy (Paul Newman) and the Sundance Kid (Robert Redford) are trapped on a mountain ledge. In front of them a posse is closing in; behind them, a sharp drop into a chasm. "If we fight," Butch reckons, "they can stay where they are and starve us out. Or they could start a rock slide and get us that way. What else could they do?" "They could surrender to us," Sundance offers. – *Butch Cassidy and the Sundance Kid* (1969)

2913 Train robber and killer Claude Akins gets arrested in a small western town for littering and is put in jail. "Is this going on my record?" he inquires. – *The Great Bank Robbery* (1969)

2914 A villain hires an assortment of outlaws, gunmen and other culprits to attack a frontier town. The prospective miscreants line up for their interviews. "What's your crime?" the chief villain asks one man. "Stampeding cattle." "That's not much of a crime." "Through the Vatican?" the outlaw adds. – *Blazing Saddles* (1974)

2915 Luckily for captured outlaw Jack Nicholson the town in which he committed his crime has an ordinance that allows a woman to claim a prisoner for her husband. Spinster farmer Mary Steenburgen saves him from the gallows, and the couple ride off together to her farm. "A good husband is hard to find," Nicholson reassures her. "You weren't hard to find," she replies. "You were standing in front of the whole town with a rope around your neck." – *Goin' South* (1978)

2916 Elderly western outlaw Richard Farnsworth is released from prison in 1901, after serving thirty years. Now a social anachronism, he boards a train and meets a salesman who asks him his line of business. At first he replies that he is between jobs, but he is pressed further. "I robbed stagecoaches," he replies softly. – *The Grey Fox* (1984)

Pain

2917 Gus the jockey (Al Jolson in blackface) has just taken quite a few falls while trying to ride a wild horse. "I think I got inferno complications," he says to the owner. "No, you mean internal complications. 'Inferno' means the lower regions. "The lower regions?" Jolson repeats. "Brother, that's where I got them." – *Big Boy* (1930)

2918 "Wait!" exclaims Robert Woolsey to pal Bert Wheeler. "I've just given birth to an idea." "My," responds Wheeler, "how you must have suffered!" – *Hook, Line and Sinker* (1930)

2919 Nightclub owner Eugene Pallette has had all his teeth removed by a dentist friend and returns to his club where he boasts about his dental work. "Did it hurt?" an acquaintance asks. "Did it give you any pain?" "Only when I got the bill." – *Bordertown* (1935)

2920 "I don't mind the suffering – it's just the pain I can't stand," remarks master sleuth Charlie McCarthy. – *Charlie McCarthy, Detective* (1939)

2921 Charlie McCarthy thinks he has swallowed his Boy Scout pin and goes to doctor Edgar Bergen. "Are you sure you swallowed it?" Bergen asks. "I get sticking pains in my stomach," explains McCarthy. "What have you eaten lately?" "One Boy Scout pin," McCarthy answers. – *Look Who's Laughing* (1941)

2922 Bud Abbott leads Lou Costello, who is suffering from a painful toothache, into a dentist's office. The dentist feels around Costello's face until he hits a sore spot that sends his patient flying off the chair in pain. "I had to find out where the pain is," the dentist explains. "Why didn't you ask me?" returns Costello. "It's no secret!" – *The Noose Hangs High* (1948)

2923 Oscar Levant prescribes the parameters of his toughness to Fred Astaire and Nanette Fabray: "I can stand anything but pain." – *The Band Wagon* (1953)

2924 Danny Kaye volunteers to enter an illegitimate king's castle posing as a jester, but fellow rebel Glynis Johns fears that he may be captured and tortured. "After months of pleading for just this type of action," Kaye protests, "what makes you think that they could force me to reveal the identity of my confederates?" "Because they'd put you on the rack, crack your every bone, scald you in hot oil and remove the nails from your fingers with flaming hot pincers," she informs him. "I'd like to withdraw the question," Kaye says. – *The Court Jester* (1956)

2925 A high-school teacher tries to use a school gym dance to bring together two hostile gangs – the Jets and the Sharks. "It won't hurt to try it," the teacher offers. "It hoits! It hoits!" a Jet blurts out. – *West Side Story* (1961)

2926 Jack Weston, a government agent working undercover to expose corruption in a Southern town, is brutally beaten by thugs. Weston, who happens to be Jewish, ends up in a local hospital with an elderly Jewish patient in the next bed. Both exchange groans as a result of their pain. "Two Jews in pain," muses Weston at the irony. "Let my people go already." – *Gator* (1976)

2927 Alvy Singer and Annie Hall (Woody Allen and Diane Keaton) talk about *The Sorrow and the Pity,* a film they have just seen. "I wonder how I'd stand up to torture," Keaton muses. "The Gestapo would take away your Bloomingdale's charge account," Allen replies, "and you'll tell them everything." – *Annie Hall* (1977)

2928 An excited auto worker rushes into a supermarket to inform fellow employee Michael Keaton that the Japanese have arrived to take over the town factory. As the man runs down the aisle, he collides with an elderly woman's shopping cart which smashes into his groin. "My eggs!" the woman cries. "*Your* eggs!" – *Gung Ho* (1986)

Parents

2929 After many years, former pals Bert Wheeler and Robert Woolsey unexpectedly meet in a mythical European kingdom and immediately begin to reminisce. "Good old Brooklyn," Wheeler recalls. "You know, I could see my mother now, standing at the window." "How do you know she's standing?" Woolsey asks. "I sold the chairs before I left home." – *Cracked Nuts* (1931)

2930 Rich, beautiful and blithe Kay Francis learns from her new assistant (Miriam Hopkins) that her mother has passed away. "That's the trouble with mothers," Francis sighs, "you get to like them and then they die." – *Trouble in Paradise* (1932)

2931 Crooked arms dealer Louis Calhern, determined to sabotage an international peace conference, confides to accomplice Hugh Herbert: "I shall get the greatest criminal mind in Europe to assist us." "Why not get your father?" Herbert suggests. "He must have had a criminal mind when he thought of you." – *Diplomaniacs* (1933)

2932 A corrupt mayor meets resistance from the citizenry and their spokesman, the village clown (Eddie Cantor). Cantor suspects the crooked mayor of getting a kickback for a proposed new jail. "The old jail was good enough for your father," Cantor insinuates, " – it ought to be good enough for you." – *Roman Scandals* (1933)

2933 Ethel Merman, in league with a con man, impersonates the long-lost mother of Eddie Cantor, son of a dead millionaire. She walks into his room, arms extended, a tear in her eye, and announces herself. "Kiss me, darling," she cries, embracing the stunned, wide-eyed Cantor, who is soon smothered by her long kiss. "Now I know what killed my father," he says. – *Kid Millions* (1934)

2934 Social reformer Margaret Dumont makes the acquaintance of Charles Ruggles, a crook traveling incognito aboard an ocean liner. "Surely you don't believe in capital punishment?" she asks. "What was good enough for my father is good enough for me," Ruggles replies. – *Anything Goes* (1936)

2935 W. C. Fields demonstrates an invention which provokes questions from observers. "Say," one asks, "do you know anything about electricity?" "My father occupied the Chair of Applied Electricity at State Prison," Fields replies, announcing his credentials. – *The Big Broadcast of 1938* (1938)

2936 Jean Arthur, a member of the eccentric Sycamore family, tries to explain her parents to James Stewart, who has met them for the first time. "Dad makes fireworks because there's a sense of excitement about it," she says. "And Mother – know why Mother writes plays? Because eight years ago a typewriter was delivered to the house by mistake." – *You Can't Take It with You* (1938)

2937 "I bet your father spent the first year of your life throwing rocks at the stork," Groucho Marx says to Chico Marx. – *At the Circus* (1939)

2938 "Papa was the biggest, but he was awful genteel," gangster Cyrus Kendall recalls. "He'd never slap mom with nothing but the back of his hand." – *Twelve Crowded Hours* (1939)

2939 Wealthy bachelor Charles Butterworth laments to Paulette Goddard: "I said 'music' and Father said 'bottle caps.' Father won." – *Second Chorus* (1940)

2940 Radio show host Kay Kyser asks a contestant to define a weasel. "A

weasel is a little man," the young woman answers. "Are you sure?" Kyser questions her. "That's what I heard my mother call my father." – *You'll Find Out* (1940)

2941 Bob Hope down and out and stranded in Morocco, sees slaves bearing a chair pass by him. Suddenly a hand sensually reaches out, grabs his and guides it inside the enclosure. "Mother told me there'll be moments like this," Hope says. "I wonder how she knew." – *Road to Morocco* (1942)

2942 When Spencer Tracy tells wife Joan Bennett of his anxiety and concern that their future son-in-law will not have the means to provide for their daughter, she becomes agitated. "Funny," he observes. "If you get someone else to start worrying, you stop worrying yourself." – *Father of the Bride* (1950)

2943 Narrator Arthur Kennedy describes his father, who left a long time ago: "He was a telephone man who fell in love with long distance." – *The Glass Menagerie* (1950)

2944 Richard Widmark's ex-wife Audrey Totter returns after abandoning him and their baby son four years earlier and demands money from him. In court Widmark's lawyer establishes that she has never tried to see her son. "I don't understand that type of devotion," the lawyer says. "You wouldn't," the witness says. "You're not a mother." "There, I suspect, we're in the same boat," the lawyer fires back. – *My Pal Gus* (1952)

2945 A crusty old cowpoke describes Bob Hope's father to him: "He was the lyingest crook, the mangiest, rottenest, low-down critter that never drew a silver breath." "You really knew my daddy, didn't you?" Hope affirms. – *Son of Paleface* (1952)

2946 When Harry the Horse (Sheldon Leonard) informs two Broadway cronies that he has five thousand dollars and is looking for a crap game, he is asked where he got so much money. "I got nothing to hide," Leonard says. "I collected the reward on my father." "It is an advantage to have a successful father," comments one associate. — *Guys and Dolls* (1955)

2947 "That is a 'B,' darling," Auntie Mame (Rosalind Russell) assists her nephew, "the first letter of a seven-letter word that means your late father." — *Auntie Mame* (1958)

2948 James Garner, divorced for several years, lives with his mother, whose only wish is that he remarry so that she can have grandchildren. "I'm practically the only one in my class who hasn't got any," she complains, referring to an upcoming school reunion. "And I was voted the girl most likely to succeed." — *Boys' Night Out* (1962)

2949 Dick Van Dyke's widowed mother (Maureen Stapleton) frowns upon her son's thoughts of marriage. "Mother, speaking of marriage—" "A wonderful institution," she interjects. She then looks up and histrionically addresses her deceased husband. "Don't worry, Lou, our only child is taking care of me. He wouldn't do anything to break my heart." — *Bye Bye Birdie* (1963)

2950 Dick Van Dyke has been courting Janet Leigh, his pretty secretary, for six years, while his clinging widowed mother (Maureen Stapleton) has been using every ploy to keep him from straying. "Oh, I don't believe it!" she exclaims, studying Leigh's face. "What happened to you? You had a fatal sickness or somethin'? I wonder some older man hasn't snatched her away." — *Bye Bye Birdie* (1963)

2951 First comic: "Was that one of your father's jokes?" Second comic: "What are you—one of your mother's?" — *The Night They Raided Minsky's* (1968)

2952 Tevye (Topol) agrees to the marriage of his oldest daughter (Rosalind Harris) to a middle-aged butcher. "I always wanted a son," Tevye says, "but I wanted one a little younger than myself." — *Fiddler on the Roof* (1971)

2953 Barbra Streisand and her husband and two children travel from their New York City apartment to the New Jersey suburbs to spend the day with her oppressive mother, who continually harps on their moving near her. "If this is what it's like to be a mother," Barbra finally explodes, "I'll turn in my ovaries!" — *Up the Sandbox* (1972)

2954 Gene Wilder, as private detective Sigerson Holmes, takes on the case of music-hall singer Madeline Kahn. "What does your father do?" Wilder inquires. "He's a janitor at the Browning Bank at Clearwater Street." "Browning doesn't have a bank at Clearwater Street." "Poor Papa," Kahn sighs. "I wonder if he knows." — *The Adventures of Sherlock Holmes' Smarter Brother* (1975)

2955 Quinn Cummings asks her mother, Marsha Mason, why she does not like Richard Dreyfuss. "I wouldn't like him if I liked him," Mason replies. — *The Goodbye Girl* (1977)

2956 Gabriel Kaplan has an argument with his wife and decides to sleep at his mother's house. "Ma, it's me," he announces after ringing the doorbell. "Me who?" "Me your son." "My son who?" "How many sons do you have?" "Give me your name," the voice persists. — *Fast Break* (1978)

2957 When Woody Allen complains to Diane Keaton that his son is being raised by two women, she counters that she read in a psychoanalytic quarterly that "two mothers are absolutely fine—just fine." "Oh, really?" questions Allen. "Because I always feel very few people survive one mother." — *Manhattan* (1979)

2958 Henry Winkler on his parents: "My mother goes to a seance every Friday night since my father died—so she can yell at him." — *Night Shift* (1982)

2959 Stand-up comic Robert De Niro, making his television debut, eulogizes his mother and then adds: "If she were only here today, I'd say: 'Hey, Mom, what are you doing here? You've been dead for nine years.'" – *The King of Comedy* (1983)

2960 Teenager Lance Guest returns home from another galaxy where his unusual skill in galactic arcade games helps to destroy an alien force. "I've just been to another planet," he informs his mother. "That's nice, dear," she replies. – *The Last Starfighter* (1984)

2961 "I didn't talk to my father for three months once," college student Rick Overton says, "and he took my birth certificate and destroyed it." – *Odd Jobs* (1985)

2962 Embittered elderly salesman Jackie Gleason, whose wife has just left him, telephones his son Tom Hanks to tell him what has happened. Hanks, preoccupied with his own advertising career, is in bed with one of his girlfriends. "This is Max Basner, your father," Gleason says. "You heard of me?" – *Nothing in Common* (1986)

2963 Con artist Richard Pryor, posing as a doctor at a hospital, is asked by intern Dr. Joffe (Bob Saget) for a second opinion concerning a patient who is critically ill. "You want a second opinion?" Pryor flares up. "Is that why your parents worked so hard to send you to medical school?" "My parents are wealthy," the intern retorts. – *Critical Condition* (1987)

2964 Danny DeVito, completely dominated by his overbearing mother, invites his creative-writing instructor Billy Crystal to meet her. At first, Crystal doesn't believe DeVito's horrible descriptions of the woman, but following a series of mishaps in which Crystal is almost killed, he more than concurs with his student's earlier remarks. "She's not a woman," Crystal concludes. "She's The Terminator!" – *Throw Momma from the Train* (1987)

2965 Members of an exclusive country club question prospective member, building developer Jackie Mason, about his background. "My father was Armenian, my mother was half–Jewish, half–English, half–Spanish," Mason replies. "That's three halves," a member questions. "Oh," Jackie explains, "she was a big woman." – *Caddyshack II* (1988)

2966 Movie extra Alan King says to his son, Billy Crystal, whom he hasn't seen for years: "It's no big news to know that I wasn't a great father; let's say I was miscast." – *Memories of Me* (1988)

2967 A school psychiatrist and a principal suggest to Steve Martin and his wife that Kevin, their overly tense eight-year-old son, be placed in a class with emotionally disturbed students. "You should not look upon the fact that Kevin will be going to a special school as any kind of failure on your part," the psychiatrist says to Martin and his wife. "No," Martin replies, "I'll blame the dog." – *Parenthood* (1989)

2968 Bride-to-be Molly Ringwald is unhappy when her future in-laws disapprove of her outlandish taste in clothes. "My parents aren't real free spirits," her prospective husband explains. "To them, being creative is buying low and selling high." – *Betsy's Wedding* (1990)

2969 Billy Crystal's mother awakens him at 5:15 a.m. with a phone call to wish him a happy birthday. She then inquires about his wife. "Is Barbara with you?" she asks. "No," jokes Billy, "she's walking the streets and she likes to have breakfast with her pimp." – *City Slickers* (1991)

2970 Father-of-the-bride Steve Martin has problems facing his twenty-two-year-old daughter's engagement. Treating his future son-in-law with suspicion, he betrays his inner fears when he calls out to the young couple as they leave his house: "Drive carefully, and don't forget to fasten your condom – seatbelt – I mean seatbelt!" – *Father of the Bride* (1991)

2971 An adult Peter Pan (Robin Williams), blatantly preoccupied with his business and neglectful of his son (Charlie Korsmo), boasts that his word is his bond. "Yeah—junk bond!" cries his disappointed son.—*Hook* (1991)

Philosophy

2972 Stan Laurel tries to explain his philosophy of survival to Oliver Hardy. "It's the law of conversation," Laurel states. "What do you mean?" "Well," Laurel elaborates, "as you cast your bread on the waters, so shall you reap." —*The Devil's Brother* (1933)

2973 Chinese philosopher Hugh Herbert offers a little oriental epigram to his villainous partner Louis Calhern. "It is written . . . rest today and make haste tomorrow." "Why?" Calhern asks. "Don't ask me," Herbert replies. "Did I write it?"—*Diplomaniacs* (1933)

2974 W. C. Fields philosophizes to his cronies at a bar: "It's a funny old world. A man's lucky if he gets out of it alive." —*You're Telling Me* (1934)

2975 As a publicity stunt, Robert Woolsey wants his assistant, Bert Wheeler, to crash one locomotive into another. But Wheeler hesitates. "It's only a question of mind over matter," Woolsey reassures him. "Mind over matter?" "Yeah, I don't mind and you don't matter."—*The Rainmakers* (1935)

2976 "I'm a firm believer in democracy," Walter Connolly says to Francis Compton, "provided that it lets me alone."—*Soak the Rich* (1936)

2977 Two children (Peter Holden and Virginia Weidler) run away from home and arrive in a rural area where their questions about their grandparents' farm are answered harshly by a truck driver. "It seems to me," the boy construes, "people are as mean in the coun-try as they are in the city." "People are mean all over," his sister adds. "The nice thing about the country is there aren't so many people."—*The Great Man Votes* (1939)

2978 "I always say," announces gregarious Mary Boland, "the time to enjoy people is before you find them out."—*He Married His Wife* (1940)

2979 Broderick Crawford conceives a daring plan in which he and Mischa Auer will shoot their way into an outlaw hideout to rescue their friend Franchot Tone. Auer, however, doesn't think much of the idea. "To die is noble," he asserts, "but to live is divine!"—*Trail of the Vigilantes* (1940)

2980 "Love is like champagne," announces Charlie McCarthy at a party, "marriage is the headache and divorce is the aspirin tablet."—*Look Who's Laughing* (1941)

2981 A famous Russian opera singer visiting America longs for his tailor, hotel, food and other niceties. "At least it's warmer than Siberia," his servant suggests. "Please," the singer says, "if there's anything I can't stand, it's a Russian philosopher."—*Tonight We Sing* (1953)

2982 A village drugstore owner fires his young helper who went to visit his child-bearing wife in the hospital. "How can you be so mean?" says Jackie Gleason. "Because I enjoy it," the owner replies. "A man can't do anything well unless he enjoys it."—*Papa's Delicate Condition* (1963)

2983 Inept Police Inspector Clouseau (Peter Sellers) falls into a pool as he is about to enter an estate to investigate a murder. Dripping wet, he privately questions suspect Elke Sommer, a maid, who is concerned about his health. "You should get out of these clothes immediately," she suggests. "You'll catch your death of pneumonia, you will." "Yes, I probably will," he acknowledges. "It's all part of life's rich pageant, you know." —*A Shot in the Dark* (1964)

2984 "I love Eastern philosophy," Woody Allen confesses to Louise Lasser. "Metaphysical and redundancy—abortively pedantic." "I know just what you mean," she responds.—*Bananas* (1971)

2985 Absent-minded musicologist Ryan O'Neal is completely dominated by his shrewish girlfriend. "I'm not looking for romance," she announces. "I'm looking for something more permanent than that—something stronger. As the years go by, romance fades and something else takes its place. You know what that is?" "Senility," he offers.—*What's Up, Doc?* (1972)

2986 "I have a pessimistic view of life," Woody Allen affirms to Diane Keaton. "I feel that life is divided up into the horrible and the miserable. The horrible would be like . . . criminal cases and blind people, the crippled. I don't know how they get through life. It's amazing to me. The miserable is everyone else."—*Annie Hall* (1977)

2987 Producer William Holden muses over his failure to bring an actress out of seclusion: "Well, as Sam Goldwyn used to say: 'You have to take the bitter with the sour.'"—*Fedora* (1978)

2988 Struggling cab driver Bill Murray, to cheer himself up, has his shoes shined. "My philosophy," he announces, "is a hundred-dollar shine and a three-dollar pair of boots."—*Stripes* (1981)

2989 Arch-villain Gene Hackman's dizzy moll helps him escape from a maximum security prison in a hot-air balloon. "Why am I here?" she cries out as they move with the wind. "What am I doing here?" "Is this a philosophy seminar?" Hackman snaps. "No, this is a getaway!"—*Superman II* (1981)

2990 Young Matthew Broderick's mother has taken in boarder Jason Robards, who is actually the boy's grandfather. Robards, using a pseudonym, tells the boy he knew his grandfather. "What business was my grandfather in?" the curious teenager asks. "Philosophy." "Can you make money in philosophy?" Broderick asks. "Oh, sure," Robards replies, "if you have the right one."—*Max Dugan Returns* (1983)

2991 Mia Farrow expresses her modus vivendi to Woody Allen: "You know what my philosophy of life is? It's over quick so have a good time. You see what you want, go for it. Don't pay any attention to anybody else. And do it to the other guy first, 'cause if you don't, he'll do it to you." "This is a philosophy of life?" Allen unbelievingly questions. "It sounds like the screenplay of *Murder, Incorporated.*"—*Broadway Danny Rose* (1984)

2992 "Everything ends badly," states cynical bartender-philosopher Bryan Brown; "otherwise it wouldn't end." —*Cocktail* (1988)

2993 Sleazy businessman Joe Pesci involves his brother-in-law Alan Alda in a shady real-estate deal with a member of organized crime. Alda, who wants to back out, meets with his silent partner. "This is my philosophy of business managing," the hoodlum explains to Alda and Pesci. "When everybody is happy, then it is very unusual that anybody is unhappy. But you can't be happy with unhappy people contributing miserableness." "Pay attention to this," Pesci says to Alda. "This is wisdom." —*Betsy's Wedding* (1990)

2994 F.B.I. agent Rick Moranis is bringing smalltime, flashy hoodlum Steve Martin back to New York to testify against mob leaders. "You tip a flight attendant?" the agent asks. "I tip everybody," Martin boasts. "That's my philosophy. Actually, it's not tipping I believe in, it's overtipping." – *My Blue Heaven* (1990)

2995 "If life is meaningless," muses Lily Tomlin, "then why the hell bring up the subject?" – *The Search for Signs of Intelligent Life in the Universe* (1991)

Places

2996 "Here's Cocoanut Grove and here's Cocoanut Heights," Groucho Marx says, explaining a blueprint to Chico. "It's a swamp. And here where the road forks is Cocoanut Junction." "Where's Cocoanut Custard?" asks Chico. "Over the forks," ripostes Groucho. – *The Cocoanuts* (1929)

2997 A philanthropist announces that he will soon sail to Uruguay. "Well," responds Groucho Marx, "you go Uruguay and I'll go mine." – *Animal Crackers* (1930)

2998 A suspicious sheriff suspects disguised Eddie Cantor as the culprit who ran off with his girlfriend. "Where are you from?" the sheriff asks gruffly. "We moved," Cantor replies. – *Whoopee!* (1930)

2999 Former vaudeville performer Aline MacMahon opens an elocution school to help silent screen stars make the transition to sound while her dim-witted partner Jack Oakie confesses his ignorance on the subject. "You don't know anything about anything," she says, "but if what they say about Hollywood is true, you'll go far." – *Once in a Lifetime* (1932)

3000 Constance Bennett, as a famous London hostess: "If one wants to be a success in London, one must have looks, wit or a bank balance." – *Our Betters* (1933)

3001 A proud mayor, escorting a tour of prominent women through the corridors of the local museum, finds town vagrant Eddie Cantor sleeping in the concaves of a reclining Roman statue. "What's the meaning of this?" the indignant mayor asks. "You can't sleep here!" "It *is* a bit noisy," Cantor agrees. – *Roman Scandals* (1933)

3002 "You were born in St. Louis," says John Miljan to Mae West. "What part?" "Why, all of me," she replies. – *Belle of the Nineties* (1934)

3003 Con artist Warren Hymer has trouble finding Africa on a world map until his accomplice Ethel Merman points it out to him. "It's green!" he utters in surprise. "I always thought Africa was black." – *Kid Millions* (1934)

3004 Newspaper columnist Jack Benny comments to his assistant Sid Silvers that when a rich socialite and a Broadway producer flirt with each other, "one of them's got something the other wants." "Same as in The Bronx," Silvers quips. – *Broadway Melody of 1936* (1935)

3005 "I understand you were born in Brooklyn," sailor Sid Silvers' captain remarks. "What part?" "All of me," replies Silvers. – *Born to Dance* (1936)

3006 Charlie Chan (Warner Oland) to number one son (Keye Luke) who wants to see the Big Apple at night: "New York like mouth of great river: many reefs in channel to wreck small boat from Honolulu." – *Charlie Chan on Broadway* (1937)

3007 In the small village of Warsaw, Vermont, doctor Charles Winninger informs Carole Lombard he had made a mistake in a previous diagnosis in which he had given her only a few weeks to live because of radiation poisoning. "It's kind of startling to be brought to life twice," she replies equably, "and each time in Warsaw." – *Nothing Sacred* (1937)

3008 Aspiring actress Katharine Hepburn boasts to fellow thespians about her grandfather's pioneering spirit. "If he hadn't crossed the country in a covered wagon, there'd still be Indians in Wichita," Hepburn concludes. "Who do you think is living there now?" Eve Arden quips. – *Stage Door* (1937)

3009 New York police lieutenant Sam Levene is about to enter a house to investigate a possible murder. "The murderer might still be in there," warns Barbara Stanwyck. "The murderer could be in Brooklyn by now," he returns, "that is, if anybody wants to be in Brooklyn." – *The Mad Miss Manton* (1938)

3010 "This picture," announces a narrator, "takes place in Paris in those wonderful days when a siren was a brunette and not an alarm." – *Ninotchka* (1939)

3011 Detectives Larry, Moe and Curly are hired by a museum to retrieve a valuable mummy in Cairo, Egypt. "I got an uncle in Cairo," Curly announces. "He's a chiropractor." – *We Want Our Mummy* (1939)

3012 A cyclone blows Dorothy (Judy Garland) and her little dog Toto right "over the rainbow" and deposits them rudely in the exotic land of Oz. "I've a feeling," says Dorothy, "we're not in Kansas anymore." – *The Wizard of Oz* (1939)

3013 Norma Shearer and friends meet in Nevada's capital for their divorce when one makes the following toast: "To Reno, beautiful emblem of the great divide." – *The Women* (1939)

3014 Andy Hardy's parents (Fay Holden and Lewis Stone) take their family to New York where Judy Garland shows Andy (Mickey Rooney) the sights of the city. "Do you think it's all right for Andy to walk around with Betsy?" his mother asks. "I mean, there are gangsters; they may take him for a ride –" "Well," Stone interrupts, "Betsy is a New Yorker, so of course she carries a gat." – *Andy Hardy Meets Debutante* (1940)

3015 "I've just been to Canada – Pocupine, Ontario," announces Reginald Owen. "Sounds like a very uncomfortable place, and it jolly well is." – *The Earl of Chicago* (1940)

3016 World War I goldbricking soldier James Cagney meets Father Duffy (Pat O'Brien), the unit's chaplain, but is unaware of his position. Brooklyn-raised Cagney tries to involve the priest in his schemes, claiming the "world's our 'erster.'" "What?" O'Brien asks. "Erster, you know –" Cagney tries to explain. "You eat 'em – ersters." "Oh," O'Brien responds. "How did you leave things in Brooklyn?" "Fine," Cagney says, then adds: "How did you know I was from Brooklyn?" – *The Fighting 69th* (1940)

3017 The citizens of a frontier town are prepared to hang W. C. Fields, believing he is the masked bandit terrorizing the community. He is asked if he has any final words. "This will be a great lesson to me," he mutters. "Do you have any last requests?" "I'd like to see Paris before I die – Philadelphia will do." – *My Little Chickadee* (1940)

3018 "The nation is behind the Fuhrer!" announces loyal Nazi officer Paul Henreid after Hitler invades Poland. "Yes," says a Czech citizen, "but how far behind?" – *Night Train to Munich* (1940)

3019 Dorothy Lamour, the daughter of an army colonel, visits a Hollywood movie studio. "It must be some struggle to achieve success in Hollywood," she says to her guide, film agent Lynne Overman. "Oh, no," he replies. "You just have to know which fork to use and which knife to stick in whose back." –*Caught in the Draft* (1941)

3020 In Casablanca, just before Pearl Harbor, swaggering Nazi Major Strasser (Conrad Veidt) boasts about the fall of Paris; he suggests London will be next, perhaps even New York. American adventurer Rick Blaine (Humphrey Bogart) remains unimpressed. "There are certain sections of New York, major," Bogart warns, "that I wouldn't advise you to try to invade." –*Casablanca* (1942)

3021 Mary Wickes complains to boyfriend Millard Mitchell about his standing her up. "Do your talent scouting closer to home," she orders. "What's the matter with Brooklyn?" "Now I ask you: did anybody ever find anything good in Brooklyn?" "Well, you found me there." "So," he concludes, "I should make the same mistake twice?" –*The Mayor of 44th Street* (1942)

3022 Leo Gorcey and his East Side Kids ambush smalltime hoodlum Billy Gilbert and try to get him to talk about his mob. "You're a man without a country," Gorcey threatens. "I am too," Gilbert insists. "I live in Brooklyn." "That's the same thing." –*Mr. Wise Guy* (1942)

3023 Bob Hope and Bing Crosby are lost in the desert. "Where do you suppose we are?" Crosby asks. "This must be the place where they empty all the old hour glasses," replies Hope. –*Road to Morocco* (1942)

3024 Radio scriptwriter Dick Powell meets waitress Mary Martin in a small diner in a New York City borough. Thinking he is broke, she gives him a full meal "on the house." Powell wonders about her inherent trust in strangers.

"It's sort of an investment in the bank of life," she explains. "You plant seeds and you get flowers." "How long have you been in New York?" he asks. –*True to Life* (1943)

3025 Red Skelton, held captive by a gang of murderers, offers his guard, Sam Levene, a large sum of money. "You can go where the days seem like weeks and the weeks seem like years–" "I've been to Philadelphia!" Levene replies. –*Whistling in Brooklyn* (1943)

3026 Bud Abbott disputes Lou Costello's remark that a young aspiring singer is a neighbor of his. "Didn't you hear him say he's right from Des Moines, Iowa?" Costello asks. "Ain't that near Patterson, New Jersey?" "Des Moines, Iowa, is two thousand miles from Patterson, New Jersey," Abbott corrects his pal. "Well," explains Costello, "can I help it if I have a big back yard?" –*Abbott and Costello in Hollywood* (1945)

3027 Carmen Miranda: "I cannot be in two different places at the same time." Groucho Marx: "Why not? Boston and Philadelphia are in two different places at the same time." –*Copacabana* (1947)

3028 Friend George Sanders meets widow Gene Tierney in a driving London rainstorm. "It is easy to understand," he wryly observes, "why the most beautiful poems about England in the spring were written by poets living in Italy at the time." –*The Ghost and Mrs. Muir* (1947)

3029 Amateur sleuth William Powell and wife Myrna Loy return from a fruitless search for a murder suspect. "I don't believe there is any such person as Buddy Hollis," she comments. "There must be," adds Powell. "The missing persons' bureau reported him seen in Chicago, Denver, Palm Beach and Hollywood, all at the same time." "Oh, darling," Loy returns, "how could he be in all those places at the same time?" "Split personality." –*Song of the Thin Man* (1947)

3030 Trusting fortune hunter Marilyn Monroe informs friend Lauren Bacall that her beau is going to take her to Atlantic City next Saturday to meet her mother. "We'd better put a check on that one," her friend cautions. "Nobody's mother lives in Atlantic City on Saturday." – *How to Marry a Millionaire* (1953)

3031 American entertainer Danny Kaye, posing as a sportsman and world traveler, is asked what he thinks of the Himalayas – a question which baffles him. "Loved him, hated her," he finally answers. – *Knock on Wood* (1954)

3032 "In Rhode Island," Vivian Blaine informs Nathan Detroit (Frank Sinatra), "people do not remain engaged for fourteen years. They get married." "So how come it's such a small state?" he asks. – *Guys and Dolls* (1955)

3033 Nightclub comic Joe E. Lewis (Frank Sinatra) to his audience: "Las Vegas is the only place I know where money really talks – it says, 'Goodbye.'" – *The Joker Is Wild* (1957)

3034 Rosalind Russell reveals that actress friend Coral Browne is not English. "She sounded English," says Jan Handzlik. "Well," explains Russell, "when you're from Pittsburgh, you have to do something." – *Auntie Mame* (1958)

3035 Rejected suitor Tony Randall tries to keep Doris Day close at home. "In Texas there's nothing but a bunch of prairie dogs and stuff," he reminds her. "And even the air out there – there's nothing in it but air. New York you've got air you can sink your teeth into." – *Pillow Talk* (1959)

3036 Paul Newman, as Butch Cassidy, the leader of the Hole-in-the-Wall gang – named after their hideout in a desolate valley – returns with pal Robert Redford at his side. "You know," Newman says, "every time I see Hole-in-the-Wall again, it's like seeing it fresh for the first time. And whenever that happens I ask myself the same question: 'How can I be so darn stupid as to keep coming back here?'" – *Butch Cassidy and the Sundance Kid* (1969)

3037 Ohio couple Jack Lemmon and Sandy Dennis arrive in New York by plane several hours late because of fog. They are then mugged and kidnapped and abandoned in Central Park. Lemmon offers to carry his wife, whose foot is bleeding. "You can't walk on a bleeding foot!" he insists. "I would fly, but New York is fogged in," she says wryly. – *The Out of Towners* (1970)

3038 Ukrainian Jews, evicted from their homes by the Czar's edict, plan their new lives. "I'm going to Chicago, America," one villager announces. "I'm going to New York, America," Tevye (Topol) interjects. "We'll be neighbors!" – *Fiddler on the Roof* (1971)

3039 Television personality Bob Hope is falsely accused of a murder in a small southwestern town and promptly arrested. An influential citizen soon effects his release. "You're still under suspicion," local sheriff Keenan Wynn warns Hope, "so don't leave the town." "I may have to," Hope returns. "It's only fifty feet long." – *Cancel My Reservation* (1972)

3040 Young Alvy Singer (Jonathan Monk) will not do his homework. He despairs that the expanding universe will someday doom cosmic life. "What is that your business!" his mother shouts. "Brooklyn is not expanding!" – *Annie Hall* (1977)

3041 General Douglas MacArthur (Gregory Peck), now retired, had graduated from West Point with the highest honors and later became its superintendent. "When I left the hotel this morning," he opens a speech to the cadets, "the doorman asked me where I was going. I told him 'West Point.' He said that it was a beautiful place and asked whether I had ever been there before." – *MacArthur* (1977)

3042 On board an airplane, former World War II pilot Robert Hays regales a fellow passenger about his past. "I used to hang out at the Mogambo Bar," he begins. "It was a rough place – the seediest dive on the wharf – populated with every reject and cutthroat from Bombay to Calcutta. It was worse than Detroit." – *Airplane!* (1980)

3043 Aging, smalltime hustler Burt Lancaster recalls Atlantic City in its heyday. "Yeah," he says to a young disciple, "the Atlantic Ocean was something back then." – *Atlantic City* (1980)

3044 Supreme Court justice and part-time mountain climber Walter Matthau describes California as Disneyland to Jill Clayburgh, a former California judge. "You don't think much of California, do you?" Clayburgh says. "Why don't you try climbing some of our mountains?" "I have, I have," he acknowledges. "I admire your mountains. It's your valleys that make me nervous." – *First Monday in October* (1981)

3045 Vacationing New York clothing manufacturer Jack Fine (Jack Warden), lounging in a gondola in Venice, wonders: "How long have the streets been screwed up like this?" – *So Fine* (1981)

3046 In a trendy Los Angeles restaurant overrun with flora and fauna, diner Burt Reynolds asks a waiter: "You have a problem finding your way back?" "We just leave a trail of crumbs," the waiter quips. – *Best Friends* (1982)

3047 Los Angeles writer Walter Matthau receives a visit from his nineteen-year-old daughter Dinah Manoff, who has been raised in New York by her mother. "How come you never see any people in the street out here?" she asks. "They're all in their cars," Matthau explains. "Well," she continues, "how do you meet anyone? When you crash?" "You meet at filling stations and red lights." – *I Ought to Be in Pictures* (1982)

3048 In this satire, gangster Johnny Dangerously (Michael Keaton) and night-club entertainer Marilu Henner fall in love and she tells him her life story. "Then I decided to leave Pittsburgh and come here to Chicago," she concludes. "This ain't Chicago," he enlightens her. "We're in New York." – *Johnny Dangerously* (1984)

3049 "My agent is always telling me I'm negative about everything," narrates screenwriter Charles Grodin. "Being negative about ideas in Hollywood is a safe way of life. You'll be right ninety percent of the time." – *Movers and Shakers* (1985)

3050 Army disc jockey Robin Williams in Saigon describes a search-and-destroy patrol into Viet Cong territory: "That's like Newark after dark." – *Good Morning, Vietnam* (1987)

3051 A big-city truck driver, lost in the maze of New England's back roads, pulls up and asks a local resident for directions. "Hey Mac, which way to Redbud?" "How'd you know my name is Mac?" the inhabitant asks. "I just guessed." "Then why don't you guess your way to Redbud?" – *Funny Farm* (1988)

3052 Los Angeles surgeon Michael J. Fox has had a car accident in a small, obscure Southern town and is forced to spend some time there. The proud mayor escorts him to the local café to meet some of the town's more distinguished citizens. "Well, doc," one begins, "what do you think of our town?" "I don't know," Fox replies. "I haven't seen all of it yet." "Oh, yes you have," the mayor interjects. – *Doc Hollywood* (1991)

3053 Linguistics tutor Tim Curry has fallen in love with slow-witted Marisa Tomei, daughter of mobster Sylvester Stallone. "I'll be leaving next month on the *Ile de France* for a linguistics symposium in Brussels –" Curry begins. "Brussels?" she ponders. "The one in Europe?" – *Oscar* (1991)

3054 Forest Whitaker, a very proper bookkeeper in a Harlem funeral parlor, loses patience with two fellow workers and their antics, calling them "philistine heathens." "Man," one of the pranksters protests, "I'm not from Philly. Who you talkin' to?"—*A Rage in Harlem* (1991)

3055 Albert Brooks is killed in an auto accident. When he awakens, he meets Rip Torn and asks him if he is in Heaven. "No, this isn't Heaven." "Is it Hell?" "No, it isn't Hell either. Actually, there is no Hell—although I hear Los Angeles is getting pretty close."—*Defending Your Life* (1991)

Police

3056 Looking for a murder weapon, a police officer begins to search male cast members of a Broadway show. "What are you lookin' for, flatfoot?" an irate entertainer asks. "A gun." "If you had been more careful, you wouldn't have lost it."—*Forty Naughty Girls* (1937)

3057 Ham movie star and amateur sleuth Jack Oakie constantly ridicules the local police. "I read in the morning papers," he says to several officers, "where one of your boys caught a robber singlehanded. Of course, he was a new policeman on the force. I guess he didn't know any better."—*Super-Sleuth* (1937)

3058 A mayor storms into the press room of a city jail looking for his crooked sheriff. "Have you seen Sheriff Hartwell?" he shouts. "Well, it's hard to tell," reporter Cliff Edwards replies. "There are so many cockroaches around here." —*His Girl Friday* (1940)

3059 Police inspector Richard Lane arrives at an art gallery where an important auction is about to commence. "I didn't expect the department to send its best man," the gallery owner comments. "I'll bet you say that to all the cops," Lane jokes.—*Confessions of Boston Blackie* (1941)

3060 Amateur sleuth George Sanders and his assistant Allen Jenkins leave a

police precinct after wrapping up a complex murder case. "You're on your own now," Jenkins addresses the officers. "What a break for crime!"—*A Date with the Falcon* (1941)

3061 Police inspector James Gleason and his not-too-bright assistant Ed Gargan try to pressure amateur sleuth George Sanders' chauffeur Allen Jenkins into confessing his role in a recent murder. "We got enough on you to send you up for a hundred years," Gleason threatens. "We might even make it life," Gargan adds.—*The Falcon Takes Over* (1942)

3062 A police officer searches amateur sleuth Boston Blackie (Chester Morris) for a weapon. "Don't you know that people who carry guns must have inferiority complexes?" Morris quips. "Is that a fact?" the policeman responds. "And all the while I thought they only had to have permits."—*Boston Blackie's Chinese Venture* (1949)

3063 When reporter Allyn Joslyn, at a local bar, sounds off about his editor, calling him an "imbecile, half-baked nitwit," he invokes the interest of a fellow customer, an off-duty police officer. "I can't understand how a man with them qualifications," the officer wonders, "didn't get to be commissioner of police." —*It Shouldn't Happen to a Dog* (1958)

3064 "Inspector Clay's dead," observes a policeman. "Murdered. And somebody's responsible."—*Plan 9 from Outer Space* (1959)

3065 A narrator explains the relationship between petty criminals—pimps, prostitutes, hustlers—and the police of a particular section of Paris: "The attitude of the police is live and let live—and some of them make a pretty good living at it."—*Irma la Douce* (1963)

3066 When Arlo Guthrie illegally dumps a load of garbage over the side of a road in Stockbridge, Massachusetts, the incident becomes the town's crime of the century. Obie, a local cop, arrests and jails Guthrie and his buddy—but not before he confiscates their belts. "Kid," the officer explains, "we don't want any hangin's." "Obie," Guthrie returns, "do you think we're gonna hang ourselves for littering?"—*Alice's Restaurant* (1965)

3067 When tycoon Jerry Lewis meets with an underworld figure to arrange for the purchase of guns, the man denies any knowledge of the subject. Lewis has his secretary read aloud part of the mobster's background: "From 1928 to 1935 Mr. Colonico lived in Boston. He committed twelve murders, ran an extortion racket, and was a master at armed assault. Then Mr. Colonico quit the police department and came to New York."—*Which Way to the Front?* (1970)

3068 A police precinct comes under attack by a group of thieves who are using the assault as a diversion. The stunned police officer in charge deploys his forces and paraphrases President Johnson during the Vietnam War. "I'm not going to be the first American policeman to lose a station," he promises.—*The Hot Rock* (1972)

3069 Undercover cops Elliott Gould and Robert Blake, fed up with the power of a local drug lord and the corruption in their department, consider switching to the other side. "We could be good bad guys," suggests Gould. "The

pay is better, better hours, more cooperation from the police."—*Busting* (1974)

3070 Undercover cops Elliott Gould and Robert Blake arrest a hooker whose appointment book lists and rates the performance of her "Johns." Gould discovers two fellow cops have been her customers. "How did they do?" asks Blake. "Good." "Terrific," Blake breathes a sigh of relief. "I wouldn't want our department to get a bad name."—*Busting* (1974)

3071 When a patrol car receives an emergency call, the officer inside ejects a sexy young woman from the passenger seat and hurriedly drives off. "You coppers are all alike!" the disheveled woman cries out. "All holster and no gun!"—*Off Your Rocker* (1980)

3072 An angry crowd begins to gather outside a police precinct, and a policeman urgently breaks into the office of captain Edward Asner. "We got a bit of a riot building up, captain," he informs Asner. "Where?" the captain asks. "In The Bronx," the officer replies. "I wouldn't bother you if it was Philadelphia."—*Fort Apache, The Bronx* (1981)

3073 Two of their own have been shot, and a police clerk remarks to detective Nick Nolte that "there are a lot of bad people out there in the world." "Look at it this way," Nolte returns, "if there weren't, what would we be doing today?"—*48 Hours* (1982)

3074 To help capture a serial killer in a gay community, police officer Ryan O'Neal is selected to pose as a gay lover—much to his dissatisfaction. "Why did you choose me for the job?" he asks his superior. "Because you're a good cop—and you have a cute ass." —*Partners* (1982)

3075 When harried schoolteacher Marsha Mason reports at a police precinct that her beat-up car has been stolen, an officer asks for a description of the vehicle. "The parking lights don't work," she says. "That's a violation," he announces mechanically. "Well, when you catch the thief, you can give him a ticket." – *Max Dugan Returns* (1983)

3076 Government law-enforcement functionary Kurtwood Smith confides to Texas border patrol officer Kris Kristofferson: "Every morning I wake up and thank God for drugs and subversion and murder – because without them we'd all be out of a job." – *Flashpoint* (1984)

3077 Chicago cops Billy Crystal and Gregory Hines chase a suspect to his apartment where he blocks their entrance by pressing his body against the door. "I have this gun here," Hines addresses the young hoodlum on the other side. "I'm gonna take this gun out and I'm gonna shoot a lot of holes in this door. If you're standing in front of the door, what can I tell you? Some of the holes are gonna be in you." – *Running Scared* (1986)

3078 Pompous, strait-laced police officer Dan Aykroyd and his partner Tom Hanks, working under cover, pose as members of a secret cult at one of its outdoor meetings. In disguise, they watch as the masked leader begins the evening's ritual. "Prepare the virgin," the leader calls out. "'Prepare the virgin,'" Hanks echoes while looking at his partner. "I don't like the sound of that. Let's just hope they're not referring to you." – *Dragnet* (1987)

3079 A hail of bullets almost claims the life of police officer Mel Gibson, who is saved by his bulletproof vest. "Two inches higher they would have gotten your head," remarks his partner Danny Glover after examining the vest. "Yeah," Gibson adds, "two inches lower I would have been a falsetto for life." – *Lethal Weapon* (1987)

3080 Police officer Richard Dreyfuss and his partner get a particularly bad stakeout assignment in a dingy abandoned house. "What the hell did we do to deserve this?" Dreyfuss's pal asks. "It was the stripper we sent to the captain on his birthday," Dreyfuss offers. "I told you we should have sent the woman." – *Stakeout* (1987)

3081 "I hear police work is dangerous," a sultry blonde secretary says to police detective Leslie Nielsen. "It is," he acknowledges. "That's why I carry a big gun." "Aren't you afraid it might go off accidentally?" "I used to have that problem." "What did you do about it?" "I would just think about baseball." – *The Naked Gun* (1988)

3082 Undercover cop Kiefer Sutherland, pursued by a Native American (Lou Diamond Phillips), at one point stops an elderly woman in the street and asks her if there is an "Indian" chasing him. "Yeah," the suspicious pedestrian replies, "a whole tribe." – *Renegades* (1989)

3083 Police officer Bruce Willis, in pursuit of criminals at an airport, apprehends an employee who has one of their "beepers." "How about giving me twenty bucks for it?" "How about I let you live?" "The man knows how to negotiate," the employee says as he surrenders the beeper. – *Die Hard 2* (1990)

3084 "You know what you guys in vice ought to do?" suggests a fellow police officer to detective Gene Hackman. "Every time you bust a whore, you ought to paint a little tit on the side of your car to keep score." – *Loose Cannons* (1990)

3085 Veteran police officer Clint Eastwood is saddled with a new partner, rookie Charlie Sheen, who is quick to draw his gun, holstered at his hip. "Why don't you holster that thing?" Clintwood advises. "In fact, why don't you get yourself a shoulder holster? You don't want to go around half-cocked, do you?" – *The Rookie* (1990)

3086 Police detective Leslie Nielsen wonders why a suspect is spending much of his time in a red light district. "Sex?" a fellow officer suggests. "No, not right now," Nielsen replies. "We got work to do." – *The Naked Gun 2 1/2: The Smell of Fear* (1991)

3087 To avenge his cop-brother's murder, drifter Christian Slater joins the police force but finds the physical training exhausting. During one running exercise, he drops out and approaches the drill instructor. "Why are we running?" he complains. "Don't we always ride?" – *Kuffs* (1992)

3088 Undercover cop Mel Gibson has just knocked senseless a dangerous criminal. "You have the right to remain unconscious," he addresses his captive, adding: "Anything you say ain't gonna be much." – *Lethal Weapon 3* (1992)

Politics and Politicians

3089 "Pocahontas saved John Smith," an Indian reminds Eddie Cantor. "Why didn't he do something for his brother Al?" Cantor quips, referring to New York Governor Alfred Smith, who in 1928 lost the Presidential election to Herbert Hoover. – *Whoopee!* (1930)

3090 "The first thing I learned in politics," admits Judge Priest (Will Rogers), "is when to say 'ain't.'" – *Judge Priest* (1934)

3091 "There's a picture down the street where the villain kidnaps a politician and tortures him with a red hot poker," Fred Allen says. "It sounds like the sort of thing I'd enjoy seeing." – *Thanks a Million* (1935)

3092 Singer Dick Powell has antagonized a group of state politicians, and his boss, band manager Fred Allen, fears reprisals. "A woman scorned has no fury like a politician who's been double-crossed," warns Allen. – *Thanks a Million* (1935)

3093 Band manager Fred Allen introduces himself to a group of small-town politicians. "Always happy to see a politician with his hands in his own pocket," he says to one politico. – *Thanks a Million* (1935)

3094 Joan Fontaine leads a small political rally for the local mayor. Preston Foster speaks out, calling Mayor Olsen corrupt and a scoundrel. "Perhaps you don't know who I am?" Fontaine asks him. "No, I don't." "I'm Trudy Olsen, Mayor Olsen's daughter." "Perhaps you don't know who I am?" Foster asks. "No, I don't." "Well, thank heaven for that!" Foster quips. – *You Can't Beat Love* (1937)

3095 Governor John Barrymore, on the telephone with an architect, turns to college president Donald Meek, standing nearby, and asks him what style architecture he prefers for the new football stadium. "Classic Greek would be most appropriate," Meek states. "Classic Greek," Barrymore repeats into the telephone. "Get some of the Greek boys down in the Sixth Ward to help you." – *Hold That Co-ed* (1938)

3096 Corrupt Governor John Barrymore delights in the series of football victories achieved at his state's college until he learns that some of the players are professionals hired by one of his cronies. "We shouldn't let a little technicality like this upset us," he says to football coach George Murphy. "Let's keep a skeleton like this in our own little closet." "Do you think there's room for it?"

Murphy questions. – *Hold That Co-ed* (1938)

3097 Una Merkel: "Do you believe in reincarnation – like dead people coming back?" Bob Hope: "You mean like the Republicans?" – *The Cat and the Canary* (1939)

3098 Political stooge William Demarest reads the details of a newspaper headline about dozens of indictments in a city hall shakeup and treats the news incredulously. "If it wasn't for graft," he comments, "you get a very low type of people in politics – men with ambition, jellyfish." – *The Great McGinty* (1940)

3099 Bob Hope and Bing Crosby bring in a marlin during their fishing venture. "It's still alive!" Hope cries. "It won't give up!" adds Crosby. "He must be a Republican," concludes Hope. – *Road to Singapore* (1940)

3100 Bing Crosby: "He's a philanthropist." Bob Hope: "I don't care who he votes for." – *Road to Zanzibar* (1941)

3101 Bob Hope accuses his pal Bing Crosby of reneging on his promise he made to Aunt Lucy to look after Hope. "The dead have a way of coming back, you know," Hope warns. "Get out," Crosby says. "When they're dead, they're dead." "Not Aunt Lucy," Hope argues. "She was a Republican." – *Road to Morocco* (1942)

3102 Rookie Wally Brown and two of his buddies try to escape from an army hospital. "I'm going to see what's around the corner," one suggests. "I hope it's prosperity," Brown quips. – *Adventures of a Rookie* (1943)

3103 Politics is a very peculiar thing," explains William Demarest. "If they want you, they want you. They don't need no reasons anymore. They find their own reasons. It's just like when a girl wants a man." – *Hail the Conquering Hero* (1944)

3104 "It's no use," laments an elderly amateur thief. "When I lie, everybody knows it. Maybe I ought to go into politics where it doesn't matter." – *Heartbeat* (1946)

3105 Dorothy Lamour is put under the hypnotic spell of Gale Sondergaard. "I find myself saying things, and I don't know why I'm saying them," she confides to Bob Hope and Bing Crosby. "Why don't you run for Congress and leave us alone?" Hope suggests. – *Road to Rio* (1947)

3106 Publisher Lee J. Cobb confides to journalist Tyrone Power that he wants to enter politics. "You know the oldest and noblest occupation of them all?" "I think so." "I mean politics," Cobb clarifies. "Well, you'll admit there are certain points of similarity." – *The Luck of the Irish* (1948)

3107 Producer Robert Montgomery grouses to playwright John Payne: "Our theater cannot compete with life in these melodramatic times. Politicians have stolen our tricks and blown them up into earth-sized, untidy productions and discarded the happy ending." – *The Saxon Charm* (1948)

3108 Political party boss Adolphe Menjou is approached by wealthy backer Angela Lansbury, who is willing to invest in his candidate's campaign. "What's your stake in all this?" Menjou asks. "I want nothing." "People who want nothing worry me," Menjou says. "The price isn't right." – *State of the Union* (1948)

3109 Publisher Angela Lansbury has backed candidate Spencer Tracy for the Presidency. "He is beginning to wonder if there's any difference between the Democratic and the Republican party," she says to party boss Adolphe Menjou. "That's a fine question for a Presidential candidate to ask," Menjou replies. "There's all the difference in the world. They're in and we're out." – *State of the Union* (1948)

3110 Amateur sleuth Boston Blackie (Chester Morris), in the course of investigating a murder, impersonates a drunk at a bar. "I'm a prestidigitator," he announces. "I don't know about that," the bartender replies. "I've always been a Democrat myself." – *Boston Blackie's Chinese Venture* (1949)

3111 Bob Hope to Lucille Ball: "Presidents can be fooled. They vote for themselves, don't they?" – *Fancy Pants* (1950)

3112 During the Mexican Revolution, Pancho Villa wins in the North while Zapata (Marlon Brando) triumphs in the South. At their victorious meeting, Villa asks Zapata if he can read and the latter nods. "You're the President," Villa states decisively. – *Viva Zapata!* (1952)

3113 Recently elected New York City mayor Jimmy Walker (Bob Hope) disregards a list of office seekers and invites an independent reporter to join his staff. "I didn't even vote for you," the reporter admits. "Why do you want an enemy in your own office?" "I just got a good look at my friends." – *Beau James* (1957)

3114 During the early 1930s New York Mayor Jimmy Walker's administration comes under fire with charges of corruption, and Fiorello LaGuardia's challenge is heard off-screen: "I could run on a laundry ticket and beat those political bums anytime." – *Beau James* (1957)

3115 Political boss Frank Skeffington (Spencer Tracy) lies on his deathbed. "There's one thing we can be sure of," remarks a long-time foe. "If he had to do it all over again, there's no doubt in the world he'd do it very, very differently." "Like hell I would," the crusty Tracy murmurs. – *The Last Hurrah* (1958)

3116 East German communist firebrand Horst Buchholz makes his case against the West's economic structure: "Capitalism is like a dead herring in the moonlight – it shines, but it stinks." – *One, Two, Three* (1961)

3117 Peter Ustinov, President of Concordia, a small European community, is accosted by a battery of reporters as he leaves U.N. headquarters in New York City. "Where is Concordia?" a reporter inquires. "Why should I tell you?" Ustinov replies. "Maybe the reason it still survives is because no one can find it." – *Romanoff and Juliet* (1961)

3118 "In an atomic age, it's wiser to remain a small target," Peter Ustinov remarks. – *Romanoff and Juliet* (1961)

3119 Political low-life Bill Russell (Cliff Robertson) competes for his party's nomination for the Presidency. "The women are behind Bill Russell," someone remarks. "Under him is their more usual position," another comments. – *The Best Man* (1964)

3120 First woman President of the U.S. Polly Bergen, becoming pregnant and forced to leave office, analyzes the sex vote with "First Man" Fred MacMurray. "Do you realize," he says, "that it took forty million women to get you into the White House – " "And one man to get me out," she interjects. – *Kisses for My President* (1964)

3121 A prison warden asks inmate Peter Ustinov why he chose to embezzle funds from the Conservative Central Office. "I'm a Conservative," Ustinov explains. – *Hot Millions* (1968)

3122 The facade of an entire western town and cardboard inhabitants have been erected overnight. "These people are dummies," someone points out to governor Mel Brooks. "I know that," he returns. "How do you think I got elected?" – *Blazing Saddles* (1974)

3123 "You know the ethics those guys have," Woody Allen says of politicians. "It's a notch below child molester." – *Annie Hall* (1977)

3124 Detective Richard Dreyfuss on a political candidate: "I thought my razor was dull before I heard him speak."
– The Big Fix (1978)

3125 Unemployed and depressed circus clown Jerry Lewis comes to live with his married sister who hopefully offers: "They must need clowns somewhere." "Sure," responds Lewis, "but who wants to get into politics?" *– Hardly Working* (1981)

3126 Three detectives on stakeout of a high-priced hooker watch her at work with a powerful candidate for governor. "He has his head in her crotch!" exclaims the first officer. "I ask you," says the second, "should that man be governor?" "That's the human touch," quips the third. *– Sharky's Machine* (1981)

3127 Russian policeman Arnold Schwarzenegger, on temporary assignment in Chicago, relates to local cop James Belushi that in the Soviet Union drug dealers and users are rounded up and summarily shot. "It'll never work here," Belushi educes. "The politicians would never go for it." "Shoot them first," his Russian counterpart advises. *– Red Heat* (1988)

3128 Paul Newman, as powerful Governor of Louisiana Earl Long, is accused of "buying" politicians. "I never bought a Congressman in my life!" he bellows. "I rent them – it's cheaper." *– Blaze* (1990)

3129 "You are singlehandedly responsible for the whole resurgence of political humor for my generation," a sexy college graduate greets outspoken political cartoonist Gene Wilder. "Thanks," Wilder replies, "but I think you have to give a little credit to Ronald Reagan and maybe Dan Quayle." *– Funny About Love* (1990)

3130 Police lieutenant Leslie Nielsen, while pursuing a murderer, accidentally crashes through a zoo wall, allowing all the animals to escape. That evening, at a cocktail party, the police commissioner reproaches him. "Do you realize that because of you this city is being overrun by baboons?" "Isn't that the fault of the voters?" *– The Naked Gun 2 1/2: The Smell of Fear* (1991)

3131 Congressional candidate John Cusack reminds his Department of Justice friend James Spader about surviving in Washington: "There are only two things that could wreck a man's career: getting caught with a live boy or a dead girl." *– True Colors* (1991)

3132 At a veterans' hospital where shortages, bureaucracy and ineptness are commonplace, several rebellious doctors raid the research department for supplies – and wonder why the lab containing monkeys is so well equipped. "I guess they vote Republican," a doctor cracks. *– Article 99* (1992)

Poverty

3133 Bert Wheeler and Robert Woolsey are down and out on their luck. "Have you ever stopped to wonder what you would do if you had Rockefeller's money?" Wheeler asks. "No, but I've stopped to wonder what he'd do if he had mine." *– Caught Plastered* (1931)

3134 Groucho Marx touts his credentials to prospective employer Rockliffe Fellowes: "I've worked myself up from nothing to a state of extreme poverty." *– Monkey Business* (1931)

3135 In rural Italy struggling tavern owner Henry Armetta forbids his daughter to marry an impoverished soldier; instead, he arranges for her to marry a wealthier prospect. "But father," she pleads, "I love Lorenzo. I'm not afraid of poverty." "But I am," replies Armetta. – *The Devil's Brother* (1933)

3136 Three unemployed, penniless showgirls sharing an apartment hear a knock on their door. It is Ginger Rogers, a fellow trouper. "Who did you think it was–the wolf?" she jokes. "If it was, we'd eat it," quips Joan Blondell. – *Gold Diggers of 1933* (1933)

3137 "I wasn't always rich," Mae West confides to her maid (Louise Beavers). "There was a time when I didn't know where my next husband was coming from." – *She Done Him Wrong* (1933)

3138 Mae West and her maid Louise Beavers discuss their experiences with poverty. "But you ain't been in the circumstances where de wolf was at your door," the maid asserts. "The wolf at my door?" West questions. "Why, I remember when he came into my room and had pups." – *She Done Him Wrong* (1933)

3139 Bert Wheeler and Robert Woolsey, down on their luck, pose as millionaires to impress their girlfriends Dorothy Lee and Thelma Todd. The boys telephone to say they can't keep their date because they're riding with the hounds. "Yeah," Wheeler quips to Woolsey in the phone booth, "we're going to the dogs." – *Hips, Hips, Hooray* (1934)

3140 Rich, spoiled Carole Lombard accidentally meets down-and-out homeless tramp William Powell, who resides in the city dump and finds him interesting. "Can you tell me why you live in a place like this when there are so many other nice places?" "Because my real estate agent thought the altitude would be very good for my asthma," he quips. – *My Man Godfrey* (1936)

3141 "My little plum," W. C. Fields says to adopted daughter Poppy (Rochelle Hudson), "I am like Robin Hood; I take from the rich and give to the poor." "What poor?" "Us poor," Fields replies. – *Poppy* (1936)

3142 Arriving at a train depot followed by an entourage of porters carrying his luggage, Groucho Marx asks them if they have change for ten cents. When they shake their heads, he says, "Well, keep the baggage." – *Go West* (1940)

3143 Major Barbara (Wendy Hiller), in charge of a Salvation Army kitchen, introduces her wealthy father, Undershaft (Robert Morley), to a destitute but proud worker. "Poverty, my friend, isn't a thing to be proud of," the industrialist asserts. "I wouldn't have your conscience, not for all your income," the poor man replies. "And I wouldn't have your income, not for all your conscience." – *Major Barbara* (1941)

3144 Red Skelton: "He's so poor he don't have a pair of shoestrings that match." – *DuBarry Was a Lady* (1943)

3145 "If the poor can get satisfaction out of being proud," offers Frank Morgan, "why not? It costs nothing." – *Casanova Brown* (1944)

3146 Penniless Groucho Marx tries to sneak into his hotel but is caught and forced to make out a check for his back rent. "You didn't sign it," the desk clerk points out. "Naturally," Groucho replies. "Without your signature it's worthless." "That's what you think," Groucho tries to explain. "It's perfectly good now, but if I sign it, it *would* be worthless." – *Copacabana* (1947)

3147 Board members confront Charles Coburn, dean of a small Catholic university, and inform him that his school is in debt for $170,000. "When I take the vow of poverty," Coburn says, "I go all the way." – *Trouble Along the Way* (1953)

3148 Wealthy college student George Hamilton and financially strapped Jim

Hutton discuss girls and marriage during their spring vacation in Fort Lauderdale. "They don't realize what a risk marriage is for a man," Hamilton says. "Not for you," Hutton adds. "You can afford to be wrong. I can't even afford to be right."—*Where the Boys Are* (1960)

3149 Tony Randall: "What is this obsession you have with girls?" Rock Hudson: "Remember, I was a poor kid. I didn't have toys to play with."—*Lover Come Back* (1961)

3150 Impoverished East German youth Horst Buchholz marries flighty Atlanta Southerner Pamela Tiffin, who is accustomed to the good life. "We'll have breakfast in bed," he promises his bride, "also lunch and also dinner." "Lunch and dinner, too?" she questions. "There are no table and chairs."—*One, Two, Three* (1961)

3151 Financially pressed Broadway producer Zero Mostel, dressed like a man of substance, including an ivory-tipped cane, invites accountant Gene Wilder to dine "alfresco"—and takes him to a hot dog stand. "This is alfresco?" a disappointed Wilder asks. "Excellent!" Mostel exclaims after tasting a hot dog. "Please send my compliments to the chef." "Please send half-a-buck," the vendor replies.—*The Producers* (1968)

3152 A peasant in a Ukrainian village declares: "If the rich could get others to die for them—we, the poor, would make a nice living."—*Fiddler on the Roof* (1971)

3153 "It's no shame in being poor," Tevye (Topol) the milkman says to the Lord, "but it's no great honor either." —*Fiddler on the Roof* (1971)

3154 Aerospace engineer George Segal loses his job, and his wife (Jane Fonda) informs him that they are dead broke. "We don't have any assets?" he asks. "Other than the sun in the morning and the moon at night," she replies whimsically.—*Fun with Dick and Jane* (1977)

3155 Struggling prizefighter Harry Hamlin needs thousands of dollars to send his sister to Vienna for an eye operation. On a tenement roof he confides his dilemma to his girlfriend. "You know what they charge for an eye?" he says. "An arm and a leg."—*Movie Movie* (1978)

3156 Impoverished Steve Martin writes to his adopted parents that to stay alive he has been giving pints of blood in exchange for meals. He ends the letter with the following: "I decided to quit when I cut myself shaving and nothing came out but air."—*The Jerk* (1979)

3157 Cloris Leachman, as a ragged French peasant during the reign of Louis XVI, declares: "We are zo poor we don't even 'ave a language, joost a stoopid accent."—*History of the World—Part I* (1981)

3158 Widowed schoolteacher Marsha Mason invites her peripatetic father (Jason Robards), who has only a few months to live, to move in with her and her teenage son Mike. "You can live here with Mike and me for as long as you want," she offers. "All three of us living on your salary," he muses. "Heart failure doesn't frighten me, but malnutrition does."—*Max Dugan Returns* (1983)

Prejudice

3159 A brutal, bigoted Southerner threatens Al Jolson, as the jockey Gus. "You're scared," a fellow black man rebukes Jolson. "You're just a coward." "Now wait a minute," Jolson objects. "He called *me* a coward. He didn't say anything about any of my kin."—*Big Boy* (1930)

3160 Groucho Marx to a Native American: "If you don't like this country, go back to where you came from."—*Monkey Business* (1931)

3161 Dentist Bert Wheeler and assistant Robert Woolsey are captured by hostile Native Americans. "That's the trouble with this country," Wheeler muses, "too many foreigners."—*Silly Billies* (1936)

3162 Irish bartender to customer Dr. Kildare (Lew Ayres): "I don't care what nationality a man is—as long as he's Irish."—*Young Dr. Kildare* (1938)

3163 "Don't the French accept the half-castes?" an American tourist in pre–World War II Saigon asks missionary Ernest Cossart. "No," replies Cossart, "they only create them."—*Lady of the Tropics* (1939)

3164 When boss Mr. Dithers (Jonathan Hale) learns that Blondie (Penny Singleton) is on voluntary patrol as a fire watcher at a local dam, he expresses strong disapproval to her husband, Dagwood (Arthur Lake). "It's up to you," he orders, "to convince Blondie a woman's place is in the home, not by a dam site."—*Blondie for Victory* (1942)

3165 A matronly woman from a family steeped in riches remarks: "I don't mind being equal with anybody as long as they don't start being equal with me." —*This Above All* (1942)

3166 A traditional pillar of Boston society, family man Ronald Colman learns that his son is receiving letters from a love-interest outside of Boston. "Oh, good heavens!" Colman exclaims. "It's postmarked Worcester! The girl's a foreigner!"—*The Late George Apley* (1947)

3167 J. Carrol Naish, as Sitting Bull, is censorious of the white man's reporting of the fighting: "When the white men win a battle they call it victory. But when we win they call it a massacre." —*Sitting Bull* (1954)

3168 An old bigoted Southern landowner has daily confrontations with his college-educated son who believes in integration and African Americans' rights. The father fumes at this talk of "Nigras'" rights. "Four years in college," he grumbles to his son, "and you still can't say the word right."—*Gone Are the Days* (1963)

3169 Eight G.I.s during World War II billet down in a luxurious French castle. "Do you think my living here will lower the real estate value?" a black soldier quips.—*Castle Keep* (1969)

3170 A white mayor attempts to cool some overheated black demonstrators: "We've given you everything you needed! I let you use the swimming pool every Fourth of July!"—*Medium Cool* (1969)

3171 In a Ukrainian village at the turn of the century, a judge says to a local village milkman (Topol): "You're an honest and decent man—even though you are a Jew." "Thank you, your honor," Topol replies. "It's not often that a man receives such a compliment." —*Fiddler on the Roof* (1971)

3172 Joseph Bologna, who has just graduated from college, berates his father (Paul Sorvino) for interfering with his future plans. "I just figured you needed some pull," Sorvino explains, "graduating at twenty-nine and majoring in 'colored people's studies.'" "It's African studies!" Bologna explodes, "and if I hear one more bigoted remark from you, you'll never see me again!"
—*Made for Each Other* (1971)

3173 Several G.I.s are separated from their units and are lost during a battle with the Germans. One soldier asks for suggestions. "We could surrender," Billy Pilgrim (Michael Sacks) proposes. "Listen," the soldier says, "me and the corporal and the Dago—we're Americans. We don't surrender. You got that?"—*Slaughterhouse Five* (1972)

3174 Hooded members of the Ku Klux Klan approach a bus of orphan kids driven by Richard Pryor. "They're all blind," Pryor explains in an effort to protect his charges. "We're going to the Ray Charles Institute for the Blind."
—*Bustin' Loose* (1981)

3175 The President has appointed the first woman to the Supreme Court, and justice Walter Matthau resents the move. "It's like the Jesuits going coed," he quips to his fellow justices.—*First Monday in October* (1981)

3176 Hired killer Kathleen Turner quotes her ex-husband to Italian-American gangster Jack Nicholson: "The Sicilians would rather eat their children than part with money—and they're very fond of their children."—*Prizzi's Honor* (1985)

3177 Ally Sheedy, the spoiled daughter of a millionaire, is forced to work as a maid but has difficulty getting along with her coworkers. "I don't know how to talk to maids," she confesses to the black cook. "I know just how you feel," the cook answers sardonically. "One once tried to move into my neighborhood."—*Maid to Order* (1987)

3178 F.B.I. agent Rick Moranis offers hoodlum Steve Martin, who is under the witness protection program, tickets to a baseball game. "You folks would probably be Yankee fans," Moranis presumes. "It's been my experience that most organized crime people are."—*My Blue Heaven* (1990)

3179 An English researcher discovers the next person in line to sit on the throne and reports to the royal secretary (Peter O'Toole). "He has his strengths and his weaknesses," the clerk states. "You see, he's an American." "Quickly," O'Toole asks, "the strengths." —*King Ralph* (1991)

3180 A bigoted salesman in a chic men's clothing store rejects the patronage of customer Eddie Murphy. "We don't have layaway," he snipes. "And we don't keep cash in the store." —*Boomerang* (1992)

3181 Fast-talking, two-bit lawyer Robert De Niro is accused by an incensed bar patron of philandering with his wife. A fight ensues and De Niro is tossed out into the street with the epithet "Jewish bastard." "I'm not Jewish!" he fires back.—*Night and the City* (1992)

3182 New Yorker Luis Caballero gripes about police logic: "If you're Puerto Rican and have a beautiful white woman in your car, you're selling drugs. If you have an ugly white woman in your car, you must be using drugs." —*Puerto Rican Mambo* (1992)

Prostitution

3183 A World War I army officer in France studies the local maps of a province and bellows: "Bring me the lay of the land!" Doughboy El Brendel responds by presenting the local prostitute. – *The Cock-Eyed World* (1929)

3184 At a dinner party social-climber Jean Harlow tries to ingratiate herself with dowager Marie Dressler. "I was reading a book the other day –" Harlow begins. "Reading a book?" the surprised Dressler interjects. "Yes, it's all about civilization or something," Harlow continues. "You know, the guy said that machinery is going to take the place of every profession." "Oh, my dear," retorts Dressler after perusing Harlow, "that is something *you* need never worry about." – *Dinner at Eight* (1933)

3185 Mae West, the Belle of the Bowery, steps out of her carriage and swaggers down the street under the appreciative wide-eyed stares of saloon patrons. "A fine woman," one assesses. "One of the finest women that ever walked the streets," another adds. – *She Done Him Wrong* (1933)

3186 Groucho Marx enters a western saloon and recognizes one of the bar girls. "Lulubelle, it's you!" he exclaims. "I didn't recognize you standing up." – *Go West* (1940)

3187 "I started at Amherst," muses high-class prostitute Elizabeth Taylor, "and I worked my way through the alphabet to Yale. I'm stuck there." – *Butterfield 8* (1960)

3188 Naive gendarme Jack Lemmon, his first day on duty in a Paris district noted for its prostitutes, observes streetwalker Irma la Douce (Shirley MacLaine) walking her dog without a leash. "Pardon me," he approaches her. "Do you have a license?" "No," she replies, thinking he is inquiring about her profession. "It's a violation of Ordinance No. 56," he explains. "Well, usually they let us get away with it." "Not me!" he objects. "And another thing: You're supposed to keep it on a leash." "On a leash?" MacLaine exclaims. – *Irma la Douce* (1963)

3189 Shirley MacLaine, as Irma, a sweet Parisian prostitute, says apologetically to Jack Lemmon, whom she had met earlier: "Sorry, I never remember a face." – *Irma la Douce* (1963)

3190 English aristocrat Sophia Loren reminisces about her early years when, as a young woman, she worked as a laundress for a French house of prostitution. She describes the wanton women as an international mixture. "Oh, I see," her English companion concludes, "a sort of finishing school." "Is that what they call them in England?" Loren inquires. – *Lady L* (1965)

3191 Prostitute Lee Grant caters chiefly to disgruntled and neglected husbands in her apartment and knows her clients well. "Men don't grow up," she muses, "they just grow old." – *Divorce, American Style* (1967)

3192 Dance-hall hostess Shirley MacLaine tells her fellow workers that she's gone sweet on a very decent fellow. "Have you told him that you're in the rent-a-body business?" one hostess asks. "I told him! I told him!" MacLaine emphatically exclaims. "When?" another skeptically asks. "Tomorrow, that's when I told him." – *Sweet Charity* (1969)

3193 Call girl Barbra Streisand claims she turned only a few tricks, and those only in an emergency and with the best clientele. "I may be a prostitute," she admits, "but I'm not promiscuous." – *The Owl and the Pussycat* (1970)

3194 Writer George Segal and hooker Barbra Streisand, originally neighbors, soon become friendly enemies. "You're a fine example of capitalism at its most efficient," he says sarcastically. "You merely take natural resources, add the cost of labor and sell the product for a reasonable profit." – *The Owl and the Pussycat* (1970)

3195 Enterprising housewife Barbra Streisand reluctantly turns hooker to help her husband raise money. "I've never cheated before, you know," she explains to her madam (Molly Picon). "Cheated?" the elderly madam echoes. "Cheating is when it's for fun. This is business, like a doctor seeing a patient." – *For Pete's Sake* (1974)

3196 Ambulance driver Bill Cosby, during a visit to a sex parlor, asks what a "Tahitian titillation" is. "That's the same thing you're getting," a young woman replies, "except that I wear a sarong." – *Mother, Jugs and Speed* (1976)

3197 Teenager Brooke Shields and photographer Keith Carradine plan to marry and go to a preacher who must fill out the proper form. He asks about Shields' mother, who has abandoned her. "And she was a Caucasian or other?" "She was a whore." – *Pretty Baby* (1978)

3198 Chief inspector Clouseau (Peter Sellers) narrowly escapes assassination although the press announces his death. He returns to his apartment to find that Kato, his servant, has turned it into an elaborate brothel. "So," Sellers angrily charges, "as a tribute to my memory, you open up this Chinese nookie factory!" "I had to do something to keep busy," Kato rationalizes. – *Revenge of the Pink Panther* (1978)

3199 Lesley-Anne Down, as a high-class prostitute, promises a nervous

customer: "I will take care of every little thing – and every big thing." – *The Great Train Robbery* (1979)

3200 Three women, having problems with their husbands or ex-husbands, find themselves strapped for money. They suggest different plans to raise hard cash. "Why don't we just become hookers and run a hotel room?" one suggests. "We'd starve to death," another replies. "There's twelve thousand college girls in this town giving it away." – *How to Beat the High Cost of Living* (1980)

3201 Dom DeLuise shocks his friend George Segal when he announces that his third wife is a hooker. "I mean," DeLuise adds, "it's not so terrible, really. At least I know where she is at night." – *The Last Married Couple in America* (1980)

3202 Broadway gambling figure Bob Newhart recommends a woman to look after an orphan to friend Walter Matthau. "She always kept a very clean house," Newhart explains. "She wouldn't even let her girls smoke." "This is a whole different kind of house," Matthau quickly corrects him. – *Little Miss Marker* (1980)

3203 Crusading newspaper columnist John Belushi meets many admirers as he walks the streets of his beloved Chicago. "That was a great piece!" a prostitute calls out to him, referring to his latest column. "It's about time you said that about *me!*" he returns. – *Continental Divide* (1981)

3204 Private detective Steve Martin's latest case takes him to a seedy part of the city, and he describes the neighborhood as follows: "It was a street of frustrated hopes and broken dreams. Everything was cheap and cut-rate. Even the prostitutes were having a sale." – *Dead Men Don't Wear Plaid* (1982)

3205 In a posh restaurant where several hookers are dining, one regales the others with her latest role-playing act in which she is dressed as a sailor. "It's 1931 and we're in a long bar in Shanghai–" "That sounds like fun," another interjects. "Until we play 'find the gunboat,'" the first speaker continues. *– Doctor Detroit* (1983)

3206 Naive professor Dan Aykroyd innocently befriends a bevy of hookers and asks: "You're in the entertainment business?" "Well," one call girl replies thoughtfully, "you could call it public service." *– Doctor Detroit* (1983)

3207 Naive professor Dan Aykroyd asks a bevy of prostitutes: "Where did all this money come from?" "The old-fashioned way," one of the hookers quips. "We earned it." *– Doctor Detroit* (1983)

3208 In Vienna a prostitute boasts to Steve Martin that she is an American. "I guess you could say I'm a member of the Peace Corps," she adds. *– The Man with Two Brains* (1983)

3209 Business-minded prostitute Jamie Lee Curtis confides to Dan Aykroyd: "I've saved forty-two grand,

and it's in T-bills earning interest. I figure I've got three more years on my back and I'll have enough to retire on." *– Trading Places* (1983)

3210 A New York assistant district attorney picks up a prostitute for questioning and takes her to his swank apartment for questioning. He notices that she is impressed with the building. "It's got a waiting list to get in," he says. "Yeah," she replies. "I got the same problem. *– Street Smart* (1987)

3211 Hooker Julia Roberts asks business tycoon Richard Gere about the people in the companies he is buying and selling. "People have nothing to do with it," he explains. "It's strictly business." "Oh," she perks up, "then you do the same thing I do." *– Pretty Woman* (1990)

3212 Milquetoast East European clerk Woody Allen becomes acquainted with circus sword swallower Mia Farrow, who confesses to him that though she has just slept with a student for seven hundred dollars, she is not a whore. "Do I care what your hobbies are?" Allen shrugs. *– Shadows and Fog* (1992)

Psychiatry

3213 Jimmy Durante and Buster Keaton go to a banker–who knows Durante–to borrow money for a business. "Do you know your partner long?" the man asks Durante. "Yeah," Durante replies, "we were shell-shocked over in France, but I got over mine." *– What! No Beer?* (1933)

3214 Bert Wheeler confides to Robert Woolsey that he is a kleptomaniac. "Well," counsels Woolsey, "take something for it!" "I've already taken everything," replies Wheeler. *– Cockeyed Cavaliers* (1934)

3215 "I'm a psychiatrist," George Brent introduces himself to Alan Mowbray. "Do you know anything about psychiatry?" "No," replies Mowbray, "only that it's expensive." *– In Person* (1935)

3216 "I like the cuckoos," admits one asylum guard to a fellow officer. "They're the same as everyone else, only they're smart enough to admit they're nuts." *– Charlie Chan at the Opera* (1936)

3217 Merle Oberon reluctantly visits the office of Park Avenue psychoanalyst

Alan Mowbray and asserts: "I'm sure there's absolutely nothing wrong with me." "I'm sure you'll think differently after you leave this office," he counters. –*That Uncertain Feeling* (1941)

3218 Patient Merle Oberon, faced with marital problems, admits to psychoanalyst Alan Mowbry that she has trouble sleeping whereas her husband sleeps very well. "Aha!" Mowbray comments suggestively. "Are you trying to break up my marriage?" she questions. "No," he answers confidently, "only wake up your husband." –*That Uncertain Feeling* (1941)

3219 "Women make the best psychoanalysts till they fall in love," a psychoanalyst teases colleague Ingrid Bergman. "After that, they make the best patients." –*Spellbound* (1945)

3220 A psychiatrist in the employ of mobsters tries to convince private eye Bob Hope that a Miss Montaigne (Dorothy Lamour) is unbalanced. "For the past six months," the doctor begins, "Miss Montaigne has been suffering from an acute form of schizophrenia accompanied by visual aberrations with increasingly severe paranoiac delusions." "And how is she mentally?" Hope inquires. –*My Favorite Brunette* (1947)

3221 When private detective Lou Costello tries to tell the police about a man disappearing before his eyes, they send him to the precinct psychiatrist. "Do you always see things?" the doctor questions him. "Only with my eyes open," Costello responds. –*Abbott and Costello Meet the Invisible Man* (1951)

3222 "Do you know where the subconscious man comes from?" a psychiatrist asks Lou Costello. "The subway?" Costello hazards a guess. –*Abbott and Costello Meet the Invisible Man* (1951)

3223 "The doctor thinks my cold might possibly be caused by psychology," Vivian Blaine explains to boyfriend Nathan

Detroit (Frank Sinatra). "How does he know you got psychology?" Sinatra asks. –*Guys and Dolls* (1955)

3224 Actor Dan Dailey says to psychoanalyst David Niven, who is seeing Dailey's wife: "Any psychoanalyst who would take a woman for a patient should see a psychoanalyst." –*Oh, Men! Oh, Women!* (1957)

3225 Straitlaced psychoanalyst David Niven, who is having problems with fiancée Barbara Rush, over-intellectualizes everything and refuses to respond to his emotions. His old friend and former professor tries to enlighten him. "As a very wise old man once said," the professor begins, "–it was myself, now that I come to think of it–'the distance between the library and the bedroom is astronomical.'" –*Oh, Men! Oh, Women!* (1957)

3226 Advertising executive Henry Jones confides to coworker Tony Randall that he takes his teenage daughter to a psychoanalyst three times a week, adding that the cost is staggering. "The man must be building a monument to Freud," Jones quips. –*Will Success Spoil Rock Hunter?* (1957)

3227 Secretary Joan Blondell confides to her employer, movie sex queen Jayne Mansfield, why she lost faith in psychiatry: "The psychiatrist I went to had a couch, but it was built for two." –*Will Success Spoil Rock Hunter?* (1957)

3228 Jerry Lewis tells about the time he went to a psychiatrist. "He told me I had a dual personality," Lewis explains. "Then he lays an eighty-two-dollar tab on me. So I give him forty-one bucks and say, 'Get the other forty-one bucks from the other guy.'" –*The Nutty Professor* (1963)

3229 "My uncle said I was a psychoceramic," Jerry Lewis tells an audience. "I said, 'What's that?' He said, 'a crackpot.'" –*The Patsy* (1964)

3230 Actuary John McMartin explains to dance-hall hostess Shirley MacLaine that he just missed his last session of group analysis. "What was your problem?" she asks. "Well," explains McMartin, "one of my problems was I was painfully shy." "And now you're cured?" "I never had the nerve to bring it up," he answers, "so I quit." – *Sweet Charity* (1969)

3231 Utilizing a Rorschach Test, a prison psychiatrist probes the source of Woody Allen's criminality. "That looks to me," says Woody while studying one of the test cards, "like two elephants making love to a men's glee club." – *Take the Money and Run* (1969)

3232 Joseph Bologna takes his Jewish girlfriend Renee Taylor to meet his conservative Italian family and she says she met Bologna at a group encounter session. "Gig and I are so good for each other," she continues, "because we're two self-destructives confronting the life-force." – *Made for Each Other* (1973)

3233 Locked in a mental hospital, Jack Nicholson describes the electric sexual charge he derives from shock treatments: "They were giving me ten thousand watts a day, and, you know, I'm hot to trot. The next woman who takes me out is going to light up like a pinball machine and pay off in silver dollars." – *One Flew Over the Cuckoo's Nest* (1975)

3234 Jack Lemmon is having an anxiety attack. "Why don't you see the analyst again?" wife Anne Bancroft proposes. "Dr. Peke is dead," he returns. "Six years of my life and twenty-three thousand dollars. What does he care if he gets a heart attack?" – *The Prisoner of Second Avenue* (1975)

3235 Woody Allen tells Diane Keaton that he has been in analysis for fifteen years. "I'm going to give him one more year," he adds, "and then I'm going to Lourdes." – *Annie Hall* (1977)

3236 "I was suicidal, as a matter of fact," Woody Allen relates to an audience, "and would have killed myself. But I was in analysis with a strict Freudian, and if you kill yourself, they make you pay for the sessions you miss." – *Annie Hall* (1977)

3237 Mel Brooks, as a distinguished psychiatrist, is hired to run an institute. "I'm curious," he addresses the acting director. "What exactly is the patient rate of recovery here at the institute?" "The rate of recovery?" the man repeats, checking his calculator. "Once in a blue moon." – *High Anxiety* (1977)

3238 Mel Brooks, as a noted psychiatrist, meets one of his old professors who questions him about the field of psychiatry: "And the most important thing?" "Never take a personal check," Brooks answers proudly. – *High Anxiety* (1977)

3239 Airline pilot Stryker (Robert Hays) is on trial, accused of mental incompetence. The prosecutor calls a psychiatrist as a witness. "Doctor," the prosecutor begins, "can you give the court your impression of Mr. Stryker?" "Sorry," the witness replies, "I don't do impressions. My training is in psychiatry." – *Airplane II: The Sequel* (1982)

3240 Woody Allen, posing as a doctor, tells his psychiatrist: "I have to get back to town. I have an interesting case treating two sets of Siamese twins with split personalities. I'm getting paid by eight people." – *Zelig* (1983)

3241 Zelig (Woody Allen), suffering from an acute identity crisis, takes on the professions of eminent people in his life. Of his association with Freud, he explains: "I broke on the concept of penis envy. Freud felt it should be limited to women." – *Zelig* (1983)

3242 At a hectic New York City high school, where chaos rules, a staff member suddenly goes berserk. "Who is that?" a visiting lawyer (JoBeth Williams)

asks. "Oh, the school psychologist."
—*Teachers* (1984)

3243 A psychiatrist examines aging hippy Cheech Marin. "I'm going to say a word," the psychiatrist begins, "and I want you to give me the first word that comes into your mind." "Pussy," Marin willingly offers. "No, we haven't started yet."—*Far Out Man* (1990)

3244 According to his psychiatrist-priest, police officer Dan Aykroyd, resting at a religious retreat, has fully recovered from a nervous breakdown.

"You're the sanest man I know," the doctor reassures his patient. "Actually, that's not very encouraging, coming from you," Aykroyd challenges. "You're a psychiatrist. Everyone you know is crazy—or a celibate."—*Loose Cannons* (1990)

3245 Twenty-one-year-old student Juliette Lewis becomes enamored of college professor Woody Allen and urges him into a tryst. "Why do I hear fifty thousand dollars' worth of psychotherapy dialing 911?" he muses.—*Husbands and Wives* (1992)

Religion

3246 Retired con artist John Barrymore compliments a bishop on his recent sermon. "And what did you bring away with you?" the bishop asks. "Someone else's umbrella," Barrymore replies. —*Long Lost Father* (1934)

3247 During the Third Crusade, Loretta Young cheers on Richard the Lion-Hearted (Henry Wilcoxon): "You've just gotta save Christianity, Richard! You gotta!"—*The Crusades* (1935)

3248 Sister Helen Eddy tries to swing Mae West back into line. "Too many girls follow the line of least resistance," she sermonizes. "Yeah," West returns, "but a good line is hard to resist." —*Klondike Annie* (1936)

3249 Millionaire munitions maker Robert Morley visits his daughter Wendy Hiller, who works as a volunteer in a Salvation Army mission. "By the way, Papa," she asks, "what is your religion, in case I have to introduce you again?" "My religion?" Morley responds. "My dear, I'm a millionaire—that's my religion."—*Major Barbara* (1941)

3250 Young Jimmy Lydon's mother (Irene Dunne) wants to know why he didn't kneel in church today. "I just couldn't," he says simply. "Has it anything to do with Mary?" she asks, referring to their pretty house guest. "I know she's a Methodist." "Oh, no, Mother," Lydon replies. "Methodists kneel. Mary told me. They don't get up and down so much, but they stay down longer."—*Life with Father* (1947)

3251 Irene Dunne continually pleads with husband William Powell to allow himself to be baptized. "You've got to make your peace with God," she asserts. "Until you stirred Him up," the adamant husband retorts, "I had no difficulty with Him!"—*Life with Father* (1947)

3252 Charlie Chaplin, as Verdoux, a dreaded Bluebeard who murders his wives for money, is to be guillotined; he receives a visit from a priest. "I've come to ask you to make your peace with God," the chaplain announces. "I am at peace with God," Chaplin replies. "My conflict is with man."—*Monsieur Verdoux* (1947)

3253 Opportunistic reporter Kirk Douglas, at the site of a mine cave-in, requests that Jan Sterling, the wife of a trapped man, simulate a praying position. "I don't pray," the resentful Sterling replies. "Kneeling bags my nylons." *– Ace in the Hole* (1951)

3254 Father Brown (Alec Guinness) discusses car engines with a stranger who suggests jokingly: "You should have been a salesman, Father." "I already am," Guinness replies. *– The Detective* (1954)

3255 Arab horse owner Hugh Griffith learns about Judaism from his friend, Ben Hur (Charlton Heston). "One wife?" Griffith questions. "One God – that I can understand. But one wife? That is not civilized. It is not generous!" *– Ben Hur* (1959)

3256 Evangelist troupe manager Dean Jagger confronts opportunistic newcomer Elmer Gantry (Burt Lancaster): "I hope you know who's boss here." "Why, God is," Lancaster craftily answers. "I'm only his messenger." "I'm sure God will be relieved," Jagger ripostes. *– Elmer Gantry* (1960)

3257 Three cowboys stop at a pious man's farm for rest and food. "If you can spare us a few eggs, we'll be glad to pay for them," their leader (Joel McCrea) says. "One you can have because the Lord's bounty is not for sale," the farmer replies. "The rest are a dollar each." *– Ride the High Country* (1962)

3258 Two hoodlums working for a notorious gambler enter a poolroom and pick up a bookie their boss wants for questioning. "Gee, fellas," the bookie says, "I was ahead seventeen dollars." "You may never get to spend it," one hood replies. "Fellas, please," their captive pleads, "can I go to St. Vincent's? I want to light a candle." "You're Jewish, ain't you?" "Sure," the bookie answers, "but I like to play the percentages." *– Who's Got the Action?* (1962)

3259 House-of-pleasure owner Phil Silvers announces to his courtesans before he leaves: "I'll be back to lead you in noonday prayers." *– A Funny Thing Happened on the Way to the Forum* (1966)

3260 In ancient Rome a citizen prepares to ignite a bier on which allegedly lies a dead virgin. "Wait!" Zero Mostel cries. "The gods will be angry if you send up a smoked virgin." *– A Funny Thing Happened on the Way to the Forum* (1966)

3261 Con man Zero Mostel, disguised as a minister, tries to impress a town clergyman by quoting from Hebrews forty, Verse eighteen. "Hebrews forty?" the clergyman questions. "There are no forty chapters in Hebrews." "And they said he wasn't up on scripture," Mostel retorts. "You have passed the test, my son." *– The Great Bank Robbery* (1969)

3262 A religious army doctor in Korea finds nurse Sally Kellerman with similar theological leanings. "God meant us to have each other," he intones. "His will be done!" she exclaims, opening her bathrobe. *– M*A*S*H* (1970)

3263 Ohio couple Jack Lemmon and Sandy Dennis, who have suffered a series of disasters in New York City, decide to enter a Central Park West church to pray, only to be told they can't pray inside at this time. "I got my orders from the network," says a television crewman. "This is a closed TV rehearsal. There is no one allowed in this church until two o'clock." "In other words," challenges Lemmon, "you're denying my divine rights to worship the God of my choice in the house of the Lord of my desired faith?" "Yeah," the technician replies, "until two o'clock when you'll get your divine rights back." *– The Out of Towners* (1970)

3264 During World War II a reverend notes that General George Patton (George C. Scott) has a Bible alongside his bed. "Do you actually have time to read it?" "Every goddamn day," the general replies. – *Patton* (1970)

3265 Con man James Garner and partner Susan Clark pose as a clergyman and a nurse respectively as they journey about the South bilking their victims. "I do hope we run into a Catholic or two," Garner remarks. "What for?" asks Clark. "I'd love to hear a confession." – *Skin Game* (1971)

3266 "Do I believe in God?" Woody Allen questions rhetorically. "I'm what you call a teleological, existential atheist. I believe there is intelligence in the universe with the exception of certain parts of New Jersey." – *Sleeper* (1973)

3267 "Indians don't fight in the dark," someone informs Gregory Peck. "It's against their religion." "They don't seem that religious to me," Peck replies. – *Billy Two Hats* (1974)

3268 Before Woody Allen dances with Death, he imparts to the audience what he has learned: "If it turns out there is a God, I don't think He's evil. The worst thing you can say about Him is that He's basically an underachiever." – *Love and Death* (1975)

3269 God charges King Arthur (Graham Chapman) and his knights with a most sacred mission – to seek and find the Holy Grail. "Good idea, O Lord," says Arthur. "'Course it's a good idea!" God storms. – *Monty Python and the Holy Grail* (1975)

3270 "I don't do miracles," God (George Burns) says to John Denver. "They're too flashy. Maybe now and then, to keep my hand in. The last miracle I did was the 1969 Mets. Before that you have to go back to the Red Sea. That was a beaut." – *Oh, God!* (1977)

3271 Immediately preceding a church wedding, a religious leader enlightens a fellow member of the cloth: "There is also the capital gains element. But you

can always handle that by setting up an eleemosynary trust in the Bahamas and laundering it back through Switzerland." – *Semi-Tough* (1977)

3272 George Burns, as God, visits little Tracy, a precocious child from a broken home. "I expected you to look much older," she comments. "Thanks, Tracy. I take care of myself." "How old are you?" "Who knows?" Burns replies. "After the first two million years I stopped counting." – *Oh, God! Book II* (1980)

3273 Director Woody Allen tells a studio executive that the "whole point of the movie is that nobody is saved." "This is an Easter film," the executive explains. "We don't need a movie by an atheist." "To you – to you I'm an atheist," Allen retorts. "To God I'm the loyal opposition." – *Stardust Memories* (1980)

3274 As Moses (Mel Brooks) descends from the mountain, carrying the cherished tablets, he says over his shoulder: "Yes, Lord, I will pass unto thy people your fifteen" – a tablet falls and shatters – "er, your Ten Commandments." – *History of the World – Part 1* (1981)

3275 Struggling songwriter Jeff Wass, who has alienated his wife after making a pact with the Devil in return for fame, seeks to cancel the contract. Failing to reach God in a church, he decides to try a synagogue. "I'm looking for God – the Person," he says to a caretaker within. "I'm trying to get my wife back." "You want God or a lawyer?" the man asks. – *Oh, God! You Devil* (1984)

3276 "Catholicism for me was die now, pay later," remarks neurotic television executive Woody Allen. – *Hannah and Her Sisters* (1986)

3277 "Are you religious?" acquaintance Cleavon Little asks Chevy Chase, who has been investigating an unscrupulous television evangelist. "I believe in a God that doesn't need heavy financing." – *Fletch Lives* (1989)

3278 A fellow police officer asks detective Gene Hackman about his ex-wife. "Claire's a born-again Christian," Hackman says. "Every time I go over to see my son, she calls me the anti-Christ and hides under the bed." – *Loose Cannons* (1990)

3279 A gossipy tenant in a Harlem tenement, noticing a young bachelor taking a sexy young woman up to his apartment, cries out: "If Christ knew what kind of Christians He had up here in Harlem, He'd climb back up on the cross and start over." – *A Rage in Harlem* (1991)

3280 Madonna, portraying a tart on an all-women's baseball team, emerges from a confessional followed by a shaken priest. "That's the second time he's dropped the Bible since she's been in there," observes a fellow teammate. – *A League of Their Own* (1992)

Revenge

3281 Bert Wheeler and Robert Woolsey become embroiled in a Kentucky feud. As Noah Beery, leader of the Wakefields, plots revenge upon the Milfords, Wheeler overhears his plans. "Get the horses!" Beery orders. "We're gonna do some killin'!" "I wonder what kind of horses they're going to kill," Wheeler says. – *Kentucky Kernels* (1935)

3282 Gangster Alan Ladd is gunning for Gates (Laird Cregar), who has paid Ladd off in counterfeit bills. "You don't want to kill Gates," nightclub singer Veronica Lake says to Ladd. "What do you want me to do – send him some candy?" – *This Gun for Hire* (1942)

3283 "You wouldn't kill me in cold blood, would you?" an enemy of gangster James Cagney snivels, fearing the worst. "No," a vindictive Cagney replies, "I'd let you warm up a little." – *White Heat* (1949)

3284 Mob boss Dan Hedaya assembles his gang to devise a suitable revenge for "wise guys" Danny De Vito and Joe Piscopo who have double-crossed him. "Do we really hurt them by killing them?" Hedaya ponders. "It's a start," one hood blurts out. – *Wise Guys* (1986)

Rivalry

3285 A woman spurned by her lover meets innocent Clara Bow, his new love interest, at a party. "I suppose you know you broke up my home," the woman charges. "I didn't know you were in a home," Bow says coyly. "When did you get out?" – *Call Her Savage* (1932)

3286 Ben Lyon, on a date with the beautiful Constance Bennett, warns one of her admirers that men go out of their minds thinking about her. "I'd go out of anything for her!" the man declares. "Good," Lyon replies. "Going out of your mind wouldn't be much of a sacrifice." – *Lady with a Past* (1932)

3287 "I had four girls chasing me down the street," sailor Ted Healy boasts to rival Nat Pendleton and other fellow seamen. "What did you do," asks Pendleton, "steal a pocketbook?" — *Murder in the Fleet* (1935)

3288 Just as Bert Wheeler is romancing pretty Dorothy Tree, his rival enters the garden. "I had a run-in with him this morning," Wheeler says. "I told him plenty. I called him everything I could think of." "What did he say?" she asks. "He didn't hear me." — *The Rainmakers* (1935)

3289 Aspiring dancer Ginger Rogers and an actress, residing at a boarding house, battle for the same beau. "May I come in?" the actress says, knocking at Rogers' door. "Sure," she calls out. "I guess you'll be safe. The exterminators won't be here until tomorrow." — *Stage Door* (1937)

3290 Rather than the one-man fixation of Loretta Young, her friend Eve Arden presents a broader perspective: "What the heck, darling, competition is the life of trade." — *Eternally Yours* (1939)

3291 Rosalind Russell goes to Reno for her divorce and meets Paulette Goddard, who has seduced Russell's estranged husband. "How much did he settle on you?" Russell asks. "I made Howard pay for what he wants," Goddard rejoins. "You made him pay for what he doesn't want." — *The Women* (1939)

3292 W. C. Fields to Charlie McCarthy: "Quiet, or I shall cut you and use you for a Venetian blind." "That gives me the shutters," quips McCarthy. — *You Can't Cheat an Honest Man* (1939)

3293 Jealous Frenchman Fritz Feld, suspecting Leon Errol of having an affair with his girlfriend, challenges him to a duel. "You mean you actually want to fight me a duel?" the incredulous Errol asks. "Your weapons, monsieur?" "Boxing gloves at six paces," suggests Errol. — *Mexican Spitfire's Baby* (1941)

3294 Ruth Warrick's fiancé barges into her hotel room and finds her with Edmond O'Brien. "Stand on your feet!" the man challenges O'Brien. "And get knocked down?" O'Brien replies. "Don't be silly!" — *Obliging Young Lady* (1941)

3295 "I want to have a talk with you — man to man," Bing Crosby says to Bob Hope. "Yeah?" Hope replies. "Who's going to hold up your end?" — *Road to Morocco* (1942)

3296 Rivals Betty Grable and "Brazilian bombshell" Carmen Miranda parry with each other. "Is that a diamond?" Miranda asks. "Yes," Grable responds. "Did the size of it startle you?" "Yes," Miranda counters. "In Brazil we throw that kind away." — *The Gang's All Here* (1943)

3297 Gildersleeve's (Hal Peary) romantic escapades begin to catch up to him when one of his love interests suspects another woman. "Who is that little tomato?" she asks angrily. "That's my mother," he replies. "Mother?" "I was born very young," he explains hopelessly. — *Gildersleeve on Broadway* (1943)

3298 Fred MacMurray, as photographer Claudette Colbert's assistant, deliberately picks a fight with a jealous male model and decks him by dropping a spotlight on his head. "Now clear this mess out of the way," Colbert demands. "You just told me not to touch him," MacMurray replies. — *No Time for Love* (1943)

3299 Suspecting that her husband Walter Pidgeon is having an affair with a Lady Nora in England, Greer Garson as Mrs. Parkington crosses the Atlantic and discovers the pair during a hunting game. "How long are you planning to stay?" Lady Nora asks. "Until the hunting season is over," Mrs. Parkington replies. — *Mrs. Parkington* (1944)

3300 A squeamish Dolores Moran has fainted at the sight of blood, and Humphrey Bogart picks her up. Lauren Bacall enters the room and asks acidly: "What are you trying to do–guess her weight?" – *To Have and Have Not* (1944)

3301 Philip Terry has fallen in love with Audrey Long, who is engaged to another man. "Is he good-looking?" Terry asks grudgingly. "You know," she answers, "there are such things as mental and spiritual attractions as well as physical." "Oh, sure," he persists, "but I can't understand a woman who'd settle for less when she can have all three in the same guy." – *Pan-Americana* (1945)

3302 Elderly Dorothy Lamour, married to Bob Hope for thirty-five years, hears the old, familiar voice of Bing Crosby, Hope's longtime rival, singing outside their home at night. "That voice!" she cries. "What voice?" "Listen," she says. "What does it sound like?" "Who'd be selling fish at this hour?" Hope asks. – *Road to Utopia* (1945)

3303 Bob Hope is convinced that Dorothy Lamour is in love with him. "Don't just stand there," the jubilant Hope addresses Bing Crosby. "You want to be best man, don't you?" "Always was," Crosby smoothly replies. – *Road to Rio* (1947)

3304 Greer Garson, separated from husband Walter Pidgeon for years, tries to get him jealous by playing up to her admirer, acrobat Cesar Romero, whom she compliments on a difficult feat he performs nightly. "The trick took seven years to perfect," Romero boasts. "I must say," Pidgeon says wryly, "that's one way to spend seven years." – *Julia Misbehaves* (1948)

3305 A tough cowpuncher, finding his gal in the arms of Bob Hope, threatens: "I don't like anybody fooling with my girl!" "I got news for you," replies Hope. "I ain't foolin'." – *The Paleface* (1948)

3306 An advertising executive (Dennis Morgan) enters a posh nightclub and joins his partner, Holmes (Zachary Scott), and his date, Betsy Drake, at their table. Both men are competing for Drake's affection. "Here's ten dollars for your trouble," Morgan furtively approaches the waiter. "Tell Mr. Holmes he has a phone call." "Sorry, sir," the waiter replies. "Mr. Holmes gave me twenty dollars not to call him to the phone." – *Pretty Baby* (1950)

3307 Beautiful young islanders hover about Bob Hope and Bing Crosby when two native muscle men appear behind them. "Don't look now," Crosby says. "Tabu and his brother." "Don't worry about them," Hope replies. "Let them get their own girls." – *Road to Bali* (1952)

3308 To placate Bob Hope, rival Tony Martin concedes that Hope is a better lover when it comes to wooing Arlene Dahl. "To the victor belong the spoils," Martin declares. "Who's spoiled?" questions Hope. – *Here Come the Girls* (1953)

3309 Ladies' man Rock Hudson is supposedly going alone to theatrical investor Tony Randall's country home to score a musical. But he is surreptitiously taking with him Doris Day, the woman Randall loves. "Here's to make sure you do plenty of scoring up there," Randall says, handing Hudson a packet of sheet music. "I'll do my best." – *Pillow Talk* (1959)

3310 Jerry Lewis watches from behind a bush as his mean stepbrother romances the princess Lewis loves. "Isn't he holding my future wife a little too close?" he asks Ed Wynn. "Stop worrying, she's all yours–every bit of her." "Yeah," Lewis mutters, "but I'd like to have the bits he's holding." – *Cinderfella* (1960)

3311 U.S. Marshal James Stewart confides to cavalry officer pal Richard Widmark why he doesn't trust his mistress Belle. "You know," Stewart says, "she carries a stiletto right there in her garter–" "I know," Widmark acknowledges. "And we were sitting around the place," Stewart continues, when suddenly he turns to his friend and asks: "How do you know?" "You just told me." "You didn't know about the stiletto?" Stewart asks suspiciously. *– Two Rode Together* (1961)

3312 Middle-aged dentist Walter Matthau, dating the much younger Goldie Hawn, finds her with a handsome, young hippy neighbor. Despite Matthau's protestations, she invites her neighbor to join them for dinner. "I'll put on a tie," the young man says. "Why?" Matthau asks. "You're having your beads restrung?" *– Cactus Flower* (1969)

3313 Hooker Barbra Streisand exhibits an unprofessional interest in neighbor George Segal but soon learns that he already has a fiancée. "Does she have a nice body?" Streisand asks. "Very delicate," he replies softly. "She's extremely fragile." "Does she have a sticker on her saying, 'This End Up'?" *– The Owl and the Pussycat* (1970)

3314 Kooky Barbra Streisand meets staid musicologist Ryan O'Neal in a hotel and immediately falls in love with him. However, he is presently engaged to a shrew named Eunice. "You don't want to marry Eunice," Streisand says. "You don't want to marry someone who's going to get all wrinkled, lined and flabby." "Everybody gets wrinkled, lined and flabby," he counters. "By next week?" Streisand asks. *– What's Up, Doc?* (1972)

3315 Cranky ex-vaudeville comedian Walter Matthau fires off a venomous barb at his erstwhile partner George Burns: "You know the expression 'You don't know what you're talking about'? It comes right before the expression 'You'll never know what you're talking about.'" *– The Sunshine Boys* (1975)

3316 Shirley MacLaine, distraught over her husband Adam's (Anthony Hopkins) affair with a college student, meets her rival (Bo Derek). "We have so much in common," Derek says. "What?" "Adam." "Yes," MacLaine replies, "Adam is common." *– A Change of Seasons* (1980)

3317 Bounty hunter Robert De Niro nettles his long-time rival, F.B.I. chief Yaphet Kotto. "You're going to spend ten years for impersonating a federal agent," Kotto promises De Niro. "Ten years for impersonating a federal agent?" De Niro echoes. "How come no one's after you?" *– Midnight Run* (1988)

3318 Tess Trueheart (Glenne Headly) walks in on boyfriend Dick Tracy (Warren Beatty) while he is entertaining the sexy Madonna, who soon departs. "I'll bet she does some nifty undercover work," Headly remarks to Beatty. *– Dick Tracy* (1990)

Romance

3319 "Just think," Groucho Marx coos to Margaret Dumont, "tonight – tonight when the moon is sneaking around the clouds, I'll be sneaking around you. I'll meet you tonight under the moon. Oh, I can see you now – you and the moon. You wear a necktie so I'll know you." *– The Cocoanuts* (1929)

3320 "Ever since I met you," Groucho Marx woos Margaret Dumont, "I've swept you off my feet. Something keeps throbbing within me. Oh, it's been beating like the incessant beat of a tom-tom in a primitive jungle. There's something I must ask you." "What is it, captain?" she asks anxiously. "Would you wash out a pair of socks for me?" *– Animal Crackers* (1930)

3321 Strong-minded Edna May Oliver is determined to break up the romance between her niece and Bert Wheeler, but the young woman persists in defending her beau. "He said with prudence, two can live as cheaply as one." "Why doesn't he marry Prudence?" her aunt suggests. – *Cracked Nuts* (1931)

3322 Groucho Marx becomes wildly enamored of sexy Thelma Todd. "Oh, why can't we break away from all this," he pleads, "just you and I, and lodge with my fleas in the hills – I mean, flee to my lodge in the hills?" – *Monkey Business* (1931)

3323 Groucho Marx is busily engaged in wooing Margaret Dumont. "What are you thinking of?" she asks romantically as he snuggles up to her. "All the years I wasted collecting stamps," he replies. – *Duck Soup* (1933)

3324 Fredric March, who meets Claudette Colbert at a ball and is enchanted by her beauty, says: "I want this moment to last." "How long?" she asks. "At least until breakfast." – *Tonight Is Ours* (1933)

3325 Fred Astaire awaits a telephone call from newly found love Ginger Rogers. "You pining for that girl?" Edward Everett Horton asks. "Men don't pine," Astaire explains. "Girls pine – men just suffer." – *The Gay Divorcee* (1934)

3326 "You know, you'd look beautiful with blonde hair," Fred MacMurray mutters to Carole Lombard. "I have blonde hair," she says. "I know it," he replies. – *Hands Across the Table* (1935)

3327 "Where did you learn to kiss like that?" a startled Sally Eilers asks Eddie Cantor. "I used to blow a bugle for the Boy Scouts." – *Strike Me Pink* (1936)

3328 A forty-year-old servant has been waiting by the window for fifteen years, hoping someday to meet her true love. "Fifteen years?" her mistress Fay Bainter repeats. "And you're still –"

"Hopeful? There's not a more hopeful woman in all the king's dominion." – *Quality Street* (1937)

3329 Madcap heiress Katharine Hepburn has innocently and inadvertently overturned the quiet, orderly life of paleontologist Cary Grant into a chaotic frenzy. He diplomatically explains to her why their relationship has not blossomed: "Now it isn't that I don't like you, Susan, because after all, in moments of quiet, I'm strangely drawn toward you. But – well – there haven't been any quiet moments." – *Bringing Up Baby* (1938)

3330 Love-disillusioned Laurence Olivier is fleeing Merle Oberon, who checks his office and finds him gone. "Did he say when he's coming back?" she asks his colleague. "Yes." "When?" she asks anxiously. "Never." – *The Divorce of Lady X* (1938)

3331 Newspaperman Henry Fonda woos kooky socialite Barbara Stanwyck. "Before I knew you I disliked you immensely," he admits; "when I met you I disliked you intensely; even now I dislike you intensely. But there's an insane side of me that acts a little violent every time I think of you." – *The Mad Miss Manton* (1938)

3332 Mexican secretary Martha Raye tries to tell writer Ray Milland that his Hollywood girlfriend does not really want to marry him. "Whose business is it?" he snaps. "Yours," Raye retorts. "She's been giving it to you for months." – *Tropic Holiday* (1938)

3333 Groucho Marx asks stately Margaret Dumont to recall their romantic times on the Riviera. "We were young, gay, reckless," he begins, and ends with, "Ah, Hildegard –" "My name is Susannah," she corrects him. "Let's not quibble over a name," Groucho continues, unruffled. – *At the Circus* (1939)

3334 Commissar Ninotchka (Greta Garbo) explains to Count Léon (Melvyn

Douglas) that she is a "tiny cog in the wheel of evolution." "You're the most adorable cog I ever saw in my life," a moonstruck Douglas interjects. *–Ninotchka* (1939)

3335 When Bud Abbott sees Lou Costello eating a hot dog without mustard, he rebukes him. "The hot dog and mustard go together." "Let 'em go together," declares Costello. "I don't want to spoil any romance." *– One Night in the Tropics* (1940)

3336 James Stewart confides to avuncular fellow employee Felix Bressart about his unseen pen pal (Margaret Sullavan) and the high intellectual plane of their correspondence: "We came to the subject of love, naturally on a very cultural level." "What else can you do in a letter?" Bressart asks. *– The Shop Around the Corner* (1940)

3337 Bob Hope makes a necklace for Dorothy Lamour, who he thinks has fallen in love with him. "It's for a certain party," Hope confides to Bing Crosby. "It's a token of my steam." "Esteem," Crosby corrects him. "No, no – steam," Hope insists. "I was hot that night." *– Road to Zanzibar* (1941)

3338 Divorcee Mary Astor befriends Claudette Colbert. "We can look for husbands together," Astor proposes. "I'm looking for an American at the moment. It's so much more patriotic." *– The Palm Beach Story* (1942)

3339 "I suppose I can't get along without you," saloon entertainer Marlene Dietrich teasingly says to gold prospector John Wayne. "Sure you can," Wayne replies, "which also goes for me. We can do with a lot less food too, but we'd get awfully hungry." *– The Spoilers* (1942)

3340 Van Johnson, as an air force pilot during World War II, returns from a mission into the arms of his sweetheart (Irene Dunne) and exclaims: "You're the prettiest girl I ever saw.

You're even prettier than a P-38!" *– A Guy Named Joe* (1943)

3341 A young man of modest means woos an older woman with a large income: "I dream a little picture of retiring to one's home in the evening – " "Where have you been in the afternoon?" the woman inquires. "And there, seated at one's dinner table, a divine lady – " "To whom you address a few kind words before going out to dine with someone else," she charges. *– On Approval* (1943)

3342 Flighty Jane Wyman convinces Jack Carson that they should leave New York and get married in Baltimore. "It's more romantic eloping like this," she beams. "Eloping from what?" Carson fires back. "Who's stopping us? You're an orphan and my family disowned me for voting Democratic." *– The Doughgirls* (1944)

3343 In World War II London, a middle-aged English colonel falling in love with American actress Kay Francis gently takes her hand in his. "Will you forgive me?" he asks. "It was quite by accident. But, you kow, if I had held this hand ten years ago, I might have had a full house by now." *– Four Jills in a Jeep* (1944)

3344 "In the spring," Jack Carson notes, "a young man's fancy lightly turns to what he's been thinking about all winter." *– Mildred Pierce* (1945)

3345 British secret agent Ray Milland, on the run in Europe from the Nazis, encounters tempestuous gypsy Marlene Dietrich, who finds him irresistible and begins her pawing advances. "Please," Milland protests, "your hands – couldn't you learn to sit on them or something?" *– Golden Earrings* (1947)

3346 "I have loved you since the beginning of time," Don Juan (Errol Flynn) says, romancing Mary Stuart. "But you only met me yesterday." "That was when time began." "But you made love to so many women." "Catherine," Flynn explains, "an artist may paint a thousand canvases before achieving one work of art. Would you deny a lover the same privilege?" – *Adventures of Don Juan* (1948)

3347 "What are you so glum about?" Oscar Levant asks Gene Kelly. "I got woman trouble," Kelly explains. "Good," his friend returns. "It proves you're a man." – *An American in Paris* (1951)

3348 "You're a regular rooster," Maureen O'Hara says to cocky army officer Errol Flynn. "You seem to be a high-spirited chick yourself," Flynn ripostes. – *Against All Flags* (1952)

3349 William Holden spots Maggie McNamara as the girl of his dreams, and the chase is on. She enters a building and disappears into an elevator. Holden in pursuit enters another elevator. "Follow that car!" he orders the operator. – *The Moon Is Blue* (1953)

3350 Dapper Hollywood producer Fred Astaire, falling in love with Soviet agent Cyd Charisse, has his affections marginally reciprocated as her icy, repressed womanhood begins to thaw. "The arrangement of your features," she says in a cold monotone, "is not entirely repulsive to me." – *Silk Stockings* (1957)

3351 To fend off matrimony, debonair playboy Cary Grant tells European actress Ingrid Bergman that he is married. But she soon discovers the truth. "How dare he make love to me," she fumes, "and not be a married man!" – *Indiscreet* (1958)

3352 For years, Jerry Lewis has idolized his childhood sweetheart Marilyn Maxwell, now a famous movie star. When she returns to their home town, he finally admits his true feelings for her. "I even took a muscle-building course so you wouldn't laugh at me when we went swimming," he recalls. "That didn't do very much good because I couldn't find my muscles to build them up." – *Rock-a-Bye Baby* (1958)

3353 Quixotic Polish colonel Curt Jurgens, traveling with Jewish refugee Danny Kaye during World War II, romantically delivers to a bevy of European women his charmer-line: "In the cathedral of my heart a candle will always burn for you." "That must be the best lit cathedral in the world," Kaye quips. – *Me and the Colonel* (1959)

3354 A rescued nurse aboard a submarine during World War II tries to help machinist's mate Arthur O'Connell, a confirmed woman-hater, make repairs, but he resists. Eventually he succumbs first to her mechanical skills and then to her charms. "You're different," he rhapsodizes. "You're not a woman. You're more than that. You're a mechanic." – *Operation Petticoat* (1959)

3355 To ensnare handsome basketball star Anthony Perkins, college student Jane Fonda takes the same course as Perkins with professor Ray Walston. When the instructor reveals Fonda's scheme to his wife, she laughs. "It isn't *your* classroom she's using as a matrimonial agency," Walston protests. "And, if that isn't bad enough, she's now extending her field of operations to my home. I am a professor of ethics, not a madam!" – *Tall Story* (1960)

3356 Romantic complications arise between student Troy Donahue and librarian Suzanne Pleshette. "You mean we'll never meet again?" he asks. "There's never and there's never." – *Rome Adventure* (1962)

3357 "You know what's wrong with you?" a smitten Audrey Hepburn says to Cary Grant. "What?" "Nothing." – *Charade* (1963)

3358 Elke Sommer of the Swedish foreign ministry, assigned to keep Nobel Prize winner Paul Newman safe from foreign entanglements, succumbs to his charms. While visiting his hotel room, Newman gently removes her cloak. "I never should have listened to you," she purrs. "What did I say?" "About defrosting in the bathtub." "Did you?" "Much too long." "Well," Newman adds, "I've been getting into hot water all my life." – *The Prize* (1963)

3359 A fashion model confides to her gay photographer that she is dating and falling in love with Robin Stone (John Phillip Law), a handsome television personality. "Funny, isn't it?" she says, "to be hung up on someone and have to hide it." "When it comes to Robin Stone, I know exactly how you feel," the photographer agrees. – *The Love Machine* (1971)

3360 "What's happening to me?" Marsha Mason says to new beau James Caan. "Suddenly I can't stand anything cultural." "Yes, I know," replies Caan. "It's infatuation that makes you stupid." – *Chapter Two* (1979)

3361 After living together for several years, Burt Reynolds and Goldie Hawn decide to buy a house. Reynolds proposes marriage, but to his surprise,

Hawn turns him down, preferring not to lose her identity. "That's great!" Reynolds exclaims. "They moved into their dream house and they dated happily ever after." – *Best Friends* (1982)

3362 In Paris, Englishman Cary Grant and American Jim Hutton tease Samantha Eggar about her English fiancé, both claiming that the English make poor lovers. "What about Henry VIII?" she counters. "He was promiscuous, not romantic," Grant quips. – *Walk, Don't Run* (1986)

3363 Big-time gambler-gangster James Caan, with a mile-wide romantic streak, woos stunning Sarah Jessica Parker. "If I were a medieval knight, I would have jostled for you," he vaunts. "Jousted," she corrects him. "I mean," he continues, "we're up there with Romeo and Juliet, George and Gracie – all the big ones." – *Honeymoon in Vegas* (1992)

Rooms

3364 "I want a large room," a stocky woman demands of hotel manager Bert Wheeler. "You'll need it," he cracks. – *Hook, Line and Sinker* (1930)

3365 "He wants a room with exposure," hotel manager Robert Woolsey says to desk clerk Bert Wheeler about a guest. "Are we going to allow that here?" Wheeler inquires. – *Hook, Line and Sinker* (1930)

3366 "I can give you a nice room with a bath," hotel clerk Irving Bacon offers guest Charles Ruggles. "You give me the room," replies Ruggles. "I'll take a bath myself." – *Six of a Kind* (1934)

3367 Stan Laurel and Oliver Hardy check into a hotel in a small village in

Scotland. "We'd like for you to give us a room and a bath, please," Oliver announces. "I can give you the room," the desk clerk replies, "but you'll have to take the bath yourself." – *Bonnie Scotland* (1935)

3368 Well-known financier Edward Arnold checks into a fashionable Park Avenue hotel and says to its owner Luis Alberni: "Give me a room with a bath." "Naturally with a bath," the offended owner replies. "You don't think we use a rain barrel, do you?" – *Easy Living* (1937)

3369 Archaeologist Cary Grant arrives at the apartment of erratic socialite Katharine Hepburn and is startled by her pet leopard. "You've got to get out of this apartment!" Grant shouts frantically. "But I can't," Hepburn calmly replies. "I have a lease." – *Bringing Up Baby* (1938)

3370 Magazine editor Otto Kruger, always seeking new faces for the cover of his periodical, is dissatisfied with the photos supplied by his assistant, Eve Arden, and other members of his staff. "I want a girl with a story in her eyes," he demands. "Drawing room or smoking room?" Arden quips. – *Cover Girl* (1944)

3371 Columnist Clifton Webb cavalierly presents his extravagantly furnished apartment to police detective Dana Andrews: "It's lavish, but I call it home." – *Laura* (1944)

3372 A foreign agent thinks entertainer Danny Kaye knows where a secret formula is hidden and approaches him in the hallway of a hotel. Kaye has just returned from the men's shower room. "Where is it?" the stranger asks him. "Third door on the right," Kaye answers. "But lock the door. They'll walk right in on you." – *Knock on Wood* (1954)

3373 Desi Arnaz and Lucille Ball, about to marry, consider buying a trailer, a long-time dream of the bride-to-be. She shows the reluctant Arnaz a brochure of a particular model. "It's kind of roomy at that," he admits. "Wonderful closet space." "That's the living room," she corrects him. – *The Long, Long Trailer* (1954)

3374 On board a ship, a pretty woman comments to Huntz Hall that his stateroom is charming. "Exclusive, huh?" he replies. "There's only two hundred more exactly like it." – *In the Money* (1958)

3375 Navy lieutenant Steve McQueen persuades two buddies to join him in a

scam to beat the roulette wheel at a Venice gambling casino. He rents a lavish hotel suite which impresses his two fellow officers. "It kind of looks like a place I promised my wife I'd stay out of," one officer says. – *The Honeymoon Machine* (1961)

3376 Unconventional Jason Robards is visited by the social worker of his nephew (Barry Gordon). "You'd better go to your room," Robards says. "This is a one-room apartment," Gordon reminds him. – *A Thousand Clowns* (1965)

3377 Jane Fonda's mother (Mildred Natwick) arrives exhausted after climbing five flights of stairs to her newlywed daughter's New York apartment. "I feel like we've died and gone to heaven," the mother gasps, "only we had to climb up." – *Barefoot in the Park* (1967)

3378 Cicely Tyson, in charge of a group of eight orphans whom she is taking to a farm, stops at a motel and assigns rooms. "I ain't staying alone with Julio!" protests a blind boy. "He always makes me bump into furniture!" – *Bustin' Loose* (1981)

3379 Suburbanite Sid Caesar grumbles about his wife's covering all the living-room furniture with plastic. "I haven't sat in that room since my son was born," he says. "I keep sliding off everything." – *Over the Brooklyn Bridge* (1984)

3380 In crowded Paris during the Olympics, businessman Cary Grant responds to an ad about sharing an apartment, but attractive apartment owner Samantha Eggar frowns upon the idea of having him as a roommate. "I prefer sharing an apartment with a woman," she explains. "Well," replies Grant, "so do I." – *Walk, Don't Run* (1986)

Royalty

3381 Bert Wheeler has just become king of a mythical dominion, and a flirtatious young woman tries to gain his affection. "Your royal highness is so cute," she says. "Yeah," he replies, "well, yours isn't so bad either." – *Cracked Nuts* (1931)

3382 The Grand Duke of Russia informs Czar Nicholas (Ralph Morgan) of the army's desperate state of affairs: "They have no bullets for their rifles, no bread for their bellies, no coats for their backs and no belief in their officers. "Well," says the surprised Nicholas, turning to his wife, "I didn't know that." – *Rasputin and the Empress* (1932)

3383 Bert Wheeler and Robert Woolsey, diplomats aboard a luxury liner, are invited to dine at the captain's table where a matronly guest is about to make a speech. "She's a countess," the captain whispers to Woolsey. "Her husband is in the peerage." "Fine woman!" Woolsey frowns. "She rides first class and puts her husband down in the peerage." – *Diplomaniacs* (1933)

3384 Vagabonds Bert Wheeler and Robert Woolsey surreptitiously hitch a ride under the stagecoach of a duchess. "I hope she doesn't find us here," Woolsey muses. "She's liable to have us beheaded." "Beheaded?" Wheeler echoes. "Can she do that?" "Sure, she can be head." – *Cockeyed Cavaliers* (1934)

3385 Movie star Lucille Ball, on a personal tour to promote her latest film, is about to go on stage in a packed movie theater. She asks traveling companion Ruth Donnelly if there is any royalty in the audience. "Yeah," Donnelly replies, "the duke of the stockyards and the king of the underworld." – *Annabel Takes a Tour* (1938)

3386 Professor of phonetics Henry Higgins (Leslie Howard) makes flower girl Eliza Doolittle (Wendy Hiller) an offer she can't refuse: "Yes, you squashed cabbage leaf, you disgrace to the noble architecture of these columns, you incarnate insult to the English language, I can pass you off as the queen of Sheba." – *Pygmalion* (1938)

3387 Leon Errol, as the eccentric Lord Epping, enters a room to find all the guests bowing to his lordship. "Oh," he comments, "a bunch of squatters." – *Mexican Spitfire at Sea* (1942)

3388 When Red Skelton, as King Louis XV, captures the Black Arrow (Gene Kelly), his mortal enemy, he resists cries to kill the revolutionary. "What kind of a king do you think I am?" Skelton exclaims. "We'll give him a fair trial – and then we'll hang him." – *DuBarry Was a Lady* (1943)

3389 "Don't you ever want to do anything for anyone?" a young woman at a social event asks a duke (Clive Brook). "My dear," Brook replies, "the most that can be expected from any duke is to think." – *On Approval* (1943)

3390 Bob Hope, as Louis XIV's private barber, is plying his trade as the king and queen discuss affairs of state. At one point Hope interjects his opinion, only to be cut short by the queen, who orders: "Shut up, you idiot!" "He didn't say anything," Hope replies, looking at the king. – *Monsieur Beaucaire* (1946)

3391 Imperious Nero (Peter Ustinov) is beside himself with rage when he learns that his court arbiter (Leo Genn) has taken his own life: "Petronius, dead? By his own hand? I don't believe it . . . I shall never forgive him for this, never!

Without my persmission? It's rebellion! It's blasphemy!" – *Quo Vadis* (1951)

3392 Criticized for his boorish table manners, Marlon Brando as Stanley Kowalski explodes at his wife Stella and sister-in-law Blanche DuBois. "What do you think you are?" he exclaims. "A pair of queens? Now, just remember what Huey Long said – that every man's a king – and I'm the king around here." – *A Streetcar Named Desire* (1951)

3393 Wounded horseman Alan Ladd falls unconscious before King Arthur (Harry Andrews). "Merlin, quickly, Merlin," the King cries. "By my eyes, that magician is never around when you need him." – *The Black Knight* (1954)

3394 Deposed European king Charlie Chaplin, residing in New York, is invited as a guest of honor to a social event. "What's all this business about curtsying to the king?" a guest inquires. "Why, of course," the host affirms. "Haven't you ever been presented at court?" "Only for speeding," the man returns. – *A King in New York* (1957)

3395 Charlie Chaplin, as a deposed European king, is falsely accused of running off with his country's treasury, which his crooked ministers have stolen. "To think you're accused of absconding with the funds," his aide muses. "It's just as well," Chaplin replies. "I'd sooner be thought of as a successful crook than a destitute monarch." – *A King in New York* (1957)

3396 At a ski resort, playboy David Niven invites princess Claudia Cardinale to his room. "Are you – what they call you – the 'virgin queen'?" he asks jokingly. "I am not a queen," she replies. – *The Pink Panther* (1964)

3397 World-famous sex queen Didi (Elke Sommer) says to her director-boyfriend who has been mistreating her: "You know that I am of royal blood! Everybody knows that Didi comes from a noble line!" "You come from a noble

line, all right. A noble line a sailor gave your foolish mother!" – *Boy, Did I Get a Wrong Number!* (1966)

3398 Donald Sutherland, posing as one of the notorious Corsican brothers at Louis XIV's palace, meets the pretty Princess Christine of Belgium. "You're very well known in my country," the princess says. "And you are very well known in your country," Sutherland replies. – *Start the Revolution Without Me* (1970)

3399 Russian patriots and self-appointed assassins Woody Allen and wife Diane Keaton confront Napoleon (James Tolkan), who has invaded their land. "You're a tyrant! A dictator! And you start wars!" Allen exclaims. "Why is he reciting my credits?" the French general asks. – *Love and Death* (1975)

3400 Minister Harvey Korman: "The people are revolting!" King Louis XVI (Mel Brooks): "You said it! They stink on ice!" – *History of the World – Part 1* (1981)

3401 The King of mythical Druidia, whose daughter is about to be kidnapped by villains from the planet Spaceballs, hires Lonestar (Bill Pullman) to rescue her. Lonestar asks for a description of her spaceship. "A brand new white Mercedes," the King replies. "I got it at a very good price. I paid cash. My cousin, Prince Murray, has a dealership in the valley...." – *Spaceballs* (1987)

3402 Eddie Murphy, as the prince of a mythical African kingdom, has been raised in a state of luxury. Now, on his twenty-first birthday, he is tired of all the pampering and complains to his father, the king (James Earl Jones), that he is not even permitted to tie his own shoelaces. "I've tied my shoes once," his father consoles him. "Believe me, it's an overrated experience." – *Coming to America* (1988)

3403 A marriage is arranged between Princess Anna of Finland and King Ralph

(John Goodman) of England. "You are unsophisticated, ignorant and totally lacking in social grace," she says to the English king in private, "but I console myself in the fact that you have nice buttocks." – *King Ralph* (1991)

Sales and Salespeople

3404 Robert Woolsey, in an attempt to sell a policeman a life insurance policy, proclaims: "Why, people are dying this year who have never died before!" – *Hook, Line and Sinker* (1930)

3405 Salesperson Patsy Kelly, tending a women's wear counter in a department store, is confronted by an indecisive customer who has Patsy remove many nightgowns from shelves but still cannot make up her mind. "Will the colors run?" the woman asks about one of the items. "Not till they see you in it," Patsy mumbles. – *Babes in the Goods* (1934)

3406 Penniless W. C. Fields and his daughter approach a hot dog stand. He orders two franks, which they partially devour. Fields then returns the remains to the vendor. "You tramp!" the owner shouts. "How am I going to sell these dogs?" "First you insult me, then you ask my advice concerning salesmanship?" Fields retorts indignantly. – *Poppy* (1936)

3407 G.I. Richard Conte in Italy during World War II tells his buddy about his dream of becoming a traveling salesman in the States. "*You're* a traveling salesman," his pal points out. "What do you mean, I'm a traveling salesman? I'm a murderer," Conte jokes. "You're a traveling salesman," his buddy insists, "selling democracy to the natives." – *A Walk in the Sun* (1945)

3408 Joan Davis asks soap salesman Andy Devine, who has just returned from a stint on the road, if he got any orders. "Well," he replies, "in one town I got two orders." "That's better than nothing," she says. "What were they?" "Get out and stay out." – *The Traveling Saleswoman* (1950)

3409 "People are always fighting each other," a munitions salesman says. "We are the only salesmen who are actually pursued by our customers." – *Flame Over India* (1960)

3410 "After all," the spirit of Woody Allen reports back to the audience, "there are worse things than death. If you ever spent an evening with an insurance salesman, you know exactly what I mean." – *Love and Death* (1975)

3411 Car designer Thomas Gottschalk, recently arrived from Germany, asks hotel doorman Billy Dee Williams to help him sell his experimental vehicle. "I was a thief, not a salesman," Williams explains. "Oh, that is a difference?" – *Driving Me Crazy* (1991)

Science and Scientists

3412 "You know, I crossed the goldenrod with poison ivy once," Joan Davis relates. "What do you think I got? Hay fever and the seven-year itch." — *Josette* (1938)

3413 Austere Russian agent Greta Garbo boasts to romantic American Melvyn Douglas about one of her country's great scientists: "He has proved beyond any question that physical attraction is purely electrochemical." — *Ninotchka* (1939)

3414 Law partners and pals Pat O'Brien and Broderick Crawford are baffled by a series of murders. When O'Brien suddenly claims he can crack the case, Crawford laughs. "All right," O'Brien says, "they laughed at Marconi, too." "I don't know why," Crawford quips. "I didn't think his stuff was funny." — *Slightly Honorable* (1940)

3415 Amateur scientist and inventor Victor Moore explains his new discovery, invisible paint, to a visitor. "You paint something with it and you can't see it," he begins. "I'm worried about it, though.... I painted the can with it, and now I can't find it." — *True to Life* (1943)

3416 At a laboratory, Broadway producer Cary Grant, who has discovered a dancing caterpillar, refuses to part with his find until he gets a price. "This worm must remain here for the advancement of science," an entomologist insists. "A phenomenon like this occurs once in a million years!" "Then sit down and wait for the next one," Grant suggests. — *Once Upon a Time* (1944)

3417 A well-meaning scientist (James Stewart) suspects the plane he is on is going to crash—at least, according to his mathematical calculations. He sidles up to unsuspecting woman passenger Marlene Dietrich. "If anything happens," he whispers, "you have three minutes before the plane crashes. Go into the men's room, sit on the floor with your back against the partition. It's bolted down." — *No Highway in the Sky* (1951)

3418 Detective Shemp Howard of the Three Stooges discovers he is being attacked by a crazed scientist named Dr. Jekyll. "Dr. Jekyll?" he cries. "We must hide!" — *Spooks!* (1953)

3419 Mad scientist Whit Bissel pulls teenager Gary Conway from an auto wreck and puts him back together. "Answer me!" Bissel orders. "You have a civil tongue in your head! I know—I sewed it in there!" — *I Was a Teenage Frankenstein* (1957)

3420 Garbage collector Lou Costello tinkers with chemistry, hoping one day to be famous. "They also laughed at Einstein and his theory of relativity," he proclaims. "Now everybody has relatives." — *The 30-Foot Bride of Candy Mountain* (1959)

3421 "Your brain will be electronically simplified," a scientist threatens Woody Allen. "My brain is my second favorite organ," Allen declares. — *Sleeper* (1973)

3422 At a science lab a technician trying to demonstrate to British agent James Bond (Roger Moore) a deadly weapon in the guise of an umbrella is having problems with the release mechanism. "Having problems keeping it up?" Moore jests. — *Octopussy* (1983)

3423 "If you played your cards right," obnoxious television comic Alan Alda propositions Mia Farrow, "you could have my body." "Wouldn't you rather leave it to science?" she ripostes. — *Crimes and Misdemeanors* (1989)

Secretaries

3424 Con artist Robert Woolsey decides to impersonate the president of a railroad. "Can I be your secretary?" his assistant Bert Wheeler asks. "No," Woolsey replies. "You wouldn't fit on my lap." – *The Rainmakers* (1935)

3425 "You'll have to talk to my secretary," announces George Burns on the telephone. "You'd better call about twelve o'clock. She'll be in then to go out to lunch." – *A Damsel in Distress* (1937)

3426 George Burns: "If you're not here on time, I'll have to get another secretary." Gracie Allen: "Do you think there'll be enough work for both of us?" – *A Damsel in Distress* (1937)

3427 To help him trap a killer, amateur sleuth Boston Blackie (Chester Morris) wants his pal's slow-witted girlfriend to impersonate a secretary. "Have you ever been a secretary?" Morris asks her. "Why?" she questions. "You want me to sit on your lap?" – *A Close Call for Boston Blackie* (1946)

3428 Ladies' man and novelist Kirk Douglas learns that his former secretary is now working for a publisher. "Has he been questioning you about me?" Douglas asks. "Only the normal questions," she replies. "About my experience—" "You didn't talk, did you?" Douglas' pal Keenan Wynn asks sarcastically. – *My Dear Secretary* (1948)

3429 Broadway producer Zero Mostel hires a secretary who appears in a yellow, tight-fitting mini dress and who responds to work directives with a wild, gyrating dance. "Would you believe it?" Mostel says to his accountant (Gene Wilder). "I met her at the public library." – *The Producers* (1968)

3430 Publisher Gene Wilder meets attractive secretary Jill Clayburgh aboard a train. "I can't even read my own writing," she admits. "I don't do shorthand and I can't type." "How do you keep your job?" he wonders. "I give good phone." – *Silver Streak* (1976)

3431 Secretary Dolly Parton, who has bound and gagged her boss with a telephone wire after he tried to attack her, takes an incoming call. "He's tied up at the moment," she intones. – *9 to 5* (1980)

Seduction

3432 Doughboy Bert Wheeler, stationed in Paris, poses as an officer to attract the women. "You look like a million dollars," his buddy Robert Woolsey says. "I may look like a million dollars," Wheeler returns, "but I'm going to be much easier to make." – *Half Shot at Sunrise* (1930)

3433 Jean Harlow, dressed in a sheer evening gown with a low-cut back, slinks toward her bedroom and turns at the threshold to face her "Hell's Angel" pilot Ben Lyon. "Would you be shocked," she asks, "if I put on something more comfortable?" – *Hell's Angels* (1930)

3434 Groucho Marx romances the married Thelma Todd: "I've respected your husband for many years, and what's good enough for him is good enough for me." — *Monkey Business* (1931)

3435 Assertive Charlotte Greenwood seductively embraces stranger Eddie Cantor whom she plans to marry. "All my life I've been waiting for this moment," she coos. "Well," replies Cantor, escaping her hold, "you've had your moment. Goodbye." — *Palmy Days* (1931)

3436 Valet Edward Everett Horton politely informs his employer, Wall Street wizard Douglas Fairbanks, Sr.: "There's a vast difference, sir, between the art of making money and the art of making — a lady." — *Reaching for the Moon* (1931)

3437 President of Huxley College Groucho Marx, learning that his son Zeppo has been dallying with seductive widow Thelma Todd, promptly pays her a visit. "I tell you, you're ruining that boy!" he berates her. "You're ruining him! Why can't you do as much for me?" — *Horse Feathers* (1932)

3438 "Do you mind if I get personal?" Cary Grant asks Mae West. "I don't mind if you get familiar," she ripostes. — *I'm No Angel* (1933)

3439 Maurice Chevalier tries to seduce rich widow Jeanette MacDonald, but she gently maneuvers herself away and turns on the lights. She points out a portrait of Napoleon on the wall to the frustrated Chevalier. "A great man," she says. "His only trouble was he attacked too soon." — *The Merry Widow* (1934)

3440 Small-town mechanic Randolph Scott shows his invention to film star Mae West, who is passing through the area. However, she seems more interested in developing the handsome mechanic than his invention. "I can be of great assistance to you," she offers. "I can't tell you the number of men I've

helped to realize themselves." — *Go West, Young Man* (1936)

3441 Roguish baron Douglas Fairbanks, Jr., attempts to seduce Mary Astor, a prince's mistress. "Someone once said," he notes, addressing her, "fidelity is a fading woman's protection and a charming woman's weakness." — *The Prisoner of Zenda* (1937)

3442 Irene Dunne sidesteps a compromising situation with Charles Boyer. "It's not that I'm prudish," she says warily, "it's just that my mother told me never to enter any man's room in months ending in 'R.'" — *Love Affair* (1939)

3443 Ladies' man Francis Lederer, trying to woo Claudette Colbert, escorts her to the home of Mrs. Flammarion, his mistress, who has invited them for a weekend party. "We have very good news," a servant addresses him. "We found your cufflink." "You did?" Lederer asks uncomfortably. "Yes," the servant continues. "It was in Madam Flammarion's sitting room." "The wind probably blew it in," Colbert adds wryly. — *Midnight* (1939)

3444 During a picnic in the woods, Cesar Romero takes advantage of the romantic setting and begins to woo pretty Nancy Kelly. "I'll cut some pine bowers and build a fire," he offers, "and we'll sit here alone under the stars and watch the fire die out and the night close in." "Watch the wolves close in, you mean," she corrects him as she begins to leave. — *He Married His Wife* (1940)

3445 Womanizer Groucho Marx invokes the suspicions of husband Henry Armetta. "Hey," Armetta complains, "press-a the grapes, no press-a my wife." — *The Big Store* (1941)

3446 Sailor Dennis O'Keefe meets a nightclub singer who thinks he is a numerologist. "I don't suppose you do anything except on certain days," he

remarks. "Well," she replies suggestively, "that all depends on the induce-
ment. Why don't you try tempting me?"
–*Hi Diddle Diddle* (1943)

3447 A crook's sexy girlfriend, assigned to seduce Jack Benny, gets him
alone in a hotel room. "Look at me, darling," she whispers, "can't you see what
my eyes are saying?" "Yes," Benny
replies, "and you ought to watch your
language!"–*The Horn Blows at Midnight* (1945)

3448 A woman, trying to poison Lou
Costello to cover up a murder, first tries
to seduce him. "Gee," Costello says as
she prepares to make love to him,
"you're pretty." "I'll bet you say that to
all the girls." "Yes," he replies. "It don't
go over so good with the boys."–*Abbott
and Costello Meet the Killer* (1949)

3449 Ultra-dumb blonde Judy Holliday
is rattled by the cultivated demeanor of
her handsome tutor William Holden.
"Let me ask you something," she says,
getting right down to basics. "Are you
one of these talkers or would you be interested in a little action?"–*Born
Yesterday* (1950)

3450 French movie actress Corinne
Calvet tries to seduce fledgling singer
Dean Martin. "I think you have a
beautiful voice," she says as she embraces him. "Lady," Jerry Lewis interjects, "where are you looking for the
vocal cords?"–*My Friend Irma Goes
West* (1950)

3451 A man-hungry nurse, who someday hopes to meet a rich husband by
way of her profession, sees a wealthy
hospital board member enter the
hospital building. "Oh, if he'd only break
his leg or something," she says excitedly, "and I could have him for just
about two weeks."–*Half Angel* (1951)

3452 "You made a hit with the girl," a
meteorologist says to his colleague.
"How did you do it?" "My training as a
meteorologist," his friend replies. "I can

take one look at a girl and tell whether."
–*Destination Gobi* (1953)

3453 Bob Hope, disguised as the great
lover Casanova, enters the chambers of
a beautiful young woman. "Señor
Casanova," she warns, "you must not be
found in my room. If necessary, I will
scream for help." "Oh, I don't need any
help," Hope replies confidently.–*Casanova's Big Night* (1954)

3454 While artist Dorothy Malone
demonstrates to model Dean Martin how
to romantically embrace a woman, he
kisses her. "That was uncalled for!"
Malone protests. "I could have sworn I
heard you call," Martin teases.–*Artists
and Models* (1955)

3455 Ensign Jack Lemmon has his
cabin "ready for action" in preparation
for a social evening with a voluptuous
nurse. Fellow officer Henry Fonda reads
the inscription on one of Lemmon's
pillows positioned prominently on his
cot: "Tonight or never. Compliments of
American Harvester Company. We plow
deep while others sleep."–*Mister
Roberts* (1955)

3456 Jack Lemmon, an officer aboard
a cargo ship in the Pacific during World
War II, has an opportunity to invite a
nurse to his quarters. Fellow officers
Henry Fonda and William Powell help to
make Lemmon's evening a success. "All
right," Powell says, "Doug and I made
the scotch. The nurse is your department."–*Mister Roberts* (1955)

3457 "I'm starved for your kisses,"
seductive Anita Ekberg whispers to Bob
Hope. "I'm famished for your love."
"You don't want me," Hope replies. "You
want the Diner's Club."–*Paris Holiday*
(1958)

3458 During the Civil War Southern
belle Constance Towers uses all her
feminine wiles to gain the confidence of
Union soldiers billeted on her estate.
Serving a special dinner she has prepared, she suggestively leans over officer

John Wayne with a platter of delicacies. "Now what is your preference," she asks, "the leg or the breast?" – *The Horse Soldiers* (1959)

3459 Submarine commander Cary Grant rescues several American nurses during World War II, and his junior officer Tony Curtis forthwith maneuvers a pretty nurse into a rubber raft and rows off with her. Another officer warns Grant that they are missing. "When a girl's under twenty-one," Grant explains, "she's protected by the law; when she's over sixty-five, she's protected by nature; anywhere in between, she's fair game." – *Operation Petticoat* (1959)

3460 A proper Doris Day lambastes a licentious Rock Hudson: "This may come as a shock to you, but there are some men who don't end every sentence with a proposition." – *Pillow Talk* (1959)

3461 Janis Paige has always displayed a sexual interest in David Niven, even though he is happily married. "I'm thinking of going on the make for you," she confesses. "But why?" he wonders. "The usual," she returns. "I like the way you look." "Since when?" "Does it have to be retroactive?" she asks. – *Please Don't Eat the Daisies* (1960)

3462 James Mason, English college lecturer in the U.S., considers renting a room for the summer in the home of widow Shelley Winters, whose sexual interest is aroused by the handsome prospective boarder. "If what you're needing is peace and quiet," she promises laughingly, "I can assure you you couldn't get more 'peace' anywhere." – *Lolita* (1962)

3463 Seductive Joan Collins tries to get Bob Hope to reveal a secret formula he has memorized. "I could love you body and soul," she pants. "They're available," he responds, "in that order." – *The Road to Hong Kong* (1962)

3464 Gentlemanly Cary Grant escorts widow Audrey Hepburn, who has fallen in love with him, to her apartment. "Won't you come in?" she asks. "No, I won't," he replies. "I don't bite, you know – unless it's called for." – *Charade* (1963)

3465 American Nobel Prize winner Paul Newman, during his visit to Sweden, removes the jacket of his beautiful liaison officer (Elke Sommer). "What are you doing?" she purrs. "Inspecting the foreign ministry," he explains. – *The Prize* (1963)

3466 Womanizer Walter Matthau tries to seduce Debbie Reynolds, who is reduced to running around a living room to avoid him. "I beg of you," she cries, "don't waste your life in the endless pursuit of pleasure, just running from woman to woman!" "Don't worry about my running," he replies. "I'm in terrific condition." – *Goodbye Charlie* (1964)

3467 Tony Curtis' servant (Lionel Jeffries) explains that a now wealthy and widowed contessa had met her rich husband while she was a hotel maid: "She took his breakfast up one morning and stayed for lunch – as you might say." – *Arrivederci, Baby* (1966)

3468 A sexy young woman invites secret agent Matt Helm (Dean Martin) into her bedroom where she seductively places herself on the bed. "Oh," she murmurs, "I am a terrible hostess. I haven't offered you a thing." "I wouldn't say that," Martin replies. – *The Wrecking Crew* (1969)

3469 Young Goldie Hawn returns with lecherous, middle-aged Peter Sellers to his apartment where he attempts to seduce her. But she parries his thrusts until he is forced to retreat. Slightly discouraged, he makes one last verbal attempt. "And if I made a pass at you now," he asks cautiously, "what would your reaction be?" "You want the result before you place the bet!" she protests. – *There's a Girl in My Soup* (1970)

3470 A sexy party girl flirts with rodeo rider Cliff Robertson and, as she leaves, hips swinging provocatively, she attracts the attention of a fellow rider. "I wish I had a swing like that in my back yard," he remarks. "No, you don't," another says. "That's a public playground." – *J.W. Coop* (1971)

3471 Forward middle-aged Alice Ghostley is drawn to government agent Jack Weston: "You're a very masculine man. I'll bet you think I've never been married." "I don't care," Weston replies. "Well," she continues, "I've never been married. In fact, I've never even been–" "Lady!" – *Gator* (1976)

3472 A well-dressed college student, shopping in a local supermarket, approaches a middle-aged woman selecting cucumbers at the vegetable bin. The student doesn't know she is the college dean's wife. "Mine's bigger than that," he says. "I beg your pardon." "My cucumber is bigger," he continues, selecting a large cucumber. "I have a husband named Dean Wermer," she enlightens him. "You still want to show me your cucumber?" – *National Lampoon's Animal House* (1978)

3473 James Caan asks Marsha Mason if she would like a tour of his place. "What time does it leave?" she asks. "We could start with the bedroom." "You start with the bedroom, you could end with the bedroom," she reasons. "Endings are just beginnings backwards," he concludes. – *Chapter Two* (1979)

3474 Happily married George Segal is surprised when his wife's divorced friend arrives in his office and tries to seduce him. "You guys have been coming on for what – ten thousand years?" she whispers. "Now it's our turn." – *The Last Married Couple in America* (1980)

3475 When James Bond (Roger Moore) returns to his hotel room and finds a youthful blonde ice skater in his bed, he is reluctant to proceed. "But you're in training," he reminds her. "That's a laugh," she returns. "Every-

body knows it builds up muscle tone." – *For Your Eyes Only* (1981)

3476 Brenda Vaccaro, as the wife of a petty tyrant terrorizing an old California province, tries to seduce local landowner George Hamilton. "The people only see the part I play in public," she confides to him. "Only a few select friends know my private parts." – *Zorro, the Gay Blade* (1981)

3477 British secret agent James Bond (Roger Moore) attends a meeting arranged by arch villain Louis Jourdan. His seductive mistress, Kristina Waylord, has been sent to represent Jourdan. "Does he have a proposition for me – or do you?" Moore inquires – *Octopussy* (1983)

3478 On a Rio beach, middle-aged Michael Caine is seduced by adolescent nymphet Michelle Johnson, the daughter of his best friend. In the cold light of the following day, Caine would like to bury the regrettable roll in the sand. "Last night never happened," he says to her. "I know," she replies. "I was there when it never happened." – *Blame It on Rio* (1984)

3479 "Do you want this body?" seductive Sigourney Weaver entices innocent Bill Murray. "Is this a trick question?" he replies. – *Ghostbusters* (1984)

3480 Tom Hanks has devoted a lot of time romancing sexy Rita Wilson, all the while trying to seduce her. "You mean you've just been trying to get to bed with me?" she finally discovers. "Well," Hanks acknowledges, "I think I've put in the hours, don't you?" – *Volunteers* (1985)

3481 Straitlaced police officer Dan Aykroyd and his free-spirited partner Tom Hanks interview a porno publisher at his lavish home where one of the magnate's playmates indirectly tries to seduce Aykroyd. As the two officers leave, the more worldly Hanks berates his partner for not jumping at the proposal. "Now let me tell you something," the uptight Aykroyd replies angrily.

"There are two things that clearly differentiate the human species from animals. One, we use cutlery; two, we control our sexual urges." – *Dragnet* (1987)

3482 Sexy Priscilla Presley tires to lure police detective Leslie Nielsen up to her apartment. "Can I interest you in a nightcap?" she asks seductively. "No thanks," Nielsen replies. "I don't wear them." – *The Naked Gun* (1988)

3483 Struggling nightclub singer Beverly D'Angelo questions whether her latest boyfriend is in love with her. "He maybe just has an ulterior motive," she confides to her eight-year-old daugther Jenny Lewis. "You mean like he wants to get in your pants?" the child asks. – *Trading Hearts* (1988)

3484 Woody Allen is collaborating with Mia Farrow on a documentary film about television comic Alan Alda, who invites Farrow to his hotel room. Allen, aware of Alda's many amorous affairs, warns her not to go. "He's interested in producing something of mine," she

counters. "Your first child," Allen quips. – *Crimes and Misdemeanors* (1989)

3485 California reporter Chevy Chase, journeying to the South to take over his deceased aunt's run-down plantation, meets a pretty real-estate agent. He returns with her to her home where she prepares a complete dinner. "Would you like some dessert?" she asks suggestively. "What do you have in mind?" "How about something sweet and Southern?" – *Fletch Lives* (1989)

3486 Architect Tom Selleck, visiting England, attracts a sex-starved headmistress who studies him as he looks out the window of a manor where workmen are raising a large tent. "Not so splendid as your mighty erections, I imagine?" she remarks. – *Three Men and a Little Lady* (1990)

3487 The Devil tries to tempt Ellen Barkin to join him in his domain, but she resists. "Sooner or later I'm going to get you anyway," he continues. "Come along now and I'll guarantee you a hell of a time." – *Switch* (1991)

Self

3488 Mae West: "When I'm good, I'm very, very good, but when I'm bad, I'm better." – *I'm No Angel* (1933)

3489 Self-effacing poetess Elizabeth Barrett (Norma Shearer) worries that she will not make a favorable impression upon poet Robert Browning (Fredric March). "You're very interesting and picturesque," one of her sisters says encouragingly. "Isn't that how a guidebook describes a ruin?" Elizabeth asks. – *The Barretts of Wimpole Street* (1934)

3490 Aging eccentric millionaire George Arliss complains about his worth-

less relatives to lifelong friend Ralph Morgan. "Why are you exciting yourself?" asks Morgan. "Here, let me feel your pulse." "Go away," the cranky Arliss protests. "I don't enjoy holding hands with you." – *The Last Gentleman* (1934)

3491 "Any man's a fool who's certain about anything," Hugh Herbert instructs his servant Eric Blore. "Are you sure, sir?" Blore inquires. "Positive." – *To Beat the Band* (1935)

3492 A forty-year-old servant, still dreaming of finding a husband, conveys her thought to her mistress Fay Bainter. "It would be idle to pretend that you are – especially handsome," Bainter suggests delicately. "Well, that may be, ma'am. But my face is my own. The more I see in the glass, the more it pleases me. I never look at it without saying to myself: 'Who's to be the lucky man?'" – *Quality Street* (1937)

3493 "I'm the kind of fellow when you first meet me you don't like me," writer Lee Tracy confesses to Joan Woodbury, "but after you get to know me better – you hate me." – *Crashing Hollywood* (1938)

3494 Groucho Marx announces himself to Eve Arden: "It's me or it's I or, at any rate, it's one of us." – *At the Circus* (1939)

3495 "I've always looked for someone like you," Eve Arden says to Groucho Marx. "Like me, eh?" Groucho challenges. "I'm not good enough?" – *At the Circus* (1939)

3496 Howard da Silva is rejected by Linda Hayes, who thinks he is cute but not for her. "I'm not pretty, but I'm cute," he acquiesces. – *I'm Still Alive* (1940)

3497 Two wealthy businessmen have just been hoodwinked out of thousands of dollars by con artist Kay Francis. "There's something pathetic about a woman struggling on her own," one of the victims rationalizes. "It arouses the protective instincts in a man," the other adds. "We must keep this quiet. People might think we were a couple of old fools." "And most emphatically we're not," says the first. "We're just a couple of blasted liars!" concludes his companion. – *Play Girl* (1940)

3498 In a notions shop, Felix Bressart commiserates with fellow employee James Stewart, both chafing from the abrasiveness of their boss, Frank Morgan. "He picks on me, too," Bressart complains. "The other day he called me

an idiot. What could I do? I said, 'Yes, Mr. Matuschek, I'm an idiot.' I'm no fool." – *The Shop Around the Corner* (1940)

3499 Sleazy Mayor Lovett (Gene Lockhart) learns that John Doe (Gary Cooper) plans to commit suicide by jumping off a roof. "What about me!" the politician grouses. "It's my building he's jumping off of – and I'm up for re-election, too." – *Meet John Doe* (1941)

3500 John Barrymore, playing himself, comments on his own reputation: "I've been in the public eye so long, it's permanently bloodshot." – *Playmates* (1941)

3501 Marjorie Main, as housekeeper of a small boarding house, rings the dinner bell for the guests. Young Bonita Granville comes charging down the hall stairs and rushes into the dining room. "One of these days," Main gripes, "you're gonna fall down and get blood all over my nice clean stairs." – *The Wild Man of Borneo* (1941)

3502 During World War II in Casablanca, nightclub owner Rick Blaine (Humphrey Bogart) forcibly enlists the aid of Vichy police captain Claude Rains in an escape plan. "Remember," Bogart warns, "this bullet is pointed right at your heart." "That's my least vulnerable spot," Rains quips. – *Casablanca* (1942)

3503 Lord George Sanders comforts Hurd Hatfield when Angela Lansbury, because of unrequited love, takes her life: "I do wish that I had had such an experience. The women who have admired me ... have always insisted on living on long after I ceased to care for them." – *The Picture of Dorian Gray* (1945)

3504 Groucho Marx, on the run from police, seeks refuge in a showgirls' dressing room and pleads with its occupants to hide him. "I'm as innocent as a babe – even more innocent. I know some babes who ain't so innocent." – *Copacabana* (1947)

3505 Clarence Day (William Powell), determined to hire a maid for his family, storms into an employment office and selects one prospect waiting to be hired. "Sir," the woman in charge announces, "before I can let any girl go from this establishment, I must know the character of the home in which she will be employed." "Madam," Powell replies, "*I am the character of my home.*"–*Life with Father* (1947)

3506 Bob Hope inadvertently becomes the target of foreign assassins. Trapped in a department store, he collars the manager for help. "There are guys after me in this store," Hope cries. "They're trying to kill me. You gotta do something. You gotta help me." "Please, please," the manager replies, "you're crushing my carnation."–*Where There's Life* (1947)

3507 Recently married veteran William Holden tells wife Jeanne Crain that he is thinking of dropping out of college and becoming a used-car salesman. "In a recent survey," she responds, "sixty-four percent of all used-car dealers said they wished they'd gone into some other field." "You made that up!" Holden exclaims. "You're always making up statistics. Why?" "Of course I made that up. Someone is always making up statistics. It might as well be me."–*Apartment for Peggy* (1948)

3508 Witty piano-thumping Oscar Levant introduces himself to the audience: "It's not a pretty face, I grant you, but underneath its flabby exterior is an enormous lack of character."–*An American in Paris* (1951)

3509 When their plane develops engine trouble, married couple Macdonald Carey and Anne Baxter cancel their vacation and return home. Their housekeeper, however, is less than enthusiastic about returning to work. "Some month off!" she mutters. "Nice you weren't killed, though, jobs being what they are."–*My Wife's Best Friend* (1952)

3510 Unlucky gambler Dean Martin is dragged to the den of big-time gambler-mobster Sheldon Leonard because of Martin's pile of I.O.U.s. "It's nice to know you," Martin says nervously. "It's not nice to know me," Leonard replies. "I know me, and believe me, it is not nice to know me."–*Money from Home* (1953)

3511 Impoverished, aging film star Bette Davis, swallowing hard and taking a position as a salesperson in a department store, overhears one dowager ask another, "Isn't that Margaret Elliot?" "I *am* Margaret Elliot," Davis, humiliated, straightens up and huffs, "and I intend to *stay* Margaret Elliot."–*The Star* (1953)

3512 "You're a real likable guy," Mister Roberts (Henry Fonda) says to Ensign Pulver (Jack Lemmon). "I also think you're the most hapless, lazy, disorganized, and in general the most lecherous guy I ever saw." "I am not disorganized!" Lemmon protests. –*Mister Roberts* (1955)

3513 "Everybody thinks of me as a sexpot," complains aspiring, buxom singer Jayne Mansfield, holding two milk bottles against her breast. "Nobody thinks of me as equipped for motherhood."–*The Girl Can't Help It* (1956)

3514 Working as a map maker in Cairo, D. H. Lawrence (Peter O'Toole) chafes his superior. "I can't make out whether you're bloody bad-tempered or just half-witted," the officer snipes at O'Toole. "I have the same trouble, sir." –*Lawrence of Arabia* (1962)

3515 Naive Jack Lemmon has been dismissed from his job as gendarme. His friend Lou Jacobi, a bistro owner, encourages Lemmon, now depressed, to become a pimp. "They let the girls work for them," Jacobi explains. "I'm afraid I wasn't cut out for a life of crime." "There you go again," Jacobi says, "selling yourself short."–*Irma la Douce* (1963)

3516 Zero Mostel and Gene Wilder, in search of a certain playwright, find the tenement in which he lives. "He's up on the roof with his boids," janitor Madlyn Gates informs them. "Doity, disgusting, filthy, lice-ridden boids. You used to be able to sit on the stoop like a person. Not any more. No, sir. Boids! You get my drift?" "Thank you, madam," says Wilder. "I'm not a madam," she replies indignantly. "I'm a concierge." – *The Producers* (1968)

3517 Famous Italian actor Ricardo Montalban takes dance-hall hostess Shirley MacLaine to an exclusive nightclub. "This place is crawling with celebrities," the awed MacLaine says to herself. "I'm the only person here I never heard of." – *Sweet Charity* (1969)

3518 General MacArthur (Gregory Peck), returning to the Philippines, disembarks with the Filipino president a few yards from shore. "My people are going to laugh if I fall in the deep water," the president says. "I cannot swim." "That's not so bad, Mr. President," Peck replies. "Everyone is about to see that I cannot walk on water." – *MacArthur* (1977)

3519 African killer bees have invaded the American Southwest, and the first attempts by the military to wipe them out have been disastrous. "I'm going to be the first officer in U.S. battle history to get his butt kicked by a mess of bugs," grumbles Richard Widmark. – *The Swarm* (1978)

3520 Without a search warrant, police detective Dick Shawn, accompanied by doctor Richard Benjamin, hesitates to break into Dracula's apartment where Benjamin's sweetheart is being held against her will. "If we don't," Benjamin pleads, "her immortal soul will be lost forever." "If we do," Shawn counters, "I'll lose my pension." – *Love at First Bite* (1979)

3521 Woody Allen criticizes his married friend Tony Roberts for seeing Diane Keaton behind his back. "You are so self-righteous, you know," Roberts retorts. "I mean, we're just people, we're just human beings. You think you're God!" "I – I gotta model myself after someone," Allen returns. – *Manhattan* (1979)

3522 Policeman Paul Newman, in a self-deprecating mood, complains to partner Danny Aiello, who advises Newman to get in touch with his feelings. "I'm trying," Newman replies, "but my line is always busy." – *Fort Apache, the Bronx* (1981)

3523 "I have this problem with my self-esteem," Richard Dreyfuss' attractive girlfriend admits. "The minute I turn away from a mirror I think I'm short and fat." "That's funny," replies Dreyfuss. "Every time I turn away from a mirror I think I'm tall and irresistible." – *The Buddy System* (1984)

3524 A serial killer has struck again, and an investigator from the district attorney's office arrives at the scene of the crime, asking if there are any witnesses. "Only this bum here," replies a police officer. "I'm not a bum," the witness protests, "I'm homeless." – *Party Line* (1988)

3525 Unemployed television actress Jacqueline Bisset denigrates her own sitcom, "Hillary," now in syndication: "I hear in El Salvador you get your choice of torture – genital clamps or 'Hillary.'" – *Scenes from the Class Struggle in Beverly Hills* (1989)

3526 A drug addict, pleading with musician Cheech Marin for some cocaine, insists that he is not addicted. "Some people can handle it and some people can't," the addict asserts. "Me, personally – I can handle it. I've been doin' coke for years. I ain't got no habit." – *Far Out Man* (1990)

3527 When Joan Plowright learns that son-in-law Kevin Kline is cheating on her daughter, she arranges with the son of a friend to kill Kline. "You're a very good boy," she says to the young killer. "Today, many young people have no respect. I think because of T.V. and all—so much sex and violence." "Yeah," the young man agrees. "Who can figure what this world is coming to."—*I Love You to Death* (1990)

3528 "I know you think I'm a sleaze bag," porno king Dom DeLuise admits to police detective Gene Hackman. "Maybe I am a sleaze bag. Maybe all my life I've been a sleaze bag. Somebody had to be the sleaze bag. If it hadn't been me, it might have been you. Maybe you should thank me. Did you ever think of that?"—*Loose Cannons* (1990)

3529 Kirstie Alley's sister explains why she has left her husband: "He cut

my allowance; he makes me drive his old Jaguar." "Some people have worse problems," Alley replies. "Like what?" her sister asks.—*Madhouse* (1990)

3530 Bill Murray, disguised in a clown's costume, holds up a bank. "What the hell kind of clown are you?" an elderly guard asks. "The crying-on-the-inside kind, I guess," Murray quips. —*Quick Change* (1990)

3531 Browbeaten secretary Michele Pfeiffer, with a zero self-esteem, laments to her tyrannical tycoon employer Christopher Walken: "How can you be so mean to someone so meaningless?"—*Batman Returns* (1992)

Sex

3532 Wise-guy William Haines tries this line on hard-to-get Leila Hyams: "Say, did you ever hear the story—the egg has no sex, but the banana has a peel?"—*Way Out West* (1930)

3533 The morning after one of bachelor Lowell Sherman's nights of revelry, his servant discovers a necklace in the living room. "I found this, sir," the servant says to a groggy Sherman. "Do you suppose the lady lost anything else, sir?" "Well, if she did," Sherman quips, "she didn't lose it here."—*Bachelor Apartment* (1931)

3534 Robert Woolsey, upon hearing Edna May Oliver's off-key singing, asks her where she learned to sing. "I spent four years in Paris," she says proudly. "Of course, I'm not a virtuoso." "Not after four years in Paris," Woolsey quips.—*Hold 'Em Jail* (1932)

3535 Wealthy Constance Bennett, in Paris to make a name for herself in

society, enlists the aid of fellow American Ben Lyon, who refers her to a popular playboy. "Say," Lyon explains, "that fellow is one of the great chasers in Paris. If he chases you, you're made." "What?" Bennett asks.—*Lady with a Past* (1932) .

3536 Myrna Loy flaunts an inordinate fascination for the opposite sex, inducing princess Jeanette MacDonald to wonder if Loy thinks of anything else besides men. "Oh, yes," Loy replies. "Of what?" "Schoolboys."—*Love Me Tonight* (1932)

3537 "Goodness," Alison Skipworth says, admiring Mae West's jewelry, "what lovely diamonds." "Goodness had nothing to do with it, honey," West returns.—*Night After Night* (1932)

3538 At a world peace conference in Geneva, Bert Wheeler and Robert Woolsey boast of their accomplishments. "The nations didn't want peace," Wheeler asserts. "But we made them," adds Woolsey. "They didn't want to disarm." "But we made them." "The girls were a little tough at first." "But we–come on, let's get out of here."–*Diplomaniacs* (1933)

3539 Margaret Dumont, in a telephone conversation with Groucho Marx, asks to see him. "It's a long story," she explains. "I can't tell it to you on the phone." "Oh," says Groucho. "It's that kind of story. You should be ashamed of yourself."–*Duck Soup* (1933)

3540 Groucho Marx has just been made President of Freedonia, and Mrs. Teasdale (Margaret Dumont) congratulates him. "This is a gala day for you." "That's plenty," Groucho returns. "I don't think I could handle more than a gal a day."–*Duck Soup* (1933)

3541 A chorus girl says of fellow trouper "Anytime Annie" (Ginger Rogers): "Who could forget her? She only said 'no' once–and then she didn't hear the question."–*42nd Street* (1933)

3542 "Where are you sitting?" a male dancer asks a pretty blonde on his knee. "On a flagpole, dearie," she replies. –*42nd Street* (1933)

3543 An experienced dancer is trying to help newcomer Ruby Keeler learn a new step. A stagehand wants to know what's going on. "I was just trying to make her–" the hoofer begins to explain. "Yeah," the stagehand interjects, "'make her' is right."–*42nd Street* (1933)

3544 "You were born in August," someone remarks to Mae West. "Yeah," she acknowledges, "one of the hot months."–*I'm No Angel* (1933)

3545 "I see a man in your life," a circus mystic, looking into a crystal ball, reveals to Mae West. "What, only one?" she challenges. "I see a change . . . a change of position," he continues. "Sitting or standing?" West asks.–*I'm No Angel* (1933)

3546 Gilbert Roland, trying to restrain his hot-blooded mistress (Violet Kemble-Cooper), asks: "Why don't you leave me to do the lovemaking?" "If I did," she replies, "there wouldn't be any lovemaking."–*Our Betters* (1933)

3547 Reporter ZaSu Pitts, to win the confidence of radio singer Ginger Rogers, says that all the Hollywood stars trust her. "I know them all," Pitts boasts. "I eat with them, I sleep with them–" "You sleep with them?" Rogers asks.–*Professional Sweetheart* (1933)

3548 Eddie Cantor, as a Roman slave placed on the auction block, is rejected by the bidders. Afraid he will be fed to the lions if he is not bought, he pleads with prospective buyers: "I can cook a little, I can take care of the children. If there are no children, I can take care of that."–*Roman Scandals* (1933)

3549 "This is your horoscope," someone says to Mae West. "Consult it frequently." "All right," she agrees. "I'll take it to bed with me."–*She Done Him Wrong* (1933)

3550 I wouldn't want no policeman to catch me with no petticoats on," admits Louise Beavers, Mae West's housekeeper. "No policeman?" questions West. "How about a nice fireman?"–*She Done Him Wrong* (1933)

3551 Detective Cary Grant prepares to handcuff underworld figure Mae West. "Is that necessary?" she asks, looking disdainfully at the manacles. "I wasn't born with them." "A lot of men would be safer if you had," Grant replies. "I don't know," West says. "Hands aren't everything."–*She Done Him Wrong* (1933)

3552 Cary Grant: "Haven't you ever met a man who could make you happy?" Mae West: "Sure. Lots of times."–*She Done Him Wrong* (1933)

3553 Douglas Fairbanks, Sr., as an aging Don Juan, is infatuated with sultry dancer Merle Oberon. "A lovely little girl," he confides to his servant Melville Cooper. "She'd look awful by daylight," Cooper says. "Who wants a girl in daylight?" – *The Private Life of Don Juan* (1934)

3554 "What were you doing on the night of October 5, 1902?" Nick Charles (William Powell) jokingly asks his wife (Myrna Loy). "I was just a gleam in my father's eye," she replies. – *The Thin Man* (1934)

3555 Groucho Marx is outraged that wealthy dowager Margaret Dumont has signed an opera star to a one-thousand-dollar-per-week contract. "Why," he asserts, "you can get a phonograph of Minnie the Moocher for seventy-five cents. And for a buck and a quarter, you get Minnie!" – *A Night at the Opera* (1935)

3556 Stan Laurel causes his pal Oliver Hardy to land on the second-story window ledge of a married couple. Hardy had earlier fought with the husband, who accused Hardy of having an affair with the man's wife. The wife then helps Hardy exit from the apartment. "I've never been in a position like that before," Hardy later remarks. – *Tit for Tat* (1935)

3557 Handsome small-town auto mechanic Randolph Scott straightforwardly begins to read a map to Mae West. "This curved portion is the main body," he points out, "and this is the undeveloped territory." "Hm-m," West intones suggestively, "we'll have to do something about that." – *Go West, Young Man* (1936)

3558 Mae West, on her way to the Klondike, hitches a ride on Victor McLaglen's boat. "If there's anything you want," he says innocently, "just yell for it." "Do you have to yell for it?" West asks. – *Klondike Annie* (1936)

3559 "I haven't got any relations anywhere," showgirl Jean Harlow says, "but I've got a rich uncle." – *Suzy* (1936)

3560 Edward Everett Horton cannot find his roommate, Fred Astaire, aboard a ship. "He might be in someone else's stateroom," suggests a steward who has just completed a search. "What would he be doing in someone else's stateroom?" Horton questions. "That would be entirely up to him, sir." – *Shall We Dance* (1937)

3561 Egbert Sousé (W. C. Fields) takes prissy bank examiner Franklin Pangborn to the Black Pussy Café to forestall his auditing of the books. "Can't we, uh, pull the shade?" Pangborn says nervously. "You can pull anything you want in here," Fields replies. "It's a regular joint." – *The Bank Dick* (1940)

3562 Saloon owner Joseph Calleia, charmed by Mae West, wants to take her under his wing. "Every man I meet wants to protect me," she remarks. "I can't figure out what from." – *My Little Chickadee* (1940)

3563 "I understand you need a guide," W. C. Fields inquires. "I need more than that, honey," Mae West replies. – *My Little Chickadee* (1940)

3564 Bob Hope, posing as a physician, is questioned by a worried mother. "Doctor, I have a girl of nine that never listens to what's right. She's always doing the wrong thing. What should I do?" "Well," Hope answers, "wait another ten years, and if there's no improvement, mail me her phone number." – *My Favorite Blonde* (1942)

3565 During World War II, Frank Morgan, posing as a navy doctor, interviews Ann Sothern, who wants to join the WACS. "Phone number?" Morgan asks. "I beg your pardon, doctor." "It's just a formality," he quickly adds. "The navy likes to know where they can get a hold of you." He then mumbles under his breath: "And I wouldn't mind knowing, either." – *Thousands Cheer* (1943)

3566 "Is there anything I can do for you?" Marilyn Monroe asks Groucho

Marx. "What a ridiculous statement!" he exclaims after weighing the offer. – *Love Happy* (1949)

3567 Leo G. Carroll discusses with his daughter the murder of a promiscuous woman. "Even the most unworthy of us has a right to life and the pursuit of happiness," he says graciously. "From what I hear," his daughter responds cattily, "she pursued it in all directions." – *Strangers on a Train* (1951)

3568 Outspoken and innocent Maggie McNamara has been sounding off to architect William Holden on the subjects of virgins, mistresses and seduction. "How come you're so preoccupied with sex?" he asks. "Don't you think it's better for a girl to be preoccupied with sex than occupied?" – *The Moon Is Blue* (1953)

3569 When Dean Martin suspects a beautiful woman of being a spy, he notifies the F.B.I. An agent encourages him to go "all out" with her so that he can meet her accomplices. "If I had known that," Martin confesses, "I would have joined the F.B.I. instead of the Kangaroo Patrol." – *Artists and Models* (1955)

3570 Henry Fonda as Mister Roberts derides the limited reading material of Ensign Pulver (Jack Lemmon). "He's been reading *God's Little Acre* for over a year now," Fonda scoffs. "He's underlined every erotic passage and added exclamation points – and after a certain pornographic climax, he's inserted the words 'well written.'" – *Mister Roberts* (1955)

3571 Scantily dressed dancer Milly Vitale enters vaudeville entertainer Bob Hope's dressing room several times on various pretexts. "In Milano we do this all the time," she explains. "No wonder Italy is so overpopulated," Hope cracks. – *The Seven Little Foys* (1955)

3572 Dance director Gene Kelly complains to his troupe about a dancer who is about to marry: "Do you have any idea how much time I put in day and night teaching her how to dance?" "Especially nights," someone quips. – *Les Girls* (1957)

3573 Outlaw Henry Silva tells fellow desperado Skip Homeier how he romanced half the women in Sonora. "I would have been there yet," Silva continues, "if I hadn't pulled a leg muscle." – *The Tall T* (1957)

3574 Gruff machinist Arthur O'Connell, aboard a damaged submarine during World War II, does not countenance any meddling with the vessel's machinery – especially from a rescued nurse who outranks him. "Lady," he replies angrily, "Congress made you an officer, but God made you a woman! And a woman shouldn't mess around with a man's machinery!" – *Operation Petticoat* (1959)

3575 Doris Day has fallen in love with New York songwriter Rock Hudson but hesitates to rush headlong into marriage. Her housemaid Thelma Ritter dismisses caution. "It takes only one sip of wine to tell if it's a good bottle," Ritter says. – *Pillow Talk* (1959)

3576 When U.S. Marshal James Stewart invites his friend, cavalry officer Richard Widmark, into Belle's gambling house and saloon for a drink, Belle chases them out because her place is not open for business so early in the morning. "You can have anything you want – out on the veranda!" she exclaims. "Now that's a pretty broad statement," Stewart quips. "That takes in a lot of territory." – *Two Rode Together* (1961)

3577 "When it comes to sex," observes Kim Novak, "men can't keep from lying and women can't keep from telling the truth." – *Boys' Night Out* (1962)

3578 Gambler's mistress Nina Talbot relates to Lana Turner that Tony, her lover, communicates with her chiefly by messages: "Everything's done through a

middleman – well, nearly everything."
– *Who's Got the Action?* (1962)

3579 Naive gendarme Jack Lemmon, his first day on duty in a notorious section of Paris known for its prostitutes, grows suspicious when he sees several couples enter a local hotel. "Would you have even a vague idea of what they're doing in there?" he asks bistro owner Lou Jacobi. "I have a very definite idea," Jacobi replies. – *Irma la Douce* (1963)

3580 The carefree, spirited Tom Jones (Albert Finney), hunting in the verdant countryside, discovers buxom wench Molly Seagrim (Diane Cilento) hiding behind a tree. Tom turns to the audience and remarks: "It's a good night to be abroad and looking for game." – *Tom Jones* (1963)

3581 "My films add dignity and culture to the movie industry," a producer remarks. "And three starlets a week to your bed," adds another. – *The Carpetbaggers* (1964)

3582 James Bond (Sean Connery) is under the covers with a supple blonde (Shirley Eaton) when he receives a telephone call from another guest for an important meeting. "Felix," Bond replies, "I can't. Something big has come up." – *Goldfinger* (1964)

3583 Dean Martin, who desires Kim Novak, keeps Ray Walston busy while he takes Novak into the garden. "She can show me her parsley," Martin quips lasciviously. – *Kiss Me, Stupid* (1964)

3584 Sean Connery, as the resourceful James Bond, takes his lovemaking where he can find it – including under water. "I hope we didn't frighten the fish," he cracks. – *Thunderball* (1965)

3585 Bachelor Rock Hudson watches as the young woman who has just made him breakfast leaves his apartment hugging a skillet. "She says my eggs will touch no pan but hers," he sighs. – *A Very Special Favor* (1965)

3586 "In America they don't have sex, they commit it," someone observes. – *A Very Special Favor* (1965)

3587 At a gambling casino, ladies' man Tony Curtis picks up wealthy and beautiful Zsa Zsa Gabor, who temptingly confides to him: "I love a man who plays all night, but not on the table." – *Arrivederci, Baby* (1966)

3588 Doris Day, an employee at a space project, is suspected of being a spy. An army general (Edward Andrews) decides upon a course of action. "One of us will just have to spend the night with her," he confides to space executive Dick Martin. "We've got to fight fire with fire." "May I volunteer, sir?" Martin suggests. "I admire your spirit," the general replies, "but this is one mission I may have to take on myself." – *The Glass Bottom Boat* (1966)

3589 Vassar graduate Jessica Walter continues her relationship with school friend Shirley Knight. "Come over and gab," Jessica proposes. "I can't," Shirley says. "I'm going to bed early." "Are you tired or just boasting?" – *The Group* (1966)

3590 "Small college and all," disillusioned professor Richard Burton describes his school. "Musical beds is the faculty sport around here." – *Who's Afraid of Virginia Woolf?* (1966)

3591 A woman instructor aims a ray gun at Dean Martin's belt buckle and dissolves it, causing his pants to drop. "That's when the danger usually starts," remarks one female student. "I like my way better," says a second student. – *The Ambushers* (1967)

3592 Psychiatrist and marriage counselor Martin Gabel enlightens troubled husband Dick Van Dyke about marital sex. "You know," Gable begins, "I always suggest that we think of the sex drive as we would of a fine violin. Play it regularly, as it were, and it stays in tune, responding to your slightest touch." – *Divorce, American Style* (1967)

3593 Outlaw Richard Boone says to the wife of a corrupt Indian agent: "My mom told me to take off my hat and my cigar in the presence of a lady. What else I take off depends on how lucky I get." – *Hombre* (1967)

3594 Mrs. Pollifax (Rosalind Russell), a patriotic widow, volunteers her services to the C.I.A. "Since I lost my husband and my children moved away," she explains to the department chief, "I managed to fill my days. The problem is – with the nights." "That goes for all of us," the officer adds. – *Mrs. Pollifax – Spy* (1967)

3595 British agent James Bond (Sean Connery) undresses a nubile beauty. "The things I do for England," he utters. – *You Only Live Twice* (1967)

3596 A shapely Japanese maiden says to James Bond (Sean Connery): "It will be a pleasure serving under you." – *You Only Live Twice* (1967)

3597 Barbarella (Jane Fonda) in a space adventure is enclosed in a machine designed to kill its victims by means of sexual pleasure. Instead, she destroys the machine. "What kind of girl are you?" the shocked operator demands. "Have you no shame?" – *Barbarella* (1968)

3598 C.I.A. agent James Garner radios his bureau chief from a banana republic in South America that his return will be slightly delayed. "No, it's not official," he says, with beautiful Eva Renzi at his side. "But you may call it undercover activity." – *The Pink Jungle* (1968)

3599 "Danger really turns me on," teenager Joan Delaney boasts to an ambassador's son. "Do you know how many babies were born during the blitz?" – *Don't Go Near the Water* (1969)

3600 Neal (Richard Benjamin) reaches out for Brenda (Ali McGraw). "Later," she says. "What if I can't wait?" "Start without me." – *Goodbye, Columbus* (1969)

3601 "Not every woman is a lesbian," Susannah York remarks. "I'm aware of that unfortunate fact," lesbian companion Beryl Reid replies. – *The Killing of Sister George* (1969)

3602 "I once stole a pornographic book which was written in Braille," Woody Allen confides to his psychoanalyst. "I used to rub the dirty parts." – *Take the Money and Run* (1969)

3603 U.S. secret agent Matt Helm (Dean Martin), in Denmark on a case, has trouble ditching klutzy Sharon Tate. "My orders from the insurance bureau are to work directly under you," she persists. "Directly under me?" Martin echoes. – *The Wrecking Crew* (1969)

3604 Mae West is informed by an aspiring actor that he is six-feet, seven-inches tall. She peruses his well-structured body and mutters: "Forget about the six feet. Let's talk about the seven inches." – *Myra Breckinridge* (1970)

3605 Mae West: "Is that a gun in your pocket or are you just pleased to see me?" – *Myra Breckinridge* (1970)

3606 Guitar-plucking ex-marine Glen Campbell visits Brooklyn flame Tisha Sterling, who calls out from her bath: "Does your guitar play under water?" "No," he replies, beginning to disrobe, "but I do." – *Norwood* (1970)

3607 "You got your terminology confused," George Segal says to Barbra Streisand. "We did not make love." "Whatever the hell it was," she replies, "it beats drying the dishes." – *The Owl and the Pussycat* (1970)

3608 Lascivious Peter Sellers, a guest at an afternoon wedding, discovers that he and the bride had once been lovers. He persuades her to go to bed with him one last time. "Isn't it better to end with a bang than a whimper?" he asks. – *There's a Girl in My Soup* (1970)

3609 A married couple are about to go to bed when the wife kneels down and begins to pray. "Don't you ever say your prayers after?" the impatient husband remarks. "Don't get dirty," she replies. –*Made for Each Other* (1971)

3610 Attractive Goldie Hawn enters her regular bank where the manager Gerde Frobe begins to escort her to her safety deposit box. "I've got no will power," Hawn admits. "So twice a week I go shopping, then business with my private box." "Oh," leers Frobe, "I would give anything to see your private box." –*$ (Dollars)* (1971)

3611 Jester Woody Allen, desiring the forbidden pleasures of a woman of the Medieval court, is stymied because her treasure is locked within a chastity belt. "I must think of something quickly," he announces, "or before we know it, the Renaissance will be here and we'll all be painting." –*Everything You Always Wanted to Know About Sex (But Were Afraid to Ask)* (1972)

3612 Court jester Woody Allen repins a piece of fallen jewelry onto the dress of queen Lynn Redgrave and rewards himself with an extra touch. "Did I feel thy two hands upon my royal body cop a feel?" she inquires. –*Everything You Always Wanted to Know About Sex (But Were Afraid to Ask)* (1972)

3613 Cybill Shepherd suggests to Charles Grodin that they take their clothes off and get as close as they can without touching. "I love it, I love it!" Grodin cries ecstatically. "All my life I wanted to be in a place like this, with a girl like you, playing games like this." "I don't know if I can go through with it," she suddenly hesitates. "Oh, yes you can," he cajoles. "Sure, it's just a game. The worst that could happen, you'd lose." –*The Heartbreak Kid* (1972)

3614 "I was really great last night," Woody Allen touts his sexual prowess. "I didn't once have to sit up and consult the manual." –*Play It Again, Sam* (1972)

3615 Divorced from his wife, Allan Felix (Woody Allen) withdraws from the outside world as he ponders over a visit to the analyst: "No matter what I'll say, he'll say it's a sexual problem. Isn't that ridiculous? We don't even have relations anymore." –*Play It Again, Sam* (1972)

3616 "When I go with a man I don't bother him," entertainer Renee Taylor tells her audience. "I don't wake him when it's over, I don't wake him in the middle. I have to wake him to start, though." –*Made for Each Other* (1973)

3617 Diane Keaton: "Do you want to perform sex with me?" Woody Allen: "I'm not up to a performance. But I'll rehearse with you." –*Sleeper* (1973)

3618 After George Segal and Glenda Jackson bed down, she characterizes the experience in English understatement as "very nice." "'Very nice,'" Segal echoes, "is hardly the phrase to describe two bodies locked in heavenly transport . . . 'Very nice' is when you get a get-well card from your butcher." –*A Touch of Class* (1973)

3619 Doctor Walter Matthau informs accountant George Burns, who has come to examine the doctor's books, that he has to make an appointment with his nurse. "I did," replies Burns. "I'm seeing her Friday night for dinner." "Don't fool around with my nurse," Matthau shouts. "She's a Virgin-ian." "She ain't goin' back," Burns ripostes. "I'll tell you that." –*The Sunshine Boys* (1975)

3620 Horse thief Jack Nicholson reports back to his gang's hideout after visiting a town and is asked to tell about some of his evening experiences. "I picked up this chubby little girl off some sod buster's outfit." "How was she?" "About like a Swiss clock – the same exact movement over and over again." –*The Missouri Breaks* (1976)

3621 While Harvey Keitel and Raquel Welch are under the sheets in a stolen ambulance, they receive a call from their boss, Allen Garfield, asking for its return. "If you can't face me for some reason," he pleads, "at least report your position." – *Mother, Jugs and Speed* (1976)

3622 Detective Wang (Peter Sellers) notices that David Niven has placed his hand on his wife's derriere. "Getting to the bottom of things?" Sellers quips. – *Murder by Death* (1976)

3623 Inspector Clouseau (Peter Sellers), while making love in bed to a Soviet agent, mentions his days in the French Resistance during World War II. "Was it hard for you in the Resistance?" she asks. "Very hard," he replies, "but not as hard as it is now." – *The Pink Panther Strikes Again* (1976)

3624 Woody Allen after having sex with Diane Keaton: "That was the most fun I ever had without laughing." – *Annie Hall* (1977)

3625 Nick, a delivery boy, asks "madam" Xaviera Hollander, the "happy hooker," what she wants for breakfast. "You have any danish?" she asks. "No," he replies, "how about a little Greek?" – *The Happy Hooker Goes to Washington* (1977)

3626 Happy hooker Xaviera Hollander (Joey Heatherton) is brought up before a Senate hearing where she is accused of undermining the morals of the nation. "Our committee investigations," charges one senator, "have come up with an even more shocking piece of evidence regarding the spread of your pernicious influence." "That's one of the few things I never spread," Heatherton ripostes. – *The Happy Hooker Goes to Washington* (1977)

3627 Before Mel Brooks can speak to Madeline Kahn, an intruder enters his phone booth and begins to strangle him with the telephone wire. Kahn hears Brooks' gasps and groans. "Listen, mister," she says, "I don't go for this sort of thing. I know a lot of other girls

are turned on to kinky phone calls, but I don't go in for this...." – *High Anxiety* (1977)

3628 A pompous, devious publisher, seeking to exploit football player Burt Reynolds, proposes a book on the sport. At first frowning upon sensationalism, the executive says he would like material on drugs and corruption and especially information about gay players – whether they prefer the defense or offense. "Defense," Reynolds replies wryly. "You're allowed to use your hands on the defense. Gives you a better chance to grope somebody." – *Semi-Tough* (1977)

3629 Spy Barbara Bach informs James Bond (Roger Moore) that she learned in a Siberian survival course several defenses against a drop in temperature, including a "positive mental attitude" and the importance of food. "What else?" Bond asks. "When necessary, shared body warmth." "That's the part I like," he replies. – *The Spy Who Loved Me* (1977)

3630 "Is there anything you would like – anything at all?" sexy Barbara Bach asks James Bond (Roger Moore). "Well," he replies, embracing her, "I had lunch, but I seemed to have missed dessert." – *The Spy Who Loved Me* (1977)

3631 Private eye Peter Falk calls upon a prospective client whose sexy wife bares her cleavage as she leans forward to pour some drinks. "What's your pleasure?" she asks silkily. "What you got looks good," he replies. "I know, but I thought you'd like a drink first." – *The Cheap Detective* (1978)

3632 Several neighbors visit newly married couple Jack Nicholson and Mary Steenburgen, and the wives offer Mary some advice in private. "A husband has certain rights," one woman hints, "and a wife has certain duties. It's not as much of a chore as you may have heard. But if it does become one, the best thing to do is just think about cannin' apricots." – *Goin' South* (1978)

3633 "There are only two things to do on a rainy day," says the madam of a New Orleans whorehouse, "and I don't like to play cards." — *Pretty Baby* (1978)

3634 In a New Orleans whorehouse a man carries a young virgin to a private room while others look on. "Let him have his young peach," says another customer. "I like my fruit ripe." — *Pretty Baby* (1978)

3635 Frustrated wife Ellen Burstyn complains about her spouse: "He can't get it up. You know, when I married a C.P.A., I thought it would be his eyes that would go first." — *Same Time, Next Year* (1978)

3636 In a London bank Sean Connery and an acquaintance ogle a pretty woman at one of the windows. "I wouldn't mind making a deposit in that one, I dare say," the acquaintance remarks. "If she didn't provoke a hasty withdrawal," Connery adds. — *The Great Train Robbery* (1979)

3637 When Steve Martin discovers that Bernadette Peters, the young woman he loves, has a boyfriend, he asks: "Do you think it possible that someday you can make love with me and think of him?" "Who knows?" she answers. "Maybe you and he can make love and you can think of me." — *The Jerk* (1979)

3638 American college instructor George Segal perversely offers this example of "great" literature: "There once was a harlot named Sue,/ Who filled up her whozis with glue./ She said with a grin, 'They could pay to get in,/ They could pay to get out again, too.'" — *Lost and Found* (1979)

3639 Woody Allen and his teenage girlfriend Mariel Hemingway imagine their lives nineteen years from now. "You'll be at the height of your sexual prowess," he says to her. "Of course, I will, too, probably. You know, I'm a late starter." — *Manhattan* (1979)

3640 "I once played nurse with a boy next door and got sued for malpractice," admits a high-school student. — *Rock 'n' Roll High School* (1979)

3641 Songwriter George (Dudley Moore) and his neighbor have been training their telescopes on each other's home for assorted sexual escapades, but the results have been one-sided. "That's it, George!" the neighbor explodes. "For one year now we've been providing X-rated entertainment, and you reciprocate with PG! It's an iniquitous arrangement!" — *10* (1979)

3642 A worker at a local country club comments on a sexy, flirtatious guest of the club: "She's been plucked more times than the Rose of Tralee." — *Caddyshack* (1980)

3643 "Remember," Richard Benjamin says to his wife, "a good man is hard to find, and a hard man is good – good to find." — *How to Beat the High Cost of Living* (1980)

3644 A maid describes to a group of women how she spent last evening with her husband: "He brought home a six-pack, I made pizza, we watched Merv Griffin, then he looked at his watch like he always does and says: 'Well, it's time to play Hide the Salami.'" — *Serial* (1980)

3645 In ancient Egypt Dudley Moore, who thinks God has chosen him to lead the slaves out of bondage, enters a house where an orgy is in progress. "Beware," he announces. "Turn from evil ways before God destroys you and your city with fire from the skies – and put some clothes on." — *Wholly Moses* (1980)

3646 "Premature ejaculation means always having to say you're sorry," a sex-clinic doctor begins his lecture. — *Buddy Buddy* (1981)

3647 James Bond (Roger Moore) cautions a young and sexy blonde ice skater with a strong sexual appetite: "Don't grow up anymore. The opposite sex will never survive it." – *For Your Eyes Only* (1981)

3648 Gum-chewing Empress Nympho (Madeline Kahn), in a reclining position, holds out her wine cup to her steward. "Say when," her steward inquires. "Eight-thirty," she replies. – *History of the World – Part 1* (1981)

3649 Karen Black complains to former suitor George Hamilton about her sex life with her husband Ron Leibman. "Do you realize that we only make love twelve times a year?" "Once a month is not so bad." "I mean twelve times in one night!" she exclaims. "And then for the rest of the year – nothing." – *Zorro, the Gay Blade* (1981)

3650 Married couple Paul Bartel and Mary Woronov arrive at a swinging party and are greeted by Howard, the boyfriend of the hostess. "Hi, swingers!" he exclaims. "I'm Howard Swine, your hearty host and hung with the most. Though I hate to boast, I'm as big as a post and as warm as toast." – *Eating Raoul* (1982)

3651 Oversexed nurse Julie Hagerty, invited to spend a summer weekend in the country, is shown around by hostess Mary Steenburgen. "Oh, a hammock!" Hagerty exclaims. "That's so nostalgic. I lost it in a hammock. You really have to have good balance." – *A Midsummer Night's Sex Comedy* (1982)

3652 Nightclub owner James Garner, unable to perform in bed with his svelte blonde girlfriend, sits up as she tries to soothe his male pride. "If there's one thing I know for sure," she says, "you can't let it get you – you should excuse the expression – down." – *Victor/Victoria* (1982)

3653 The soul of dead spinster Lily Tomlin enters the body of lawyer Steve Martin. A sexy young woman tries to comfort the disconcerted Martin, assuring him that a swami can make Tomlin's spirit "leave your body and enter mine."

"I think I envy her," Martin says. – *All of Me* (1984)

3654 Maureen Stapleton, the mother of gangster Johnny Dangerously (Michael Keaton), embraces her son's girlfriend (Marilu Henner). "You've gotten to be like a daughter to me," the mother confesses, "and I want to share something with you." "What's that, Mom?" Henner asks. "I go both ways." – *Johnny Dangerously* (1984)

3655 "Can you point out the nymphomaniacs to me?" Tom Conti asks the hostess at a party. "They'll make themselves known," she replies. – *Reuben, Reuben* (1984)

3656 John Candy's brother, Tom Hanks, who has a real live mermaid for a girlfriend, becomes the object of his fellow workers' curiosity. "What are you looking at?" Candy bellows at the men. "You never saw a guy that slept with a fish before?" – *Splash* (1984)

3657 Dentist Bruce Fleckstein (Joe Mantegna), who had been having affairs with many of his patients, is found murdered. The police locate nude photographs of his patients in his instrument drawer. "Where did you find the pictures?" Susan Sarandon, one of the suspects, asks a police officer. "Stuck behind the drawer," the officer replies. "You know – those funny little drawers dentists keep their tools in?" "Oh," suggests another woman, "Brucey should have kept *his* tool in the drawer." – *Compromising Positions* (1985)

3658 In this farce, a police precinct captain, seeking to increase his force, contacts his slow-witted police academy commander who is also his brother. "I got a problem here," the captain explains. "I need to get my hands on some healthy young men." "I guess there are places you can go," the commander suggests. "Certain bars and so on. Does Martha know about this?" – *Police Academy 2: Their First Assignment* (1985)

3659 Richard Dreyfuss catches house guest Nick Nolte sleeping with the maid. "She asked me to come in and fix her T.V.," Nolte begins to explain. "The cable holder came off the cable, so I put some paper on the cable and reinserted it in the female receptacle. That's when she crawled all over me." – *Down and Out in Beverly Hills* (1986)

3660 "It's an old joke, really," shapely blonde Theresa Russell begins. "How do two porcupines make love? Very carefully." – *Black Widow* (1987)

3661 Kim Basinger, to help boyfriend Bruce Willis out of his legal problems, consents to marry lecherous lawyer John Larroquette, who has offered to defend Willis in court. "I don't like you anymore," she confesses to the lawyer. "And I certainly don't love you. Do we have to have sex?" "Oh, yes," he insists. "Okay, but no kissing." – *Blind Date* (1987)

3662 A twelve-year-old boy in the body of a thirty-year-old (Tom Hanks) is out on the town with an adult friend. "You see that woman over there?" the friend says. "Just say hello to her and she's yours. She'll wrap her legs around you so tight, you'll be begging for mercy." "Well," Hanks construes, "I'll stay away from her then." – *Big* (1988)

3663 Baseball team groupie Susan Sarandon believes it is her mission in life to give her all for a winning season by sleeping with one pivotal player each summer. "I'd never sleep with a player hittin' under 200," she explains, "unless he had a lot of RBIs and was a great glove man up the middle." – *Bull Durham* (1988)

3664 Robert Stack tries to teach Jackie Mason how to ride a horse. "Nothing to it," Stack says. "Hold on tight, grip with your knees, let the animal do all the work." "Sounds like my wedding night," Mason cracks. – *Caddyshack II* (1988)

3665 Several television executives are viewing previews of future shows, including a typical family program in which a young son asks his mother where Father is. "If I know your father," she replies, "he's out chasing beaver." – *Scrooged* (1988)

3666 Radio talk-show host Eric Bogosian, who attracts a bizarre audience, listens to a caller obsessed with cats. "Take my advice," Bogosian says. "Stop hanging around with pussy. Go out and find some." – *Talk Radio* (1988)

3667 In a New York delicatessan, Harry (Billy Crystal), discussing orgasms with Sally (Meg Ryan), boasts that he can always differentiate between the real thing and the deception. Disputing his claim, Sally simulates the mother of all orgasms – replete with moans, groans, ohs and ahs – to the astonishment of nearby customers. A matronly woman at another table, after observing Sally's performance, addresses her waiter. "I'll have what she's having." – *When Harry Met Sally . . .* (1989)

3668 Widow Cybill Shepherd's husband, dead for twenty-three years, returns in the form of young Robert Downey, Jr. "I haven't done it in twenty-three years," she confesses. "That's okay," he says affectionately. "It's like riding a bike. You never forget." – *Chances Are* (1989)

3669 After a lengthy sexual abstinence Woody Allen admits: "The last time I was inside a woman was when I was inside the Statue of Liberty." – *Crimes and Misdemeanors* (1989)

3670 Neophyte troop leader Shelley Long, seeing honor achievement patches on other Wilderness Girls' uniforms, would like them for her own troop of girls. "Where can I buy them?" she asks. "You don't buy them," a camper replies. "You have to earn them." "Like jewelry!" she exclaims. – *Troop Beverly Hills* (1989)

3671 Warren Beatty, as Dick Tracy, wants Madonna to testify against an underworld kingpin. "You know," he threatens her, "it's legal for me to take you down to the station and sweat it out of you under the lights." "I sweat a lot better in the dark," Madonna purrs. − *Dick Tracy* (1990)

3672 "Dames!" a World War II soldier exclaims. "They're like poison ivy. You rub up against them, and everything starts to swell." − *A Man Called Sarge* (1990)

3673 Escaped convict James Belushi, after impersonating advertising executive Charles Grodin, reveals that he, in the guise of Grodin, slept with the daughter of the ad man's employer. "You mean I slept with Walter's daughter?" Grodin asks. "Yeah." "How was I?" "You were great!" Belushi replies. "I knew I could be great in bed!" Grodin says ecstatically. − *Taking Care of Business* (1990)

3674 Gangster Bugsy Siegel (Warren Beatty) and his moll Virginia (Annette Bening) are about to make love. "Do you always talk this much before you do it?" "I only talk this much before I'm going to kill someone," he replies. − *Bugsy* (1991)

3675 "Women need a reason to have sex, men just need a place," Billy Crystal asserts. − *City Slickers* (1991)

3676 During World War II, the comedy team of James Caan and Bette Midler are in England entertaining the troops. Midler says that she was alone for two hours with a serviceman. "Two hours alone with you?" Caan echoes. "I think that boy deserves a Purple Heart." "It was purple all right," she replies, "but I don't think it was his heart." − *For the Boys* (1991)

3677 On stage, ninety-one-year-old ex-entertainer James Caan invites his former partner Bette Midler to his bedroom. "Then we can get undressed?" Midler asks. "Yes," Caan replies. "And then we get into bed?" "Yes." "And then what?" she asks. − *For the Boys* (1991)

3678 Short-order cook Al Pacino falls in love with waitress Michelle Pfeiffer and attempts to woo her with a string of similes. "We fit like a hammer and a nail, like a lock and a key," he says. "I'm not so sure I like where the key has been," she retorts. − *Frankie and Johnny* (1991)

3679 A sexy enemy agent is assigned by her master to kill American student Richard Greco, who they think is a C.I.A. agent. While seducing him in his hotel room, she places a poisonous scorpion on his body. "You see, my sweet," she purrs, "you have only begun to get hard." − *If Looks Could Kill* (1991)

3680 Harlem architect Wesley Snipes confides to friend Spike Lee that he's seeing a young white woman. "H bomb," says Lee in a tone of awesome respect, "but I know you didn't bone her." "I threw her on the table," Snipes admits. "Nuclear holocaust!" exclaims Lee. − *Jungle Fever* (1991)

3681 Chevy Chase rushes into his apartment building and finds a fellow tenant holding the elevator door for him. "I saved it for you," she announces. "That's what she says to all the guys," quips her brother. − *Nothing but Trouble* (1991)

3682 "Me and Andy got entrepreneurial plans," Lily Tomlin confides to a friend. "Telephone sex with millions. No germs and no hand-to-hand contact." − *The Search for Signs of Intelligent Life in the Universe* (1991)

3683 A mild-mannered clerk (Woody Allen) in Kafka country visits a brothel and confesses that he had never before paid for sex. "You just think you haven't," replies prostitute Jodie Foster. − *Shadows and Fog* (1992)

3684 In an outtake from *The Voice of the Turtle* (1947), wry Eve Arden asks Ronald Reagan: "Getting any lately?" "You mean overtime?" he replies, smiling. − *Wisecracks* (1992)

Show Business

3685 "The manager said he didn't allow any profanity in his theater," vaudeville comic Bert Wheeler warns partner Robert Woolsey about a past performance. "We didn't use any profanity," says his partner. "No," replies Wheeler, "but the audience did." —*Caught Plastered* (1931)

3686 "It was all a mistake," Jimmy Durante's writer pleads when the comic's radio ratings topple. "Please forgive me." "Did Napoleon forgive Waterloo?" Durante fires back. "No! Then why should I forgive you? The cases are parallel."—*Strictly Dynamite* (1934)

3687 Overindulged and fiery theater director John Barrymore threatens to slash his throat if his leading actress Carole Lombard doesn't return. "If you did," she says, mindful of his histrionics, "greasepaint would run out of it." —*Twentieth Century* (1934)

3688 Theatrical producer John Barrymore fires all who cross him with the same bellowing reprise: "Out! I close the iron door on you."—*Twentieth Century* (1934)

3689 A man who wants to get on the Broadway stage approaches publicity agent Sid Silvers. "What do you do?" Silvers inquires. "I snore." "Oh, you're part of the audience," Silvers quips. —*Broadway Melody of 1936* (1935)

3690 Playwright Frank Albertson arrives from Oswego, New York, to meet with down-and-out producer Groucho Marx and director Chico Marx in New York City. "I still have some cinders from the train ride," Albertson grumbles. "Save them," Groucho responds. "It looks like a hard winter." —*Room Service* (1938)

3691 "Whatever became of that cute little blonde you used to saw in half?" bookie Victor Moore asks a magician. "I just couldn't make both ends meet," the man replies.—*She's Got Everything* (1938)

3692 Teenage Mickey Rooney, son of unemployed vaudeville star Charles Winninger, argues with his father and his fellow troupers that he, Mickey, would like to join their show with his new, untried routines. "Our acts are routines," one seasoned entertainer objects. "They're standards." "Standards?" Rooney echoes. "I'll say they're standards. They're so standard that when you miss a line the audience can prompt you."—*Babes in Arms* (1939)

3693 Circus impresario W. C. Fields introduces two perfectly normal men of average stature to the crowd: "Two brothers who baffle science, side by side—the world's smallest giant and the world's largest midget."—*You Can't Cheat an Honest Man* (1939)

3694 Broadway director Allyn Joslyn is critical of fledgling playwright James Stewart, who has just arrived from Redfield, Minnesota: "What right does a rube from Redfield have to write high comedy? What does he know about Park Avenue?" "It doesn't mean a thing," the producer replies. "I don't know anything about Park Avenue either, and I live on the darn street."—*No Time for Comedy* (1940)

3695 A new drama has opened on Broadway, and opening night proves a disaster. "Pretty awful, isn't it?" remarks director Allyn Joslyn during intermission. "It wouldn't be so bad if people didn't laugh so much," his friend Charlie Ruggles adds. "It keeps waking me up."—*No Time for Comedy* (1940)

3696 Studio acting coach Charlotte Greenwood inveighs against talent scout Roland Young's newest discovery – a football player. "What – a football player?" she questions. "Nothing doing. You brought a Notre Dame tackler in here once, and when I got through coaching him, I was black and blue in places you don't use in rehearsing love scenes." – *Star Dust* (1940)

3697 As part of their carnival act, Bing Crosby persuades Bob Hope to act as a "human bullet" by being shot out of a cannon. "I don't mind being drafted," Hope complains, "but not as ammunition." – *Road to Zanzibar* (1941)

3698 "I know you'll enjoy the next act," announces the emcee at a nightclub. "She's an osteopathic soprano. She sings in all the joints." – *The Fleet's In* (1942)

3699 Madeleine Carroll reveals to vaudeville performer Bob Hope that she is a British agent. "Too late, sister," Hope fires back, "I've already got an agent." – *My Favorite Blonde* (1942)

3700 "In this spot," announces emcee Joe E. Lewis, "I'm supposed to introduce the Andrews Sisters, but that won't be necessary. I found out that they knew each other." – *Private Buckaroo* (1942)

3701 Theatrical producers S. Z. Sakall and Edward Everett Horton are overwhelmed by Eddie Cantor's plans for a spectacular show. "It's chaos, utter chaos!" Horton exclaims. "He wants us to dress the dancing girls as boiled potatoes and have them dive into a tank of sour cream." "Ridiculous," Sakall agrees. "It would splash." – *Thank Your Lucky Stars* (1943)

3702 Ex-vaudevillian Charles Butterworth and his dog visit fellow entertainers George Raft and his family at a small vaudeville theater. "How did you find us?" Raft's sister asks, surprised. "Oh, Fifi picked up your trail on 46th

Street," Butterworth replies. "From then on it was easy. She could smell ham a mile away." – *Follow the Boys* (1944)

3703 Performer Bob Hope informs princess Virginia Mayo about his profession. "My act is known all over Europe – that's why I'm taking it to America." – *The Princess and the Pirate* (1944)

3704 "You must have the theater in your blood," showman veteran George Murphy says to amateur performer Eddie Cantor. "Yes," Cantor replies, "and I have a little of my blood in many theaters." – *Show Business* (1944)

3705 During a World War II air raid over London, the cast and audience of a musical show are forced to take refuge in the basement. As explosions are heard outside, someone rushes in to announce: "The last one got the Cumberland Theater – a direct hit!" "That's the first hit they've had in ten years," Florence Bates quips. – *Tonight and Every Night* (1945)

3706 Bob Hope has been bamboozled into riding a bicycle on a high wire. "We're getting two hundred dollars for this," Bing Crosby explains enthusiastically. "Let me hold it," Hope replies. "At least I won't die poor." – *Road to Rio* (1947)

3707 Dean Martin and Jerry Lewis make a successful television debut, but the sponsor pays off only in a dozen cans of spaghetti. "Would you be good enough to open a can?" Lewis asks. "I'd like to pour some in my wallet so that I can see that I was working this week." – *My Friend Irma Goes West* (1950)

3708 U.S. government agents try to persuade Bob Hope to impersonate a notorious international spy. "Please, fellas," Hope pleads, "you got the wrong guy. This ain't my line of work. I tell jokes. That's dangerous enough." – *My Favorite Spy* (1951)

3709 Sailors Dean Martin and Jerry Lewis volunteer to entertain in a

Honolulu nightclub and step up to the microphone. "How would you like to do a song in unison?" Martin asks. "No," Lewis protests. "Let's do it here in the club." – *Sailor Beware* (1951)

3710 While entertainer Bob Hope is performing on stage, a killer hurls several knives at him, barely missing him. "This is the toughest audience I've ever met," Hope deduces. – *Here Come the Girls* (1953)

3711 "That was the worst act I ever saw," Phil Silvers says of an old-time vaudeville team. "They didn't close theaters; those people closed cities!" – *Top Banana* (1954)

3712 "Do you know any of my soft-shoe routines?" legendary entertainer George M. Cohan (James Cagney) asks singer-dancer Eddie Foy (Bob Hope). "I know all the routines you ever did," Foy replies. "I did them first." "And I did them right," Cohan quips. – *The Seven Little Foys* (1955)

3713 Nightclub comedian Joe E. Lewis (Frank Sinatra) reminisces about the Roaring Twenties. "They didn't fool around in those days," he recalls. "It was a different kind of show business. If they didn't like you, they didn't throw you out of the show; they threw you out of a speeding car." – *The Joker Is Wild* (1957)

3714 "Well, that's it for tonight, folks," Joan Shawlee, band leader of an all-girl band, closes the evening. "This is Sweeet Sue saying 'good night,' reminding all you daddios out there that every girl in my band is a virtuoso, and I intend to keep it that way." – *Some Like It Hot* (1959)

3715 Broadway producer Zero Mostel is confounded when his fraudulent scheme to make a bonanza by selling an overabundance of shares in a flop show backfires; the show becomes a smash hit. "I picked the wrong play, the wrong actors, the wrong director," he moans.

"Where did I go right?" – *The Producers* (1968)

3716 In the early, hectic days of vaudeville, Ryan O'Neal is hired to ride a horse on stage. "If you fall off or get hurt," the manager notifies O'Neal, "don't expect no extra pay, and if you get killed, we don't supply the funeral." "Mighty encouraging, sir," O'Neal sardonically returns. – *Nickelodeon* (1976)

3717 "How much time till the final curtain?" producer George C. Scott asks anxiously on opening night. "Eighteen minutes we'll be in clover," director Red Buttons replies. "Or under it," Scott rejoins. – *Movie Movie* (1978)

3718 Second-rate comic Rip Taylor picks up hitchhikers Cheech Marin and Thomas Chong and regales them with some of his best material: "I just made a killing in the market – I shot my butcher." – *Things Are Tough All Over* (1982)

3719 Overly impassioned actor Dustin Hoffman's recalcitrance about how to play a tomato in a commercial has resulted in his becoming persona non grata in the acting field. "I was a stand-up tomato – a juicy, sexy beefsteak tomato!" he remonstrates to his agent (Sydney Pollack). "Nobody does vegetables like me! I did an evening of vegetables off Broadway!" – *Tootsie* (1982)

3720 Theatrical agent Woody Allen tries to negotiate a deal for a client who plays melodies on drinking glasses: "I'll let you have her at the old price, which is anything you want to give her." – *Broadway Danny Rose* (1984)

3721 The manager of the rock group Spinal Tap queries a booking agent: "This time you booked the group in a theater with a capacity only of one thousand four hundred. Does this mean their popularity is waning?" "No," the agent answers. "It means they're attracting a more select audience." – *Spinal Tap* (1984)

3722 An aspiring actor at a Hollywood party with his friends is amazed at the number of celebrities that are present. "Five feet from where we're sitting," he observes, "there are three directors that I would sell my mother to meet." "You sold your mother last year," his girlfriend quips. "They returned her," he retorts. – *The Marrying Man* (1991)

3723 Albert Brooks is killed in a car accident and is sent to Heaven where he enters a small club with a stand-up comic who is not getting any laughs from his small audience. "Hi," the comic addresses Brooks. "How'd you die?" "On stage," Brooks replies, "like you." – *Defending Your Life* (1992)

3724 Fretful Michael Caine, director of a comedy opening on Broadway, walks out after five seconds, grumbling that there are no laughs. "Anything wrong with the seat?" an usher asks. "Yes," replies Caine, "it faces the stage." – *Noises Off* (1992)

Sleep and Dreams

3725 On a steaming Saigon rubber plantation Jean Harlow is informed of the difficulties of comfortable slumber. Unruffled, she replies: "Guess I'm not used to sleeping nights anyway." – *Red Dust* (1932)

3726 Stan Laurel and Oliver Hardy are in danger during the night, and Stan is to take the first shift of guard duty. He soon falls asleep, however, and is awakened by Hardy. "Well, I couldn't help it," Laurel says sheepishly. "I was dreaming I was awake and then I woke up and found myself asleep." – *Oliver the Eighth* (1934)

3727 Mae West shares a cabin on board a tramp steamer with a woman missionary, and as they bed down for the night West asks: "Oh, you don't snore, do you?" "I don't know," the young woman says. "Do you?" "Well," West retorts, "I haven't had any complaints." – *Klondike Annie* (1936)

3728 When Robert Woolsey's wife catches him in another woman's bedroom, he feigns sleepwalking. "So," exclaims his wife, "you were walking in your sleep!" "Yes, it saves time," he explains. "You see, I'm so busy during the day, I don't get any exercise, so I take it at night." – *On Again, Off Again* (1937)

3729 "I didn't rest well last night," Dagwood (Arthur Lake) says to his wife, Blondie (Penny Singleton). "How could you say that?" inquires Blondie. "You slept like a log." "But I dreamed I was awake," Dagwood explains. – *Blondie Plays Cupid* (1941)

3730 Red Skelton, who dreams he is King Henry XV, receives a note from the rebellious Black Arrow (Gene Kelly), which warns: "The longer you delay, the greater the price you will have to pay." "The finance company," Skelton concludes. "I used to get a lot of these things." – *DuBarry Was a Lady* (1943)

3731 Muggs (Leo Gorcey) tells Glimpy (Huntz Hall) about a dream he had. "Was I in it?" Hall wonders. "I said a dream, not a nightmare." – *Docks of New York* (1945)

3732 "Do you know anything about walking in your sleep?" guest George Murphy asks a hotel maid. "No," she replies, "I work nights." – *Having Wonderful Crime* (1945)

3733 "It seems we've met before," Dorothy Lamour says seductively to Bob Hope, trying to win his confidence, "perhaps in your dreams." "You wouldn't be seen in those kinds of places," Hope returns. – *Road to Utopia* (1945)

3734 "How about a story, Dad?" little Dean Stockwell asks his father, William Powell. "No story for you tonight," Powell explains. "You've got to get some sleep." "But your stories always put me to sleep," the boy replies. – *Song of the Thin Man* (1947)

3735 Book salesman Lou Costello meets alluring Hillary Brooke and is immediately infatuated. "That's the kind of girl I dream about," he swoons, "but you should see the kind I get." – *Africa Screams* (1949)

3736 Huntz Hall complains that Leo Gorcey snores. "I don't snore," Gorcey objects. "I know because I stayed awake one night to find out." – *The Bowery Boys Meet the Monsters* (1954)

3737 Reveling in capitalistic excesses, Peter Lorre, as a Russian emissary in Paris, telephones his crony Jules Munshin. "I just got your call," he says. "I–I was having a manicure." "At two o'clock in the morning?" Munshin questions. "I cannot sleep with long fingernails." – *Silk Stockings* (1957)

3738 Investigator Clint Eastwood, trailing Bernadette Peters, who has jumped bail, drives into a remote gas station. "Have you seen a blonde in a pink Cadillac?" he asks the attendant. "Only in my dreams," comes the reply. – *Pink Cadillac* (1989)

3739 Soap-opera writer John Candy dreams he is imprisoned in one of his own plots. "I'm dead, and I'm in Hell," he laments. "And I have to spend eternity on my own show." – *Delirious* (1991)

Spies and Spying

3740 Spies Harpo and Chico Marx report to their boss Louis Calhern that they shadowed Groucho Marx all day. "What day was that?" Calhern asks. "Shadowday," replies Chico. – *Duck Soup* (1933)

3741 The Ritz Brothers, posing as the famous Three Musketeers, try to retrieve a secret message which Lady De Winter, Cardinal Richelieu's spy, has hidden down her dress. They turn her upside down and shake her. To their surprise, numerous messages fall from her cleavage. "She's a walking post office!" exclaims one of the brothers. – *The Three Musketeers* (1939)

3742 British secret agent Madeleine Carroll appeals to Bob Hope for help. "Do you know what it feels like to be followed, hounded and watched every second?" "I used to," Hope returns. "Now I pay cash for everything." – *My Favorite Blonde* (1942)

3743 Vaudeville entertainer Bob Hope balks at helping secret agent Madeleine Carroll. "I'm not getting involved with any murders," he states, "especially mine." – *My Favorite Blonde* (1942)

3744 Foreign Legion recruits Abbott and Costello are called in by their commander to carry out a secret mission. "Us?" Abbott asks, unbelievingly. "Oui," the commandant confirms. "Oh," Costello says excitedly, "all three of us are going?" – *Abbott and Costello in the Foreign Legion* (1950)

3745 As two American spies for the Soviet Union, Alan Napier warns Gayne Whitman to be on his guard. "And for security reasons," he reminds Whitman, "don't call me 'comrade.'" – *Big Jim McLain* (1952)

3746 During the Cold War, F.B.I. chief George Murphy assigns agents to film every person who visits Virginia Gilmore's apartment. After several weeks of surveillance, the agents study the processed films which reveal Gilmore wildly kissing a Soviet agent. Her passions aroused, she seizes her lover's hair, ears, neck, then pulls him down out of camera range. Murphy shuts off the projector. "Poor kid," he mutters. "Doesn't she know she's being used?" – *Walk East on Beacon* (1952)

3747 A young, pretty cryptologist in Istanbul contacts British Intelligence and says that if James Bond, whom she loves, will personally take her back to England, she will turn over a secret decoding machine. "What if I don't measure up?" Bond asks, cracking a smile. "See that you do," his supervisor replies dryly. – *From Russia with Love* (1963)

3748 A huge mural of an actress's face on the facade of a building in Istanbul hides a window. A Soviet agent tries to escape through this window which happens to be set in the mouth of the portrait. A Turkish police chief shoots the figure who then falls to his death. "She should have kept her mouth shut," James Bond (Sean Connery) quips. – *From Russia with Love* (1963)

3749 American Nobel Prize winner Paul Newman, in Sweden to receive his prize, becomes entangled in a plot by Communists to kidnap an American scientist. Newman is thrown from a bridge and almost drowned. When he tells his story to the police, they think he has had too much to drink and fail to believe him. "I'm surprised you don't arrest me for drunk driving," he quips to the police inspector. – *The Prize* (1963)

3750 An English intelligence network chief negotiates with an international kidnapping ring's contact for the return of an important scientist. "My principals are prepared to buy," the British agent begins. "Shall we say – fifteen thousand?" "My dear sir," the contact replies, "this is not a clearance sale." – *The Ipcress File* (1965)

3751 Cliff Robertson learns from an enemy agent that his colleague (Jack Hawkins) has been caught and neutralized. "You mean you killed him?" Robertson asks. "Killed him?" the agent replies. "I should say not. I'm a professional. The next time he may have the drop on me. No, tit for tat. That's what I always say." – *Masquerade* (1965)

3752 After seducing a ravishing enemy agent (Luciana Paluzzi), James Bond (Sean Connery) sets the record straight: "You don't think I enjoyed what we did this evening, do you? What I did tonight was for Queen and country." – *Thunderball* (1965)

3753 Laurence Harvey, as a double agent working for both the East and the West and about to be exposed, comments: "I feel like a whore in a creaking bed." – *A Dandy in Aspic* (1968)

3754 Jacques, one of the major leaders about to launch the French Revolution, asks one of his chief spies – a blind peasant – how many new troops have moved into the palace. "How do I know? I'm blind!" "All right, all right," Jacques replies. "Go back to your observation post and keep your eyes open." – *Start the Revolution Without Me* (1970)

3755 James Bond (Sean Connery) returns from his vacation and is forthwith assigned to track down a diamond smuggler in Holland. "Do we know who his contacts are?" he asks his chief. "We do function in your absence, sir," his superior retorts. – *Diamonds Are Forever* (1971)

3756 British secret agent Nicky Henson, seated in a barber's chair, almost has his throat cut by a hired assassin posing as a barber. Henson disposes of his adversary and quips: "That was a close shave." – *Number One of the Secret Service* (1977)

3757 An attractive agent informs fellow agent Maxwell Smart (Don Adams) that she has reviewed every one of his cases. "Oh," he says defensively, "wouldn't you like to hear my side of the story?" "I think you're wonderful." "She has heard my side of the story." – *The Nude Bomb* (1980)

3758 James Bond (Roger Moore) reports to the British secret service laboratory where he notices the development of a clever but gruesome device – an umbrella that when closed releases a circle of sharp blades around the victim's throat. "Stinging in the rain?" he quips to the agent in charge. – *For Your Eyes Only* (1981)

3759 C.I.A. agents James Belushi and John Ritter are trapped in an abandoned house as Soviet agents direct a hail of bullets at them. "You want the good news first or the bad news?" asks Belushi after surveying their predicament. "Give me the bad news," Ritter replies. "There's no way out of here alive." "What's the good news?" "Doesn't look as if we're going to be here for long," Belushi answers. – *Real Men* (1987)

3760 Ladies' man Michael Caine and his pal Roger Moore, both of whom resemble captured smugglers, are enlisted to help the C.I.A. crack an international smuggling ring. However, the man whom Caine resembles escapes and Caine is forced to subdue him. "You'll never guess who I've got tied up in my cabin," Caine says, reporting to Moore. "Only you could think of sex at a time like this," Moore remarks. – *Bullseye!* (1990)

Sports

3761 Chico Marx, playing for the Huxley College football team, blares out his own set of signals: "Hey diddle diddle, the cat and the fiddle, this time I think-a we go up-a de middle. Hike!" – *Horse Feathers* (1932)

3762 Jimmy Durante visits taxidermist Buster Keaton and sees a stuffed skunk. "Last year when I went hunting I shot at one of them and I missed," Durante says. "Boy, was I incensed! For days I was incensed!" – *What! No Beer?* (1933)

3763 Knobby Walsh (Jimmy Durante), disappointed that his fighter has been kayoed, resigns himself to the loser's purse – fifty dollars. But the ring owner offers him only "twenty bucks or nothin'." "I'll take the twenty," Durante replies. "I was reachin' for the moon. What an eclipse!" – *Palooka* (1934)

3764 Novice prizefighter Joe Palooka (Stuart Erwin) has just won the championship bout, and his elated manager, Knobby Walsh (Jimmy Durante), grabs the radio microphone. "Palooka will meet all comers in physical combat as faithfully as faithfully permits," he announces. "And if faithfully don't show up soon enough, we'll go lookin' for him!" – *Palooka* (1934)

3765 Radio emcee Jack Benny jokes with his audience about his sponsor: "Did you ever hit a Platt Air-Flow golf ball? Well, you don't know what you're missing." – *The Big Broadcast of 1937* (1936)

3766 Two inmates are enjoying a baseball game between their penitentiary and a rival prison. "Did you see that guy steal second?" one points out.

"I didn't see nothin'," the other insists. "I ain't no stool." – *Back Door to Heaven* (1939)

3767 Dagwood (Arthur Lake) requires two hundred dollars for membership in a "trout club," a request his wife, Blondie (Penny Singleton), finds incredulous. "You're asking for two hundred dollars to join a club of fish!" she questions. – *Blondie on a Budget* (1940)

3768 Coach Knute Rockne (Pat O'Brien) directs Gipp (Ronald Reagan), at his first practice session, to carry the ball. "How far?" Reagan asks, cracking a smile. – *Knute Rockne, All American* (1940)

3769 Franchot Tone and young Peggy Moran watch Mischa Auer perform some awe-inspiring stunts on a horse. "How on earth does he do things like that?" Peggy wonders. "Probably with mirrors," replies Tone. – *Trail of the Vigilante* (1940)

3770 "This is gonna be a great fight," a fan at a wrestling match says to William Powell. "How do you know?" Powell questions. "Were you at the rehearsals?" – *Shadow of the Thin Man* (1941)

3771 Broadway gamblers Humphrey Bogart and William Demarest search a house used by Nazi spies. Demarest clunks one enemy agent with an axe handle, and Bogart congratulates him. "Joe DiMaggio couldn't have done better." "I used to bat three-twenty in reform school," Demarest proudly replies. – *All Through the Night* (1942)

3772 Patsy Kelly: "There's a fly in my ice cream." Bert Lahr: "The flies in here go in for winter sports." – *Sing Your Worries Away* (1942)

3773 During a boxing match, Huntz Hall acts as Leo Gorcey's second. "Gee," Hall muses, "I wish I was in there. I remember my first fight, my last fight. It was the same fight." – *Kid Dynamite* (1943)

3774 Prissy Jerome Cowan, representing the bank that owns a baseball team, complains to the team's manager about expenses. "It's an outrage the way these players soil their uniforms," Cowan says. "Is it necessary for the boys to slide from base to base? Can't they just run?" "Maybe I can get them to tiptoe," the manager suggests, "so they won't wear their shoes out either." – *Ladies' Day* (1943)

3775 Leo Gorcey, leader of the East Side gang, takes charge of the boxing matches between the boys. He soon notices one of the participants fighting dirty. "What are you doing?" Gorcey intercedes. "Don't you know that's an infatuation of the rules?" – *Come Out Fighting* (1945)

3776 Bud Abbott describes the lineup of a baseball team, mentioning that Who's on first, What's on second and I Don't Know's on third. Costello is bewildered but finally gets the players' positions right without realizing what he is saying, and Abbott compliments him. "I don't give a damn!" the exasperated Costello shouts. "Oh, he's our shortstop." – *The Naughty Nineties* (1945)

3777 Fight manager Walter Abel and his assistants plan to make a prizefighter out of milkman Danny Kaye. "Loosen up his muscles," Abel orders Steve Cochran. "Loosen them?" replies Cochran, groping around Kaye's legs. "It will take a week to find them!" – *The Kid from Brooklyn* (1946)

3778 Artist Dane Clark has just flattened a bully in a nightclub brawl. Boxing promoter Zachary Scott is impressed and considers matching Clark against Carney, the present champ. Scott then learns that Clark is an artist. "Maybe that's what it takes to put Carney on canvas," Scott smirks. – *Whiplash* (1949)

3779 Racehorse owner Bing Crosby, proud of his entry, announces to a rival owner that the horse in back of Crosby's truck will win the forthcoming derby.

"Want a tip?" the rival offers, after scanning the competition. "What?" Crosby asks. "Enter the truck instead." – *Riding High* (1950)

3780 Lou Costello, led on by his pal Bud Abbott, volunteers to impersonate a tough prizefighter. When he has to enter the ring, Costello has reservations, despite a gambler's offer of fifteen thousand dollars to take a fall in the fifth round. "People work a lifetime and never get fifteen thousand dollars," Abbott reminds him. "You're getting it for just lying down." "Lying down – that's what's got me worried," Costello returns. "The big question is – will I be able to get up?" – *Abbott and Costello Meet the Invisible Man* (1951)

3781 Jerry Lewis tries to imitate an experienced prizefighter by employing bobbing and weaving. "What are you, a boxer?" Dean Martin asks. "What do I look like," Lewis replies, "a cocker spaniel? I was fighting Gene Tierney once – " "You mean Gene Tunney," Martin corrects Lewis, who has just referred to a popular movie actress. "You fight who you want, I'll fight who I want." – *Sailor Beware* (1951)

3782 "Must you wear glasses?" a football coach asks Junior (Jerry Lewis). "Oh, no, sir," Lewis answers dutifully, "only when I want to see." – *That's My Boy* (1951)

3783 Charles Coburn, as a priest and dean of a small college, attempts to hire a football coach. "You know my salary?" the coach asks. "Twenty-five thousand a year." "Einstein gets ten," Coburn reminds the coach. "If Einstein could figure a way to beat Michigan State, he'd get the twenty-five," the coach explains. – *Trouble Along the Way* (1953)

3784 Comedian Joe E. Lewis (Frank Sinatra) to a nightclub audience: "If Paul Revere had ridden the horse I bet on today, we'd all be speaking in a British accent." – *The Joker Is Wild* (1957)

3785 Tony Curtis, posing as a millionaire and champion water polo player, impresses gullible Marilyn Monroe with his prowess in the water. "Isn't that dangerous?" she asks. "I'll say," he replies. "I had two ponies drown under me." – *Some Like It Hot* (1959)

3786 A local reporter interviews the basketball coach of Custer College, the school most likely to play the Russian all-star team. "Well, as coach, how do you feel about Custer being tapped to play the Russians?" "Very proud," the coach states, and then adds: "and very humble." – *Tall Story* (1960)

3787 At a football game a shot is heard, and the ball carrier goes down. "My God!" cries nurse Sally Kellerman. "They shot him!" "Hot Lips, you incredible nincompoop," snaps colonel Roger Bowen, "it's the end of the quarter!" – *M*A*S*H* (1970)

3788 Old Jewish gangster Hyman Roth (Lee Strasberg) reflects: "I loved baseball since Arnold Rothstein fixed the World Series in 1919." – *The Godfather, Part II* (1974)

3789 Ex-football player Burt Reynolds, now serving time in a state prison, tells fellow convict Jim Hampton that he hasn't thrown a football in seven years. "It's just like making love," Hampton explains. "Once you've done it, you never forget how." – *The Longest Yard* (1974)

3790 Robert Mitchum as gumshoe Philip Marlowe recalls the news headlines of June 22, 1941: "'Russia Invaded by Germany.' So what? So did Napoleon. It was a lot harder for DiMaggio to hit in thirty-three straight." – *Farewell, My Lovely* (1975)

3791 "If you can't be an athlete, be an athletic supporter," school principal Eve Arden announces to the student body. – *Grease* (1978)

3792 Marsha Mason describes the end of her ex-husband's football career to writer James Caan. "He was out in the beginning of the second year. Bad hands, I think they called it. He couldn't hold on to the football." "Yeah," Caan says philosophically, "some coaches can be very demanding." – *Chapter Two* (1979)

3793 Passenger: "Do you have anything light to read?" Stewardess: "How about this leaflet, 'Famous Jewish Sports Legends'?" – *Airplane!* (1980)

3794 An elderly husband cannot understand his wife's obsession with karate. "To me," he says in frustration, "karate doesn't make sense. You spend hours hitting boards. When was the last time you were attacked by a piece of wood?" – *Off Your Rocker* (1980)

3795 Ex-prizefighter Jake LaMotta (Robert De Niro) is relegated to doing comedy routines in seedy nightclubs. "It's a thrill to be standing here before you wonderful people tonight – well, in fact, it's a thrill to be standing." – *Raging Bull* (1980)

3796 An attractive client collapses in gumshoe Steve Martin's office. "I must apologize for my dramatic entrance," she says after being revived. "It was when I saw the newspaper headline – " "You must be quite a Dodger fan," Martin remarks, mistakenly looking at the headline of the sports page. – *Dead Men Don't Wear Plaid* (1982)

3797 Albert Brooks and Julie Hagerty have sold their home and purchased a larger one. While lying in bed one night, a nervous Brooks expresses concern about the decision. "We didn't get a tennis court," he complains. "We don't play tennis." "We don't have a court," he persists. "If we had a court we'd learn." – *Lost in America* (1985)

3798 "I finally figured this game out," a college student remarks while watching a golf game in progress. "There's something very primitive about it.

Young men with clubs trying to prove their manhood in the open field. They're following their animalistic urges – struggle for survival with nothing but a stick. They're beasts." – *Odd Jobs* (1985)

3799 California reporter Irwin Fletcher (Chevy Chase) joins a Southern coon hunt to learn more about a local murder. "A coon hunt is like an English fox hunt," one of the men informs him, "except we cut through all the baloney – the fancy clothes, the music, the beautiful women. We've reduced the experience to its essence." "Yeah," ripostes Chase, "a bunch of sweaty drunks chasing a scared animal." – *Fletch Lives* (1989)

3800 "What do you do with an elephant with three balls?" a female psychologist asks top-gun pilot Charlie Sheen and then, supplying her own answer, adds: "You walk him and pitch to the rhino." – *Hot Shots!* (1991)

3801 Teammate Jumpin' Joe Dugan (Bruce Boxleitner) advises Babe Ruth (John Goodman) to "hit 'em where they ain't." "Well," the Babe replies grandly, "they ain't over the fences, so that's where I hit 'em." – *The Babe* (1992)

3802 Someone informs Babe Ruth (John Goodman) that he earns more than the President. "Why not?" Goodman returns. "I had a better year than he did." – *The Babe* (1992)

3803 One-time New York Yankee slugger Tom Selleck, whose life of bad booze and fast women has taken its toll, joins a Japanese team. On his first day he is put through calisthenics – and he rebels. "Athletes?" he gripes. "We aren't athletes. We're baseball players." – *Mr. Baseball* (1992)

3804 American Tom Selleck, playing for a losing Japanese baseball team, says encouragingly to an interpreter: "It ain't over till the fat lady sings." The message is then carried to the dugout and relayed to the sullen players: "If you win, a fat lady will come and sing to you." – *Mr. Baseball* (1992)

Structures

3805 Con artist Lee Tracy brings carnival entertainer Lupe Velez to New York, hoping to pass her off as a princess. In their hotel room Velez shouts her objections to his scheme. "If you don't keep still," Tracy threatens, "I'm going to reach out that window and get the Flat Iron Building and rap you over the head with it." – *The Half Naked Truth* (1932)

3806 At a social gathering, English duchess Violet Kemble-Cooper suggests that the National Gallery is being used as a rendezvous for lovers: "It's a marvelous place for that, I've heard. You never meet any of your friends there. And if you do, they're there for the same purpose and pretend not to see you." – *Our Betters* (1933)

3807 Robert Woolsey, caught in a Midwest dust storm, enters a shack where Bert Wheeler emerges from a storm cellar. "What do you got down there?" Woolsey asks. "A cyclone cellar. You'd better come down." "Why would I come down there for a cyclone when I got a dandy one going on right here?" – *The Rainmakers* (1935)

3808 Laurel and Hardy discover they've given a deed to a gold mine to the wrong party. "That's the first mistake we've made since that guy sold us the Brooklyn Bridge," Laurel claims. "Buying that bridge was not a mistake," Hardy corrects his friend. "That's going to be worth a lot of money to us someday." – *Way Out West* (1937)

3809 Russian commissar Greta Garbo, who has arrived in Paris straight from Russia, stops playboy Melvyn Douglas at an intersection. "I'm looking for the Eiffel Tower," she inquires. "Good heavens!" he replies. "Is that thing lost again?" – *Ninotchka* (1939)

3810 Free-spirited Holly Golightly (Audrey Hepburn) innocently becomes a messenger between a gangster in Sing Sing and the outside world. "Sing Sing," she remarks, pondering the famous prison. "Sounds more like it should be an opera house or something." – *Breakfast at Tiffany's* (1961)

3811 U.S. gangster George C. Scott shows his complaining moll Shirley MacLaine the Tower of Pisa. "So it leans," she whines. – *The Yellow Rolls Royce* (1965)

3812 Young Texan Jon Voight, intent on succeeding as a stud in New York City, approaches a blonde prospect walking her dog. "I'm looking for the Statue of Liberty," Voight announces confidently. "It's up in Central Park taking a leak," the woman replies. – *Midnight Cowboy* (1969)

3813 Diahann Carroll, ghetto mother of six, visits the middle-class apartment of sanitation worker James Earl Jones. "It's a nice building," she comments. "You get a better class of cockroaches." – *Claudine* (1974)

3814 Chevy Chase, who has inherited his aunt's Southern plantation and one thousand acres, discovers that the property consists of one dilapidated, run-down and abandoned building. "I can see you're disappointed," the real estate agent remarks. "No, not at all," Chase replies. "A little speckling and some napalm and this place could make a nice mausoleum." – *Fletch Lives* (1985)

3815 Smalltime hoodlums Danny DeVito and Joe Piscopo question an excessively overweight member of their gang why he doesn't place large bets at the racetrack. "I'm too well known down there," the obese man explains. "You could disguise yourself," Piscopo suggests. "As what?" "The Time-Life Building," DeVito whispers to Piscopo. —*Wise Guys* (1986)

Stupidity

3816 Bert Wheeler: "You know, I'm not as big a fool as I used to be." Robert Woolsey: "Oh, did you diet?"—*Hook, Line, and Sinker* (1930)

3817 "Don't stand there acting like a fool," says Edna May Oliver to Bert Wheeler. "I'm not acting," he protests. —*Cracked Nuts* (1931)

3818 "My father sells bulldogs for twenty-five dollars apiece," George Burns informs Gracie Allen. "A piece?" she asks. "That's very cheap," she declares. "How big is a piece?"—*Once Over, Light* (1931)

3819 Carnival barker Lee Tracy complains about the show's press agent: "That guy we got is so dumb he couldn't sell a fat boy to a tribe of cannibals." —*The Half Naked Truth* (1932)

3820 Groucho Marx to Chico: "Why don't you bore a hole in yourself and let the sap run out?"—*Horse Feathers* (1932)

3821 "What do you take me for, a fool?" Edgar Bergen exclaims during an argument with Charlie McCarthy. "No," McCarthy replies. "Of course, I may be wrong."—*At the Races* (1934)

3822 Eddie Cantor, as the heir to a fortune, is compelled to go to Egypt to claim his money. He meets a sheik's daughter, a mixed blessing for Cantor. "Go away," Cantor orders, exasperated by her shrill giggle. "I can't talk to an idiot." "Come here," she cackles. "I can." —*Kid Millions* (1934)

3823 Broadway bookie Adolphe Menjou assigns two not-too-bright toughs to play nursemaid to little Shirley Temple. Later, in the betting parlor, a barber charges in to complain to Menjou that two hoodlums stole his striped barber pole. "What is this?" Menjou questions his cronies. "Well," explains one (Warren Hymer), "you told us to mind her, and she wanted it."—*Little Miss Marker* (1934)

3824 "You have an aunt that sees with her mouth?" George Burns questions Gracie Allen. "Yeah," Gracie replies, "she sees if the soup is hot."—*Six of a Kind* (1934)

3825 A big-shot gangster warns some small-time hoodlums not to pick on gambler Joe E. Brown. "He's got scruples," the gangster explains. "I didn't know he had them things," one hoodlum confesses.—*A Very Honorable Guy* (1934)

3826 The entire opposing football team tackles Charlie McCarthy, knocking him unconscious. When he recovers, Edgar Bergen's dimwitted girlfriend asks him how it feels to be unconscious. "Well, you ought to know," he replies. "You've been that way all your life." —*All American Drawback* (1935)

3827 A young woman asks cab driver Allen Jenkins where she can find William Gargan, but Jenkins remains silent. "Playing dumb, hey?" she remarks. "Who, me? I never play dumb." "You're darn right. It comes natural." —*A Night at the Ritz* (1935)

3828 Lawyer Aline McMahon reads the will of Hugh Herbert's wealthy aunt and then explains that the deceased considered her nephew "a perfect idiot." "She's wrong, she's wrong," Herbert protests. "Of course she's wrong. None of us are perfect." – *To Beat the Band* (1935)

3829 Newly hired, half-witted bodyguard Parkyakarkus gleefully demonstrates his skill on boss Eddie Cantor by handcuffing him in record-breaking time. He then announces he doesn't have the key. "You're the most moronic, imbecilic, idiotic nincompoop I've ever seen!" Cantor shouts. "This is no time for compliments," Parkyakarkus replies. – *Strike Me Pink* (1936)

3830 In San Quentin prison, a returning prisoner reports the latest news to his fellow inmates: "You remember Louie? He got himself a job on the dock and fell into the drink. He's still standing on the bottom waiting for someone to tell him to come up." – *San Quentin* (1937)

3831 "Look at this new design for a cell block," a not-too-bright bank robber says to a fellow crook, referring to a newspaper picture. "That's not a cell block," his friend says looking at the newspaper. "That's a crossword puzzle." – *Go Chase Yourself* (1938)

3832 Japanese detective Mr. Moto (Peter Lorre) catches brawny, dim-witted Maxie Rosenbloom picking someone's pocket. "I can't help taking things that attract my eyes," Maxie confesses. "He's a kleptomaniac," Moto's nephew explains. "Thanks, pal, thanks," Maxie says as if complimented. – *Mr. Moto's Gamble* (1938)

3833 Penniless Broadway producer Groucho Marx introduces simple-minded Faker Englund (Harpo) to a young playwright: "This is Mr. Englund, the brains of the organization. That'll give you some idea of the organization." – *Room Service* (1938)

3834 Gangster Alan Baxter reads a newspaper story about the capture of a bank-robber pal. "Why should Duke be mixed up with a soda jerk?" he asks feather-brained girlfriend Lyda Roberti. "Maybe he was thirsty," she replies. – *Wide Open Faces* (1938)

3835 In an Egyptian desert the Three Stooges have destroyed a mummy coveted by a murderous gang of criminals. Moe thinks of a way of replacing the mummy. "I got an idea," he says to Curly. "We'll make a mummy of you." "I can't be a mummy," Curly protests. "I'm a daddy." – *We Want Our Mummy* (1939)

3836 As Edgar Bergen and Mortimer Snerd sail through the air in a balloon, Bergen tries to explain the aeronautic principles of balloon flight. Mortimer listens carefully and concludes: "I don't think it'll work." – *You Can't Cheat an Honest Man* (1939)

3837 "How could you be so ignorant?" Edgar Bergen addresses his dummy Mortimer Snerd. "It ain't easy," comes the reply. – *You Can't Cheat an Honest Man* (1939)

3838 Simple-minded bank teller Grady Sutton listens to his future father-in-law W. C. Fields and "borrows" bank money to buy worthless mining stocks. Suddenly, a bank examiner arrives. "I knew this would happen," Sutton cries. "I must have been a perfect idiot to have listened to you." "Listen to me," Fields reassures Sutton. "There's nothing in this world that is perfect." – *The Bank Dick* (1940)

3839 Abandoned at a deserted inn during a stormy night, Bud Abbott and Lou Costello are forced to fend for themselves. Abbott sends Costello out for fresh water. "I don't want to go outside all by myself with nobody to talk to," Costello protests. "Why don't you talk to yourself?" "I get too many stupid answers," admits Costello. – *Hold That Ghost* (1941)

3840 During World War II, patriotic Blondie (Penny Singleton) invites a women's organization to meet in her home and introduces them to her husband, Dagwood (Arthur Lake). "These are the Housewives of America," she announces. "All of them?" Dagwood asks. *– Blondie for Victory* (1942)

3841 "Look at that bunch of cows!" cries Lou Costello. "Herd of cows," Bud Abbott corrects him. "Certainly I heard of cows! What do you think I am, a dummy!" – *Ride 'Em Cowboy* (1942)

3842 "How can you be so stupid?" G.I. Wally Brown addresses bemused buddy Alan Carney. "It ain't easy," comes the reply. – *Adventures of a Rookie* (1943)

3843 Gangster Frank Jenks proposes to a fellow hoodlum that they bribe a juror by means of a letter which they will sign "anonymous." "Anonymous?" his crony asks. "Who's he?" "Anonymous is somebody nobody knows." "Well, how come you know him?" – *Gildersleeve's Bad Day* (1943)

3844 Radio actor Red Skelton, falsely accused of murder, wants to borrow a meddlesome reporter's press card to help him prove his innocence. "You can't impersonate me," she objects. "Oh, yes I can," Skelton insists. "I can act very stupid." – *Whistling in Brooklyn* (1943)

3845 "He's the most famous bibliophile in the country," police inspector Richard Lane enlightens his slow-witted assistant. "Bibliophile?" echoes the cop. "He don't look in shape to go six rounds." – *Boston Blackie Booked on Suspicion* (1945)

3846 "Are you stupid," a tavern keeper berates Lou Costello, "a nincompoop, moronic, idiotic, imbecilic? What are you laughing at?" "You went right by me and didn't even know it," Costello replies playfully. – *Abbott and Costello Meet Captain Kidd* (1952)

3847 Dining in a fancy restaurant, Lou Costello notices a waiter carrying a skewer of flaming meat and douses it with water. "How stupid can you get?" remarks Bud Abbott, who has received much of the splash. "How stupid do you want me to be?" asks Costello. – *Abbott and Costello Meet the Mummy* (1955)

3848 Jayne Mansfield, as a movie sex symbol, compares herself to "that Communist queen." "Catherine the Great?" asks advertising agent Tony Randall. "She wasn't a Communist, she was a czarina." "I don't care what was wrong with her," Mansfield declares. – *Will Success Spoil Rock Hunter?* (1957)

3849 U.S. Navy brass accuses lowly lieutenant Jerry Lewis of "misplacing" a "fully equipped, seaworthy and battle-ready destroyer escort." "I didn't take her," Lewis pleads, "I haven't got her. Frisk me." – *Don't Give Up the Ship* (1959)

3850 An admiral suspects lieutenant Jerry Lewis, who has "misplaced" a destroyer escort, of being a spy. "This man is the shrewdest, cleverest undercover agent we've ever been up against," he says to intelligence officer Dina Merrill. "But sir," she interjects, "I think he's too dumb to be that smart to play it that stupid." "Say that again," the admiral orders. – *Don't Give Up the Ship* (1959)

3851 Gangster Telly Savalas sends his feather-brained girlfriend to take his money out of his safety deposit box, but she returns empty-handed. She explains that there was an eagle on the box, and she was unable to open it. "You birdbrain!" he bellows. "That was the great seal of the United States!" "It was not a seal," she persists. "It was an eagle!" – *The Man from the Diner's Club* (1963)

3852 Philip Marlowe (Robert Mitchum), tracking down a lead, encounters an acid-tongued madam (Kate Murtagh). "I think you're a very stupid person," she rasps. "You look stupid, you're in a stupid business – and you're on a stupid case." "I get it," he says.

"I'm stupid." – *Farewell, My Lovely* (1975)

3853 "Where did you find these two oafs?" a friend asks Michael Caine about James Caan and Elliott Gould. "Oh," Caine explains, "they're not oafs. They would require practice to become oafs." – *Harry and Walter Go to New York* (1976)

3854 Dim-witted henchman Ned Beatty reports to the underground hideout of his boss, the demonic Lex Luthor (Gene Hackman). "Got the newspaper I asked you to get me?" Hackman asks. "Yeah," Beatty replies. "Why am I not reading it?" "Because I haven't given it to you yet?" Beatty asks after a long pause. – *Superman* (1978)

3855 "There is one thing all of us have in common," Bill Murray announces to fellow soldiers. "We were all stupid enough to join the army." – *Stripes* (1981)

3856 A group of friends at a diner are discussing man's origins, and one states that mankind emerged from some sort of slime or swamp. "People don't come from swamps," insists another. "They come from Europe." – *Diner* (1982)

3857 During the Vietnam War small-town mayor Brian Dennehy has hidden his dim-witted nephew, an army deserter, on a remote farm. Dennehy, in an angry mood, berates the boy for deserting. "I wouldn't have deserted if you had kept me out of the draft," the boy asserts. "What draft!" Dennehy explodes. "You enlisted!" "Oh, yeah. That's right." – *Finders Keepers* (1984)

3858 A corrupt police lieutenant, coveting his precinct captain's job, can only be promoted if a group of new recruits fail. "If they fail," the lieutenant says to his assistant, "that makes me the captain. And if I'm the captain, I'm going to need somebody to be the new watch commander." "So?" asks the confused assistant. "So we make sure they

fail." "Who?" "The new recruits!" "Why?" the assistant questions. "If they're out, I'm in, and I'm going to need a new watch commander. And you know who that's going to be?" "Who?" – *Police Academy 2: Their First Assignment* (1985)

3859 The captain of a school for armed guards greets the new recruits, many of whom seem to be lacking in intelligence or education or both. To instill a sense of importance in the trainees, he announces that they are entering a "twelve-billion-dollars-a-year industry." "You mean we're actually going to earn twelve billion dollars a year?" one student asks. – *Armed and Dangerous* (1986)

3860 Jewel thief Kevin Kline hates to be called stupid, but his own girlfriend (Jamie Lee Curtis) finally tells him he *is* stupid – and cites one telling example: "The London underground is not a political movement." – *A Fish Called Wanda* (1988)

3861 Vincent Spano, the son of a successful building contractor – who has set up Vincent with a sinecure – abandons his soft job at a construction site. "The only guy stupid enough to quit a no-show job," his pal muses. – *City of Hope* (1991)

3862 Two outlaws in Sherwood Forest plan to rob two unwary travelers. "You take the one on the left," one says to his fellow brigand. "Which one's left? Which one are you taking?" "What do you mean which one am I taking! If you're taking the one on the left I'm taking the one on the right." "Which one's the one on the right?" – *Robin Hood: Prince of Thieves* (1991)

3863 The incensed mother of Macaulay Culkin berates the manager of a posh New York hotel for accepting her child by himself as a guest. "What kind of idiots do you have working here?" she demands. "The finest in New York," he proudly returns. – *Home Alone 2: Lost in New York* (1992)

Success and Failure

3864 Hotel proprietor Groucho Marx tries to encourage his unpaid, disgruntled staff with an Horatio Alger introduction. "Three years ago I came to Florida without a nickel in my pocket," he boasts. "Now I have a nickel in my pocket." – *The Cocoanuts* (1929)

3865 A severe, no-nonsense Ninotchka (Greta Garbo) has been sent to Paris to investigate laxities involving three envoys. Fellow Russian Felix Bressart meets her at the railway station. "How are things going in Moscow?" he asks. "Very good," she replies. "The last mass trials were a great success. There are going to be fewer and better Russians." – *Ninotchka* (1939)

3866 A femme fatale tries to get Bert Lahr, a failed songwriter and prospective heir to a fortune, to commit suicide. "Gosh!" Lahr ponders. "I'll go down in history – statue in the parks – a bust in the Hall of Fame!" "A bust is right," the woman mumbles aside. "I'll be immoral!" Lahr concludes. – *Sing Your Worries Away* (1942)

3867 Charlotte Greenwood, as the man-hungry confidante to Betty Grable, has returned from one of her prowls. "Where have you been?" Betty asks. "Fishing." "Any luck?" "No," Charlotte concedes, "but you should have seen the one that got away." – *Springtime in the Rockies* (1942)

3868 "Why are you always chasing women?" Carmen Miranda asks Groucho Marx. "I'll tell you as soon as I catch one," he quips. – *Copacabana* (1947)

3869 When Cary Grant's dream house turns into a fiasco, Melvyn Douglas offers some friendly advice: "The next time you're going to do anything or say

anything or buy anything, think it over very carefully. When you're sure you're right, forget the whole thing." – *Mr. Blandings Builds His Dream House* (1948)

3870 When Joan Davis, who wants to be a traveling saleswoman, tells her father her idea, he says that people would laugh at her. "People always laugh at anything new," she says. "Why, they laughed at Fulton when he invented the cotton gin." "Eli Whitney invented the cotton gin," her father corrects her. "No wonder they laughed at Fulton." – *The Traveling Saleswoman* (1950)

3871 Bob Hope, as the "oldest living chorus boy," has bungled every stage opportunity offered to him. "Failure is the only thing I've ever been a success at," he muses. – *Here Come the Girls* (1953)

3872 "If talent had anything to do with success," cynical advertising executive Henry Jones remarks to Tony Randall, "Brooks Brothers would be out of business, television studios would be turned into supermarkets." – *Will Success Spoil Rock Hunter?* (1957)

3873 Millionaire Tony Randall grumbles to his friend Rock Hudson: "I started out with eight million dollars, and I still have eight million. I just can't seem to get ahead." – *Pillow Talk* (1959)

3874 Inept Jerry Lewis cannot seem to hold a job. He even failed a civil service examination for a letter carrier's position. "How could anyone fail a mailman's test?" his girlfriend's mother wonders. "Sloping shoulders," someone volunteers. "The bag kept falling off." – *Who's Minding the Store?* (1963)

3875 Max Bialystok (Zero Mostel), a once-famous Broadway producer, cries to his accountant, Gene Wilder. "Look at me – I'm drowning," Mostel laments. "Other men sail through life. Bialystok has struck a reef. I'm going under. I'm being sunk by a society that demands success when all I can offer is failure." – *The Producers* (1968)

3876 Wife Janet Margolin is interviewed on the criminal failings of husband Woody Allen. "I think he would have felt better if he had been a successful criminal," she explains. "He never made the Ten Most Wanted list." – *Take the Money and Run* (1969)

3877 Smalltime thief George Segal gets brother-in-law Robert Redford, just released from prison, involved in another crooked caper – which fails after several attempts. Redford in disgust calls it quits. "You take failure too hard," Segal tries to comfort him. "I don't mind it so much any more." – *The Hot Rock* (1972)

3878 Cab driver Carroll O'Connor explains to his wife how all his life he has missed golden opportunities. "I ain't a failure," he concludes. "I just ain't on time." – *Law and Disorder* (1974)

3879 Beautiful Soviet agent Barbara Bach, who blames James Bond (Roger Moore) for her lover's death, threatens to kill him at the end of a mission for which they have joined forces. "I have never failed a mission, Commander, any mission," she declares with an air of finality. "In that case, Major," Bond replies, "one of us is bound to end up gravely disappointed." – *The Spy Who Loved Me* (1977)

3880 Successful sports car dealer Richard Crenna tries to steer his young protégé Matt Dillon away from college and into a sales career. He takes Matt for a ride in a spanking red Ferrari – a dream car at the top of Matt's "most-wanted" list. "Socrates rode around on a donkey," Crenna concludes, driving home his point. – *The Flamingo Kid* (1984)

Suicide

3881 "Yesterday I tried killing myself," Eddie Cantor admits. "I walked in front of a taxi cab and dared the taxi to run over me. But the taxi wouldn't do it. You know why? Because it was yellow." – *Palmy Days* (1931)

3882 On board a train W. C. Fields sees an attractive young woman with a bottle of iodine next to her. Thinking she is about to commit suicide, he removes the bottle and gives her a sermon. "What are you up to?" he asks. "Don't do it, little lady. When you wake up in the morning and find you're dead, it's too late to regret it." – *You're Telling Me* (1934)

3883 Robert Woolsey, who thinks he is a failure, asks farmer Bert Wheeler for

some poison. "What kind is it?" "Rat poison." "Rat poison?" the disappointed Woolsey replies. "No good. If I can't die like a man, I'm not going to die like a rat." – *The Rainmakers* (1935)

3884 A band leader tries to talk suicidal Roger Pryor out of jumping out of a window. "Why," he explains, "your legs would be on one side of a street, your arms on the other. One half of your body would be in one place and the other half on the opposite side. What would you say if that happens?" "I'd say it was me all over," Pryor rejoins. – *To Beat the Band* (1935)

3885 Friend David Tree intercepts Wendy Hiller after she has had a falling out with Leslie Howard. "Where are you going?" he asks. "To the river." "What for?" "To make a hole in it."–*Pygmalion* (1938)

3886 "Now that I've met you again," vaudevillian Joan Davis says to Eddie Cantor, "I feel that I've led a full life. I think I'll go home and kill myself." –*Show Business* (1944)

3887 For court favors Bob Hope's servant girlfriend is willing to give herself to the King of France. A distraught Hope laments to a confidant: "I threw myself at her feet, told her if she went through with this, I'd hang myself." "And what did she do?" "Loaned me the rope."–*Monsieur Beaucaire* (1946)

3888 Charlatan swami Boris Karloff, trying to get Lou Costello to commit suicide by hypnotizing him, proclaims: "You'll kill yourself if it's the last thing you do."–*Abbott and Costello Meet the Killer, Boris Karloff* (1949)

3889 Anne Baxter storms into friend Catherine McLeod's apartment, distressed about a farewell note her husband left. Baxter suspects the worst.

"He hasn't killed himself," McLeod reassures her. "Otherwise he would have said, 'Don't blame yourself, darling.' They always do, so you will."–*My Wife's Best Friend* (1952)

3890 "In my family nobody ever committed suicide, nobody," Woody Allen says. "This was just not a middle-class alternative. My mother was too busy running the boiled chicken through the deflavoring machine to think about shooting herself or anything."–*Stardust Memories* (1980)

3891 In ancient Egypt, Dudley Moore, the pharaoh's stargazer assigned to a battlefield, urges a fanatical general not to fight to the death. "There are some wonderful things we'll be giving up–" he pleads with the general, "sunsets, flowers, the love of a good woman, breathing. I've always been particularly fond of breathing."–*Wholly Moses* (1980)

3892 Bette Midler's husband (Rip Torn) has just committed suicide by electrocuting himself while taking a shower. Bette, almost hysterical, peruses his still body and says: "He looks just like a hard-boiled egg."–*Jinxed!* (1982)

Supernatural

3893 Count Dracula (Bela Lugosi) acknowledges the astuteness of Professor Van Helsing (Edward Van Sloan), who observes that the Count casts no reflection upon a mirror–a characteristic of a vampire. "For one who has not lived even a single lifetime," Dracula notes, "you are a wise man."–*Dracula* (1931)

3894 The sounds of wolves howling outside the castle of Count Dracula (Bela Lugosi) strike a chord within him. "Listen to them," he utters responsively

as he ascends a cobwebbed staircase, "children of the night. What music they make!"–*Dracula* (1931)

3895 Claude Rains, as a chemist who has found the secret of making himself invisible, wants a colleague to join him in "setting the world right." "We'll begin with a reign of terror," Rains elaborates, "a few murders here and there...." –*The Invisible Man* (1933)

3896 On a remote island, crazed scientist Charles Laughton transforms animals into half-human, half-beast forms. "The natives are restless tonight," he sniffs one moonlit night. – *Island of Lost Souls* (1933)

3897 When daughter Marguerite Churchill confides to racketeer Ricardo Cortez that her father (Boris Karloff) seems somewhat different, Cortez takes her by the shoulders. "Darling, darling," he explains, "when a man as sensitive as your father has been hung by the neck, pronounced officially dead and brought back to life, he's bound to be affected by the experience." – *The Walking Dead* (1936)

3898 As a full moon lights Lon Chaney's bedroom, he grows fangs while fur covers his body. With bestial cries he rips apart his bed, knocks over tables and flings a chandelier into a huge mirror. His father (Claude Rains), hearing the clamor, knocks softly at his son's door. "Larry, Larry, my boy," he inquires, "is something troubling you?" – *The Wolf Man* (1941)

3899 On their wedding night a bewitched Veronica Lake begins to disclose her dark secret to bridegroom Fredric March: "I think I'd better tell you. You'll never forgive me if you found out later." "Ah, confession," March notes. "Well, I haven't exactly been a saint myself." – *I Married a Witch* (1942)

3900 After Bing Crosby sells Bob Hope to an Arab slave trader, the ghost of Hope's Aunt Lucy (Hope in drag) appears in Crosby's dream. She chastises him for not trying to find his friend. "He was resold," Crosby explains sheepishly. "I don't know to who." "To whom, Jeffrey, to whom," Aunt Lucy's ghost corrects him. – *Road to Morocco* (1942)

3901 After Dr. Watson (Nigel Bruce) returns from a visit to a spooky manor, Sherlock Holmes (Basil Rathbone) facetiously asks him whether he's seen any ghosts. "Ghosts don't stab people in the neck, do they?" Watson questions. "Not well-bred ghosts," replies Holmes. – *Sherlock Holmes Faces Death* (1943)

3902 Swami Edgar Bergen gazes into his crystal ball. "Do you know what I see when I look into that?" he asks Charlie McCarthy. "Goldfish?" McCarthy asks. – *Stage Door Canteen* (1943)

3903 "It's not hard to die. It's the coming back that's hard." – *The Phantom Speaks* (1945)

3904 Publisher Jonathan Hale, interested in spiritualism, learns that his artist friend James Ellison has just died in a fire. "We'll arrange for a seance right away," he proclaims to Ellison's servant. "It's a wonderful opportunity to get some really first-hand information from the other world – hot off the griddle, as you might say." – *The Ghost Goes Wild* (1947)

3905 Lou Costello to Bud Abbott: "I know there's no such thing as Dracula. You know there's no such thing as Dracula. But does Dracula know it?" – *Abbott and Costello Meet Frankenstein* (1948)

3906 A seductive vampire under the influence of Dracula tries to seduce Lou Costello. "Don't you know what's going to happen now?" she asks, closing in for the kill. "I'll bite," Costello says innocently. "No," she contradicts, "I will." – *Abbott and Costello Meet Frankenstein* (1948)

3907 Count Dracula (Bela Lugosi) to Lou Costello: "What we need today is young blood." – *Abbott and Costello Meet Frankenstein* (1948)

3908 "You don't understand," Lon Chaney tries to confess to Lou Costello about his predicament of turning into a werewolf. "Every night when the moon is full I turn into a wolf." "You and fifty million other guys," Costello returns. – *Abbott and Costello Meet Frankenstein* (1948)

3909 A princess, wishing to be changed into a bird so that she can join Sinbad, visits a wizard. When he tells her to remove her clothes, she demurs. But he insists, explaining that he cannot grow feathers on silk. "There are three men in a woman's life she should not be afraid to undress in front of," he says. "Her husband, her doctor, and her magician." —*Captain Sinbad* (1963)

3910 "There's still so much more of life to taste," a female vampire muses. —*Daughters of Darkness* (1971)

3911 A speaker addresses his fellow townspeople: "Ladies and gentlemen, there is a herd of killer rabbits coming this way."—*Night of the Lepus* (1972)

3912 Court jester Woody Allen enters the bleak lair of a swarthy and sinister-looking sorcerer, busily stirring a gurgling cauldron. "I think your eggs are done," Woody says.—*Everything You Always Wanted to Know About Sex (But Were Afraid to Ask* (1972)

3913 Woody Allen, illegally awakened by scientists in 3173, is being hunted by the authorities. "I can't believe this!" a bewildered Allen exclaims. "I go into the hospital for a lousy ulcer operation, I wake up and suddenly I'm on the 'ten most wanted' list. I knew it was too good to be true. I parked right near the hospital."—*Sleeper* (1973)

3914 At a train station young Dr. Frankenstein (Gene Wilder) requests a confirmation from a youngster. "Pardon me, boy. Is this the Transylvania station?"—*Young Frankenstein* (1974)

3915 Servant Arte Johnson suggests to Dracula (George Hamilton): "If you're hungry, master, we can ring for the night maid."—*Love at First Bite* (1979)

3916 George Hamilton, as Count Dracula, induces fashion model Susan St. James to join his world of vampirism. In the last scene they happily fly off together. "There is one small disadvantge," Hamilton confesses. "We can only live by night." "That's all right," his partner responds. "I can only get it

together by ten anyway."—*Love at First Bite* (1979)

3917 American youths David Naughton and Griffin Dunne, vacationing in England, are attacked by a werewolf and Dunne is killed. His mangled figure appears before Naughton, who is recuperating in a London hospital. "The supernatural? The powers of darkness?" Dunne says. "It's all true. The undead surround me. Did you ever talk to a corpse? It's boring!" —*An American Werewolf in London* (1981)

3918 An experiment gone awry transforms scientist Ray Wise into the Swamp Thing—a grotesque mass of dripping vegetation. In a confrontation with thugs, they riddle him with machine-gun bullets and hack off one of his arms. "Does it hurt?" his girlfriend (Adrienne Barbeau) solicitously asks. "Only when I laugh," he replies.—*Swamp Thing* (1982)

3919 Ghostbuster Bill Murray hears a report about eggs leaping out of their shells and frying themselves and blinding lights emanating from a refrigerator. "Generally, you don't get that kind of behavior in major appliances," he states.—*Ghostbusters* (1984)

3920 Alien creature John Candy is sent to rescue a princess. "What are you?" she asks. "I'm a mog," he explains, "half man, half dog. I'm my own best friend."—*Spaceballs* (1987)

3921 "I know this sounds crazy," young Nicholas Strouse says to Andrea Thompson, "but it's the truth. I'm an extraterrestrial genetic accident born on earth. Tomorrow night I'm taking off for my home planet with those friends of mine in the revolving Rotunda Room which is actually a space ship, which is generated by a collective extraterrestrial energy. I'm their navigator. Are you with me so far?" "There's more?" she asks.—*Doin' Time on Planet Earth* (1988)

3922 Woody Allen, visiting a clairvoyant, enters the mystic's quarters where the woman, all alone, is engaged in a strange ritual. "What are you doing?" he inquires. "I'm speaking to a dead friend of mine." "Would you rather talk privately?" Woody suggests. "I could wait in the other room." – *New York Stories* (1989)

3923 A demonic hand – the pet of the Addams family who admire it for its cuteness – scurries along on a five-fingered exercise. "Thing, you're a handful," says Morticia (Anjelica Huston) fondly. – *The Addams Family* (1991)

Transportation

3924 Bert Wheeler and Robert Woolsey board a trolley car and present the conductor with an outdated transfer. "Hey, this transfer is two days old." "It just goes to show you," Woolsey declares, "how long we've been waiting for this car." – *Caught Plastered* (1931)

3925 On a dark night a mysterious figure lurking in the shadows steps toward a parked taxi as another vehicle pulls away. "Hey," he awakens the dozing driver, "follow that car!" "Why?" – *Murder on a Bridal Path* (1936)

3926 "Follow that cab, quick!" Myrna Loy orders as she rushes to a waiting taxi. "Yes, ma'am," the driver says, darting off without her. – *Shadow of the Thin Man* (1941)

3927 A luxury liner docks at a port in Rio de Janeiro where reporters are conducting interviews. "I came here on my own private boat," one beautiful young woman says. "Yeah," another cattily adds, "a tramp steamer." – *The Thrill of Brazil* (1946)

3928 "There is one reassuring thing about airplanes," wealthy Rudy Vallee declares. "They always come down." – *Unfaithfully Yours* (1948)

3929 A young prince on horseback stops Jack (Lou Costello) and inquires:

"Tell me, will this road take me to the princess' palace?" "No," replies Costello, "but your horse will." – *Jack and the Beanstalk* (1951)

3930 Joan Fontaine, trying to persuade reluctant Bob Hope to pose as Casanova and accompany her to Venice, cuddles up to him and lists the pleasures that await him in that city, such as fine restaurants and beautiful women. "If this is the way they live in Venice, let's hurry," he says. "We can still catch the 7:15 gondola." – *Casanova's Big Night* (1954)

3931 Television star Phil Silvers questions his writer (Jack Albertson) on the whereabouts of a company vice-president: "Ain't he supposed to be flyin' in from St. Paul? Well, where is he?" "Well, maybe his arms got tired." – *Top Banana* (1954)

3932 Gregory Peck, inadvertently finding himself entangled in an international plot, orders a cab driver: "Follow that car!" "All my life I've been waiting for someone to say that!" exclaims the elated driver. – *Arabesque* (1966)

3933 Super-salesman Tom Hanks, aboard an airplane, is discovered under a blanket with a pretty flight attendant. "I'm a frequent flier," he quips to an inquisitive passenger. "They gave me a bonus." – *Nothing in Common* (1986)

3934 "Does the sheriff always drive around in a taxi?" Chevy Chase asks a local resident. "Yep," the man replies, "since he flunked his driving test."
—*Funny Farm* (1988)

3935 On a steamy summer day in New York, Gene Wilder and Christine Lahti are trapped in a taxi which is caught in a traffic jam on a bridge. The driver refuses to turn on the air conditioner until his two customers complain

vehemently about the heat. "I'm in traffic here," the driver replies. "You're going to buy me a radiator when this one burns out?"—*Funny About Love* (1990)

3936 Chevy Chase exits from a taxi and comments on the driver: "Driven ten blocks in fifteen minutes. Not bad for a one-eyed Russian immigrant."
—*Nothing but Trouble* (1991)

Travel

3937 A philanthropist announces that he will be sailing shortly for Uruguay. "Well," says Groucho Marx, "you go Uruguay and I'll go mine."—*Animal Crackers* (1930)

3938 "Where're you going?" Robert Woolsey broken-heartedly asks his girlfriend. "Abroad." "Yeah, but what part of abroad?" "The answer is nonessential," her aunt interjects. "Is that far?" Woolsey asks.—*Cracked Nuts* (1931)

3939 On board the Peking-Shanghai Express, oriental bandit chief Warner Oland questions Shanghai Lily (Marlene Dietrich) as to the purpose of her journey to Shanghai. "To buy a new hat," she replies.—*Shanghai Express* (1932)

3940 W. C. Fields lands his aircraft "Spirit of Brooklyn" on top of a roof garden and discovers he is in Wu-Hu, China. "Well, what is Wu-Hu doing where Kansas City ought to be?" he demands of the manager. "Maybe you're lost," the manager suggests. "Kansas City is lost!" Fields declares. "I am here!"—*International House* (1933)

3941 "I do adore Paris," Alice Brady says to Ginger Rogers. "It's so much like

Chicago. It's such a relief when you travel to feel that you've never left home at all."—*The Gay Divorcee* (1934)

3942 While listening to a tour guide describe a gargoyle, a tired Lucille Ball blurts out: "I don't want any more culture. It makes my feet hurt."—*I Dream Too Much* (1935)

3943 A roving radio reporter enters a trailer camp and asks one trailer owner to tell the listening audience about the "beauties of this glorious country." "I didn't see any," the owner declares. "You mean you traveled three thousand miles and didn't see anything?" "We had a little trouble with our sink in Atlanta; the bed broke down in St. Louis; worst of all, the bumps went bad in Idaho. To tell the truth, I never did get a chance to get out of the trailer."—*Go Chase Yourself* (1938)

3944 "I have to go to New York," Judge Hardy (Lewis Stone) says to his son Andy (Mickey Rooney). "If the mountain won't come to Mohammed, Mohammed must go to the mountain." "What would he want with a mountain anyway?" Rooney questions.—*Andy Hardy Meets Debutante* (1940)

3945 Chico and Harpo Marx enter a ticket office in a train station. "All we want to know is where's the train," Chico asks Groucho Marx. "It's on the tracks," Groucho replies. "It seldom comes in here."–*Go West* (1940)

3946 "Travel broadens one so, don't you think?" Leon Errol's stocky wife remarks. "Oh, yes," Errol returns, "you must have traveled a great deal." –*Mexican Spitfire* (1940)

3947 "Have you traveled much lately?" worldly June Preisser asks fellow high-school student Mickey Rooney. "A little," he answers. "My uncle took me to Chicago once." "Oh, no," she interrupts. "I mean the Continent." "Which one?" inquires Mickey.–*Strike Up the Band* (1940)

3948 Clifton Webb and wife Myrna Loy, driving their brood of twelve children in their open touring car, stop in a town. "Hey, Noah! What are you doing with that ark?" a heckler calls out. "Collecting animals like the good Lord told us, brother," Webb returns. "All we need now is a jackass. Hop in!"– *Cheaper by the Dozen* (1950)

3949 Huntz Hall approaches a travel agent: "You handle all types of travel, don't you? Well, I'd like you to fix my roller skates."–*In the Money* (1958)

3950 Although author Bob Hope has written several books about Africa, he has never set foot on that continent. "Why don't you go to Africa?" his servant proposes. "The only wild animal I want to see is the cigarette girl at the Stork Club," Hope ripostes.–*Call Me Bwana* (1963)

3951 Dean Martin, on his way to Hollywood, passes through the town of Climax, Nevada, and quips: "The only way to go."–*Kiss Me, Stupid* (1964)

3952 At a hotel pool Matt Helm (Dean Martin) and his attractive date meet a young woman also staying at the hotel.

"Are you on vacation?" Helm's date asks. "I was on tour–a sightseeing tour," the woman explains. "But the man in charge kept taking me places that were not in the brochure." "Where was that?" Helm asks. "His room."–*The Silencers* (1966)

3953 Peter Lawford takes his wife on vacation to Italy, where she experiences her first brush with Italian customs. "Oh!" she exclaims. "I've just had my bottom pinched!" "Welcome to Southern Italy," says Lawford jokingly. "Do I acknowledge it in any way?" she asks. "Just turn the other cheek."–*Buona Sera, Mrs. Campbell* (1969)

3954 American tourist Shelley Winters, visiting Italy, confides to fellow tourists that she is looking forward to the art treasure tour in Florence. "I hear you can pick up the most beautiful, marvelous bargains there," she says. "Really?" interjects a listener. "What are you interested in, painting or sculpture?" "Bedroom slippers," replies Winters. –*Buona Sera, Mrs. Campbell* (1969)

3955 Hunted by a relentless posse, Butch Cassidy (Paul Newman) and the Sundance Kid (Robert Redford) head for Bolivia. When they get off the train, they find themselves surrounded by a bare, desolate landscape dotted only by a few small huts, some pigs and a muddy road. "Just think," Newman says wryly, "fifty years ago there was nothing here."–*Butch Cassidy and the Sundance Kid* (1969)

3956 New Jersey caterer Jackie Gleason, traveling reluctantly in Europe with his wife and daughter, cannot get excited about the sites of the Old World. "If you like ruins," he mutters to his family, "take a look at my business when you get back."–*Don't Drink the Water* (1969)

3957 The Hollanders, on their way to Paris, discover that their plane has been hijacked to East Europe and that they are accused of spying. "First no movie in the plane and now this!" Mrs. Hollander complains. "Nobody can be dragged out and shot without written consent of the American government," her husband offers as consolation. – *Don't Drink the Water* (1969)

3958 On board a passenger plane that is circling New York and waiting to land, Jack Lemmon asks a flight steward for a cup of coffee for his wife Sandy Dennis – only to learn it is all gone. "Is it possible to make some more?" he asks. "We're not allowed to have the burners on during landing." "Yes," Lemmon continues, "but we're not landing, we're circling." "We're circling prior to landing," the steward explains. "Yes, but if we keep circling and circling," Lemmon persists, "that's not circling, that's flying. Is it possible to make coffee during flying?" – *The Out of Towners* (1970)

3959 "What brought you from Chicago to Ohio?" Peter Boyle asks Candice Bergen. "An airplane," she replies. – *T.R. Baskin* (1971)

3960 Steve Martin, an orphan raised by a poor black family in the rural South, decides to strike out on his own.

He spends all day hitchhiking from in front of the remote family shack without success. Finally, a truck stops, and Martin announces that he is hitchhiking. "How far are you going?" he asks the driver. "To the end of this fence." "Okay," Martin agrees. – *The Jerk* (1979)

3961 Ex-pilot Robert Hays aboard a passenger plane appears nervous to his fellow passenger. "Nervous?" the woman asks, trying to comfort him. "Yes." "Your first time?" "No," he replies. "I've been nervous lots of times." – *Airplane!* (1980)

3962 "I'm terrified of flying," Burt Reynolds confides to psychiatrist Julie Andrews during one of his weekly sessions. He then adds: "I'm not so terrified of flying as I'm terrified of crashing." – *The Man Who Loved Women* (1983)

3963 Chevy Chase is annoyed by a fellow passenger aboard an airplane and treats her with derision. The plane hits some turbulence which disturbs the woman. "Oh, Lord, what was that?" she questions. "We clipped a Piper Cub," he explains. "Pilot's okay. I just saw him parachuting." – *Fletch Lives* (1989)

Vanity

3964 Charlie Chan (Warner Oland): "Big head is only good place for large headache." – *Charlie Chan Carries On* (1931)

3965 One of Mae West's many admirers: "I'll never forget you." Mae West: "No one ever does." – *I'm No Angel* (1933)

3966 Leslie Howard, as the "damned elusive Scarlet Pimpernel" who keeps his identity hidden by posing as a fop, toys

with Robespierre's ambassador to England (Raymond Massey). "I've just been to Bath to be cured of the fatigue," Howard sighs. "And now I'm so fatigued by the cure that I really think I shall have to go back to Bath to be cured of the fatigue." – *The Scarlet Pimpernel* (1935)

3967 Dentist Bert Wheeler, traveling to the West by stagecoach, engages in conversation with some of the passengers. "Are you going to Littletown to practice?" a young teacher asks. "I don't have to practice," Wheeler replies. "I'm perfect." – *Silly Billies* (1936)

3968 Police inspector Grant Mitchell investigates the theft of a valuable necklace. He questions several guests, including a famous European conductor (Alan Mowbray). "Another musician!" Mitchell says in frustration. "In America today, I am probably the *only* musician," declares Mowbray. – *Music for Madame* (1937)

3969 "Of course, I would have to read the script," a ham movie actor remarks before committing himself to a contract. "I couldn't consider a *small* part." "No matter how small it is," quips Lee Patrick, "you'll fit it." – *Crashing Hollywood* (1938)

3970 Con artist Erich von Stroheim describes to his two partners their next wealthy victim: "Astrologically speaking, he's a Virgo – very fine and clever people. I was born under the same sign." – *I Was an Adventuress* (1940)

3971 At a ball the wealthy Mr. Darcy (Laurence Olivier) rejects an opportunity to meet Elizabeth Bennet (Greer Garson). "She looks tolerable enough," he explains, "but I'm in no humor tonight to give consequence to the middle class at play." – *Pride and Prejudice* (1940)

3972 Princeton football player Richard Carlson tries to persuade Desi Arnaz to sign with his college, but young Arnaz boasts that other schools are trying to recruit him. "There's no sense in being conceited," Carlson says. "I'm not conceited," Arnaz objects. "I am the greatest player in fifty years, but I'm not conceited." – *Too Many Girls* (1940)

3973 Bob Hope, portraying a movie star, worries that the draft might keep him off the screen for a year. "What would my fans do?" he asks. "Maybe they're the ones who put the draft through," quips his agent Lynne Overman. – *Caught in the Draft* (1941)

3974 "I'm doing the work of ten men," a Washington bureaucrat boasts to a group of women during World War II. "Who are they?" Jane Wyman asks innocently. – *The Doughgirls* (1944)

3975 "In my case, self-absorption is completely justified," flaunts columnist Clifton Webb. "I have never discovered any other subject quite so worthy of my attention." – *Laura* (1944)

3976 During World War II Russian soldier Paul Muni captures a group of Nazi soldiers and, finding a monocle, surmises one of them is an officer. "You feel naked without it, huh?" he asks a likely suspect. "It's the difference between a man like me and a goat like you," the German returns. "It's the officer," Muni says, nodding with a wry smile. – *Counter-Attack* (1945)

3977 Dapper Clifton Webb applies as babysitter for Maureen O'Hara's three rambunctious children. "May I ask what is your profession?" she inquires. "Certainly," he responds. "I am a genius." – *Sitting Pretty* (1948)

3978 Immediately after Don Juan (Errol Flynn) has sworn off women, he exchanges social pleasantries with a charming young woman in a passing coach – and then decides to ride after her in hot pursuit: "There is a little bit of Don Juan in every man, but since I am Don Juan, there must be more of it in me!" – *Adventures of Don Juan* (1948)

3979 Pretty Rhonda Fleming volunteers to get Bob Hope out of a jam. As she departs, she gives him a passionate kiss, leaving him stunned. "I'm not worth it," Hope says to himself. "But if I'm not, who is?" – *The Great Lover* (1949)

3980 "To those of you who do not read, attend the theater, listen to unsponsored radio programs, or know anything of the world in which you live," theater critic George Sanders opens a speech, "it is perhaps necessary to introduce myself. My name is Addison DeWitt." – *All About Eve* (1950)

3981 Ambitious young actress Anne Baxter confides to theater critic George Sanders that he would probably find her boring. "You won't bore him, honey," Sanders' protégée (Marilyn Monroe) interjects. "You won't even get to talk." – *All About Eve* (1950)

3982 The murderous pirate Captain Kidd (Charles Laughton) is forced to make a deal with waiter Lou Costello, who happens to know where a buried treasure is hidden. "The things I have to do to go down in history," Laughton sighs. – *Abbott and Costello Meet Captain Kidd* (1952)

3983 Toulouse-Lautrec (Jose Ferrer), tired of hearing pretentious art critics expounding opinions as God's truth, asks one: "How do you know it's the greatest painting in the world? And how do you know it was painted by Leonardo?" "Because I feel it," the critic answers vaguely. "I feel it here in my heart." "I feel it in my heart that you're a pompous ass," Lautrec replies, "but that doesn't make it so." – *Moulin Rouge* (1952)

3984 "Oh," muses Bob Hope, "I wish I was a girl so I could fight over me." – *Here Come the Girls* (1953)

3985 Chorine Mitzi Gaynor comments on the love life of her boss Gene Kelly: "Barry fell in love with himself the first time he looked in the mirror and he's been faithful ever since." – *Les Girls* (1957)

3986 Nightclub singer Frank Sinatra is rejected by wealthy widow Rita Hayworth. "By the way," he observes, "if you knew what you were throwing away, you'd cut your throat." – *Pal Joey* (1957)

3987 Chemist Jack Oakie balks at advertising executive Rock Hudson's proposal that Oakie create a product for

his agency. "Nothing can induce me to associate myself with that dull, insipid group of people called the human race," Oakie asserts. "I'm merely happy and content, and I have the companionship worthy of my company – myself." – *Lover Come Back* (1961)

3988 A conceited waiter at the Grand Hotel in Stockholm, Sweden, condescendingly instructs his assistant. "There is much to learn by observing me," he crows. "I agree," his assistant admits. "You should be placed under observation." – *The Prize* (1963)

3989 A representative from Georgia arrives at Congress and, seeing the eminent Benjamin Franklin (Howard da Silva), stares in admiration. "What are you staring at?" Franklin asks. "Haven't you ever seen a great man before?" – *1776* (1972)

3990 President Harry Truman (Ed Sanders), who has been feuding with the imperious General Douglas MacArthur (Gregory Peck), travels to Hawaii for a face-to-face meeting and undergoes the indignity of being kept waiting by his general. "They probably had to get him down off his cross," Truman fumes. – *MacArthur* (1977)

3991 Luciano Pavarotti, playing a married Italian opera superstar – and accustomed to doting admirers – meets and dates independent American doctor Kathryn Harrold. "You must promise you will not fall in love with me," he says. "I know it will be hard." – *Yes, Giorgio* (1982)

3992 At a women's club poetry reading, one matron approaches poet Tom Conti. "Who is your favorite author?" she asks. "I am," he replies. – *Reuben, Reuben* (1984)

3993 "I like to talk to myself," says construction millionaire Jackie Mason. "You know why? I like to deal with a better class of people." – *Caddyshack II* (1988)

3994 Police detective Gene Hackman, proud of his restored station wagon, shows it off to a fellow officer. "You know what this car represents?" Hackman asks.

"It's an extension of your penis," his friend offers. "Actually, I think you're flattering yourself. You ought to be driving a compact." –*Loose Cannons* (1990)

Villains and Villainy

3995 An actor caught in a thieves' hideout must pass a test involving picking a pocket from a dummy without ringing attached bells. "Can *you* do it?" the captive demands of vagabond leader Thomas Mitchell. "I'm above this sort of thing," Mitchell fires back. "I cut throats. I don't cut purses." –*The Hunchback of Notre Dame* (1939)

3996 The Wizard of Oz (Frank Morgan) looks on as the Wicked Witch fades away after Dorothy (Judy Garland) douses her with water. "She's been liquidated," Morgan quips. –*The Wizard of Oz* (1939)

3997 Vladimir Sokoloff, as a Soviet chief of police, acknowledges his role in the elimination of the man he has replaced. "How quickly fortune changes," he quips, "when we help it a little." –*Comrade X* (1940)

3998 Two killers, searching for Bob Hope and Bing Crosby, are directed to a room where a stick of dynamite is about to explode. "We'll hear from them later," Crosby says. "Yeah," Hope wisecracks, "they'll be men about town." –*Road to Utopia* (1945)

3999 During a peace pow-wow between Apache chief Cochise and Major Thursday (Henry Fonda), the chief unleashes a torrent of Apache epithets against a crooked Indian agent named Beacham. "What did he say?" Fonda asks the interpreter. "Well, sir," the trooper replies hesitantly, "a free translation would be that Beacham's a

yellow-bellied polecat of dubious antecedents and conjectural progeny. Cochise's words, of course, sir." –*Fort Apache* (1948)

4000 Danny Kaye, posing as a jester, is mistaken for an assassin by villainous knight Basil Rathbone. Meanwhile, Kaye thinks the knight is his accomplice in stealing a strategic key from the king. "When do we start?" Kaye asks. "Tonight." "Good. I'd like to get in, get on with it and get out. Got it?" "Got it," Rathbone replies. "Good," Kaye concludes. –*The Court Jester* (1956)

4001 "The explosion," villain Victor Buono informs an adversary, "will raise a cloud of radioactive dust that will settle over vast areas of the Southwest ... Beautiful!" –*The Silencers* (1966)

4002 Master criminal Karl Malden castigates his bodyguard Tom Reese for killing a "perfect stranger." "Nobody's *perfect*," Reese retorts. –*Murderer's Row* (1967)

4003 Arch-villain Woody Allen proposes to his captive, Daliah Levi: "I'll unlock you immediately and we'll run amok. If you're too tired, we can walk amok." –*Casino Royale* (1967)

4004 On an inhabited planet somewhere in space, a crazed villain, plotting to take control, confides to Barbarella (Jane Fonda), an agent from Earth, that he faces a formidable obstacle. "The Black Queen must first be destroyed," he explains. "Whoever succeeds in killing her will be put immediately to a horrible death. Hence my prudence. I find horrible the idea that one could do to me that which I do to others." – *Barbarella* (1968)

4005 An arch-villain whispers to one of his hatchet men: "Look after Mr. Bond. See that some harm comes to him." – *Moonraker* (1979)

4006 A peasant-spy, after revealing to town tyrant Ron Leibman a scheme for capturing the rebel Zorro, tells about his own squalid living conditions in a crowded household. "I pray for a small room of my own," he entreats Leibman as his little reward. "Your prayers are answered," says the town villain, and, turning to his soldiers, orders: "Lock him up in solitary!" – *Zorro, the Gay Blade* (1981)

4007 The villainous Dr. Lizardo (John Lithgow) captures the heroic titular hero (Peter Weller) and has him taken to the Shock Tower where a complex electrical machine will be used to torture him. "More power to him!" Lizardo gleefully commands. – *The Adventures of Buckaroo Banzai Across the 8th Dimension* (1982)

4008 Evil orphanage supervisor Carol Burnett cruelly seizes little Annie (Aileen Quinn) by the collar of her dress and muses: "Why anyone would want to be an orphan is beyond me." – *Annie* (1982)

4009 The Corsican brothers (Cheech Marin and Tommy Chong) meet in a French forest after several years of separation, and Chong relates that the country is ruled by villains. "They rape the fields and pillage the women," he says. – *Cheech and Chong's The Corsican Brothers* (1984)

4010 Arch-villain Christopher Plummer has kidnapped detective Joe Friday (Dan Aykroyd) and a female witness, but the officer cannot be silenced as he eulogizes the formidable Los Angeles Police Department: "Just like every foaming rabid psycho in this city with a foolproof plan, you've forgotten that you're facing the single, finest fighting force ever assembled." "The Israelis?" Plummer asks. – *Dragnet* (1987)

4011 Arch-villain Ricardo Montalban, after failing to assassinate the Queen of England, uses his secretary Priscilla Presley as hostage to make his getaway. "Now we're going to take a little walk," he says, holding a gun to her head. "To think I respected you!" she utters. "How could you do something so vicious?" "It was easy, my dear," explains Montalban. "Don't forget, I spent two years as a building contractor." – *The Naked Gun* (1988)

4012 Captain Hook (Dustin Hoffman) struggles to devise a plan to destroy Peter Pan. "I think I'm having an apostrophe!" announces his right-hand man Smee (Bob Hoskins). "I think you mean 'epiphany,'" says Hook. – *Hook* (1991)

4013 The arch-villain of an international gold plot captures innocent Richard Greco, whom he mistakes for a C.I.A. agent. "I want to talk to him," the villain says to his assistant Linda Hunt. "Why?" "I never get to talk to anyone." – *If Looks Could Kill* (1991)

4014 The villainous Sheriff of Nottingham (Alan Rickman), in one of his more disagreeable moods, snarls: "Cancel the table scraps for lepers and orphans!" – *Robin Hood: Prince of Thieves* (1991)

War

4015 A group of raw German recruits, fresh out of high school, are sent to the front during World War I. They join a handful of battle-weary soldiers. "We haven't eaten since breakfast," Lew Ayres, leader of the hungry young innocents, announces. "We thought maybe you could tell us what we could do about it." "Eat without further delay," one of the soldiers replies. – *All Quiet on the Western Front* (1930)

4016 Louis Calhern, as President of his nation during a war with Freedonia, announces to Chico Marx: "There's a machine-gun nest on hill twenty-two. I want it cleaned out." "Good," Chico replies. "I'll tell the janitor." – *Duck Soup* (1933)

4017 The status of the battle is grave, and Groucho Marx selects Harpo to break through enemy lines. "Remember," Groucho says, "while you are risking life and limb, through shot and shell, we'll be thinking what a sucker you are." – *Duck Soup* (1933)

4018 During a war with Sylvania, Groucho Marx receives a messenger at headquarters who announces that a general is undergoing a gas attack. "Tell him to take a teaspoon of soda and half a glass of water," Groucho advises. – *Duck Soup* (1933)

4019 An American submarine during World War I is sitting on the ocean floor while German warships rain depth charges about her. "Chief," a sailor utters to Walter Huston, "I wonder what port we're in." "What's the difference?" Huston returns. "There's no liberty today." – *Hell Below* (1933)

4020 Peasant-poet Francois Villon (Ronald Colman), having been capriciously appointed as constable by Louis XI, proposes an attack against the Burgundians who have surrounded Paris. "It's quite apparent you have no knowledge of military maneuvers," a defeatist general objects. "You're right, general," Colman ripostes. "I've only studied yours and I've learned nothing from them." – *If I Were King* (1938)

4021 During World War I, vain chorus girl Margaret Sullavan asks her maid for a cup of coffee with two lumps of sugar. "The second lump is for the second cup," her maid says. "What?" the entertainer exclaims, perturbed. "Only one lump per cup," her boyfriend (Walter Pidgeon) interjects. "There's a war going on." "What are they doing?" Sullavan asks. "Throwing cubes of sugar at each other?" – *The Shopworn Angel* (1938)

4022 "I had a nephew in the last war," Leon Errol regales fellow dinner guests, "who brought down twelve planes – and he was in every one of them." – *Mexican Spitfire* (1940)

4023 "I had an uncle who was a hero in the last war," agent Lynne Overman relates to movie actor Bob Hope. "He broke up a gas attack singlehanded." "How?" asks Hope. "With bicarbonate of soda?" – *Caught in the Draft* (1941)

4024 American pilot Tyrone Power is late for a date with girlfriend Betty Grable because of a night bombing run over Berlin. "Sorry, I'll be a little late," he apologizes over the telephone. "I was held up by a traffic light in Berlin." – *A Yank in the R.A.F.* (1941)

4025 French underground leader Paul Henreid asks German major Conrad Veidt for permission to speak to Ugarte (Peter Lorre). "You will find the conversation entirely one-sided," Veidt replies. "Monsieur Ugarte is dead." – *Casablanca* (1942)

4026 During World War II, downed English fliers behind German lines overpower some German soldiers and begin donning their uniforms. Pilot Ronald Reagan pulls at one soldier's trousers which won't come off. "I've never seen a man so attached to his uniform," he quips. – *Desperate Journey* (1942)

4027 World War II pilot John Carroll says to commanding officer John Wayne at the end of a mission briefing: "I'm not going to ask you what to do if your chute doesn't open, because you'll say – " "Take it back to the factory," all the airmen chime in. – *Flying Tigers* (1942)

4028 German fighter-bombers attack an American cargo ship somewhere in the North Atlantic, and one sailor scores a hit on one of the planes. "You knocked him down!" one of the gun crew shouts. "Yeah," his buddy cracks, "that's for makin' me miss the World Series." – *The Navy Comes Through* (1942)

4029 U.S. Marine William Bendix is bombarded with orders from his sergeant. "The dumber those guys are," Bendix confides to buddy Robert Preston, "the more stripes they get." "You ought-a look like a zebra," Preston rejoins. – *Wake Island* (1942)

4030 On Wake Island during World War II, leatherneck Robert Preston, during a Japanese bombing attack, takes refuge in a foxhole where he complains to buddy William Bendix that the Japs are blowing everything to bits. "What d'you care?" Bendix returns. "It ain't your island, is it?" – *Wake Island* (1942)

4031 Alan Hale, as the cook aboard a World War II liberty ship which is being mercilessly tossed about by a raging storm, says: "This is the kind of day I'd like to be home with a blonde and a book." "Since when can you read?" a fellow sailor reminds him. "Who said I

could read?" – *Action in the North Atlantic* (1943)

4032 Aboard a troop ship headed for Guadalcanal during World War II, U.S. Marine sergeant Lloyd Nolan notices that William Bendix is sporting a blackjack as part of his array of weapons. "Hey, wait a minute," Nolan says. "That ain't government issue." "No," Bendix acknowledges, "that's Flatbush issue." – *Guadalcanal Diary* (1943)

4033 During World War II, U.S. Marine chaplain Preston Foster informs some troops about to storm Guadalcanal that there are thousands of natives on the island. "Cannibals?" asks a nervous William Bendix. "No, strictly vegetarians," Foster replies, then smilingly adds: "Then, of course, they never tasted Marine meat." – *Guadalcanal Diary* (1943)

4034 Three Japanese planes attack a diving U.S. submarine. The sub rocks with each explosion, and it is touch and go whether any of the crew will make it out alive. "A guy could get killed in here!" cracks sailor Sam Levene, breaking the silence. – *Gung Ho!* (1943)

4035 A freighter is torpedoed by a German submarine during World War II, and William Bendix, one of the few surviving seamen, is angry. "This is the fourth time I shipped out since the war and I ain't got no place yet," he complains. "I wish I could make the complete round trip just once." – *Lifeboat* (1944)

4036 During World War II, two G.I.s aboard a troop ship peer down upon a lower deck where more than one hundred nurses are sunbathing and playing deck games. "We never had anything like this in the last war," says one soldier. "We don't have anything like it in this war either," adds the other. – *Up in Arms* (1944)

4037 In an airplane over Burma during World War II, nervous reporter

Henry Hull tremulously questions battle-weary paratroopers. "What if my chute doesn't open?" he asks. "You'll be the first one down," a soldier replies. –*Objective, Burma* (1945)

4038 U.S. soldiers escaping pursuing Japanese are forced to hack their way through the Burmese jungle. "I don't go in for this," a worried reporter says. "Who does? This is muck and mire," G.I. George Tobias offers. "Hello, Muck," one soldier pipes. "Hello, Mire," Tobias responds. –*Objective, Burma* (1945)

4039 In the dead of night a group of U.S. Marines on Guadalcanal await a Japanese counterattack. "You know something?" one soldier whispers to buddy John Garfield. "We've been here two weeks already. It's our anniversary." "Remind me later," Garfield says. "I'll bake a cake." –*Pride of the Marines* (1945)

4040 "You know," a G.I. fighting in Europe muses, "after this war is over, I'm gonna get me a map and find out where I've been." –*The Story of G.I. Joe* (1945)

4041 During World War II on the Italian front, Richard Conte and his buddy are assigned to man a machine gun. "You ever go to Coney Island?" Conte asks. "You ever shoot those electric guns that shoot down those airplanes? I never could hit those airplanes." "Maybe you ain't safe to be with," his buddy suggests. "How did you ever get to be a machine-gunner?" "I bribed a guy," replies Conte. "I want a transfer." –*A Walk in the Sun* (1945)

4042 During World War II in Italy, American soldiers give K-Rations to captured Italian soldiers. "When they get a load of this," cracks G.I. Richard Conte, "they'll wish Italy never got out of the war." –*A Walk in the Sun* (1945)

4043 During the Battle of the Bulge, all available troops – cooks, clerks, and even the wounded – are given a rifle and sent to the front. "This is a thirty caliber, gas-operated, quick-set, semi-automatic rifle," a battle-hardened G.I. explains to an untried soldier. "Look," the soldier returns, "you ain't selling it to me. You're only showing me how it works." –*Battleground* (1949)

4044 During World War II, England is stacked with armaments in preparation for D-Day, and the narrator issues the American caveat: "We'd better get off this island before it sinks with the weight of this stuff." –*Breakthrough* (1950)

4045 Aide Dean Jagger steals aboard a bomber to man one of its guns during a mission over Germany in World War II. Upon Jagger's return, group commander Gregory Peck rebukes him, then asks if he hit anything. "Well, sir, my glasses were frosted over some, but I think I got a piece of one." "Ours or theirs?" Peck asks. –*Twelve O'Clock High* (1950)

4046 When a patrol of French Foreign Legionnaires are attacked by a horde of Riffs, their sergeant, Burt Lancaster, leads them out of danger during a blinding sand storm. "I can see nothing with the sand blowing in my eyes," one soldier admits. "How does the sergeant know where we're going?" "He keeps his eyes closed," explains another. –*Ten Tall Men* (1951)

4047 A squad of battle-weary G.I.s in a war-torn, virtually flattened European town receive some good news. "We're getting relieved," one G.I. announces. "Yeah," says another, "we're giving them the keys to the city. Too bad there are no doors to unlock." –*Eight Iron Men* (1952)

4048 Guard Sig Rumann enters a barracks in a World War II German prison camp. "Am I interrupting something?" he asks the Americans. "Yeah, we were just passing out guns," one G.I. quips. "Ah," Rumann returns, "you're alvays mit de vise crackers." "Vise crackers?"

another prisoner questions. "Where did he pick up his English – in a pretzel factory?" – *Stalag 17* (1953)

4049 American prisoners of war, stationed in a German camp, are surprised when fellow prisoner William Holden volunteers to test out their new escape route. "I'd like to know what made him do it," a prisoner muses after Holden succeeds. "Maybe he wanted to steal our wire cutters," a fellow prisoner cracks. – *Stalag 17* (1953)

4050 Captured American air crews in a German prisoner-of-war camp make guard Sig Rumann the butt of their jokes. "How do you expect to win the war with an army of clowns?" Rumann asks. "We sort of hope you'll laugh yourselves to death," one prisoner returns. – *Stalag 17* (1953)

4051 During the Korean War, American pilot Frank Lovejoy knocks out a North Korean supply train and cracks: "Due to technical difficulties, the Wonton Limited will be a few minutes late." – *Men of the Fighting Lady* (1954)

4052 After a suicidal kamikaze attack upon his ship, tough navy captain Jeff Chandler sustains punctured lungs, internal bleeding, shrapnel wounds, a ruptured spleen and a fractured rib cage. "Cap," medic Keith Andes advises, "you really shouldn't be moving around now." – *Away All Boats* (1956)

4053 American serviceman William Holden walks past some English training exercises on his way to a conference during World War II and is mistakenly attacked by a Commando. "I thought you were the enemy," the soldier apologizes. "I'm an American," Holden replies, "if that's what you mean." – *The Bridge on the River Kwai* (1957)

4054 During World War II, German officer Marius Goring, stationed in Greece, ponders about his nation's military successes: "The Fuhrer leads us from victory to victory, and each victory

leads us farther away from home. A few more such victories and we may never return." – *The Angry Hills* (1959)

4055 Polish colonel Curt Jurgens, escaping from Nazi-occupied France, intends to leave leisurely in a manner befitting a Polish officer. Jewish refugee Danny Kaye, traveling with Jurgens, is more realistic than his quixotic savior and wants to make a dash for the border. "He lives in fear of death, this man," says Jurgens with bravado. "I know I am a superfluous man," Kaye explains with sarcastic humility, "but even a superfluous man wants to go on being superfluous." – *Me and the Colonel* (1959)

4056 Captain Cary Grant's submarine is seriously damaged during World War II, but he pleads with his superior officer to give the *Sea Tiger* another chance to get back into action. "It's like a beautiful woman dying an old maid," Grant explains. – *Operation Petticoat* (1959)

4057 Near the end of the Korean War, G.I.s are ordered to retake Pork Chop Hill. After one battle, as the men dig in, gutsy lieutenant Gregory Peck, assessing the casualties, extends a box of raisins to those around him. "Had your iron today?" he asks. – *Pork Chop Hill* (1959)

4058 Seven female prisoners break out of a Japanese prison camp in New Guinea during World War II and, after a series of hardships, they run into American troops. "Yanks!" they cry out in joy. "Broads!" the soldiers shout in reply. – *Seven Women from Hell* (1961)

4059 During World War II, two reporters land in France with the English on D-Day and send off two carrier pigeons with the news of the invasion. But the creatures fly off in the opposite direction. "Not toward the Germans, you idiots! The other way!" one reporter shouts. "Damn traitors!" the other adds. – *The Longest Day* (1962)

4060 On Omaha Beach, D-Day, colonel Eddie Albert rallies his men, paralyzed under a heavy barrage of fire. "We're getting murdered here!" he cries out. "Let's get inland and get murdered!" – *The Longest Day* (1962)

4061 After Merrill's Marauders accomplish their mission behind Japanese lines in Burma, one soldier anxiously asks his sergeant when they are going home. "When we get replaced by the British," comes the reply. "What's holding them up?" "The enemy, you meathead!" – *Merrill's Marauders* (1962)

4062 "He was the first dead man on Omaha Beach," navy officer James Coburn announces with pride. "Was there a contest?" Julie Andrews asks. – *The Americanization of Emily* (1964)

4063 Allied prisoners of war, on their way to a German prison camp, capture the train they are on and head for the Swiss border. A British chaplain discovers a young Italian woman, a German officer's mistress, dressed only in a negligee. "What are you doing here, my child?" he asks innocently. "You are a pragmatist," British major Trevor Howard quips as the other officers smile. – *Von Ryan's Express* (1965)

4064 During World War II American forces sweep into an Italian town to hear an Italian officer call out: "Do you surrender?" "Hell, no!" an American tank commander fires back. "Do *you* surrender?" "Of course," the Italian replies. – *What Did You Do in the War, Daddy?* (1966)

4065 When the U.S. Fifth Army liberates Rome in June 1944, an Italian princess is anything but exhilarated. "Do you realize," she rebukes a staff officer, "you are the first of the barbarians to have taken Rome from the south?" – *What Did You Do in the War, Daddy?* (1966)

4066 During World War II, an American general devises a near-suicidal mission behind German lines involving twelve soldiers imprisoned for serious crimes. Major Lee Marvin is selected to train and lead them. "What do you say, Major?" the general asks. "I'd say it confirms a suspicion I've had for some time now," Marvin replies. "One of the men we're working for happens to be a raving lunatic." – *The Dirty Dozen* (1967)

4067 U.S. major Lee Marvin, using twelve volunteer army convicts, plans to attack a chateau filled with Nazi officers. "Kill every officer in sight," he orders. "Ours or theirs?" one asks. – *The Dirty Dozen* (1967)

4068 A wounded soldier, stretched out on a litter and looking as though he's been through Hell, is comforted by a well-meaning nurse who promises: "Don't worry. We'll soon have you back at the front." – *Oh! What a Lovely War* (1969)

4069 Burt Reynolds, as the nineteenth-century western drifter Sam Whiskey, elaborates upon General Sherman's comment that "War is hell." "Worse than that," Reynolds says, "the pay is bad." – *Sam Whiskey* (1969)

4070 Conversation in a field operating hospital during the Korean War: "Is he an enlisted man or an officer?" "Enlisted man." "Okay, then make the stitches big." – *M*A*S*H* (1970)

4071 During World War II, General George S. Patton (George C. Scott) poses before a giant American flag as he addresses his troops: "I want you to remember that no bastard ever won a war by dying for his country. He won it by making the other poor bastard die for his country... I don't want to get any messages that we are holding our position. We're not holding anything. We are advancing constantly. We are not interested in holding onto anything except the enemy... We're going to go through him like crap through a goose." – *Patton* (1970)

4072 As General Patton (George C. Scott) is moving his Third Army to relieve Bastogne, an officer informs him of General McCulloch's answer to the German surrender offer. "He said, 'Nuts!'" the officer reports. "Keep 'em moving, colonel!" Patton shouts orders to his advancing troops. "A man that eloquent has to be saved."—*Patton* (1970)

4073 A rebel leader in a Latin American country, holding a batch of straws, declares that the drawer of the short straw will lead a raid. Without further ado, he hands the short straw to Woody Allen. "As long as it was fair," Woody muses, resigning himself to the fortunes of war.—*Bananas* (1971)

4074 During Napoleon's war with Russia, a Russian officer explains the rules of war to his men. "If the Frenchmen kill more Russians, they win," he announces. "If the Russians kill more Frenchmen, we win." "What do we win?" soldier Woody Allen inquires. —*Love and Death* (1975)

4075 "In order to be grounded," World War II pilot Alan Arkin begins to summarize, "I must be crazy, and I must be crazy to keep flying. But if I ask to be grounded, that means I'm not crazy anymore, and I have to keep flyin'." "You got it!" base doctor Jack Gilford exclaims. "That's 'Catch-22'!"—*Catch-22* (1977)

4076 Tough, battle-hardened World War II sergeant Lee Marvin corrosively wisecracks to a booby-trapped soldier: "Just one of your balls, Smitty. You can live without it. That's why they gave you two."—*The Big Red One* (1980)

4077 A retired British cavalry unit is sent into action during World War II. Intelligence officers Gregory Peck and Roger Moore watch the middle-aged,

pot-bellied volunteers and, echoing Tiny Tim in *A Christmas Carol*, Peck proudly says: "God bless us all, every one." "Or help us—take your pick," chimes in Roger Moore.—*The Sea Wolves* (1980)

4078 In war-torn Vietnam, U.S. army disc jockey Robin Williams, dripping with sarcasm, announces: "Another morning in vacationland."—*Good Morning, Vietnam* (1987)

4079 Mel Gibson and Robert Downey, Jr., are civilian pilots working for the C.I.A. in a covert operation in Laos. While flying their helicopter over a dense jungle, they are suddenly fired upon by ground forces. "Friendlies, unfriendlies, everyone is unfriendly here," Downey complains. "Even the friendlies are unfriendly. Why are they so unfriendly?" "They haven't got to know us yet," the more experienced Gibson offers. "Why are they shooting at us?" "Because they're unfriendly."—*Air America* (1990)

4080 During the Vietnam War a pompous U.S. Senator arrives at a secret C.I.A. base in Laos where American pilots are engaged in covert military operations. That evening the Senator visits a local red light district where the off-duty Americans are carousing. "Even though none of you will ever be wearing any shining medals or be mentioned in any history books," the Senator proudly announces, "there are a few of us back in Washington who know exactly what you are doing for the war effort." "Can you explain it to us?" one tipsy pilot asks.—*Air America* (1990)

Wealth

4081 Stan Laurel and Oliver Hardy, making a delivery to a wealthy home,

receive the key from the rich owner who is busy bathing. "These millionaires are peculiar," says Hardy. "They think just the opposite to other people. Even now he's taking a bath, and it's only Monday." – *Wrong Again* (1929)

4082 Unemployed Ginger Rogers has befriended wealthy manufacturer Walter Connolly and soon learns about his family problems. "I guess rich people are just poor people with money," she muses. – *Fifth Avenue Girl* (1939)

4083 Young playwright James Stewart meets wealthy Wall Street broker Charles Ruggles at a party. "What do you do?" Ruggles asks Stewart. "Write plays . . . what do you do?" "I'm in Wall Street." "Where's that?" "I don't know," Ruggles replies, "but my chauffeur finds it every morning." – *No Time for Comedy* (1940)

4084 Reporter James Stewart observes the rich in their habitat and comments sarcastically to socialite Katharine Hepburn: "The prettiest sight in this fine, pretty world is the privileged class enjoying its privileges." – *The Philadelphia Story* (1940)

4085 Richard Carlson's aunt, who runs a small restaurant in Maine, is surprised and overwhelmed when a millionaire enters her establishment. "Do you know who that man is?" she whispers nervously to her nephew. "One of the richest individuals in the country. They say he has $7.50 more than Henry Ford." – *Too Many Girls* (1940)

4086 Wealthy Cecil Cunningham confides to Greer Garson: "My husband and I have decided to give the advantage of our home to one of your foundlings. . . . Of course, we wouldn't want one that cries." – *Blossoms in the Dust* (1941)

4087 Heir to one of the richest silver mines in the world, Charles Foster Kane (Orson Welles) invests in a newspaper that is losing money, much to the consternation of his banker. "I know I lost a million dollars this year," Kane says flippantly. "I lost a million dollars last year,

and I expect to lose a million dollars next year. At this rate, I'll have to close this place – in sixty years." – *Citizen Kane* (1941)

4088 Munitions millionaire Undershaft (Robert Morley) learns that his daughter Barbara (Wendy Hiller) is a major in the Salvation Army. "I'm rather interested in the Salvation Army," he announces. "It's motto might be my own – 'Blood and Fire.'" – *Major Barbara* (1941)

4089 Columnist Clifton Webb cavalierly presents his extravagantly furnished apartment to police detective Dana Andrews: "It's lavish, but I call it home." – *Laura* (1944)

4090 Wealthy Tony Randall reproaches his friend Rock Hudson. "The trouble with you," Randall says, "is you're prejudiced against me because I'm part of a minority group – millionaires. You outnumber us, but you'll never get us. We'll fight for our rights to the bitter end. We've got the money to do it." – *Pillow Talk* (1959)

4091 Advertising agency president Tony Randall bemoans his lot: "Wealthy people are hated and resented. Look what's written on the Statue of Liberty. Does it say, 'Send me your rich'? No. It says, 'Send me your poor.' We're not even welcome in our own country." – *Lover Come Back* (1961)

4092 A young caddy, worried that he will not have enough money to go to college, reveals his predicament to wealthy golf player Chevy Chase. "I'm gonna end up working in a lumber yard the rest of my life," he says. "What's wrong with lumber?" Chase asks. "I own two lumber yards." "I notice you don't spend too much time there." "I'm not sure where they are." – *Caddyshack* (1980)

4093 Spoiled millionaire Dudley Moore must choose between a dull woman selected by his parents and his dream-working girl (Liza Minnelli), the latter choice resulting in his loss of the family fortune. At one point he gamely agrees to get a job, eat tuna fish sandwiches and ride the subway. "Where's the subway?" he suddenly wonders. –*Arthur* (1981)

4094 A wealthy Beverly Hills booking agent and his wife confess to a charity executive: "We feel a little guilty. There are children in China starving, and here we are. It's uncomfortable. We haven't even been to a Chinese restaurant in over a month." –*Maid to Order* (1987)

4095 Rapacious Wall Street corporate raider Danny DeVito assumes the role of a modern-day Robin Hood. "I take from the rich and give to the middle class," he announces proudly. Then, close to the mark, he adds: "Well, the upper middle class." –*Other People's Money* (1991)

Widows and Widowers

4096 Concupiscent baron Leon Errol has a keen eye for W. C. Fields' daughter (Marilyn Miller), and Fields intercedes on his behalf. "He's rich and old," Fields informs her. "What more do you want? You can look forward to a happy widowhood." –*Her Majesty, Love* (1931)

4097 W. C. Fields describes an old widow: "She's all dressed up like a well-kept grave." –*The Old Fashioned Way* (1934)

4098 Throckmorton P. Gildersleeve (Hal Peary), much to his regret, meets eccentric widow Billie Burke aboard a train. "Henry is really much nicer since he died," she confides about her deceased husband. "He lets me put flowers all around him, and it doesn't bother his hay fever one bit." –*Gildersleeve on Broadway* (1943)

4099 Bachelor Wallace Beery and widow Marjorie Main continue their twenty-eight-year running feud. "Now that we're dealing with unpleasant subjects," Beery remarks, "allow me to mention your husband." "He never left me," Main declares. "Well, he did the next best thing – he died." –*Rationing* (1944)

4100 Pirate Hillary Brooke tries to seduce Lou Costello, who knows where a buried treasure is hidden, but warns him about trifling with her. "Sometimes my men become foolish and tire of me before I tire of them." "Then what happens?" Costello asks. "I make a lovely widow." –*Abbott and Costello Meet Captain Kidd* (1952)

4101 "I notice you're not wearing your wedding ring," an attractive former rival says to widow Debbie Reynolds. "Now that I'm a widow, there's no need to cramp my style." –*Goodbye Charlie* (1964)

4102 A dying Ali McGraw makes a grand, loving gesture to husband Ryan O'Neal: "I want you to be a merry widower." –*Love Story* (1970)

4103 Gene Wilder visits his family's old estate and meets his old servant who inquires whether Wilder's uncle Francis is still married. "Widower," Wilder says. "Widower than what?" the servant asks. –*Haunted Honeymoon* (1986)

4104 Eccentric widow Shirley MacLaine vents some of her orneriness upon her acquaintances, including Sally Field, who suggests she visit the local guidance center. "I'm not crazy," MacLaine protests. "I've just been in a very bad mood for forty years." –*Steel Magnolias* (1989)

Winners and Losers

4105 Charlotte Greenwood, unlucky in love, visits fortune-teller Charles Middleton in search of a husband. "You are a woman who is much sought after," Middleton announces. "I may be sought after, but nobody ever finds me." —*Palmy Days* (1931)

4106 A Roman empress tries to lure slave Eddie Cantor to help her poison the emperor. "Have you ever been fired by passion?" she asks. "No," Cantor admits, "but I've been fired by everyone else." —*Roman Scandals* (1933)

4107 On a pistol range F.B.I. instructor Robert Armstrong laughs at neophyte James Cagney until, to Armstrong's amazement, Cagney shoots five straight bullseyes. "I used to be marble champion of The Bronx," explains Cagney. —*G-Men* (1935)

4108 Dagwood (Arthur Lake) decides to try his luck at a talking weight-and-fortune machine. "You weigh one hundred sixty-three pounds. You are a very stupid fellow and not very likely to succeed," the machine announces. Unconvinced, he deposits another coin only to hear the same message. When another man steps up to the machine and gets a very positive message, Dagwood decides to try again. "Save your money, sucker," the machine advises. "I've told you twice already." —*Blondie* (1938)

4109 Edgar Bergen questions Ophelia the spinster about her marital prospects. "Are you thinking of marrying anyone?" he asks. "Uh-huh," Ophelia replies. "Who?" "Anyone." —*Look Who's Laughing* (1941)

4110 The tendency for inept reporter Bob Hope to botch things up has brought girlfriend Dorothy Lamour to the end of her rope. "Nobody likes me at first," Hope explains. "I'm an acquired taste. I was fourteen years old before my mother let me in the house." —*They Got Me Covered* (1943)

4111 Eddie Bracken, an innocent, overly good-hearted rejectee from the army, does not have any better luck with the opposite sex: "I knew a girl once who told me to jump in the lake–and when I came back she was gone." —*The Miracle of Morgan's Creek* (1944)

4112 Nephew Ralph Bellamy learns during the reading of a will that his deceased uncle has left him only one dollar. "Aren't you disappointed?" someone asks him. "On the contrary," Bellamy replies. "He once threatened to cut me out of his will entirely." —*Lady on a Train* (1945)

4113 Groucho Marx: "I've had lots of pin-up girls but I've never been able to pin one down." —*A Night in Casablanca* (1946)

4114 Masseur Red Skelton at an exclusive country club is called for an assignment but wants to hear the end of a radio quiz program. "This is an important program," he explains. "They give away a lot of prizes. Last week there was an old maid from Pomona, and she won a two-week vacation in a Tibet monastery–with all expenses paid." —*Neptune's Daughter* (1949)

4115 "Once in school there was a bully," Jerry Lewis recalls. "One time I dared him to knock a chip off my shoulder. And five minutes later the chip was still there–but my shoulder was gone." —*Money from Home* (1953)

4116 Dejected and rejected Tony Randall cannot win back lost love Barbara Rush, who is about to marry David Niven. Randall enters a bar where Dan Dailey, who knows of Randall's problem, offers him a drink and a smoke. "I can't drink alcohol," Randall explains. "I've got a weak stomach . . . Smoking makes me sicker than whiskey." "And you can't make the grade with a dame either, Dailey adds. "I know a lot of guys who got their crosses to bear, but you sound like you carry around a whole cemetery." – *Oh, Men! Oh, Women!* (1957)

4117 Navy lieutenant Jerry Lewis describes to ensign Dina Merrill a costume party he had once attended dressed as a skinless frankfurter. "I won first prize," he announces proudly. "How lucky!" "It was a case of skinless frankfurters." – *Don't Give Up the Ship* (1959)

4118 Self-appointed Southern black preacher Ossie Davis complains about the stars of a radio program: "Take Amos 'n' Andy. Them jokers put black on their faces fifteen minutes a day and make millions. I'm born with the stuff and I ain't got a dime." – *Gone Are the Days* (1963)

4119 Jerry Lewis tells an audience about his rabbit's foot: "I never thought it was lucky because I figured if it was so lucky, how come the rabbit lost it?" – *The Patsy* (1964)

4120 After being robbed and kidnapped in New York City, Ohio couple Jack Lemmon and Sandy Dennis find themselves stranded in Central Park at 3:00 a.m. Dennis, exhausted and frustrated, wants to sleep in the park. "It's not safe in the park at night," Lemmon warns. "We've already been robbed and kidnapped," she reminds him. "We have nothing to lose but four cents." "We will probably be attacked by squirrels," Lemmon quips. – *The Out of Towners* (1970)

4121 A police detective, holding a prisoner, remarks to a fellow officer about his "collar": "The best damn pickpocket in the precinct, and he chooses a cop for a mark." – *Fuzz* (1972)

4122 "I had my face slapped many times," the spirit of Humphrey Bogart admits to a vacillating, anxious Woody Allen. "Yeah," Allen retorts, "but your glasses don't go flying across the room." – *Play It Again, Sam* (1972)

4123 "Treason," reflects Benjamin Franklin (Howard da Silva), "is a charge invented by winners as an excuse for hanging the losers." – *1776* (1972)

4124 Robin Williams has just been fired by a trained parrot while the boss is away on a business trip. Williams sulks at a lunch counter – to the annoyance of customer Walter Matthau. "I'm not the most sensitive guy in the world," Matthau explains. "But if you got some kind of trouble – and you'll probably feel a lot better if you unload it on somebody – so if you want to talk about what's bothering you – go do it someplace else. Okay?" – *The Survivors* (1983)

4125 Fred and his domineering wife have come from New Jersey to visit with John Larroquette and wife Kirstie Alley in Los Angeles. Larroquette, observing how subservient and reticent his friend Fred acts, questions him when they are alone. "What the hell happened to the Fred I knew in high school?" Larroquette asks. "Or the Fred who could have any girl in the senior class he wanted to when he was a freshman? A guy who could break up any class without even trying?" "I don't know," Fred replies meekly. "Anywhere between graduation and the Jerry Lewis telethon I just lost it." – *Madhouse* (1990)

4126 Anthony LaPaglia loses his job with the New York City subway system – information department. "I never had to look at the board," he says to his parents. "I always knew which trains went where. I knew every schedule by heart. You know what that means?" "Yeah," his father, Danny Aiello, replies, "you got a natural talent for useless information." – *29th Street* (1991)

Work and Workplace

4127 Florida hotel owner Groucho Marx explains to his help that he is doing them a good turn by not paying them. "You want to be wage slaves?" he asks. "Answer me that. No, of course not. Well, what makes wage slaves? Wages! I want you to be free." – *The Cocoanuts* (1929)

4128 Robert Woolsey: "My grandfather was an old Southern planter." Bert Wheeler: "A Southern planter?" Woolsey: "Yes, he was an undertaker in Alabama." – *Dixiana* (1930)

4129 The owner of a failing carnival show finds a scapegoat. "What kind of a press agent are you?" he barks. "What do I pay you for?" "I wouldn't know," the agent retorts. "I ain't been paid for four weeks." "All right," the owner says, "quit!" "I'd rather get fired. Then you'd have to pay me." – *The Half Naked Truth* (1932)

4130 Chico Marx explains to Groucho that since he could no longer afford a chauffeur and a car, he sold the car. Groucho replies that he would have kept the car and sold the chauffeur. "That's-a no good," Chico explains. "I gotta have a chauffeur to take me to work in the morning." "Well, if you've no car," Groucho reasons, "how can he take you to work?" "He don't have to take me to work. I gotta no job." – *Horse Feathers* (1932)

4131 Plantation owner Clark Gable shows new arrival Mary Astor how rubber is processed. "Why, it's milk," she concludes, observing the white latex. "Oh, no, no, it's rubber," Gable corrects her. "But you could drink it – if you wanted to stretch a point." – *Red Dust* (1932)

4132 Hoboes Al Jolson and his pal decide to go to work in a bank. At the end of the week they receive their first pay check and are elated. "It certainly feels good having money in your pocket," Jolson confesses. "Yes," his pal agrees, "but you waste so much time gettin' it." – *Hallelujah, I'm a Bum* (1933)

4133 Circus handyman Joe E. Brown, who hopes someday to become a performer, doesn't know that his new job is that of target for a knife-thrower. "It looks like things are beginning to come my way at last," he says joyfully. "My boy," his boss adds, "you've got no idea of the things that are going to come your way." – *The Circus Clown* (1934)

4134 Lawyer Edward Everett Horton at a swank resort hotel café cannot seem to decide what to order. "You know," waiter Eric Blore remarks to Horton, "I hate to leave you like this – you torn with doubts, me with my duty undischarged." – *The Gay Divorcee* (1934)

4135 When Judge Priest (Will Rogers) sends his messenger Stepin Fetchit on an errand, Fetchit complains that his feet will wear out. "As much sittin' around as you do," Rogers quips, "it won't be your feet that wear out." – *Judge Priest* (1934)

4136 Groucho Marx has failed to bring Margaret Dumont into high society. "You've done nothing but draw a very handsome salary," she charges. "You think that's nothing?" he retorts. "How many men are drawing a handsome salary these days, my good woman?" – *A Night at the Opera* (1935)

4137 Small-town judge Raymond Walburn is running for mayor. "In me you see a self-made man," he pronounces proudly to Fred Allen. "Showing the horrors of unskilled labor," Allen ripostes. – *Thanks a Million* (1935)

4138 "I put my whole heart in my work," a religious social worker confesses to "the San Francisco Doll" (Mae West). "So do I," West quips. – *Klondike Annie* (1936)

4139 Impoverished Russian aristocratic immigrants Charles Boyer and his wife Claudette Colbert are down and out in Paris. He decides that the only solution for them is to find work. "Work!" Colbert exclaims. "Even for fun you must not say things like that!" – *Tovarich* (1937)

4140 Ninotchka (Greta Garbo), recently arrived in Paris from Moscow, questions a French porter at the train depot. "Why should you carry other people's bags?" "Well," the man replies politely, "that's my business, madam." "That's no business; that's social injustice." "That depends on the tip," the porter returns. – *Ninotchka* (1939)

4141 Assigned to cover a frivolous social event for a magazine, writer James Stewart protests to photographer-coworker Ruth Hussey: "It's degrading! It's undignified!" "So is an empty stomach," she returns. – *The Philadelphia Story* (1940)

4142 Teenage messenger William Tracy tries to inflate the importance of his job at a department store. "I'm a contact man," he announces proudly to a local doctor. "I keep contact between Matuschek & Company and the customers – on a bicycle." "You mean an errand boy," the doctor remarks. "Doctor," Tracy persists, "did I call you a pill peddler?" – *The Shop Around the Corner* (1940)

4143 Alan Hale, who cannot hold a job, has just been fired. "I wasn't cut out to be a street cleaner," he says, "and it's no use reaching for the stars." – *Strawberry Blonde* (1941)

4144 Joan Blondell and Carole Landis travel to an eerie old mansion to claim the latter's inheritance. "How long have you been here?" Blondell asks an ancient housekeeper. "Twenty years," the woman answers. "It might turn out to be a steady job," Blondell quips. – *Topper Returns* (1941)

4145 A nightclub waiter accidentally spills a large salad on wealthy patron Douglass Dumbrille. "You clumsy idiot, you'll pay for this!" Dumbrille shouts. "I'll have your job!" "What do you want his job for?" stranger Rags Ragland asks. – *DuBarry Was a Lady* (1943)

4146 Radio writer Dick Powell, to get ideas for his show, takes a job in a bakery. "Did you ever do heavy work before?" the supervisor asks. "No," Powell answers, "but I like to watch other people do it." – *True to Life* (1943)

4147 "Remember one thing," Bud Abbott says to Lou Costello. "A good agent doesn't even know the meaning of the word 'capitulation.'" "Then I must be a *great* agent," Costello returns. "I never heard of the word." – *Abbott and Costello in Hollywood* (1945)

4148 Eve Arden says to nonworking, independently wealthy cad Zachary Scott: "You were probably frightened by a callus at an early age." – *Mildred Pierce* (1945)

4149 Judge Myrna Loy introduces artist Cary Grant to her venerable uncle (Harry Davenport). "Judge Turner is an associate justice of the state supreme court," she explains. "Good for you," Grant remarks. "It's better than working for a living." – *The Bachelor and the Bobby-Soxer* (1947)

4150 "I'm a union man," delivery worker Lou Costello explains to a customer who wants several cartons sent to his museum. "I work only sixteen hours a day." "A union man works only eight hours a day," the man corrects him. "I belong to two unions," returns Costello. – *Abbott and Costello Meet Frankenstein* (1948)

4151 "I'm a concert pianist," Oscar Levant announces to an audience. "That's a pretentious way of saying I'm unemployed at the moment." – *An American in Paris* (1951)

4152 Racetrack tout Bob Hope addresses some hoodlums who have volunteered to play Santa Claus: "Now don't look like you're handling hot reindeer. We have a license to collect. Just get out there and put your heart into your work just like you would if it was a shady deal." – *The Lemon Drop Kid* (1951)

4153 Frontier trader Jack Oakie is offered a job to scout for the U.S. Cavalry at five dollars a day. "Five dollars a day!" he exclaims. "It'll cost me more than that for whiskey to drown the boredom." – *Tomahawk* (1951)

4154 "My, you're here early this morning," chemist Cary Grant remarks to secretary Marilyn Monroe. "Mr. Oxie complained about my punctuation," she explains, "so I made sure I got here before nine." – *Monkey Business* (1952)

4155 Bob Hope remarks on his employment record: "I haven't looked for work since I was night watchman at Vassar." – *Road to Bali* (1952)

4156 "I like a man who is punctual," Huntz Hall's boss compliments him. "And I'm on time, too," Hall says. – *In the Money* (1958)

4157 Fast-talking con artist Professor Harold Hill (Robert Preston) arrives in River City, Iowa, and meets old crony Buddy Hackett, who is now working for a living. "So you've gone legitimate?" Preston sadly notes. "I knew you'd come to no good." – *The Music Man* (1962)

4158 Cafeteria employee Audrey Meadows provides free lunches for her unemployed friends. One day her super-visor catches her. "Are you familiar with the company policy regarding giving away free food?" he asks sternly. "No," she replies. "Are we for or against it?" – *That Touch of Mink* (1962)

4159 Writer Lana Turner, trying to work on her novel, is disturbed by Margo, her cleaning woman, who has begun vacuuming the apartment. "Do you have to do that every time I start to write?" "You got your work, I got my work," Margo says indignantly. "That's show business." – *Who's Got the Action?* (1962)

4160 Former gendarme Jack Lemmon says to hooker Irma la Douce (Shirley MacLaine): "You have one advantage. At least you get indoors once in a while and off your feet." – *Irma la Douce* (1963)

4161 The wealthy owner of a department store calls on the manager to learn how runaway daughter Jill St. John is progressing as an elevator operator. The manager, to ingratiate himself with his employer, gives a satisfactory report. "She makes smooth stops," he beams. – *Who's Minding the Store?* (1963)

4162 Fred MacMurray, as the husband of Polly Bergen, the first woman President in the U.S., is assigned his own office and both a social and a personal secretary. "There are separate buzzers for each of us," Mrs. Currier explains. "I'm all white. Mrs. Dissendorf is all white with a black dot in the middle." "Well, thank you very much," MacMurray responds sarcastically. "I'm looking forward to some jolly times when I get to know your buzzers better." – *Kisses for My President* (1964)

4163 No-nonsense factory manager Paul Ford explains his predilections for serious fun: "Fun is when I go through that gate and the men say, 'Morning, sir,' and I say, 'Morning, men.'" – *Never Too Late* (1965)

4164 An English boy whose father clandestinely works for the secret service is required to write a composition about the latter's occupation. Told that his father works in an office, the disappointed youth shouts: "I won't say my father has a rotten office job ... I'll say he got killed trying to escape from a German prison camp hanging on the barbed wire with his gut hanging out." *– The Spy with the Cold Nose* (1966)

4165 A former cigarette girl at a nightclub, attractive Maureen Arthur, aspires to a secretarial job at a large corporation. "What was your last position?" executive Robert Morse inquires. "I was in the tobacco business," she replies. *– How to Succeed in Business Without Really Trying* (1967)

4166 Ambitious Robert Morse, starting in the mailroom of a large corporation, learns that his supervisor has been there for twenty-five years, after which time he has won a medal. "It's not easy to get this medal," the man admits. "It takes a combination of skill, diplomacy and bold caution." *– How to Succeed in Business Without Really Trying* (1967)

4167 Teenage Barry Gordon is looking for a summer job and inquires in a local drugstore. The proprietor, however, says he doesn't need anyone. A customer, before leaving, suggests Barry try a local pub called Mother's Bar. "How do I get to Mother's Bar?" the boy calls out to the owner of the drugstore. "Young man," the owner replies, "just because there's no job, there's no reason to turn to drink!" *– The Spirit Is Willing* (1967)

4168 Widower Henry Fonda, left with ten children, describes one of his many problems – retaining a housekeeper. "The first one lasted an entire day," he says. "The second one lasted seven days. We discovered she was hiding from the police. After a week with us, she turned herself in." *– Yours, Mine and Ours* (1968)

4169 "Follow that car!" Claudia Cardinale orders a cabby. "You know, lady," the taxi driver acknowledges, "I gave up my career as a stockbroker just to hear someone say: 'Follow that car.'" *– A Fine Pair* (1969)

4170 A narrator depicts Woody Allen's ventures before he turns to a life of crime: "He takes to the street and for a while he earns a meager living – selling meagers." *– Take the Money and Run* (1969)

4171 "You can't open the windows," secretary Candice Bergen says about her workplace. "We're hermetically sealed like instant coffee." *– T.R. Baskin* (1971)

4172 When housewife Jane Fonda volunteers to find work, unemployed spouse George Segal suggests various positions to match her limited skills. "Interesting that the only two jobs you consider me qualified for are secretary and hooker." "You're not qualified to be a secretary," he reconsiders. *– Fun with Dick and Jane* (1977)

4173 A companion employed by Bette Davis tells how a wealthy Englishman ruined her family, forcing her to work as a servant. "Well," Davis says, "you should be grateful. If he hadn't, you would have missed the pleasure of working for me." *– Death on the Nile* (1978)

4174 Simpleton Steve Martin gets his first job as a gas station attendant working for owner Jackie Mason, who lets Martin sleep in the back of the garage. "Take a look," Mason points out. "No kitchen, no windows, no chairs, no tables – a masterpiece of understatement." *– The Jerk* (1979)

4175 "I'm no fool," agitated secretary Lily Tomlin frets about losing her job. "I killed the boss. You think they're not going to fire me for a thing like that?" *– Nine to Five* (1980)

4176 Sexist Supreme Court justice Walter Matthau opposes the appointment of a woman (Jill Clayburgh) as the newest member of the body. Matthau, whose own office is disorderly, reluctantly visits his colleague and observes her clean, organized desk. "It's quite a desk," he says sarcastically. "So neat. Do aircraft land here frequently?" – *First Monday in October* (1981)

4177 Unemployed circus clown Jerry Lewis reports for an interview for a post office job. "Have you ever been in the military?" the interviewer asks. "I visited Arlington once," Lewis offers. – *Hardly Working* (1981)

4178 Beatrice Arthur portrays an interviewer of the unemployed in ancient Rome. "Did you kill last week?" she brusquely asks a jobless gladiator. "Did you try to kill last week?" – *History of the World – Part 1* (1981)

4179 A well-known hooker asks a policewoman–traffic cop if she has met her quota. "I had it covered by lunch," the officer replies. "How about yourself?" "Still working on it." – *Crackers* (1984)

4180 A moving man asks his young helper (Paul Reiser) what the key word is in the moving field. "Teamwork?" "Them's two words," the mover laughs. "The key word is 'chain of command.'" – *Odd Jobs* (1985)

4181 Chicago cops Billy Crystal and Gregory Hines inform their precinct captain that they are both resigning from the force at the end of the month. "We're looking for some new career challenge," Hines says. "Show me another career that lets you shoot people," the captain replies. – *Running Scared* (1986)

4182 Smalltime hoodlum Danny DeVito confesses to fellow crook Joe Piscopo that he is fed up with his life of crime, but his pal is more optimistic. "Hey, we're in a growth industry," Piscopo says cheerfully. "Did you know that organized crime is the fourth largest employer in the state of New Jersey?" – *Wise Guys* (1986)

4183 Overly correct police officer Joe Friday (Dan Aykroyd), confronting three tough street hoodlums about to rob him, offers them an alternative: "If you're that strapped for cash, then I would suggest a part-time job. How about a paper route? It builds character. It did in my case." – *Dragnet* (1987)

4184 Woody Allen, as a small boy, endures his father's concerns for his future and warnings about failing in school, although his father has never revealed what he does for a living. "You think I want you working at the job I do?" his father says. "I don't even know what your job is!" the boy replies. – *Radio Days* (1987)

4185 Movie extra Alan King says to a fellow extra who is afraid of losing his job: "I warned you. Never play a coma. Comas are the first to go when they lay off." – *Memories of Me* (1988)

4186 Young Daryl Hannah, fresh out of beauty school, lands a job in Dolly Parton's beauty parlor. "I'm so excited, I can't believe this is happening!" she cries. "I'm a beautician!" "A glamour technician, glamour technician," Parton corrects her. – *Steel Magnolias* (1989)

4187 Unscrupulous New York contractor Joe Pesci has involved family member Alan Alda, a building developer, with a silent partner – a member of organized crime. Alda, now burdened with a collection of phony workers, complains to Pesci. "Look, I got a consultant at five thousand a week," Alda explains. "He doesn't even come to the site. He lives in Toledo. What kind of consultant is that?" – *Betsy's Wedding* (1990)

4188 Paul Newman, as Governor Earl Long of Louisiana, witnesses sexy Blaze Starr's (Lolita Davidovich) striptease performance and goes backstage to proposition her. "Some show you got there, gal," he says. "Powerful expression of basic human needs." "Well," Blaze explains, "I think of myself as a storyteller." – *Blaze* (1990)

4189 Joan Plowright hires two stoned amateur thugs to kill her son-in-law, but they hold out for more money. "If we've got to waste the dude," says one, "we ought to get paid for it. That's the American way, right?" "Yeah," adds his pal, "we're not Communists, you know. We're Americans who've got a right to make a living." – *I Love You to Death* (1990)

4190 Frustrated F.B.I. agent Rick Moranis discusses his job with a fellow agent. "I want to go under cover . . . eat a lot of take-out food. I want to wear a windbreaker." "Once when I went under cover," his friend says, "I got to drive a BMW. It was the highlight of my life." – *My Blue Heaven* (1990)

4191 A hit man for the mob is having trouble convincing stubborn deputy district attorney Gene Hackman to cooperate. "The people I work for are very determined," the well-dressed hoodlum warns. "They sound like very interesting people," Hackman says. "Very interesting." "You have a good dental plan, do you?" Hackman adds wryly. – *Narrow Margin* (1990)

4192 A city official berates a lethargic inspector: "You don't put in *time*. How

can you put in overtime?" – *City of Hope* (1991)

4193 A crazed man who has just murdered his wife and children offers to tell detective Bobby Gold (Joe Mantegna) the nature of black deeds. "Would you like to know how to solve the problems of evil?" he asks. "No, man," the police officer replies, "'cause then I'd be out of a job." – *Homicide* (1991)

4194 Undertaker Dan Aykroyd has just ruined some food on the charcoal broiler during a backyard barbecue. "You've cremated it," a neighbor complains. "That's what I do," Dan cheerfully replies, referring to his business. – *My Girl* (1991)

4195 "I've got a lot of job pressure," Lily Tomlin acknowledges. "I've got to find one." – *The Search for Signs of Intelligent Life in the Universe* (1991)

4196 Police sergeant Michael Madsen, investigating a murder in a private development, asks the manager what he does all day when nobody is around. "When there's no murders," the feisty manager fires back, "what do *you* do all day?" – *To Kill For* (1992)

Writers and Writing

4197 Elizabeth Browning (Norma Shearer) asks poet Robert Browning (Fredric March) to clarify an obscure passage from one of his works. "When that passage was written," the stymied poet replies, "only God and Robert Browning understood it; now only God understands it." – *The Barrets of Wimpole Street* (1934)

4198 "You're a poetess?" private detective James Stewart asks Claudette Col-

bert. "Yes." "Well, I don't know," Stewart deliberates. "I guess some people are just born unlucky." – *It's a Wonderful World* (1939)

4199 Two English tourists in Berlin on the brink of World War II prepare to leave for home. One buys a copy of Hitler's *Mein Kampf* to read on the train. "I understand they give a copy to all the bridal couples over here," he remarks. "I don't think it's that sort of book, old man," his friend says. – *Night Train to Munich* (1940)

4200 A young saleswoman interrupts columnist Clifton Webb while he is dining and asks him to endorse a pen. "I don't use a pen," he quips. "I use a goose quill dipped in venom." – *Laura* (1944)

4201 During the turn of the century the genteel George Apley (Ronald Colman) is asked by his wife what Freud's book is about. "I hardly know how to put it," Colman says. "I shall have to resort to a word I have never used in your presence. It seems to be a book very largely about – sex." "But how could he write a whole book about – that?" his wife questions. – *The Late George Apley* (1947)

4202 Secretary Laraine Day suspects her employer Kirk Douglas' motives in inviting her to his beach house to "work" on his novel. Douglas' friend Keenan Wynn mentions Douglas' last novel. "Did you like *Last Year's Love?*" he asks. "Very much," she admits. "Well," Wynn continues, "most of *Last Year's Love* was done down there." – *My Dear Secretary* (1948)

4203 Comic Phil Silvers introduces his writer to an aspiring actress (Judy Lynn). "I can tell he's a writer," she says, "by the lines on his face." – *Top Banana* (1954)

4204 Martha Hyer praises successful writer Frank Sinatra on his last novel. "It might have lacked something in craftsmanship, but it was really a powerful setting of rejection." "That it was," Sinatra agrees. "It was rejected by forty-two publishers and almost all of the English-reading public." – *Some Came Running* (1958)

4205 Publisher James Stewart has just rejected Ernie Kovacs' manuscript, *Magic in Manhattan* – a tale of witches and warlocks in the Big Apple. "I don't suppose you'd be interested in a sequel I have in mind," Kovacs asks before leav-

ing, "about the islands in the Caribbean – uh, *Voodoo Among the Virgins?*" – *Bell, Book and Candle* (1959)

4206 Woody Allen wakes up two hundred years in the future to discover most of the world has been destroyed and that scientists are trying to piece together an historical past. "Norman Mailer," says Allen, identifying a photo. "Donated his ego to the Harvard Medical School." – *Sleeper* (1973)

4207 Navy officer Robert Redford, in town on a pass, finds that Barbra Streisand has a copy of the book he wrote. "You must've gotten one of the two copies sold," he remarks. "It came in a Crackerjack box," she wryly corrects him. – *The Way We Were* (1973)

4208 A fan of writer-director Sandy Bates (Woody Allen) charges that Allen seems threatened by intellectuals. "Threatened?" Allen questions. "You're kidding. I've always said they're like the Mafia. They only kill their own." – *Stardust Memories* (1980)

4209 Working wife Julie Walters, taking an evening course in literature, asks her college instructor, poet Michael Caine, about his ex-wife. "A very noble woman, my wife," Caine begins. "She left me for the good of literature. And remarkably it worked." "What, you wrote a lot of good stuff, did you?" she asks. "No," he returns, "I stopped writing altogether." – *Educating Rita* (1983)

4210 Creative-writing instructor Billy Crystal is strangling his former student Danny DeVito, who has just had a book published, for stealing Crystal's plot. "I can't breathe," DeVito sputters. "That's because I'm choking you, you moron!" Crystal explains. – *Throw Momma from the Train* (1987)

4211 Former night-school student Danny DeVito, who has just had his own children's pop-up book published, criticizes the ending of his creative-writing instructor's (Billy Crystal) novel. Crystal flares up when his girlfriend agrees with Devito's assessment: "I can't believe you're taking criticism from someone who had his book-signing at Toys-R-Us." – *Throw Momma from the Train* (1987)

4212 During lunch in a small restaurant, mystery writer Tom Selleck tries to impress his waitress. "My name is Phil," Selleck says, and pointing to one of his novels, he beams: "I wrote this." "Mine's Karen," she replies cheer-

fully, handing him the check, "and I wrote this." – *Her Alibi* (1989)

4213 Free-spirited Jami Gertz criticizes sister Kirstie Alley, wife of a domineering doctor, for giving up her dream of becoming a writer. "You used to love to write," the younger sister reminded her. "That was a long time ago," Alley recalls. "And I never was a real writer." "You wrote short stories." "Those weren't short stories," Alley confesses. "Those were novels. I just never finished them." – *Sibling Rivalry* (1990)

Youth

4214 In 1906 free-thinking youth Eric Linden, walking home from the school prom, complains to girlfriend Cecilia Parker. "I'm afraid I was born a hundred years before my time," he says. "I was born ten days ahead of mine," she replies earnestly. – *Ah, Wilderness* (1935)

4215 "You must have been full of fire in your youth," an elderly female admirer says to W. C. Fields. "I had to carry fire insurance until I was over forty," Fields replies. – *Mississippi* (1935)

4216 Andy Hardy (Mickey Rooney) complains to his no-nonsense but understanding father (Lewis Stone) about "modern girls." "Well, Polly, for instance," Rooney begins. "Sometimes she won't let you kiss her at all. But there's Cynthia: oh, she'll let you kiss her whenever you want. She doesn't want to swim; she doesn't want to play tennis, go for walks; all she wants to do is kiss you. I'm a nervous wreck!" – *Love Finds Andy Hardy* (1938)

4217 Andy Hardy (Mickey Rooney) joins the high school drama group, an interest which soon results in his affected

speech. "That accounts for your voice sounding like molasses dripping down the stairs," his sister (Cecilia Parker) quips. – *Andy Hardy Gets Spring Fever* (1939)

4218 Andy Hardy (Mickey Rooney) has romantic problems during his visit to New York. At Grant's Tomb, teenage Judy Garland tries to take his mind off his dilemma. "Let's go inside," she suggests. "Maybe the coffins will cheer you up." – *Andy Hardy Meets Debutante* (1940)

4219 Energetic high school bandleader Mickey Rooney is urged by his mother to become a doctor. "Do I look like a doctor?" he queries girlfriend Judy Garland. – *Strike Up the Band* (1940)

4220 "Did you ever find someone," Mickey Rooney asks Judy Garland, "and then all of a sudden you felt like you were taking off right into space?" "Uh-huh. I've had that feeling, and it all started in a drugstore." "Oh," Rooney sighs after kissing her, "isn't it wonderful what you can find these days in a drugstore?" – *Babes on Broadway* (1941)

4221 Muggs (Leo Gorcey) gets into trouble with the law and is assigned to a reform school. "Young man," a tough, matronly director of the home announces, "before we're through with you, you'll learn to have respect for authority." "If you're the best example they've got," Gorcey fires back, "I'll give you odds." – *Bowery Blitzkrieg* (1941)

4222 W. C. Fields informs teenage niece Gloria that she will soon be going back to school, but the news disheartens her. "Don't you want to be smart?" Fields asks. "No," she returns, "I want to be like you." – *Never Give a Sucker an Even Break* (1941)

4223 "You know what I need in my life?" a teenage girl confides to Kay Kyser. "I need light, warmth and fire." "Well," Kyser replies, "why don't you call the gas company?" – *Around the World* (1943)

4224 When do-gooder socialite Betty Blythe hires Leo Gorcey as a chauffeur with the rough-hewn East Side Kids helping out, it's not long before her husband deplores their shenanigans. "We must give these poor unfortunates a chance to express themselves," she counters. "I'd like to express them –" he snaps, "to Africa!" – *Mr. Muggs Steps Out* (1943)

4225 Real estate agent Harry Langdon threatens to evict the East Side Kids from the clubroom if they don't keep the place clean and quiet. "You can't throw us out," protests leader Leo Gorcey. "We got a ninety-nine-year lease." "Yeah," adds Huntz Hall, "we would have made it a hundred, but we didn't think we'd live that long." – *Block Busters* (1944)

4226 Leo Gorcey and his East Side gang are engaged in boxing lessons in their cellar club. The noise brings a police officer onto the premises. "I'm putting a padlock on the place," he threatens. "We already have one," Huntz Hall blurts out. – *Come Out Fighting* (1945)

4227 "Everybody worries about my future," muses college student Andy Hardy, "but nobody worries about me now." – *Love Laughs at Andy Hardy* (1946)

4228 Bobby-soxer Shirley Temple likes her boyfriend Hugo, but also develops a crush on artist Cary Grant. "A few minutes ago I liked Hugo better," she confides to Grant, "now I like you better. It's funny how men change." – *The Bachelor and the Bobby-Soxer* (1947)

4229 "Now there's a guy who never goes out of a girl's mind," teenager Veda Ann Borg coos after seeing Cary Grant. "He just stays there like a heavy meal." – *The Bachelor and the Bobby-Soxer* (1947)

4230 Spencer Tracy expresses his disapproval of early marriages to daughter Elizabeth Taylor. "I didn't marry your mother till I was twenty-five," he says. "I know, Pop," Taylor replies. "But that was millions of years ago." – *Father of the Bride* (1950)

4231 Hollywood writer Dick Powell becomes involved with juvenile delinquent Debbie Reynolds, whom the police have charged with hitting a sailor over the head with a beer bottle. "Maybe she was trying to launch him," quips Powell. – *Susan Slept Here* (1954)

4232 "Do you know that beetles actually kiss?" young Bobby Darin says to Sandra Dee. "The boy beetle rubs his antennae against the girl beetle's." "What does the girl beetle do?" she asks. "Well," he explains, "if he doesn't rub her the wrong way, they start making plans for their future." – *Come September* (1961)

4233 Ingenuous Debbie Reynolds characterizes fiancé Tab Hunter to her debonair father, Fred Astaire. "He's very progressive," she explains. "He has all sorts of ideas about artificial insemination and all that sort of thing. He breeds all over the world." – *The Pleasure of His Company* (1961)

4234 Teenage Ann-Margret has just been "pinned" by boyfriend Bobby Rydell, and her friend asks her how she feels. "Like I've been reborn," she exclaims. "Like all my life, till this very moment, I was nothing. And now, I'm alive, fulfilled. I know what it means to be – a woman!" – *Bye Bye Birdie* (1963)

4235 Teenage Hayley Mills, on board a train on the way to St. Francis Academy, decides to light up a cigarette. "Really!" a shocked matronly fellow passenger exclaims. "A child your age – smoking!" "I'm not a child, madam," returns Mills. "I'm a midget with bad habits." – *The Trouble with Angels* (1966)

4236 "Will you buy me a car when I'm sixteen next week?" Barry Gordon asks father Sid Caesar. "No!" "I didn't ask to be born," the boy protests. "Well," his father replies, "you've asked for everything else!" – *The Spirit Is Willing* (1967)

4237 Fifteen-year-old Barry Gordon's parents have rented a seacoast house that happens to be haunted. After a battle with the ghosts, Barry steps outside and is tapped on the shoulder by his uncle (John McIver) who has come to visit. "Uncle George!" exclaims the startled boy, poised to strike the man. "I didn't know it was you. I thought it was one of the other nuts." – *The Spirit Is Willing* (1967)

4238 Folk singer Arlo Guthrie picks up a teenage girl whose nose is running and whose eyes are all red. "I want to make it with you because you'll probably get to be an album," she says. – *Alice's Restaurant* (1969)

4239 Teenage boys study a medical sex manual during World War II. "Do you believe all this stuff?" one says. "It's called foreplay. Everyone takes off their clothes and they play foreplay." – *Summer of '42* (1971)

4240 Preadolescent, snippy Mackenzie Phillips and her young driver, Paul Le Mat, cruise the streets of a northern California town. She spots a familiar hangout. "Some of my friends might be here," she boasts. "Probably a couple of weeks past their bedtime," Le Mat adds. – *American Graffiti* (1973)

4241 In a burst of eloquence, high-school cheerleader Cindy Williams pleads with boyfriend Ronny Howard not to go off to college. "It doesn't make sense," she says, "to leave home to find a new home, to leave friends to find new friends, to give up your old life for a new life." "Could you say that again?" the dumbfounded Howard asks. – *American Graffiti* (1973)

4242 Con artist Leo McKern attributes the lack of social amenities displayed by teenage orphan Jodie Foster to her "deprived childhood." "I ain't deprived," she corrects him. "I'm delinquent. There's a difference, you know." – *Candleshoe* (1977)

4243 Karen Allen, girlfriend of college student Peter Riegart, urges him not to attend a party sponsored by his Animal House "sickies." "It's a fraternity party," he explains. "I'm in the fraternity. How can I miss it?" "I'll write you a note," she suggests wryly. "I'll say you're too well to attend." – *National Lampoon's Animal House* (1978)

4244 Twelve-year-old Trini Alvarado, suspecting that her parents are about to get a divorce, asks student friend Jeremy Levy what she can expect. He describes how his parents took him to MacDonald's and offered him a dog before they told him they were filing for divorce. "Listen," Jeremy counsels Trini, "if they ask you to pick your favorite restaurant, pick a restaurant you really hate. I haven't been able to eat a Big Mac since." – *Rich Kids* (1979)

4245 Twelve-year-old Trini Alvarado stays overnight at schoolmate Jeremy Levy's apartment where their physical playfulness soon leads to their kissing. Trini suddenly pulls away. "What's wrong?" Levy asks. "Nothing." "Well, something's the matter," Jeremy insists. "Don't you like it?" "I like you, but – " "But what?" questions Jeremy. "Your braces hurt," Trini finally says. – *Rich Kids* (1979)

4246 "I only use my math book on special equations," cracks a high-school student. – *Rock 'n' Roll High School* (1979)

4247 When the daughter of parents Anthony Hopkins and Shirley MacLaine learns that her mother is having an affair with a young man, she exclaims: "It's going to be hard to accept a father who's too young to shave and too old for Little League." – *A Change of Seasons* (1980)

4248 Skinny groupie Kaki Hunter has one singular passion in her life – to "make it" with Alice Cooper. "Isn't she one of 'Charlie's Angels'?" her boyfriend Meat Loaf asks. "I can't believe you never heard of Alice Cooper," says Kaki incredulously. "Don't you read T-shirts?" – *Roadie* (1980)

4249 Teenage Tom Cruise becomes involved with a hooker and barely escapes in his father's car from Guido, the young woman's pimp, who soon gives chase. The wild ride is too much for Tom's high-school buddy rolling around in the back seat. "I don't believe this," Tom's pal mumbles. "I got a trig midterm tomorrow and I'm being chased by Guido, the killer pimp." – *Risky Business* (1983)

4250 In a parking lot outside a school dance, class clown Anthony Michael Hall asks sweet-sixteen Molly Ringwald to help him win a bet he made with his friends. "I bet I could do it with you," he explains, "but this was before I knew you as a person. I can get proof of that without being physical." "How?" Ringwald wonders. "Can I borrow your underpants for ten minutes?" – *Sixteen Candles* (1984)

4251 "By night's end," a teenager boasts, "I predict that me and her will interface." – *Sixteen Candles* (1984)

4252 While hitchhiking to California, John Cusack and Daphne Zuniga are caught in a heavy downpour at night on a desolate road with no shelter. "I have a credit card," Daphne offers. "My dad told me I can only use it for an emergency." "Well, maybe one'll come up," John returns. – *The Sure Thing* (1985)

4253 Young stockbroker Jon Cryer, hiding out from the mob, joins his sixteen-year-old cousin Keith Coogan and poses as a fellow high school student. "Let's get something straight," Coogan prompts Cryer. "You've got to orient your thinking. You've got to think oppression, think humiliation, despair." – *Hiding Out* (1987)

4254 Teenagers Randall Batinkoff and Molly Ringwald, with visions of college and careers, are suddenly faced with the problem of unwanted pregnancy. "Let's keep it!" Randall blurts out at a family conference. "Keep it?" his father (Kenneth Mars) angrily echoes. "Last year you had a gerbil and you forgot to feed it!" – *For Keeps* (1988)

4255 The bored teenage daughter of a wealthy family confides to her mother's friend: "My life is so-so. What have I got to show for it? Nothing. My idea of taking a risk is losing my birth control pills or shopping at Saks without a sale." – *Scenes from the Class Struggle in Beverly Hills* (1989)

4256 Administrators of the Wilderness Girls, a camping organization, are considering disbanding the Beverly Hills chapter, a rebellious group of spoiled, undisciplined young girls. "They've had more leaders than a banana republic," one executive comments. – *Troop Beverly Hills* (1989)

Name Index

References are to entry numbers, not pages.

Abbott and Costello 12, 17, 18, 19, 22, 224, 255, 257, 323, 327, 336, 345, 396, 397, 398, 468, 564, 685, 853, 857, 872, 874, 875, 878, 880, 964, 966, 987, 1002, 1069, 1089, 1132, 1139, 1140, 1143, 1194, 1238, 1314, 1438, 1441, 1512, 1520, 1598, 1599, 1600, 1602, 1605, 1618, 1706, 1708, 1722, 1723, 1791, 2057, 2139, 2227, 2287, 2451, 2533, 2544, 2661, 2670, 2718, 2795, 2802, 2804, 2922, 3026, 3221, 3222, 3335, 3420, 3448, 3735, 3744, 3776, 3780, 3839, 3841, 3846, 3847, 3888, 3905, 3906, 3907, 3908, 3929, 3982, 4100, 4147, 4150

Abel, Walter 508, 627, 1770, 1966, 3777

Ackland, Joss 675

Adams, Don 3757

Adams, Nick 415, 885, 2241

Adams, Tom 716

Addams, Dawn 352, 1654

Adu, Frank 427

Aherne, Brian 1217, 1828, 2641

Aiello, Danny 1761, 1898, 2103, 2267, 3522, 4126

Akins, Claude 2913

Alberni, Luis 3368

Albert, Eddie 1870, 2259, 2332, 2435, 4060

Albertson, Frank 2622, 3690, 3931

Alda, Alan 61, 121, 184, 1874, 2089, 2993, 3423, 4187

Allen, Fred 160, 261, 869, 1329, 2063, 2290, 2626, 2627, 2643, 2715, 3091, 3092, 3093, 4137

Allen, Gracie 238, 759, 760, 839, 1061, 1375, 1376, 1379, 1381, 1386, 1392, 1433, 1435, 1692, 2127, 2203, 2276, 2656, 2780, 3426, 3818, 3824

Allen, Karen 1361, 4243

Allen, Woody 119, 197, 268, 272, 371, 427, 470, 534, 590, 591, 691, 946, 973, 1057, 1079, 1098, 1101, 1102, 1103, 1158, 1161, 1173, 1225, 1267, 1268, 1412, 1458, 1460, 1467, 1563, 1736,

1739, 1741, 1873, 1885, 1918, 1940, 1975, 1976, 1977, 1978, 2016, 2087, 2109, 2150, 2368, 2369, 2426, 2430, 2439, 2462, 2499, 2574, 2575, 2580, 2647, 2724, 2731, 2768, 2771, 2873, 2927, 2957, 2984, 2986, 2991, 3123, 3212, 3231, 3235, 3236, 3240, 3241, 3245, 3266, 3268, 3273, 3276, 3399, 3410, 3421, 3484, 3521, 3602, 3611, 3612, 3614, 3615, 3617, 3624, 3639, 3669, 3683, 3720, 3876, 3890, 3912, 3913, 3922, 4003, 4073, 4074, 4122, 4170, 4184, 4206, 4208

Alley, Kirstie 138, 732, 2111, 3529, 4125, 4213

Allgood, Sara 2612

Alton, John 947, 2388, 2903

Alvarado, Trini 4244, 4245

Ameche, Don 673, 1513, 1548, 1961, 2649, 2695

Anderson, Eddie "Rochester" 1591, 1592, 1617

Andes, Keith 4052

Andress, Ursula 637, 2245

Andrews, Dana 1518, 1720, 1963, 3371, 4089

Andrews, Edward 3588

Andrews, Harry 3393

Andrews, Julie 130, 1228, 1745, 2694, 3962, 4062

Andrews Sisters 3700

Ann-Margret 488, 535, 583, 4234

Annabella 2324

Anspach, Susan 723

Arden, Eve 40, 508, 567, 627, 862, 1842, 2350, 2351, 3008, 3290, 3370, 3494, 3495, 3684, 3791, 4148

Arkin, Alan 2258, 4075

Arliss, George 295, 1541, 3490

Armetta, Henry 3135, 3445

Armstrong, Robert 2128, 4107

Arnaz, Desi 442, 3373, 3972

Arnold, Edward 6, 983, 3368

Arthur, Beatrice 1358, 1939, 2014, 2570, 4178

361

Levant, Oscar 261, 318, 1330, 1965,
2492, 2923, 3347, 3508, 4151
Levene, Sam 996, 1190, 2403, 3009,
3025, 4034
Levi, Daliah 4003
Levine, Emily 1886
Levy, Jeremy 4244, 4245
Lewis, Jenny 3483
Lewis, Jerry 171, 350, 579, 1005, 1146,
1403, 1404, 1408, 1567, 1604, 1776,
2119, 2180, 2234, 2235, 2243, 2314,
2628, 2721, 2887, 3067, 3125, 3228,
3229, 3310, 3352, 3707, 3709, 3781,
3782, 3849, 3850, 3874, 4115, 4117,
4119, 4177
Lewis, Joe E. 3700
Lillie, Beatrice 507
Linden, Eric 2446, 4214
Linn-Baker, Mark 1055, 2502
Lithgow, John 1247, 4007
Little, Cleavon 2389, 3277
Lloyd, Christopher 1923
Lloyd, Harold 1331, 1582, 2668
Lockhart, Gene 3499
Loggia, Robert 139, 1476, 2443
Lollobrigida Gina 588
Lom, Herbert, 28, 1226, 2182, 2186
Lombard, Carole 606, 776, 997, 1121,
1299, 1387, 1930, 2167, 2704, 2757,
3007, 3140, 3326, 3687
Long, Audrey 1649, 1842, 3301
Long, Shelley 386, 952, 1177, 2107,
2189, 2592, 2696, 2878, 3670
Loren, Sophia 2559, 2812, 3190
Lorre, Peter 999, 1829, 2525, 2839,
3737, 3832
Lovejoy, Frank 4051
Lowe, Edmund 73, 779, 1645, 1993
Loy, Myrna 146, 344, 769, 871, 1186,
1252, 1320, 1445, 1553, 1694, 1848,
2030, 2031, 2055, 2304, 2346, 2717,
3029, 3536, 3554, 3926, 3948, 4149
Lucas, Wilfred 2126
Lugosi, Bela 3893, 3894, 3907
Luke, Keye 1821, 3006
Lund, John 784
Lundigan, William 573, 1486
Lunt, Alfred 86
Lutter, Alfred 718
Lydon, Jimmy 3250
Lynde, Paul 1154, 1223, 1937
Lynn, Diana 707, 1402, 1969
Lynn, Judy 4203
Lyon, Ben 3286, 3433, 3535

MacBride, Donald 2171
McCarthy, Charlie 314, 813, 1125, 1442,

1926, 2447, 2452, 2487, 2534, 2920,
2921, 2980, 3292, 3821, 3826, 3902
McCarthy, Kevin 2263
McClelland, Fergus 2251
McCormick, Myron 2240
McCrea, Joel 1234, 1837, 2327, 2386,
3257
McCullough, Paul 2865
McDaniel, Hattie 1281, 1282, 2116
McDonald, J. Farrell 2491
McFarland, Spanky 1500
McGann, Paul 393
McGillis, Kelly 1471
McGiver, John 225, 484, 1799
McGraw, Ali 1531, 2814, 3600, 4102
McHugh, Frank 989, 2301
McIver, John 4237
McKenna, Virginia 658
McKeon, Doug 193
McKern, Leo 4242
McKinnon, Mona 2064
McLaglen, Victor 779, 1698, 2396, 2404,
3558
MacDonald, Jeanette 70, 1252, 1632,
1808, 3439, 3536
MacLaine, Shirley 56, 126, 390, 445,
540, 611, 1105, 1180, 1422, 2425, 3188,
3189, 3192, 3230, 3316, 3517, 3811,
4104, 4160, 4247
McLeod, Catherine 1777, 3889
McMahon, Aline 35, 763, 1811, 2280,
2999, 3828
McMahon, Ed 1921
McMartin, John 3230
MacMurray, Fred 979, 1127, 1917, 2067,
2167, 2757, 2810, 2883, 3120, 3298,
3326, 4162
McNamara, Maggie 969, 1075, 1523,
2002, 2408, 3349, 3568
McQueen, Steve 1798, 2248, 3375
Madonna 604, 2833, 3280, 3318, 3671
Madsen, Michael 4196
Magnani, Anna 2080
Magnuson, Ann
Main, Marjorie 312, 1233, 1554, 1773,
1832, 2289, 2336, 3501, 4099
Malden, Karl 661, 1011, 4002
Malina, Judith 1758
Malone, Dorothy 515, 2628, 3454
Mandel, Howie 1174
Manoff, Dinah 1568, 1569, 2876, 3047
Mansfield, Jayne 578, 1859, 2239, 3227,
3513, 3848
Mantegna, Joe 64, 3657, 4193
March, Fredric 606, 942, 1121, 1301,
1485, 1778, 2207, 2306, 2472, 2779,
3324, 3489, 3899, 4197

Title Index

References are to entry numbers, not pages.